a p l i c o r
inc

Aplicor is a global software publisher of on-demand CRM (Customer Relationship Management) and ERP (Enterprise Resource Planning) business software solutions for high growth, middle-market, and enterprise organizations. The CRM application benefits clients by improving marketing effectiveness, increasing sales win rates, growing customer share, and decreasing customer churn. Aplicor is the most independently awarded hosted solution, has achieved the highest average user count in the hosting industry, and is the only CRM and ERP hosting provider with a 100 percent uptime history. More information is available at **www.aplicor.com.**

SELF–ASSESSMENT LIBRARY (SAL)

Content

Our Self-Assessment Library offers 67 assessments. The 18 **new assessments** we have added cover:

- Personality Insights
- Motivation Insights
- Values and Attitude Insights
- Mood and Emotion Insights
- Leadership and Team Skills
- Organization Structure

Delivery

In your copy of Sales Management, you will find an Access Code Card. By using this code at **www.pearsonhighered.com/tanner**, you will gain access to the SAL program.

D0146111

Sales

Management

Shaping Future Sales Leaders

SALES
Management
Shaping Future Sales Leaders

JOHN F. TANNER JR.
Baylor University

EARL D. HONEYCUTT JR.
Elon University

ROBERT C. ERFFMEYER
University of Wisconsin – Eau Claire

Prentice Hall
Upper Saddle River, NJ 07458

Library of Congress Cataloging-in-Publication Data

Tanner, John F.
   Sales management: shaping future sales leaders / Jeff Tanner, Earl Honeycutt, Robert C. Erffmeyer.
      p. cm.
   Includes bibliographical references and index.
   ISBN-13: 978-0-13-232412-0
   ISBN-10: 0-13-232412-1
   1. Sales management.   2. Selling.   3. Sales management—Case studies.   4. Selling—Case studies.
I. Honeycutt, Earl D.   II. Erffmeyer, Robert C.   III. Title.
   HF5438.4.T36 2009
   658.8'1—dc22

                                                                          2008039596

Editorial Director: Sally Yagan
Acquisitions Editor: James Heine
Product Development Manager: Ashley Santora
Editorial Project Manager: Melissa Pellerano
Editorial Assistant: Karin Williams
Marketing Director: Patrice Lumumba Jones
Marketing Manager: Anne Fahlgren
Marketing Assistant: Susan Osterlitz
Media Project Manager: Denise Vaughn
Permissions Project Manager: Charles Morris
Associate Managing Editor: Suzanne DeWorken
Production Project Manager: Ann Pulido
Senior Operations Specialist: Arnold Vila
Art Director: Jonathon Boylan

Designer: Kathy Mrozek
Cover Designer: Kathy Mrozek
Cover Illustration: © iStockphoto/A-Digit:
Director, Image Resource Center: Melinda Patelli
Manager, Rights and Permissions: Zina Arabia
Manager, Visual Research: Beth Brenzel
Image Permission Coordinator: Angelique Sharpes
Manager, Cover Visual Research & Permissions: Karen Sanatar
Composition: GGS Book Services PMG
Full-Service Project Management: Ann Courtney/GGS Book Services
   PMG
Printer/Binder: King Printing Co., Inc.
Typeface: 10/12 Times New Roman

Credits and acknowledgments borrowed from other sources and reproduced, with permission, in this textbook appear on appropriate page within text.

Pearson Education Ltd., London
Pearson Education Singapore, Pte. Ltd
Pearson Education, Canada, Inc.
Pearson Education–Japan
Pearson Education Australia PTY, Limited
Pearson Education North Asia, Ltd., Hong Kong
Pearson Educación de Mexico, S.A. de C.V.
Pearson Education Malaysia, Pte. Ltd
Pearson Education Upper Saddle River, New Jersey

Prentice Hall
is an imprint of

www.pearsonhighered.com

2 3 4 5 6 7 8 9 10 V0CR 15 14 13 12
ISBN-13: 978-0-13-232412-0
ISBN-10: 0-13-232412-1

To Karen, and to my favorite "students,"
Emily, Ted, John, and Travis

—Jeff

To Laura, Travis, Andrea, Cole, and Raine

—Earl

To Gretchen and Hannah

—Bob

Brief Contents

Contents

PART SEVEN   Cases   373

Preface

How firms manage their selling functions has changed tremendously over the past 20 years. The Internet has had a significant impact on sales management, but at the same time, so have customer contact centers, customer relationship management (CRM) technology, knowledge management technology, increased global competition, greater cultural and generational diversity, the importance of ethical responsibilities, and a myriad of other factors. Developments such as these have greatly changed how sales teams are led.

We wanted you to understand these changes and how today's sales managers actually manage their personnel. But in spite of what we knew about what was going on in the field, we realized existing sales management textbooks had changed very little over the years. No new major sales management textbook has entered the market in more than two decades. We believed it was time for something new.

Our goal is to offer a book that prepares you for the exciting challenges related to leading sales organizations in today's hyper-competitive global economy. Of course, we want to provide you with a basic theoretical foundation that will enable you to adapt to the economy as it continues to evolve, but we will balance the theory with the practical applications one will need to know in order to lead top-performing sales teams.

What Makes This Book Different?

Our textbook emphasizes *how* sales management gets done. You will see the following cutting-edge material integrated not only into the textbook and end-of-chapter questions and problems, but the book's accompanying instructor's manual, test bank, PowerPoint slides, and other materials.

Chapter-Opening Profiles

Unique to the book are the chapter-opening profiles featuring actual sales managers. The profiles explain the day-to-day challenges these managers face, which are related to the chapters in which they appear. We want students to get a sense of the world sales managers live in. Our goal is to engage and inspire students to explore possible sales management careers, as well as to hear from the sales managers who helped shape this textbook. In addition to the chapter-opening profiles, the book's website features numerous video interviews with sales executives featured in the *Selling Power Daily Report*.

Technology Coverage

CRM and knowledge management technology are two software applications that can dramatically affect how both salespeople and sales managers spend their time. The question is, how do sales managers and their reps make the most of these systems? Not only will you find an entire chapter devoted to using technology to manage sales organizations, but you'll also find technology woven throughout the book. Furthermore, adopters will be able to use Aplicor, the most awarded hosted sales force automation tool on the market today. This software is available at www.pearsonhighered.com/tanner. Aplicor contains CRM features and a database set up with student exercises. For example, you'll find Aplicor exercises that will give you hands-on experience when it comes to forecasting sales, establishing territories, tracking the activities of salespeople, and evaluating their performance. No other textbook on the market today does this.

Coverage of Culture and the Global Sales Environment

Technology has greatly impacted the global environment of sales today, but so have other influences such as new trade agreements and changing political alignments. Sales executives know foreign markets are their future "bread and butter." And they are counting on their sales managers to find ways to capture market share abroad via the day-to-day interactions they have with their firms' global partners as well as sales representatives who perhaps grew up or are living in other cultures. Because the sales environment has truly become a "flat world," the book contains a "Global Sales Management" feature that addresses the topics discussed in each chapter, but on a global scale. There are also detailed sections of a chapter that discuss how to understand and manage buyers and salespersons from different cultural backgrounds. The feature is also integrated into the chapter, the discussion questions and problems, and the test bank, resulting in more complete coverage than any other sales management text.

Ethics Coverage

Many textbooks largely emphasize the law in their ethics chapters. Our ethics chapter covers the legal aspects of sales management. However, you will also find more coverage on people's actual ethical beliefs and why they believe what they do. For example, can you really "train" sales representatives in terms of their ethics? What is the difference between a gift and a bribe? Also included is a discussion about how successful sales managers go about developing an ethical framework to guide the behavior of their salespeople. This is especially important when their salespeople don't have the same ethical or cultural backgrounds as they do—a common situation with global sales forces. In addition to a separate ethics chapter, an "Ethics in Sales Management" feature is woven throughout the book.

Coverage of the Sales Force's Structure

In the past, devoting a few paragraphs to distributors and manufacturer's reps might be all an instructor would need to cover the topic of outsourcing. Now, however, a company might outsource its prospecting to a call center service bureau, have another contact center of its own working with independent field salespeople, and then outsource its customer service to yet another service bureau—all in addition to managing self-serve channels via the Web. As a result, what a chapter on selection or training should look like in terms of today's best practices is vastly different than what it was 20 years ago. You'll still find chapters devoted to recruiting, selecting, socializing (on-boarding), and training salespeople in our book, but the content more closely reflects the reality of the many different positions and sales force structures that exist within the realm of selling today.

Coverage of Leadership

Leadership concepts and practices have changed as professionals and academics alike recognize that there is more to leading than motivating the sales force. Leadership isn't just about getting someone to do what you want, but, among other things, it is about what you do for your followers. The material in this book lies at the forefront of sales leadership thought and practice. Not only does the book include best practices material when it comes to U.S. leaders, but information about what sales executives and representatives abroad believe good leadership is.

Acknowledgments

No book is solely the work of its authors. Although we take full responsibility for any errors or omissions, we could not have accomplished this project without a lot of help. We greatly appreciate their contributions.

Because we wanted a book that reflected the best practices that lie at the forefront of sales management, we involved successful sales executives and consultants. These people reviewed outlines, made suggestions on topics to cover, and gave us access to their thought processes and their companies' practices. These executives and consultants include:

Jill Amerie, Xtreme Xhibits by Skyline, Inc.

Jeffrey Bailey, Oracle Corporation

Melaney Barba, Liberty Mutual

Bill Bencsik, Bencsik Associates, Inc.

Charlie Cohon, Manufacturers Representatives Educational Research Foundation

Tait Cruse, Northwestern Mutual

Bruce Culbert, BPT Partners

Ken Deakman, Slipka-Deakman Associates, Inc.

Ken De Meuse, Lominger International

Susan Denny, Cisco

Antoine Destin, Hormel Foods Corporation

George Dudley, Behavioral Science Research Press, Inc.

Bill Febry, Miller Brewing Company

Jeanne Frawley, University Sales Education Foundation

Josie Gall, Pearson/Prentice Hall

Mary Gros, Teradata

Gerhard Gschwandtner, Selling Power

Bill Haas, LabCorp

Tricia Jennings, Merck & Co., Inc.

Mike Kapocius, Takeda Pharmaceuticals America, Inc.

Jerry Kollross, Top Golf Products

Richard Langlotz, Konica-Minolta

Rick Makos, NCR-Canada

Joe Matton, Vistakon (Johnson & Johnson)

Paul Nelson, IBM

Ram Ramamurthy, Sri-IIST, Inc.

David Riegel, Teradata

Chuck Schaefer, Aplicor

Tom Sherrill, B.W. Wilson Paper Company

Howard Stevens, H.R. Chally Group

Katherine Twells, Coca-Cola Company

Ken Vance, Ken Vance Automotive

Larry Vopahl, Hormel Foods Corporation

Kevin Yoder, AstraZeneca

We greatly appreciate the efforts of Jerry Kollross in the development of six of the cases used in this book. Jerry utilized his vast sales and sales management experiences and his understanding of the needs of the educational environment to produce realistic cases. His contribution adds a tremendous amount of value to this book.

Several faculty members also provided input into the design and content of the book. We especially appreciate the early input of Andrea Dixon at the University of Cincinnati. Also, Shawn Thelen at Hofstra University and Peter LaPlaca at the University of Hartford provided valuable advice and support to the author team. In addition, many professors diligently reviewed the manuscript, including:

Mary Albrecht, Maryville University

Ned J. Cooney, University of Colorado at Boulder

Darrin C. Duber-Smith, Metropolitan State College of Denver

Andrew Feldstein, Virginia State University

Tyrone W. Jackson, California State University, Los Angeles

Richard Leibert, Iona College

Joshua D. Martin, Villanova and Arcadia Universities

Chip E. Miller, Drake University

James J. Mullen, Jr., Villanova University

James W. Nall, Gardner-Webb University

Concha Neeley, Central Michigan University

Dominic Nucera, LaSalle University

Peggy Osborne, Morehead State University

Eric Popkoff, Brooklyn College

David Schumaker, Texas State University

Kevin Shanahan, University of Texas at Tyler

Craig Shoemaker, St. Ambrose University

Jeff Strieter, SUNY College at Brockport

Judy Jones Tisdale, University of North Carolina at Chapel Hill

Andrea Wills, Johns Hopkins University

A number of students pretested the book and provided us with feedback on its content. These students included Raul Benavides, Joanna Browne, Lindsey Coker, Jacqueline Simpson, and John Tanner. Research assistance was provided by Travis Tanner, Mandy McGowan, and Heidi Raynes. Jeri Weiser was instrumental in conceptualizing some of our graphics and in reviewing different parts of the manuscript.

The team from Pearson/Prentice Hall included some great talent. Amy Ray did an awesome job as the book's developmental editor. Our production editor Ann Courtney helped manage hundreds of details and kept us on schedule. We especially appreciate and acknowledge Melissa Pellerano, James Heine, and Sally Yagan's contributions and Rachel Lucas, who expertly researched the photographs for the text.

We very much appreciate three other supporters of collegiate sales education. We would like to thank Gerhard Gschwandtner, who allowed use of the outstanding videos he produces for the *Selling Power Daily Report.* Howard Stevens at HR Chally and Jeanne Frawley at The Sales Education Foundation are truly advocates of college sales education. We greatly appreciate their assistance and their support of all college educators teaching sales-related courses.

We would also like to acknowledge Richard Wonderling and his associates at Think^{TV}Network for their work on *The NEW Selling of America* video.

About the Authors

John F. "Jeff" Tanner Jr. is professor of marketing at Baylor University's Hankamer School of Business. Dr. Tanner spent eight years in marketing and sales with Rockwell International and Xerox Corporation. In 1988, Dr. Tanner earned his Ph.D. from the University of Georgia and joined the faculty at Baylor University, where he serves as the Co-Director of the Center for Professional Selling and the Associate Dean for Research and Faculty Development.

Dr. Tanner has received several awards for teaching and research, including the Business Deans Association Innovative Achievement Award. He is author or co-author of 13 books, including *The Hard Truth About Soft Selling* with George Dudley. His books have been translated into several languages, and distributed in over 30 countries. Dr. Tanner has published over 100 articles in trade publications such as *Business Marketing, Marketing Management,* and *Exhibitor Times* and over 70 research articles in academic journals such as the *Journal of Marketing, Journal of Business Research, Journal of Personal Selling and Sales Management*, and others. His research has won numerous awards, including "Best Paper of the Year, 2000" from the *Journal of Personal Selling & Sales Management*.

A founding partner in BPT Partners, Dr. Tanner is an active consultant. He helps fast-growing companies deploy sales strategies and quickly grow sales forces. In addition, he teaches marketing and sales to executives in France, Canada, Mexico, Trinidad, Colombia, Australia, and India.

Dr. Tanner and his wife have four children, and live on Jett Creek Farm, where they raise thoroughbred racehorses.

Earl D. Honeycutt, Jr. is Professor of Marketing, Marketing Coordinator, and Director of the Chandler Family Professional Sales Center at the Love School of Business, Elon University, NC. He was formerly Professor of Marketing, Chair of the Department of Business Administration, and Director of the Ph.D. program at Old Dominion University,

Norfolk, VA, and he was also a tenured faculty member at UNC-Wilmington, where he was designated a Cameron Fellow.

Before entering academia, Dr. Honeycutt served as a U.S. Air Force B-52 flight officer (SAC) and worked as an industrial salesperson for an electronics division of TRW, Inc. He holds the Ph.D. in Business Administration–Marketing from the University of Georgia, an M.B.A. with a management concentration, an M.A. in European history, and a B.S. in history/Asian studies. Earl has taught classes in Japan and the Philippines and has led numerous study abroad groups to Asia, Australia, and Europe.

Dr. Honeycutt was honored with the Elon University Distinguished Scholar Award in 2008. He also received the 2007 United Sales Center Alliance Innovative Sales Educator Award and the Marvin Jolson 2005 Award for Best Contribution to Selling and Sales Management Practice by the *Journal of Personal Selling & Sales Management*. In 2002, he was honored with the National Conference in Sales Management Outstanding Conference Paper. Dr. Honeycutt serves on the Editorial Review Boards of the *Journal of Personal Selling & Sales Management*, *Journal of Selling & Major Account Management*, and *Journal of Business-to-Business Marketing*. He is also Associate Editor of *Industrial Marketing Management*. Earl has published over 175 articles in national and international outlets and has co-authored three books on business-to-business marketing, global sales management, and cross-cultural selling.

Dr. Honeycutt and his wife, Laura, reside in Chapel Hill, NC, near their son, Travis; daughter-in-law, Andrea; and their two grandchildren, Cole and Raine. The entire Honeycutt family spends time together surfing and seeking adventure in Costa Rica as well as enjoying quiet times at their house in Wrightsville Beach, NC.

Dr. Robert C. Erffmeyer earned his Ph.D. in Industrial/Organizational Psychology from Louisiana State University in 1981 and worked in various human resource positions in the areas of selection and training. He returned to LSU to complete a post-doctorate in marketing and has worked in marketing and sales training for Deere & Company, Wausau Insurance Companies, and other organizations. In 1990, he joined the faculty at the University of Wisconsin–Eau Claire where he teaches marketing, sales, and sales management courses to undergraduate and graduate students.

He is the MBA Director for both the University of Wisconsin – Eau Claire and the University of Wisconsin Consortium MBA Programs, an online graduate program. He is a leader in distance education, conducting research and teaching distance classes for 15 years using various technologies for delivery. Dr. Erffmeyer helped to establish the Great Northwoods' Sales Warm-Up, a regional sales competition for Midwestern Business Schools held annually at the University of Wisconsin–Eau Claire. He is the chapter advisor for Pi Sigma Epsilon, a national sales fraternity for university students.

He has been a visiting professor in the Asian Studies Program at Kansai Gaidai University in Osaka, Japan, and has lectured in China and Vietnam.

Dr. Erffmeyer has served in numerous officer and board positions in the Society of Marketing Advances and the Marketing Management Association. In 2006, he was named a Fellow of the Marketing Management Association.

He has published over 30 articles in outlets such as the *Journal of Personal Selling and Sales Management, Marketing Education Review, Industrial Marketing Management, Journal of Business Ethics, Journal of International Marketing,* and *Journal of Business & Industrial Marketing*. He was the first recipient of the Marketing Education Review Award. He serves on the Editorial Review Boards for the *Journal of Personal Selling and Sales Management, Direct Marketing: An International Journal*, and on the Advisory Board for the *Journal of Advancement of Marketing Education*.

Dr. Erffmeyer and his wife, Gretchen, reside in Eau Claire, WI, with their daughter, Johannah. They enjoy traveling, biking, and kayaking in the Northwoods.

PART ONE

Strategic Planning

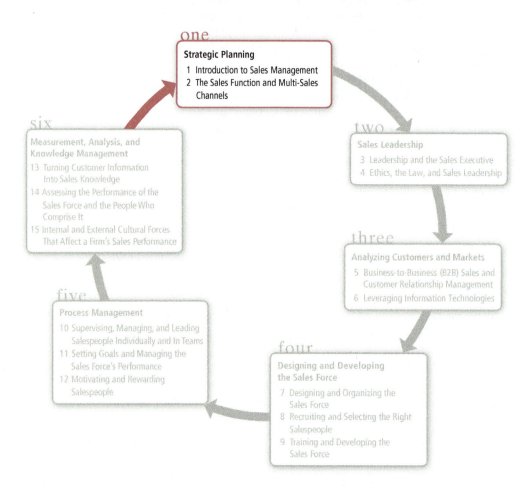

one

Strategic Planning
1 Introduction to Sales Management
2 The Sales Function and Multi-Sales Channels

six

Measurement, Analysis, and Knowledge Management

13 Turning Customer Information Into Sales Knowledge
14 Assessing the Performance of the Sales Force and the People Who Comprise It
15 Internal and External Cultural Forces That Affect a Firm's Sales Performance

two

Sales Leadership

3 Leadership and the Sales Executive
4 Ethics, the Law, and Sales Leadership

three

Analyzing Customers and Markets

5 Business-to-Business (B2B) Sales and Customer Relationship Management
6 Leveraging Information Technologies

five

Process Management

10 Supervising, Managing, and Leading Salespeople Individually and In Teams
11 Setting Goals and Managing the Sales Force's Performance
12 Motivating and Rewarding Salespeople

four

Designing and Developing the Sales Force

7 Designing and Organizing the Sales Force
8 Recruiting and Selecting the Right Salespeople
9 Training and Developing the Sales Force

Of all the functions in an organization, none has changed as much in the past decade as sales management, except perhaps purchasing! The Internet; mobile technology; globalization; a greater focus on ethical behavior; and a host of other social, economic, and political changes have altered selling and sales management to such an extent that the textbook had to be written over from scratch.

No other function in the organization has the same impact on a firm's strategy as sales management. Salespeople talk directly with customers, testing the company's strategy in every sales call. Information gathered from customers by salespeople feeds directly into company strategy. These, and other factors, make sales management a critical part of an organization's success.

This book presents sales management in six parts. The first part, *Strategic Planning*, orients you to the role of sales in the strategy of the organization. Part Two, *Sales*

Leadership, defines the leadership roles needed to create the right sales culture. Part Three, *Analyzing Customers and Markets*, examines the market, recognizing the importance of using technology to understand customers. Part Four, *Designing and Developing the Sales Force*, contains three chapters that focus on the organizational issues of sales force design, recruiting and selecting, and training salespeople. In Part Five, *Process Management*, the emphasis is on supervision, goal-setting, motivation, and compensation issues. Finally, Part Six, *Measurement, Analysis, and Knowledge Management,* considers performance evaluation, but also internal and external cultural issues and how those affect sales management.

Successful companies don't become that way by accident. They became successful because they had a plan and executed it well. The beginning of a company is its purpose, and from that purpose flows its strategy. That's why Part One, *Strategic Planning*, illustrates how the sales force and the sales function fit into the company's strategy and how the sales force serves the company's mission.

Chapter 1, *Introduction to Sales Management*, introduces you to the activities of sales managers and sales force leaders, placing the sales force into the strategic picture of the firm. This chapter also serves as an overview of the rest of the book.

Chapter 2, *The Sales Function and Multisales Channels*, explores the selling function further, examining the different types of salespeople and sales organizations that are used to reach customers. In addition, we continue the dialog regarding strategy, relating how each of these sales force alternatives can serve a company's strategy.

1

INTRODUCTION TO SALES MANAGEMENT

LEARNING OBJECTIVES

After completing this chapter, you should be able to:

- Define the strategy hierarchy and understand how a firm's sales and marketing strategies affect its overall strategy.
- Identify the different types of selling strategies and how the selling process varies across those types.
- Describe the sales management process and the responsibilities and activities of sales managers.

What should we make? What should we sell? At what price? To whom? What kind of people should we hire, and how will we manage them? These are the questions that define a company's strategy. In turn, the answers to these questions define the company. Yet in the minds of a company's customers, salespeople define the company. Why? Because salespeople are often the only face of the company that customers ever see.

In essence, this book is about how those corporate strategic questions and answers become sales practices that affect customers. Today, people recognize that aligning a firm's sales practices with its sales strategy, and its sales strategy with its corporate strategy, is central to success. Thus, in this chapter, we not only introduce the basic sales management process but show how a firm's sales force is a central part of the broader marketing strategy pursued by the firm.

JILL AMERIE

**SALES MANAGER, XTREME XHIBITS
BY SKYLINE INC.**

Jill Amerie, a sales manager for the Austin, Texas–based company Xtreme Xhibits by Skyline Inc., didn't grow up wanting to become a sales executive or entrepreneur. In fact, looking back, Amerie didn't remember knowing what an entrepreneur was. "Sure, I knew people had their own businesses, but I didn't think about what it took to start, manage, run, and grow a business," she says. "One thing that I did know though was that I needed to be my own boss. A sales career offered me that opportunity."

Raised by an artistic mother and a father who was in sales, Amerie has always been a people person with a passion for creativity. She says she walked into the trade-show world by accident and quickly realized that sales was the career she wanted to pursue. "A career in the trade-show industry isn't a career that I even knew existed. What I did know was that this career combined my creativity and my people skills while allowing me to have fun and make a great income." She says the characteristics of the job have kept her motivated, passionate, and focused.

As Amerie worked in her field, she continued to perfect her skills. "A mentor once told me to continue learning everything I could about my field (my passion) so my clients would look to me as their trusted advisor," she says. "So, over the years, I learned to be a 'student' of my industry. He also shared with me that if I was not enthusiastic about what I was doing and selling, I could not convince my prospects to be excited about what I was about to offer them." These words of wisdom have stuck with her throughout her career.

After achieving her personal goals as a sales representative, Amerie became a sales manager. She says most successful sales representatives feel pressured to eventually make the transition to sales management. "This is a decision that must be carefully analyzed because it's not an easy transition to go from being a player to a coach," she says. "Most sales professionals want to be on the front lines and have a hard time watching from the sidelines. As I mentor my team, I try to stand on the sidelines and watch as they take the lead and develop their accounts. I struggle with this role but realize that this is the only way to build a successful sales operation."

A case in point: One day when she was still a representative, Amerie ran into her sales manager, who had tears running down her face. Her manager said she was frustrated with the members of her sales team—including Amerie—because they didn't listen to her. "They've seen

3

that I was successful [as a salesperson], so I don't understand why they just don't do exactly what I did so they'll be successful," her boss told her.

Amerie pondered this statement and replied, "Have you asked them if they want to be just like you?" She says the experience still resonates with her today as she mentors her own team. That's why she prefers to call herself a sales mentor rather than a sales manager. "My advice to other sales mentors who were former sales executives is not to lose sight of where you came from," she says. "Remember what it was like when you were the sales rep, and use those positive and negative experiences to make you a better mentor/manager. Take time to learn about your team. Learn what motivates them. Learn what their passion is and coach them on how they can integrate that passion into their career."

In addition to her managers and mentors over the years, when Amerie looks back at what brought her to where she is today, she can sum it up to two words: passion and perseverance. "If you are passionate about what you are doing and have the perseverance to continuously push yourself forward, you will be successful in whatever you do—be it sales, sales management, or business ownership." ■

One of the oldest truisms of business is that "nothing happens until someone sells something." Clearly, without salespeople, some businesses would cease to exist. Nonetheless, many people believe the sales profession is not a noble endeavor. Visions of cheesy, aggressive, badly dressed product pushers dominate their view of what sales is about. Professional buyers know better though. These buyers rely on salespeople to bring them solutions to the business problems that challenge them. Product knowledge, technical expertise, and business acumen are all required to satisfactorily serve the customer and the company's needs.

Companies recognize the importance of having the best salespeople possible. According to a recent study by Manpower, a company that helps people find jobs, sales positions are the hardest jobs to fill.[1] Sales is also one of the most expensive activities a company undertakes, consuming more than 20 percent, on average, of a firm's revenue.[2] For these reasons, managing the sales force is one of the most important jobs in a company.

As a career opportunity, starting in sales is an excellent choice. The starting salaries for salespeople are significantly greater than for other positions (about 20 percent greater than other marketing positions).[3] Many CEOs, such as Mark Hurd of Hewlett-Packard, got their start in sales. Moreover, along the way, sales managers tend to earn more than their counterparts in other areas. Experts predict that the number of sales jobs will grow at a much faster rate than other professions, at least as far into the future as 2014.[4] The future for sales and sales force management is pretty bright!

From Sales Rep to Sales Manager

We will discuss the different types of sales management and leadership positions later; some discussion is needed about the sales management career to reach the right perspective. Sales managers are *not* super salespeople—in fact, many of the characteristics of successful salespeople, such as the ability to work independently, may not be useful characteristics for sales managers. Pat Metz, sales manager for Abbott Laboratories, realized being a sales manager was different the first day after his promotion from salesperson. His boss ordered him to fire a salesperson he had never met. That's when he realized that being a sales manager means "you're a manager of people."[5]

Sam Mays, of Konica-Minolta Business Systems, discovered that his gift for selling did not transfer to sales management. After several years as a sales manager, doing a poor job and hating every minute of it, he was demoted by his boss. "It was the best move for everyone," says Mays. Within a month, he was back on top of the sales lists and much happier. Mays now laughs about it, "When I was promoted, the company lost a good salesperson and gained a bad manager. Now the company has a good salesperson again and the opportunity to hire a better manager."

Being a sales manager means coaching salespeople so they can improve; developing strategies and delegating the responsibility for implementation to others; trying to figure out how to motivate people, some who are nearly twice your age; and convincing others in the organization that what is right for the sales force is right for their departments, too. Because being a sales manager can be so different than being a salesperson, sales success is not the primary reason for promotion. In fact, research has consistently shown that sales success is a poor predictor of success as a sales manager.[6] Companies have to have the right skill set and abilities in a sales manager, skills and abilities that differ from sales.

This is a book about sales force management, or sales management, for short. We define **sales management** as the activities required to lead, direct, or supervise the personal selling efforts of an organization. This definition has several important aspects. The first aspect relates to what sales managers do to manage sales*people*. Our primary objective of the book is to explain this function of managing salespeople. However, because strategy is so crucial, we also discuss many of the day-to-day tasks that sales managers do to further a firm's strategy goals. Once we've laid this foundation, a framework for the rest of the book is developed.

Establishing the Parameters of the Firm's Strategy: The Mission Statement

A **strategy** is a plan designed to accomplish a mission. A **mission** is a set of objectives. In military terms, a mission might be the objectives set for a unit, such as a brigade, for a campaign or for a longer-term goal, such as Operation Enduring Freedom, the mission for the coalition forces of building peace in Afghanistan. Because most companies are in business for the long haul, they tend to think of missions in longer terms rather than as a single campaign. Often companies summarize their goals in what's called a **mission statement**, such as those found in Exhibit 1.1. (You can usually figure out what a company's mission statement is by looking at its public financial statements or going to its Web site.) Corporate planners, which include a variety of personnel from upper management, such as employees from finance, manufacturing, and sales, are responsible for creating the mission of the organization and the mission statement.

Mission statements should serve to inspire the members of an organization, give purpose to their actions, and guide them when they are making decisions. A good mission statement does more than simply organize the company's objectives; it also serves as a standard against which the decisions and actions employees take can be compared to ensure that they are the right decisions and actions for the organization. Once the mission's objectives are set, strategy can be created.

The Strategy Hierarchy

A firm's corporate strategy encompasses its plans and goals for the entire organization. The corporate planners are responsible for creating the mission of the organization, such as the mission statements described in Exhibit 1.1. The corporate strategy will also address questions, in a general sense, such as what markets and sourcing options (such as manufacturing) the company should engage. For example, the company's corporate planners might choose to outsource sales by hiring distributors versus hiring a sales force. Or the firm might outsource its manufacturing function and focus the bulk of its efforts on marketing the products.

Once the company's strategy is formulated, it is then communicated to the firm's various business units—marketing, sales, manufacturing, and so forth—who create their

EXHIBIT 1.1

Company Mission Statements

IBM

IBM will be driven by these values:
- *Dedication to every client's success*
- *Innovation that matters, for our company and for the world*
- *Trust and personal responsibility in all relationships*

Coca-Cola

Everything we do is inspired by our enduring mission:
- *To Refresh the World . . . in body, mind, and spirit.*
- *To Inspire Moments of Optimism . . . through our brands and our actions.*
- *To Create Value and Make a Difference . . . everywhere we engage.*

Pulte Homes

Committed to building solid homes and lifelong relationships

NCR

Transforming Transactions into Relationships

Dell

Dell's mission is to be the most successful computer company in the world at delivering the best customer experience in markets we serve.

Southwest Airlines

The mission of Southwest Airlines is dedication to the highest quality of Customer Service delivered with a sense of warmth, friendliness, individual pride, and Company Spirit.

Chick-Fil-A

Be America's Best Quick-Service Restaurant

AstraZeneca

The people of AstraZeneca are dedicated to:
- *Discovering, developing, and delivering innovative pharmaceutical solutions*
- *Enriching the lives of patients, families, communities, and other stakeholders*
- *Creating a challenging and rewarding work environment for everyone*

own plans to support the corporate strategy. The flow of the strategy from the organizational level to the unit level is called the **strategy hierarchy**. The strategy hierarchy is shown in Exhibit 1.2. Note that the firm's marketing plan is likely to precede its sales plan. This order does not imply that sales executives do not participate in the process until after the firm's marketing plan is done. Rather, marketing and sales work together to create an overall marketing strategy. Then the sales executives must create the action plans specifically for salespeople to carry out the strategy.

At the marketing level, planners have to answer the following four questions with much greater specificity than was done at the corporate level:

- What markets do we serve with what products?
- What types of relationships do we form and with whom?
- What level of investment will be required, and how will we locate and allocate the needed resources?
- What are the detailed objectives and action plans?

What Markets Do We Serve with What Products?

In certain situations, the product defines the company. Consider, for example, Xerox, which was built around xerographic technology. At other times, a natural market such as a geographic area might define a company. An example might be steel mills in Pennsylvania, located near iron ore and coal deposits needed to manufacture steel. Yet, when market conditions changed, both Xerox and the mills had to carefully consider what markets they wanted to serve and with what products. Xerox, for example, had to add digital technology to its lineup in order to compete. Steel mills had to address global competition and, in some instances, begin making other products such as fiberglass. These changes required careful consideration of potential markets.

Cisco Systems' corporate strategy flows to each functional area, such as sales, which then determines the sales strategy to support that corporate strategy. (AP Wide World Photos)

The implications of a firm's product and market choices can be dramatic. Consider IBM, Apple, and Dell. All three companies sell personal computer (PC) products, but the product and market strategies of the firms are very different. IBM ultimately chose to leave the PC market and focus on services; Apple, with products like the iPod, has become a niche player in several new electronics markets; in order to grow, Dell has discovered that it needs to add new products such as digital cameras to its lineup.

The challenge is to find a **sustainable competitive advantage**, something that gives a company an edge in the market over time. To achieve a competitive advantage, you need expertise, technology, or a patent that is difficult for others to copy. If the product is easy to copy and not patented, others will imitate it. If the advantage is based on price, the most efficient company wins. Finding a sustainable competitive advantage is perhaps the most difficult aspect of any strategic plan.

If the strategic planner creates a product-market grid like the one shown in Exhibit 1.3, there are four ways a company can grow. First, a firm can seek increased **market penetration**; that is, it can try to gain more market share with its existing products. Market penetration is often about trying to find more customers like the ones who are already buying your products. Finding new customers is an important task for salespeople, and it is

EXHIBIT 1.2

Strategy Hierarchy

An abbreviated example of how a firm's strategy might be different at different levels of the organization.

CORPORATE STRATEGY

"To be a leader in womometer technology"

MARKETING STRATEGY

"To sell womometers to space engineers and to hydraulic engineers at a premium price"

SALES STRATEGY

"To sell to NASA, Boeing, and Rockwell International using a key account structure, a consultative approach, with account executives on straight salary..."

EXHIBIT 1.3

Achieving Growth via Products and Markets

Source: Based on Igor Ansoff, *The New Corporate Strategy* (1988), John Wiley & Sons, Inc., p. 83.

MARKETS

	CURRENT MARKETS	NEW MARKETS
CURRENT	Market Penetration — HP creates "full line contracts" to encourage customers to buy all HP products	Market Development — Intel sells computer chips for use in John Deere tractors
NEW	Product Development — Dell adds consumer electronics such as cameras	Diversification — Carlson Marketing expands from selling promotional trips to promotional products, such as cups and caps

PRODUCTS

vital to the ongoing success of a firm. Hewlett-Packard (HP) is following this strategy. HP tries to focus on the markets in which it does well. Recently it spun off, closed, or sold its poorer-performing operations so it could focus on capturing market share in areas in which the company has a competitive advantage.

Second, a company can grow through **product development**, which involves creating new products in order to get more business out of the company's existing customers. Another term for this strategy is **account penetration** because it involves selling more products to the same accounts. Dell is trying to implement this strategy by adding consumer electronics that interact with computers—products such as digital cameras and DVD players that hook up to and sell alongside the company's computers.

Third, a company can try to find new markets, which is called the **market development** approach. Examples of potential new markets can include new countries or new industries in which to sell the company's existing products. An example is the computer-chipmaker Intel. Intel found a way to increase its sales by putting computer chips in John Deere tractors: Today, the same type of chips used to measure the pressure of the tires on your car are now used to measure the pressure of the tires on tractors. In the Global Sales Management feature in this chapter, the market development strategies of QuadRep and Empire Technical Group are explored.

Fourth, combining new products and new markets is called **diversification**. For example, Carlson Marketing Group began as a travel agency selling trips to companies that wanted to reward their top salespeople or favorite customers by sending them on exotic trips. Carlson then expanded into other areas, such as the market for promotional products.

However, the risks associated with diversification are far greater than with other market expansion approaches because it requires developing *both* new products and new markets. The company cannot leverage its existing relationships with its customers, and it may not be able to leverage its existing technology. Indeed, the annals of business history are littered with failed diversification attempts. But when the strategy works, it can pay off tremendously.

What Types of Relationships Do We Form and with Whom?

Companies do not operate in a vacuum—they have suppliers, customers, and competitors who operate in a network: Touch one and, like ripples in a pond, others are affected. A strategic plan should consider the network of relationships within which the company operates or wants to operate. This includes its relationships with (potential) investors, bankers, suppliers of raw materials or components, sources of personnel (like your university), government regulatory agencies, and many more. For example, with which distributors will the company attempt to form close relationships so that its products have a greater likelihood of success? What

GLOBAL SALES MANAGEMENT

Going Global to Achieve Growth

Savvy salespeople closing major deals know they must contact everyone who has a say in a sale, but what do you do when the buyer's engineer is in California, the decision maker is in Taiwan, and the final destination of your product is a PC board manufacturer in Thailand? And you don't speak Chinese or Thai?

When QuadRep (www.quadreptech.com) opened its doors in 1970, QuadRep sold International Semiconductor chips to Hewlett-Packard (HP) to one location in Palo Alto. As HP expanded beyond the Silicon Valley, so did QuadRep, locating in Washington, Oregon, and Idaho.

As president Tom McCarthy says, "In the mid-1980s, a number of our customers, like Hewlett-Packard, Apple, Seagate, and Western Digital, established manufacturing operations in Singapore. These customers, especially Apple, wanted local support for their Singapore operations. QuadRep's principals (companies like International Semiconductor that QuadRep sold for) told us that if we could not provide local support in Singapore that they would have to find a local Singapore rep, so in 1987 we opened our Singapore office, and it worked beautifully."

Coordinating international sales efforts requires cooperation and meticulous attention to detail, but QuadRep proved itself up to the task. Since then, QuadRep has followed customers across the globe, opening offices in Malaysia, China, Taiwan, Thailand, the Philippines, and Mexico. If you are carrying an iPod, for example, you are carrying electronic components supplied by QuadRep.

Empire Technical Group (www.etgsales.com) also started with U.S.-based companies. But more and more of salesperson David Rossi's customers moved manufacturing and purchasing functions to Asia. Rossi, now president, saw this trend was undermining his business model and jeopardizing his company, and he knew he had to take action.

Rossi embraced the changing manufacturing environment and changed his business model accordingly. He and several other companies formed a consortium and included Asian partners where Asia/Pacific resources were required. What started out as a means to locate suppliers of component parts that the group could not supply from its existing sources turned into an opportunity to pursue contracts to build entire assemblies as well as just parts.

Rossi and his associates now control manufacturing of complete assemblies, turning "a $3 (part) sale to a $103 sale" for a complete assembly, explains Rossi. "We've morphed into an international design and assembly house," says Rossi.

Although McCarthy and Rossi found different solutions to the challenges of international commerce, each is an example of the role that creativity, flexibility, and tenacity play in building a successful sales career when the customers' needs and even the customers' geography are a moving target.

Source: Charles Cohon, Vice President of Research of Manufacturers' Representatives Educational Research Foundation. He can be reached through his Web site, www.cohon.com.

---

customers are better served through transactional strategies and transactional channels? These are the types of questions that must be answered as part of a company's relationship strategy.

A firm's relationship with its customers is perhaps the most important aspect of its relationship strategy. In the United States today, more firms are in the business of providing services than ever before. In part, this is because sustainable competitive advantages are more likely to be gained by providing intangible resources such as expertise and relationships—things that are hard to imitate. Called the **service dominant logic**, the idea is that being in

This salesperson is providing service after the sale. This is an example of how the service-dominant logic of today's companies enables them to compete more effectively. (Comstock Complete)

business is essentially about serving the needs of others. Whether or not the company actually makes a tangible product, the real advantage lies in how the organization serves its customers' needs. Therefore, all companies, no matter what line of business they are in, should try to gain a service advantage.

Frequently, a service advantage is a function of the quality of relationships a firm has with its customers. Relationships are the vehicles by which their needs are understood—the stronger the relationship, the more that is known by both parties about both parties. The more that is known, the better able one is to serve the other. As an example, consider the fashion industry. At the retail level, products are often similar. Stores that sell to college students, for example, will have similar styles. These stores are competing for a share of the average college student's expenditures on clothing. Some students claim that they spend $500 per month on clothing. A more reasonable average figure might be $200. At $200 per month, or $2,400 per year, the average college student will spend more than $10,000 before graduating, given that the average time to graduate is now 4.5 years. Now walk into any store near campus—do they treat you like a $10,000 customer? Yet the average college student's **customer lifetime value**, or the sum of all of the purchases made over a customer's lifetime, is worth a significant amount.

What these figures illustrate is that your lifetime value to that local store is worth far more than the average single purchase. Consequently, it would make sense to build a stronger relationship with its customers than most stores try to create. Salespeople at the Men's Wearhouse understand this: They treat customers with far greater personal care, knowing that good service today means repeat sales tomorrow. Each customer gets his or her own salesperson, who then works to manage the relationship. For example, the salesperson maintains a file on the customer's tastes and calls him when new styles he might like are in stock.

Customer Relationship Management (CRM) is the process of identifying and grouping customers in order to develop an appropriate relationship strategy so that the organization can acquire, retain, and grow the business. A firm's sales and marketing teams are responsible for customer relationship management. **Customer acquisition strategies**, or plans to obtain new customers, can include marketing activities such as telephone prospecting and attending trade shows to identify potential customers. **Customer retention strategies**, or plans designed to keep customers, might include making quarterly visits to current customers or inviting them to technology shows to see the firm's newest products. **Growth strategies** are plans that are designed to increase sales to the same customers. (Recall the earlier discussion on account penetration.) These strategies might include offering special discounts to customers when they make larger purchases.

What Level of Investment Will Be Required, and How Will We Allocate the Needed Resources?

Another important aspect of strategic planning involves finding the capital, or resources, necessary to accomplish the firm's plan. This includes money, of course, but it can also take the form of human and social capital. **Human capital** refers to the people that make up an organization. For example, a firm that has more highly skilled employees will have a greater degree of human capital. **Social capital**, or the ties that the firm has with others, can also be drawn upon as a resource. At its simplest, social capital is who owes you a favor or who can be asked a favor. An historic example dating from the early eighties concerns Chrysler. At one point, the firm was within days of declaring bankruptcy when David Kearns, the CEO of Xerox Corporation, called Lee Iacocca, the CEO of Chrysler. Kearns asked Iacocca how many cars needed to be sold for the company to stay afloat—Chrysler, after all, was a good Xerox customer. Iacocca told him, and he responded by placing an order for that many. The social capital between the two firms saved Chrysler long enough for other financing to be put into place and for them to return the firm to solid footing.

The question is not just one of sourcing capital but also allocating it. For example, Hewlett-Packard's (HP) CEO Mark Hurd has trimmed personnel and shed various components of HP's business in his attempts to remake the company. His decisions involve focusing the company's limited resources where they will have the greatest impact but, at the same time, starving or eliminating less productive areas so that they won't drain resources needed for more productive activities.

For the sales executive, human capital decisions include determining how many salespeople the firm needs, what skills and experience they must have, and what training they require. Other decisions might include whether to hire telephone prospectors or to outsource that activity, decide who handles customer service (a sales rep or a customer service rep), and so forth.

What Are the Detailed Objectives and Action Plans?

Review again the mission statements in Exhibit 1.1. What is NCR's business? Coca-Cola's? IBM's? Notice that these mission statements do not answer questions about what products the company will produce or markets they will serve. Nor do the statements answer questions about the firm's objectives and plans. Again, it is at the marketing and sales levels in the strategy hierarchy that these objectives and plans become more specific. For example, a strategic plan might include such objectives as achieving a market share of 10 percent by the end of the year, or sales of $500 million in the firm's fourth quarter.

One set of criteria for establishing objectives is the **SMART** format. According to the SMART format, the objectives of firms need to be:

- **S**pecific
- **M**easurable
- **A**chievable, yet challenging
- **R**ealistic
- **T**ime-based

For example, an objective to simply "increase market share" is not *specific* enough. As a manager, you need to ask yourself, by how much do we need to increase market share? If the objective is to increase customer loyalty, you need a way to *measure* customer loyalty, perhaps by recording the number of repeat purchases customers make. If the objective is to double market share, you need to ask yourself whether such an ambitious goal is *achievable* or even *realistic*. Finally, the objective needs to be *time-based*. When will it be met? In the next month, year, or decade?

SMART objectives can motivate managers and salespeople alike. These objectives can also be used to hold managers accountable. After all, without deadlines and other specifics, managers might claim they've achieved the firm's objectives when in fact they have not. **Milestones**, or important short-term objectives, can help mark the company's progress toward achieving its objectives. Milestones can be used to also determine when the plan is off course so that adjustments can be made. For example, a company might set a goal to become the leader in a market, even though it's currently in fifth place. The company's milestones might include taking over the third spot in the market this year, moving up to second spot the year after, and so forth. The ultimate goal is still to be first, but milestones help the company determine whether it is on track to reach that ultimate goal.

Along with setting objectives, a good strategic plan has detailed action plans, or steps, that will be taken in order to accomplish those objectives. These action plans include who will undertake each activity, when that activity will occur, and so forth. It is at this point that the firm's strategy begins to involve salespeople and the sales process.

> ### S SELF-ASSESSMENT LIBRARY
>
> Every successful businessperson sets goals for her or his own performance. What are yours for this class? Go to http://www.prenhall.com/sal/ and log in using the access code that came with your book. Then click on:
>
> Assessments
>   I. What About Me
>   C. Motivation Insights
>   5. What Are My Course Performance Goals?
>
> As you complete the instrument, you can see that there are different potential motivators for students. The overall score will give you an indication of your overall motivation to achieve in this course, but you should also consider how you answered individual questions.

Selling Approaches

A recent study of over 1,500 sales executives found that more than half, or 55 percent, have no formal sales process or sales model in their organization.[7] This finding is disturbing because it means that a lot of companies just throw salespeople out into the field and hope they will figure out how to perform their jobs. Moreover, how can sales supervisors manage salespeople if there is no standard approach? How can one rep's performance be compared to that of another? Of course, a manager can simply look at sales levels and tell if one rep is doing better than another. But how would that manager help either rep improve?

A company should have a standard sales method. However, because customers make buying decisions differently, there will obviously be variations in the selling techniques successful salespeople use. That said, most markets are comprised of buyers who tend to make decisions in similar ways. Buyers can be grouped by how they make decisions, and formal sales processes can be designed for each group.

Research shows that there are four basic models of selling: transactional, problem solving or consultative, affiliative, and enterprise selling. The first method, **transactional selling**, is designed to get the sale over with as quickly and as easily as possible. The key to success is making as many calls as possible to as many people as possible; little thought is given to the lifetime value of customers. An example might be life insurance salespeople who have only one product to sell—once a buyer has bought it there is nothing else to sell so the salesperson moves on. Simple products also tend to be sold this way: The buyer is well aware of her options and can make a decision without a lot of help.

Affiliative selling is based on the friendship between the salesperson and the individual buyer. Tupperware and Premier Jewelry parties rely heavily on affiliative selling. Friendships are also an important component of business-to-business selling. For example, if all products a buyer is considering are the same, but post-sales service is critical, the buyer will be inclined to purchase products sold by a friend who can be counted upon. An example is heavy mining equipment, for which there are only a few manufacturers. Because there are only a few manufacturers, the distributors of the equipment all carry a similar lineup of machines. But if a machine goes down, a mine might come to a halt, costing the buyer thousands of dollars a day. In such a situation, trust is likely to be more important than product specs, so a buyer will tend to purchase machinery from a trustworthy friend.

Consultative selling involves identifying and solving a client's problems; for this reason, it is also called **needs-satisfaction selling** or **problem/solution selling**. The process typically involves asking prospective clients a number of questions in order to determine their needs and then presenting solutions to those needs.

Enterprise selling is a business-to-business (B2B) concept that reflects, at its best, a strategic partnership between the buying and selling organizations. It is called enterprise selling because it is based on not only person-to-person relationships but on company-to-company relationships. An account manager (salesperson) initially captures, maintains, and grows a customer's business. However, the account manager's firm knows it takes an entire enterprise to satisfy the customer. Moreover, the customer is not just one person but an entire company (or at least a large portion of it). When engaged in enterprise selling, a salesperson will, at times, utilize affiliative sell-

Most business-to-business salespeople use some form of consultative selling, which involves helping buyers understand what they need and then providing them with the solutions that solve those needs. (Photos.com)

ing, transactional selling, and consultative selling all within an enterprise-level strategy. The salesperson's choice of selling model in this case depends on how the buyer needs to buy at that time. For example, a buyer who is well informed and knows exactly what she wants does not want to waste time with a consultative approach; a transactional approach will work just fine. Or the buyer might work in an organization that has an enterprise-level relationship with the vendor. Regardless of the model of selling, there is a basic structure to a sales call. In the next section, we will review that structure and identify how it varies for each selling model.

The Selling Process

There are eight steps to the sales process, as illustrated in Exhibit 1.4. These steps are prospecting, the pre-approach, approach, needs identification, presentation, handling objections, closing, and implementation/follow-up. Note that at times these steps will

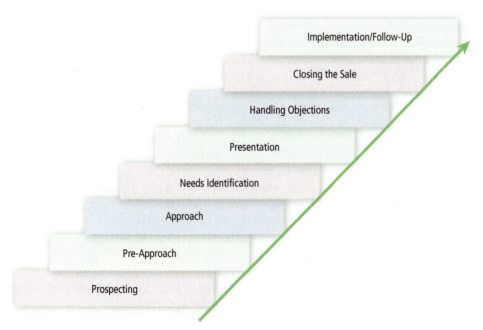

Prospecting

Pre-Approach

Approach

Needs Identification

Presentation

Handling Objections

Closing the Sale

Implementation/Follow-Up

EXHIBIT 1.4

Eight Steps in the Selling Process

occur sequentially, one after the other. In other situations, however, salespeople might find that the steps occur in a different order, they repeat, or they are skipped. We'll discuss how this works when we discuss each step in more detail.

Prospecting

Prospecting involves identifying potential customers for a particular product or service. A **prospect** is a MAD buyer, someone with the **M**oney to spend, the **A**uthority to buy what you are selling, and the **D**esire to buy it. (Although the buyer's desire might not be specifically for *your* product, at least she *has* a desire.) The process of finding prospects involves several steps. The first step is to identify a **lead**, or someone who appears to have the characteristics of a prospect. That is, the person *appears* to have a need (desire), money, and authority. The salesperson must still qualify the lead—determine that the person has the money, authority, and desire to purchase, which happens later.

Pre-Approach

During the pre-approach stage, the salesperson tries to learn everything he can about the account. Perhaps using contact management software, the account's history with the firm can be explored and the salesperson can tell what the customer needs. Or, using the internet, the salesperson can examine the account's financial strength, future strategies, and the like. The salesperson might also try to find out what can be learned about the industry in which the account operates.

Because the pre-approach stage can take a significant amount of time, in the prospecting stage a salesperson might do little if any pre-approach planning. That's because the needed information is held by the buyer (versus, say, a database). Later in the process, pre-approach planning becomes more necessary to ensure that progress is made toward an eventual sale. Note that a well-prepared salesperson is more likely to be trusted. Preparation signals that the salesperson is knowledgeable, competent, and cares about the customer.

Approach

The approach step can be difficult because at this stage the salesperson must ask the buyer to commit to a meeting without really knowing what she needs or wants. To obtain this commitment, the salesperson must make an opening statement that gets the buyer's attention. A good opening statement causes the buyer to focus on the salesperson, dropping all other activities or thoughts. For example, a salesperson might say something like, "Hi, my name is Dave from BPT Partners, and our firm is helping companies increase sales by upwards of 20 percent. May I have a few minutes to explore whether BPT could do that for you?" This statement is a good one because the seller is focusing on the potential of increasing sales. Alternatively, if the seller had said, "Hi, my name is Dave, and I'd like to sell you CRM software," the focus is entirely on the seller's goal. This statement is not likely to get that salesperson anywhere.

How does the approach differ when the salesperson and buyer are meeting for the third or fourth time? A good opening statement is still needed. In other words, you still need a good reason, or opening statement, to get a time commitment from your customer. (The thirtieth sales call can probably begin with more of a social greeting.)

Needs Identification

The next step is the needs identification step, the step in which the salesperson confirms that the prospect has money, authority, and desire to purchase. The needs-identification step is comprised of three important elements. The first element is the use of SPIN®, New Base®, or some other questioning technique in order to figure out the customer's needs. The following is a series of questions that might be asked using the SPIN questioning technique:

SELLER (SITUATION QUESTION):	How far do you have to go to make copies?
BUYER:	*It is about a 10 minute drive.*
SELLER (PROBLEM QUESTION):	Do you ever encounter problems because you are gone from the office so long?
BUYER:	*Yes, sometimes customers call and I'm not there to answer.*
SELLER (IMPLICATION QUESTION):	Have you ever lost a customer because you weren't there when they called?
BUYER:	*Yes, I once lost a pretty good account that way.*
SELLER (NEEDS-PAYOFF QUESTION):	So a copier in your office, would that eliminate that problem?
BUYER:	*Yes, I really need to get one for my office.*

The questioning process can take quite a while in a complex, custom sales situation. This is the situation Bell Helicopter salespeople face when they are selling helicopters. Or, the questioning process can take just a few minutes when a simple product is being sold.

The second element is the identification of the decision process elements facing the customer (authority to purchase). The third is gaining pre-commitment. A **pre-commitment** is an agreement that all of the customer's needs have been identified, a budget has been identified, and the decision process is known. In other words, the pre-commitment sets the "rules" for the sale and confirms that the buyer is MAD (has money, authority, and desire). In a transactional sale, there might be no needs-identification portion to the sales call. In many instances, the buyer already understands what is needed, or the needs are so similar across customers that the salesperson can simply focus on the presentation.

Qualifying buyers for MAD is important. Failing to do so can have many negative consequences. The most obvious consequence is that the salesperson wastes time with someone who might like the product but isn't allowed to make that decision. Sri-IIST is a business that scans documents for electronic indexing. Byron Williams, salesperson for Sri-IIST, had just such an experience. "I spent several hours with the office administrator of a law firm, even doing several sample jobs at no cost, only to find out the decision had to be made by the managing partner. I had to start over with her, so it took twice as long to sell this account as it should have." Williams notes that he could have made another sale somewhere else, too, had he started with the managing partner.

Presentation

During the presentation, the salesperson describes the product and how it meets the buyer's needs. Now the salesperson is playing by the rules: presenting how those needs can be met and providing the right information to the right people so a decision can be made. A sophisticated product such as a Cessna Citation executive jet has many features—so many, in fact, a salesperson could put the buyer to sleep explaining everything the plane does. Thus, during the presentation, the seller focuses on only those features that buyer needs.

One approach to presentations is to string together a series of **FEBAs**, or statements of Feature, Evidence, Benefit, and Agreement. Using this approach, the salesperson begins with a characteristic of the product or feature. For example, a pharmaceutical salesperson might say something like, "Placron reduces cholesterol to safe levels." Then evidence is provided: "As you can see in this clinical study, the reduction has been well under 200 in about 85 percent of all patients who did not respond to competitive drugs." Note that the evidence is written or visual. Whenever possible, the salesperson should offer tangible evidence that is credible. (A clinical study is usually completed by an objective third party and is published in a journal or as a monograph. It is thus both credible and tangible.) The salesperson then ties that feature back to the need mentioned by the customer; in this case, "So as you noted, you would have fewer patients with difficulty lowering their cholesterol." Describing how a feature satisfies a need is a **benefit**. Finally, the salesperson asks the customer if the product meets the need, gaining agreement: "Is this the type of cholesterol-reducing program you are looking for?"

One advantage of the FEBA approach is that the potential buyer participates in the process; the presentation is not just one-sided. Furthermore, the salesperson is checking to ensure the customer agrees that the product will meet her needs. This reduces the likelihood of her raising objections, which we discuss next.

Handling Objections

Objections are reasons a buyer offers to not buy your product. They can occur anytime during the sales call, not necessarily during or immediately after the presentation. For example, a salesperson might hear an objection as soon as introductions are made: "You are with what company? Oh, you guys are terrible—I hate your products!"

Most objections, though, come near the end of the sales call. Even with good needs-identification and strong FEBA statements, customers sometimes realize they left out a need earlier, they conclude that the product won't meet their needs, they misunderstand something the seller says, or they simply do not want to buy the product at the present time. No matter the reason behind the objection, the salesperson should probe to determine what lies at the root of the concern and then seek to resolve it. In some instances, the concern is legitimate; only when the product's other benefits outweigh the concern should the buyer go ahead and make the purchase.

Closing the Sale

A salesperson asks the buyer for the sale during the **close**, but that's not the only time the salesperson asks for commitment. When a salesperson asks for an appointment, permission to make a presentation, or some other commitment, the request is a form of closing.

Closing the sale should be a natural part of the selling process and no surprise to the buyer. At this point, the buyer has already said several times that the features of the product meet the stated needs, a budget has already been discussed, and an implementation schedule for the product's delivery has been developed. When the seller asks for the order, the asking should be a logical conclusion of the selling/buying process.

In addition to asking for the order, though, a good close accomplishes several other objectives. The decision should be reinforced by the seller and the implementation schedule confirmed. In this way, the buyer leaves the meeting feeling secure in her decision and aware of what will happen next. In addition, a good salesperson always thanks the buyer for the business and asks for a referral.

If the salesperson reaches the close of the sales call but is turned down, a "thank you" is still appropriate. Most experienced salespeople are disappointed with a rejection, but they have learned not to take it personally. One way to view such a situation is that the buyer is not saying, "No, not ever," but rather, "No, not now." Like an athlete who lost a game but has the rest of the season, these salespeople know that there will be more decisions made by that buyer, so it is important to treat the buyer with respect and lay the groundwork for future sales.

Implementation/Follow-Up

Following the close and assuming a sale has been made, the customer has to accept the delivery of the product. The salesperson's job may then be to ensure that the customer has a good experience with the product. This responsibility might include training the buyer on how the product works, how to obtain service, and any policies or procedures of which the buyer should be aware.

Follow-up does not stop with the initial training, however. Richard Langlotz of Konica-Minolta Business Systems realized that he could achieve his quota by simply selling current customers a new system. Therefore, he instituted a practice of regular follow-up to ensure that the products were still meeting customers' needs, there were no service or billing problems, and everything was going smoothly. His regular follow-up set him apart from competitors who would sell but then forget customers. As word of his service spread, he found it easier to sell to new clients, too.

The Selling Process versus the Selling Approach

The selling process is a constant cycle of prospecting, presenting, and closing. Whether the model is transactional, consultative, affiliative, or enterprise, the basic process is similar. As we explained, in a transactional situation, little time is spent on needs identification. You might simply have to ask customers which products they need and how many of them. The emphasis in the selling process is on the presentation and a key to being successful is to make as many presentations as possible.

Similarly, affiliative selling may not require a long needs identification process. Yet, there is a relationship-building process that is ongoing, within which the selling process takes place. More emphasis is given to follow-up because it is during this step that the relationship with the customer is built. Consultative selling emphasizes the needs-identification stage. The complexity of the buyer's situation will make it necessary for the salesperson to spend a great deal of time, relatively speaking, on understanding the situation and needs. With enterprise selling, the seller will engage in consultative, affiliative, and transactional selling at different times and with different products. The result is that the emphasis shifts, depending on the situation within the account.

These different models and their variations on the process of selling create many challenges for sales leaders. These executives and managers have a number of responsibilities in order to create, prepare, and lead an effective sales force. In the next section, those responsibilities are introduced, many of which merit a full chapter later in the book.

Sales Leaders

There are different levels of sales managers. Near the bottom of the organizational chart are field sales force managers who directly manage the firm's salespeople and may even have some customers to handle. (Most experts agree that sales managers should only manage, not sell.) At the top of the organizational chart are sales executives who lead the company's sales efforts, sometimes across several different sales divisions who may sell different product lines or call on different markets. A sales executive might also be responsible for choosing the company's distributors, deciding how the firm's products are sold on the Web site, and making other broad sales-related decisions. How the responsibilities of a sales leader are divided up and organized can vary by the size of the organization, the industry in which it operates, or the scope of the market. The levels in the organization can include local, regional, or other operating units. For example, Exhibit 1.5 describes the organizational charts of two sales organizations, thereby illustrating how companies can vary. Konica-Minolta has several levels of

managers, whereas Elk really only has two. For our purposes of understanding the roles and responsibilities of sales managers and leaders, we focus on the two ends of the spectrum, beginning with those tasks and responsibilities typically carried out by a sales executive.

The Sales Executive

The first responsibility of the sales executive is to lead the sales force in achieving sales goals. In doing so, the sales executive also sets the policies the firm's sales managers and salespeople must follow. In general, though, sales executives complete four activities—they plan, organize, implement, and monitor.

PLANNING We've already discussed how sales executives are involved in the overall strategic planning process. However, they are also responsible for making specific sales plans. Basically, the sales executive must take the company's strategic plan and devise an appropriate sales plan to meet the objectives set forth in the strategy.

The sales plan might include **quotas**, or minimum levels of acceptable performance. For example, the executive might assign a quota directly to each salesperson. More likely, though, the executive will assign regional, or divisional, quotas and allow the sales managers in those areas to set quotas for the individual salespeople they supervise.

The executive will also outline a general sales strategy to achieve those objectives. These general strategies will specify the sales approach—transactional, affiliative, consultative, or enterprise—that will be used in each market. For example, the sales executive might allocate how much effort will be dedicated to any particular product or market. Product positioning strategies, such as the key features emphasized for each product, will be determined by the firm's marketing strategy. However, the sales executive must translate that strategy into a sales strategy. This translation might involve creating guidelines about which customers to call and how to open sales calls and structure presentations.

ORGANIZING Organizing involves determining what type of sales force will be utilized. (The types of sales positions are detailed in Chapter 2.) For example, the executive might determine that one product should be the responsibility of a field sales force whereas another product should be sold by telemarketing. Organizing also includes creating policies and strategies regarding how salespeople should be hired and trained. Recruiting and selecting the right people for the different sales positions is also critical to a company's success. (We will discuss all of these sales management aspects in upcoming chapters.)

IMPLEMENTING Rolling out the plan to the sales force is a key activity for the sales executive. The plan must be communicated in such a way that sales managers and salespeople can implement it without constant supervision by the executive. Implementation also means creating the right sales environment or culture. The sales executive is responsible for making sure that salespeople operate ethically and engage in selling practices consistent with the company's mission and desired image. Creating the right culture is a delicate balance. For example, if you pressure salespeople to close a deal at any cost, they are more likely to use unethical and possibly illegal methods. At the same time, however, sales targets have to be met or the company suffers. The Ethics in Sales Management feature in this chapter explores the delicate balance between the two.

 ## ETHICS IN SALES MANAGEMENT

Maintaining NCR's Ethical Sales Culture

Quick! Name the most and the least honest professions. Some would say that the most honest professionals are preachers and professors whereas the least honest professionals are politicians and salespeople. Because people often expect salespeople to be dishonest, how does a company create a sales culture that dispels such a notion?

NCR, originally known as National Cash Register, is one of the pioneers in ethical selling. For example, NCR claims to be the first company to have developed a standard sales process as early as the 1880s. Today, NCR still has a strong sales culture. The company sets high performance standards for its salespeople, holds them in high esteem, *and* demands that each of them behave ethically. These expectations for high performance and high ethics are laid out during a salesperson's first job interview with NCR. They continue through training and management.

According to Rick Makos, president of NCR-Canada, "Everyone in our organization understands that NCR and its people can only thrive if we sell. Everyone contributes to the selling process in some way. But we don't put salespeople ahead of customers. We also recognize that selling only works when everything is right for the customer—when we deliver value."

Over the course of 120-plus years, NCR has proven that high sales performance doesn't require shortcuts, double dealing, manipulation, or high pressure tactics. Makos believes training has a lot to do with it: "NCR has a strong culture of training all of our people on the industries they sell into, and to be the best on the solutions we sell and implement." High-performance selling and high ethics can peacefully coexist; indeed, both can thrive in the right sales culture.

Choosing a compensation method for salespeople is critical when it comes to implementing a sales plan. The balance between a salesperson's commission and salary, for example, can support or destroy a sales culture. Why? Because salespeople are generally very attuned to how they are being paid. As a result, reaching the proper compensation balance can speak far louder than any sales executive's memos or exhortations at meetings.

MONITORING Sales executives, of course, monitor sales levels, but they also are responsible for monitoring other aspects of the firm, such as customer satisfaction levels. Monitoring customer satisfaction levels can provide executives with insight about whether the right sales methods are being followed. Other aspects sales executives monitor include how salespeople are recruited, selected, and trained.

When monitoring systems indicate problems exist or are arising, the sales executive must then take corrective action. For example, if sales quotas aren't being met, an executive might need to determine whether the firm's product(s) is competitive or its salespeople are unprepared. If the latter is the case, then more training may be the answer. Or, if the problem lies in one region and nowhere else, the executive might find it necessary to replace a regional manager. These and other corrective actions have to be taken swiftly or sales and the company's reputation may suffer.

The Field Sales Manager

Field sales managers are first-line managers to whom the firm's salespeople report. The primary responsibility, though, for all sales managers is to achieve a sales quota. The sales manager achieves that sales quota by implementing the plans, policies, and procedures set forth by the sales executive. Thus, the executive determines the general profile of the salesperson to be hired, whereas the field sales manager conducts the actual interviews and makes the final hiring decision. Or the executive creates a compensation plan whereas the field sales manager makes specific salary recommendations for each salesperson. Similarly, the executive sets overall sales targets, and the sales manager allocates a sales quota to each salesperson.

Sales managers are also responsible for either directly training salespeople or ensuring they get training. For example, by traveling with the salesperson in the field, observing her in action, and providing coaching, the sales manager can evaluate how she's doing and offer suggestions for improvement. The sales manager must also understand what motivates each salesperson. Many people pursue sales careers because the earnings can be lucrative. But more people pursue sales careers for other reasons: the desire to help others, to work independently, or compete with other salespeople.[8] It's the sales manager's job to adapt, or frame, the firm's policies in a way that motivates each individual salesperson yet creates the culture sought by the sales executive.

The sales manager also plans, organizes, implements, and monitors, but only for her particular sales team. As illustrated in Exhibit 1.6, the sales manager carries out similar tasks under the guidelines established by the sales executive.

EXHIBIT 1.6

Examples of a Sales Executive & Sales Manager's Duties

Activity	Sales Executive	Sales Manager
Plan	Set overall sales targets for each product	Set quotas for each salesperson for each product
Organize	Decide what type of people to hire for sales positions	Interview and hire specific people for sales positions
Implement	Determine the compensation plan	Identify each person's motivators and find ways to reward good performance for each person
Monitor	Track sales by region; take corrective action such as additional training if sales are too low	Observe each salesperson's actions in the field and offer suggestions for their improvement

Both sales managers and sales executives rely on technology to keep them informed as to what is happening in the field. Technology can be used to monitor a salesperson performance, but it can also be used to identify trends in the marketplace. These trends can then be incorporated into plans. Technology is also an important factor in increasing sales performance while managing costs. We focus on technology in Chapter 6, although technology is so ubiquitous in the management of salespeople that the topic permeates the rest of the book.

Summary

Sales managers serve a vital position in most companies, given the importance of the sales function to a company's success. Sales is a growing profession, and the people in it are highly compensated, with great prospects for the future.

Sales leaders participate in the creation of a firm's strategy. The strategy starts with developing the firm's objectives. The process usually begins with the formulation of a mission statement that describes the firm's overall reason for being. The hierarchy of strategy begins with the corporate strategy, from which a marketing strategy and a sales strategy flow.

A marketing strategy determines what products are sold to which customers and at what price level. These decisions are then used to create a sales strategy. Companies seek to grow through one or more strategic approaches: market development, market penetration, product development, and account penetration. The firm's salespeople must then develop customer relationship strategies in order to maximize the customer lifetime value of the firm's clients.

Salespeople take one of four selling approaches: a transactional selling approach, an affiliative selling approach, a consultative or needs-satisfaction selling approach, or an enterprise selling approach. Irrespective of the approach, the selling process generally follows eight steps; however, the relative length or importance of each step varies depending on which approach is used.

Key Terms

account penetration   8
affiliative selling   12
benefit   16
close   16
consultative selling   13
customer acquisition strategies   10
customer lifetime value   10
Customer Relationship Management (CRM)   10
customer retention strategies   10
diversification   8
enterprise selling   13
FEBAs   15
growth strategies   10
human capital   10
lead   13
market development   8
market penetration   7
milestones   11

mission   5
mission statement   5
needs-satisfaction selling   13
objections   16
pre-commitment   15
problem/solution selling   13
product development   8
prospect   14
prospecting   14
quotas   18
sales management   5
service dominant logic   9
SMART   11
social capital   10
strategy   5
strategy hierarchy   6
sustainable competitive advantage   7
transactional selling   12

Questions and Problems

1. In this chapter, we calculated the average lifetime value of a college student to a clothing store. Why is the lifetime only 4.5 years? Don't you expect to live longer than that?
2. Think about your past buying experiences, especially your purchases of expensive clothing such as suits, prom dresses, and the like. How were you treated? Could you tell if your sales clerks worked on commission? Would you expect someone working on commission to treat you differently than the store owner or someone who received only a base salary?
3. Estimate your lifetime value to Starbucks (if you never visit Starbucks, then pick a fast-food restaurant that you do visit). Then estimate your lifetime value as a car owner. Is the concept of lifetime value of equal importance to your car dealer as it is to Starbucks? What is the growth strategy of both?
4. How might the process vary for selling the following products?
   a. Large specialty computers, such as active data warehouses, that cost millions of dollars
   b. Copiers that cost $5,000
   c. Campbell's Soup sales to a grocery chain
   d. PVC pipe fittings sold to a plumbing distributor
5. Examine the mission statements in the exhibit in the chapter. Pick the best and the worst ones. Then go to the Web site of your school and find your school's mission statement. Assess your school's mission statement and compare it to the best and worst statements in the exhibit.
6. What does a "service dominant logic" mean to salespeople? Why would that concept be important to a salesperson or a sales organization?
7. "Nothing happens until a salesperson sells something." This statement has been around for decades. What does it mean? How does it relate to the strategy hierarchy?
8. "I want to be the best salesperson this company has ever had." Is that a SMART goal? If not, rewrite that statement into the SMART format.
9. Write down your goals for this semester's classes, using the SMART format.

Role Play

T&G Supply

You are about to graduate and are interviewing for jobs. You come across an opportunity to sell for T&G Supply, a company that serves manufacturers by providing maintenance, repair, and operations items. These items include janitorial products, hardware products to fix machines (like nuts, bolts, and the like), and other products commonly found in a maintenance shed. Another opportunity to sell is with Columbia Leasing, a car rental and leasing company. Your job would be to visit companies and convince them to sign a corporate contract as their exclusive car rental or vehicle leasing company.

Assignment

Break into pairs, with each student picking one company. You are the sales manager for that company. Take a moment and think about issues that reflect a service dominant logic in each situation. Then, using the other concepts discussed in the chapter, identify three characteristics that, as a sales manager, you would want each new salesperson to have. Then take turns interviewing your partner for a sales position.

Caselet 1.1: Killebrew Manufacturing

When Harry Killebrew was killed in a small plane crash, his widow, Francine, took over the company. A maker of plastic patio products (chairs, tables, etc.), the company had provided the Killebrews with a comfortable living. But its annual growth rate was only about 5 percent for the past ten years. With the Killebrew's three children now grown and entering the company, Francine was worried that the company needed to grow in order to provide a good living for all three children.

To try to fuel the growth of the company, Francine authorized a 10 percent introductory discount that salespeople could use to gain new accounts. That put Killebrew's prices at the same level as their biggest competitor. The quality of Killebrew's products, though, is much better. The idea was that stores would see the better quality and want to enter into long-term contracts with the company. The problem was that few of the new accounts were reordering.

Francine wondered if salespeople were too quick to sell price and not sell quality. If so, she knew that customers wouldn't see the quality; it had to be demonstrated and sold. So what sales process or approach should she consider?

Caselet 1.2: Morton's Ice House

Morton's Ice House began as a grill and microbrewery near the University of Georgia in Athens, Georgia, in 2004. In two years' time, the company opened two locations in Athens as well as a location in Clemson, South Carolina. Sherry Morton, the founder of the company, then hired Trey Denton to sell franchises in other college towns. Trey, after a successful career selling Subway franchises, sold 12 franchises in the company's third year.

Sherry thought that was a good first year, but her goal was to have 200 franchises in the next two years. So she hired five more salespeople and asked Trey to manage them. She would then do franchisee training, franchisee support, and corporate marketing. Quickly a number of problems arose: Salespeople were calling on the same prospects, which led to confusion. By contrast, other prospects were not getting called upon even after requesting information from Morton's. After six months, the sales staff had sold a total of 22 franchises. Worse, two of the salespeople quit, and 10 franchisees wanted out of their contracts, saying they had been misled as to what the company offered.

At this point, it was pretty clear that there were problems. Why? What should Sherry do?

References

1. "Talent Shortage Survey: 2007 Global Results," Manpower.
2. Dwyer, Robert F., and John F. Tanner, Jr. (2005). *Business Marketing: Connecting Strategy, Relationships, and Learning,* 3rd ed. Burr Ridge, IL: McGraw-Hill.
3. U.S. Department of Labor, Bureau of Labor Statistics, Occupational Outlook Handbook, http://www.bls.gov/oco/ocos020.htm, last modified Aug. 4, 2006. Data are from 2004.
4. Ibid.
5. Marchetti, Michele (2006). "Moving on Up," *Sales & Marketing Management,* 158(1), 24.
6. Ziyal, Leyla (1995). "Why the Best Salesperson is Not the Best Sales Manager," *Journal of Managerial Psychology,* 10(4), 9–20.
7. Dickie, Jim, and Barry Trailer (2006). "The Impact of CRM and Sales Process: Monetizing the Value of Sales Effectiveness," CSO Insights.
8. Tanner, John F. Jr., and George W. Dudley (2003). "International Differences: Examining Two Assumptions About Selling," in *Advances in Marketing*, William J. Kehoe and Linda K. Whitten, eds., *Society for Marketing Advances,* 236–239.

2

THE SALES FUNCTION AND MULTI-SALES CHANNELS

LEARNING OBJECTIVES

After completing this chapter, you should be able to:

- Explain what the sales function consists of and how salespeople affect a firm's supply chain.
- Identify the various channels in which the sales function can be carried out.
- Explain how effective sales management efforts can align a firm's sales strategy in a multi-channel environment.

How companies sell their products and services in the marketplace—via the Internet, direct mail, retail stores, distributors, telemarketing, field salespeople, or some combination of all of these—is one of the most important decisions a firm will make. In most situations, choosing a sales force will be the most expensive option. Consequently, it is important that when a sales force is chosen, it is managed well.

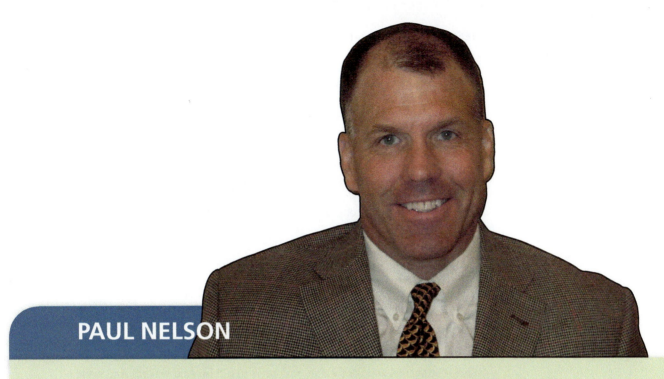

PAUL NELSON

SALES MANAGER, IBM

Paul Nelson, a sales manager at IBM, says, "The most important characteristic to have as a sales representative is the understanding of sales and how to create value for the customer and company in a win-win situation." Creating value for both the customer and IBM is often about adapting the company's strategy to the customer's situation. Nelson explains, "IBM has a competitive edge because of both the quality and the breadth of its products and services as well as an approach that adds tangible business value to its customers."

IBM accomplishes its marketing tactics by educating its salespeople about the competitive environment of the industry in which the company operates, involving customers in product development, pricing its products appropriately, and gathering business intelligence that affords the company a competitive advantage in the marketplace. This competitive advantage leads to key strategic alliances that benefit IBM and the customer by positioning the firm for long-term success.

IBM employs a series of channels to reach its market. The company uses a direct sales force, a Web channel, and two telesales channels. One telesales channel sells one-time deals to customers who call while the other is a tele-relationship channel, meaning each salesperson manages one to four large accounts. In addition, the firm has a "business partner" channel and a systems integrator channel, both of which work with other companies to provide joint solutions to IBM customers. IBM manages the relationships between the six different channels by using a segmentation strategy. The company's sales organization divides customers into groups based on similarities and then matches the segments to the right channels. IBM salespeople then apply the appropriate skills, resources, and technologies to customers in each.

"Having all of these different sales channels could result in conflict," notes Nelson, but he says that IBM avoids conflicts between the channels by sales planning so everyone knows whose accounts are whose, compensating the salespeople selling in the different channels fairly and training them so that customers are treated appropriately no matter what channel they are placed in. For example, to help employees make good decisions with regard to its business partner channel, IBM implemented a business partner "charter." This document specifies what each channel partner's role is, whether the partner is a division of IBM or one of IBM's distributors.

Nelson believes it is imperative that a sales organization thoroughly understands the strengths and weaknesses of each channel. The firm's sales managers should also understand what motivates their salespeople and know the right channels in which to sell to customers. This is where Nelson's experience as a salesperson and as a manager comes into play.

"Someone at corporate will come up with a strategy for IBM. I've got to figure out how to make that work for my customers and for my salespeople. No strategy fits all situations perfectly, but when I do my job well, I have happy customers and motivated employees, and that's a wonderful feeling."

(Meghan Derrick contributed to this profile.) ■

The Sales Function

When Herbert Ruppman woke up one cloudy morning, he quickly grabbed a pencil and some paper and started scribbling madly. His wife sleepily asked what was wrong, and he quickly replied that he had seen a vision in his sleep, a vision for a new breakfast food. A wonderfully healthy and tasty concoction, he and his wife made hundreds of pounds of the breakfast cereal and then waited for orders to roll in. And waited. And waited.

Of course, orders just don't roll in. Contrary to what the author Henry David Thoreau said, no matter how good of a mousetrap you invent, customers won't beat a path to your door to get it. Someone, in some way, must first go sell the mousetrap to them. Henry Kellogg knew this. Kellogg was a great salesperson, as he recognized what people wanted and found many ways to show and convince them that he had it; as a result, the Kellogg's brand name is familiar around much of the world.

The sales function includes locating potential buyers, persuading them, and consummating the transaction. Not to be confused with the selling process, the sales function can be undertaken by salespeople but can also be carried out in other ways. For example, a company might run advertisements to attract customers to its Web site where they can purchase its products. The firm's service department might then take care of any post-sales issues these customers have. In all likelihood, however, a firm's sales force will be responsible for providing market information to the firm's strategic planners by capturing and sharing information about potential customers, as well as information about competitors. Other tasks the sales force is likely to be responsible for include creating the sales forecasts used to schedule the firm's manufacturing, inventory, and shipping functions. These responsibilities indicate the salesperson's key role in the supply chain.

Kellogg's brand of cereals is well known, in part, because Henry Kellogg, the firm's founder, was an outstanding salesperson. (Bill Freeman/Photo Edit, all rights reserved)

The **supply chain**, as illustrated in Exhibit 2.1, is the complete process of events and people needed to bring a company's product to the customer. Most students initially think that salespeople only push products forward into the supply chain. But salespeople can also play an important role in managing the supply chain itself. This role can be passive, as is the case when a salesperson turns in a sales forecast. A **sales forecast** is simply what the salesperson expects to sell in a particular period of time. Other employees in the supply chain then use that information to determine what needs to be ordered and delivered to customers. In this case, the sales forecast influences what happens in the supply chain, but the salesperson is not taking an active role in influencing the chain's activity.

Taking an active role, though, means that the salesperson actively seeks to influence what the supply chain does. The

EXHIBIT 2.1

An Example of a
Supply Chain

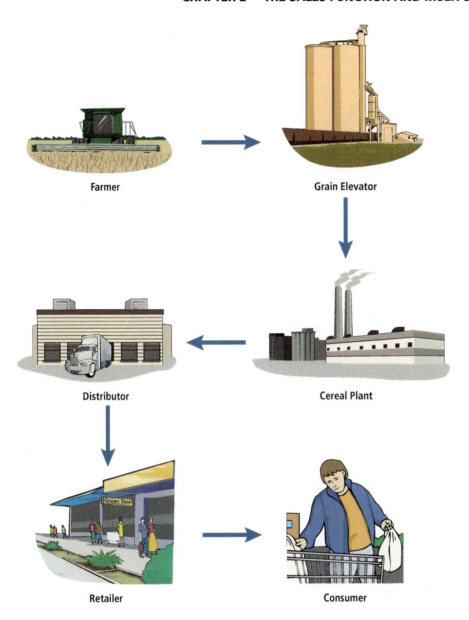

Farmer

Grain Elevator

Distributor

Cereal Plant

Retailer

Consumer

salesperson might need to marshal resources both inside and outside the firm in order
to consummate the sale or serve the customer. For example, a buyer that needs special
payment terms will need the salesperson's help in securing those terms from the company.
Or the salesperson might need to arrange expedited delivery in order to meet a buyer's
needs. Bell Helicopter's salespeople take an active role in their firm's supply chain
management: Because each helicopter sold by Bell is customized, salespeople involve
engineers in their sales calls so that the final product meets the customer's exact
specifications.

   With the advent of technology, however, more functions are being automated, including the selling function. Today, more customers want to be able to buy over the Internet or
by phone or by any number of methods. Companies are turning to a multi-channel
approach as a result.

Selling in a Multi-Channel Environment

If a company is selling in a **multi-channel environment**, it is using a number of methods, or channels, to accomplish the selling function, as illustrated in Exhibit 2.2. The Internet, for example, can actually be used in several ways. **Electronic data interchange (EDI)** takes advantage of the Internet by directly connecting the customer's inventory management system with the seller's order entry system. When the inventory management system notes that the buyer's inventories are low, it automatically places an order for replenishment. No human intervention is required. Wal-Mart is a company that extensively utilizes EDI to manage its inventory so as to drive cost out of the system.

Alternately, the customer can enter an order on a special Web site, much the same way you might use Amazon.com. This special **customer portal**, though, is a Web site that only customers can enter, because it provides them with customized information, such as their order history, shipping status, and other personalized data. Or the customer can use **reverse auctions** on the Web by posting their needs and letting companies bid on that sale; the company with the lowest bid wins. These auctions are called reverse auctions because sellers are bidding. This is just the opposite of what happens on eBay where sellers post items and buyers bid. Save33.com, for example, is an eBay for reverse auctions.

Customers may want to order from a catalog by calling a toll-free number. Dell, for example, has mastered multi-channel sales to its business customers. A business buyer can order a Dell product on the Web either through Dell's small business site or a customer portal. Or the buyer can call a toll-free number or request a personal visit by one of Dell's salespeople. Dell has recently suffered somewhat because it does not utilize retailers like Best Buy or Circuit City to sell its computers. This would enable buyers to obtain their computers right away versus waiting for them to be delivered. That said, Dell does manage its other channels very well—so well, in fact, that it can charge lower prices. This gives the company a competitive advantage.

But it's not just price that's important to consumers. Companies today have come to realize that a competitive advantage can be created by selling the *way* a customer wants to buy. Of course, a competitive advantage can also be created if a company is the only one to have *what* the customer wants to buy. Customers buy to satisfy their needs, of course. Some of their needs are fulfilled by the product itself, but other needs, such as the need for convenience, are fulfilled by how the product is bought.

A key issue, then, for salespeople is to provide value to customers. As we have explained, salespeople are expensive—the most expensive way to reach customers, in fact.

EXHIBIT 2.2

Sales Channels

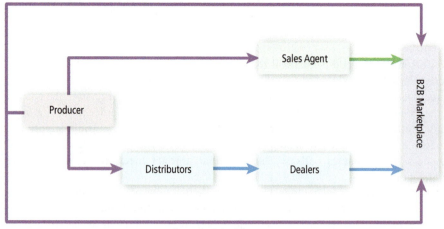

All other channels—the Internet, call centers, retail stores, catalogs, trade shows—are cheaper. So salespeople have to provide additional value to the customer, or the customer will refuse to pay the premium needed to cover the cost of the salesperson.

Because salespeople are the most expensive option to reach customers, companies pursue two strategies to reduce costs without sacrificing performance. The first strategy is to "purify" the sales job, or shift non-selling activities to lower-cost alternatives. For example, creating a Web site that allows customers to track their own orders can eliminate phone calls to the firm's salespeople, freeing up their time for more selling activity.

The second strategy is to outsource selling activity. **Outsourcing** means hiring another company to carry out a task or set of tasks. Outsourcing, sometimes to another country as the Global Sales Management feature in this chapter discusses, can be a challenging proposition. To a large extent, these two strategies, purifying and outsourcing, have proven very successful for many companies. The cost per sale has declined in the last decade, whereas the average compensation

OfficeMax gives its customers the ability to buy online or at a retail store, but the company also has field salespeople. Online stores are less expensive to operate, but salespeople are more effective when it comes to capturing the business large accounts have to offer.

GLOBAL SALES MANAGEMENT

Outsourcing to India

Most business executives think of outsourcing as sending jobs to another country. In sales, that's exactly what it might mean. For example, call an 800 number to make a purchase and you might find yourself talking to someone in India, the Philippines, or Ireland. EDS, one of the world's largest services provider with headquarters in Dallas, Texas, manages some 500 call centers across all of those countries, the United States, and other countries. Managing these centers provides a number of unique challenges to sales leaders.

India, for example, has only 20 percent of its population holding a college education, but that's more college-educated adults than all of the adult population in the United States. These adults speak English but with an accent that is difficult for Americans to understand. If the market to which they are selling is American, they have to learn to speak with an American accent and to learn American slang. EDS provides these workers training in the American accent and slang, in addition to product training.

A critical aspect for EDS is setting the appropriate metrics. The EDS account representative and the call center manager both meet with the client (the company that is outsourcing to EDS) to determine the right set of metrics, such as call length, sales quotas, satisfaction scores (taken through surveys), and other performance objectives. The client and the EDS team also write the scripts that salespeople will use. These scripts are then programmed into a computer system that enables the reps to access the right script as the conversation moves along.

In addition to getting the people in place, EDS also has to match its customer tracking system to the client's. Data captured by the contact center rep has to be entered in a system that can then move that information to the client's system, especially if the client also has a field rep who has to call on the same customer. If a sale is made or a service request is taken, that also has to be transferred to the right client systems.

All of these preparations are tedious and tricky. Yet companies continue to outsource because the cost is lower and a willing and highly educated workforce can be found in other countries.

per salesperson has doubled.[1] In other words, salespeople, as well as the companies for which they work, are now operating more efficiently—it's costing them less to sell products, and they are making more money.

There are many ways to outsource the selling function; in the next section, we'll explore the different types of salespeople or sales jobs that represent these two strategies of purifying the position or outsourcing.

To Outsource or Not to Outsource the Sales Function

Hire salespeople as employees or hire a company to sell for you? For most companies, the choice is not that simple. There are, however, advantages and disadvantages of employing company salespeople or contracting with independent representatives. In a later chapter, we'll discuss how many salespeople a firm needs and the formula for determining whether it is more economical to outsource or hire company salespeople. Here, we focus on the broader strategic issues of outsourcing.

In general, there are a number of advantages to having company-employed salespeople. First, the company can exert greater control over their efforts, telling them what to sell and enforcing requirements to carry out non-selling activities. For example, if the salespeople are company employees, then they can be required to attend training sessions. Second, there is also greater control over who is hired to represent the company. Finally, a company salesperson will focus on only the company's products whereas an outsourced representative might be free to sell many companies' products. The latter might lead to less time being spent selling the firm's individual products or product line.

With an outsourced sales force, the firm's selling costs can be shared with other manufacturers thereby reducing the cost per sales call. In addition, the outsourced sales force has established relationships with customers from which the manufacturer can benefit. Both of these benefits can then yield greater coverage of the market for the manufacturer. The question for the sales executive is whether outsourcing is right for that company's situation. First, we will explore the different types of outsourcing; then, we will briefly examine the types of company sales positions.

Types of Outsourced Salespeople

Hilti outsources some of its selling activities to distributors, such as this distributor, HD Plumbing. (Landov Media)

A common solution to the sales question is to hire a manufacturer's representative or agent. The **manufacturer's representative**, **manufacturer's agent**, or rep is an independent contractor who does not take ownership of the product and does not maintain an inventory. Many reps will sell for several non-competing principals, a **principal** being the manufacturer. For example, in the furniture business, a rep might sell furniture for one principal, lamps for another, and decorative accessories for yet another. The same buyer needs all three types of products, so it saves time for the buyer to meet with one salesperson instead of three.

Another option is a distributor. **Distributors** sell for many manufacturers, much like manufacturer's reps do. The difference is that distributors take ownership of the products, sell them on consignment, or otherwise maintain an inventory of them. Hilti, for example, sells fasteners and other construction products through distributors. These distributors sell Hilti's products directly to contractors at their job sites, or the contractors can visit the distributors' locations to purchase and pick up the products they want. Distributors carry many products made by many manufacturers, some of which compete with one another.

A **broker** represents either buyer or seller and sometimes both. A broker can carry an inventory of products but does not take ownership

of them. Brokers are common in the furniture business as a way of buying from overseas: a U.S. company can work through a broker to locate furniture manufacturers in China, for example. Brokers are not always used in international settings, though. They are common in industries such as the market for domestic produce, too. Grocery stores, for example, need to be able to buy the best produce they can get as quickly as possible so it stays fresh. Buying produce is often easier for them to do through a broker than to try to find sellers themselves.

Purifying the sales job, as mentioned earlier, often means moving non-selling activities to other people or to other channels such as the Web. Another strategy is to break the sales process down into parts and outsource only parts of the process. For example, Intrep (www.intrep.com) is a company that only calls potential prospects and sets up appointments for company salespeople to follow up. GC Services (www.gcserv.com), however, operates at the other end of the spectrum, providing only customer support services for other firms. A company could use both Intrep and GC Services in addition to its own company-employed salespeople.

Types of Company-Employed Salespeople

Whether a company outsources some or all sales tasks, there are different types of sales positions possible. Unlike the sales types described earlier, these positions can be part of an outsourced sales force or kept within the company.

One distinction that should be made is inside versus outside or field salesperson, a distinction that has nothing to do with outsourcing. An **inside salesperson** is someone who sells at a company's facilities, either by telephone or in person. Jeff Moss, for example, was hired by Paul Nelson at IBM straight out of college to sell on the telephone. Moss handles four accounts that generate a total of $1 million in revenue for IBM. Although Moss might visit each account three or four times a year in person, he is considered an inside salesperson. Inside salespeople can include salespeople who sell in a distributor's location, like a retail sales rep. Other inside salespeople, like Moss, work in a **contact center** or **call center**, an office where customers communicate with salespeople only by telephone or electronically by e-mail or live chat. (The term *call center* is now somewhat archaic, as it predates the use of the Web to talk to customers, but the terms are used interchangeably.) In some contact centers, a representative might handle as many as four chat conversations and a voice conversation at the same time. Contact centers can be either outbound, inbound, or both. An **inbound center** handles calls that customers initiate while salespeople initiate the contact in an **outbound center**. Most outbound centers handle inbound contacts.

A **field representative**, however, sells at the customer's location. Many distributors have both inside and outside salespeople, as do companies like IBM, Dell, and others. Paul Nelson, who we featured in the chapter-opening profile, currently manages a team of outside salespeople for IBM, but he used to manage a team of inside salespeople, including Jeff Moss.

Sales managers look at a number of factors, including costs, when they are choosing between inside salespeople and field salespeople. Inside salespeople cost less, especially on a per-call basis. A field salesperson might see only three to ten people a day; the rest of the field person's contacts are made by phone or e-mail in between field calls. In contrast, an inside salesperson can visit with many more people without the costs of travel. Other reasons, such as a need for customers to be able to physically see a product or for the representative to build closer personal relationships with customers (by taking them to lunch and so forth), might also influence whether a sales manager chooses a field salesperson versus an inside salesperson.

In addition to whether they are inside or outside, salespeople can be **account managers**, meaning that they have the responsibility for building sales within specific accounts or accounts within a specific area. The latter type of account manager is more commonly called a **geographic rep**. Jeff Moss is an account manager because he is responsible for whatever is sold from IBM to his four accounts. However, he is a **vertical market rep**, meaning that his accounts all operate in the same industry, in this case, the healthcare industry. Unlike geographic reps, a vertical market territory consists of accounts from the same type of business, such as banking, finance, the government, and so forth.

Some account managers have only one customer—usually a large corporation—that spans the globe. These global account managers usually have the support of geographic reps in certain areas to help cover the needs of the customer. By contrast, other salespeople can have limited responsibilities and serve mainly as support salespeople. For example, some might primarily prospect for new customers, whereas others might handle service and repeat business for existing customers. Still other support salespeople might specialize in a particular product line or technology. These people might be brought into a sales call only when an account manager thinks it is necessary. For example, when Moss needs an expert in customer relationship manager (CRM) software, he calls in an IBM specialist who sells only CRM applications. Moss can't be expected to know everything about each product. That's why IBM uses specialists, salespeople who have a special expertise and only sell to an account when an account manager asks them to.

There are also different sales positions based on the product being sold, how it is sold, and where it is sold. For example, **retail sales representatives** sell to consumers who come into stores. Like inside selling at a distributor, these salespeople work directly with consumers and rely heavily on product demonstrations. Some work solely on commission. This is especially true in the high-fashion, electronics, and furniture industries.

Trade representatives sell to organizations in the supply chain, usually retailers. Hilti, the fastener company, has its own salespeople (trade reps) who sell its products to distributors. These salespeople also help the distributors with their marketing efforts—especially when it comes to selling to big customers. Hershey salespeople who sell Kisses to grocery stores are also trade reps.

Missionary salespeople sell to people who recommend or prescribe a product to others but do not personally use it. Pharmaceutical salespeople are missionary salespeople. They call on doctors, who, in turn, prescribe the representatives' medications to patients. Furniture salespeople who call on architects or textbook salespeople who call on your professors are also missionary salespeople. Sometimes they are called detailers, or **detail reps**, because their primary activity is to detail, or describe, the product.

A company is not likely to have missionary salespeople, retail salespeople, *and* trade salespeople. However, the firm *could* have a mix of inside, outside, outsourced, and company salespeople. It might also have account managers of various types as well as specialists. Add this complex picture to a multichannel environment, and the potential combinations become astounding and confusing. Decisions about what types of salespeople to use in certain situations will be discussed in greater detail in Chapter 7; however, understanding how to integrate all of these possible combinations so that customers are served properly and the company makes money is the topic of the next section.

Aligning the Organization

You order a book from BarnesandNoble.com but receive the wrong book. You then try to return it at your local Barnes & Noble store, but the store won't refund your money. Instead, personnel at the store say to send it back to the Web site. Aren't the store and its Web site the same company?

Yes, they are the same company, and actually Barnes and Noble does a good job of providing **seamless integration**. Seamless integration occurs when a firm's customers can easily shift their transactions across the company's various channels. The goal is to allow customers to choose the method of doing business that makes the most sense for them. "Doing business" refers not only to buying products the way they want to but taking care of their billing, service, and shipping the way they want to. Unfortunately, seamless integration is probably more of a goal than a reality for most organizations, as the cartoon in Exhibit 2.3 illustrates.

For example, you can buy a ticket directly at an American Airlines ticket counter, over the telephone, at AA.com, or through a travel agent. You will pay a premium to have a live person involved in the transaction; for example, it might add $15 if American handles the transaction over the phone and $25 if in person. American passes on their costs to the consumer because self-service over the Web is the cheapest for everyone. That said, consumers *do* have the ability to choose the communication channels they most desire. It matters not, however, which channel you choose. The American Airlines agent can pull up all of the necessary information and handle your requirements.

Imagine, then, the challenges that arise when your company engages in an enterprise selling strategy with General Motors (GM), your largest and only account. GM spends more than $50 billion per year in total purchases; the company has offices literally all over the world, and 3,000 or more of its employees may be authorized to order products from your

Aligning a sales organization can include making sure that the firm's salespeople around the world operate as one team in order to meet the needs of the company's global customers. (Getty Images, Inc./Gallo Images)

company. An IBM buyer in Bogota, Columbia, for example, might want to have a salesperson from your company personally take her order and then track the order's shipment on the Web herself. If a problem arises, she might want to call and resolve the problem over the phone or via another method, such as e-mail. And, she expects whomever she talks to at your firm to be able to give her the information about her account that she wants. If your company succeeds in providing that information, your customer is experiencing seamless integration.

Achieving Alignment

You, as the account manager for GM (or another company) must track all of this activity in order to make the right sales pitch to re-win the contract every time it comes up, even if you are based in Detroit and not Bogota, Columbia. Moreover, you have a responsibility to make sure that every part of your organization services this account appropriately. Getting all of the functional areas of a firm to work together, including the company's various salespeople—its inside reps, geographic reps, customer service reps, and so forth—is called **alignment**. Achieving alignment is a major challenge in all organizations. However, as the multichannel environment and sales organizations become more complex, achieving alignment becomes more difficult. As a result, the challenges associated with achieving alignment continue to grow.

TECHNOLOGY AND ALIGNMENT   Technology can aid in aligning functional areas and multiple sales organizations. Certain types of software, as we discuss in Chapter 6, can make customer data, inventory information, financial data, and other forms of information available to all of the areas of the organization that need the information required for serving the customer. American Airlines has a reservation system, for example, that can be accessed at a ticket counter, by a ticket agent working in a call center, or by the customer over the Web. Each American representative knows immediately if they are working with a Platinum Executive flyer (someone who travels more than 60,000 miles per year with American) or an infrequent traveler. Not only does the agent have information on the current flight but historical passenger information, too.

ALIGNING A COMPANY'S PROCESSES AND GOALS   Alignment is not achieved by just having the right information, though; a firm's objectives must also be aligned so that its processes result in the right outcomes. For example, a credit clerk in charge of extending credit to the firm's customers might have all the necessary information to accept or reject their credit applications. But suppose the clerk's performance is rewarded based on customers paying their bills. If this is the case, the clerk is likely to have such high credit standards that the firm will lose some sales—sales it otherwise would have made to customers who have only good, but not great, credit. Or if a shipping manager is paid for having the highest shipping completion rate, he's not likely to drop everything to help you expedite a particularly important order, even if it is for a big customer like GM.

Thus, alignment requires that people in various areas work together and independently toward the same goals. For example, there are times when an account manager and shipping manager have to meet to settle on a strategy for a particular account—times when their two functional areas have to work together, in other words. However, there are also times when the two managers have to work independently but still toward the same goal. For example, the sales manager does not need to look over the shipping manager's shoulder to see what deliveries are scheduled first. The shipping manager works independently of the sales manager but under policies and procedures tied to goals that both share.

SALES AND ALIGNMENT   Salespeople would like to think that customer satisfaction is important to everyone in the firm. Do you think it is? Paul Greenberg, an author and CRM guru, describes visiting a call center in which a large banner reading "Customer Satisfaction is Our Goal!" was hung. Next to the banner, however, was a large digital clock showing the average length of the center's calls. Customer service reps manning the phones in the center were under strict orders to keep every call under three minutes. So which objective do you think was more likely to be closely monitored and met? Customer satisfaction or length of the call? Yes, you guessed it—length of the call. If resolving a customer's needs took five minutes, the CSR would try to finish the call in three minutes or less, even though customer dissatisfaction resulted.

Three minutes in that case was a **metric**, or performance measurement, used to determine if an objective was being met. A firm's metrics have to be aligned so that its work processes will be aligned. Employees will find ways to meet the firm's metrics because they will be evaluated on them. Consequently, alignment requires having the *right* metrics.

We will discuss more about metrics in Chapter 14. Suffice it to say here that alignment is, perhaps, more important to the salesperson than anyone else in the organization. A salesperson has to make promises to the customer that other people in the organization fulfill. Every time a salesperson tells a customer, "You'll receive your order on Tuesday," that salesperson is relying on an order entry clerk to do his job, a shipping scheduler to do his job, the credit clerk to do his job, and so on, and so forth. If any one of these people fails, then the customer's shipment is delayed and the salesperson's promise is broken.

Because alignment is so critical to sales success, the sales leadership of an organization has to take proactive action to ensure that alignment occurs. Although everyone in an organization might, in theory, recognize the importance of customers to the firm's health, each person in each department has a budget to watch and will get in trouble if more is spent; each person has a set of metrics to achieve and risks getting fired if he fails; and each person has problems and demands that must be resolved that may have nothing to do with the customer. A key function of the sales executive is to work with other areas of the firm to ensure that the leaders in those areas (like the leader in the call center we just mentioned) understands how their metrics and budgets support or sabotage the company's larger goals of sales and customer satisfaction.

For companies that have purified their sales positions, alignment is becoming a bigger issue. Once upon a time, the salesperson was the only person a customer would talk to.

 SELF-ASSESSMENT LIBRARY

Not everyone who gets into sales wanted to be in sales to begin with. The same is true for sales managers. How much do you want to actually *do* management? Go to http://www.prenhall.com/sal/ and log in using the access code that came with this book. Then click on:

Assessments
   3. Life in Organizations
     B. Careers
       4. How Motivated Am I to Manage?

As you complete the instrument, you can see that there are different potential motivators for managers. The overall score will give you an indication of your overall motivation to actually manage, but you should also consider how you answered individual questions.

Today, customers are encountering **customer-facing personnel**—people that have frequent and direct contact with customers. These people may or may not have been trained to sell to customers, yet they are expected to say and do the right things to make sure that the customer is persuaded. Many companies have gone so far as to give customer-facing personnel sales quotas. The logic is that each contact with a customer is an opportunity to sell something. Imagine, then, how a customer might react if he calls with a billing problem he can't seem to get fixed until he agrees to make another purchase! Not only is the customer unhappy, but so is the billing clerk who got into accounting because she didn't want to be a salesperson!

Remember, one of the reasons for the multi-channel environment is to gain a competitive advantage by selling the way the customer wants to buy. When a customer engages in an interaction with a seller, the customer expects to obtain a desired outcome. If that desired outcome is to resolve a billing problem, the interaction is not enhanced by selling something else. For example, the Ethics in Sales Management feature in this chapter, "Stuck in AOHell" illustrates how negative the consequences can be for a company that tries to sell when it should be trying to service.

Take care of the customer's objective first and take care of it completely, then ask permission to make an additional offer. For example, if a customer has a certain product that has

---

 ETHICS IN SALES MANAGEMENT

Stuck in AOHell

Most companies, when faced with the loss of a customer, will try diligently to save that customer. AOL, however, seems to have taken customer retention to a new low. The company seems to be unable to take no for an answer.

One customer, Vincent Ferrari, tried to cancel his AOL service 21 times. Finally, on his last try, he was subjected to a four-minute hassle that seemed like hours. So Ferrari fought back—he recorded the call and posted the conversation on the Web. Within hours, the cyberblitz started, and before it was over, Ferrari appeared on major television talk shows.

But stories of AOHell began circulating among CRM professionals long before Ferrari recorded his call. In fact, the State of New York fined AOL $1.25 million for its hassling of customers who wanted to cancel and then billing them anyway.

The sad thing about the Ferrari situation is that the call center rep was simply doing what the AOL sales manual said. For example, "If you stop and think about it, every Member that calls in to cancel their account is a hot lead. Most other sales jobs require you to create your own leads, but in the Retention Queue the leads come to you! Be eager to take more calls, get more leads, and close more sales. More leads mean more selling opportunities for you and cost savings for ⓘ AOL." Of course, the leads they refer to are people who are trying leave AOL!

One customer reported lying to AOL, saying he was going to move to France and would not have a phone for dial-up. As it was, it took talking to "the manager" before AOL would let the customer cancel, even though the customer had fulfilled any contracts.

Did AOL benefit because some customers became afraid to cancel, not wanting to enter AOHell? And what does that say about sales practices that not only ambush the customer but also ask non-salespeople to sell?

Source: Keith Dawson, "Your Call is Not Particularly Important to Us," *Call Center Magazine* (Oct. 2006), p. 4; Anonymous, "Customers Complain of Cancellation Problems," *FinancialWire* (July 2, 2006), p. 1.

accessories that can enhance its performance, the customer service rep could say something like, "You know, the XYZ 500 operates much faster with the rotary feeder accessory. Have you ever considered adding that?" This approach is an example of **suggestive selling**, where a suggestion is made to consider an accessory to the main purchase. Retail salespeople use this approach when selling ties to go with a suit or a handbag or shoes to go with a dress.

In addition, recognize that employee satisfaction is directly tied to customer satisfaction. In order for non-salespeople to remain happy with their job, they have to be able to carry out the required tasks. If sales is one of those tasks, these people need training, compensation, and an environment that supports their completion of the tasks. What they don't need is excessive pressure to sell something.

Summary

Selling in a multi-channel environment means that salespeople and sales managers have to integrate their activities with the other channels through which the company sells. The selling function can be accomplished through other channels such as the Web or call centers. Many salespeople also have to take an active role in the supply chains of their firms.

The multi-channel environment means buyers want to buy and be serviced through the channels most convenient for them. These channels might not always be the same. In other words, the customer might prefer one set of channels for purchasing and different ones for receiving service. The various channels can include EDI, customer portals, reverse auctions, and others.

The multi-channel environment also means that firms can choose to outsource some or all of their sales activities. Manufacturer's reps, distributors, and brokers are different types of outsourced salespeople. Similarly, companies can choose to operate their own contact centers or outsource their operation to other firms.

Whether or not a firm outsources some its sales positions or functions, achieving seamless integration, or alignment, among them is important. Customers want to be served appropriately, no matter what channels they choose. Sales managers need to make it their business to facilitate this alignment.

Key Terms

account managers   31

alignment   34

broker   30

call center   31

contact center   31

customer-facing personnel   36

customer portal   28

detail reps   32

distributors   30

electronic data interchange (EDI)   28

field representative   31

geographic rep   31

inbound center   31

inside salesperson   31

manufacturer's agent   30

manufacturer's representative   30

metric   35

missionary salespeople   32

multi-channel environment   28

outbound center   31

outsourcing   29

principal   30

retail sales representatives   32

reverse auctions   28

sales forecast   26

seamless integration   32

suggestive selling   37

supply chain   26

trade representatives   32

vertical market rep   32

Questions and Problems

1. In many companies, there is little trust and collaboration between their marketing departments and sales forces. Some salespeople believe that marketing costs money without generating enough leads to cover the costs; some marketing managers believe salespeople are overpaid and want all the credit for any sale, in spite of what marketing has done. What effect would such conflict have on the firm's alignment?

2. At EMC, a computer storage company, the joke is that EMC stands for "Everybody Makes Calls," as in *everybody makes sales calls*. Similarly, at the Miami Heat office (the professional basketball team), every employee is given a list of season ticket holders to have as their customers. What benefits are there to having everyone in the company call on customers? What possible problems could arise from such a policy?

3. Have you ever been on a Web site that seemed to be operated by a separate company other than the one you intended to do business with—either because the prices or service policies were different on the site? Why would such policies occur? Why is alignment across different channels so difficult to achieve?

4. Of the types of selling identified in the chapter, which one holds the most appeal for you in terms of a job after graduation? Why? Which has the least appeal? Why?

5. In the pharmaceutical industry, booking time with doctors to present drug information to them is the most difficult task. Yet, companies seem to continue to invest in salespeople to book doctors' time instead of other sales methods. Why do salespeople continue to be the most effective method of reaching doctors? What other methods might be used to help pharmaceutical salespeople book time with doctors?

6. In some companies, customer service is carried out by the salesperson. In others, it is the responsibility of a separate department. When would a separate department make more sense? When would it not?

7. How do salespeople affect the supply chains of their firms?

Role Play

Mechanix Illustrated

Mechanix Illustrated is a small, family-owned magazine that serves diesel mechanic shops. The magazine, which has about 5,000 subscribers, has seen a 10 percent increase in subscribers over the past two years and expects to see more. The magazine's advertising sales, though, which is really what brings in the revenue, have been stagnant. So far, Bill North has tried to do all of the advertising sales himself, in addition to serving as the editor of Mechanix Illustrated. But today, Sandy Lake is calling on Bill to convince him to let her company do the advertising sales for him. Her company, Lake Sales, will also take over the subscriber management. There are more than 15,000 diesel mechanic shops in the United States, so there is plenty of room for growth in the market.

Assignment

Break into pairs, with one person playing the role of Bill and the other Sandy. Bill should develop a list of objectives (use the SMART format from Chapter 1) as well as a list of concerns regarding outsourcing the selling effort. Sandy should develop a particular sales format (telephone, field, etc.) and prepare a list of advantages for that format. Once those lists are prepared, then role play the sales call by Sandy to Bill.

Sales Manager's Workshop: Promedia Technology (PMT)

Promedia Technology (PMT) is a software company that sells to companies of all types. The software packages PMT sells include media (advertising) management applications that encompass Web media as well as printed media. Specifically, the company's products include:

- Financial project tracking software, an application that tracks and allocates costs to projects. This product helps PMT's client companies establish budgets for their projects using different "what-if" scenarios.
- Media buying and tracking software automates the routine media purchases client firms make.
- Creative (ad) management software archives and makes various ads easy for client firms to retrieve.
- Lead management software is an application that tracks a client company's sales leads by the media channels that generated them. The software also develops models that compare the effectiveness of various channels relative to their costs.
- Project management software is an application that allows a client company's teams to share information about the firm's various projects in development and ensure they are completed on time.
- A media research service is a daily summary with links to all articles or stories about a company that uses PMT's services.
- Public relations tracking software is an add-on to PMT's media research service. This application scores the PR effectiveness of a client company's various media placements.

Companies can buy any or all of the applications and pay a monthly subscription rate. The rate varies by the size of the account, or client firm, and is priced either by the number of projects being tracked for the firm (via PMT's financial project tracking software) or by the number of pages being stored for the firm (via PMT's creative management application), and so forth.

A company might have only one account with PMT, but the account can actually involve many decision makers. In large companies, buyers can include a director of creative services, an advertising executive, the head of PR, and others. In addition, the information technology department also gets involved, either by providing some of the budget for the subscription or by aiding in the selection of a product or vendor. In some companies, Promedia has to get approval from the firm's finance or operations committee and be on the company's approved vendor list before any subscriptions can be purchased from them.

Exercise

You are one of six regional sales managers for PMT, and you have four branch offices. Each branch office has three to five salespeople and one sales manager who may or may not also be responsible for individual customer accounts. You report directly to PMT's chief revenue officer, Terry Baker.

PMT uses software called Aplicor to manage its sales relationships with its customers. A critical component of the effectiveness of the software is the data that your salespeople enter into the system.

Today, you personally made three sales calls. Your first call was with Benjamin Howard at Kerr-McGee, the energy company. You found out that Ben, as he prefers to be called, has two sons playing Little League baseball and that Ben played two seasons himself with the Oakland A's. Currently, to manage its media purchases, Kerr-McGee uses MarketingPilot (www.marketingpilot.com), a product that competes with PMT's products. You don't know much about this company, so you need to look it up on the Web. All of Kerr-McGee's advertising is created by an outside advertising agency, so the energy firm hasn't stored any of it digitally anywhere. Consequently, when you brought up Promedia's creative management application—which does just this—Ben was very interested. He asked you to send him some information via PDFs and to call him on the first Friday of next month.

Charlyn Sanz, of Levi-Straus, was your second appointment. She also introduced you to China Deng, the company's vice president of sales, and Edda Hevey, its CFO (chief financial officer). You had never met China or Edda before. Both women were just leaving Charlyn's office when you arrived. You spent about an hour with Charlyn going over all of the services you have to offer and trying to find out about her needs. Levi-Straus has two marketing directors, of which Charlyn is one, and her responsibility is U.S. marketing. The other director handles marketing outside of the United States. Charlyn told you that she needs to reduce her overall marketing costs as well as get better results for what she does spend marketing money on. She asked you what you knew about Levi-Straus and you said, "Nice jeans." She didn't laugh but suggested you go online and see how well the company has done lately. She also said that after you do that, call her back and provide her with some specific ideas as to what she should do first.

Jenice Anderson is the director of marketing at Medtronic, a company that develops medical-technology products. Jenice already subscribes to media buying and project tracking services. She does not, however, use your media research product. Instead, she uses Arbitron. She's heard that your service misses a lot of articles and doesn't have a good blog mention reporting capability. You offered to provide her with a research report and a demo; she wanted Ima Moreno, who reports to her, to see it, but Ima was out today.

Now that you've made these calls, you need to report them in Aplicor. We've actually already done this for you for those calls so that you can see how this information is made available once it has been input. To access the Aplicor software, go to https://baylor.aplicor. net and log in using a password your professor will give you. Log into Aplicor and view the data for these sales calls. Once you've done that, create a new record for a new account of your own creation. For this account, you need to put in all of the contact information. Use your teacher's name as the chief marketing officer and your last name as the company name. You can make up everything else. Once you are done, print the record to turn in.

Caselet 2.1: Hereford Promotions

Sandy Hereford looked at the numbers and blinked. Her company, a small promotional products agency with three salespeople, had grown little over the past year. Sales were up only 8 percent, but customer complaints had doubled. Over the past quarter, 12 new customers were added, but 15 had switched suppliers.

A promotional products agency typically represents a number of manufacturers. One manufacturer, for example, might make cups and glasses while another may make shirts and jackets. All of these products are then printed or embroidered with the client's name and advertising message. Salespeople are typically paid a 10 percent commission on each sale and can earn an average of $10,000 per month. Each rep that earns that much adds another $5,000 in profit margin to the company, which is used to pay expenses, benefits, and Sandy's salary.

Sandy had considered adding a salesperson, but no new salesperson would work for straight commission, at least not until sales were high enough to cover his expenses. Sandy estimated that would require paying the salesperson a salary of $3,000 per month, a major investment when the company's net income (after paying Sandy's salary) was averaging only a little over $1,000 a month.

The company averaged 40 large customers per salesperson. A large customer was any customer that billed $20,000 per year. Small customers accounted for about $20,000 per month in revenue per rep. Each rep might have 100 small customers to manage.

Questions

1. What alternatives for growth might Sandy consider?
2. Can you think of some multi-channel options she might pursue?

Caselet 2.2: Marchetti Machines: One Big Happy Family

Emily was steaming. Even for a Monday, this one was proving to be one of the worst. The first thing she did every Monday was a conference call with the other three regional sales managers and her boss, the VP of sales. While on the call, she read an e-mail from one of her best salespeople, Frank McCaslin. Frank had worked for weeks to land a large account, traveling from Chicago to LA three times to meet with various members of the client's executive team. They loved his in-depth analysis of their situation and the solution he had crafted. They also seemed happy with the price. All it took was for the president to sign off on the deal. Then he got the following e-mail from his client's chief financial officer, which he had forwarded to Emily:

"Frank—I played golf with Louis Ruggieri from your office. I think he's your service manager. Anyway, he says the service team hates to work on the system you proposed. I think if that is the case, we're going to have to open our search up to some other companies to try to find something more reliable."

Frank added this note to the e-mail: "This is one of the biggest sales of the year! What was Ruggieri thinking?" Emily wondered that herself.

About this time, Jerry, the VP, said, "Okay, we've got a reorganization coming up. We're going to take the bottom 10 percent of accounts and give those to inside sales. Further, inside sales will no longer report to me, but will be part of a new division that will include Web sales and sales through distributors."

Emily interrupted, "So we won't have distributor sales in our division anymore? We're already having problems with distributors selling to our accounts; how can we resolve these problems if they are part of another division?" The way the current structure works, distributors are only allowed to sell to certain types of accounts: accounts under $100,000 in annual revenue, accounts that require engineering that Marchetti doesn't do, and any account they find first. Distributors cannot sell to the government or any accounts that are already on Marchetti's customer list, but sometimes, company names are not obvious or divisions operate under different names, and it is difficult to know who owns the account. Marchetti Machines has a sales force that helps distributors sell, in addition to those, like Emily's sales team, that sell direct. But prior to this reorganization, all sales reported to Jerry, whether inside, distributor, or direct. Now that was about to change.

Questions

1. How should Emily handle the problem with Louis Ruggieri? What should she do about the account? What should she tell Frank if the account is lost completely?
2. What problems are likely to occur because of the reorganization? Did these issues exist before the reorganization, and will these issues be better or worse as a result of the change in structure?

Reference

1. Tanner, John F., Jr., and Shannon Shipp (2005). "Sales Technology Within the Salesperson's Relationships: A Research Agenda," *Industrial Marketing Management*, 34(4), 305–312.

PART TWO

Sales Leadership

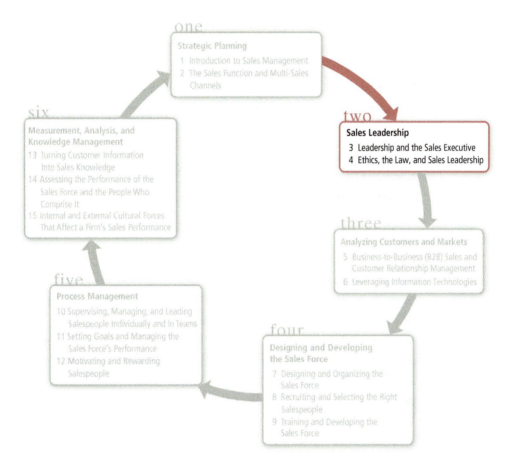

In Part One, you were introduced to the concepts of mission and strategy, as well as the multichannel reality that is sales today. You also have an idea of how complicated those channels can be, with salespeople who are company employees calling on independent distributors or contact centers supporting field salespeople who in turn support manufacturer's agents. Somehow, these channels must also be integrated with the company's web channels and any other channels they may choose.

Simply managing in this reality is insufficient; leadership is also required. In Part Two, we explore *Sales Leadership,* beginning with Chapter Three, *Leadership and the Sales Executive.*

Are leaders born or made? What would it be like if you wanted to be a leader or were thrust into that position and you weren't sure if you were one of the born leaders? Yet we all know people we think are natural-born leaders. Can anyone lead? Can anyone manage? We don't claim that one chapter will enable everyone to become a leader or a manager. This chapter does identify those actions that separate leadership from management, but not necessarily leaders from managers. After all, as you will see in the chapter, managers must lead and leaders must manage, and there are things you can learn to do that will make you a better leader or manager.

In today's reality, ethics are extremely important. Chapter Four, *Ethics, the Law, and Sales Leadership,* explores the role of sales leadership in creating an ethical sales climate. First, we explore the more common approaches to ethics, such as the Golden Rule and the Protestant ethic, that individuals can adopt. Carefully considering one's own approach to ethics is a good first step but it takes more than one's good intentions to create an ethical climate. The chapter discusses policies and procedures that a sales leader can enact and enforce that should yield the proper climate, as well as considers legal issues that will confront sales managers. The right for a company to exist is a privilege extended by society. That is one reason why sales executives must create the right ethical climate so that the firm can serve its customers well.

3

LEADERSHIP AND THE SALES EXECUTIVE

LEARNING OBJECTIVES

After completing this chapter, you should be able to:

- Understand the historical development and different approaches to examining leadership.
- Recognize the contributions made by contemporary leadership approaches.
- Identify issues today's sales leaders face.
- Use the information in this chapter to develop your own leadership skills.

Effective leadership is vital to guiding your sales organization. Are leaders born, or can leadership skills be developed? If they can be developed, what is the best way to do this? Can everyone be a leader?

Although there are many definitions for the term "leadership," there is agreement that having sales personnel with leadership skills to guide your sales organization is critical. A sales organization with these skills can overcome many challenges in a competitive workplace.

LARRY VORPAHL

**GROUP VICE PRESIDENT, HORMEL FOOD CORPORATION;
PRESIDENT OF CONSUMER PRODUCTS SALES DIVISION**

Larry Vorpahl knew he wanted to be involved in management of a Fortune 500 company when he graduated with a marketing degree. Vorpahl started out as a sales merchandiser, became a sales representative, and then went on to hold a series of product management positions. Later he became a director and marketing vice president. Today he is the group vice president of Hormel Foods Corporation as well as the president of the company's consumer product sales division. As the president of the consumer product sales division, he is responsible for a sales team of 300 people who sell approximately $2.2 billion in grocery and refrigerated products annually. ■

In his first management position, Vorpahl recalls spending his first six months on the job listening to and learning from his subordinates. Gradually he gained confidence with regard to his own skills as a manager. Although he didn't have a formal mentor, he did observe the leadership styles of other managers around him. He describes his own leadership style as collaborative and team-based with an emphasis on teaching.

As part of a team, he asks questions and then asks group members for their recommendations. After a decision has been reached, he spends time reviewing the basis for his decision with team members. This helps prepare them to be able to make the decision next time. "A leader has to have integrity. If people trust that you are being straightforward and honest with them and are not going to hang them out to dry on their own, they will respect you as the leader of the team and will follow you."

One of the biggest challenges those who manage sales forces face is making sure everyone is motivated to do their absolute best every day: "Each salesperson is motivated by their own unique thing—a big bonus, to live in a specific geography, no travel away from home, to be left alone as long as they are meeting their sales goals, lower levels of administrative work, etc. You've got to do your best to identify those factors that motivate them to do their best."

When asked what someone approaching a career as a sales manager should look for in an employer, Vorpahl identified several things: He encourages people to look at a firm's initial and ongoing training opportunities and any opportunities for educational assistance. His own formal training consisted of both managerial and leadership skill development programs, and each of his job promotions involved a broader scope of responsibilities.

Even if you are still in school, Vorpahl says you should try your hand at sales in various organizations. This will give you a sense of what it is like to sell different products or services to different customers, learn different selling techniques, and be supervised by people with different managerial styles. "Get experience working and leading others," he suggests.

What Is Leadership?

The topic of leadership receives a great deal of attention these days. It seems like you can almost always find a headline discussing the leadership of a country, a company, or an organization. Sometimes it is because a positive, notable event has occurred—for example, a company has successfully launched a new product or service or reached an important milestone. Oftentimes, however, it is because of just the opposite—because of a lack of leadership, something negative has occurred. For example, perhaps a customer or a group of customers was treated poorly or a product or service did not function as expected.

People agree that every organization needs good leadership, especially good sales managers. The question is: How does an organization get good leadership? Is leadership a trait you identify when hiring employees? Is it a skill that can be developed in existing employees? Can good managers be good leaders, and are the two one and the same?

In an effort to answer questions like these, the formal investigation of leadership has been going on for years. As a result, today there are nearly as many definitions of leadership as there are researchers who have studied the topic. Researchers generally agree, however, that leadership is a process whereby an individual influences other group members to move toward or achieve a common goal. There are several key points implicit in this definition. The first is that *leadership is a process*—not a trait or characteristic of a person. Second, *leadership involves influence*. Third, *leadership occurs in a group*. Fourth, *leadership involves movement toward a goal or goals*.

Leading versus Managing

Based on the previous definition, ask yourself this question: If a sales manager attempts to persuade her employees to accomplish a shared goal, is she engaging in leadership? Or just management? Harvard Business School Professor John Kotter, widely regarded as an authority on leadership, has tried to answer this question. In the late 1980s and early 1990s, Kotter spent several years interviewing, observing, and analyzing questionnaire data from nearly 200 leaders in business organizations. He noted that leadership can be defined two ways: first, *as a process* that helps direct and mobilize people and ideas, and second, it can refer to a person in *a formal position* whose job is to be the group's leader. The first definition describes a leader; the second describes a manager. *Leaders* are involved with establishing direction, aligning and communicating direction, and motivating and inspiring. *Managers* are involved with planning and budgeting, organizing and staffing, and controlling and problem solving.[1] A summary of these differences is presented in Exhibit 3.1.

Kotter identified a number of similarities between leading and managing. They both include deciding what needs to be done and working with people to make sure action is taken. However, leadership focuses on change whereas management focuses on results that

Leadership Practices
- Direction – development of a vision to guide the organization in the future
- Aligning people – communication and community building to support the organization's goals
- Motivating and inspiring – working to overcome political, bureaucratic, and economic setbacks by appealing to human needs, values, and emotions
- Change – results in useful and sometimes dramatic change

Management Practices
- Planning and budgeting – setting and achieving targets, allocating appropriate level of resources
- Organizing and staffing – structuring and staffing the organization with needed people
- Controlling and problem solving – monitoring the implementation of plans and making needed adjustments
- Predictability – results in an orderly, predictable pattern of results

EXHIBIT 3.1

Leadership Practices versus Management Practices

Source: Based on John P. Kotter, *A Force for Change: How Leadership Differs from Management* (1990), pp. vii–6, New York: Free Press.

keep things working efficiently. But an organization needs both if it is to prosper. When an organization has only strong leadership (without strong management), the firm's executives might advocate change for change's sake ("Let's try a different approach to this issue"). By contrast, with doses of heavy management (and no leadership), the organization might become too bureaucratic and produce order for order's sake ("We've always done it this way").

It was Kotter's opinion that in years past most organizations did not need many people in leadership positions. However, with the advent of complex technology, increasing educational opportunities, changing demographics, and the intricacies of operating in a global marketplace, this is no longer the case. More change requires more leadership. Compounding this situation are the following research findings from two of Kotter's studies and a third study conducted by another research team:

- Respondents from two-thirds of companies surveyed indicated they had too many people with strong management skills but weak leadership skills.
- Over 95 percent indicated having too few people with both strong leadership and management skills.
- Over 80 percent of respondents indicated that their firms did less than a very good job at attracting, developing, and motivating people with leadership potential.[2]
- Two-thirds of sales vice presidents indicated that less than 60 percent of their sales managers were meeting expectations.[3]

Given the challenges that exist in today's marketplace, organizations need their employees to be both good managers but also good leaders as well. Much of the remainder of this book will focus on management skills. However, this chapter obviously focuses on leadership. We'll begin this process by examining the findings of some past leadership researchers in their chronological order and reflect on the contributions they have made. As we review each of the different approaches, consider how to apply their contributions to your leadership style.

Understanding Leadership: An Historical Perspective

Over the years a number of different approaches to studying leadership have developed. As shortcomings to each theory were identified, a new, improved perspective developed. In this section we'll describe some of the major approaches, some of the shortcomings of each, and how this has led to a better understanding of leadership. Exhibit 3.2 outlines these approaches.

EXHIBIT 3.2

Leadership Research Approaches

Trait Approach—1900s to 1940s; 2000s *"These are the traits you need to be a leader"*
- Leaders are different from followers.
- Leaders tend to display more intelligence, self-confidence, determination, integrity, and predictability.

Behavioral Approach—1950s to 1960s *"This is how leaders behave"*
- Leaders should use a combination of behaviors focused on group relations (consideration) and tasks (initiating structure).
- Group-level supervision is preferred to supervising employees at the individual level.
- Groups report more satisfaction with higher levels of consideration.

Situational Approaches—1960s to 1970s *" Assess the situation and adjust behavior to it"*
- Different situations require leaders with different styles. One size/trait does not fit all in this case.
- Different types of leaders will operate more effectively in different situations.
- Leaders should consider the situational characteristics and the backgrounds of their groups and adapt their behavior to best fit the group.

Contemporary Perspectives of Understanding Leadership—1980s to 1990s *"Motivate your followers through your leadership"*
- Leaders should work with all group members to help them develop their leadership skills.
- Good leader/member relationships result in increased job satisfaction, productivity, and decreased turnover.
- Leaders should strive to be role models.

Emerging Theories of Leadership—1990s to 2000s *"Develop your followers"*
- Leaders should be proactive, work to be good listeners, and build on the contributions of others.
- Leaders should work to support and advance each individual.
- Leaders should be humble, diligent, driven to produce sustained results, and ambitious for their organizations—not themselves.

Is there one trait that makes a person a good salesperson or sales manager? Would it be an ability to communicate with people and motivate them, the ability to analyze information and prioritize it, or some other trait? During the first part of the twentieth century, many researchers examined the traits or characteristics that leaders shared. Often referred to as "The Great Man Theory of Leadership," it examined (primarily male) leaders such as Thomas Jefferson, Abraham Lincoln, Napoleon Bonaparte, Mahatma Gandhi, and Martin Luther King. The assumption was that people were born with certain traits that lent themselves to the development of leadership skills and consequently were more likely to become leaders. Identify the traits and you can then identify a person who either will be or is a leader.

Initially these traits included a wide array of characteristics such as height, intelligence, dominance, and social skills. After a massive review of hundreds of trait studies, Stogdill criticized them for lacking universality.[4] He demonstrated that a leader with one set of traits in one situation was not a leader in another. He did observe that leaders differed from followers in that they had the following traits: intelligence, alertness, insight, responsibility, initiative, persistence, self-confidence, and sociability.

For years, further investigation into the trait approach languished. However, during the 1990s and into the twenty-first century, a more sophisticated statistical analysis procedure, called a *meta-analysis*, was developed. Meta-analysis allows the results of different studies to be compared. Using this procedure, earlier data was re-analyzed to identify differences between leaders and followers. Researchers were able to make strong cases that leadership traits explain what makes some individuals leaders.[5, 6]

One summary of the major characteristics that have a positive relationship to leadership is as follows:[7]

- **Intelligence**—Higher verbal, perceptual, and reasoning skills are important. However, a leader's general intelligence should not greatly differ from his or her followers, as it can be counterproductive.
- **Self-confidence**—The ability to be certain about one's competencies and skills helps produce self-confidence. These skills assist the leader in conveying appropriate and sincere messages that influence followers.
- **Determination**—Leaders demonstrate the ability to get the job done. They must have drive, dominance, and persistence in achieving their goals.
- **Integrity**—Leaders must demonstrate honesty and trustworthiness. Followers don't want to be deceived; they need to see these traits in a leader's actions.
- **Sociability**—The ability to interact in a comfortable, outgoing, and pleasant manner in social relationships is critical. Demonstrating good social skills helps leaders develop strong relationships with their followers.

The trait leadership approach can be observed in the success of Mary Jurmaine and her company Realityworks. Faced with a young family, limited job prospects, and a husband about to be laid off from his position as an aerospace engineer, Mary's sheer determination to succeed blossomed. Utilizing her husband's engineering skills, the couple developed a computerized, lifelike infant to simulate the challenges of caring for a newborn. (The simulator is used in high school parenting education classes.) Mary was responsible for the firm's public relations, advertising, and sales. She was so successful that the product received coverage in *USA Today* and on *The Oprah Winfrey Show*. Her strong determination trait has certainly been a leadership asset for Reality Works.

The trait approach has several limitations. Most notably it lacks a universal list of traits. Furthermore, it's not evident which trait is more important than another and how they interact with one another. For example, can a shortage of one trait be compensated for with an excess of another? Finally, a person's traits and the strength of them change over time. However, the effect of these changes doesn't appear to reverse a person's leadership ability.

Even with these shortcomings, the trait approach does offer several useful applications. Some organizations will look closely at these traits and incorporate them in their selection tools when they recruit and select individuals for employment. Students interested in a sales leadership position should work to develop these traits and have them reflected in their resumes. The biggest beneficiary of this research, however, is the area of training: Knowing what characteristics and experiences are important when it comes to developing better leaders is very important. Using this information, organizations can help develop the leadership skills of their employees. The Global Sales Management feature in this chapter discusses this benefit further.

The Behavioral Approach: "This is How a Leader Behaves"

Unable to overcome the limitations of the trait approach, researchers pursued a new school of thought. World War II was ending, and there was an invigorated interest in studying leadership. Instead of focusing on leaders' characteristics, this approach examined how a leader interacted, or behaved, with his or her subordinates. In other words, the approach looked at different leadership styles. Three groups of researchers pursued this approach with complementary findings.

Researchers at Ohio State identified two dimensions of behavior: *consideration behavior* and *initiating structure*.[8] Consideration behaviors dealt with maintaining good social interactions and relationships with a group's members and building respect and trust within a group.

GLOBAL SALES MANAGEMENT

Identifying Leaders in a Global Marketplace

Dr. Ken De Meuse, the vice president of research for Lominger International, has a big challenge these days. Lominger International is one of the largest providers of leadership development tools for individuals, groups, and companies. The firm's tools can be used to help identify individuals with high leadership potential as well as areas of development for aspiring leaders. This is important because the cost of poor leadership can be monumental when a "bad" decision is made—say, a product is developed that no one wants to buy or personnel have been hired that alienate customers. Moreover, with the expanding internationalization of the marketplace, firms need leaders who can help guide the future of their organizations in every corner around the globe.

"Much of the early research on identifying leadership traits was conducted in U.S. companies with U.S. employees. Yet today, many high-potential growth opportunities for businesses have locations in Asia, in countries such as China, Japan, Singapore, South Korea, New Zealand, Australia, as well as in Europe and South America," says De Meuse. Therefore, using North American leadership measures for employees who have grown up in other parts of the world has significant drawbacks. "We can't assume that experiences present in aspiring leaders in Peoria are the same as those growing up in Shanghai or Tokyo."

A recent study of leaders from North America, Europe, New Zealand, Australia, and Asia revealed that although there are more similarities between those thought to be competent leaders in different nations, there are also some differences. For example, all regions considered integrity and trust as the number-one competency of a leader, except North America, where the trait ranked third. Intellectual "horsepower" ranked first in North America, but only third and fourth in Europe and New Zealand and Australia, respectively, and only sixth most important in Asia. Another interesting finding was that managing diversity was ranked the seventh most important leadership competency in North America, but only the seventeenth most important in Europe, the fourteenth most important in New Zealand and Australia, and a distant fortieth in importance in Asia. De Meuse's efforts seem to be paying off. Lominger's initial success following the refinement of its leadership instruments is a reflection of the fact that international companies believe the instruments will greatly help them when it comes to identifying leaders and fostering better leadership behaviors among them—no matter where they are located.

The second dimension, initiating structure, dealt with behaviors that focus the group on accomplishing its task. These behaviors included giving directions, keeping people focused, and staying on schedule. It was theorized that each dimension was independent of the other—that is, a leader could exhibit a high amount of consideration and a low amount of initiating structure or vice versa. Conversely, the leader could exhibit either a low or high amount of both behaviors. Leaders exhibiting a high amount of both behaviors were thought to be preferred.

A second group of researchers at the Survey Research Center at the University of Michigan were examining the behavior of leaders from highly productive work groups and those whose groups had low productivity. They found that leaders of the productive groups were more *employee centered* rather than *production centered*, and they exercised supervision at the group level, rather than at an individual level.[9] In other words, these leaders were less likely to micromanage individual employees but concentrated instead on the efforts of the group as a whole.

Building on the foundation laid out by these early researchers, a third behavioral approach was developed by Blake and Mouton.[10] Initially called the Managerial Grid®, it was later renamed the Leadership Grid®.[11] This approach is based heavily on the previous findings dealing with the importance of leaders demonstrating a *concern for people* and a *concern for production*. Individual and group assessments of a leader's style results in a score that is displayed on a grid. The axes for the grid reflect the leader's concern for people and concern for results (originally production) and are scaled 1 to 9. Each corner of the grid portrays a different leadership style: Impoverished Management (1,1—low concern for people, low concern for results); Country Club Management (1,9—low concern for results, high concern for people), Authority-Compliance Management (9,1—high concern for results, low concern for people), Team Management (9,9—high concern for results and people). An additional style, Middle of the Road Management (5,5—was a midpoint of both axes).

All three behavioral approaches have an intuitive appeal. They describe behaviors that leaders need to engage in on both a social level and a task level. If you were to subscribe to these leadership approaches, you would want to engage in behaviors addressing both the social needs of the individual group members and all those that focus on accomplishing the task. The more you can display behaviors that demonstrate "consideration," the more satisfaction your group should report.

Aligning a sales organization can include making sure that the firm's salespeople around the world operate as one team in order to meet the needs of the company's global customers. (AP Wide World Photos)

An example of this leadership style can be observed in Meg Whitman, the former CEO of eBay. Whitman has seen the company go from 30 to 13,000 employees while presiding over its rapid growth. She knows that her style balances the dimensions of working with people (the "No. 1 job of a CEO," she says) and being able to focus on the tasks related to eBay's current challenges at hand.[12]

Nonetheless, all three behavioral approaches have been criticized on several grounds. None of them found that there was one best way to lead. The testing of the theories has consistently indicated that leadership depends upon the characteristics of the situation—not just the person doing the leading. Additionally, the theories lacked empirical evidence linking leadership styles and effectiveness. Though the theories implied that leaders with a high concern for both people and production are the most effective, this has never been demonstrated in all situations.[13]

S SELF-ASSESSMENT LIBRARY

Leadership is a behavior that each of us can engage in with a unique approach. The first step toward understanding our leadership practices is to reflect on what behaviors we prefer to use and which behaviors we prefer to avoid. Take the following assessment quiz. After you have completed the assessment, you will have a better idea of your own leadership style, based on your people and task orientations. To access the assessment, go to http://www.prenhall.com/sal/ and log in using the access code that came with your book. Then click on:

Assessments
  II. Working with Others
    B. Leadership and Team Skills
      1. What's My Leadership Style?

Situational Approaches: "Assess the Situation, then Adjust Behavior to It"

The lack of empirical evidence linking trait and behavioral approaches with the effectiveness of leaders underscored the importance of examining *the situation* that the leader faced. As a result, instead of focusing on leaders' traits and patterns of their behavior, research shifted to improve the understanding of different situations and how leaders should best respond.

The pioneer in this area was Fred Fiedler [14] whose **contingency theory of leadership** incorporated both an assessment of the leader's style and characteristics of the situation. Similar to his predecessors, Fiedler considered a leader's style along the dimensions of relationships (concern for people) and task orientation (concern for production). Fiedler believed that a leader's style was stable and not open to major changes. In other words, only the situation could change, and this, in turn, impacted the leader's effectiveness. Each leadership situation was evaluated based on three characteristics. Each of these three characteristics was considered either favorable or unfavorable in contributing to the leader's effectiveness. The dimensions were:

- *Leader-member relations*—Were the relations between the leader and group members good or poor?
- *Task structure*—Were the steps to solving the problem structured or was the approach to solving the problem unclear?
- *Position power*—To what extent did the leader have formal authority to reward or punish the followers?

Task-oriented leaders will be most effective in either well-structured settings or disorganized settings (settings in which they can provide structure to their followers). Relationship-oriented leaders are generally more effective in situations that the theory considers less favorable. Such a leader can work to develop strong relations and use them effectively as the group tackles a less-structured, more ambiguous task.

Because the demands of different situations are not identical, they will require leaders with different skill sets. This line of thought led to the concept of *organizational engineering*, where efforts are made to match tasks to people with the prerequisite skills for success.

Fiedler was applauded for his pioneering efforts, but his theory was not without some weaknesses. For example, replicating some of Fiedler's initial findings has not been accomplished. Additionally, because Fiedler's position was that a leader's style was stable or not likely to change, the model doesn't consider the fact that a leader could learn from past experiences and adapt his style to the situation. [15]

A second leadership approach that incorporates the leader with the characteristics of the situation is the situational leadership model offered by Hersey and Blanchard. [16] Contrary to Fiedler's approach where the style of the leader does not change, this model assumes that the leader can adapt her behavior to the constraints of the situation. In order to determine how to respond to a group, the leader must diagnose the group's level of task competency and commitment on a continuum from "developing" to "developed." Once this diagnosis has been made, the leader must then adapt her behavior along two dimensions: directive behaviors (those that are task-oriented) and supportive behaviors (those that are relationship-oriented). Depending upon a group's level of development, the leader should utilize one of four leadership approaches when working with the group. These styles include:

- Directing—providing a high degree of direction and a low degree of support to the group's members. In other words, simply instruct the members on what to do.
- Coaching—providing a high degree of direction and support to the group's members. In other words, help structure the group and work with its members.
- Supporting—providing a low degree of direction and a high degree of support to the group's members. In other words, work with members but give them the opportunity to make their own decisions.

■ Delegating—providing a low degree of direction and support to the group's members. In other words, give members a high degree of authority.

The Situational Leader® approach is a popular training program for leadership. A version of the program has been developed specifically for sales leaders. The popularity of the Situational Leader® approach reflects the fact that it is easy to understand and offers guidance about which style(s) a leader should incorporate, depending upon the level of development of the followers. Although this seems to be an easy approach for leaders, such as a sales manager, to use, questions remain as to whether or not the data backs up the theory's assumption. For example, do leaders truly have the ability to diagnosis the level of development of their followers?

Introduced in the 1970s, a third contribution to the situational leadership approach focuses on the level of involvement in decision making that a leader should obtain from group members. The **Vroom and Yetton model** [17] examines each situation in terms of its structure, information available, and how important the decision's acceptance is to its implementation. It then proposes the level to which followers should be involved in the decision making. Group decision making has both benefits and drawbacks: When followers are allowed to make decisions, they typically will be more committed. Moreover, they might have additional information that the leader does not know about, which can help them make better decisions. However, making group decisions often takes more time. And as anyone who has ever been involved in a group decision knows, it can result in conflict when a clear course of action is not evident.

Advocates of situational leadership believe leaders should alter their styles depending upon the situation. (Getty Images/PhotoAlto)

In sum, the situational approach to leadership says that there is no one "best style." As a leader, you need to consider the characteristics of the situation you're in and adapt your behaviors to each unique challenge. Consider Johan Hjertonsson who received a call at home from his boss, the CEO of consumer product giant Electrolux. Hjertonsson's boss told him that "things weren't moving fast enough" and that sales were falling. He wanted Hjertonsson to fix the problem as soon as possible. Faced with this challenging and changing situation, Hjertonsson adapted a leadership style that included the use of tight timetables. He also sought input from many parties and used both "carrots and sticks" with his team to make things happen—fast. His success can be seen in the multitude of new products recently introduced by Electrolux.[18]

Contemporary Perspectives of Leadership: "Motivate Your Followers Through Leadership"

The next two approaches to understanding leadership appeared in the decades of the 1980s and 1990s. Neither of these approaches focuses on the situation. Instead, they emphasize the relationships that exist between leaders and individual group members. These approaches theorize that if a leader fosters the development of the members of the group, the members will grow and, in turn, move more toward shared leadership roles.

The first such theory is the **leader-member exchange (LMX) theory**, which has evolved over the course of the last 25 years.[19, 20] The focus of LMX is on the unique relationship that exists between a leader and each group member. This relationship is referred to as a *dyad*. The theory proposes that two different relationships can develop as a result of these interactions: *in-group* and *out-group* exchanges. In situations in which the leader and a member develop high levels of interaction, support, trust, and respect, the member is considered part of the in-group. In situations in which that type of interaction fails to develop, an out-group relationship develops. The out-group relationship is based more on the formal roles of the organization, whereby a leader assigns job responsibilities and ensures that the follower completes them. These relationships are characterized as being more formal or impersonal. As a result, followers are less satisfied and less productive.

The distinction between in- and out-group membership is measured through the use of a questionnaire that addresses the level of affection, loyalty, contribution to work, and respect.

Further development of this approach resulted in the concept of *leadership making*.[20, 21] This approach suggests that every leader should work to have as many in-group relationships as possible with their followers and few or no out-group relationships. Leadership making recognizes however that a leader's qualities, such as trust, respect, and the ability to make a contribution to one's job, develop over time.

According to the **transformational leadership theory**, a leader is someone who is determined and has the charisma to inspire, change, or otherwise transform their followers.[22, 23] Transformational leaders do this by stimulating their followers intellectually, encouraging them, and supporting their development. Leaders give personal attention to their followers and make each of them feel valued and important. As a result, their followers trust and respect them and want to be like them.

Research has generally supported many of the tenets of transformational leadership and found evidence that it positively correlates with job satisfaction and better performance on the part of employees. However, transformational leadership takes a very broad-based view of how a leader should act. It does not prescribe how a leader should act in a particular situation.

To adopt this style of leadership, a sales manager would focus on building trust and respect among all of his employees. In some situations that might mean focusing on improving a relationship with a member of the sales force, and in another, it might mean helping a member lay out the activities needed to be successful in a sales call. Over time, followers develop increased job satisfaction, become more productive, and take on actions similar to those of the leader. Michael Brown, the vice president of sales for Kodak, exemplifies this style. "How you recognize and treat salespeople is something I've focused on," says Brown. "You need to communicate with them en mass, but also on a one-to-one basis." Even during tough times, Brown keeps them motivated by constantly communicating his vision to his team. They trust him and support him because they feel like he's one of the members of the team.[24]

Emerging Leadership Concepts: "Develop Your Followers"

Several leadership approaches popular with the general public might be thought of as having a somewhat "self-help" orientation. The final three approaches, developed in the 1990s and early 2000s fall into this category. However, these approaches have also found acceptance in the business community.

Business professor Steven Covey has gained worldwide recognition for having developed the **principle-centered leadership model**. Covey outlines his approach in his book *Seven Habits of Highly Effective People*.[25] The seven habits (and an additional eighth one added in 2004) are briefly outlined below:

1. **Be proactive.** You can either take an active or a passive role in your environment. Take responsibility and initiative in your actions.
2. **Begin with the end in mind.** Make plans for where you want to go.
3. **Put first things first.** Manage your time and schedule your priorities in order to execute your plan (see #2).
4. **Think win-win.** Adopt a philosophy based on cooperation.
5. **Seek first to understand, then to be understood.** Be a good listener. Learn to diagnose before you prescribe.
6. **Synergize.** Respect differences and build on the contributions of others.

7. Sharpen the saw. Practice self-renewal, including the four dimensions of your nature: physical, social/emotional, mental, and spiritual.[25]

8. Find your voice and inspire others to find theirs. Look for the potential in people.[26]

Although not designed to be a theory, Covey's "principles" have won wide acclaim from individuals and organizations alike.

In the 1970s, the **servant leadership model** grew out of the writings of teacher and management consultant Robert Greenleaf.[27] Greenleaf believed that leaders should serve their followers. By serving their followers, they set an example for them. Some observers have commented that this approach has its origins in the teaching of Jesus Christ. This approach emphasizes collaboration, empathy, and the ethical use of power. It was never designed as a theory.

A number of characteristics of the servant-leader have been identified; they include listening, empathy, healing, awareness, persuasion, stewardship, commitment to the growth of people, and building community.[28] A growing number of companies have embraced these concepts and include service to others as an integral part of their culture. Embedded in the mission statements of companies such as Starbucks, Men's Wearhouse, ServiceMaster, and Southwest Airlines are examples of this

Listening and understanding different viewpoints is an important leadership skill sales managers need to develop. (Comstock Complete)

ETHICS IN SALES MANAGEMENT

Ethical Leadership at Ken Vance Motors

Ken Vance is the owner of an award-winning automotive dealership, Ken Vance Motors, located in Eau Claire, Wisconsin. Ken Vance Motors consists of eight different franchises and nearly 140 employees. Vance says that when a person buys a car, it is an exciting event. He has worked to keep buying and selling cars both fun *and ethical* by following a few basic principles—principles that have helped him and those who work for him achieve great success.

- Follow the Golden Rule. (Treat others the way you would like to be treated.) It's simple and it works.
- Never tell lies or distort the truth. It's easier to tell the truth from the beginning.
- Trust and respect must be central in the relationship with your customer.
- Good communication is critical, be it with your customer or your employees. Time spent listening to them is time well spent.

Although Vance says he has always enjoyed selling cars, he loves the challenges of managing people. "I really get a charge out of working with employees. Watching them grow and develop is very rewarding. I hate to see people fail."

Vance also emphasizes the importance of communicating with employees. To keep the lines of communication open, the sales managers at Vance's various dealerships meet with their employees daily to discuss what is going on and the firm's financial performance.

Does taking an ethical approach to leadership work? Apparently so. The walls of his office are filled with sales and civic awards and citations he and his firm have received. Moreover, in an industry in which turnover can be high, many of his sales and service employees have worked for him for over 25 years.

Bill Marriott believes in developing his employees. Marriott's sales force is consistently ranked as one of the best. (Landov Media)

approach. Additionally, a growing number of colleges and universities are requiring students to participate in a service learning project because they believe it to be an important part of their education. The Ethics in Sales Management feature in this chapter discusses how the owner of an award-winning automotive dealership keeps ethics at the front and center of his organization.

The **Level 5 leadership model** was set forth by another former business professor, Jim Collins.[29, 30] Collins sought to identify the characteristics of "good" companies versus "great" companies based on a number of financial performance measures over a 15-year period. Some of those identified as great companies included Abbott, Kimberly-Clark, Walgreens, and Wells Fargo. Collins discovered that the leaders of the great companies shared several common traits: They were modest and willful, humble and fearless, and they set up their successors for greater success and were diligent.

The five-level hierarchy describes the skills and abilities that individuals should possess as they move from using characteristics attributed to their position as a formal leader into the more skilled and esteemed Level 5 leadership positions. The model proposes that an individual's level of skills builds successively on the skills and abilities of those from the previous level(s). Several concepts from earlier leadership research can be observed in this framework. For example, the first two levels reflect the need for leaders to have certain traits to be successful. Leaders operating at Level 1, termed the Highly Capable Individual, are hard working and display the knowledge, skills and abilities needed to master their particular job. At Level 2, the Contributing Team Member level, leaders contribute interpersonal skills that allow them to work effectively with others in groups. To be classified in the hierarchy's three highest levels, individuals need to increasingly incorporate more transformational leader characteristics into their leadership repertoire. The Level 3 leaders, labeled the Competent Manager, have the skills needed to organize followers and resources to achieve goals. Level 4 leaders, the Effective Leader, can convincingly articulate a vision and motivate followers to achieve it. The Level 5 leaders, labeled the Level 5 Executive, are capable of executing all of the previous skills with a style that demonstrates humility and determination. Although the model is conceptually intuitive, additional research is needed to confirm Collin's hierarchy.

Leadership Challenges for the Sales Executive

Today's sales management leaders are faced with many challenges when leading their organizations. Having good leadership at all levels in the organization can make the difference when it comes to meeting and exceeding these challenges. The following are some leadership challenges frequently cited by sales executives.

- *Recruiting and selecting good employees.* Finding and hiring the right person for your organization is vital to its future growth. The impact of a bad hire can be significant in terms of lost goodwill and sales, as well as training costs.
- *Keeping good employees.* Once you have identified good employees, you must work to ensure they want to continue to work for you and not be hired away by another firm.

- *Executing virtual leadership.* Sales managers may go long periods without being physically together with their employees. Communicating via phone, e-mail, and text messaging with their employees is therefore essential.
- *Diversifying the sales force.* Customers usually don't have the same cultural backgrounds. Having a diverse sales force better positions a company to understand its existing customers and attract new ones.
- *Removing limitations facing females.* Women occupy CEO positions at many companies including PepsiCo, Xerox, eBay, ADM, and Kraft Foods. During the past five years, over half of the top winners in the *National Collegiate Sales Conference were women.* Making sure women are an integral part of every level in your organization is essential.

Sales leaders face many challenges, including removing the barriers women employees face. (Comstock Complete)

- *Avoiding ethical mistakes.* Although the bar has been raised, ethical mistakes will occur. Through training and good leadership; making sure that lapses in ethical decision making isn't happening in your organization is a constant challenge.
- *Maintaining motivated sales teams.* By nature, sales involves rejection. Sales leaders need to create and sustain an environment that maintains high levels of individual and group motivation.
- *Integrating technology in sales.* Integrating technology into sales and sales management processes will oftentimes be the difference between the most successful company and those who follow it.

Summary

The leadership research conducted to date suggests there is no one best way to lead a sales force. A person who wants to be an effective sales manager will have to focus on a variety of behaviors. Being a good manager does not necessarily make you a good leader and vice versa. Oftentimes it isn't a matter of finding the best theory or approach as much as it is finding one that you are comfortable with and that works best for you.

The trait approach would suggest that certain traits are the earmark of someone with leadership characteristics or potential. These traits include self-confidence, determination, and sociability. The behavioral approach distinguishes between leaders on the basis of their concern for people versus production, or task behaviors.

The nature of the situation dictates how leaders should respond when using situational approaches. According to this approach, depending upon the characteristics of the situation, a leader should display a corresponding level of social and task behaviors. The more contemporary approaches to situation leadership encourage leaders to motivate their followers. Developing their trust and respect helps improve their job-related satisfaction and performance.

Lastly, new emerging leadership approaches offer a set of principles for leaders to embrace. According to these approaches, sales managers who aspire to be leaders should work to support their salespeople and should experience satisfaction when their salespeople are successful. Regardless of the leadership approach a person utilizes, there will be no shortage of challenges for the next generation of sales executives.

Key Terms

contingency theory of leadership 52	principle-centered leadership model 54
leader-member exchange (LMX) theory 53	servant leadership model 55
leadership 46	transformational leadership theory 54
Level 5 leadership model 56	Vroom-Yetton model 53

Questions and Problems

1. Think of one person you know who is an effective leader. What actions or traits does the person demonstrate? What behaviors does he or she engage in? Now do the same for an ineffective leader.
2. What behaviors or actions can you engage in to help develop your leadership skills while you are still in school?
3. What is the difference between managing and leading? Give some examples of each for a sales manager. How are the two concepts interrelated?
4. If leadership can be developed, how well are organizations doing with this challenge? Identify their strengths and/or weaknesses.
5. What traits are considered important for a leader's success? What are the shortcomings of the trait approach to leadership?
6. Describe the central tenets of the behavioral approach to leadership. Provide examples of each in a sales management situation.
7. According to situational theorists, what characteristics of a leadership situation need to be considered? Describe organizational engineering and provide an example of it.
8. What are in-groups and out-groups? Why is it beneficial to develop more in-group relationships?
9. What types of activities do transformational leaders engage in? Describe someone you believe displays these characteristics.
10. What is the focus of Covey's principle-centered leadership? How can you apply these principles to your situation as a student? As a sales manager?
11. Visit the Web sites for ServiceMaster, Starbucks, and Men's Wearhouse. How is the servant leadership approach conveyed in the mission statements of these firms? What servant-leader behaviors might a sales manager engage in?
12. How would you describe the leadership behaviors exhibited by a person in Collins' Level 5? What behaviors can you personally improve on to approach this level?
13. What are the most important leadership challenges you believe today's sales executives face, and how do you think they are meeting those challenges?

Role Play

Jackson Kramer Clothiers

Jackson Kramer Clothiers (JKC) is a company that sells business suits directly to busy managers and executives. Jackson Kramer, or "JK" as he is known, started selling men's clothing for a large department store during college and joined the store after he graduated. He did well and moved up in the company.

Seven years ago, JK launched his own company based on the premise that successful businesspeople don't have much time to shop for clothes because of their busy schedules. In fact, more companies are providing their executive-level personnel with wardrobe allowances. JKC reps want to be selected by these organizations as their "wardrobe provider of choice." The salespeople meet their clients at their workplaces or homes, take their measurements, and help them with wardrobe decisions. This service, combined with the custom-tailored, high-quality suits and business-causal wear the company provides, is viewed by many companies as a valuable service for this unique customer niche.

The salespeople JK employs are experienced, former department-store personnel. However, because one of the company's strategic goals is to grow its younger-client business segment over time, new hires without experience have been added to the firm's sales force.

JK has asked the firm's youngest sales managers to complete a campus recruiting assignment. He always advocates hiring people with leadership potential, and he wants the managers to try to identify candidates with those traits. He believes the traits help salespeople develop good rapport and trust with their clients and will help position the company for future growth.

Assignment

Break into groups of three. Have two people play the roles of recruiting sales managers. Develop a list of at least four or five questions that can be used to identify the leadership potential in each candidate examined.

The third person should play the role of JK and develop his or her own list of questions. The two sales managers need to convince the third person (JK) why the questions they have chosen should be asked of candidates.

Caselet 3.1: "I Never Thought About It"

Elena Shomos was looking forward to a preliminary interview for a job as a sales manager with Italia Optics. Elena had done well working as a sales representative for Italia. She nearly always was able to meet or surpass her sales, profitability, and customer service goals. In addition she had enjoyed her training and leadership development experiences with the company. People often told her she was a natural leader. Not surprisingly, her manager Liz Mercer had encouraged her to consider a sales management position.

Liz called Elena in and was helping her to prepare for her interviews with some additional sales executives. "Now, Elena, you've done the training and are showing good prospects for being a terrific saleswoman," Liz said. "If you are interested in becoming a leader at Italia, you need to have some idea about how you'll get there. So when they ask you in your interview about your style of leadership, what will you tell them?"

Elena thought a moment and then commented: "Style of leadership? Hmmm, I've never thought much about it. I've just done things."

As Elena left the office, Liz offered the following comment and suggestion: "If you don't think about your leadership style, how can management get a handle on what it is? Why don't you take some time and think about it."

Question

1. Put yourself in Elena's position. Based on what you know about different leadership approaches, how would you describe your leadership style?

Caselet 3.2: "Coach" Charlie Hustle

Michael Messina and David Fong graduated from college together. After graduation, both accepted job offers with the same company. Michael went to the company's Pittsburg office, and David went to the firm's San Francisco office.

During a refresher training course held one year later, the two finally got to see each other again. Michael listened for a couple of days as David, a competitive tennis and basketball player, sung the praises of his sales manager, Chuck Houser. David commented that Chuck's employees called him "Charlie Hustle" or "Coach" because of his style. "We come in, and Coach tells us what to do," David said. "I never have to wonder what's up or how to deal with a problem. He tells me what to do. He is super results-oriented. You always get pats on the back, and he even has a miniature scoreboard in his office where he can display our sales. He calls them 'points.' If you don't produce points, he'll be on your case and tell you what to do. Reminds me of my old tennis coach."

Michael wondered about a supervisor who was always telling his salespeople what to do. "Man, David, Chuck sounds like a high school coach—not the leader of your sales team."

"What do you mean?" countered David. "He seems like the perfect leader. What else should he be doing?"

Question

1. Put yourself in Michael's shoes. What should he tell David about other leadership behaviors Coach could use?

References

1. Kotter, John P. (1990). *A Force for Change: How Leadership Differs from Management*. New York: Free Press.
2. Kotter, John P. (1988). *The Leadership Factor*. New York: Free Press.
3. Wellins, Richard S., Charles J. Cosentino, and Bradford Thomas (2004). "Building a Winning Sales Force," White paper published by Developmental Dimensions, Inc. (DDI).
4. Stogdill, R. M. (1948). "Personal Factors Associated with Leadership: A Survey of the Literature," *Journal of Psychology*, 25, 35–71.
5. Lord, R. G., C. L. DeVader, and G. M. Alliger (1986). "A Meta-Analysis of the Relation Between Personality Traits and Leadership Perceptions: An Application of Validity Generalization Procedures," *Journal of Applied Psychology*, 71, 402–410.
6. Kirkpatrick, S. A., and E. A. Locke (1991). "Leadership: Do Traits Matter?" *The Executive*, 5, 48–60.
7. Northouse, P. G. (2007). *Leadership: Theory and Practice*, 4th ed. Thousand Oaks, CA: Sage Publications, Inc.
8. Flesishman, E. A. (1953). "The Description of Supervisory Behavior," *Personnel Psychology*, 37, 1–6.
9. Katz, D., N. Maccoby, and N. C. Morse (1950). *Productivity, Supervision, and Morale in an Office Situation*. Ann Arbor: University of Michigan, Institute for Social Research.
10. Blake R., and J. Mouton (1964). *The Managerial Grid*. Houston: Gulf Publishing Company.
11. Blake, R., and A. McCanse (1991). *Leadership Dilemmas: Grid Solutions*. Houston: Gulf Publishing Company.
12. Lashinsky, A. (2006) "50 Most Powerful Women: Building eBay 2.0," *Fortune*, (154) 8, October 16, 161–164.

13. Yukl, G. (1994). *Leadership in Organizations*, 3rd ed. Englewood Cliffs, NJ: Prentice Hall.

14. Fiedler, F. E. (1967). *A Theory of Leadership Effectiveness*. New York: McGraw-Hill.

15. Vroom, V. H., and P. W. Yetton (1973). *Leadership and Decision-Making*. Pittsburg: University of Pittsburg Press.

16. Hersey, P., and K. H. Blanchard (1969). "Life Cycle of Leadership," *Training and Development Journal*, 23, 26–34.

17. Vroom V. H. (1976). "Leadership" in *Handbook of Industrial and Organizational Psychology*, M. D. Dunnette, ed. Chicago: Rand McNally.

18. Sains, A., and S. Reed (2006). "Electrolux Redesigns Itself," *Business Week* Inside Innovation supplement (4011), November 27, 12–15.

19. Dansureau, F., G. B. Graen, and W. Haga (1975). "A Vertical Dyad Linkage Approach to Leadership in Formal Organizations," *Organizational Behavior and Human Performance*, 13, 46–78.

20. Graen, G. B., and Uhl-Bien, M. (1991). "The Transformation of Professionals into Self-managing and Partially Self-designing Contributions: Toward a Theory of Leader-making," *Journal of Management Systems*, 3(3), 33–48.

21. Graen, G. B., and Uhl-Bien, M. (1995). "Development of Leader-Member Exchange (LMX) Theory of Leadership over 25 Years: Applying a Multi-level Multi-domain Perspective," *Leadership Quarterly*, 6(2), 219–247.

22. Bass, B. M. (1985). *Leadership and Performance Beyond Expectations*. New York: Free Press.

23. Bass, B. M. (1997). "Personal Selling and Transactional/Transformational Leadership," *Journal of Personal Selling & Sales Management*, 17(3), Summer, 19–28.

24. Ehmann, L. C. (2006). "A Team of Winners," *Selling Power*, 26(9), November/December, 40–43.

25. Covey, S. R. (1989). *Seven Habits of Highly Effective People*. New York: Simon and Schuster.

26. Covey. S. R. (2003). *The 8th Habit: From Effectiveness to Greatness*. New York: Free Press.

27. Greenleaf, R. (1977). *Servant Leadership*. Ramsey, NJ: Paulist Press.

28. Spears, L. C. (1995). *Reflections on Leadership: How Robert K. Greenleaf's Theory of Servant-Leadership Influenced Today's Top Management Thinker*. New York: John Wiley & Sons.

29. Collins, J. (2001). *Good to Great: Why Some Companies Make the Leap . . . and Others Don't*. New York: Harper Collins Publishers.

30. Collins, J., and J. Porras (2004). *Built to Last: Successful Habits of Visionary Companies*. New York: Harper Collins Publishers.

31. Gschwandtner, L. (2007). "Great Managers," *Selling Power*, 25th Anniversary Issue, 27(1), 33–35.

4

ETHICS, THE LAW, AND SALES LEADERSHIP

LEARNING OBJECTIVES

After completing this chapter, you should be able to:

- Identify the more common ethical dilemmas that face salespeople, sales managers, and sales executives.

- Distinguish between those organizational policies and practices that support ethical behavior and those that enable unethical behavior.

- Explain how principled leadership can foster a firm's ethical principles and corporate culture.

- Develop an appropriate course of action when you're personally faced with an ethical dilemma.

Does the profit motive create opportunistic values and morals? Does greed drive every salesperson to engage in unethical behavior whenever possible? Of course not. Nonetheless, the sales profession has developed a reputation for being unsavory. Yet any sales professional who is in business for the long haul knows that unethical sales practices and unethical salespeople can't last. Even without legal safeguards and judicial recourse (not to mention the potential for negative word-of-mouth and reduced future sales), most salespeople are still good people. They do the right thing because they want to, not because they have to. In this chapter, we will explore ethics in the sales profession and the actions sales managers can take to support ethical behavior by their employees.

TAIT CRUSE

MANAGING PARTNER, NORTHWESTERN MUTUAL

After graduating from college with a finance and economics degree, Tait Cruse thought he wanted to work with money and took a job in finance. Quickly, though, he realized that he was in the wrong part of the business and that what he really wanted to do was to work with people. After some trial and error, he said, "I thought I should make another move, preferably into financial services sales."

A friend suggested Northwestern Mutual, so Cruse sent his resume to the home office. A year later, they called, hired him, and put him to work in Dallas. "Everything seemed fine for about eight months, but suddenly it all crashed," recalls Cruse.

Driving into work one morning, he was run off the road and totaled his car. The night before, his girlfriend had broken up with him, telling him he was going nowhere and had no career. He walked from the accident to the office and sat in his cubicle, watching as the wrecker towed his car off and realizing that he was failing. With no leads, no appointments, and nothing to do, he just sat there all day and reflected, reaching some important conclusions.

"First, I realized that I should have been committed from day one to being successful. I hadn't been committed to the training, to the sales process, and to my customers. I realized I needed to be a student of people, relationships, and sales."

Cruse goes on to say that he was carrying a "fake it until you make it" mentality. To him, this meant he wasn't being true to himself because he was pretending to be something he wasn't. And that wasn't ethical—it wasn't right. "One important discovery that day was that I was trying to be like the big names in my business rather than just being myself," Cruse explains. "At the same time, I also realized that not only was I not being honest with my clients by not being myself, I wasn't being honest with myself." Cruse realized that while he could inflate the number of calls he made or exaggerate the quality of those calls when talking with a manager, he was really only hurting himself. "I had the 'fake it until you make it' mentality, and I wasn't making it."

Two other factors that he realized were important were passion and vision. "I had to ask myself if I was passionately pursuing helping people or only worried about my quota. I realized that if I focused on truly helping people, then the quota would take care of itself." The vision was simply keeping this passion in front of him. "I had to write my goals down, track my activities, and make sure that I was doing the right things so that I could help as many people as I could."

He went into his boss's office at 5:30 that evening and described the factors that he thought he needed to focus on to be successful. "My boss was surprised, and he told me that he was actually in the process of writing me a letter telling me I had 30 days to bring my numbers up or I was going to be fired. I asked him for a year to prove myself." A year later, Tait Cruse was the top rep in the country among those with under two years of experience.

From this beginning, he has built a sales career that put him in the elite of his company's salespeople. His growth was so stellar that the same manager that was about to fire him asked him to help others. Starting with one salesperson, Cruse began to work with struggling salespeople. Quickly, his team became three, then five, then seven, then more. By 2003, he was managing half of the office, or 45 salespeople. In 2004, the company made him managing partner, responsible for 150 salespeople.

Cruse was financially set for life as a sales representative. Becoming a managing partner did not necessarily mean he would make more money. Rather, it was the opportunity to help others grow and develop that triggered his decision to move to management. "In 2005, we grew core insurance 15 percent, group health 45 percent, and investments 50 percent. In 2006, we expect the same trajectory for growth." These numbers are incredible for the entire industry, not just Northwestern Mutual. But it isn't the numbers alone that get Cruse excited. As he says, "My passion has always been about helping people. When I became focused on helping others, I freed myself to be honest and ethical. That is what turned my career around as a salesperson; that is what is making my career as a sales executive successful." ■

In the business world, the issue of ethics is a constant. True, there are periods of time when unethical or illegal activities grab the headlines and people wonder if business is becoming more ruthless and less honest. True, there are also cycles in behavior that lead to increases in law-breaking or increases in honesty and decent behavior. At the same time, however, when making their purchasing decisions, buyers are increasingly taking into account how ethical salespeople and the companies they represent appear to be.[1] Ultimately, though, the question is whether or not *you* will do the right thing when faced with an ethical dilemma.

What exactly is the right thing? Is the Golden Rule, "do unto others as you would have others do unto you," the best guide? Or is "do whatever is legal, whether it is right or not" all that is required of salespeople and their managers?

For the sales executive, there are many dimensions to "doing the right thing." Questions about the right thing to do can involve the right thing to do for customers, salespeople, shareholders, vendors, and many, many others.

Ethics are the moral principles of right and wrong that guide people's behavior. What is and isn't ethical varies from culture to culture. In terms of business it can vary from industry to industry. What is believed to be ethical can also change over time. For example, it was once considered unethical for doctors and lawyers to advertise their services. Today, many doctors and lawyers are still reluctant to do so, but the practice has become more widely accepted. (We are all familiar with television and radio commercials touting the LASIK skills of doctors and the big awards attorneys have won for their clients.)

Problems arise, however, when people's values conflict with what they see going on around them. When the problems are large enough, the responses to them are then codified into law. For example, there are laws regarding how prices can be set, laws that proscribe how long a buyer has to rethink a purchase (such as a car), and still other laws that govern salespeople's behavior. All of these laws were created to stop practices that people thought were problematic.

Of course, not everyone agrees about what is ethical and how people should and should not behave. As a result, different salespeople and sales managers have different ethical philosophies. In the following section, we review some of these approaches to ethics.

Approaches to Ethics

We mentioned a couple of approaches to ethics in the introduction to this chapter—the Golden Rule, do as much as the law allows, and so forth. Other common approaches include the conventionalist approach, the market imperative, the Protestant ethic, the Libertine ethic, and the utilitarian ethic.[2] These approaches are summarized in Exhibit 4.1. Next, we will discuss each approach.

The Golden Rule

The Golden Rule is familiar even to schoolchildren: *Do unto others as you would have them do unto you.* To treat others as you want to be treated changes what might be considered the natural order of things. After all, isn't putting someone else's needs on a par with your own needs only fair? The challenge arises when there are multiple "others," and their needs or wants conflict with one another. For example, assuming you do not want to be cheated, you would therefore not cheat your customer. But you also want to buy as much as you can at the lowest price, so you lower your price to your customers; this action damages your company and your manager gets into trouble. You wouldn't want to be in trouble, so you don't want your manager to be in trouble. Thus, the Golden Rule often works well in situations with only two parties, but because most salespeople are responsible to several different people who all want different things, the Golden Rule is not always helpful.

EXHIBIT 4.1

Approaches to Ethics

Approach	Summary	Pros and Cons
Golden Rule	Treat others as you would like to be treated	• Personalizes ethical decisions, making it easy to determine what to do • Fails to account for situations in which "others" are in conflict
Conventionalist Approach	Acts are OK as long as its legal or if everyone is doing it	• Fails to account for gray areas, in which acts are not specified as either "legal" or "illegal"
Protestant Ethic	Do what you can defend to a committee of peers	• What's "ethical" is based on the intended, not actual, outcome • Can lead to more concern about doing what can be defended than what is right
Market Imperative Approach	The market will determine what is right	• Provides clear responsibilities for individuals • Can devolve into "might is right" scenario
Libertine Ethic	Do what you want, as long as no one gets hurt	• Outcomes are important, and a responsibility for others is assumed • Can lead to problems when others are harmed indirectly or harm is not obvious
Utilitarian Ethic	Do what has the best outcome for all involved	• Outcomes, and honorable intent, are important; requires taking responsibility for others • It's unclear who gets to decide what outcomes are "best"

S **SELF-ASSESSMENT LIBRARY**

How do your ethics compare to those of business professionals? Go to http://www. prenhall.com/sal/ and log in using the access code that came with your textbook. Then click on:

Assessments
  I. What About Me?
    D. Decision Making Insights
      3. How Do My Ethics Rate?

After you have completed the assessment, your answers are then compared to those offered by a group of 243 businesspeople. Because the instrument presents both philosophical positions and individual situations, your answers could vary greatly from the managers' average. That does not necessarily mean you are more or less ethical; just not average!

Furthermore, the Golden Rule assumes that the way you want to be treated is the way others want to be treated, too, when maybe that's not the case. For example, you might not want a salesperson to call your friends, so you don't give out referrals. Then a friend gets mad because she finds out you've been using this great new product for weeks and wants to know why you didn't just have the salesperson call her.

The Conventionalist Approach

The conventionalist approach is entirely different. It suggests that people should take any and all actions allowed by law or by convention.[3] In a sense, the conventionalist approach is a variation of the phrase "Everybody's doing it, so it must be okay." Thus, people shouldn't feel the need to act on a higher principle than other people.

The problem with this approach is that it really doesn't consider what's ethical and not ethical. For example, if someone were harmed by a practice considered to be the norm, then the practice would still be considered okay according to the conventionalist approach. For example, not selling homes in certain areas to people of color was once considered standard practice in the real estate business. But the negative, unethical outcomes of the practice are precisely why laws were passed to ban it. Another way to view the conventionalist approach to behavior is as follows: "Do it until they say you can't." But that does not make the behavior right.

A conventionalist ethic means assuming that because everyone is doing something, it is the right, or "OK," thing to do. (Shutterstock)

Recently, it seems a similar philosophy has arisen in the business world—one that is based on the expression: "It is easier to ask for forgiveness than permission." Although such a philosophy might be appropriate when it comes to dealing with red tape that can slow down doing what is right, some have observed salespeople and managers using this philosophy as an excuse to engage in questionable activity. Giving free service to a customer when your company prices that service at several thousand dollars is an example. Although there may be a good business reason to do such a thing, problems arise when the outcome damages someone, such as a customer or the company. In this case, the company will have lost out on a significant amount of sales revenue it is due. If you fail to ask permission first before you do it, your company might not consider it a forgivable mistake.

The Protestant Ethic

Most students associate the term "Protestant ethic" with "work ethic." However, when discussing approaches to moral choices, these terms are not the same. The Protestant ethic is an approach to considering an ethical dilemma and can be summed up as follows: "Could I satisfactorily explain this choice to a committee of my peers?"

Such was the case in the early development of the Protestant church. If you were a Protestant accused of a sin, you had to appear before a committee of your brethren who would decide upon your punishment. A similar question related to this approach is the following: "Could I explain the action to my spouse or to the public?"

You can probably see how the Protestant ethic can end up mirroring the conventionalist approach. Pick the right committee (don't put any customers on it, for example), and you can probably explain away anything. In addition, your explanation could focus on your intent rather than your actions, but the committee would have to consider your intent to be more important. (Recall that the origin of Protestant ethic lies in understanding sin; thus, your intent is very important.) Providing evidence that your intent was honorable, though, can be difficult.

Pilgrims brought the Protestant ethic with them when they came to the United States; assessing the ethics of a behavior requires understanding intent. (Corbis/Bettman)

For example, suppose a customer's shipment of a product is delayed. If the firm's sales rep has some of the product on hand, she might give it to the firm to tide it over until the shipment arrives. The problem is that the firm might consider the product the sales rep supplied to be free, whereas the sales rep's manager might consider the handout to be a form of stealing on the salesperson's part. So, even though the rep's intentions were honorable, she would have to prove it to a committee of her peers.

The Market Imperative

The market imperative stems from Adam Smith's classical economics approach to capitalism. The imperative states that the market requires a person to act in his or her own best interest. Similar to Darwin's approach to understanding the natural world, Smith believed that the notion of the "survival of the fittest" dictated the economic world. This is somewhat similar to Nietzsche's "might makes right" approach—that the strongest deserve to rule. However, all of us know that modern civilizations have decreed that such an approach is not appropriate. Laws are created to protect the defenseless and one's strength does not determine one's rights.

Nonetheless, isn't the purpose of an organization to maximize the wealth of its shareholders? This vision of an organization's purpose holds if you accept Smith's view of the market. The salesperson, therefore, works for the organization, and it is the organization's needs that must come first, according to this ethic. A counter-argument to the market imperative is that the corporation is an entity that is granted the right to exist by society. Therefore the corporation must be governed by what is best for society *in addition to* maximizing shareholder wealth. Moreover, what is best for society must balance the interests of the different people within it—those of shareholders, employees, and customers alike. Smith, though, might argue that these three groups should fight it out to see who comes out on top. As a result, sometimes labor will win (labor laws will be passed, for example); sometimes customers will win (as was the case when the Consumer Rights Act of 1962 was passed); and sometimes companies will win (as was the case when the Robinson-Patman Act—a law that protects retailers from powerful manufacturers—was passed).

The Libertine Ethic

According to the Libertine approach, ethics are based on the principle of individual freedom. Specifically, the principle is that customers should be free to make their own decisions, as they best see fit. The Libertine ethic grew to prominence in the 1960s and is best

The Libertine ethic developed in the 1960s. It essentially says you can do whatever you want, as long as no one is hurt. (Getty Images/Time Life Pictures)

expressed as the notion that one should be free to do whatever one wants, as long as no one else gets hurt.

On the face of it, the Libertine approach appears to work very well with sales. A salesperson can do whatever he or she wants as long as no one (the customer) is hurt. So, for example, if the salesperson were to manipulate the selling situation in a way that it eliminated or narrowed the customer's choices, this would clearly be unethical because it would adversely affect the customer. What about bribing customers with kickbacks? At first glance, it would appear that according to the Libertine view of things, bribery would be okay. After all, bribery doesn't influence the buyer's *ability* to choose, just his willingness to do so.

As you can see, if bribery is acceptable, there must be drawbacks to the Libertine ethic. After all, fairness isn't just what is fair for the customer but also what is fair for the competition, and a bribe eliminates competitors unfairly. Furthermore, a bribe isn't fair in a business-to-business setting because the person doing the buying, although he represents the customer, personally benefits from the bribe. This is the difficulty of the Libertine ethic—it identifies as important only the two actors in the transaction; in this case, the person selling and the person buying. Conflicts among other groups are rarely considered, much less resolved.

The Utilitarian Ethic

The utilitarian ethic, like the Libertine ethic and the Golden Rule, focuses on outcomes—do what has the best outcome. There are different forms of the utilitarian ethic (situational ethics, the Bentham/Mills proportional ethic, and so forth). All of them, however, come down to the basic question of whether or not an action's positive consequences outweigh its negative consequences.

The difficulty of this approach becomes immediately apparent: After all, who gets to decide what the value, or weight, of the positive and negative outcomes are? Of course, it has to be the person making the decision about whether or not to engage in the act—in this case, the salesperson. The salesperson's temptation, therefore, would be to minimize the weight given to the negative outcomes experienced by others and maximize the value of the positive outcomes she herself experienced.

Hence, we return to the Golden Rule: The salesperson must consider her customer's needs to be as important as her own. Ultimately, however, we know she not only has to consider her own needs and the needs of her customer but also the needs of the organization and society. They, too, come into play. This means that neither the Golden Rule nor the Libertarian ethic adequately address all situations a salesperson faces.

The Salesperson as a Boundary Spanner

Is sales among the most unethical professions? Actually, there are people in many professions who are more likely to exaggerate, which is another form of manipulation. According to several studies conducted by noted psychologist George Dudley, politicians (no surprise there), psychologists, preachers, and professors are more likely to exaggerate than are salespeople. So are Web designers, architects, and others.[4] Another study found that business students are more likely to engage in unethical behaviors than sales professionals do.[5] Salespeople are unique, however, in that they are **boundary spanners**, meaning that they operate both outside of and within an organization's boundaries—that is, they work within their companies but they also work outside of their companies with customers. Because salespeople are boundary spanners, they encounter ethical dilemmas not only externally with customers but internally with other employees.

If salespeople are boundary spanners, who, then, do they ultimately represent? The organization for whom they work, obviously. However, in a sense, they also represent their customers. You can probably see how a salesperson might represent a customer. For example, if the customer needs an order expedited, it is the salesperson who argues the customer's case to her firm's shipping department.

Does the salesperson represent different people within her company? At times, yes. Suppose a company's sales managers want certain products produced faster in order to make more sales. Now suppose personnel in the company's manufacturing department want the products produced more slowly so they're not defective. With whom should the salesperson side in this case? After all, if the products are defective, it will be the salesperson who has to listen to customers' complaints.

Also, doesn't the salesperson, in some respects, represent her own family? Suppose not enough of the product is produced and the salesperson doesn't make her quota. Obviously her performance will suffer, she will earn less money, and her family will have less to live on.

As you can see, trying to understand ethics from a simple dyadic (seller/buyer) perspective or from an organizational perspective (do whatever you want as long as it is best for the company) doesn't work. In the real world, things are obviously more complex than that.

Representing multiple parties simultaneously is what causes salespeople difficulty, and problems can obviously ensue when the salesperson emphasizes one party's needs over another. When selling is done right, however, great things can happen. The Ethics in Sales Management feature in this chapter describes one such situation.

 ETHICS IN SALES MANAGEMENT

Done Right

September 15 was Laura Johnston's last day at Travelocity. She had accepted a new job at Bank of America. The job came as a huge promotion, with great increases in her salary, incentives, and benefits, such as vacation days. As in many cases, her coworkers gathered at a reception to say good-bye and to wish her well.

David Riegel organized the reception, ordered the food, reserved the reception room at the hotel, and hired the bartenders. At the appropriate moment, he offered a few words regarding Laura's contribution to Travelocity and how much he appreciated her work. He then gave her a small parting gift and presented a toast to her future. While wiping away a few tears, Laura described how much she appreciated all that Dave had done for her over the past years.

This wasn't your usual going-away party, though. Why? Because not everyone in the room worked for Travelocity. In fact, Dave works for Teradata; Laura was his customer at Travelocity. At Bank of America, Laura would be someone else's customer—not Dave's.

Dave made it clear that while Laura worked for Travelocity, he worked for *both* her and the company. The collaboration and respect between the two was unmistakable; it was clear that they had become a team, and it saddened them both that Laura was leaving.

When sales is done right, friendships can develop and great things can be accomplished. Moreover, the issue of ethics never comes up. But that's the way it should be.

Common Ethical Issues Facing Salespeople

In this section we examine ethical dilemmas salespeople most commonly face with regard to their customers. Then we examine the dilemmas they commonly face with regard to their firms.

ETHICAL ISSUES ASSOCIATED WITH THE SALESPERSON'S CUSTOMERS Exhibit 4.2 summarizes the more common ethical issues salespeople face with customers. When a salesperson lies about a product, making claims for it that are not true, the salesperson is guilty of **misrepresentation**. Misrepresentation can lead to lawsuits, the recovery of damages by injured parties, and other negative consequences. The insurance industry offers such an example: In a notable case in the 1990s, registered nurses believed they were buying retirement accounts because the Met Life insurance salespeople with whom they were dealing used terms like "deposit" during their sales pitches. Actually, however, the nurses had been sold life insurance policies and were paying "premiums" on them—not making deposits into retirement accounts. Met Life was fined, and the salespeople involved lost their licenses.[6]

Misrepresentation is not the same as puffery. **Puffery** is an allowable exaggeration as long as it is vague and general, with no specific facts. For example, a salesperson can be reasonably expected to claim that his firm's product is the best because "best" is a general term and can mean different things to different people. However, if he claims the product will process 200 packages per hour, and it only processes 100, then that is misrepresentation.

Bribery is another common temptation (and illegal in a number of countries. We discuss bribery laws later). We can officially define **bribery** as any offer of a gift that secures undue influence. Xerox once offered the following: When a company purchased a Xerox copier, the person buying it received a free round-trip ticket to fly anywhere in the United States. This would not have been a problem if the people buying the copiers gave the tickets to their companies to use for business travel. There were no mechanisms in place, however, to ensure that this happened. Competitors complained that the free airline ticket amounted to bribery. As a result, Xerox pulled the plug on the promotion. What is interesting about this example is that the program was created by Xerox's sales managers, not its salespeople. This example illustrates how sales managers can unwittingly put their salespeople at risk by devising poorly conceived sales strategies.

As you can probably tell from the Xerox discussion, offering customers overly expensive entertainment and gifts can get companies and their sales reps into trouble. Pharmaceutical companies once gave lavish trips to doctors—weekend hunting trips, for example, during which time they would listen to a half-hour presentation about a new drug. Would you want to know that the medicine you take was chosen on the basis of which company had the best hunting trip? Thankfully, the practice was halted by government regulations.

Salespeople can also get into trouble if they offer buyers gifts when selling to government entities. One Waco, Texas, schoolteacher found that out the hard way when she accepted $750 in gift cards from a salesperson selling a computer-based English learning software product. Even though the teacher claimed she was going to use the gift cards to

EXHIBIT 4.2

Common Ethical Issues between Customers and Their Salespeople

> **Misrepresentation:** The salesperson exaggerates benefits or minimizes problems, leading a customer to draw erroneous conclusions about a product or service.
>
> **Bribery:** The salesperson attempts to influence a buyer unfairly by offering a gift or money.
>
> **Privacy:** The salesperson fails to protect the privacy of another customer by giving the customer's confidential information to another customer; the salesperson invades the customer's privacy with spam or unwanted calls.

buy iPods for the classroom, she lost her job, as did the salesperson, when the gifts came to light in 2006. The former teacher also faces possible criminal charges.[7]

So that there can never be any question about undue influence being exerted as a result of gifts or entertainment, some companies, such as IBM and Wal-Mart, will not allow their employees to accept so much as a cup of coffee from a vendor.

This doesn't mean that it's always wrong to reward your customers. It just depends on how it is done and whether or not it's excessive. For example, as a thank-you to its customers, e-Rewards, a Dallas-based marketing research company, provides them with a catalog of gifts to choose from. However, e-Rewards' salespeople are given guidelines suggesting how much business a customer needs to do with the firm in order to receive certain gifts. In addition, e-Rewards' marketing staff determines what holiday gift to give customers at the end of the year. This approach eliminates guesswork for the salesperson as to what gift is appropriate for which customer and when.

What about an offer from a customer to a salesperson? One student once reported how his father had accepted a month-long vacation on a private Caribbean island from a customer—his only customer. Was this simply a gift from one friend to another or an attempt to generate special offers, lower prices, and the like?

Recall that earlier, we pointed out that a bribe can harm the competition. Salespeople are sometimes tempted to hamper their competitors in other ways, though. Julie Featherston, a sales representative for Revlon, described how her competitors would sometimes move Revlon's products off of store shelves, which interfered with displays she had set up. When it happened in one part of her territory on a regular basis, Featherston brought it to the attention of the store managers there. The managers determined who the guilty party was and removed that company's products from their stores.

Salespeople also have access to a lot of confidential information that needs to remain confidential. It's not unusual for buyers to want to know what their competitors are doing and to try to obtain that information from salespeople. For example, a buyer in one store might ask Featherston how well Revlon's products sell in a competing store. If Featherston says, "Walgreen sells an average of five cases of Revlon products per store," she just gave Walgreen's confidential sales figures to the competitor. The competitor might also be reluctant to do business with Featherston in the future because she obviously can't be trusted to keep trade secrets confidential. Similarly, salespeople sometimes pressure buyers to give them information about their competitors. For example, customers sometimes find themselves in situations in which they know about new, soon-to-be-released products but are asked by the makers of the products to keep the information private until market announcements are made. During that time, it would be inappropriate for a customer to share that knowledge with a salesperson employed by another vendor.

The issue here is privacy. (Recall the controversy that Facebook got into because it began sending information subscribers thought was private to everyone on the subscribers' contact lists.) The Federal Trade Commission requires financial institutions that collect personal information to have a privacy policy. Any company, though, that has a privacy policy has to abide by it, whether or not the firm is a financial institution. Salespeople have to recognize that they are bound by these policies, too. No one wants their private information published or shared with others without permission.

Another issue is not following established policies your customer's company sets. For example, Diamond Shamrock requires all salespeople calling on the firm to register with its purchasing office before making a visit to the company's corporate headquarters. Even a visit to drop off supplies or a sales proposal means the salesperson has to register. If the salesperson doesn't comply, he can be banned from doing business with the company. What Diamond Shamrock is trying to do via this policy is to prevent **rogue purchasing**— the practice of purchasing products from nonapproved vendors.

EXHIBIT 4.3

Common Ethical Issues Involving the Salesperson's Company

> **Stealing:** The salesperson fails to work a full day, stealing time that he or she is paid for; the salesperson pads his or her expense accounts.
>
> **Claiming Credit:** The salesperson steals other people's leads; the salespeople misrepresent the location of a customer in order to receive credit for an order belonging to someone else.
>
> **Sexual Harassment:** The salesperson experiences unwanted sexual offers or inappropriate physical contact.

In summary, most students, when asked, say that they would neither accept nor offer a bribe. Yet, as you can see, rarely are ethical issues as obvious as a buyer saying, "Here—take this bribe and give me a cheaper price." Ethical issues are generally much more complex than that.

ETHICAL ISSUES ASSOCIATED WITH THE SALESPERSON'S COMPANY Not all ethical issues are associated with the salesperson's customers. Salespeople can also find themselves either tempted or pressured to engage in unethical activity at their own companies. Exhibit 4.3 summarizes the ethical issues that involve the companies of salespeople.

It's obvious that salespeople shouldn't steal from their companies by taking things that don't belong to them—say, taking office supplies home for their own personal use. But more subtle forms of "stealing" can occur. Consider the salesperson who spends money on office supplies while traveling but company policy prohibits reimbursement for those expenses. In this case, the salesperson might be tempted to recover the money for the supplies by inflating her other allowable expenses. Or consider a salesperson that takes a day off without telling anyone. These types of behaviors can be considered stealing.

In some situations in which salespeople do not have defined territories, stealing "leads," or contacts, from other salespeople can be a problem. Jeff Hostetler, the sales director at Tele-Optics, a telecommunications firm, likens the behavior to "wolves fighting over a chunk of meat. Not only will reps kill each other, but they will kill the business, too," Hostetler says.[8] Similarly, some reps will falsify customers' orders. They do this by shipping products to their customers and then their customers send the products on to customers outside their territory. The rep whose customers ultimately receive the product is cheated out of the sale. The rep who took the order gets the credit, even though credit for the sale is supposed to go to the rep whose customer placed the real order. Either way, it is stealing and wrong.

Sexual harassment (unwelcome sexual advances, jokes, and so forth), even if it's unintentional, can obviously occur within a salesperson's company as well as with one's customers. To be sure, salespeople can be vulnerable to important customers who seek sexual favors in exchange for their business. Overall, however, sexual harassment is rare. One study found that the average company experiences just over one case of sexual harassment per year.[9] Nonetheless, companies need to prepare their employees, including their salespeople, to deal with unwelcome sexual advances.

Creating an Ethical Sales Climate

A recent study of salespeople in France found that high-performing salespeople are far more likely to leave a company if the ethical climate of that company is poor. A firm's **ethical climate** is the degree to which its corporate culture supports ethical business practices. (Or, stated in the obverse, an unethical climate is the degree to which unethical business practices are tolerated or encouraged.) From this study we can conclude that high-performing salespeople prefer high ethical standards and want to work for companies that support such standards.[10] Although the culture of the firm is the subject of another chapter, suffice it to say here that a company's sales leaders are responsible for ensuring that its salespeople operate in an ethical environment.

A company outlines its standards for ethical behavior in its **code of ethics**. According to the Ethics Resource Center, a nonprofit educational organization whose mission is to foster ethical practices among individuals and institutions, some 90 percent of U.S. organizations have a written code of ethics.[11] A code of ethics is established in order to:

- Provide salespeople and other employees with guidelines and standards for conduct.
- Help salespeople inform others that they intend to conduct business in an ethical manner.
- Support salespeople's intentions to remain ethical, offering salespeople an "out" when under pressure. (In other words, make it easy for salespeople to say, "I can't do that because it's against my company's policy, and I would get fired.")
- Attract high-quality salespeople.

Therefore, the first step to creating an ethical climate is setting standards and listing these standards in a code of ethics. Companies are not the only groups with codes of ethics; professional organizations also set codes for their members. For example, the Direct Selling Association (comprised of companies like Mary Kay, Premier Jewelry, and other companies that sell direct to consumers) has established a code of ethics for its member companies. Of the 12 standards, 9 focus squarely on the salesperson. Codes of ethics exist for purchasing, too; the Institute for Supply Management (formerly the National Association of Purchasing Managers) has a code of ethics for its members. The Caux Round Table offers a code for businesses operating internationally.

An important aspect of these codes is the clarity with which they are written. The more specific the codes are, the greater assistance they can be to salespeople and sales managers. Salespeople and sales managers don't have to worry about whether a decision is right or wrong if the decision is spelled out in the code.

The U.S. **Federal Sentencing Guidelines (FSG)** were enacted in 1987 and updated in 2007 as a response to an increase in white-collar crime, specifically crime committed by businesses. The FSG is a set of suggested guidelines for sales organizations developing programs for preventing, detecting, and halting unethical or illegal misconduct by their employees. If a company has an employee engaging in illegal behavior, it is liable if it has not followed the FSG; however, a company that follows the guidelines can avoid severe penalties. In this case, it's assumed the company did all it could to prevent the behavior and that the employee simply acted of his or her own accord.

These guidelines include:

- Developing a clear and complete code of ethics capable of reducing misconduct.
- Securing top management's support for high ethical standards and charging an executive-level officer of the company with responsibility for establishing and managing a compliance program.
- Establishing and managing a compliance program that includes mandatory training and regular communication.
- Creating internal auditing systems to monitor behavior and detect misconduct.
- Enforcing standards and punishing violations consistently.
- Reviewing and modifying the compliance program on a regular basis to demonstrate a focus on continuous improvement.

GLOBAL SALES MANAGEMENT

The Caux Round Table

Excessive imbalances in trade and the disparities between developed and developing nations create a number of problems in the world. Countries with greater economic power can easily abuse those with less by building sweatshops, using child labor, and other practices designed to take advantage of people in these countries. Even companies that want to do the right thing sometimes find themselves criticized for their business practices in other countries. To provide guidance for companies operating globally, the Caux Round Table (CRT) was developed.

The CRT was founded in 1986 by Frederick Phillips, the former chair of Phillips Electronics, and Olivier Giscard d'Estaing, the former vice-chair of INSEAD, an international business school. The primary purpose of CRT was to reduce trade tensions between countries, but it was soon clear that more than reducing tensions needed to be done. Ryuzaburo Kaku, then chair of Canon, Inc., urged executives from Europe, the United States, and Japan to help the worldwide business community take steps to reduce social and economic threats. Out of this work, in 1994, came the CRT principles, which codified the most comprehensive set of responsible business practices that exists today.

Although there are many CRT principles, several are particularly important to sales organizations:

- The value of a business to society is the wealth it creates for shareholders and employees, as well as the marketable products and services it provides to consumers *at a price commensurate with quality.*
- Businesses should *respect international and domestic rules*, and avoid behavior that, even if legal, has adverse consequences to society. Thus, salespeople have to consider the impact of their behavior on society, rather than the legality of such behavior.

Most recently, Nissan Motor Co. adopted the CRT's vision for socially responsible businesses. The firm is just one of many organizations that subscribe the CRT's principles of moral capitalism.

Source: **www.cauxroundtable.org**

As you can see from our discussion of the Federal Sentencing Guidelines, simply establishing a code of ethics is not enough. Sales leaders must also clearly and regularly remind salespeople of what is considered ethical and what is not, as well as monitor their behavior. Furthermore, sales leaders can't say one thing and do another. When unethical dealings are identified, the personnel involved have to be punished, and the punishment has to be consistent across people and situations.

IDENTIFYING AND RESPONDING TO ETHICAL BREACHES How are unethical dealings identified? Many times, an unethical event or incident is not identified unless an employee or customer reports it. When an employee reports unethical or inappropriate behavior, it is called **whistle-blowing**. Whistle-blowing is the primary method by which companies identify breaches of policy.

Another method is to use technology. Edward Jones, the stock brokerage firm, uses sophisticated statistical modeling techniques that help the company's compliance department identify when an investment representative (IR) is engaged in questionable behavior. Such behavior might include buying and selling stocks in an account far too frequently only for the purpose of earning commissions. A compliance department employee might, in this case, call the customer who owns the account in order to determine if she really wanted to make those transactions or if the IR had acted independently.

DUE PROCESS SYSTEMS FOR RESPONDING TO ETHICAL BREACHES Once a breach is identified, there are four types of due process systems used to evaluate and respond to ethics violations complaints: (1) investigation and punishment systems; (2) grievance and arbitration systems; (3) mediator/counseling systems; and (4) employee board systems.[12] As you will see shortly, some of these systems are better at punishing violators than they are at reinforcing ethical behavior or improving a firm's policies.

Companies need to have procedures for evaluating complaints about potential ethics violations committed by their salespeople or anyone else in their organizations. (Comstock Complete)

Compliance investigation and punishment systems are characterized by an upper manager who investigates potential violations, determines guilt, and assesses punishment to the guilty. This person can be an ethics officer but is probably more likely to be a line officer, or someone in the chain of command. For example, within the firm's sales force, a sales manager is likely to handle the resolution of any complaint. In this system, there is no intentional examination of the appropriateness of policies or potential biases in the company's policies that might be at least partially responsible for the violation having occurred; only the behavior is considered. For example, if a company's policy is to determine a customer's financial status and then to use that information to determine how much to charge, the policy might encourage unethical price setting. For example, someone with more money might get charged more simply because he or she is wealthier. An investigation and punishment system would not explicitly consider the policy as part of the problem. However, such a system is fast and inexpensive to administer; a disadvantage of the system is that most managers are not trained well enough to give employees a fair hearing.

A **grievance and arbitration system** is similar in that guilt and punishment are investigated and discussed by progressively higher levels of management and labor—the difference being that labor is involved. If management and labor cannot agree on guilt or on the amount or type of punishment, then an outside arbitrator resolves the case. Again, however, the appropriateness of the company's policies and practices are not considered. Grievance and arbitration systems generally require that more procedures, or due process, be followed than compliance and punishment systems do. On the upside, the extra amount of due process gives people a sense that they are being treated more fairly. The downside is that the system can be expensive and slow, and it requires employees to have a labor contract with their companies, which most salespeople don't have.

The mediator/counselor system is somewhat different in that the goal is not punishment so much as it is determining what is right both now and into the future. In **mediator/counselor systems**, a manager (typically an ethics officer) investigates, leads discussions, and builds consensus about the potential guilt of an accused person, as well as the need for any changes in the organization's practices or policies. This system is widely accessible to employees and typically fast and inexpensive. The degree of due process administered, though, depends on the mediator/counselor's expertise and may vary. If a consensus is not reached in the mediator/counselor system, then some other form of governance, such as compliance investigation and punishment, has to finish the job.

An **employee-board system** operates in much the same way as a mediator/counselor system, except that the mediator/counselor role is taken on by a board of the accused employee's peers. These people are formally able to make decisions about the violation as well as formal recommendations for change. The process, as one might expect, is slow and cumbersome, making it expensive. On the positive side, the system typically offers high levels of procedural fairness and is widely accessible to employees. Furthermore, it allows not only for the investigation of violations and the determination of guilt but it can also bring about changes in the organization's policies.

DEALING PERSONALLY WITH ETHICAL BREACHES   What choices does a person have when faced with pressure to engage in questionable tactics? Of course, one choice is to quit and leave the organization. However, this is not always possible, at least not right away, without a significant sacrifice being made.[13] After all, quitting might mean having to take a pay cut, move to another city, or otherwise burden your family with a loss of income and stability. Thus, leaving might seem like the obvious, simple solution, but life is rarely that simple.

Another simple and obvious choice is to just say no—that is, to refuse to engage in unethical tactics. Taking a stand and trying to influence policies is a moral high ground that few people are willing to take. Yet once such a stand is taken, a salesperson is likely to find many others willing to support it. Taking a stand is more likely to be effective when the organization has a code of ethics and an ethics officer responsible for enforcing the code. The salesperson or sales manager faced with the challenge can refuse to follow along and can put the blame on the ethics code, a tactic that can help alleviate the stress associated with such situations.

Organizations with a code of ethics often have, as part of that code or the policies that support the code, a reporting mechanism that allows victims to report ethics violations. Usually, an ethics officer is available to hear concerns about ethics violations. The victim can simply threaten to inform the ethics officer or the manager of the person engaging in the violation. If the threat does not work, then the victim can file a complaint.

Sometimes, the victim can negotiate for an alternative course of action. Assuming the pressure is coming from above, what is the manager's objective? More sales of a certain product? If the victim can identify an alternative and ethical course of action to achieve that objective, and the objective is ethical, then the manager is likely to allow the victim to proceed with that action.

Another alternative is to appear to agree with the tactic but then choose to remain ethical. The risk here is that if the manager encouraging the unethical behavior is caught, the victim might also be culpable. For example, suppose your sales manager tells you to tell a customer that a product is safe to operate underwater when really it isn't. You say okay, but then choose to tell the customer the truth. If your customer then inadvertently operates the product underwater, is hurt, and sues, you might be in trouble. Why? Because as far as your company knew, you promised your manager you would tell the customer the product, indeed, worked underwater. To defend yourself against such a charge, you must document whatever actions you took.

Sales-Related Laws

In the field of selling and sales management, there are a number of laws that apply. There are laws that apply to salespeople and how they treat customers, and there are labor laws that apply to how salespeople are treated by sales managers. We will

EXHIBIT 4.4

Some of the Laws Affecting Sales

Law	Comments
Uniform Commercial Code	Defines key elements of a sale, such as what is a "sale" and a "warranty"
Business Defamation	State laws that govern what businesses (and salespeople) can say about competitors
Gramm-Leach-Bliley Act	Federal law regarding privacy policies
Can-SPAM Act	Federal law prohibiting spam and governing how companies can contact customers; related is the Do-Not-Call registry
Foreign Corrupt Practices Act	A U.S. law that makes bribery and other activities illegal in other countries for American companies
Civil Rights Act	Governs hiring practices, among others, for sales managers
Robinson-Patman Act	Federal law regarding fair pricing

briefly review both sets, beginning with the salesperson (a summary can be found in Exhibit 4.4).

THE UNIFORM COMMERCIAL CODE In the United States, one of the most important set of laws salespeople must follow is the **Uniform Commercial Code, or UCC**, because it is the legal guide to commercial practices. For example, the UCC determines who has the ability to make a binding agreement for a company; this person is called an **agent**. Not all salespeople are agents, although a company cannot escape the consequences of its sales representatives by simply claiming they are not agents.

Another important element is that the UCC defines the term **sale** as the transfer of title from the seller to the buyer in exchange for consideration (money). The date of a title transfer can be very important in determining who is responsible for what and when. For example, if the motor quits on a car as the customer is driving it off the lot, who is responsible?

Another factor that determines who is responsible is the warranty. A **warranty** is an assurance by the seller that the product or service will do what it was sold to do. The warranty might also outline how any performance issues the product might have must be resolved. Warranties can be both written and *implied*. For example, when you buy a car, it's implied that the car will be at least drivable. As agents of their companies, salespeople can even create warranties through their statements to customers: A chemical company was once held liable for a product that did not do what the salesperson promised, even though the company's own printed brochures contradicted the salesperson's claims.[14] Laws in other countries, such as Canada or in European countries, are often tougher about what can be said about a product. Even puffery is illegal in Canada.

OTHER IMPORTANT LAWS There are other laws, too, that affect salespeople. For example, **business defamation** occurs when salespeople (or other company representatives) make unfair or untrue statements to customers about a competitor, its products, salespeople, or other aspects of that organization. These are state laws and therefore vary from state to state. In general, however, they involve false public statements about a firm's products, salespeople, or other employees, service levels, and any other actions. What constitutes a "public statement" is open to interpretation. Nonetheless, if a salesperson defames a competitor's product to a customer, those comments can be used to prosecute both the salesperson and the salesperson's company. Typically, if a business is found guilty, the punishment is to pay the victim an amount equal to the estimated business losses caused by the defamation.

We mentioned the issue of privacy earlier, but there is also a law that governs privacy policies of which sales leaders must be aware. The Gramm-Leach-Bliley Act requires companies to notify their customers regarding their privacy policies. Importantly, although the law was written to protect information provided on credit applications or posted on the Web, it does not distinguish between sources of information. Therefore, a salesperson who gathers any information from a customer is under the same obligation regarding that information as is the company regarding any credit information gathered from the customer at the time of the sale.

The CAN-SPAM Act is a law that salespeople can violate without any intention. This law requires companies to clean up their e-mail lists and only contact those with whom they have an ongoing relationship. Salespeople can spam customers with blanket e-mails sent to everyone in their customer list, in violation of the law. In addition, salespeople can create other problems with blanket e-mail, such as putting every customer's e-mail address in the address line for all the other customers to see. Customers may not want their e-mail addresses publicized and might consider it a violation of the privacy policy. In addition, all it takes is for one customer to get mad about being spammed to forward the e-mail, along with the list of addresses, to a competitor. Now the rep is really in trouble! The best advice is to either send each e-mail separately and personalize it, or let your marketing department do e-mail campaigns.

Similar is the Do Not Call (DNC) list maintained by the Federal Trade Commission. This registry allows individuals to make their phone numbers off-limits to telemarketers. Now, only companies with whom a customer has a business relationship can call the person. So you can still get a marketing call from your credit card company, but not from any other credit card company, assuming you've registered your number.

An important law for salespeople who operate in other countries is the Foreign Corrupt Practices (FCP) Act. This law requires salespeople to live up to the law of the United States, even if the laws in the country they operate in are more lenient. If Lebanese law allows bribery, for example, a salesperson representing an American company cannot offer a bribe in Lebanon because it is against the law in the United States. Violations can result in large fines for the company and the persons involved. Interestingly, although Italian and German laws do not allow bribes in those countries, they do allow companies to not only use bribes in other countries but to expense those bribes when calculating Italian or German taxes! Exhibit 4.5 shows the Top Ten countries for being offered bribes, according to Transparency International, a nonpartisan organization committed to helping end worldwide corruption.

Jens Jensen, a sales representative for Dow Chemical, sells ion-exchange resins in Malaysia, Singapore, Brunei, and Thailand. These resins take minerals out of water to prevent chemical buildup in pipes, boilers, heaters, and other water-using machinery. Jensen notes that many companies in the region close their deals by providing kickbacks to key decision makers. He, however, can't offer kickbacks. Not only is it against Dow's corporate policy, but it would be in violation of the FCP act. Instead, he focuses on building friendships with buyers, thus leveraging the fact that people all over the globe like to do business with friends. As a result, Jensen has become very successful.[14]

Which nations' businesspeople were most likely to offer bribes when making deals abroad?

1. India
2. China
3. Russia
4. Turkey
5. Taiwan
6. Malaysia
7. South Africa
8. Brazil
9. Saudi Arabia
10. South Korea

Those least likely were from:

1. Switzerland
2. Sweden

EXHIBIT 4.5

World's Top Bribe Payers

Source: Transparency International survey of 11,000 executives, reported in *Parade Magazine*, December 17, 2006, p. 6.

Tying agreements are also illegal under U.S. antitrust laws such as the Sherman Act of 1890. A salesperson cannot force a buyer to purchase some products in order to be able to buy others protected by patents. For example, Microsoft couldn't force you to purchase five games in order for you to be able to buy its latest Xbox when it comes on the market.

Both state and federal laws provide buyers with cooling-off periods, periods in which they may cancel a purchase without penalty. These laws do not apply to sales made at the seller's location, such as a store, but they do apply to most purchases made in your home (including your dorm room), at the state fair, or any other location. Not all products are included, and, in some instances, even local ordinances can apply; laws can vary depending on the city or state in which the transaction took place.

Laws for Sales Managers

Most of the laws that sales managers need to worry about are labor laws. These laws relate to fair pay issues, appropriate employee selection and retention issues, and the like. (Many of these laws will be covered later in the book when we discuss recruiting and selecting salespeople.) In addition, there are laws regarding the reporting processes and legal requirements for firms in which claims of sexual harassment are made. Workplace sexual harassment is prohibited by the 1964 Civil Rights Act, and a company can be held liable even if the harassment is done by a customer. If a company forces a salesperson to continue to call on an account in which harassment (either in terms of unwanted contact or negative work environment) occurs, the firm can be found guilty of contributing to that harassment. At the same time, however, if a company has a procedure for preventing sexual harassment and the worker does not avail herself of those procedures, the company is not liable.[15]

Another set of laws that affects sales leaders are market laws designed to promote fair competition. The Foreign Corrupt Practices Act, mentioned earlier, is one of those laws. Another is the Robinson-Patman Act and the antitrust acts that forbid price discrimination. **Price discrimination** is defined by the law as a seller giving unjustified special prices, discounts, or services to some customers and not to others. Differences in pricing are acceptable if there are differences in the quality of the product or service delivered, if the prices have to be different to meet the prices offered by competitors in particular markets, or if the cost of doing business is different. For example, the buyers of large quantities can be given discounts for their purchases because they cost less per unit to process, ship, and so forth.

Some prices, like car prices, are negotiated. Does this mean that the Robinson-Patman Act is violated when one person pays one price for a car and another person pays a different price? Or why doesn't an airline have to charge the same price for every seat on a flight? The answer is that every customer had the same opportunity, either to negotiate the price or to buy on the date that a certain price was valid.

Antitrust laws also prohibit certain forms of noncompeting agreements. For example, two competitors cannot agree to divide up a territory in order to create a monopoly for each within their territory. A company can hire another company to be an exclusive dealer in a particular area, but that same company cannot conspire with a competitor to create a monopoly.

We've also discussed whistle-blowing and responses individuals can take if asked to do something illegal or unethical. There are also laws protecting the whistle-blower. A whistle-blower who is treated badly by a company can win literally millions in compensation for damages; the largest claim to date is $77 million. That was the amount won by a whistle-blower who notified federal prosecutors of a scheme to bribe doctors to prescribe a particular medication.[16]

As you can probably tell, sales executives are very concerned with all of the laws that apply directly to salespeople's activities. But if a salesperson does something wrong, was it only the fault of the salesperson? Or is the salesperson's company also guilty? As we mentioned earlier in this chapter, the Federal Sentencing Guidelines specifies that a company has to create the right policies and procedures to ensure that its salespeople act appropriately. These policies and procedures can be used to justify that the company acted appropriately. Such policies and procedures include creating a code of ethics, conducting training so that salespeople and sales managers know what is right and wrong or legal and illegal, and other practices. If a company has successfully developed such policies and procedures, judges are more likely to assume that the salesperson is at fault, not the company; however, if a company is found to have created a culture that encourages illegal activities, then under the FSG, the consequences can be huge. TAP Pharmaceuticals, for example, had to pay over $875 million in fines because the federal government determined that the firm's salespeople acted in accordance with the company's culture, which encouraged deception.[17]

Summary

Although there are many approaches to developing ethics guidelines, common ones are the Golden Rule, the conventionalist approach, the Protestant ethic, the market imperative, the Libertine ethic, and the utilitarian ethic. These different approaches are likely to lead different salespeople faced with ethical dilemmas to make different decisions. As boundary spanners, salespeople are likely to face many ethical challenges because they represent both their companies and their customers. Misrepresentation, bribery, and encouraging rogue purchasing are common ethical breaches salespeople face. Companies and sales managers can reduce unethical behavior by creating the right ethical climate within their firms. Ethics codes are also useful tools, not only because these guide salespeople when they're faced with ethical challenges but also because they help foster an ethical climate. Companies also create different types of systems for identifying and responding to ethical breaches by their employees. These systems include mechanisms for whistle-blowing, compliance investigation, and punishment. Such systems include grievance and arbitration processes, mediator/counselor systems, or employee-board systems.

Laws also govern salespeople's and sales managers' actions. In the United States, these laws include the Uniform Commercial Code, which defines when a sale occurs, the limitations of warranties, and other important elements in selling. Also important are laws such as state laws governing business defamation, the CAN-SPAM Act, the FTC's Do Not Call registry, and the Federal Corrupt Practices Act. Managers also have to worry about labor laws, such as those that protect employees from sexual harassment.

One challenge is determining whether a company should be liable when one of its employees, who acts alone, commits an ethical violation. The Federal Sentencing Guidelines specify the actions, such as creating codes of ethics and conducting training programs that companies must take to demonstrate that they have taken all of the necessary steps to create the right culture within their firms.

Key Terms

agent   77
boundary spanners   68
bribery   70
business defamation   77
code of ethics   73
compliance investigation and punishment
   systems   75
employee-board system   76
ethical climate   72
ethics   64
Federal Sentencing Guidelines (FSG)   73

grievance and arbitration system   75
mediator/counselor systems   75
misrepresentation   70
price discrimination   79
puffery   70
rogue purchasing   71
sale   77
sexual harassment   72
Uniform Commerial Code (UCC)   77
whistle-blowing   74
warranty   77

Questions and Problems

1. The different approaches to ethics discussed in this chapter focus on the salesperson's actions. Now consider what buyers might consider appropriate or inappropriate behavior under each of the different approaches.
2. Likewise, consider each of the different approaches and review the ethical challenges faced by sales managers. How might a sales manager's response to an ethical challenge differ under the different approaches?
3. Jim Stradinger, a sales manager for Holland 1916, argues, "Do what's right for the customer and everything else will take care of itself." Discuss the pros and cons from the perspectives of the sales representative, the customer, and the sales manager.
4. The Federal Trade Commission has generally ruled that puffery is acceptable. What is not acceptable is deception that is subjectively interpreted as injurious to consumers— that is to say, the claim can be interpreted in a way that harms the buyer. Review the following claims. Are they puffery or deceptive misrepresentation?

   a. This sinus medication was developed by a scientist to alleviate his own sinus headaches!
   b. There is no other wrench like it!

    c. You can't buy a faster copier in this price range.

    d. I've sold lots of other customers this same product at the full list price.

5. A sales manager listened to a customer complain about a salesperson and thought, "This is the third complaint like this I've gotten this week. We've got a code of ethics. Why aren't my people following it?" Discuss some reasons why her sales team is acting unethically and what she can do about it.

6. Your university has probably established multiple ethics violation investigation systems. An honors council, for example, often acts like an employee board when it comes to the actions of students. Ethics violations by a professor, however, are likely to be addressed in another system. As a student, if you were treated unethically by a professor, which type of system (discussed in the chapter) would you want and why? Would it make a difference to you if the unethical behavior involved a professor claiming your work was his or her own versus a situation involving sexual harassment?

7. Which of the following are legal practices and which might be considered illegal? If you determine that not enough information is provided, what would make the practice legal or illegal?

    a. A salesperson offers a discount to a small drugstore if the store will set up a special display of his product at its entrance.

    b. A salesperson sends two bottles of wine, valued at $100 each, to a customer as a thank-you gift after making a large sale.

    c. The buyer asks the salesperson out for drinks after work.

    d. A buyer provides a salesperson with as competitor's proposal, including pricing information.

8. As a sales manager, you find yourself faced with the following situations. Identify the ethical or legal issue in each and discuss how you would handle the problem. (All of these were experienced by former students.)

    a. The regional sales manager, your boss, forwards several ethnic jokes and lewd e-mails to you and your entire sales and support staff. Two of your salespeople complain to you.

    b. A customer has called and asked you to send someone else to his office as he does not want to be called on by his currently assigned salesperson. When you ask why, it is because he doesn't want someone of that sexual orientation calling on him.

    c. You've asked a salesperson to create a training session for the entire sales team, a task that will require the salesperson to spend about $60 on materials that company policy expressly prohibits salespeople from charging on their expense report. She agrees and then submits an expense report with the $60 down as entertainment of a client, an acceptable expense. You notice it on the expense report; she hasn't said anything about it but you know she was conducting a training session on the day in question and couldn't have entertained the client that day.

    d. The company has introduced a new product and requires all salespeople to memorize a demonstration script. To encourage salespeople to learn it, a contest was developed by your boss to award a new HDTV to the best presentation of the demonstration. Two salespeople come to you and say, "Let's just let Beverly represent our team. We don't have time for this. We need to be out selling."

9. Look at the article describing the Caux Round Table principles. Which model of ethics would you say most aptly describes those principles? What is the impact on salespeople and sales managers if they ascribe to the CRT principles?

Role Play

Magnum Performance

You are an account manager with Magnum Performance, a company that finds salespeople jobs. Hiring companies pay Magnum to handle all of their sales recruiting. Shoshiba Manufacturing is a foreign company that has just entered the U.S. market. Shoshiba has asked Magnum Performance to hire 500 salespeople across the nation. For your office, this represents about 20 salespeople, easily making Shoshiba your biggest client. Arnold Jackson was hired by Shoshiba to be the company's U.S. vice president of sales. He recently called your office and spoke to Jackie, the general manager of the office, and said, "Just get us warm bodies—we've got to get people into the field. I don't care if they're not that good. We'll sort out who can sell later." The only problem is that if the salespeople don't remain with Shoshiba for six months, the company doesn't pay Magnum for the hire. In addition, the office is behind its quota by 15 salespeople overall. That means that Jackie won't get a bonus for the first time in two years. The bonus is substantial, about $10,000, and Jackie has counted on it. But more importantly, the regional vice president is likely to come down pretty hard on Jackie when she learns that there is an open order for 20 salespeople and it didn't get filled because there weren't enough good salespeople available to send to the client. The best estimate is that there might be 8 qualified candidates that can be sent to Shoshiba. If qualifications don't matter, there are 30 candidates that could go.

Assignment

Break into groups of three. In each group, one person should play Jackie, the office general manager, and another should play the salesperson who is responsible for the Shoshiba account (and for finding the salespeople to fill Shoshiba's jobs). Don't worry about matching your genders to the names in the case. Discuss strategies for how to handle Arnold Jackson (the client) and how to respond to Magnum's regional vice president. The third person in your group should play the role of "devil's advocate." This person's job is to suggest unethical strategies to each person. The devil should call time-out and whisper suggestions to each person, who must then propose that suggestion. The other two people in your group should respond to the unethical suggestions in terms of their implications and then present ethical alternatives to them.

Caselet 4.1: Patman Paper Co.

Jared Hernandez graduated from college and went to work as a salesperson for Patman Paper Company, a provider of office supplies in Indianapolis. Then he got married to his college sweetheart, and life seemed good. But sales were slow initially, and after six months, Jared had sold only 80 percent of his quota. At this point, he was expected to be at 100 percent. After a brief meeting with his manager, he knew he had better gain another 10 percent in the next month or find a new position.

What really bothered Jared was that he knew he had an account worth 30 percent of his quota sitting out there for him to get. He had made the first call to the account on a Friday afternoon; he met Suzy McDermott, the firm's purchasing director. The call seemed to go well, and he got a small order.

"There's a lot more where that came from," winked Suzy at Jared. An attractive woman in her mid-thirties, she leaned over and put a hand on his knee. "What do you say we head over to O'Malley's for happy hour and talk it over?"

Jared declined, but later wondered if he was an idiot. Entertaining clients was not unusual. He needed the sale. What should he have done?

Caselet 4.2: Callahan Car Parts

Tommy Callahan took over the manufacturing firm Callahan Car Parts after his father died of a fatal heart attack. The company had 12 salespeople, each responsible for a region of parts stores. The firm also has two account executives who handled the big parts retailers, either NAPA or O'Reilly's. Callahan's three manufacturing plants in the United States were unionized, but its sales force was not.

The company has never had many complaints about its salespeople. However, one of its competitors had been hit with a multimillion-dollar fine for resale price maintenance (setting minimum prices its distributors could charge for its products). The competitor's lack of policies prohibiting the practice was cited as a contributing factor, which made the fine much larger than it would have been otherwise.

Tommy trusted his salespeople, but he knew that without an effective ethics policy and a procedure for investigating complaints, Callahan's was at risk. So he asked three of his senior salespeople, the firm's vice president of human resources, and the company's attorney to form a committee and set up policies and procedures.

The sales staff, however, revolted. "We're honest people—we don't need this!" they claimed. Worse, one of the senior salespeople told Tommy privately that if the policy were truly effective, it might identify some real problems Tommy would rather not learn about!

What type of approach to monitoring, investigating, punishing, and improving ethics policies should Tommy suggest to the committee? What should he do to get salespeople to support the need for clear ethics policies?

References

1. Anonymous (2003). "Sales Ethics," http://www.salesfocusinc.com/newsarchive/ 0319_sales_ethics.htm, dated June 13, 2003.
2. A good resource is *Ethical Decision Making in Marketing* written by Lawrence B. Chonko (1995), Sage Publications. Although becoming somewhat dated, the fundamental principles and approaches covered are truly timeless.
3. Carr, A. Z. (1968). "Is Business Bluffing Ethical?" *Harvard Business Review,* (January/February), 4–10.
4. Dudley, George, and John F. Tanner, Jr. (2005). *The Hard Truth About Soft Selling: Restoring Pride and Purpose to the Sales Profession.* Dallas: Behavioral Sciences Research Press.
5. Nill, Alexander, and John A. Schibrowksky (2005). "The Impact of Corporate Culture, the Reward System, and Perceived Moral Intensity on Marketing Students' Ethical Decision Making," *Journal of Marketing Education,* 27(1), 68–80.
6. Chonko.
7. Doerr, David (2006). "WISD Official Finds Pitfall in Gifts," *Waco Tribune-Herald* (December 17), 1A, 10A.
8. Weitz, Barton A., Stephen B. Castleberry, and John F. Tanner, Jr. (2007*). Selling: Building Partnerships,* 6th ed. Burr Ridge, IL: McGraw-Hill.
9. Henneman, Todd (2006). "After High Court Ruling, Firms May Want to Take a Long Look at Anti-Harassment Strategies," *Workforce Management,* 85(14), 33–35.

10. Tanner, Jr., John F., and Christophe Fournier (2008). "Revisiting Antecedents of Propensity to Leave: The Moderating Role of Ethical Climate," presented at the 7th International Marketing Trends Congress, Venice, Italy (January 15).

11. Joseph, Joshua, Lee Van Weer, and Ann McFadden (2000). *Ethics in the Workplace*. Washington, DC: Ethics Resource Center.

12. Much of this section is based on Richard P. Nielsen (2000). "Do Internal Due Process Systems Permit Adequate Political and Moral Space for Ethics Voice, Praxis, and Community?" *Journal of Business Ethics,* 24(1), 1–27.

13. Much of this section is based on Richard P. Nielsen's work, including "What Can Managers Do About Unethical Management?" *Journal of Business Ethics,* (1987), 6, 309–320: "Negotiating as an Ethics Action (Praxis) Strategy," *Journal of Business Ethics,* (1989), 9, 383–390: and "Dialogic Leadership As Organizational Ethics Action (Praxis) Method," *Journal of Business Ethics,* (1990), 9, 765–783.

14. Weitz, Castleberry, and Tanner (2007).

15. Weitz, Castleberry, and Tanner (2007), p. 75.

16. Haddad, Charles, and Amy Barrett (2002). "A Whistle-Blower Rocks the Industry," *Business Week,* (June 24), 126–130.

17. Cron, William L., and Thomas DeCarlo (2006). *Dalrymple's Sales Management,* 9th ed. Hoboken, NJ: John L. Wiley & Sons.

PART THREE

Analyzing Customers and Markets

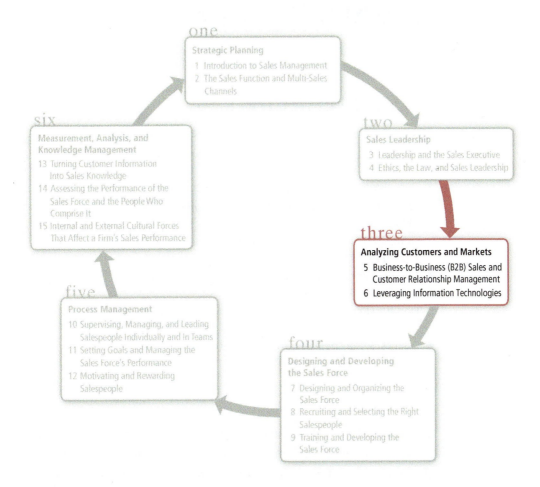

Now that you understand that sales leadership strategies are influenced by ethics and legal issues, we discuss sales strategies and information technologies for managing customer relationships. Sales firms and their sales leaders must invest time and energy into profitably serving their best customers. Sales technology allows the sales leader to identify profitable customers and understand their needs. The more accurate customer information firms possess, the easier it is to manage customer relationships.

Chapter 5 discusses how business-to-business salespersons sell to and serve buyers. Salespersons must understand buyer needs and goals in order to provide value and form long-term relationships with their best customers. Business relationships vary from transactional to strategic, depending upon the level of trust and cooperation between the two firms. We explain how salespersons come to know their buyers and gauge the roles played by individuals in the buying firm. Selling firms compute customer lifetime value to prioritize customer service levels.

Information technology is also essential to manage customer relationships, which is the focus of Chapter 6, *Leveraging Information Technologies*. Imagine, for example, if General Motors was your customer. GM buys more each year than most countries and they need products shipped to hundreds of locations all over the world. How do you keep up with that? Or with the hundreds of people who may be involved in various purchase decisions? This chapter examines technologies that help salespeople manage their markets—whether their market consists of one account or thousands. The sales strategy and customer relationship approach a firm selects greatly influences the structure of the sales force, as continued in Chapter 7.

5

BUSINESS-TO-BUSINESS (B2B) SALES AND CUSTOMER RELATIONSHIP MANAGEMENT

LEARNING OBJECTIVES

After completing this chapter, you should be able to:

- Recognize how people make organizational purchasing decisions.
- Describe and explain the three buying situations.
- Identify the different roles played by buying center members.
- Understand individual forces that influence the B2B buying process.
- Comprehend how buyer-seller relationships are established and maintained.
- Explain success factors that apply to buyer-seller relationships.
- Discuss seller performance factors that lead to successful customer relationships.

To be successful in today's highly competitive marketplace, a firm's sales force must deliver long-term customer value. In business-to-business (B2B) sales, this is particularly important. Why? Because B2B buyers are large customers in contrast to most firms that engage in retail or business-to-consumer exchanges. For example, a retailer like Target serves hundreds of thousands, if not millions, of customers each year. In contrast, airline manufacturers like Boeing and Airbus have less than 100 customers—airline companies, governments, and wealthy individuals from around the world—that can afford to buy its airplanes. The loss of any one buyer by Boeing would likely result in a significant loss of business. To minimize lost customers, a firm's salespeople and sales managers must understand what's important to B2B buyers—how and why they purchase what they do. They must also formulate a sales strategy that expands the firm's relationship with its most profitable buyers. The better they understand their buyers and form a trusting relationship, the more successful their sales efforts will be.

BILL BENCSIK

PRESIDENT, BENCSIK ASSOCIATES, INC.

Bill Bencsik is the president of the manufacturer's representative firm Bencsik Associates, Inc. (www.bencsik.com). Bencsik believes that relationships with buyers have never been more important than they are today: "The relationship our firm and sales force has with customers is one reason that manufacturers outsource their sales functions to us," says Bencsik. "Our firm has developed long-term relationships with every vertical market in the electronic-systems business in the state of Florida." Audio, video, lighting, cable television, and security are just a few industries supported by Bencsik Associates, Inc.

When an electronic system is being engineered, specified, and purchased, the difference between similarly priced components is very often a subjective matter. In effect, Bencsik Associate's relationships are what cause buyers to "give the firm the benefit of the doubt and win the business," he says.

"Many of our relationships are based upon our knowledge of electronic product lines, product applications, and the influence we have with the manufacturer that buyers believe will contribute to their success. These relationships are also based on the trust and respect that Bencsik Associates has earned due to our performance history and our position in the industry. From our perspective, relationships are based upon what the other person or company needs. Our job is to uncover that need and make it obvious we are meeting it in a trusting and dependable way."

Bencsik Associates employs GoldMine® (www.goldmine.com) customer relationship management (CRM) software to monitor buyer opportunities, make sales forecasts, target customers, analyze lead characteristics, and link all parties within the firm with consistent information. Bencsik especially likes the "caller ID" feature that identifies who is calling and automatically pulls up the correct informational screen for him or the customer service representative. The ability to add notes to the system permits Bencsik and his associates to remember what was discussed in previous personal meetings or phone conversations.

However, a firm's relationship with a customer is likely to break down if one or both parties no longer see the value of that relationship. Usually this happens slowly because one party feels neglected by the other. But when either the buyer or seller betrays a trust, fails to perform as agreed upon, or gets greedy, relationships that have taken years to foster can end quickly. "When

Technology allows today's sales teams to increase their efficiency and improve their service to buyers. (Comstock Complete)

this happens, the relationship ends since it is no longer 'good' for one or both parties," explains Bencsik. However, Bill Bencsik attempts to maintain the relationship with the buying firm if it is financially worthwhile. Bencsik says that "the quicker we try to recover from a service failure or misunderstanding often makes the difference in the firm looking like a 'hero' or losing the account." ∎

Understanding B2B Purchasing Decisions

Business relationships occur between people, so it is important to remember that personal relationship skills are an essential part of making purchases and conducting successful commerce. Forming and maintaining a relationship with a B2B customer is a complex undertaking that requires a highly skilled sales force and constant support from the firm's other functional groups—especially the salespeople's managers. Understanding buyers also requires an information technology system that's easy for salespeople to use and gives them and their managers accurate and near, real-time information that they need to serve their customers. (Chapter 6 discusses the technical aspects of CRM systems in more detail.)

The Buyer's Decision-Making Process

B2B buyers tend to engage in a specific process when making a purchase decision. This process is shown in Exhibit 5.1. The first step is recognizing that a problem or need exists that can be resolved by making a purchase. In a commercial situation, the buyer may view the situation not as a problem, but as an opportunity that can be exploited by making a purchase. For example, if a manufacturing machine wears out, it is likely that the firm will want to purchase a replacement that offers added production capacity at a lower cost.

Once a decision is made to search for a product or service, the buyer must decide upon the needed product or service specifications. They then begin to search for possible solutions offered by sales vendors. These offers are then evaluated based upon price, their adherence to the buyer's stated specifications, and quality. When a vendor passes the certification, it is placed on an **approved vendors' list** and, as the product is needed, orders are placed. The new product or solution is then evaluated based upon the buyer's original criteria—price, quality, delivery, and so forth. If the buyer is satisfied that the product offers value, future purchases are made as the need arises.

Organizational Buying Situations

The first buyer process is based upon whether the purchase situation is completely new, current business that is up for re-bid, or a routine purchase. Each of these buying situations impacts the relationship formed and the amount of information that is shared between the

EXHIBIT 5.1

The Buyer's Decision-Making Process

Problem Recognition	>	Information Search	>	Evaluation of Alternatives	>	Purchase Decision	>	Postpurchase Evaluation

EXHIBIT 5.2

The Buy-Grid Framework: Participation in the Buying Stages of the B2B Buying Process

Buying Stages	New Buy	Modified Re-buy	Straight Re-buy
1. Recognize Problem	Yes	Perhaps	No
2. Determine Product Characteristics	Yes	Perhaps	No
3. Determine Product Specifications	Yes	Yes	Yes
4. Search for Suppliers	Yes	Perhaps	No
5. Evaluate Proposals	Yes	Perhaps	No
6. Select Supplier	Yes	Perhaps	No
7. Specify Quantity Needed	Yes	Yes	Yes
8. Review the Supplier/Products Performance	Yes	Yes	Yes

buyer and seller. A **new buy** occurs when a complex or expensive product is purchased for the first time. In many organizations a new-buy product/service that has never been purchased before is a rare occurrence. For individual buyers and sellers in organizations, however, new buys happen more frequently. When a new buy occurs, the buyer engages in all eight purchase steps listed in Exhibit 5.2. If the selling firm and buyer already have a relationship, the amount of information shared regarding the new product is greater and the level of testing and scrutinizing for approval is lower. The opposite conditions will apply to sellers who have a limited or no relationship with the buyer.

A **modified re-buy** is the purchase of a product or service that is currently being bought, but for important reasons the buyer is considering different vendors or product changes. For example, a manufacturing firm that previously purchased a fleet of Chevrolet trucks to deliver automobile parts to independent repair facilities might debate whether to switch to Toyota trucks in an effort to get higher gas mileage and lower maintenance costs. Thus, the company is seeking to make a modified re-buy. A selling firm that has a relationship with the manufacturer will be aware of its changing needs and have advanced time to work out a solution for the firm. In contrast, sellers with transactional links will most likely learn about the change in purchase specifications when and if the manufacturing firm issues a **request for quotation (RFQ)**—a formal request by the buyer for a sales quote. More experienced salespeople generally participate in new-buy and modified re-buy purchase situations because these are often high-dollar sales and long term in nature, so a good relationship with the buyer and a high level and amount of information about the buyer is needed to successfully negotiate with the firm.

Last, in a **straight re-buy** situation, the buying firm moves directly from need recognition (Step 1) to ordering (Step 7). Today, many routine purchases or straight re-buys are made through automated, electronic data interchange (EDI) systems or the exchange of electronic information between buyer and seller for purchase orders, confirmations, and invoices. For example, suppose a company routinely buys printer paper and office supplies. As the firm's employees consume these supplies, the company's inventory management system tracks stock levels and electronically transmits an order to the supplier when the reorder point is reached. At Chrysler, supply analysts use a "production control portal" linked to the company's suppliers and shippers to monitor the status of orders and send out alerts when there appears to be a potential problem with inventory levels, deliveries, and so forth.[1]

Clearly, straight re-buy situations do not require a live salesperson to call upon the buyer—yet it was a salesperson who got the seller's product(s) on the buyer's approved vendors list, set up the electronic reorder system, and finalized the contract during a new-buy or modified re-buy situation. Furthermore, by maintaining a positive relationship with the buyer, the seller increases the likelihood of extending the original contract with a new agreement.

An **in-supplier**, or an approved vendor that has established a relationship with the buyer, will often try to convert all of the buyer's purchases to a straight re-buy situation. If the seller can successfully do so, it can strengthen the relationship and conduct business with the purchaser for longer. By contrast, an **out-supplier**, or a vendor who has no or only a transactional relationship with the buyer, will attempt to convert the purchase to a modified re-buy situation in order to have an opportunity to capture the business. For example, an out-supplier will try to persuade the buyer that the current product being purchased is not the best one or that a new technology or feature found in their product is superior. Unlike in-suppliers, out-suppliers often have to offer price concessions to buyers to persuade them to do business with them.

Understanding the Buyer's Criteria

An important model for the sales force to understand is the multi-attribute matrix. Buyers utilize a **multi-attribute matrix** to evaluate vendors by assigning an importance weight to categories like price, product conformance, delivery time, and manufacturing capacity. That is, a buyer might compare all vendor offerings by assigning a ranking of .5 for quality, .3 for delivery, and .2 for customer service. Then, the buyer rates each seller in terms of that category on a scale, say 1–10, and multiplies the weight times the rating. All of the sellers' scores for all of the categories are then summed up and compared. As seen in Exhibit 5.3, a multi-attribute matrix allows buyers to more objectively compare two or more vendors. In this example, Vendor A's offering receives the highest multi-attribute rating.

For certain important categories, all vendors would probably have to meet a minimum standard for their product or service to be considered. For example, sellers might have to quote a price that is below a specified ceiling amount. For the remaining features, the buyer might allow a strong performance on one dimension to compensate for a weaker performance on another. In this case, a moderate rating on one important feature will be pulled upward by stronger ratings on other categories, even when these features are less important. Salespeople that understand a buyer's weights and ratings can use this information to alter the weights (convince the buyer that other features are more important) or improve the ratings (show that the product's/service's performance is higher than the buyer originally thought). It is easier for a salesperson to modify product/service weights or ratings when a high level of trust exists between the two firms.

Buying Center, or Group, Purchases

An autonomous purchasing decision occurs when one person single-handedly moves the firm through all eight stages of the purchase process. However, it is more likely that a group of employees in the firm—either a **buying center** or **decision-making unit**

EXHIBIT 5.3

A Multi-Attribute Matrix Comparison

Attribute	Weight	Vendor A	Vendor B
Quality	.5	9 = 4.5	7 = 3.5
Delivery	.3	8 = 2.4	9 = 2.7
Customer Service	.2	10 = 2.0	8 = 1.6
Totals	1.0	8.9	7.8

(DMU)—are involved in the purchase process. These employees play a variety of "roles" in the process:[2] The **initiator** starts the purchase process by recognizing a need. For example, the purchasing manager concludes that the current copier requires maintenance too often and produces poor-quality copies. Or a design engineer may specify the need for a product to replace an existing component in an air-conditioning unit that is failing at a significant rate. At the other end of the buying process is the **decision maker**, or the person/committee that makes the final decision. Sales managers have long been taught to help their reps identify and meet with the "economic decision maker" or the person who holds ultimate purchase decision authority. To help identify the decision maker, a sales manager instructs her salespeople to ask the customer to explain the buying process to them. When the purchase is large, the salesperson can also find out who is on the buying committee and then ask who is chairing the group. There are also times when the decision maker isn't a member of the buying center at all. For example, a **controller** may approve or set the budget for the purchase.

The sales force must understand the needs and goals of a diverse group of buyers. (Comstock Complete)

The **purchaser** is any person who actually buys the product. The purchasing role can be played by anyone in the firm; for example, a person who will use the purchased product or her manager. The purchasing agent's role is to be responsible for the firm making objective purchase decisions. Purchasing agents may assume multiple roles in a purchase decision, such as coordinating meetings, sharing information, ensuring the firm's purchase process is followed, and even finalizing the purchase of a product or service. There is no absolute job description for someone who holds the purchasing agent title, but people that do are normally involved in more than simply ordering the product. Consequently, sales managers need to coach their salespeople to be careful not to confuse roles and titles.

Influencers are individuals who affect the decision maker's final choice through recommendations about which vendors to include or which products will best solve the organization's needs. The number of influencers expands as major purchases are considered that involve more people and resources. A case in point: A mining machine sales firm experienced resistance from a mining company when it came to buying a new type of machine. Why? Because the mining company's maintenance personnel, who influenced the purchase, did not want to learn how to repair a new machine or maintain an additional spare parts inventory.[3]

Users are part of the buying center because their jobs require that they implement and evaluate what was purchased. Users may also attempt to influence the decision and, at times, influencers represent the users' perspective by considering the users' needs or ability to implement the purchase decision. For example, a decision maker may choose one product over another because of the users' familiarity with the selected product; thus, shortening the user's learning curve when implementing the new product.

Gatekeepers control information, either in the form of knowledge or access into, out of, or between members of the buying group. Gatekeepers can actively influence a decision by determining the level and amount of information reaching the decision maker. Sometimes gatekeepers unintentionally exclude or overemphasize information that impacts the purchase decision. There are two types of gatekeepers: **screens**, who decide who is given access to members of the buying center; and **filters**, who control the flow of information. Secretaries who decide which salespeople can communicate with executives are one type of screen. A purchasing agent who demands that all salespeople check in with the purchasing office before visiting anyone at the account also acts as a screen.

An example of a buying center in action is a plant manager that informs the CEO that a piece of manufacturing equipment is costing more to repair than to operate and suggests that it is time to buy a new one. In this scenario, the plant manager acts as an initiator. The CEO meets with the chief financial officer (CFO) and inquires whether there is money in the budget to buy a new piece of equipment. The CFO, acting as controller, sets a budget. The CEO then asks the plant manager to request proposals from three vendors. Now the plant manager is acting as a gatekeeper. If the plant manager prefers a particular vendor, he may try to make a stronger case for that vendor, and becomes an influencer. When a proposal is made and the CEO decides to buy the recommended equipment, this makes her the decision maker. If she instructs the plant manager to order the equipment, the plant manager is the purchaser. The plant manager will also be the user, since his department installs and uses the equipment. Thus, as seen in this example, roles can and do shift as one person plays multiple roles. The number of stakeholders that participate in a buying center is usually 3–12,[4] and this number appears to be increasing.[5] In cross-cultural buying situations the number of participants can reach 30![6]

Note that at no time in our plant-equipment purchase example was a committee formed; nor was there an official designation of specific roles. A common misconception by new sales personnel is that a buying center committee is formed and individuals are assigned specific roles. In actuality, the buying center is a dynamic group of individuals whose membership changes over time. There may be a formal buying committee for certain decisions, but more frequently, the decision process is less structured and informal.

Team Selling and Multi-Level Selling

In today's business environment that is focused around customer relationships, buyers expect higher levels of service from sales organizations. One way to provide higher service levels is to form sales teams that are comprised of highly skilled members of the selling firm. An **extended selling team** is a group of specialists from the major areas of the sales organization that interact with counterparts in the buying center. Buyers report a number of advantages derived from a sales team that include quicker responses to buyer questions, an ability to speak to one's counterpart who understands technical language, and a capability to work as a group to offer multidisciplinary solutions to complex buyer problems. Depending upon the situation, extended selling teams can be formed for short or long periods. For example, an extended selling team may be formed to navigate through a modified re-buy scenario with a buyer and then be disbanded. Or, an extended selling team can be formed to handle all long-term interactions with a major account such as Wal-Mart.

At Omnicell®, a market leader of automated pharmaceutical distribution systems, the salesperson is expected to make four to five visits with prospective customers—normally hospitals—to learn their business and establish a relationship. At that point the regional sales director accompanies the salesperson and, in consultation with the client, helps formulate an expert team. For example, a pharmacist may be added to the team to evaluate and advise how drugs can be more efficiently and safely handled throughout the supply chain. Likewise, a nurse may be called upon to interview and advise how the client's nursing staff can be trained and motivated to utilize automated systems that safely distribute and protect pharmaceutical products.

In many firms the account manager serves as the official sales team captain. This means that the salesperson must demonstrate leadership and an ability to plan, coordinate, and communicate with sales team members from diverse functional areas within the firm. For example, an extended selling team may be comprised of select personnel from engineering, finance, quality control, manufacturing, management information systems, and customer service. In addition, a vice president from a functional area may serve as the executive member of the team who can weigh in with other top-level managers to expedite important requests made by the buying organization. Since buyers form centers to reduce risk, improve decision making, and increase technical expertise, the selling firm may also form a selling center to interact with the buying center and offer the highest level of service to the customer.[7]

Although essential, team selling faces coordination, communication, and compensation challenges. For example, when multiple parties within the sales force interact with members of the buying firm, promises may be made that are not communicated to the remainder of the sales team and sales organization. Also, when a sale is made, a customer is lost, or customer satisfaction decreases, the sales manager is not certain who to credit or blame.[8] Extended team selling is utilized almost exclusively for large, major accounts that purchase high volume and generate sufficient profits to cover the higher expenses of team selling.

SELF-ASSESSMENT LIBRARY

Establishing and maintaining customer relationships requires sales managers and salespeople to pay close attention to the details related to their customers and work hard to meet their expectations. Successful salespeople who are able to do this have the ability to listen. Have you ever wondered whether or not you listen well? To learn more about your listening skills, go to http://www.prenhall.com/sal/, log in using the access code that came with your book. Then click on:

Assessments
  II. Working with Others
    A. Communication Skills
      2. How Good Are My Listening Skills?

As a result of these ambiguities, managing selling teams is a complex undertaking for sales managers. First, when a sales manager creates a sales team, it is important that recruited members be adaptable, able to work together, and willing to put the good of the group above their own individual needs. Second, they must be provided with sales training that covers topics like team selling and relationship marketing. Third, as a sales manager, you must clearly communicate the team's goals and correct the various team members who perform below expected levels. Last, a team's compensation package must include a component that motivates the members to cooperate so the group's goals will be achieved.

Team compensation can consist of a significant commission or bonus tied to a group meeting its goals, and the members of the group are expected to evaluate individual contributions to the team. For example, a customer-service manager at Cisco® will have different team-selling responsibilities than a supply chain manager, even though they are on the same team. Since all sales team members must contribute their expertise if the group is to succeed, Cisco® requires sales team members to constantly evaluate other members of the team.

Sales firms also form multi-level teams from different areas of the organization to sell to their counterparts in buying firms. That is, **multi-level selling** occurs when two or more personnel from the selling firm make a sales call to their functional counterparts at the buying organization. For example, a salesperson may call upon the purchasing agent at the buying firm, while a vice president of engineering calls upon the buyer's vice president of engineering and a quality assurance supervisor visits with the buyer's chief of quality control. From a protocol perspective, each sales firm member calls upon their counterpart at equal levels of the organizational chart. As necessary, the executive team member can negotiate price agreements, policy deviations, and expedited shipping dates to win the order and establish a deeper relationship with the buying partner.

In certain industries, like computers and telecommunications, customers purchase electronic components that are manufactured by two or more suppliers. Recently, firms started forming **marketing alliances** in which two or more companies combine their technologies, unique resources and skills, and products in order to market total systems to final users. Alliances allow selling firms to combine resources that create and deliver value to buyers in response to market opportunities. Marketing alliances are most effective when mutual trust, interdependence, and cooperation exist in the partnership. Salespersons can enhance their value in a sales alliance setting by exhibiting high levels of product, market, and customer knowledge.

A marketing alliance was formed when Parke-Davis, a pharmaceutical division of Warner Lambert, introduced the drug Lipitor® to reduce lipid cholesterol. Parke-Davis combined their sales efforts with Pfizer, a pharmaceutical firm with a large and experienced sales force, and the two sales forces worked together to maximize sales of Lipitor®. A few years later, Pfizer purchased Warner Lambert.[9]

A **value-added reseller (VAR)** purchases products from one or more manufacturers and assembles these products into a system before delivering the package to specialized customer segments. A VAR might purchase a computer system from Gateway®; add software from SAS®; and have their technical staff merge, test, and install the system for the end user. When a VAR delivers a complete package, buyers may call their purchase a **turnkey operation**. VARs may also handle customer service and repair issues or if one of the manufacturers partners with the value-added reseller, then the manufacturer may assume responsibility for repair and customer service.

B2B Customer Relationship Management

Recall from Chapter 1 that customer relationship management (CRM) is the process of identifying and grouping customers in order to develop an appropriate relationship strategy so that the organization can acquire, retain, and grow the business. Progressive firms have known for years that the key to successful business means keeping customers satisfied by developing a deeper understanding of their buyers' needs and producing products and services that they truly need or want. This is often easier for business-to-business firms to do because their sales forces are very in-touch with their customers. They also have relatively fewer customers to deal with than, say, retailers do. Having fewer customers allows sellers to more readily explore and uncover what products or services buying firms need.

However, in the past, many B2B sellers were less willing to track the needs of their customers and customize products for them in part because they lacked accurate information about what their buyers wanted since it wasn't readily available. Things are much different today: Salespeople and their managers can gather a lot of information about their customers simply by looking at their Web sites. Industry-wide and firm-specific news are also available with the click of a computer mouse. Sellers today are also more willing to customize their products for their business-to-business buyers, because new technology like CRM software has made it more feasible to determine the profitability of these customers over a specific time period. In other words, the selling firm knows in advance if going through the trouble of customizing a product for the customer is worth the extra effort. As the following Global Sales Management feature shows, many firms around the world, including Dow Chemical, Inc., Clorox Co., and Kforce, utilize CRM software to analyze the profitability of short- and long-term sales and compensate their sales representatives.

TECHNOLOGY IN SALES MANAGEMENT

Technology Can Help Ensure a Firm's Sales Are Profitable

Salespeople have long been criticized for making unprofitable deals. The growing forces of globalization and competition have further increased the pressure on firms to sell items that generate revenue, but not profits. Now, however, software prevents salespeople from entering unprofitable orders without the permission of their managers. The programs analyze the orders for their profitability as they are placed.

In response to unprofitable deals, companies are dropping losing product lines and unprofitable customers. For example, one European firm audited its sales to a $5-million-a-year customer that purchased a large number of custom products. When managers factored in the account's shipping and service costs, they realized the customer was costing them $700,000 a year! As you can see, these software systems provide sales managers with valuable information that allows them and their salespeople to do their jobs better. Armed with the information, the European firm's sales force renegotiated the customer's shipping and ordering arrangements.

Such a strategy might drive unprofitable customers away, but a firm cannot serve buyers that are not profitable. Firms that are using the new software include Clorox Co., Agere Systems, Inc., Dow Chemical, Inc., and Kforce. The sales managers in these firms also changed how they compensated their sales employees. Instead of compensating them on the total sales revenues they generated, they began compensating them on the profits earned from their sales.

Source: Based on Jaclyne Badal (2006). "A Reality Check for the Sales Staff," *Wall Street Journal*, October 16, B3.

Other advances in information technology, such as e-mail and EDI, have made it much easier for sellers to communicate with their buyers, predict their purchasing needs so as to forecast future sales to them, and more accurately understand buyer behavior through data mining. Firms that **data mine** examine information collected in their CRM databases. The bulk of this information is gathered by salespeople and may include: purchase dates, incentives offered the customer, product/services purchased, selling price, the buyer's position in his or her organization, number of rep visits between buys, and samples and promotional materials requested by the company. Having such information allows both sales representatives and their managers to identify important relationships or "connections" that might not be readily apparent.[10] For example, sales managers at a large pharmaceutical company learned which sales approaches were most effective via data mining—something they didn't know before.[11] Managers are also able to conduct competitive analyses that result in higher sales revenues, lower order entry errors, and the increased acquisition of new customers.[12]

From a technological perspective, an information-based CRM system connects the organization's entire operations to function like a 24-hour nerve center that shares information in "real time"[13, 14] by sending information that alerts appropriate managers about changes in demand, inventory levels, and product movements. Consider the following example: a buyer requests that an order be delivered by FedEx®, and this is entered into the CRM system. When the shipping labels are printed by the seller's CRM system, FedEx labels are printed. The system also records when the shipment was picked up by the delivery company and provides tracking numbers to confirm the shipment arrived safely. The

EXHIBIT 5.4

A Customer Centric Firm's View

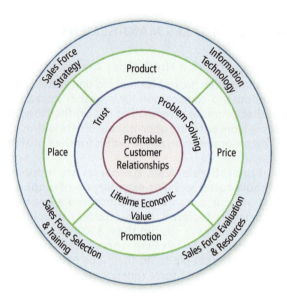

seller's intranet also permits the buyer to log into the site securely and check production schedules and delivery dates.

Cisco is a company that uses an information-based CRM system to enable its sales team. First, the CRM system at Cisco provides a single source of information for the extended selling team. In effect, the system increases accuracy and decreases confusion by allowing Cisco sales, marketing, and/or customer service employees to access historical purchases, part numbers, sales revenue, who sold the product(s), when the purchase occurred, and whether there is a service contract.

In short, CRM technology helps firms become more market- or customer-oriented.[15] Firms practice a market orientation when their business processes and functions are aligned to maximize their effectiveness in the marketplace. As Exhibit 5.4 shows, a market-oriented selling firm places the buyer at the center of all of the strategic decisions it makes. In effect, the seller becomes **customer-centric**. We will discuss more about sales information technology, including CRM technology, in Chapter 6.

The Nature of B2B Relationships

Different B2B buyers and sellers have different types of relationships with one another at different times. Exactly how a buyer and seller relate to one another will depend upon how the buyer extracts—or gets—value from the relationship. After all, the buyer is often in the "driver's seat," so to speak. Sales managers must understand business relationships in order to devise strategies and direct their salespeople to move profitable customers to deeper relationships. It is management, not the salesperson, who decides which customers are worth additional time and resources.

In a **transactional relationship**, the buyer-seller relationship can be adversarial when either party views the situation from a purely economic perspective. In this case, important and powerful buyers might play sellers off against one another to get lower prices or free services. For example, a buyer might inform the salesperson that the salesperson must lower the price of the product or service if he or she is to continue to do business with the firm. Otherwise, a competitor will receive either a larger portion or all of the business. (This does not mean that transactional situations are good or bad. Rather, in certain industries in which a product is viewed as a commodity, there is a known market price for the product, and the buyer and seller work together to reach an agreement that benefits both parties.)

But it's not only buyers who play games. Salespeople have been known to play games with their buyers. They might, say, ship products manufactured for specific buyers to new, more profitable customers and make the original customer wait for a later shipment of the products. In transactional relationships, communication and contact are funneled through a "bow tie" arrangement between the purchaser and the salesperson. This means that all information and contact occurs between the salesperson and a buyer. The information and requests are then communicated by the purchasing agent or salesperson to respective areas within their firm. Although sellers and buyers may begin to establish trust and share information in a transactional relationship, their early relationships are greatly influenced by established business practices within each firm.[16]

In a **facilitative relationship**, trust and cooperation between buyers and sellers is better. This can create value for both parties. For example, a buyer might award most of a company's business to one particular seller, allowing the seller to reduce its purchasing and marketing costs through efficiencies and economies of scale. That is, the buyer saves time and money by not having to coordinate multiple vendors and their systems, while the seller minimizes expenses needed to win new accounts.

In the facilitative relationship stage, an inside sales representative might advance the relationship with the customer by identifying who the influencers and decision makers are, solving the customer's day-to-day problems, and offering suggestive selling solutions when opportunities arise. As the relationship expands to the facilitative stage, the seller will be better able to analyze the buyer's past purchases and figure out the best contact strategies for doing business with them.[17] For example, the seller's sales managers might determine that the best way for the company to conduct business with the buyer is by assigning an external sales representative to the customer. Or, perhaps it's best for an inside sales representative to continue serving as the customer's point of contact.

Integrative relationships are the deepest relationships. They occur when the buyer decides to partner with a seller that can add a significant amount of value to the buyer's product or processes. In a deep relationship, buyers and sellers trust one another and cooperate to reduce costs and advance their mutual goals,[18] and the selling firm becomes the buyer's **sole source supplier**—the single supplier for the buyer's product or service, in other words. Google is an example of a firm that has partnered with Yahoo! and has become its sole search engine supplier.

In integrative relationships, both partners also seek out new ways to deliver and add value to one another's products and processes (see Exhibit 5.5). In certain integrative relationships, a sales manager might decide to replace an outside salesperson with an inside sales representative, who might actually go to work in the buyer's offices.[19] IBM is one company that actually has on-site consultants, or representatives, at their buyer's sites to help solve their computing problems.

When business partners trust each other, they depend on one another to achieve a goal. However, not all sales organizations receive the same level of trust from their partners because trust is earned by making and keeping your promises.[20] At Schering-Plough® Pharmaceuticals, sales managers expect their sales representatives to bring integrity and honesty to their jobs in order to establish trusting relationships with physicians. Building this relationship can take from 6–18 months.[21] Without trust, the buyer will likely be reluctant to share information the salesperson needs to recommend solutions to the buyer's problems.[22] Forming business relationships can vary significantly across cultures, as seen in the following Global Sales Management feature.

EXHIBIT 5.5

Differences in Key Variables Based upon the Stage of the Buyer and Seller's Relationship

Relationship:	Transactional >	Facilitative >	Integrative
Trust	Little trust	Increasing trust	Broad trust
Communication	Buyer-seller "bow tie"	A Few Departments Begin Communicating	Direct Communication between All Departments
Value	"Win-Lose"	Buyer: Lower Prices Seller: Lower Costs	"Win-Win" for both
Commitment	Little expectations beyond Current Contract	Growing commitment by Buyer & Seller	Long-term expectations of Partnership
Feedback	Little expectation of feedback	Growing Acceptance of Feedback	Honest feedback expected and Sought
Sales Programs	Little opportunity to cross-, up-sell	May Switch to Inside Salesperson	Expansive opportunity to cross-, up-sell
Profits	Little concern for supplier profits	More Concern	Acknowledgement that supplier Must Make reasonable profit
Competitive Advantage	Little Other Than Current Buy	Growing Competitive Advantage	Customized offering

GLOBAL SALES MANAGEMENT

Forming Business Relationships in Other Cultures

Many Americans assume you walk into a potential customer's place of business, introduce yourself, call the buyer by his or her first name, and, after a very short while, make a sale. However, in many cultures around the world, it takes years to form a relationship with a person one does not know. For example, in China *guan xi* (personal relationships) greatly influence who one buys from and trusts. In Japan, and in most Asian nations, the collectivist, or group nature, of the societies makes it difficult to get to know and learn to trust foreign businesspeople.

For foreigners who travel to Japan, the process of forming a relationship requires a significant amount of effort that involves proving to your Japanese customers that you can be trusted to provide them with the products or services they need to keep their businesses running. Americans often misunderstand this and mistakenly reject going out at night with their customers for long sessions of karaoke, drinking, and talk. All of these social niceties, however, allow the Japanese to look deeply into the character of the *gaijin*, or foreigner.

Source: Based on John B. Ford and Earl D. Honeycutt, Jr. (1992). "Japanese National Culture as a Basis for Understanding Japanese Business Practices," *Business Horizons,* 35:6, 27–34.

Customer Lifetime Value (CLV) Strategies

The goal for sales representatives and their managers is to establish and maintain mutually beneficial, long-term relationships with their *most profitable* customers. Companies that follow a CRM strategy work to provide distinct service levels to customers based upon

	One Year	Three Years	Five Years
Average Sales	$20,000	$24,000	$30,000
Sales Orders per Year	1	1	1
Referrals	0	2	4
Number of Referrals That Buy	0	1	2
Gross Sales/Year/Customer	$20,000	$72,000	$150,000
Referrals That Become Customers	0	20%	25%
Gross Sales Referrals	0	$28,800	$150,000
Computed Customer Value	$20,000	$100,800	$300,000
Minus Marketing Expenses	($2,000)	($13,600)	($25,500)
Net Lifetime Customer Value	$18,000	$87,600	$274,500

EXHIBIT 5.6

Computing a Buyer's Customer Lifetime Value (CLV)

their expected customer lifetime value (CLV). Recall that customer lifetime value refers to the profitability of partnering with a buyer for an extended period of time.[23] This involves computing the customer lifetime value for each buyer—its future profitability, that is.[24] In fact, CLV is the most effective metric for managing future customer profitability.[25]

The selling firm can compute CLV by knowing or projecting three criteria: (1) the probability of future purchases, (2) future marketing costs, and (3) future contribution margins. Depending upon the CLV of customers, selling firms can allocate resources based on how profitable sales to them are, propose the correct product to the correct buyer at the correct time, and earn and retain profitable customers. Exhibit 5.7 shows how a firm might set their sales strategies based upon CLV.

Once the customer's CLV is calculated, salespeople and their managers then develop distinct service levels, approaches, and strategies for the customer based on its CLV. Exhibit 5.6 shows how a seller that makes one sale to a customer receives $18,000 in customer lifetime value. But, if the seller works to make the buyer a long-term partner, the account could potentially generate a CLV of nearly $275,000 over five years due to lower marketing costs and additional customers being referred to the seller.

EXHIBIT 5.7

Planning a Firm's Sales Strategy Based upon Customer Lifetime Value (CLV)

	Low Percentage of Purchase Share	High Percentage of Purchase Share
High Lifetime Earning Value	Frequent Sales Force Visits Monthly Visits Direct Mail/Telemarketing Optimal Contact: Bi-weekly High Potential Customer Value	Constant Sales Force Interaction Weekly Visits Direct Mail/Telemarketing Optimal Contact: Weekly Highest Customer Value
Low Lifetime Earning Value	Extended Sales Force Visits Yearly Intervals Direct Mail/Telemarketing Optimal Contact: Quarterly Low Value Customer	Infrequent Sales Force Visits Six-Month Intervals Direct Mail/Telemarketing Optimal Contact: Bi-monthly Low Potential Customer Value

The Stages of B2B Customer Relationship Management

Firms that adopt a CRM strategy tend to follow three distinct stages. Initially, CRM sales managers view the system as a driver of income. Having accurate information about buyers allows the sales force to **up-sell** more expensive products and **cross-sell** new products to existing buyers who haven't purchased these products before. For example, at Cisco, a salesperson might gather information from customers by asking the following questions:

1. What does your computer network currently look like?
2. What is the design of the network?
3. Where does your company want to be in a year? In five years?

After gathering the information, the salesperson determines how Cisco's products can best be matched to the buyer's needs and how many years it will take for the buyer to receive a financial return on the product(s) purchased. By following this process, Cisco boosts revenue and profits by selling at a higher level to its current customers.

In the second stage, sales managers recognize that CRM allows their representatives to manage customer relationships to earn higher profits. For example, a sales executive might decide to primarily contact customers from which the firm earns less profit via less costly Internet, telemarketing, or mail campaign methods. This will give sales representatives more time to call upon more profitable clients and lower the firm's overall selling costs.

In the third stage, sales managers understand that CRM is the driver of customer lifetime value. Thus, sales managers encourage their salespeople to offer customized solutions to their most profitable buyers. The sales managers then work to coordinate the activities within the firm's sales, customer service, and marketing groups to retain buyers with the highest LCV.

A salesperson that has product and application knowledge, advocates for the buyer, and calls upon the buyer at the appropriate time and in the correct medium (in-person, phone, or e-mail) will be perceived by buyers as a professional sales consultant that adds value to their firms.[26] An excellent example of a "credible consultant" is Michael Gerrity of Action Packaging Systems®. Gerrity once promised a customer a next-morning delivery of 30,000 labels. To keep his promise, he remained in contact with FedEx® throughout the night, drove to the Boston airport at 5:00 a.m. to collect the shipment, and personally delivered the order to the customer at 7:30 a.m. to meet an eight o'clock deadline.[27]

Maximizing the Buyer's Value

Buyers look for value and satisfaction in their purchases. This value can be computed as:

$$\frac{\text{Benefit}}{\text{Costs}} = \frac{\text{Functional Benefits} + \text{Emotional Benefits}}{\text{Monetary Costs} + \text{Time Costs} + \text{Energy Costs} + \text{Psychic Costs}}$$

Salespersons can increase their product or service's value in the minds of the customer by: (1) increasing product/service benefits, (2) decreasing buyer costs, or (3) doing both. For example, the selling firm, through the salesperson, can maximize the functional benefits of their offering by ensuring that the product exceeds the buyer's expected satisfaction level. Emotional benefits are maximized through trust and shared successful business relationships. Although it may not be possible to lower the buyer's monetary costs, the seller can reduce the buyer's time and energy costs through electronic ordering, high-quality products that exceed expectations, and by assuming additional service duties like monitoring the buyer's inventory and communicating directly with the buyer's manufacturing and quality control personnel when problems arise. Likewise, the buyer's "psychic" costs are reduced when the seller exhibits high levels of trust, dependability, and honesty.

The reward for creating customer value is that buyers purchase larger amounts for longer periods and are less likely to leave the business relationship. This goal is achieved by eliminating causes of dissatisfaction and increasing the buyer's **drivers of delight**, or factors that exceed the buyer's expectations. Most sellers can list four to five categories such as perceived value, customer service, responsiveness, and quality that account for 80 percent of buyer dissatisfaction and two or three other factors that cause increased buyer satisfaction.[28]

Building trusting relationships leads to sales success. (istockphoto.com)

Risk and the Organizational Buyer

Sales managers can also help their salespeople establish trust and form deeper relationships by reducing the risk faced by the firm's customers. For example, when a professional buyer decides to order a computer system, a major piece of manufacturing equipment, or a healthcare system for their workforce, the potential risk is high because the purchase price is significant and the problems associated with such products are difficult to correct. However, if a sales manager in a computer manufacturing firm can convince the company's executives to offer customers a "no-questions-asked" return policy for newly released products, then the buyer's risk will be substantially minimized. The easiest and least expensive way to reduce risk is by sharing information. A CRM system provides common information within the sales organization that can improve the probability of higher customer service levels occurring.

When a problem occurs with your best customers, it is best to meet personally with them to be sure all of their issues are addressed. (Getty Images/Digital Vision)

Consider the following example: The buyer calls the seller's customer service department to report that a shipment arrived damaged. The customer service representative apologizes for the problem, opens the buyer's CRM account to record that the most recent shipment was damaged, and enters an expedited replacement order. This report is almost immediately visible to the salesperson, his or her sales manager, the firm's customer service manager, production manager, and shipping team leader. A replacement order is readied to be shipped overnight to the customer and an e-mail is sent to the salesperson confirming that the replacement order will arrive the next day. The salesperson calls the buyer to confirm the problem has been corrected and thanks the contact for the company's continued business. In addition, the seller's salespeople provide the buyer with excellent product information via sales presentations, product demonstrations, or product trials. In a trustful, customer-centric relationship, risk is lessened by partners that share valuable information with one another.

Sales managers are primarily concerned with the outcome of the relationships their salespeople have with customers—namely, higher sales and higher profits. However, to take these relationships to their highest levels and extract the maximum customer lifetime value, sales managers must also be concerned about the importance of the outcome for their customers. As we have said, ideally, both buyers and sellers work to attain mutually agreed-upon goals in their relationship by forming a trusting relationship and willingly resolving problems.[29]

Important Salesperson Behaviors

Behaviors that the firm's sales managers should encourage their representatives to take to create and maintain relationships with their customers include:

- Fostering a long-term perspective. The success of customer relationship programs depends on the salesperson's passionate interest in and constant efforts toward establishing and maintaining long-term relationships. The sales force cannot generate sales unless buying firms possess a true need. At Cisco, sales managers encourage their representatives to take a long-term perspective by assigning each buyer a single sales contact. This person assures the buyer he or she is available to support the buyer's needs.

- Being honest and sincere. Both qualities are important in a business relationship. To retain trust, the buyer must always be told the truth even when a promise cannot be met. Cisco salespersons are encouraged to take the time to get to know their buyers, show genuine interest in them, and truly address their needs. It is obvious to the buyer that Cisco is not simply looking for a quick sales transaction.

- Understanding customer needs and problems. A good CRM program requires fully informed and knowledgeable sales representatives. For example, Medtronic requires its senior managers to attend medical operations and discuss how the company's products work. This serves as an example to the company's sales representatives. The idea is for everyone in the company to gain an intimate understanding of what customers need and how Medtronics' products can solve those needs.[30]

- Meeting commitments. To build trust and maintain a relationship, the salesperson must keep all commitments made to the buyer. This requires support from the sales firm and the salesperson's manager so the buyer is not let down. In this way, buyers come to believe that the selling firm and their salespeople are committed for the long-term and will serve them at a higher level than other competitors. As a Cisco salesperson told one of the authors: "This is the name of the game." Cisco salespersons call and update buyers on the status of their information request or purchase. After all buyer-seller discussions, the Cisco salesperson researches questions and concerns raised by the buyer and communicates this information to the buyer.

- Providing after-sales service. The salesperson must respond positively to buyers' concerns and problems. Many customer-centric firms have established high-quality customer service centers that resolve buyers' problems quickly and efficiently. Even so, the salesperson must be made aware of customer concerns expressed to his or her firm's customer service center and ensure the buyer receives valued service and remains satisfied. For example, all of Cisco's sales quotes contain an after-sales service contract supported by a "Follow the Sun" service center setup. This means the customer can call Cisco anytime day or night and, depending upon where the sun is shining, a service center in Virginia, California, Australia, India, or Belgium will take the call, consult the CRM system, help troubleshoot the customer's problem, order replacement parts, or send in a certified local partner to repair any nonfunctioning equipment the buyer might have. Cisco believes that selling a product without after-sales service is not responsible selling.

Why Business Relationships End

Business relationships unravel or come to an end when one or both parties feel their partner is too complacent, their goals no longer match, their cultures have diverged, or one or both parties have behaved irresponsibly. This can include acting in a way that is not trustful, being dishonest, looking out for their own interests, sharing confidential information with others, and/or taking unfair advantage of information shared with their partner. When such behavior occurs, one or both parties conclude that it is not in their best interests to maintain the business relationship.[31]

Salespersons can be "lightning rods" whenever anything goes wrong because they are boundary spanners. (Recall that we discussed boundary spanners in Chapter 4.) After all, it is a salesperson's job to bring the selling and buying firms together to conduct business for their mutual benefit. As a result, it is often the salesperson who is blamed for the loss of the relationship with a valued partner. When a salesperson makes a promise—that she will have parts air freighted to the buyer to maintain production, for example—this commitment must be honored or the buyer will rightly assume that the seller cannot be trusted and does not have its best interests at heart. In fact, research confirms that the strength of the buyer-seller relationship plays an important role in reducing buyer defection.[32]

The trouble is that salespeople can't always control everything that occurs at their firm. Sometimes the selling firm itself is responsible for "cracks" in the relationship with a B2B partner. For example, a manufacturer might assure the salesperson that a product will be delivered to the customer on a specific date; whereupon, the salesperson passes the information to the buyer. But when the product doesn't arrive on time, who do you think the customer will blame? The salesperson, of course.

Even if it's not the salesperson's fault, it is often best to have him or her resolve the buyer's conflicts instead of, say, the firm's service center. In other words, for the relationship to be maintained, it's the salesperson who should optimally break the "bad" news to customers. However, sales managers can help in situations such as this by taking speedy actions to remedy the misunderstanding.[33] For example, Bill Bencsik, featured in the opening profile, makes a special effort to correct misunderstandings that lead to broken relationships. Bencsik feels that it is important to communicate with the buyer as soon as possible and to meet personally over dinner with them, whenever possible. According to Bencsik, moving quickly to resolve misunderstandings shows the value of the relationship with the buyer and, when successful, can make the relationship stronger because he went the extra mile for his customer.

Summary

Buyers tend to engage in a specific process when making a purchase decision. The buying process is based upon whether the purchase situation is completely new, current business that is up for re-bid, or a routine purchase. Each of these buying situations impacts the relationship formed and the amount of information that is shared between the buyer and seller.

Buyers use the multi-attribute matrix in an effort to objectively evaluate sales offers. A multi-attribute matrix allows the salesperson to list and prioritize the importance of the buyer's criteria, like price, delivery, and quality. When a group of employees in the firm—either a buying center or decision-making unit (DMU)—are involved in the purchase process, these employees play a variety of "roles" in the process. They may act as initiators of the purchase, influencers, the decision maker, the purchasing agent, the gatekeeper, the financial controller, or any combination of roles. Buying centers are dynamic. That is, the group of individuals who comprises them changes over time. Certain decisions might involve a formal buying committee. More frequently, however, the decision-making process is less structured and informal.

More and more firms are adopting a customer relationship management strategy to profitably serve their current and future business partners. CRM systems allow the seller to collect information through a data-based system that helps them better understand and fulfill buyer's needs. For a B2B relationship to be nurtured to grow, both partners must act in a trustworthy manner and work to resolve the inevitable problems encountered in any relationship. However, a customer relationship means different things to different people. Not all firms want a "partner" for every purchase. Lastly, firms understand that it is not economically feasible or even desirable to turn every customer into a long-term partner.

Key Terms

approved vendors' list   90
buying center   92
controller   93
cross-sell   102
customer-centric   98
data mine   97
decision maker   93
decision-making unit (DMU)   92–93
drivers of delight   103
extended selling team   94
facilitative relationship   99
filter   93
gatekeeper   93
influencer   93
initiator   93
in-supplier   92
integrative relationship   99

marketing alliances   96
modified re-buy   91
multi-attribute matrix   92
multi-level selling   95
new buy   91
out-supplier   92
purchaser   93
request for quotation (RFQ)   91
screen   93
sole source supplier   99
straight re-buy   91
transactional relationship   98
turn-key operation   96
up-sell   102
user   93
value-added reseller (VAR)   96

Questions and Problems

1. Define customer lifetime value (CLV). What three factors comprise the formula for computing CLV? Why is CLV the most effective metric for managing future customer profitability?

2. Go to Multimedia Education Resource for Learning and On-line Teaching (MERLOT) at http://www.imrtn.com/lifetimecalc.asp and compute two lifetime customer values (CLV) based upon a one-year customer experience and a five-year relationship. First, assume you will sell $25,000 two times per year to your new customer, but for only a single year. The customer will not provide you with any referrals. Compute the total value of a satisfied customer given this scenario. Second, run the same calculation, but make these new assumptions: The customer continues to buy $25,000 twice a year for five years; in addition, the customer provides two referral customers that result in one additional customer. Based upon this information, recompute the total value of a satisfied customer. What are the financial differences between a one-year and five-year customer? How can sellers increase their profitability by computing the expected CLV?

3. What actions can a sales manager propose, other than lowering the price, to increase value for the customer?

4. A bank wants to purchase a new PC-based computer system. Who do you think would play each of the roles in the buying center? What would the president's role be? What about that of the office manager, the average teller, the manager of customer service, or any other manager? What characteristics or personal interests

might influencers have? How might the size of the bank influence the purchase? That is, compare and contrast the different purchase decisions for a bank that wanted to purchase 25 PCs and had one location and $50 million in assets versus 125 locations and $2 billion in assets?

5. Discuss the differences between a new buy, a modified re-buy, and a straight re-buy situation in respect to time, information required, and role of the salesperson. How does a relationship influence the roles played by the in-supplier and the out-supplier?

6. Use the multi-attribute matrix below to compute the assigned list of attributes for a machine.

Product		A	B
Price	(.5)		
Dependability	(.3)		
Warranty	(.2)		
Totals			

Machine A costs $12,000 and Machine B costs $14,000. A is considered to be average dependability and warranty, and B is considered to have above-average dependability and warranty.

7. Why is it important for a salesperson to properly identify the decision maker in a buying center? How should a sales manager go about coaching his or her reps to find out who this person really is?

8. Define multilevel selling. Give an example of a marketing alliance and explain why such a partnership benefits both parties.

9. What is a value-added reseller (VAR)? How should VAR sales managers coordinate their service and repair issues with their manufacturing partners?

10. Why have B2B firms been shifting to a customer relationship management perspective? What are the benefits of pursuing a CRM strategy? How does such a shift in a company's focus impact its sales force and sales managers?

11. What are the three levels of B2B customer relationships? How do they differ?

12. What actions should a sales manager take when a firm adopts a CRM strategy? What sales force skills are driven by a CRM strategy, and how does it affect the type of people sales managers hire and how they're trained?

13. What types of behaviors lead to the demise of a business relationship? How can a sales manager minimize the loss of profitable partners? What role should a sales manager play in terms of dealing with dissatisfied partners? Why?

14. Some firms have tried to form and maintain relationships with all their customers. Is it a wise strategy for a sales manager to emphasize? Why or why not?

Role Play

Managing a Sales Team at Alamance Associates

Henry Conner is the sales manager at Alamance Associates, a firm that manufactures B2B goods that are sold globally. Recently, a major customer, Four Part Solutions, asked Jerry Phillips, its sales representative, to meet with them to begin discussions about purchasing a new line of machinery, plus contracting for installation and services for the new equipment. As a first step, Conner appointed a sales team that was comprised of Phillips; Linda Lu, who is a design engineer; and Devin Jackson, who supervises the services for Alamance Associates. Conner has scheduled a meeting with Phillips, Lu, and Jackson to listen to their concerns and suggestions about the forthcoming meetings with Four Part Solutions. At the conclusion of the meeting, Conner must appoint a sales team leader and determine what questions the team will propose to the customer when they meet. Also, Conner must decide how he will evaluate the team and structure the members' compensation.

Characters

Henry Conner, Sales Manager at Alamance Associates (AA)
Jerry Phillips, AA Account Manager for Four Part Solutions
Linda Lu, Design Engineer at Alamance Associates
Devin Jackson, Service Manager at Alamance Associates

Assignment

Break into groups of four, with each student in the group playing a character. Do not be concerned about matching the gender of the character with the actual gender mix of the student group. Prior to breaking into a group, work individually to summarize a list of concerns and questions that are important to your area of expertise at Alamance Associates. Then meet as a group and role-play the meeting between Henry, Jerry, Linda, and Devin. Your initial goal is to conclude the meeting with an agreed-upon list of questions that will be discussed at the initial meeting with the Four Part Solutions Buying Team. Also, work together as a group to determine who should be the team leader, how the team will be evaluated, and what type of compensation each member should receive for their contribution to the team's success.

Sales Manager's Workshop: Adjusting the Territory Sizes within a Sales District

You are Promedia's district sales manager for the North Central District that is comprised of five salespeople who are assigned to geographic territories. After three years of conducting business in this geographic area, it is apparent that some territories are growing. This has resulted in several salespeople not having enough time to properly call upon their new customers while serving their old customers. However, the sales in other territories are stagnant. As sales manager, it is your responsibility to adjust the sizes of the territories, utilizing appropriate criteria. Go to the Applicor data and compare the sales revenue, potential, and number of accounts per territory to analyze the current workload for each of the five territories. Based upon your findings, recommend the appropriate changes and, if it's requested, turn in a printed copy of your decisions to your sales management professor.

Caselet 5.1: Managing Buying Dynamics at Hughes Aircraft

Fred Johnson is a sales manager with WRT Electronics and his team of sales engineers call upon original equipment manufacturers (OEMs) located in Southern California. Hughes Aircraft is a large manufacturer with multiple government contracts for supplying helicopters, communications equipment, and weapons systems to all branches of the military that is serviced by WRT.

On a recent visit to the satellite communications components division in Los Angeles, sales engineer Ron Hartley was told by the purchasing administrator, Sharon Reynolds, that WRT will be in a bidding war for the current Request for Quotation (RFQ) and that the supplier would be selected based primarily upon price. However, later in the day when

Ron met with Matma Singh, design engineer, he was informed that conformity to design tolerances would be the criterion utilized for selection of suppliers. To his further dismay, Ralph Jackson, who is the Hughes's Quality Assurance Manager, stated that the initial contract would be for six months at which time the supplier with the fewest quality problems would receive a multi-year contract for the major share of the components.

Fred understands that participants in a buying center play distinct roles and are motivated differently. As he drives to his home in Orange County through heavy freeway traffic, Fred tries to make sense of what is motivating these three members of the Hughes buying center so that he can recommend a sales strategy for his salesperson Ron Hartley, who will visit Hughes again next week.

Questions

1. How can Fred explain Sharon, Matma, and Ralph's motivations to Ron based upon the different buying roles they play?
2. Could Fred explain each buyer's weight using the multi-attribute model?
3. What pointers should Fred offer Ron to successfully manage this major account? Why?

Caselet 5.2: Choosing a CRM System for Burlington Mechanical Solutions

Bobby Puckett, sales vice president of Burlington Mechanical Solutions (BMS), feels that it is time to introduce a customer relationship management strategy at his $500 million-in-annual-sales firm. BMS sells all types of mechanical solutions to original equipment manufacturers (OEMs) in the automotive industry. Currently, BMS employs 110 salespersons that cover nearly 400 subsidiary and independent subcontractors that manufacture components for the "Big Three" U.S. and on-shore Japanese and European automotive manufacturers.

The BMS sales force is organized by product and geography, and, because of duplication in different manufacturing areas of an account, each salesperson is assigned about 30 customers. Puckett has come to understand that not all customers are the same. That is, a small number of customers are categorized as "A" or "key accounts" and a slightly larger number are "B" or possessing potential to move to key account status. Until now, the BMS sales force has devoted significant time to "B" and even less profitable "C" accounts. Puckett is convinced that by switching to a CRM strategy BMS will see increased profits from the same group of customers. However, a number of questions remain to be answered before the new strategy is implemented.

Puckett has met with three providers of CRM software to learn about the types of systems that are available. Puckett was surprised to learn there were over 300 CRM software systems on the market that varied significantly in cost, based upon the amount of customization needed for BMS's customer group. First, what process should BMS follow to purchase a CRM system? Second, Puckett knows that any CRM system he purchases must be user-friendly for his sales force. Several articles he read and discussions with peers from other competitors convinced him that if the sales force requirement to add information to the system is too demanding, the sales force will oppose the new system. Lastly, Puckett feels that it is important to identify the type of information that will benefit the sales force and help them improve their productivity.

As Puckett sits in his office after everyone else has left for the day, he ponders how he should proceed with this very important decision. Purchasing a CRM system will be costly, but buying a system that likely will not be adopted by the sales force is fraught with risk. He would like to delay the situation while he studies the pros and cons of the new strategy, but given BMS's competitive position, there is little time to waste. Finally, Puckett decides to sleep on the problem and see how he feels when he arrives back at work in the morning.

Questions

1. How can Puckett ensure the CRM system is easy for the sales force to load and use? What role can members of the sales force play in making the CRM system "user-friendly"?
2. Is CRM an information-based system, a sales force-based strategy, or both? How does each role vary? In what ways do they vary?
3. Make a list of important information that a CRM should provide to a sales force. How should a sales manager use this information to assist the sales team? What is the likely outcome if CRM information does not help the sales force succeed?

References

1. Anthes, Gary. "It's All Global Now," *Computerworld*, February 20, 2006.
2. Jackson, Donald W., Jr., Janet E. Keith, and Richard K. Burdick (1984). "Purchasing Agents' Perceptions of Industrial Buying Center Influence: A Situational Approach," *Journal of Marketing*, 48:4 (Autumn), 75–83.
3. Bonoma, Thomas V. (2006). "Major Sales: Who Really Does the Buying," *Harvard Business Review*, July–August, 172–181.
4. Jenning, Richard G., and Richard E. Plank (1995). "When the Purchasing Agent Is a Committee: Implications for Industrial Marketing," *Industrial Marketing Management*, 24:5 (October), 411–419.
5. Trailer, Barry, and Jim Dickie (2006). "Understanding What Your Sales Manager is Up Against," *Harvard Business Review*, July–August, 48–55.
6. Honeycutt, Earl D., and Lew Kurtzman (2006). *Selling Outside Your Culture Zone.* Dallas, TX: Behavioral Science Research Press, Inc.
7. Moon, Mark A., and Susan Forquer Gupta (1997). "Examining the Formation of Selling Centers: A Conceptual Framework," *Journal of Personal Selling & Sales Management*, Spring, 31–42.
8. Brewer, Geoffrey (1998). "Lou Gerstner Has His Hands Full," *Sales & Marketing Management*, May, 36–41.
9. Cohen, Andy (1998). "Top of the Charts—Pfizer," *Sales & Marketing Management*, July, 41.
10. Magnini, Vincent P., Earl D. Honeycutt, Jr., and Sharon K. Hodge (2003). "Data Mining for Hotel Firms: Use and Limitations," *Cornell Hotel and Restaurant Administration Quarterly*, 44:2 (April), 94–105.
11. Graettinger, Tim. "Digging Up $$$ with Data Mining? An Executive's Guide, The Data Administrator's Newsletter, TDN.Com, Accessed July 8, 2007.
12. Dickie, R. James. (1999). "The Sales Effectiveness Challenge? Are We Solving the Right Problem?" *CSO Forum White Paper*, Boulder, Colorado.
13. Goldenberg, Barton (2007). "Real Time CRM the New Way of Doing Business," *Sales & Marketing Management*, June, 34–37.
14. Lee, Dick (2000). "Smarketing! Is CRM Technology Ready to Support the New Sales/ Marketing Discipline?" *Sales and Marketing Automation*, (January), 51–56.
15. Shapiro, Benson (1988). "What the Hell is 'Market Oriented?'" *Harvard Business Review*, November–December, 2–7.

16. Wilson, David T. (2000). "Deep Relationships: The Case of the Vanishing Salesperson," *The Journal of Personal Selling & Sales Management*, XX:1 (Winter), 53–61.
17. Kumar, V. (2006). "Customer Lifetime Value is the Path to Prosperity," *Marketing Research*, Fall 2006, 41–46.
18. Kalwani, Menohar, and Narakesari Narayandas (1995). "Long-Term Manufacturer-Supplier Relationships: Do They Pay Off for Supplier Firms?" *Journal of Marketing*, 59 (January), 1–16.
19. Wilson (2000).
20. Dorsch, Michael J., Scott R. Swanson, and Scott W. Kelly (1998). "The Role of Relationship Quality in the Stratification of Vendors as Perceived by Customers," *Journal of the Academy of Marketing Science*, 26:2 (Spring), 128–142.
21. Stewart, Thomas A., and David Champion (2006). "Leading Change from the Top Line," *Harvard Business Review*, July–August, 90–97.
22. Liu, Annie H., and Mark P. Leach (2001). "Developing Loyal Customers with a Value-adding Sales Force: Examining Customer Satisfaction and the Perceived Credibility of Consultative Salespeople," *Journal of Personal Selling & Sales Management*, XXI:2 (Spring), 147–156.
23. Kumar (2006).
24. Ibid.
25. Ibid.
26. Johnson, Julie T., Hiram C. Barksdale, Jr., and James S. Boles (2001). "The Strategic Role of the Salesperson in Reducing Customer Defection in Business Relationships," *Journal of Personal Selling & Sales Management*, XXI:2 (Spring), 123–134.
27. Anonymous (2007). "Proof of Delivery," *Sales & Marketing Management*, May, 46.
28. Kotler, Philip (2003). *A Framework for Marketing Management*. Upper Saddle River, NJ: Prentice Hall.
29. Leek, Sheena, Peter W. Turnbull, and Pete Naude (2006). "Classifying Relationships Across Cultures as Successful and Problematic: Theoretical Perspectives and Managerial Implications," *Industrial Marketing Management*, 35:7 (October), 892–900.
30. George, Bill (2003). *Authentic Leadership*. San Francisco: Jossey-Bass.
31. Jones, Thomas O., and W. Earl Sasser (1995). Why Satisfied Customers Defect," *Harvard Business Review*, 73:6, 88–99.
32. Johnson, Barksdale, and Boles (2001).
33. Palmatier, Robert W., Rajiv P. Dant, Dhruv Grewal, and Kenneth R. Evans (2006). "Factors Influencing the Effectiveness of Relationship Marketing: A Meta-Analysis," *Journal of Marketing*, 70:4 (October), 136–153.

6

LEVERAGING INFORMATION TECHNOLOGIES

LEARNING OBJECTIVES

After completing this chapter, you should be able to:

- Explain how common technologies used today have altered sales forces and the way they are managed.

- Explain what sales force automation technology is and what it's used for.

- Explain what a customer relationship management system is and the challenges related to implementing one.

- Describe what sales managers can do to encourage their employees to adopt and effectively utilize technology.

A customer sees a company's new product at a trade show. Later she receives a phone call from her salesperson asking what she thought about the product. The company's salesperson then visits her and makes a product recommendation. She decides to buy the product and goes online to place her order. She then gets an e-mail confirmation from her salesperson, who schedules a visit to train her to use the new product after it arrives. In this instance, the customer interacted with the company through at least three channels—trade shows, personal visits, and online. How much did technology help her salesperson close the business?

In this chapter, we explore the role technology plays in sales and sales management. Most technology supporting salespeople is not obvious to the customer, yet today's salesperson would be much less productive without it.

PATRICIA JENNINGS

BUSINESS MANAGER, MERCK & CO.

Business Manager Patricia Jennings, based in San Antonio, Texas, is a field sales business manager for Merck & Co., the global pharmaceutical firm. Jennings says that after six years as a salesperson and nine as a manager, the most important part of her job is to be of value to her 13 sales representatives during her routine coaching visits with them. "I strongly believe that similar to sales managers, sales representatives have to be of value to their customers and provide them with the most accurate and balanced information, depending on their beliefs about our products," says Jennings.

One of the overarching goals for Merck & Co. is to pursue better ways of reaching customers. Technology has been a major part of this objective. Merck's sales representatives use software that allows them to work paper-free—from obtaining signatures for pharmaceutical samples to presenting materials to physicians straight from their laptop computers. Printed product brochures have long been the gold standard within the industry to review with physicians. But Merck has far surpassed the gold standard by loading those brochures into computer software and adding graphics that enhance the visual aspect of the information. Furthermore, the computer memory of representatives' laptops allows them to reference much more material at the tap of a stylus than could be carried in any briefcase.

Jennings says that as a manager she has certain expectations that she and each of her representatives go through prior to each customer visit. "Prior to the call, I'll have the representative walk me through their plan for the customer," says Jennings. "We take the time to actually go through the product information on the laptop computer, and, in most cases, we will even role-play highlighted points in the planned discussion." This expectation is consistent for every representative, no matter their tenure, experience, or accolades. The coaching then comes into play when and if the information is appropriate, based upon what the representative identifies is important for the customer.

Depending on the circumstance, the representative has to make quick decisions and be multiple steps ahead, but move swiftly throughout the conversation with the customer. "At times, I'll coach around not just the message but around logistics—for example, on how well the representative maneuvers through each 'page' within the computer," says Jennings. "The customer's time is always unpredictable, so a representative has to be able to plan for a long visit, which is the best we can hope for, as well as a plan for a very brief opportunity to convey information."

Jennings does more coaching once the visit is complete. This "debriefing" is just as important as the review prior to the call. It helps both her and the representative assess whether or not the technology was utilized to its fullest potential during the call. Did it convey a message and address the questions the customer had?

As an observer, it is easier for Jennings to identify missed opportunities during a visit: "If I see a missed opportunity, then I'll bring it up during the debrief to see if the representative agrees with that assessment. Then we'll discuss what types of approaches could have had more meaning or made more of an impact."

Jennings notes that not only are the representatives harder on themselves, but, for the most part, they tend to already know what went well and what could have gone differently during a call. In fact, most representatives struggle to reflect on what went well and go straight to what they felt went wrong. "I simply ensure they identify positive behaviors, reinforce their assessment, plus provide my own," she says.

At the end of the coaching visit, Jennings also takes the time to assess the overall day and discuss key "takeaways" with the representative. These takeaways—or points to remember—include things that are going well for the representative as well as things that would enhance the person's sales calls from both a technical aspect as well as from the aspect of providing value for physicians and patients. The technology that Merck incorporates for the debrief is a spreadsheet that allows managers to document the highlights of the visit, including follow-up items or the representative's skill sets to be monitored for the next visit. Those items are then automatically filled in at the top of a clean document, which is then used during the next coaching visit.

In terms of managing her administrative duties, Jennings relies on the calendar, task lists, and e-mails on her computer. As manager, she can get anywhere from 15 to 30 e-mails a day about everything ranging from best practices and competitive information to requests from upper management. But it's not enough for her to use technology simply to be a proficient administrator. "Personally, it is important to not only rely on the resources I have to be organized and efficient but to utilize the technology resources to their fullest," she says. ∎

S ales technology has dramatically changed the way salespeople sell. Today, technology drives how salespeople plan their days, how they contact customers, how they manage all of the information they must know, and much more. Moreover, new technology applications are being developed continually. Some of these applications affect the sales executive or sales manager. Others address only the needs of the salesperson.

In this chapter, we explore different types of sales technology. Some of the most common forms of technology used by salespeople include things you're familiar with—cell phones, laptops, PDAs, and so forth. First, we discuss these technologies and how they've changed sales forces and the way they are managed. We then discuss software applications, including knowledge management, sales force automation, customer relationship management, and enterprise resource planning software. Finally, we discuss how sales managers can encourage their employees to get the most out of the technologies available to them.

Commonly Used Technology

Today's college student stays in touch with friends and family through technology in ways that seem incredibly foreign to their grandparents. The same is true of salespeople. David Harris, of Legacy Land and Ranch, uses his cell phone to call customers while he drives from one rural property to another. Once he reaches the property, he uses Global Positioning Systems (GPS) technology to make sure he's at the right ranch because sometimes directions are nothing more than "turn on the gravel road past the third oil well." While he's showing the property to a client, he brings up topographic maps and satellite photographs of the property on his laptop. If he sees a piece of property that is for sale by owner, he can link up via his PDA (personal digital assistant) to databases on the Internet to learn about the property before he calls the owner. Says Harris, "Before this technology, selling ranch land was a lonely business. Now I can sell many more properties and do so more efficiently because the technology gives me so many selling tools.

Salespeople use many common types of technology, such as laptops, cell phones, and GPS devices, but in unique ways. (Comstock Complete)

E-mail, which today's salespeople use to communicate with their customers, drove $8.8 billion in business-to-business sales in 2005.[1] A recent study reported that 85 percent of salespeople use e-mail to communicate with existing customers, 67 percent to prospect for new customers, 60 percent employ e-mail to communicate with the home office, and 24 percent check existing stock via e-mail messages.[2]

Cell phones, PDAs, and laptop or notebook computers can turn any location into a virtual office. With a PDA, a salesperson can access the Internet, make a phone call, or access customer records. The laptop or notebook computer also provides salespeople with access to customer records, as well as presentation materials. Mike Kunz, sales executive with St. Louis–based Kunz and Associates, believes that these technologies will lead to more virtual office-based salespeople in the future. In fact, it is because of these technologies that the average cost of a sales call declined over the past decade, even though salespeople's salaries have, on average, doubled. Salespeople can visit with more clients in less time, and the visits are more effective because of technology.[3]

Sales Management Software

Salespeople and their managers use different types of software applications to solve their problems. Some of these technologies are designed to manage the ever-growing body of knowledge they have to deal with. Others are designed to automate functions to make it less costly and time consuming to serve customers. Exhibit 6.1 briefly describes a number of more advanced software applications designed to support sales functions.

Knowledge Management, Proposal Writing, and Pricing Software

Salespeople sometimes have to manage as many as 5,000 products. In the past, a company might print a catalog, punch it with three holes, and put it in a notebook. Updates would be sent out so the old pages could be easily replaced. As one might imagine, salespeople might not get the new pages, might lose them before inserting them in the notebook, throw away the wrong ones, and so forth. Taking these catalogs online seemed like a good way to make sure salespeople always had the most current information. This online application is a form of **knowledge management**.

Of course, customers want that information too. Many knowledge management systems have mechanisms to enable customers to access portions of the knowledge base. The **knowledge base** is the data contained in the system; it can consist of data like product specifications, how to troubleshoot problems with products, or identify where the knowledge is, such as who to call in certain situations.

Octant sells knowledge management software that helps salespeople and their managers write better proposals.

Some knowledge-based information isn't available to customers but only to the firm's sales reps and other employees. This information can include things like answers to service questions, even if they are not frequently asked, how to handle customer service issues, and so forth. For example, Dell maintains a knowledge base of employees who have expertise troubleshooting certain applications, including a record of who was able to fix what problems. Then if the problem arises again, Dell's customer service reps can call these employees for help.

Companies are even building knowledge bases around selling practices. For example, if a salesperson sells a funeral home a new product, that sale is entered into the knowledge base. The next rep to try to sell to a funeral home can then access the knowledge base to find out how the sale was closed. If a proposal was created for the funeral home, it might become part of the knowledge base, and the rep can then copy appropriate portions of it. In fact, **proposal-writing software** was one of the first knowledge management applications created for salespeople and their managers. The idea was to create a library of successful proposals from which they could select portions and create new proposals. Octant (www.octantsoftware.com) and PropLibrary.com are two providers of proposal library and management software.

Pricing software was another early knowledge management application created for sales purposes. Job-costing, or putting a price together on custom jobs, can be very difficult, particularly if there are many components to the job. Pricing software made sure that all of the components were accounted for, resulting in a more accurate estimate of the job's cost. Octant's software provides pricing features, but there are other packages specific for job-costing. Most of these are industry specific; for example, Pem Software (www.pemsoftwareinc.com) is used in the construction industry.

Each industry has its own special software. For example, real estate agents use software that enables them to easily create brochures on properties for sale, whereas salespeople for contract manufacturers use animation software to show how components work in machinery.

Sales Force Automation Systems

Sales force automation (SFA) was one of the first types of information technology used by salespeople and their managers. SFA systems automate salespeople's contact management, scheduling, and reporting functions. **Contact management** is the use of customer databases to keep track of customer information, calendaring to schedule customer activities such as sales calls, follow-up, and so forth.

ACT! (marketed by Symantec Corp.) and GoldMine (sold by Front Range Solutions) are commonly used SFA software. ACT! and Goldmine are designed for small-to-medium-sized sales forces, although sometimes as many as several thousand salespeople in a firm use the software. The applications enable salespeople to not only record basic account information, such as who to contact and at what address or phone number, but also important data such as notes from each sales call. Competitors' sales to the account can also be recorded, information that can be quite useful to marketing managers, product planners, and other people in the salesperson's organization.

In the past, salespeople would send handwritten or typed call reports to their managers, listing the customers they had called on, what was discussed, and any items that they needed to follow up on. Now sales managers simply access the same data system used by their salespeople. After each sales call or at the end of the day, the salesperson downloads his or her call notes into a central system. Summary reports can be created outlining the salesperson's activities for the day, week, or month. The manager can also track salespeople's activities by the types of calls they make and suggest strategies to improve their productivity. We'll discuss reporting more in Chapter 15 when we explore how managers evaluate a salesperson's performance.

Being able to access sales reports instantly can not only help managers evaluate and coach their salespeople at critical points but also improve a firm's sales forecasts. Tom Wood, of ElkCorp, a premium roofing and construction products company, recalls meeting and working with a salesperson as part of his training before computers were commonplace. After the two men talked about what they were going to do that day, the salesperson said, "We've got to stop by a mailbox first, though." At the mailbox, the rep reached into the backseat of his car and pulled a manila envelope from a box, then dropped it into the mailbox.

"What's that?" asked Tom.

"Call reports," said the rep. (Call reports are records of what happens on a sales call.) "My family and I write out an entire year's worth every Christmas break. I keep them in that box in order, and every Monday, I mail in the one for the previous week." Obviously, if there was any element of truth to his reports of the sales calls he supposedly made, it was by sheer accident; they were all entirely fabricated the previous December. Imagine trying to forecast your company's sales and schedule its manufacturing activities using these reports!

Another benefit to managers and to their companies is the retention of customer records. Companies without SFA systems can encounter problems when salespeople resign. If the salesperson takes these records to the next job or simply throws them away, the next salesperson won't have much to work from. That makes it harder for the new salesperson to get up to speed. Customers suffer, too. For example, they might have expected their salesperson to call or service them at certain times or otherwise be familiar with their accounts. But without the data, the new salesperson is likely to fall down on the job.

For the salesperson, the benefits of an SFA system can include improved customer interaction because more information about each customer is readily available. This is especially important in large territories. Without a SFA system, keeping track of who wants what can be pretty difficult. For example, Konica-Minolta Business Systems salespeople each have 2,000 customers in their territories. Imagine trying to remember the hobbies and interests of all these customers! However, these are things that can make buying more enjoyable for customers and improve a rep's sales.

Salespeople using SFA systems also enjoy automatic reminders, called **ticklers**. Ticklers remind them to complete certain tasks. For example, if a customer tells his rep to call him back in a month's time, the salesperson makes a note in the account, and the SFA system automatically notifies her in one month to call back. SFA systems can also help salespeople manage their time more efficiently, even creating schedules for them that minimize their driving times.

Eric Williams uses GoldMine to manage his real estate business. His real estate company, Legacy Land and Ranch, focuses on selling large tracts of farm and ranch land around the world. His agents create accounts for both buyers and sellers in the GoldMine system. When one of Williams' agents lists a property, the file on the seller is also tied to other files on the property, such as topographic maps, .pdf brochures, satellite photos of the property, and other important information. Eric can show those files to the buyer on a laptop or notebook computer at the property.

Aplicor is a CRM software product that helps salespeople better manage their time and their customers more effectively.

The use of SFA is not without issues and challenges. Some of the challenges involve getting salespeople to use the system, which we will discuss later. Other issues relate to how managers should use the system. For example, how closely should sales managers monitor their salespeople's activities? Salespeople frequently enjoy working independently.[4] If using the technology results in close supervision, it is possible that some good salespeople will leave the organization. Perhaps more importantly, a salesperson often needs to adjust her approach in the field, depending upon what customers are indicating they want.[5] However, if technology is used to "script" a sales pitch or sales approach, this flexibility will be lost. In other words, greater technological control might result in less autonomy for the salesperson, which in some situations might not increase sales.

When customers' needs are similar and the selling process the same for each of them, technology can be a tool for ensuring that salespeople stick to the script. Inside salespeople frequently use scripts generated by SFA systems; even customers' responses to questions can be programmed into the script so that the dialogue the reps use sounds spontaneous.

Although SFA systems have automated some salespeople's tasks, allowing them to manage their time and their territories more effectively, it has proven to be insufficient for larger organizations and companies following a multi-channel strategy. For those situations, organizations have turned to CRM software.

Customer Relationship Management Software

Customer relationship management (CRM) is more than a software package; it has been described as a philosophy, a strategy, and even a way of life because it encompasses the types of relationships you want to create with your customers.[6] CRM software can result in more effective communication, integrating salespeople's customer communications with other channels such as their firm's Web sites, e-mail campaigns, direct mail, and others. The philosophy, though, is that companies should strategically create the right kinds of relationships with its customers. These relationships then become the foundation for customer service, product creation, product delivery, and everything else the company does to add value for the customer. Thus, CRM software has to integrate with all of the company's other software systems and cannot just automate salespeople's activities.

CRM data also needs to be visible to those who need it. For example, imagine a complicated business, such as an equipment manufacturer that has many customer contact personnel. In this situation, not only do the field salesperson, the call center salesperson, and a marketing manager need information about each buyer, but so does a technical support person, a dispatch center for field service calls, the shipping department, and the billing department. When each of these people talk with the customer, information from the dialog has to be captured into the system. Ideally, the customer should come away with the feeling that the company "knows" her and will take care of her. From the company's perspective, each conversation is an opportunity to learn more about that customer so that the company can do a better job of serving her. As the Global Sales Management feature illustrates, the same challenges of getting information to the right people at the right time are even more important when the sales team is scattered across the globe.

The more commonly used CRM software for companies with salespeople is Siebel, a product originally developed by Tom Siebel but now owned and marketed by Oracle. Other popular products are SAP, Salesforce.com, and Salesnet. One difference between Salesforce.com or Salesnet and Siebel, ACT!, or GoldMine is that these are sold as

GLOBAL SALES MANAGEMENT

Global Issues in Sales Technology

How do you manage one customer with 500 locations around the world? Or 500 customers located around the world, each with their own location? The answer to both challenges lies with technology.

WildenPump is a company that makes pumps for manufacturing processes and is located in California. According to Walter Bonnet, a global manager with the firm, the company has built a database that captures data and, using Maximizer SFA software, can distribute leads to any of its 40 distributors around the world. "Users can assign leads to certain distributors or send out e-mails with 1,000 names quickly and easily," says Bonnet. Furthermore, any sales rep in the field can access the data via a wireless portal. This portal means that they can share information about an account to reps or distributors, no matter where they're located.

BT (formerly British Telecom), which provides telecommunications services to Europe, the Americas, and Asia, experienced some challenges. One of BT's biggest issues was e-mail. As the firm's salespeople handling the same accounts across the globe communicated with each other about them, the quality of the written communication was suffering. The result was declining sales productivity.

To address the problem, BT trained its entire global sales staff on how to communicate more effectively when writing. One conclusion that Chris Smithers, BT's global communications manager, reached was that no matter how good or seemingly easy the technology, it still requires the right skills to make sure the desired outcomes are reached.

Sources: Anonymous, "Flexibility and Mobility Increase CRM Adoption Rate," *Manufacturing Business Technology* (December 2006) 24, p. 16; and Chris Smithers, "Improving Communication to Boost Sales at BT," *Strategic Communication Management* (January 2006), 18–22.

"hosted" applications, or **software as a service (SaaS)**. What this means is that the makers of the software host the program and all of the data on their own servers. The salespeople of other companies then access the data via the Internet. In other words, the entire customer database of the salespeople's firms reside on servers owned by Salesforce.com or Salesnet, rather than at the customer's location, such as is the case with Siebel.

SaaS has several benefits over software purchased and kept only on laptops or company servers. First, the vendor (Salesforce, RightNow, etc.) is responsible for making sure the software is always up and working. The vendor can also make improvements to the software and all customers (the sales organizations using the software) immediately benefit. By contrast, when the software resides on the customer's computers, new software to fix bugs has to be sent to the customer, who has to stop everything and install the new software. Also, with SaaS, salespeople can easily access customers in real time anywhere they can access the Internet. This may or may not be the case for resident software like Siebel, which depends on the salesperson to download or "sync" new data periodically from a company computer upon which the software is installed. Not all CRM software is hosted, nor is all hosted software used for CRM applications, but CRM software for sales applications is more likely to be hosted.

EXHIBIT 6.1

Sales Tools and Uses of SFA/CRM by Job Role

Source: Based on Colin Beasty, "How Sales Teams Should Use CRM," *CRM Magazine*, 30–34, February 2006.

CEO
- Sales forecast

VP of Sales
- Sales forecast
- Identify/share best practices
- Track performance—by salesperson, product, etc.
- Capture win/loss data for strategic planning/pricing
- Create or use models to understand segments

Sales Management
- Sales forecast
- Identify big impact opportunities
- Identify coaching and training opportunities by examining win/loss ratios by rep and by stage of sales process
- Monitor activities by account or by rep relative to results

Sales Representative
- Access to customer data
- Access to pricing formulas and product information for better proposals
- Integrated access to other relevant information (shipping, billing, etc.)
- Faster access to leads

WHAT CAN A CRM SYSTEM DO? Contact management is an important function of CRM software, but it is only one of many. Exhibit 6.1 lists some of these functions and how different people in the organization might make use of those functions. CRM software enables customers to interact with the selling organization via all channels in a seamless fashion. Via a CRM system, important data such as shipping information, for example, can be made available to the salesperson in the field, a customer service representative in a call center, or even perhaps to the salesperson's customer via the Internet.

A critical feature of a hosted version of CRM is the ability for salespeople and sales managers in multiple divisions or locations to access the same customer information. **Opportunity management**, which is the process of identifying prospective customers or sales opportunities and shepherding those potential customers through the sales process, is accomplished more effectively when salespeople and managers can access the information. For example, Andy Haffke, director of sales operations for LexisNexis, reports that his company uses their CRM system to identify opportunities that span different business divisions. The software can notify salespeople when their accounts are making purchases from other divisions, thus enabling salespeople to consider whether there are additional sales opportunities for these accounts.

Another key component of CRM software is that it enables managers to create predictive models using customer data. Using statistical procedures called **data mining**, analysts, marketing managers, and sales managers can build statistical models to get a better understanding of the company's customers. More advanced modeling is likely to require sophisticated statistical software like SAS or SPSS, but Siebel, Salesforce.com, and others have the ability to create simple models. These models can be used to determine the best approach for certain customers, which customers should be targeted, how offers for products and services should be priced, and even what features should be included in a new product design. For example, long before CRM technology, pharmaceutical salespeople would target doctors for sales calls based on how many prescriptions they wrote. In other words, doctors who wrote more prescriptions were called upon more often. Having a CRM system makes this information much more accessible to reps. Rather than having to figure out who to call on at what intervals, they can spend more time making actual calls.

CRM software can also manage e-mail sent by a firm's marketing department, track the activity of customers on the company's Web site, and incorporate information collected from customers at trade shows. Salespeople then have information about how their customers responded to the company's different marketing activities. This information can also be useful when it comes to finding new sales leads.

Campaign management is yet another feature of CRM systems. **Campaign management** is a rules-based way to determine which message to send to a buyer at what time. CRM systems offer campaign management because it can track customers' responses to various offers. For example, Pearson/Prentice Hall, the publisher of this book, can send an e-mail to professors about this book when it first comes out. Those who respond positively to the e-mail might then get a visit from a Pearson/Prentice Hall salesperson. Those who do not respond may get a second e-mail with a somewhat different offer or a survey asking them for their opinions. Based on factors such as class size (that affects how many books will be sold), the professor's response, and other factors, different rules are put into action. Professors with bigger classes are likely to have a salesperson drop by their offices. Professors with smaller classes are more likely to get a call from a representative via telephone. Campaign management helps Pearson/Prentice Hall determine which campaigns are more effective.

Exhibit 6.2 illustrates how a rules-based campaign might work. This example is fairly simple. In reality, campaigns can be far more complex. For example, they might begin with a salesperson visiting a customer's office or the customer visiting the company's booth at a trade show or browsing the company's Web site. The point is to engage the buyer through the channel that makes the most sense for that person, both in terms

EXHIBIT 6.2

An Example of Simple Rules-Based Campaign

In this example, actions are based on buyer response. If the buyer clicks on a button contained in the e-mail to visit the Web site, an e-mail is then sent back to the buyer, suggesting a call to the contact center. Based on the outcome of that call, a sample is sent or other information is provided by a salesperson. Many campaigns are far more complicated, with branches to different actions based on account size or CLV.

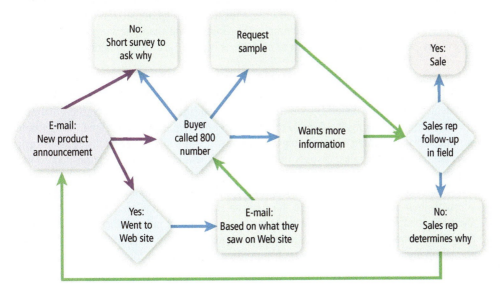

Sales managers can purchase data like Personicx to give their salespeople greater insight into the lifestyles of their consumer clients. Business-to-business sales organizations are likely to purchase data that describes their customers' industries, the sizes of those industries, and other similar, but business-oriented, information. (Ryan McVay/Stone/Getty Images)

of the cost and timing of the contact and information needed by the buyer in order to move the sale along.

CRM APPLICATIONS One of the more vital CRM applications is segmentation. **Segmentation,** or the process of grouping customers into homogeneous groups, has long been associated with marketing. What makes CRM segmentation different is that each customer is actually classified or placed into a segment. The San Antonio Spurs have purchased a database called Personicx (developed by Axiom) that categorizes people into different lifestyle segments. The club then augments that information with fan information in its own database, which gives Spurs salespeople a much better understanding of the personality and lifestyle of the season ticket holder a salesperson is talking to. For companies that sell to other businesses, segmentation tools are likely to be statistical models based on industry types, company sizes, and other factors that might influence the buyer's purchasing practices.

Once a customer is placed in a segment, the value of the customer can then be determined. Customer lifetime value (CLV) analysis is a CRM tool that calculates the value of a customer to the firm for a period of time. (Recall the example in Chapter 1 about how much clothing a student buys while in college). Theoretically, you could calculate each customer's value for the remainder of that customer's lifetime, but as with any forecast into the future, the farther you go into the future, the less accurate your forecast will be. Most companies now forecast CLV for a shorter period of time, such as three to five years.

Once CLV is calculated, it can be summed across an entire market segment. Effort can then be spent on acquiring and retaining more valuable customers and even specific customers. This concept of focusing on more valuable customers is not new. Pharmaceutical companies have long been dividing doctors into four levels: A-level doctors prescribe most of a company's drug, B doctors the next, C doctors rarely prescribe the drug, and D-level doctors never prescribe it. Salespeople might spend most of their time on A doctors, half as much on B doctors, and visit C doctors only if convenient or they had nothing else to do. D doctors would never be visited. What makes CLV different is that it is forward-looking. In some industries and settings, understanding the full buying potential of the customer over time is more important than knowing how much they buy today because companies want to capture as much of a continuous revenue stream as possible.

Think about how much information about buyers a salesperson could collect on a daily basis. A salesperson can almost build a lifestyle model of each buyer in a business-to-business setting. This additional information can then be matched to the customer's lifetime value, allowing the firm to create more effective sales campaigns, design better products, price products more strategically, and so forth. CRM spreads customer information beyond just the salesperson's head, making it available to all decision makers who can use it.

CRM data collected by an entire sales organization can also help individual salespeople with their accounts. By mining the data, sales managers can create predictive models their salespeople can use to close more business. A case in point: When Edward Jones, a financial services company, was about to sell a new Chicago O'Hare Airport bond issue, the company's CRM department built a predictive model that identified a list of people most likely to buy the bond. This list was then provided to the investment representatives (salespeople). Using the list, the sales force sold the entire bond in less than three hours, as compared to the usual three days. What that means in terms of productivity is that the salespeople were then able to sell other things for more than two and a half days, a substantial improvement in productivity.

The approach taken by Edward Jones is what managers call a guided sales tool. **Guided sales tools** are repeatable processes that managers can help salespeople implement in order to move a prospect closer to a sale.[7] Another guided sales tool is a script that a call center representative can use verbatim. Other examples are databases of proposals that can be used over and over and pop-up menus that suggest approaches salespeople can take based on the types of accounts they are calling on. A salesperson getting ready for a call can then review the suggested strategy.

CRM DATA: WHERE DOES IT COME FROM? Like SFA systems, the heart of CRM systems is data. What makes CRM more sophisticated is that additional layers of data are added to the picture in order to determine how best to treat individual customers. Again, this data includes information gathered by salespeople such as personal data.

Another layer of information that gets added to the CRM system is information that comes from **back office systems**—software systems designed to automate functions like accounting, shipping, inventory control, manufacturing, and other activities the customer doesn't see. From these databases and software systems, the CRM system would capture and use information as simple as billing addresses and payment histories or as complex as combined total shipments to every location for that company. Gathering data such as these might seem simple, but when companies have many divisions and many different names, just putting it all together can be difficult. For example, NCR may buy products and be entered in the system as NCR, National Cash Register, Teradata (a division of NCR), and so forth.

A third layer of information can also be added to the information that salespeople collect. That layer is information purchased from other sources. In the pharmaceutical industry, marketing research companies often purchase data from pharmacies about the number of prescriptions doctors write. This gives the firm's salespeople significantly more accurate information on doctors' prescribing habits.

OneSource is a company that mines data from its database of businesses in order to provide leads to other companies. Experian is a similar company that has a database of some sixteen million businesses. These two companies can create models to identify leads that sales organizations then purchase. Both systems can also be integrated with the CRM software that these organizations use.[8] Dun & Bradstreet, Standard & Poor's, and other companies offer various other kinds of databases on companies. The additional data can tell the salesperson such things as a company's size, executives' names, contact information, and more, even though the salesperson hasn't yet made a call to that account.

All of this information is intended to provide what is called a "360-degree view" of the customer—a complete picture of who that customer is and what motivates his or her purchases. Not only is the salesperson then better armed for a sales call, but the marketing person can also create more effective advertisements, stronger trade show programs, and better e-mail campaigns targeted toward the customer. All of these sales and marketing efforts should be more meaningful to the buyer, which should then increase the effectiveness of all of the firm's sales and marketing activities. Exhibit 6.3 illustrates the various sources of information and how they might be used in the firm.

EXHIBIT 6.3

Sources of Information Used in CRM

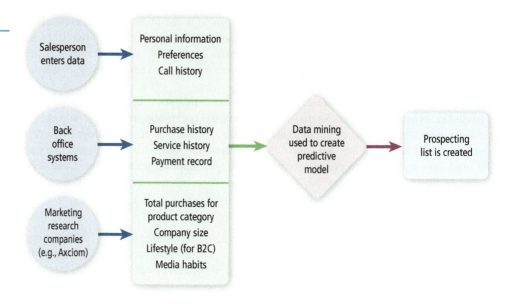

The Challenges of Implementing CRM and SFA Systems

Using CRM and SFA software is not without its challenges, nor is it a solution to all of a company's selling problems. In fact, it can create a number of problems, or issues, not all of which are simple to solve. One of the biggest challenges becomes who "owns" the relationship with the customer. As we've noted, once a CRM system is installed, many members of the firm can contact customers in addition to the customer's salesperson.

Take, for instance, a university. A university is likely to have a fund-raising department for the entire university, another for its athletic department, and yet others for each of its academic units. An individual donor might receive "sales" offers from all three departments (fund-raising, athletics, and an academic unit) independently and give to all three separately. Companies with multiple divisions selling products and services to the same buyers face the same question. Ultimately, the question of who owns the relationship should determine what offers are made and when. If athletics owns the relationship, then the athletic department gets first dibs to ask for gifts, for example.

As you can probably tell, the salesperson loses an element of control over how each account is sold, what is sold, and when once a CRM or SFA system is installed. This can be threatening to many salespeople who are used to being a customer's sole contact with the firm. Although research shows that sales technology does make salespeople more productive, it also makes them feel like their jobs are less secure.[9] A case in point: When Harris Interactive, one of the largest marketing research companies in the world, installed an SFA system in 2004, the company asked its salespeople to hand over all of their files so the data could be entered. They weren't happy about it. In fact, their resistance to the system nearly killed it. To overcome their resistance, their managers gave them a period of time to adapt to the new system without close oversight. Eventually the reps found out on their own that the system made them more productive.[10]

Another set of strategic decisions involves developing a customer data strategy. A **customer data strategy** is a company's strategy for collecting, storing, using, and distributing information about customers. Among the key questions managers have to ask themselves

SELF-ASSESSMENT LIBRARY

An important part of CRM software systems is that the systems provide data used by a lot of different departments. In order for the systems to work well, the departments also have to work together well. How well can you play the politics necessary to get other departments to work with your department? Go to http://www.prenhall.com/sal/ and log in using the access code that came with your textbook. Then click on:

Assessments
II. Working with Others
C. Motivation Insights
3. How Good Am I at Playing Politics?

Although there are four dimensions of political savvy, your score will give you an indication of your overall ability to use politics to your advantage.

when creating a customer data strategy are the following: What data are needed, and how will it be used? Where is the data? Who needs access to it?

That brings up another question: How much information should be available, to whom, and for what use? How much information should the customer service representative (CSR) have? Should the CSR have all of the same information as the salesperson? Should an accounts receivable representative trying to collect payment on a bill know that the buyer's hobby is golf, for example? While that may seem like a harmless thing to know, a buyer could feel like the seller is Big Brother if someone unknown to the buyer refers to the buyer's favorite activity or recent vacation.

In addition to these general issues, there are a number of other challenges that must be specifically addressed by the firm's sales managers. Some of the challenges occur in implementation of a new system while others are ongoing.

Salesperson/Sales Manager Issues

Encouraging Salespeople to Use Technology Effectively

Research indicates that the more salespeople use a CRM system, the more they sell.[11] Salespeople can make more calls because functions are automated, and the calls they make are of better quality because they have more information.[12] Getting them to use it, though, as well as other technology, can be quite a challenge. 3M, for example, has found that salespeople's reluctance to use the system is the biggest barrier to CRM implementation. To some extent, they believe the challenge is generational, as a large proportion of the sales force is within five years of retirement and less familiar with technology. Another issue may be success; salespeople who have been successful without technology may not perceive the need for implementing it. These are challenges endemic to any technology adoption situation, not just CRM; salespeople can be slow to adopt other software, too, such as proposal management software, for example.

There are tactics that sales leadership can implement to get salespeople to use the system. These tactics include communicating the benefits of technology to the salespeople and sales managers, eliminating opportunities to conduct work without the technology, and creating reward/punishment systems for using the system.

TRAINING Training is very important. A critical issue identified in the research is having sufficient training; too little training actually results in a decrease in the performance of the salesperson. Salespeople who have to use a program or technology, but don't know how, waste too much time trying to figure it out. Research also indicates that because they simply do not know how to make use of the system, they make poor decisions about their time. The result is fewer sales calls and lower sales, the opposite of what you want from sales technology.

Training isn't a once and done project, either. While initial training is important, ongoing training can secure more effective use of the system. Ongoing training, according to Ram Ramamurthy of DG Vault, is as much about how to get the most out of the system as it is about what buttons to push. He regularly presents the sales staff with ideas of how to use the information in the system as well as the more advanced features. Salespeople now eagerly attend these training sessions because they know they will learn something that will enhance their performance (we'll address training with greater detail in Chapter 9).

MANAGEMENT SUPPORT When SFA or CRM software is not used by a sales force, sales managers may be part of the problem. In a study of sales executives, one sales executive stated that he believed that technology had little to offer in the future. Yet this same sales executive was not using the system he had to its fullest capability; he was not using many of the applications. One conclusion of that study was that sales leaders do not always fully comprehend the value of a CRM or SFA system, nor do they have the skills needed to gain full benefit.[13]

Managerial support is critical to salesperson adoption. If managers expect salespeople to use the software, salespeople are far more likely to adopt it.[14] When managers fail to adopt the software and to support it, a significant barrier to adoption is created. Salespeople who want to use the software then report being stymied in reaching the productivity gains they expect from the software.[15] What is less important is peer use—salespeople are not as likely to use software just because their peers do.

Managers can run into some ethical challenges when they implement software. The Ethics in Sales Management feature in this chapter identifies some of these challenges, though the list of challenges is by no means complete.

TECHNICAL SUPPORT In addition to training and managerial support, postimplementation technical support is also important. Salespeople need to have easy access to help because problems can arise in the field; there is no one right there with them to answer questions. For example, Tricia Jennings has her office in her home. As a sales manager for Merck, a pharmaceutical company, she spends most of her time making sales calls with her salespeople or working at home on reports. When she encounters problems with the system, there isn't anyone in the next office to ask for help. Good technical support is important to ongoing use after the initial training.[16]

COMMUNICATING THE BENEFITS When a new system is launched, salespeople have to be sold on its benefits. Some companies have created systems that benefit marketing or sales management but have few benefits for salespeople. According to Bruce Culbert, a leading CRM consultant, a lack of real benefits for salespeople can doom a system to failure. He also says, though, that even when the benefits are real, they must be communicated to the sales force. Otherwise, using the system may be seen as just another task or responsibility added to the bottom of an already long list of things to do.

Kristin Johnson, of Wallace Welch and Willingham (WWW) Insurance, encountered a sales force happy with spreadsheets and index cards. The best salesperson, at least in terms of sales, refused to adopt the new system. "He told me," says Johnson, 'You can have all of

ETHICS IN SALES MANAGEMENT

Ensuring Salespeople Derive the Benefits of CRM Systems

E-commerce has replaced the need for human interaction in some business settings, and replacing salespeople with technology is, by itself, not an ethical issue. Yet, in some instances, companies have asked reps to populate a database with customer information so that the salespeople can ultimately be replaced. Does it matter that the salespeople had no idea that the purpose of their data input was so they could be laid off?

Another far more common scenario occurs when companies ask their salespeople to learn new technology on their own time and without pay. Is it any more or less ethical to do this if the salespeople are paid on the basis of a straight commission or a straight salary? According to Bruce Culbert, a leading technology consultant, making such a request is a poor decision from the purely practical standpoint of getting the technology adopted. But the push-back from the sales force is always about the *fairness* of the request.

"A related issue," says Culbert, "is raising quotas because of the increased productivity that should happen." He cautions against accepting a software vendor's glowing predictions that productivity will improve to justify raising the sales force's quota. "One way to get the technology adopted quickly is to let salespeople enjoy the benefit. Raising the quota kills that opportunity." It is also questionable from an ethics perspective.

Technology can be a boon for sales organizations, but the implementation of technology can present its own ethical dilemmas. For business technology to be implemented ethically, management cannot lose sight of the people issues, too. Salespeople and customers have to be treated properly, creating a win-win for all.

Sources: Culbert, Bruce, personal correspondence; Honeycutt, Earl D., Jr., Tanya Thelen, Shawn T. Thelen, and Sharon Hodge (2005). "Impediments to Sales Force Automation," *Industrial Marketing Management*, 34:4 (May), 313–322; Rangarajan, Deva, Eli Jones, and Wynne Chinn, "Impact of Sales Force Automation on Technology-Related Stress, Effort, and Technology Usage Among Salespeople," *Industrial Marketing Management*, 34:4 (May), 345–354.

the new guys change, but I'm not.' " Other salespeople then started asking why they had to use the system. This problem could have been averted had she communicated more completely with the sales team when launching the system.[17]

The system can only be as good as the data that drives it. Quality use requires the system to have quality information.[18] At the same time, there is some evidence to suggest that overuse can result in lower performance.[19] There are many possible explanations for such a fact, one of which is that there are some salespeople who find it difficult to make calls unless they are completely and totally prepared.[20] These salespeople spend far too much time getting ready, such as thoroughly overusing CRM software, so much so that they don't have as much time for making calls.

MAKING THE TRANSITION Making the transition when launching a new system requires eliminating ways to work around it, as well as rewarding good use and penalizing bad use. Even the best systems have a learning curve, and the steeper (or more difficult) that curve, the more likely that salespeople will try to revert to the old ways of doing things.

Rewarding good use can also aid in the adoption of the new system. 3M, for example, has created incentive systems to reward salespeople with small prizes for inputting their account data into new systems. The key is that 3M needs the data in the system but not at the expense of salespeople making calls; if they spend too much time putting the initial data in, their performance will suffer for a short period. The incentives encourage salespeople to put the data in over a month's time, in the evenings or other downtime, so that it doesn't affect their selling performance.

Penalizing failure to use the system can also encourage effective use. David Dubroff, with Cypress Care, put a system in place whereby salespeople's expense checks are delayed one month if they have not kept the system up to date. Johnson implemented a similar practice at WWW. She blocked salespeople from using the old financial/accounting system and forced them to run their activity reports through the new system. "That pushed everybody to use it," she noted, for if they did not use the new system for their reports, the reports were considered not filed.[21]

Summary

Technology has greatly changed how salespeople are managed and how they manage their time and their territories. Technology as common as PDAs, cell phones, wireless broadband, and laptops turn any location into a virtual office.

Salespeople use special technology, though, like knowledge management software, to manage a complex array of information, ranging from which technician knows how to fix certain problems to the details of all the products they must sell. Specialized proposal-writing and pricing software are also used.

Sales force automation software was among the first software used by salespeople. It includes contact management applications that enable salespeople to maintain detailed records on their customers. Software designed to support customer relationship management strategies evolved from SFA applications and includes many features designed to enhance customer communications and management reporting.

The data for CRM systems can come from back office software systems, from third-party providers, and from salespeople. Implementing CRM systems is fraught with challenges such as deciding who owns the customer relationship, salespeople's resistance to the systems, and improving the quality and quantity of data that systems need to function optimally.

To improve the odds of salespeople accepting and using CRM systems, many firms rely on training, management support, technical support, and communicating the benefits of the systems to their representatives. Activities such as these make it easier for salespeople and their managers to transition to new software systems.

Key Terms

back office systems   123
campaign management   121
contact management   116
customer data strategy   124
customer relationship management
   (CRM)   118
data mining   120
guided sales tools   123
knowledge base   115

knowledge management   115
opportunity management   120
pricing software   116
proposal-writing software   116
sales force automation (SFA)   116
segmentation   122
software as a service (SaaS)   119
ticklers   117

Questions and Problems

1. A salesperson says, "This new software is like Big Brother. Now my company and manager watch every move I make! As long as I make my quota, why can't they leave me alone!" As a sales manager, how would you counter an argument like this?

2. How would you characterize the difference between SFA and CRM systems?

3. In addition to contact information like name and address, what other information would you expect to see in a salesperson's database?

4. One student argued that he didn't want companies to know what he ate for breakfast, what television shows he watched, magazines he read, or Web sites he visited. Another student said she wanted companies to know that information if it meant she got better products and services as a result. What information about you is okay for salespeople to put in their database? What information would you like to keep private? As a sales manager how do you manage this private–public balance?

5. Go back to the 3M example in the chapter. How should a sales manager deal with salespeople who are resistant to technology? Does age of the sales force matter in these decisions? Or the age of the salesperson? Why or why not?

6. The Ethics in Sales Management feature in the chapter discusses several ethical issues in the use of technology. Identify two such issues raised in the feature and discuss how you would handle such situations if you were a sales manager with a sales executive pushing for such ethically questionable practices.

7. Are the benefits of CRM the same for sales executives, sales managers, and salespeople? If not, how do those differences create challenges? If so, how do companies take advantage of those similarities in benefits?

8. CRM isn't really used much in sales; at least, not as much as it is in companies that market primarily through online or other channels. Why do you think that is? One barrier to full use is that sales managers don't understand CRM. If you were a sales executive, how would you overcome this barrier?

Role Play

Blackburg Technologies

For this role play, you will need to divide into groups of three. Blackburg Technologies provides information technology consulting, hardware, software, maintenance, and training to educational institutions around the globe. Hardware, software, and maintenance are offered by the company's Solutions Division; consulting and training are offered by the Services Division. Typically, both divisions are involved in the same accounts, as it requires consulting and training to complete any major project. The Solutions Division, though, spends more time with a client because most upgrades don't require significant consulting or training, and maintenance is ongoing. The Solutions Division has 48 salespeople; the Services Division has 36.

The company is now implementing its own CRM system. The marketing department, which manages the company's exposure at trade shows, special events, and technology shows (an event in major towns where the company showcases its new products and invites customers) is really excited about the new software. The software has the capability to manage e-mail campaigns, customer tracking, and so forth. Customers will soon be able to log into the system to track the status of service calls, delivery of new products, place orders, and much more. Furthermore, if there is special negotiated pricing (and there usually is), that is the only pricing that a customer sees.

Assignment

Divide into groups of three. One person is the VP of Marketing, another is the VP of Sales for Solutions, and the third is VP of Sales for Services. The three of you will now conduct a meeting to determine who owns an account. Before you conduct your meeting, determine what you think the reasons are for your division to be in charge of a particular account (Marketing, Services, or Solutions?), including what communication is provided to an account, who should access and track the overall sales performance of an account, and who should develop strategies for it. Should there be a difference in how current accounts versus prospective clients are assigned? If Services or Solutions owns the account, how does that affect what marketing does or says at trade shows, in e-mail campaigns, or in advertising? And when conflicts in strategies or pricing decisions occur, how should they be resolved?

Sales Manager's Workshop

Promedia Technology: Familiarizing Yourself with Aplicor

What does Aplicor offer Promedia Technology managers? Review the chapter and then examine Aplicor's features. Identify and describe how Aplicor provides the following:

1. Knowledge management
2. Opportunity management
3. Campaign management

Write a short training script (write exactly what you would say) that you would use to show someone unfamiliar with Aplicor how to create an opportunity management report.

Caselet 6.1: Frisco Solutions

Marty Stubbs, the vice president of sales for Frisco Solutions, was exasperated. Stubbs had spent nearly a half million dollars on new software, including the cost of flying all of Frisco's salespeople to a nice resort for two days of training. Yet after six months, it hadn't increased sales. In fact, in some regions, sales even declined. And if the numbers were to be believed, in those regions, the salespeople were making fewer sales calls, which could explain their poor performance.

According to Tim Wagner, Frisco's IT director, those regions with higher sales actually used the software more. But in the regions with flat or slow growth, salespeople weren't using the software much. Worse yet, their sales managers were hardly using it at all. Wagner told Stubbs that one manager had not logged on to the system in over a month. "What kind of training did you do for the managers?" he asked. "It looks like some managers are using the system incorrectly, and others aren't using it at all!"

With that, Stubbs felt the bottom drop out of her stomach. She had not done any training for sales managers other than the same training done for reps. Now, with no money left in the budget, she didn't know what to do. Nonetheless, it was clear that the sales managers weren't using the system properly, if at all, and, therefore, neither were the reps. "We could create an online training program for the sales managers out of the IT budget," Wagner suggested. "But it will take more than training, now."

Stubbs wondered—should she create penalties for not using the new program or rewards for using it? And how could she make sure managers got trained?

Caselet 6.2: Zeron Corporation

Zeron Corporation sells vitamins, mineral supplements, and veterinary products to horse trainers. The company has just over 100 salespeople who call on trainers at horse tracks, rodeos, and other places they gather. These salespeople also call on feed stores to sell products through the stores.

Zeron's salespeople have gathered e-mail addresses for about 30 percent of its 200,000 accounts. Of those 60,000 e-mail addresses, probably 45,000 are for feed stores, but the company isn't sure. The company has created a Web site so that feed stores can reorder its products at wholesale without having to contact their salespeople. (New stores have to be set up with accounts by salespeople who verify that they are, indeed, stores and qualify for wholesale pricing.) The company also has a Web site that allows trainers to order products directly, which are sold at retail prices. In addition to the 60,000 e-mail addresses by Zeron's salespeople, the company has another 60,000 e-mail addresses gathered from its Web site. It does know whether these addresses belong to trainers or feed stores.

Zeron's VP of sales would like to create a campaign strategy encouraging smaller customers to always order via the company's Web site. Moving some customers to the Web site for orders would give the firm's salespeople more time to focus on larger accounts. But because customers sometimes buy from several vendors, knowing which customers are big and which customers are small can't be determined by looking just at their purchases of Zeron products. A potentially large account can look small if the customer only buys a few products from Zeron.

If you were a sales manager for Zeron, how would you go about developing a rules-based campaign for the 120,000 e-mail addresses the company has?

References

1. Magill, Ken (2006). "E-Mail Tops in ROI," www/Directmag.com/disciplines/email/marketing, November 1.
2. Clarke, Irvine, III, Theresa B. Flaherty, and Michael T. Zugelder (2005). "The CAN-SPAM Act: New Rules for Sending Commercial E-mail Messages and Implications for the Sales Force," *Industrial Marketing Management* 34:4 (May), 399–415.
3. Tanner, John F., Jr., and Shannon Shipp (2005). "Sales Technology within the Salesperson's Relationships: A Research Agenda," *Industrial Marketing Management* 34(4), 305–312.
4. Tanner, John F., Jr., and George W. Dudley (2003). "International Differences: Examining Two Assumptions About Selling," in *Advances in Marketing*, William J. Kehoe and Linda K. Whitten, eds., Society for Marketing Advances, 236–239.
5. Weitz, Barton A., Stephen B. Castleberry, and John F. Tanner Jr. (2006). *Selling: Building Partnerships*, 6th ed. Burr Ridge, IL: McGraw-Hill.
6. Greenberg, Paul (2005). *CRM at the Speed of Light,* 3rd ed. McGraw-Hill.
7. Lager, Marshall (2006). "Point to Profits," *CRM Magazine* (May), 24–30.
8. Canady, Henry (2006). "Leading to Sales," *Selling Power* (November), 88–93.
9. Johnson, Devon S., and Sundar Bharadwaj (2005). "Digitization of Selling Activity and Sales Force Performance: An Empirical Investigation," *Journal of the Academy of Marketing Science* 33(1), 3–18.
10. Cotteleer, Mark, Edward Inderrieden, and Felissa Lee (2006). "Selling the Sales Force on Automation," *Harvard Business Review* 84(7/8), 18–19.

11. Jelinek, Ronald, Michael Ahearne, John Mathieu, and Niels Schillewaert (2006). "A Longitudinal Examination of Individual, Organizational, and Contextual Factors on Sales Technology Adoption and Job Performance," *Journal of Marketing Theory & Practice* 14(Winter), 7–23; Ko, Dong-Gil, and Alan R. Dennis (2005); and "Sales Force Automation and Sales Performance: Do Experience and Expertise Matter?" *Journal of Personal Selling & Sales Management* 24(4), 311–322.

12. Hunter, Gary K., and William D. Perreault, Jr. (2006). "Sales Technology Orientation, Information Effectiveness, and Sales Performance," *Journal of Personal Selling & Sales Management* 26(2), 95–106.

13. Ahearne, Michael, Ronald Jelinek, and Adam Rapp (2005). "Moving Beyond the Direct Effect of SFA Adoption on Salesperson Performance: Training and Support as Key Moderating Factor," *Industrial Marketing Management* 34(4), 379–388.

14. Schillewaert, Niels, Michael J. Ahearne, Ruud T. Frambach, and Rudy K. Moenaert (2005). "The Adoption of Information Technology in the Sales Force," *Industrial Marketing Management* 34(4), 323–336.

15. Buehrer, Richard E., Sylvain Senecal, and Ellen Bolman Pullins (2005). "Sales Force Technology Usage—Reasons, Barriers, and Support: An Exploratory Investigation," *Industrial Marketing Management* 34(4), 389–398.

16. Ibid.

17. Beasty, Colin (2006). "Barriers to CRM Success," *CRM Magazine* (May), 32–35; quote is on p. 35.

18. Gohmann, Stephan F., Robert M. Barker, David J. Faulds, and Jian Guan (2005). "Salesforce Automation, Perceived Information Accuracy, and User Satisfaction," *Journal of Business & Industrial Marketing* 20(1), 23–32.

19. Ahearne, Michael, Narasimhan Srinivasn, and Luke Weinstein (2004). "Effect of Technology on Sales Performance: Progressing from Technology Acceptance to Technology Usage and Consequence," *Journal of Personal Selling & Sales Management* 24(4), 297–310.

20. Dudley, George, and Shannon Goodson (1999). *The Psychology of Sales Call Reluctance,* Dallas, Texas: Behavioral Sciences Research Press.

21. Ibid., p. 35.

PART FOUR

Designing and Developing the Sales Force

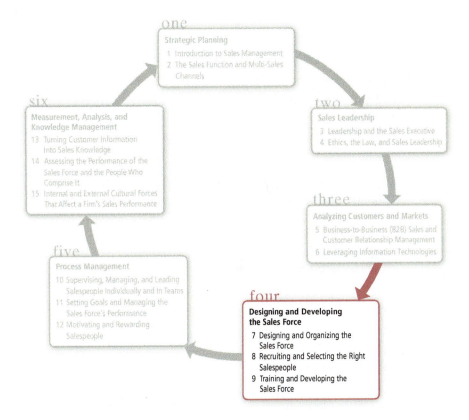

In Part Three, you learned how sales firms form relationships and manage these relationships better using technologies. Now, we provide guidance for designing the sales force structure, hiring qualified salespersons, and training them to meet both employer expectations and customer needs.

Chapter 7, examines the options sales managers and firms have when *designing and organizing the sales force*. Sales managers understand that customers must be able to buy what they want, from a convenient channel, when they want it. Today sales firms offer products and services to meet buyer expectations through multiple channels. Customers can be organized around geographic, product, market, functional, or combination criteria.

Chapter 8 looks at *Recruiting and Selecting the Right Salespeople*. Once the territory is designed, the firm must determine what characteristics are necessary for success in the sales position. Then, firms must attract qualified sales candidates and put them through an organized selection process. Sales managers handle the entire selection process in some firms, and work in concert with human resource managers in larger companies. Unless a formal selection process is followed, unqualified salespersons are hired and loss of personnel or "turnover" occurs.

Chapter 9, explains the critical role played by sales managers in ensuring their sales force receives the training and development they need for job success. Regardless of the company's size, sales managers are involved in the planning that goes into developing a training program, the issues related to the delivery of training, and the process for evaluating the effectiveness of their training investments. New technologies offer opportunities for sales training that is available in the field and on-demand.

Once the sales effort is properly designed, the correct people are hired, and salespersons receive training to insure proper skills, knowledge, and attitudes are present, managers can lead the sales force to success. Part Five offers guidance for leading individuals and teams, setting goals, and motivating and rewarding salespersons.

7 DESIGNING AND ORGANIZING THE SALES FORCE

LEARNING OBJECTIVES

After completing this chapter, you should be able to:

- Explain how a firm's goals affect the organization of its sales force.

- Understand that a sales force can be organized in multiple ways that match the way customers want to buy.

- Explain the advantages and disadvantages of different sales force organizational structures.

- Describe the various reporting relationships sales forces typically have.

- Understand the advantages and disadvantages of outsourcing a firm's sales force.

Salespeople directly impact the satisfaction and long-term relationships their organizations have with their customers. To increase the satisfaction levels of their buyers, firms must structure their sales forces so that their customers can purchase what they want, when they want it, and from the channel that is most convenient for them. Although many companies continue to employ geographical, product, market, or functional sales force structures to serve the marketplace, buyers also utilize electronic, multi-channel, or hybrid supply chains. As a result of these changes, selling firms are using inside salespersons (discussed in Chapter 2), sales alliances and sales teams (discussed in Chapter 5), and other methods to serve their buyers as well. Ultimately, the way the sales force is organized and managed determines the success of these strategic sales plans. This chapter explains the myriad options firms must navigate between to successfully serve their customers.

BILL HAAS

EXECUTIVE VICE PRESIDENT OF SALES AND MARKETING, LABCORP

In 1996, two medical diagnostic companies, Roche Biomedical Laboratories and National Health Laboratories, merged to form what is now the Fortune 500 firm Laboratory Corporation of America (LabCorp). LabCorp's customers are primarily doctors and hospitals that purchase laboratory testing for their patients. Bill Haas, LabCorp's executive vice president of sales and marketing, recalled that the two sales forces had been organized differently and pursued distinct sales strategies. Consequently, their merger required a degree of compromise by both firms. After the merger, LabCorp melded the two former competitive sales forces into a generalist sales team that achieved unprecedented and consistent double-digit sales growth for five years. But by 2004, Haas and other managers at LabCorp realized that the firm's sales force structure was being challenged by three market drivers:

- Managed Care: Several companies like Cigna, Wellpoint, and United HealthCare, offered health maintenance organization (HMO) plans that allowed them to dictate the tests physicians could and could not order for their patients and steer these tests to specific testing companies.
- Specialized Competition: LabCorp's competitors were offering specialty tests aimed at specific market segments of the healthcare industry.
- Specialty Acquisitions: LabCorp began to acquire successful specialized labs and their highly specialized sales forces.

LabCorp managers understood the importance of having the sales structure and sales compensation system aligned in a way that supported the firm's strategic plan. The company identified three strategic initiatives as part of that plan:

Managed Care: LabCorp wanted to implement a more sophisticated "partnership" approach to capture the managed care portion of the marketplace. This would require the company's executives to work with and propose various sales initiatives to managed care organizations like United HealthCare, Cigna, and Wellpoint.

Scientific Superiority: LabCorp knew that its relationship with doctors and hospitals was based upon trust and the reliability of the test results it provided them. Thus, good science and quality were essential to LabCorp's success, as was the ease with which hospitals and physicians were able to do business with LabCorp.

Customer Retention: LabCorp wanted to reduce the number of customers that switched to competitors' products each year. Consequently, a plan was devised that included several new sales force initiatives to make LabCorp its customers' "Laboratory of Choice."

With these goals in mind, Bill Haas and other LabCorp sales managers began working to transform the company's 1,000 strong "generalist" sales force into a more scientifically oriented, retention-focused specialized sales team. To accomplish this very complex structural change, LabCorp hired a consulting firm to help.

After careful consideration, the consulting firm suggested that LabCorp reorganize its "generalist" sales force to serve five customer-segmented healthcare markets:

1. Specialty Cancer I (physicians performing general cancer-related procedures)
2. Specialty Cancer II (physicians performing general cancer- and blood-related procedures)
3. Hospital Physician Specialty (physicians performing general endocrinology and allergy procedures)
4. Hospital Business Group (hospitals)
5. Primary Care (family practice, pediatric, and internal medicine physicians)

LabCorp also reorganized its other functional operations to align them with the new sales structure.

An important element of the sales reorganization was to make a single sales representative responsible for all of LabCorp's product lines within a specific customer segment. That way, no matter what a doctor needed in the form of laboratory testing, the sales representative that serviced the account could meet the physician's needs. This helped LabCorp optimize its relationships with its customers and maximized the firm's opportunity to penetrate accounts with additional product lines. The change also had the fringe benefit of lowering the firm's sales-related expenses because different salespeople weren't all calling upon the same customer.

How a Firm's Goals Affect the Design of Its Sales Force

The opening profile about Bill Haas and LabCorp shows that ideally the organization of a company's sales force is driven by its strategic goals. The seller's organizational structure dictates how many salespeople will call on the buyer, and it has an impact on how familiar the sales force will be with the purchaser's strengths, weaknesses, and buyer base. The way the seller organizes its sales force will also define the type of customers the firm's sales representatives will call upon, the array of products they will sell, and the sales activities they engage in daily. This, in turn, influences the selection, training, evaluation, and compensation decisions made by the company's sales managers, as shown in Exhibit 7.1. Ideally the firm's sales reps should be organized in a way that allows them to best respond to purchasers' needs and problems.[1]

Normally, a company's goals are set at the corporate level and then are implemented via the firm's marketing and sales plans. Thus, the setting of sales goals flows from higher to lower levels of the organization. In the end, sales managers are responsible for organizing the sales force so that sales goals are accomplished and the sales force operates as efficiently as possible. Organizational sales structures serve a number of purposes that include:

- Serving buyers effectively in ways they want to be served:
  - Contacting the buyer at preferred times
  - Allowing the customer to order when and in a way that best meets their needs
  - Providing high-quality customer service levels
  - Developing an appropriate relationship level with different types of customers, depending upon their value to the firm.

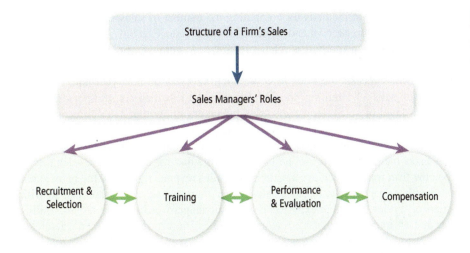

EXHIBIT 7.1

Areas Impacted by a Firm's Sales Force Structure

- Operating efficiently as measured by cost and customer satisfaction:
  - Achieving a competitive advantage as measured by the firm's market share, profits, and buyer feedback
  - Offering customers stability and sales continuity over time as measured by customer retention levels.

Firms often mistakenly design their sales structures around their current salespeople and managers rather than in response to the firm's sales activities.[2] Decisions such as this are made when a sales force is already in place, when the firm changes its mission or products, or when the firm merges with or takes over another firm. Rather, the best way to design a sales structure is to determine the necessary sales activities that must be performed to achieve the firm's goals, followed by the sales structure that affords the highest levels of service to buyers at the lowest overall cost. Then, once the sales structure is decided on, salespersons and managers can be selected, trained, and managed to become experts in their assigned duties. ■

Organizing the Members of the Firm's Sales Force

As we first explained in Chapter 2, although many customers continue to buy through a company's regular sales force, today they also purchase through multiple personal, electronic, or third-party channels. For example, Charles Schwab reaches customers daily at its offices, over the Internet, and through telemarketing calls. This multi-channel sales activity makes organizing the sales force more complex. In light of these complexities, how do sales managers and sales executives figure out how to best organize their sales forces? Let's begin by looking at some of the factors they have to consider.

The Size of the Sales Force

When firms design their sales organization, a major decision is how many salespersons are needed to serve existing and potential customers. Economic theory suggests that a firm should continue to hire salespersons as long as the marginal revenue of doing so exceeds the marginal cost. Said differently, sales managers should hire additional salespersons as long as the new salesperson generates more revenue than expenses. However, it is difficult to practically apply this economic theory since the added costs and revenue derived from hiring one additional salesperson are seldom known to the sales manager. Therefore, sales managers utilize two methods for computing the number of salespersons they should hire and maintain: the breakdown and workload methods (see Exhibit 7.2).

The **breakdown method** is relatively simple to compute. Sales managers need only divide the forecasted sales revenue by the average sales dollars per salesperson. For example, if a firm forecasts the sales force will sell $20 million next year and, on average, a salesperson sells $3.5 million, the firm would need less than six salespersons to accomplish this level of sales. However, sales managers know that sales forecasts are often inflated and that not all salespersons are equally able; that is, one or two salespersons will sell $6 million each, whereas three or four salespeople might sell $1 million or less each year. Sales managers often use the breakdown method for computing a sales force's size when the firm wants to achieve a certain total sales revenue figure and the main goal of the company's salespeople is to close sales rather than say, develop relationships with customers or service them. For example, if a sales manager were asked to sell $45 million this year and an average salesperson generates $3 million in revenue, then 15 salespeople would be needed to reach the sales goal.

A second method for computing the appropriate number of salespersons in an organization incorporates the firm's strategy and work expectations into a **workload method**. For example, how many salespersons are required to visit existing accounts, based upon the customers' wishes, to convert non-buyers to buyers and perform other duties—such as customer service and finding new customers—assigned by the sales firm? A workload computation consists of three steps:

1. computing the total sales call workload
2. determining the amount of work performed by each salesperson
3. factoring in additional work responsibilities.

EXHIBIT 7.2

Breakdown and Workload Methods for Determining Sales Force Size

Breakdown Method: $\dfrac{\text{Forecasted Sales}}{\text{Average Sales per Salesperson}}$ $\dfrac{\$20 \text{ million}}{\$3.5 \text{ million}}$ = 5.71 salespersons

Workload Method:

Step 1: Compute Total Number of Calls to Current Customers

Category of Account	Number of Accounts	Calls per Year	Total Calls
A	22	50	1,100
B	53	12	636
C	104	4	416
			2,152

Step 2: Compute Total Calls Made per Salesperson

Salespersons will average 3 calls per day	3
Salespersons will work outside office 4 days per week	4
Salespersons will work 45 weeks per year	45

$3 \times 4 \times 45 = 540$ sales calls per year for each salesperson

Step 3: Compute Total Number of Salespersons

$\dfrac{\text{Sales Calls to Service Existing Accounts}}{\text{Sales Calls Made per Salesperson}}$ $\dfrac{2,152}{540} = 3.98$

Adjust for Other Workload Factors

15 percent to call upon new accounts and 10 percent for customer service duties = 25 percent

$\dfrac{3.98}{.75} = 5.33$ salespersons needed to service existing accounts, call on new accounts, and provide customer service

The first step in the workload method requires that, based upon current or potential sales, all current buyers be placed into A, B, or C categories. "A" accounts have the highest value, "B" accounts have high potential value, and "C" accounts are of low value. According to the firm's sales strategy, "A" category accounts are to be visited weekly, "B" accounts monthly, and "C" accounts are called upon quarterly and serviced by inside telephone salespersons. Thus, as shown in Exhibit 7.2, there are 22 "A" accounts that require approximately 50 annual calls ($50 \times 22 = 1{,}100$ calls); 53 "B" accounts that a salesperson will call upon 12 times ($12 \times 53 = 636$); and 104 "C" accounts that require four annual visits ($4 \times 104 = 416$). Totaling this workload requirement ($1{,}100 + 636 + 416$) results in 2,152 total sales calls by the outside sales force.

In step 2, the sales manager computes the work expectation for an average salesperson. That is, how many sales calls can a salesperson reasonably be expected to complete in a year? The sales manager can compute this number by multiplying the total number of calls per day by the number of days worked per week by the weeks worked annually. For example, if the average salesperson makes 3 calls per day and works 4 days per week on the road, this works out to 12 sales calls per week. Few salespersons will work 52 weeks annually due to vacation time, training, and holidays. A fair estimate is 45 weeks since most U.S. workers are on the job about 220 to 225 days per year. Multiplying 12 calls per week times 45 weeks worked (12×45) results in 540 annual sales calls made per salesperson.

To calculate the total number of salespersons needed, divide the total number of calls the sales force must make (2,152) by the total number of calls completed by an average salesperson (540). That is, 2,152 divided by 540 tells us approximately four full-time salespersons (actually 3.98) are needed to call upon all existing outside accounts. The final step requires computing additional sales-related activities the salesperson will be expected to complete. Let's assume each salesperson will be directed to devote 15 percent of their time calling on new accounts and 10 percent of their time will be committed to completing customer service calls. This means each salesperson spends 75 percent of their time (100% minus 25% = 75%) on existing accounts. By dividing 4 by .75 = 5.33 salespersons are needed based upon all projected workload activities computed by the sales manager. Sales managers utilize the buildup method for determining a sales force's size when the market is large, complex, and sales success depends upon interacting with customers and building relationships with them.

Specialists versus Generalists

Sales managers like Bill Haas understand that when selling a complex service like scientific testing, it is difficult to be an expert in multiple medical specialties. Thus, a specialized sales force can give the firm the advantage of selling expertise. That said, the sales forces of many companies are not specialized. Their salespeople sell the firm's sole product or entire product line to a discrete group of customers that use the product(s) similarly. Consider Karl Strauss Brewing Company of San Diego whose representatives sell all of the firm's beverages—Red Trolley Ale, Woodie Gold, and Stargazer I.P.A.—to retailers.

Conversely, other firms find it is necessary to specialize the efforts of their sales forces. For example, computer manufacturers organize their sales forces by consumer, B2B, and education markets because each market purchases and utilizes the products differently. Likewise, sales managers also understand that, based upon internal and external conditions, partnering with distributors, sales agents, and resellers can improve the effectiveness and profitability of their own sales organization. This is what LabCorp is trying to do by partnering with managed-care companies.

A specialized sales structure offers the firm expertise advantages over a generalist sales force. That said, the sales manager must safeguard against a number of potential problems caused by overspecialization. First, all sales efforts must be coordinated and integrated

Geographic territories can increase the travel distances for the sales manager. (© Peter Beck/Corbis, all rights reserved.)

to address and satisfy buyers' needs. This is necessary because as firms increase the specialization of their sales force, the addition of personnel both inside and outside of the company that interact with the buying firm increases the complexity of its operations. Second, the sales function must be integrated and coordinated with other organizational functions—accounting, finance, production, engineering, quality control, customer service, and so forth. As explained in Chapters 5 and 6, CRM systems help firms communicate and coordinate effectively between a company's functional work areas.

Geographical, Product, and Market Structures

Sales force structures can be as simple as a generalist salesperson who sells all products manufactured by a firm in a discrete geographical area to a specialized salesperson who works with a team of experts to sell certain products to specific markets. Let's consider each type of sales organizational structure.

A firm that employs a **geographical sales structure** depends upon physical boundaries to organize its sales force with customer accounts. When the sales force is organized geographically, the sales force interacts with buyers as generalists. For example, B.W. Wilson Paper Company, which was formed in Richmond, Virginia, slowly expanded its geographical sales territories across the state and into central North Carolina. Depending upon the number of accounts located within a geographic entity, a salesperson is assigned a specified group of customers within a state, region, or nation, a single city, a county, or a zip/postal code.

Firms often favor a geographical sales organization because it is relatively easy to design, minimizes duplication of effort, and ensures a specific salesperson is assigned to each customer. Geographical sales structures also address a number of concerns for the sales firm. First, customer visits can be more efficiently scheduled based on their geographical location. Second, as sales in a geographic territory increase, the territory can simply be divided and an extra salesperson added to the force. If sales shrink, territories can be combined.

However, there are a number of potentially negative aspects of geographical sales organizations. Geographical sales territories work best when the selling firm's product line is simple. This means that the salesperson can reasonably be expected to master all the products sold by the firm and advise the potential buyer about their unique features. For example, at B.W. Wilson Paper Company, company salespersons sell all paper and industrial products to commercial printers, publishers, and government print facilities located in their geographically assigned territories. Geographical territories can also be inefficient. If you analyze most geographical territories, the sales are concentrated in one or more cities or areas, leaving large areas of the territory with only a few profitable customers. Examples of geographical, product, and market organizational charts are shown in Exhibit 7.3.

When a firm's product lines are broad and complex, it might be more effective to organize sales activities around a product or division—to specialize the sales force, in other words. An example of a sales force that sells broad and complex product lines is Applied Industrial Technologies (AIT), which distributes more than two million specific products to 156,000 customer accounts in categories that include bearings, power transmission components and systems, industrial rubber products, linear components, tools, safety products, general maintenance, and a variety of mill supply products.[3]

In a **product sales structure**, the firm organizes its sales activities around related product lines or manufacturing divisions. For example, General Electric offers consumer and commercial solutions in the areas of automotive, aviation, energy, healthcare, oil and

Geographic-Based Structure

EXHIBIT 7.3

Geographical, Product, and Market Sales Force Structures

Product-Based Structure

Market- or Customer-Based Structure

gas, and transportation to markets worldwide (www.ge.com). It's simply not feasible for a salesperson to be an expert in each of these areas of technology and customer usage. By specializing by product line or division, the salesperson can become an expert in that one area.

There are also a number of limitations to product specialization. First, a firm may unknowingly send two or more salespersons to the same account, thus confusing the buyer. A noteworthy example is Xerox®, which at one point had three independent sales forces that sold computers, copiers, and office equipment, respectively. Xerox® became aware, based on customer feedback, that its sales representatives from the different forces: (1) called upon the same accounts; (2) had little knowledge of each other's products; (3) confused buyers who had a genuine need for the company's products; and (4) did not cooperate by providing leads and information to one another.

To fix the problem, Xerox® assigned a single salesperson to sell all three product lines to accounts. As a result, customer service levels and total sales increased. However, the reorganization led to increased turnover because some salespeople were not interested in or able to learn and sell three separate product lines.

Firms that utilize a **market sales structure** assign representatives to customers based upon their markets—telecommunications, military, automotive, computer, and so forth—or by how the product being sold was used, say by individual consumers or by B2B firms. By employing a market or industry-type sales force organization, the firm is able to apply the marketing concept and be more customer-centric, which means the sales force learns more about customer's specific business needs and offers customized solutions—by recommending the right applications—that solve customers' problems.[4] Organizing by customer type appears to be gaining momentum in today's marketplace. For example, many B2B manufacturers sell similar products to commercial and governmental buyers who purchase and utilize the product(s) in very different ways.

Organizing by market also appears to be an effective strategy when a seller wants to penetrate a new market. A market structure allows a selling firm to vary the allocation of its sales efforts to specific industries by adding to or reducing the number of salespersons slotted in one area to another. For example, over the past decade pharmaceutical manufacturers like Pfizer® have added a large number of salespersons to sell to physicians, hospitals, and healthcare providers. In some markets, pharmaceutical firms have assigned more than one salesperson to the same physician to intensify the selling effort. Organizing by market or customer type also permits the sales firm to offer specialized training and develop individualized sales approaches and applications by industry unlike what is possible in other sales force structures.

The disadvantages of market sales structures are similar to those faced by product specialized sales forces. Because businesses in the same industry, or market, are often located in different parts of the country, selling expenses are higher than for geographical sales organizations. Also, when a buying firm has several divisions or offers a wide variety of products, multiple salespersons may end up calling on the same buyers. As we have explained, this results in potential buyer confusion, duplication of effort, and higher sales expenses.

In a **functional sales structure**, the selling process is divided into two or more steps that are performed by specialists. For example, a company may have one salesperson open a new account. But as soon as the buyer makes the first purchase, the account is turned over to another salesperson who manages the account. For firms that sell to grocery stores or retail outlets, the sales effort might include one salesperson who establishes a store's account, a second sales professional who manages the store's stock and its orders and resolves customer service issues, and a third sales-support person who merchandises the company's products by setting up in-store shelf and point-of-purchase displays and mailing out promotional materials.

A major problem with using a functional sales organization is coordinating the multiple sales reps that would call on a single customer. A customer relationship management (CRM) system can simplify coordination problems and allow all members of the sales team to know what the others discussed and promised, no matter who last talked to the buyer. Sales managers may also struggle to coordinate the two or three sales specialists—the one that opens the account, the one that manages customers, and the one that conducts the customers' merchandising efforts. That is, once a salesperson opens an account, the sales manager must ensure there is a smooth "hand off" to the other account manager(s). One way to help ensure a smooth transition and make sure the salesperson that opened the account remains dedicated to it, is to reduce his or her commission should the account be lost within the first year.

A firm utilizes a **combination sales structure** when its sales force is organized based on a mixture of product, market, and geographical factors. Combination sales structures work best when the market is large, the product mix is complex, and customers require different applications. An example of a combination sales force organization is a salesperson for Lenovo®. Lenovo sells sales force CRM systems to automotive parts manufacturers in the Midwest. A combination sales force structure connects the benefits of product and market structures. But combination sales structures are expensive and can result in duplicate sales efforts, too. Such a structure tends to work best for larger firms that serve many diverse and specialized markets.

As you can probably tell, sales managers face different trade-offs with different sales structures. Exhibit 7.4 outlines the major pros and cons of each sales structure.

Key Account Structures

Firms today provide their key accounts (which are sometimes called *national accounts*) with extra attention and service levels by assigning special salespeople to them. Key accounts consist of customers that are large in terms of their sales revenue and profitability and that are strategically important for the future of the sales firm. An excellent example of a key account is Wal-Mart® who purchases and distributes a significant amount of

Territory Structure	Pros	Cons
Geographical (generalist approach)	Simplicity Efficiency No Duplication	Unbalanced Territories Product and Market Knowledge More Difficult for Reps to Master Broad Product Lines Coordination Issues
Product (specialist approach)	Better Rep Product Knowledge Better Rep Product-Application Knowledge	Duplicate Sales Effort
Market (specialist approach)	Better Rep Customer Knowledge Better Rep Product-Application Knowledge Better Rep Market Knowledge	Duplicate Sales Effort More Complex to Work with Product Managers
Functional (specialist approach)	Job Expertise Achieved by Reps	Coordination Issues
Combination (specialist approach)	Better Rep Customer Knowledge Better Rep Market Knowledge	Economies of Scale Issues More Complex to Manage Duplicate Sales Effort

EXHIBIT 7.4

The Pros and Cons of Different Territory Structures

GLOBAL SALES MANAGEMENT

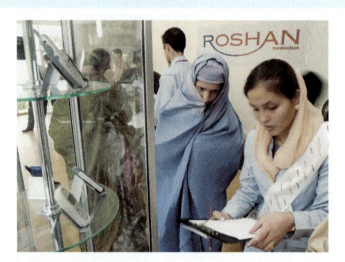

Sales assignments can vary tremendously in global markets.
(AP Wide World Photos)

Sales Structures in Global Markets

When a firm implements a global sales force, sales managers have multiple factors to consider. In global markets, sales force organizations and practices vary by country. A country's cultural context greatly influences the type of organizational sales force structure a company uses. Foreign salespeople and sales managers from the firm's home country (known as expatriates) can work well in low-context countries, like Germany, where oral and written communications are direct. By contrast, local salespeople perform more efficiently in Japan and China, due to the language and cultural knowledge they possess. Firms, such as Procter & Gamble, learned that local hires that understand both the market and the local culture work best in the growing China market.

Even though organizational alternatives are available, sales firms often employ geographical territories to structure their overseas sales forces. For example, Caterpillar organized Central America into a single region for a U.S. expatriate salesperson to manage. On the other hand, global firms that offer broad product lines, have large sales volumes, or that operate in large, developed markets tend to favor customer or product assignments. In smaller markets, like those that are found in developing areas like Southeast Asia, it is not economically feasible to structure the sales force by product or customer—thus, geographical assignments are more common.

Finally, global firms might utilize cultures, including languages, to organize their sales force. That is, a firm might divide the nation of Belgium by language—French to the south and Flemish in the north—and combine Austria and Germany because each nation speaks German. Likewise, global firms might combine the Central American countries into a single geographical territory if the sales in those countries are small, and their languages and cultures are similar languages. However, sales force managers must remain sensitive to the fact that although nations might lie geographically close to one another, one is distinct in terms of its culture, customs, and values.

Sources: Based on Samli, A. C., R. Still, and J. S. Hill (1993). *International Marketing*, New York: MacMillan; Axtell, Roger E. (1990). *Do's and Taboos Around the World*, New York: John Wiley & Sons.

Procter & Gamble® products both nationally in the United States and throughout the world. Because key accounts are so important to manufacturers, they are given higher levels of service, a more experienced sales force, and private channels to communicate with sales firm executives. IBM® reports that 75 percent of its revenues are generated by its largest customers.[5] Key account relationships also exemplify the **80/20 Rule**, which states that 80 percent of a firm's total business and profits are derived from 20 percent of its customers.

Recently, B2B buyers have reduced the number of approved sellers they work with in order to cut costs and to form closer relationships and work more closely with the vendors they retain. As a result, many suppliers now sell larger volumes to fewer key accounts.[6] This shift can be both good and bad: it can lead to lower costs for the supplier because there are fewer accounts to service. However, the supplier is also more likely to face pressure from the buyer to lower its prices so the buyer doesn't take their business to another firm.[7] To keep from falling into such a "trap," sellers must be prepared to offer the buyer something other than low prices that its competitors can't offer—for example, higher levels of service, greater product value, or both.

Sellers today understand that large, strategic accounts require higher levels of service and deeper buyer-seller relationships. Thus, sellers must develop a strategy for serving large strategic accounts. Many firms begin their key account management programs by utilizing the existing sales force. Because key account buyers require significantly higher service levels than smaller non-key accounts, sellers must restructure their sales force to best meet the needs of their strategic partners. Firms can manage national or key accounts through their existing sales force structure by assigning company executives to the accounts or by creating a separate sales force or sales division. We discuss each option next.

EMPLOYING THE EXISTING SALES FORCE STRUCTURE Firms may initially manage national or key accounts through their existing sales force. In this way, the sales force structure is simplified, and all accounts are managed under a single organizational structure. However, a number of disadvantages rise to the surface when using the regular sales force to serve key accounts. For example, a territory-based salesperson might focus on closing sales rather than fostering long-term relationships. This short-term view is prevalent when salespeople are motivated by the constant pressures of their quotas. Plus, a territory-based salesperson is unlikely to understand the broader, overall needs of the key account. For reasons such as these, many firms decide to structure their key account sales operations differently.

SELF-ASSESSMENT LIBRARY

As you have seen throughout this chapter, a sales organization's structure can vary widely based upon the firm's goals, the marketplace, and company history. Studies have shown that sales managers are more successful when they work in organizations that share their work styles and goals. In what type of sales organization do you believe you would flourish? To find out your preference for a specific type of organization, go to http://www.prenhall.com/sal/, and log in using the access code that came with your book. Then click on:

Assessments
  III. Life in Organizations
    A. Organization Structure
      1. What Type of Organizational Structure Do I Prefer?

ASSIGNING COMPANY EXECUTIVES Assigning sales and marketing executives to manage key accounts makes sense for smaller firms that cannot afford a separate sales effort. The drawback of assigning executives at small firms to singly manage key accounts is that the added assignment can take a lot of time, which leaves the executives less time for their principal duties, including overseeing the firm's sales force. Large firms like Cisco® assign their most important 15 accounts to individual executives who are responsible for managing the relationship of one key account. The Cisco® account executive also coordinates a sales team to meet the needs of the key or major account. By virtue of their influence and power, company executives at both large and small selling firms can ensure their firm addresses the needs of their key account buyers.

BUILDING A SEPARATE SALES FORCE/DIVISION As sales firms grow in size, they often create separate sales structures to serve their most important customers. This can take the form of having a senior salesperson visit the buyer's headquarters and then assign regular sales force members to service local accounts. Or, a parallel sales force structure can be formed and managed. For example, firms can establish a separate key account division to which they promote their most successful and experienced sales reps. Forming a separate sales force/division offers the benefit of integrating marketing and sales operations for key accounts under one organizational structure. However, establishing distinct sales channels for major accounts is more costly and results in duplication of effort for the sales organization. Lastly, should one or two large customers be lost to competitors, the financial viability of a separate sales force or division will be in jeopardy!

Telemarketing and Computerized Sales Structures

Recall that telemarketing was first discussed in Chapter 2. **Telemarketing** is the use of telecommunications technology by an inside salesperson to communicate with an established or potential customer to sell products or services. For business-to-business firms, telemarketing is growing at a rate of 9 percent per year and in 2007 accounted for $650 billion in sales.[8] Firms are also switching to telemarketing to service small accounts, prequalify customers, set up appointments for the outside sales force, notify customers about upcoming trade shows, and handle incoming sales calls. As sales firms rely on telemarketers to conduct sales activities for smaller accounts and to support the salesperson in the field, the sales manager must devote more time and effort coordinating the interactions of inside and outside sales personnel. In a number of instances, sales firms have recently begun to move their telemarketing operations offshore to reduce costs. However, as customers subsequently complained about the level of service they received from service providers at offshore call centers, sales firms slowed or stopped offshoring their telemarketing and customer service centers, as explained in the accompanying "Global Sales Management" sidebar.

As we initially discussed in Chapter 2, there are two basic forms of telemarketing sales structures that firms employ: incoming and outgoing. An incoming telemarketing group operates within a firm's pull strategy. That is, the firm employs advertising and promotional messages to end-users to "pull" or create buyer demand to call an 800 number and consult with an in-house telemarketing salesperson. Sales companies also utilize toll-free phone numbers that allow small accounts to contact the seller and place orders that fulfill their needs. An outgoing telemarketing group performs a variety of activities that involve pushing a firm's product line by calling current or potential customers to try to uncover needs and close the sale. Telemarketing is favored by firms because of its lower cost, higher call rate per day, and overall profitability that can be generated. Sales managers understand, however, that telemarketing salespersons require different skill sets, training, compensation, and motivation than do field sales personnel.

GLOBAL SALES MANAGEMENT

Sales managers often encounter problems coordinating the strategies of their sales forces and their overseas customer support groups. (Joel Nito/AFP/Getty Images)

Some Offshore Call Centers Go Back Home

At first, firms that built and staffed offshore call centers were praised for their cost-cutting acumen. In fact, the offshoring of services—to include telemarketing and customer service—is proving to be a global phenomenon: French-speaking Europeans are serviced by residents of former colonies in Africa, German speakers by Eastern Europeans, Scandinavians by workers in the Baltic region, Portuguese by Brazilians and residents of former colonies in Africa, and Japanese by citizens of northern China.

But the offshoring movement to lower-cost countries was quickly met by buyers who complained about miscommunications, cultural gaffes, lack of professionalism and product knowledge, and ability to solve their problems. In response, firms that offshore invested time and money training their agents and retaining the best telemarketing salespersons they could afford. Some firms purchased better voice-recognition software to make communication with customers easier and faster. Still other companies went so far as to purchase software designed to help sales managers recognize buyer dissatisfaction levels during telephone calls.

Despite these efforts, many firms decided to move call centers back to their home countries because, in the buyer's eyes, lower-cost offshore centers equates to lower-quality service. In fact, one study found that many U.S. citizens "hang up" or refuse to speak to call center representatives when they believe the telemarketer is located in another country.

Sources: Based on Ali, Sarmad. 2006. "If You Want to Scream, Press . . . ," *The Wall Street Journal*, October 30, R4; Thelen, Shawn, Tanya Thelen, Vincent P. Magnini, and Earl D. Honeycutt, Jr., *An Introduction to the Offshore Service Ethnocentrism Construct.* 2008. Services Marketing Quarterly, In Press.

EXHIBIT 7.5

The Sales Process in a Hybrid Selling Structure

Sales Process Tasks

Vendors	Lead Generation	Qualifying Sales	Presales	Close of Sale	Post-Sale Services	Account Management	Customer
Field Sales/Agent				X		X	
Telemarketing		X	X		X		
Direct Mail/ Computerized Sales	X						

Telemarketing salespeople who work in a functional sales organization might prospect for and qualify sales leads, set sales-call appointments, and handle customer satisfaction issues. Telemarketers are normally organized similarly to field representatives, by geography, product, or markets. As Exhibit 7.5 shows, a firm has the option of shifting the functional responsibility for servicing customers between its inside salespeople and its field salespeople.

Computerized sales, generated via the Internet and telephone, are increasing annually for most firms. The Internet sales process can vary greatly. For example, Prentice Hall® allows university bookstores to go online to interact with OASIS, a free Internet-based system that enables the placing and tracking of book orders 24 hours a day, 7 days a week. In addition, bookstores can look up price and availability and request copies of invoices, credit memos, and statements. If customers need to speak with a person, there is an 800 phone number they can call to reach an inside salesperson.

Another option, as we discussed in Chapters 2 and 5, allows firms to be linked to an intranet and order standard products as they are needed. Buyers order either when they are notified via e-mail by a just-in-time or EDI ordering system or when their stock reaches a designated level. No live salesperson is needed because the buyer orders from an approved vendor at a pre-negotiated price. Computerized sales systems are significantly less costly for the seller.

Firms that use computerized sales to either service buyers placing reorders or to attract new buyers have to keep in mind that customers are being inundated by e-mail and automated sales calls. Much of the e-mail buyers receive is **SPAM** ("junk" or unsolicited electronic messages). Salespersons should ask permission to send e-mail messages to buyers; otherwise, only personal electronic messages that are relevant should be sent to current or potential buyers. That is, make sure that you have permission to send "blanket" e-mail sales messages to buyers. The CAN-SPAM Act was enacted in 2003 and sets conditions for sending e-mail to current clients and potential buyers:

- The subject lines of e-mail should not be misleading.
- The "From" line should contain a functioning e-mail address.
- The body of the message should list a valid physical postal address.
- There should be conspicuous instructions to opt out of future mailings.

If these requirements are not followed, firms face penalties of up to $2 million or more imposed by the U.S. government.[9]

As far as telephone messages go, the federal law allows firms to make telemarketing calls under specific conditions. Sales firms that make telemarketing calls to business locations are not in violation of the Federal Trade Commission "No-Call" regulation; telemarketing calls are expressly permitted when a business relationship exists. However, it is a violation of the Telephone Consumer Protection Act (TCPA) for firms to make prerecorded telephone calls via automatic computerized dialers (also known as Automatic Dialing and Announcing Devices—ADAD) and to fax SPAM to any fax location.[10] Therefore, sales managers should keep in mind that although business telemarketing calls may be legal, unwanted and intrusive telemarketing calls are likely to negatively impact an existing or potential business relationship.

Reporting Relationships within a Firm's Sales Force

There are a number of ways a sales force's reporting relationships can be set up in a firm. In a **line organization**, all salespeople, from the highest to the lowest levels, report to a single manager. For example, a field or inside salesperson reports to her sales manager, her sales manager reports to the district sales manager, the district sales manager is supervised by the regional sales manager, and the regional sales manager reports to the national sales manager. To carry this line organization further, the national sales manager reports to the firm's vice president of sales and marketing, and the vice president of sales and marketing then answers to the president of the firm.

There are advantages and disadvantages to line structures. Line structures are advantageous because the chain of command is clear. For example, if the president and the vice president of sales and marketing feel that it is necessary to modify the firm's sales strategy, this action can be implemented quickly and easily through the firm's line structure. A disadvantage of the line structure is that as firms adopt customer relationship strategies, salespeople need greater authority to make quick decisions to keep customers satisfied. To make quicker decisions, companies and sales managers must *flatten* the sales organization—if not the actual reporting structure itself—then the decision making that occurs within it. That is, authority must be pushed down to lower-level salespeople who can be more responsive to buyers' needs.

Firms also must decide how other sales activities, like sales selection, sales training, buyer research, and customer service, fit into the structure. When a sales support activity falls outside of the line structure, the organization operates a line and staff structure. A **line and staff sales structure** entails using a line structure for the firm's core sales functions and then placing its support activities, like sales training and customer service, into centers or departments that reside outside of the line structure. For example, a salesperson would report directly to his district manager in a line organization. However, when undergoing training, he would be supervised by the firm's sales training manager, who is a staff member. Remember that staff managers report to and are delegated authority by line managers. The geographical, product, and market sales force structures shown in Exhibit 7.3 all provide examples of line and staff structures.

Span of Control

The **span of control** refers to the number of individuals that report directly to a sales manager. There is no rule for an "ideal" span of control; however, Exhibit 7.6 offers guidelines for sales managers. Technical sales and industrial products—both of which require customized customer solutions—result in narrower spans of control (fewer employees reporting to a sales manager), whereas routine trade sales and telemarketing activities allow a broader span of control (larger numbers of employees reporting to a sales manager).[11] For example, as the exhibit shows, the recommended number of salespeople reporting to one sales manager in a technical sales setting is seven, whereas a sales manager can supervise 12 to 16 trades salespersons that are involved in more routine sales duties.

EXHIBIT 7.6

Recommended Span of Control Ratios

By Selling Task		By Product Type	
Technical Sales	7:1	Industrial Products	6:1
Missionary Sales	10:1	Consumer Products	8:1
Trade Sales	12–16:1	Services	10:1
Telemarketing	12–18:1		

Adding Independent Sales Reps to the Sales Structure

Recall from Chapter 2 that **independent sales representatives**, or agents, often sell on behalf of manufacturers or other sellers in territories where no company sales force is present. These agents receive a commission for all sales they make within an assigned geographical sales territory. As agents, they do not take ownership of the product and do not maintain an inventory. A manufacturer's representative traditionally sells several related, but noncompeting product lines that are similar in quality and price. For example, in the furniture business, a rep might sell furniture for one principal, lamps for another manufacturer, and decorative accessories for yet another. The retail buyer needs all three types of products, so it is more efficient for the buyer to meet with a single salesperson instead of three. One study found that 50 percent of North American companies utilize sales agents for product, geographic, or market-oriented sales. Intel, Texas Instruments, Hunt Wesson, and Cirrus Logic are companies that switched from in-house sales forces to sales agents. Moreover, as we also discussed in Chapter 2, there are times when firms outsource their entire sales forces.

The relationship between company sales managers and agents in general is complex. First, a selling firm can contract with a manufacturer's agent or wholesaler's sales force to manage accounts in geographical regions. For example, a manufacturer might have a company sales force that manages larger, more profitable territories while also contracting with agents to service less developed, less profitable geographical territories. Many insurance firms utilize a combination of company and independent sales agents to sell their products.

Second, because agents are "independent," a company sales manager has little direct control over them other than dissolving the agency relationship. As a result, the sales manager must motivate the agents by appealing to their self-interests. For example, the sales manager might structure the compensation system for the agents based upon measures other than simply sales revenue generated. This may include measures that are related to growing the company's existing accounts and building higher-quality relationships with customers.

As we mentioned, when firms enter new territories with low or unknown sales volumes, it is common for manufacturers to use sales agents. This appears to be a prudent business decision for sellers because selling costs are only incurred (in the form of sales commissions) when products or services are sold. For example, a manufacturer that decides to expand into a new region but lacks the financial resources to hire, train, equip, and manage a company sales force, will likely contract with an independent sales agency that may also be called a broker or manufacturer's representative.

Independent salespeople offer firms a number of advantages, including:

- An "in-place" or existing sales force
- Established buyer relationships
- Little (or no) fixed costs
- Experienced sales personnel
- Lower costs per sales call
- Long-term stability in the territory

However, given all these benefits, firms that hire independent sales reps often complain that they do not receive equal time for their products. Or, agents are blamed for shifting their sales call focus to another product line when a buyer's need is not easily identified. Independent sales reps are also criticized for not opening new accounts, not following up on leads, representing too many manufacturers, and communicating poorly with the firms they represent. That said, there's a tendency for manufacturers to take credit for positive sales outcomes accomplished by their agents and assign blame for negative outcomes when they lack control over the outcomes. For example, if a sales agent is doing a super job, the manufacturer will assume that an internal sales force will work better at a lower cost and the agency will be dumped. This suggests that a sales agency will likely be criticized when its performance is either too high or too low.

Any written agreement a selling firm has with an agent should clearly articulate the expected level of feedback the firm wants regarding its customers, the customers' inventory levels, the customer service level the agent will provide the firm's customers, and how the firm will be represented by the agent at trade shows.[12] Otherwise, conflicts like those listed in Exhibit 7.7 are likely to occur. For example, the manufacturer might want the agent to focus on selling the firm's products at high prices, whereas the sales agent's goal might be to maximize sales revenue by selling the firm's products at a discounted price.

Sales agencies understand that once their client's sales revenues reach a certain level, the client might sever their business relationship and hire its own sales force. In effect, the sales agent is so successful that they put themselves out of business. Because both agents and the firms that contract with them realize that their relationship can change over time, it's a good idea to incorporate provisions for modifying the original agreement that created the partnership in the first place. That is, in addition to clearly stating how each partner will support the other, it is also essential to discuss and agree upon how the partnership can be amicably dissolved. Agreements between agents and manufacturers normally offer specific provisions for how the partnership can be ended, how much notice is required, and how each party will behave toward the other. It is also common practice to split commissions for a specified time period, such as one year, after the company sales force assumes responsibility for a territory's customers. Even so, ethical dilemmas can arise between the parties, as illustrated in the accompanying Ethics in Sales Management feature.

Conflict	Explanation
Goal Divergence	This conflict occurs when the objectives of the agent and the seller differ. For example, the seller might want the agent to focus on getting a high price for products, whereas the sales agent might want to maximize sales revenue by offering discounts and remaining flexible on prices.
Domain Dissension	This conflict relates to a disagreement about who owns a particular domain, like the territory served, expected duties, and the target market.
Reality Perceptions	This conflict is often observed in the very nature of human relationships: one party feels slighted while the other believes it acted in good faith.
Abuse of Power	One partner may threaten to or change a policy without consulting with the other. When challenged, the more powerful partner simply tells the other "that's the way it is."

EXHIBIT 7.7

Sources of Conflict between Firms and Their Selling Agents

Source: Based on Russell S. Winer, *Marketing Management* 2nd ed., Upper Saddle River, NJ: Prentice Hall, 2004.

ETHICS IN SALES MANAGEMENT

Ethical Dilemmas with Partners

John Orlando is a national sales manager for Exitron, a manufacturer of electronic chips utilized in alarm systems, appliances, irrigation timers, and industrial machinery. Currently Wiles & Associates represents Exitron as a manufacturer's rep in California. When Wiles agreed to represent Exitron, both parties signed an agreement that stated that either party could terminate the relationship by sending a written notice to the other party at least 90 days prior to ending the partnership.

Exitron's sales in California have been phenomenal, and Orlando calculates that the cost of servicing the accounts would decrease by 25 percent by switching to a company sales force. Exitron's attorney advised Orlando to send notification to Wiles & Associates by overnight express mail exactly 90 days from the termination date. John Orlando feels bad about not personally meeting with Mr. Wiles, thanking him for the service his company has extended to Exitron, and offering to split the sales commission for the next year. Exitron's attorney advises that nothing in the partnership agreement requires this "golden handshake," and such an action would set a bad precedent and financially impact Exitron's bottom line. Orlando wonders in this instance what the difference is between being legal and being ethical.

Epilogue

After weighing his options, John Orlando decided his best course of action was to meet with the managers at Wiles & Associates, thank them for representing his products in their territory, and offer a phase-out of commissions. His actions were well received by Mr. Wiles and Orlando believes that should sales decline significantly in this region at some time in the future, Wiles would once again partner with Exitron.

Company Salesperson or Sales Agent?

When it is important to control the sales effort, the product or its related technology is new, and buyers need a high level of sales service, most firms and their sales managers conclude that it is in their best interests to hire, train, organize, and manage a company sales force. This way, the company can exert greater control over the sales force's efforts, such as what will be sold, when, and how, as we first discussed in Chapter 2. The firm also has greater control over who is hired to represent the company. However, when the potential sales revenue is low in a territory, or will take years to become substantial and highly qualified sales agents currently operate in the area, an attractive alternative is a contract sales force.

So, exactly at what point should a sales agent and a company sales representative be switched? The simplest way to determine this is to do a **break-even analysis** that compares the fixed and variable costs associated with the two types of representatives. A break-even analysis can be conducted by using a mathematical formula (see Appendix 7A) or an economic diagram, as shown in Exhibit 7.8. First, the total cost of the agent (TC^a) line begins at zero and increases linearly as the agent sells additional units of the product. Second, a company salesperson receives a straight salary component and additional commission for each unit sold. As a result, the firm's costs for maintaining the company salesperson in the field is highest at lower sales volumes.

As Exhibit 7.8 shows, the total cost of the salesperson (TC^{sp}) starts on top of the horizontal fixed cost line because the salesperson is paid a salary and there are other fixed costs that must be expended even when there are no sales in the territory. At a specific unit of sales volume, there is a point of indifference (Q^*) where the two sales options cost the selling firm exactly the same amount. Prior to reaching the break-even point, the agent is the least costly option for the sales firm. However, once the break-even point has been crossed and sales continue to increase, it is more economically advantageous for a sales firm to operate a company sales force in a territory. Conversely, when sales revenue decreases below the switch over point Q^*, then the sales manager would need to consider changing from a company salesperson to an agent.

Firms now recognize that sales agents may be the best solution for given situations. For example, National Semiconductor and Advanced Micro Systems employ a contract sales force because their products are used in most industries and it is not feasible for a company sales force to cover the entire market. Likewise, using agents to sell services like advertising is logical because nearly anyone can advertise. However, sales agents are not practical in all sales situations. For example, pharmaceutical companies use in-house sales forces because of ethical and accountability issues.[13]

Manufacturers and wholesalers have recently begun outsourcing their sales responsibilities to independent companies. For example, firms routinely outsource their telemarketing function to independent telemarketing companies that have call center and telemarketing expertise. Likewise, insurance companies have found that independent sales reps are less expensive than hiring, training, and retaining company salespersons. As we have discussed, the "jury is still out" on the outsourcing of a firm's sales-related responsibilities. Companies that partner with other firms to perform their sales function must decide whether to stick with the partnership, depending upon the level of sales, profitability, and buyer satisfaction achieved by the independent or outsourced sales firm.

Sales managers often hire sales agents instead of in-house personnel because of cost and expertise issues. (Getty Images)

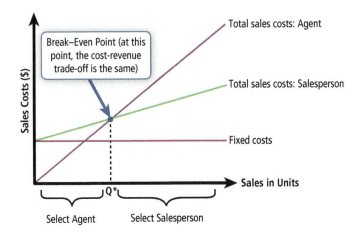

EXHIBIT 7.8

Company Salesperson or Sales Agent? Doing a Break-Even Analysis

Summary

The way the sales force is organized and managed is a major aspect of a firm's strategic sales plan. When the sales force is organized geographically, the representatives interact as generalists with buyers located in their territory. Conversely, by organizing along product, market, combination, or functional structures, buyers receive additional specialized service from the sales force. Sales managers must consider line and staff, span of control, specialization, coordination, and integration factors when deciding upon the best way to organize the sales effort. In addition to structuring their field representatives, firms also have to decide how to structure their other selling groups, such as their key account, telemarketing, and computerized sales functions and groups.

When the sales territory is unproven or when the selling firm cannot afford to hire, train, and manage its own sales force, the firm can partner with sales agents or manufacturer's representatives. Sales agents are less controllable than company salespeople, and misunderstandings between a firm and its agents can sometimes lead to conflicts between the two. Sales managers can perform a break-even analysis to compare the fixed and variable costs associated with the two types of sales representatives. There are times, however, when sales agents are not practical in a particular selling situation, no matter how large the cost differences. A clear example used earlier in the chapter is pharmaceutical firms that utilize their own sales force to ensure that ethical and accountability guidelines are followed by their sales teams.

Key Terms

breakdown method 138	line and staff sales structure 149
break-even analysis 152	line organization 149
combination sales structure 143	market sales structure 142
computerized sales 148	product sales structure 140
80/20 Rule 145	SPAM 148
functional sales structure 142	span of control 149
geographical sales structure 140	telemarketing 146
independent sales representives 150	workload method 138

Questions and Problems

1. Explain why firms organize their sales activities into a specific structure. How important is the sales structure for a business's strategic plan?
2. Using the following information, perform a breakdown and workload computation to predict how many salespersons XYZ Inc. will need to service their customers. Forecasted sales for next year are $110 million and an average salesperson sells $9 million annually. Also, the XYZ sales manager has categorized existing accounts into 41 "A," 105 "B," and 225 "C" customers. "A" accounts are visited weekly, "B" accounts monthly, and "C" accounts every other month. Salespersons are required to make four calls per day and be in the field four days per week. Because of vacation, training, and holidays, each salesperson works 48 weeks a year. In addition to calling upon existing accounts, salespersons are assigned a quota of calling upon 10 percent new accounts and devoting 5 percent of their time to information gathering duties.

3. Why does specialization lie at the heart of organizing the sales force?

4. Compose a table with five rows and four columns. List the five potential ways to structure a sales force in the left-hand column and then discuss the advantages and disadvantages of each sales structure in the middle and far right columns.

5. What are the three principal ways to manage national or key accounts? What is the best option for a smaller firm? For a large multi-divisional firm?

6. Explain team selling. What role does the salesperson play? What other functional areas are likely to be represented on the team? Why?

7. Many firms have moved their customer service and telemarketing operations offshore. How have many U.S. citizens responded to offshore sales and customer service representatives? How do you explain this reaction? What actions could a sales manager take to improve customer acceptance of offshore service?

8. What should sales managers coach their salespersons to do prior to sending blanket e-mail messages to customers and potential customers?

9. What is SPAM? What four conditions does the CAN-SPAM Act of 2003 impose on the sender of e-mails? Integrate these four conditions as you compose a sales e-mail strategy for communicating with buyers.

10. What influences do line and staff organizations and span of control have on the final structural decision with regard to decisions being made and routine vs. nonroutine sales calls?

11. Compare and contrast the advantages/disadvantages of utilizing an independent sales agent and a company sales force.

12. Draw a break-even analysis diagram and assume that Q* is 500 units. If the forecasted sales for the territory was 450 units a month, which sales structure—an independent agent or a company sales force—would be most economical? What other factors, other than costs, might influence your decision?

Role Play

Structuring the Sales Effort at Green River Software

Janet Jackson is the sales manager at Green River Software (GRS), a firm that produces custom B2B software for manufacturing equipment. Examples include software for the robotic assembly of automobiles, the mixing of precise chemical solutions at pharmaceutical and chemical plants, and the testing of assembled and manufactured goods for their quality and reliability. Green River's sales efforts have been handled by the manufacturer's representative firm, RC Associates, owned by Ronald Childress.

Childress was a computer science professor who consulted with Green River in the early days of computing when software solutions for manufacturing problems were first being developed. Childress left academia after several GRS programs were developed, and he offered to handle the sales efforts for GRS. This arrangement worked well for GRS for 10 years as sales increased; however, about a year ago, GRS adopted a relationship marketing approach for its best customers.

Jackson is trying to determine whether GRS is receiving the best support from RC Associates because its agents also sell hardware and computer peripheral equipment made by other companies to GRS customers. RC Associates receive an 8 percent commission on all sales of GRS products. Last year the sales revenues for GRS were $200 million. Besides the obvious cost of outsourcing its sales effort, GRS feels that the relationships it has with its best customers are not deepening because of the current sales agency arrangement. Jackson wants to do what is best for both RC Associates and GRS; thus she has scheduled a lunch one week from today with Ron Childress to discuss the agency relationship. The outcome of the meeting will determine what sales structure Jackson recommends to GRS's CEO and board of directors.

Characters in the Role Play

Janet Jackson, Sales Manager at Green River Software
Ron Childress, Owner and Principal of RC Associates

Assignment

Break into groups of two, with one student playing each character. Do not be concerned about matching the gender of the character with the actual gender mix of the student group. Prior to meeting, work individually for a short while to list the advantages of each option for organizing GRS's sales force. Then role-play the meeting between Janet and Ron. Each party should present what they believe are the costs and benefits of the current sales agency relationship. At the conclusion of the meeting, Jackson and Childress need to agree about the changes that should be made to meet GRS's new strategy. Alternatively, Jackson should recommend and logically justify that the contract with RC Associates be terminated and a new sales structure established for GRS.

Caselet 7.1: Jefferson Pilot Reorganizes Its Sales Force

Bradley Peters is the National Sales Manager for Jefferson Pilot (JP) Insurance Corporation. JP offers life, hospitalization, and disability insurance to both small and large companies, primarily in the Southeast United States, through its company salespeople. Each salesperson works for commission that is paid on closed sales within a geographical territory. Over the past decade, the turnover rate for JP's salespeople has increased from around 20 percent to over 50 percent annually.

Peters has asked the firm's accounting department to provide him with information about the total cost of hiring new salespeople, including the cost of advertising to attract applicants as well as interview, train, and license them. He's surprised when the figure he receives amounts to over $5 million dollars per year! With a turnover rate of 50 percent, Peters knows there's a tremendous amount of waste associated with the firm's current sales structure.

Consequently, Peters is considering partnering with independent sales agents, located in all of the company's current sales areas, because of their marketplace knowledge, market status, similarity of goals and values, and ability to create win-win situations for all parties involved in transactions. However, JP's sales managers would need to contact the agents operating in the company's various sales territories and convince them of the benefits of partnering with Jefferson Pilot. Peters also understands that utilizing this new market channel would make JP's current salespeople unhappy because the independent reps would compete at least indirectly with them. Still, as Peters thinks about all the money JP could save and how the independent reps have strong reputations and sales histories in their hometown areas, he knows partnering with them is probably the way to go.

Questions

1. What are the benefits of partnering with independent reps, as opposed to a company sales force? Can a case be made for finding a way to retain JP's current salespeople instead of hiring sales agents to replace them?
2. Why would the turnover rate be significantly lower for JP if it hired sales agents?
3. What type of resistance might JP encounter from its current sales reps if it hired sales agents?
4. How might JP integrate an independent rep strategy with its existing company sales force?

Caselet 7.2: IMC Considers Offshoring Its Call Center

International Manufacturing Corporation (IMC) produces high-quality electronic components for original equipment manufacturers (OEMs). Currently, it costs IMC about $4 million a year to operate a customer service center for its dealers and distributors located worldwide. IMC sales manager Sharon Jones has been reading about her competitors opening call centers in India, the Philippines, and in remote parts of Canada. Jones is reluctant to offshore IMC's call center, but her department is being pressured to lower its total costs.

To learn about her options, Jones contacts NCS International, which provides global site selection services specifically for the call center industry. She discovers that utilizing offshore call centers will lower her department's cost per call by 75 percent—a huge savings for IMC. But Jones wonders about the negatives she has read about in the newspaper. For example, other firms appear to have experienced the euphoria of saving money initially, only to learn that caller satisfaction and repeat purchases dropped significantly later on. As Jones drives home for the weekend, she ponders how she can make an offshore call center work for IMC.

Questions

1. Even though IMC's cost per call would decrease, what other costs should Jones consider when making her decision?
2. Do you think some of the countries Jones was thinking about offshoring to would result in potentially less caller dissatisfaction than others?
3. What criteria would you recommend that Jones consider when selecting a potential offshore location?
4. What other factors should Jones weigh as she ponders this major shift in customer service responsibilities?

References

1. Ledingham, Dianne, Mark Kovac, and Heidi Locke Simon (2006). "The New Science of Sales Force Productivity," *Harvard Business Review*, September, 124–133.
2. Honeycutt, Earl D., John B. Ford, and Antonis Simintiras (2003). *Sales Management: A Global Perspective*. London: Routledge.

3. Jordan, Jason (2006). 2006 World Class Sales Force Benchmark Executive Summary, The HR Chally Group, www.chally.com/benchmark/index.html. Accessed May 9, 2008.
4. Jordan (2006).
5. Marchetti, Michele (2001). "IBM's Marketing Visionary," *Sales & Marketing Management*, September, 52–62.
6. Sharma, Arun (1997). "Who Prefers Key Account Management Programs? An Investigation of Business Buying Behavior and Buying Firm Characteristics," *Journal of Personal Selling & Sales Management*, Fall, 27–39.
7. Piercy, Nigel F., and Nikala Lane (2006). "The Hidden Risks in Strategic Account Management Strategy," *Journal of Business Strategy* 27:1, 18–26.
8. Libey, Donald R. (2004). *Libey-Concordia Economic Outlook: Extrapolations and Implications for the Direct Marketing Industry*, MMIV:5 (July), Philadelphia, PA, www.libey.com.
9. Clarke, Irvine, III, Theresa B. Flaherty, and Michael T. Zugelder (2005). "The CAN-SPAM Act: New Rules for Sending Commercial E-mail Messages and Implications for the Sales Force," *Industrial Marketing Management* 34:4 (May), 399–415.
10. www.ag.state.mn.us/Consumer/YLR/AutoDialers.asp. Accessed August 1, 2007.
11. Honeycutt, Ford, and Simintiras (2003).
12. Zoltners, Andris, Prabhakant Sinha, and Greggor Lorimer (2005). *The Complete Guide to Accelerating Sales Force Performance*. New York: AMACOM.
13. Anonymous (2004). "Making the Case for Outside Sales Reps," Association of Independent Manufacturers/Representatives, Inc., www.aimr.net. Accessed June 7, 2007.

Appendix 7A

COMPUTING THE POINT WHEN IT IS TIME TO SWITCH FROM A COMPANY SALESPERSON TO A SALES AGENT

1. To compute Q*, a number of factors must be known or estimated:
   a. The fixed costs for the salesperson or sales force in an area. This may include straight salary, automobile costs, and cell phone costs
   b. The variable costs, such as cost of goods sold and commission
   c. The forecasted sales for the salesperson or sales team
   d. The ability to compute contribution margins or the selling price minus the variable costs. This leaves the amount from a sale that is left to pay off the firm's fixed costs.
   e. An estimation of the time the agent spends on your product in comparison to a company salesperson. This is abbreviated as "R." Since agents sell multiple products, the agent cannot spend their exclusive time on a single product.

2. Q* or the break-even point can be computed by using the following formula:

$$Q^* = \frac{\text{Fixed Costs}}{\text{Contribution Margin}_{\text{Salesperson}} - R \times \text{Contribution Margin}_{\text{Agent}}}$$

Compute the break-even point based on the following information:

Product sales price is $225; the manufactured sales cost is $110.
A sales agent receives a commission of 6 percent of the sales price.
The company salesperson receives a $3,000 monthly salary and a 2 percent commission on total sales.
Additional fixed costs = $800 a month for an auto and $150 for a cell phone.
Sales agents spend 30 percent of their time selling the firm's products.

$$\text{Fixed Costs} = \$3,000 + \$800 + \$150 = \$3,950$$
$$\text{Contribution Margin}_{\text{Salesperson}} = \$225 - \$110 - \$4.50 = \$110.50$$
$$\text{Contribution Margin}_{\text{Agent}} = \$225 - \$110 - \$13.50 = \$101.50$$

Adding numbers to the formula:

$$\frac{\$3,950}{\$110.50 - .3 \times 101.50} = \frac{\$3,950}{80.50} = 49.068 \text{ units per month}$$

If Q* is 49 units, and the sales manager forecasts a company salesperson (or team) can sell 60 units per month, the forecasted sales is greater than Q*. Therefore, from an economic perspective, the company should replace the sales agent with a company salesperson. Conversely, if forecasted sales were 45 units per month for a company salesperson, the company should retain the sales agent in the territory.

8

RECRUITING AND SELECTING THE RIGHT SALESPEOPLE

LEARNING OBJECTIVES

After completing this chapter, you should be able to:

- Understand why having a formal selection process improves the quality of newly hired salespeople.
- Discuss why it's important to analyze the skills a salesperson needs to succeed and include that information in a job description.
- Name the sources from which salespeople can be recruited both within and outside of the firm.
- Explain the five steps of the selection process.
- Explain why it's important to have a diverse sales force.
- List common recruiting mistakes and ways to avoid them.

Successfully recruiting salespeople is one of the most important functions performed by sales managers. Informed sales managers understand that when a firm conducts its selection and recruiting practices haphazardly, the company will experience higher salesperson turnover rates, higher recruiting and training costs, dissatisfied and lost customers, and lower revenues. One sales-industry expert calculated that the sum of the various costs of hiring the wrong salesperson can exceed $300,000![1] By following the process presented in this chapter, sales managers can reduce the likelihood of making incorrect decisions, improve the probability of hiring successful salespeople, and reduce costly sales force turnover.

JOSIE GALL

DISTRICT SALES MANAGER, BUSINESS & SCIENCE TEXTBOOK DIVISION, PRENTICE HALL®

In its search for highly qualified sales representatives, Prentice Hall mandates that a thorough recruitment and selection process be conducted. The firm's human resource department first writes a standardized description of the open position. Then the company's district sales managers, such as Josie Gall, publicize the job description in advertisements so that candidates can determine whether the position is of interest to them. Prentice Hall recruits applicants via numerous avenues, including college career centers, university career fairs, and Web sites like Monster® and CareerBuilder®. Gall also seeks recommendations from the company's current sales representatives, her contacts within the textbook industry, and referrals from college professors she knows.

After recruiting applicants, Prentice Hall adheres to the following selection procedures:

1. All applicants complete a standardized application form.
2. The hiring (district) sales manager then sorts as many as 200 candidate resumes into "A," "B," or "C" groupings.
3. The manager then screens, via phone, approximately "A" category candidates.
4. Personal interviews are set for the top 12 to 18 candidates.
5. The top three to five finalists are assigned campus projects whereby they interview a number of professors about their textbooks and why they chose them.
6. The manager then conducts a second interview of the top two to four candidates.
7. The top one to three candidates advance beyond the second interview, are assigned a day in the field with a sales representative, and have their references checked.
8. One to two finalists are interviewed by both Prentice Hall's director of recruiting and the national sales manager.
9. After consultations with the director of recruiting and the national sales manager, a final selection is made by the hiring sales manager.

Gall uses the applicants' resumes to formulate her interview questions, and all applicants must answer the same set of questions. This allows her to compare the quality of their responses. She also asks all interviewees to sell her something, and she expects candidates to show interest in the job by asking a lot of questions.

A candidate's day in the field with a sales representative is extremely important, Gall says. "Candidates need to witness the long days our reps spend on campus and be able to ask the reps questions about the job," she explains. The reps then provide Gall feedback about the suitability of the different candidates.

After phoning the candidate selected for a job offer, Gall gives the person a limited amount of time to either accept or reject the position depending upon the circumstances of the territory that needs to be filled. Prentice Hall does not currently require sales applicants to take tests or complete a physical exam. Although she says she has never had a candidate exaggerate his accomplishments, she believes that if she were to discover he hadn't been honest, she would exclude the person from further consideration.

Successful Hiring Requires Sales Managers to Follow a Process

By investing quality time and effort up front into a structured recruiting and selection process, a sales manager can determine the most appropriate type of individual needed for the job, attract sufficient numbers of applicants, and select the best-qualified person for the position. Aside from the huge costs related to hiring the wrong person, why is this so important? It's important because companies are discovering that every competitive advantage they have—except high-performing employees—can be duplicated by their competitors.[2] As a result, the successful recruitment and selection of salespeople has become a higher priority for sales managers.[3]

A comprehensive recruiting and selection process consists of five interrelated steps:

- determining the number of salespeople needed
- identifying the unique skills, knowledge, and attitudes a salesperson needs to do the job successfully
- attracting a sufficient number of applicants to form a pool of potential new hires
- conducting an interview process that accurately assesses the applicants' qualifications for the position
- offering a sales position to one or more applicants

Although larger firms may utilize human resource professionals to assist with the recruiting and selection process, in many organizations the task falls primarily upon the shoulders of sales managers. Therefore, sales managers should not view the selection and hiring of a new salesperson as a "knee-jerk" reaction, but rather that of following a methodical hiring process. ■

Planning to Hire

Sales managers and firms too often view the selection of representatives as a process that's initiated once there is a sales opening. But ideally, firms should have a sales selection process in place—one that considers factors such as the firm's strategy, predicted sales force turnover rate, the growth or shrinkage of sales territories, and the promotion and retirement of sales personnel. This is important because the longer a territory goes without a good salesperson working it, the more revenue the company can lose to a competitor. Moreover, good salespeople are hard to find, and turnover rates are generally high in the profession because many potential candidates have negative perceptions about working in sales. In a few industries, like the life insurance business, the turnover rates of salespeople can exceed 300 percent a year. This means that the average salesperson is hired and leaves the firm after just four months on the job! By contrast, Exhibit 8.1 shows that the turnover rate for U.S. employees as a whole is just a little over 22 percent. That's why many sales managers make recruiting an ongoing process and try to have a list of potential applicants on hand in case a sales position opens up.

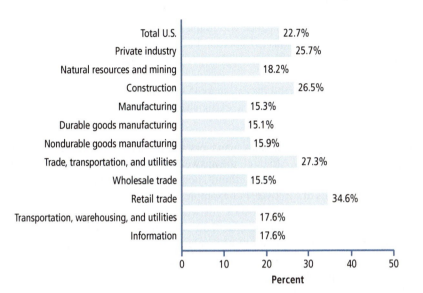

EXHIBIT 8.1

Annual Voluntary Turnover by Industry

Calculating the Turnover Rate

The **turnover rate** is the annual percentage of salespeople that leave the firm for both controllable and uncontrollable reasons, which are shown in Exhibit 8.2. The turnover rate can be computed as follows:

$$\text{Annual turnover rate} = \frac{\text{Number of salespeople that left the firm during the year}}{\text{Average sales force size during the year}}$$

$$= \frac{4}{25} = 16 \text{ percent}$$

A far more difficult task for the sales manager is determining exactly *why* salespeople are leaving the firm. To accurately understand this aspect, sales managers should ask themselves a series of pertinent questions:

- Who is leaving the firm? Are they primarily men, women, minorities, the young, or the old? If a larger percentage of salespeople in one category or another are leaving the firm, what's driving the decisions made by these people?
- How long has the average salesperson worked for the company? Are new salespeople seeking opportunities elsewhere after a short period of employment with the firm? Or are older, higher-performing workers leaving?

EXHIBIT 8.2

Controllable and Uncontrollable Reasons for Sales Force Turnover

Controllable	Uncontrollable
Retirement	Moving
Promotion	Marriage
Transfer	Death
Termination	Quitting
Territory changes	Returning to college
	Changing career

- What is the level of performance within the sales team? Are the highest-performing salespeople departing? This is important because the loss of a "sales star" to a rival firm is usually felt more deeply. Higher-performing salespeople are also more difficult to replace.
- What specific reason(s) did the salespeople give for resigning? Are they going elsewhere for higher salaries, better working conditions, management positions, or increased responsibility?

Usually firms require their sales managers and human resources personnel to jointly investigate these questions. Although the answers to these questions may reveal unpleasant truths about an organization, without such an analysis, the sales manager cannot address the root causes of turnover. For example, if the turnover rate is high among newly hired reps, a sales manager might look for ways to improve the training they receive. Perhaps mentors can help them increase their self-confidence during the first year(s) on the job. By contrast, if more senior salespeople are leaving the firm, it may be that alternate career plans can be developed to encourage them to remain with the firm. If a large percentage of salespeople are moving to positions in career fields outside of sales, perhaps the firm's current recruiting and selection process isn't painting a realistic view of what a sales job really entails.

That said, a zero percent turnover rate should also concern sales managers because they understand that some level of sales force turnover will occur no matter what policies are followed. Some salespeople will perhaps decide to move to a warmer state, get married or have children and need to work a different schedule, or choose to return to college or graduate school full-time, for example. Sales managers should also examine their firm's turnover rate in comparison to industry standards. This allows the sales manager to better understand whether turnover at their firm is higher or lower than those of competitors and whether it's being caused by the firm's environment or market forces. For example, if a sales manager finds that her company has a turnover rate of 22 percent, whereas the industry average is only 10 percent, she should consider issues like the firm's working conditions, pay, training, and the career stages of the salespeople leaving the firm.

Computing a turnover rate provides the sales manager with a starting point for understanding how many salespersons left the firm or were terminated during a defined time period. Next, we consider how a sales manager identifies the characteristics that job applicants should possess in order to succeed in the open sales position.

Conducting a Job Analysis

What personal characteristics or "objective profile" should sales managers seek when they look for candidates to fill an open sales position? One recent study found that good listening and time-management skills, the ability to follow up with customers, one's adaptability and tenacity (ability to stay on the task and keep pushing), and organizational skills are important predictors of a salesperson's success.[4] Finding sales representatives—both inside and outside the firm—with good organizational skills who can handle scores of small accounts—can be difficult. Sales managers also believe that it is important for candidates to have successful experience in the same industry.[5] Since sales jobs vary tremendously, it is essential for each firm to determine the characteristics that lead to the best representatives for the organization's purposes. Determining these characteristics or abilities requires the sales manager or human resource specialist to conduct a job analysis.

A **job analysis** is an objective examination of the duties, activities, and behaviors of people employed in a sales position. When sales managers lack the technical expertise or do not have the time to conduct a job analysis, a human resource specialist or consultant should be contacted for assistance. A comprehensive sales position analysis provides the hiring manager with an understanding of: (1) what a salesperson currently does on the job and (2) how the salesperson should ideally spend his or her time. To answer these questions, the person performing the job analysis should interview current salespeople and their sales supervisors. A job analysis may also involve conducting field observations, keeping field diaries, looking at sales reports, and getting feedback from customers. By observing how the more successful members of the sales force prioritize their time and activities, sales managers can identify successful on-the-job behavior.

Misunderstandings about what's expected of a person on the job underscore the importance of performing an accurate and current job analysis before taking actions to fill an open sales position. For example, a misunderstanding could occur if a sales manager tells a prospective salesperson that the job she's applying for involves forming a deeper relationship with the president of a purchasing firm, when, in reality, the buying firm expects the salesperson to be available 24/7 to expedite and process orders. When the expectations salespeople have about their jobs don't match the realities they face, their turnover will increase.[6]

Writing a Job Description

After conducting a comprehensive job analysis, a **job description**, like the one shown in Exhibit 8.3, is prepared. A job description for a salesperson should address:

1. The nature of the products and services the salesperson will sell.
2. Customer type(s) and the frequency with which they should be called upon.
3. The salesperson's specific tasks and responsibilities.
4. The relationship(s) between the salesperson and other people in the sales organization.
5. The intellectual and physical demands of the job.
6. Environmental factors affecting the sales position, such as the amount of travel required.
7. The compensation method used, for example, whether the salesperson will be paid a base salary plus commission, and, if so, what, or whether the position will be a commission-only position.

EXHIBIT 8.3

Job Description— Southeast U.S. Territory Manager

- Responsible for acquiring new business and developing partnerships at original equipment manufacturers (OEMs) in the Southeast United States.
- Coordinates sales, contracts, technical support teams, and internal sales assistants. Conducts long-range planning of OEMs to assure account penetration, customer satisfaction, sales growth, and profitability.
- Develops and plans account strategies and activities for assigned accounts to include: selecting accounts, selecting products for buyers, identifying buyer influences and concerns, introducing new products, making sales presentations, and negotiating contracts.
- Provides customer and competitor feedback to management.
- Attends and participates in industry sales conferences and trade shows.
- Required to operate independently and travel 50% of the time.
- Must possess strong knowledge of industry products and sales tactics, demonstrated organizational and planning skills, exceptional verbal and written communication skills, and computer proficiency.
- Bachelor's degree or equivalent in business or engineering required. Prefer an MBA degree and minimum of five years of related sales experience working with OEM firms.

Once a job description has been written and approved by management, the document can be utilized to develop a statement of job qualifications. For example, based on the identified job qualifications, the sales manager lists the necessary skills, knowledge, attitudes, and experience required of applicants. It should be clear that, without an accurate and current job analysis and job description that lists job qualifications, sales managers will have trouble selecting the best person from a pool of applicants. This initial stage of the process—that is, determining the qualifications for a new hire—is the most exacting part of the sales selection process.[7]

Sales managers make a mistake if they try to minimize the costs of recruiting salespeople in the false belief that training them can correct their individual weaknesses. This hiring strategy is fraught with danger because short-term training will seldom correct a salesperson's core deficiencies. To address this concern, some firms only hire experienced applicants who have proven track records, whereas other companies hire sales "neophytes" who require extensive training and mentoring. Thus, the sales manager must ensure—through the selection process—that the individual hired possesses the attributes listed in the job description.

Finding and Recruiting Applicants

Recruiting is the process firms use to find and hire the best qualified candidates for an open sales position. The recruiting step of the selection process is based upon accurate information gathered in the planning stage while forecasting turnover, conducting a comprehensive job analysis, and writing an accurate and concise job description. The sales manager must also determine an appropriate number of applicants that need to apply for the open position(s). To arrive at a suitable number of applicants, sales managers can employ the following formula:

$$\text{Annual turnover rate} = \frac{\text{Number of Applicants Needed}}{\text{\% of Applicants Selected} \times \text{\% of Acceptances}}$$

To estimate the number of applicants that need to be generated in the recruiting step, let's assume that a firm needs to hire two salespeople; that traditionally 10 percent of applicants who apply with the firm are offered a sales position; and 80 percent of them accept the offer. This would lead you to the following solution:

$$\text{Number of Applicants Needed} = \frac{2 \text{ open positions}}{.10 \text{ selected} \times .80 \text{ acceptance}} = 25$$

As you can see from this analysis, 25 applicants are needed to generate two quality hires. The number of applicants necessary to satisfy the total open sales position requirements is directly influenced by the total number of open sales positions, the percentage of applicants offered the position, and the percentage of applicants that accept the job offer. The number of applicants needed can be reduced by generating higher-quality candidates and offering them employment packages that result in higher acceptance rates.

Sales managers sometimes have a hard time generating a large enough pool of highly qualified applicants from which to fill an open sales position. When too few or low-quality applicants are generated, it's likely there is a problem with the sources utilized to find them. As a result, most firms look at several origins, including both internal and external sources to the company.

Recruiting Internal Applicants

Internal applicants are potential candidates for open sales positions that currently work for the company; perhaps as engineers, product managers, customer service representatives, buyers, or manufacturing managers. Many companies first look within their firms to find outstanding candidates: Managers already know a great deal about internal applicants, including their work habits, personality, and ability to assume more responsibility—information that is seldom known about external applicants. In any case, there remains a quandary about whether it is best to hire an external salesperson and teach them product knowledge or to hire an internal employee who knows little about selling. One study that looked at the pros and cons of hiring "from within" versus externally suggested that internal hires are more successful.[8] That said, internal candidates seldom possess sales experience, and managers from the firm's other functional areas will likely view internal recruiting less positively than the sales department. For example, when a first-rate engineer is selected for an open sales position, the engineering manager must subsequently initiate a job search to fill the open position created by the transfer. However, in industries in which buyers prefer purchasing from salespeople with strong engineering or scientific backgrounds, recruiting internal candidates with a technical background can be the better route to go.

External Applicants

Internal sources seldom produce either the quantity or the quality of candidates needed by the firm. In these cases a company must turn to external sources to identify applicants for open sales positions. **External applicants** are candidates for sales positions that are generated from a variety of sources that include: referrals, advertisements, private recruiters, educational institutions, job/career fairs and trade shows, and e-recruiting.

REFERRALS   There is a saying, "It's not what you know but who you know." Many sales managers look to referrals as first applicants. When current salespeople provide a sales manager with the names of friends or acquaintances that are seeking sales jobs, networking has occurred. **Networking** is the practice of forming relationships and consulting with other salespeople, executives, educational institutions, and friends to learn about positions that may or may not be publicly advertised. For example, members of the sales force sometimes know competing salespersons who have expressed a desire to be considered for future openings with the firm. Applicants can also network with contacts from the college or university they attended or with current employees at companies they are interested in

---

 ETHICS IN SALES MANAGEMENT

When Should a Sales Manager Raid Her Competitors' Sales Force?

Shannon Myers is sales manager for Rulagon, Inc., a firm that represents the largest chemical manufacturers in the world. Rulagon makes business-to-business sales to large, medium, and small manufacturers in Texas, Louisiana, Arkansas, and Tennessee. Two weeks ago, Richard Reason handed Shannon his resignation without warning to take a sales management job in Los Angeles. Since Richard was Rulagon's top salesperson, Shannon is very concerned about finding a highly competent replacement that can "hit the road running," so to speak. Yesterday, Janice Johnson informed Shannon that Jerry Hill, the top salesperson at AMC Chemical, Rulagon's biggest competitor, casually mentioned that he was looking for a better situation. Shannon would like to speak to Hill, since he is the top salesperson at AMC, but she believes this would be unethical. Shannon discusses her dilemma with the human resources director who tells her: "What is important is who contacts who. If Hill contacts you, you are obligated to speak to him." Do you agree or not with Shannon Myers about it being unethical for her to hire away a competitor's best salesperson? What are your reasons for your position?

joining at Web sites like LinkedIn (www.linkedin.com) and Ryze (www.ryze.com). Both sites promote their ability to facilitate business networking. At many firms, salespeople receive a bonus for referring applicants who eventually are offered positions with the firm and remain with it for a specific period of time. This helps motivate salespeople to provide their firms with qualified leads as well as do what they can to help the people they referred succeed once hired.[9]

Your customers can also be a good source of referrals. That is, you can ask customers with whom you have a good business relationship to refer highly qualified candidates that they come across in the course of doing business. However, take a look at the Ethics in Sales Management sidebar and, based upon the scenario, consider whether you would actively pursue competing salespeople for an open sales position.

ADVERTISEMENTS A universal method of finding sales applicants is by *advertising* in newspapers, magazines, and/or online. Technical and highly qualified applicants can be reached through trade publications or in special issues of newspapers like *USA Today* or the *Wall Street Journal*. Advertisements assume various forms, but most contain a format of information that includes:

A. The title of the job opening.
B. Minimum job qualifications.
C. Preferred job qualifications.
D. Location of the sales territory.
E. Expected travel time in field.
F. Discussion of pay and benefits.
G. Statement of core company values.
H. Who and how to contact the hiring firm.

Exhibit 8.4 shows some of the different kinds of advertisements sales managers run to generate interest in the positions they're trying to fill. **Blind advertisements** offer only a limited amount of information about the sales position and therefore tend to generate an applicant pool with a wide range of experience and qualifications. Often these jobs pay sales commissions only. In other words, the salesperson hired doesn't receive a regular salary. The sales managers hiring for commission-only jobs prefer blind ads so as not to disclose any potentially negative information because they would prefer to talk to candidates personally in an effort to stress or "sell" the more positive aspects of the job.

Advertisements that elicit a large pool of job seekers are ineffective unless a sufficient number of applicants are qualified for a personal interview. Conversely, generating too large an applicant pool can result in costly screening activities. The goal of a sales position advertisement is to generate sufficient numbers of *qualified* applicants for an open position so that managers can interview and select highly qualified applicants. In most cases, the more precisely the advertisement describes the minimum acceptable requirements, the higher the probability of attracting qualified applicants.

PRIVATE RECRUITERS For more complex sales positions, like technical and international sales, career counselors or "headhunters" from private recruiting firms are utilized to locate and conduct initial applicant screening. Examples of professional recruiting firms that specialize in sales positions include: Porter Group, Inc. (www.portergroup.com), Sales Ladder (www.sales-jobs.theladders.com), and Sales Recruiters, Inc. (www.salesrecruiters. com). Career counselors may specialize by industry or company and maintain a pool of applicants who would like to move up to higher paying and/or more challenging sales positions. Firms turn to professional recruiters to identify sales managers and sales executives more so than for finding entry-level or territory salespersons.

EXHIBIT 8.4

Open and Blind Advertisements for Salespeople: An Example of an Open Advertisement for a Sales Position

Regional Sales Manager

Bogen Communications, Inc., a leader in institutional and commercial sound, telephone paging, and business communications is currently seeking aggressive individuals to be a Regional Sales Manager in our Eastern Regions.

Must have strong history of sales success, selling through systems contractors & design community, with solid knowledge of Commercial Audio/Pro Sound markets and products. Extensive travel within the region is also required. Responsibilities include: Manage individual Sales Region to achieve business objectives by motivating, training, selling, and managing all Bogen customer types to meet the objectives of the region.

Bogen provides a competitive compensation and benefits package. Please take a look at our Web site: www.bogen.com.

If you are willing to work hard, you meet the above description, and thrive on building and maintaining excellent customer relationships and winning, send, fax, or e-mail your resume and salary requirements in confidence to:

Bogen Communications, Inc., Human Resources Manager, 50 Spring Street, Ramsey, NJ 07446. Fax 201-995-2061. E-Mail:hr@bogen.com.

An Equal Opportunity Employer

An Example of a Blind Advertisement for a Sales Position

SALES POSITION

Firm expanding territory. Salary and commission opportunity for selling technical products to small businesses. Appointments furnished. Sales experience preferred. Call 555-4303.

Sales managers sometimes criticize professional recruiters for being expensive and not producing long-term employees. In many cases, the recruiting firm receives a significant percentage of the first year's salary as compensation for finding and screening the new salesperson or manager. This means that sales managers must weigh each of these factors before signing a contract with a recruiting firm.

However, for busy sales managers at larger firms, private recruiters can save the manager significant time and frustration. To improve the likelihood of success, sales managers must provide private recruiters with specific applicant skill information that is derived from the job analysis and job description. Firms tend to reuse the same private recruiting firm when high-performing job candidates are hired and retained.

EDUCATIONAL INSTITUTIONS Colleges and universities can be excellent sources of applicants for firms seeking entry-level salespeople. This is because college graduates have demonstrated an ability to complete projects, solve problems, and remain focused on achieving long-term goals. Research shows that sales recruiters prefer collegiate applicants that are enthusiastic about selling, think outside the box, can work in a team setting, and demonstrate initiative.[10] Many colleges and universities maintain well-organized placement or career management centers that actively cooperate with potential employers.

College graduates normally require basic sales training and mentoring. However, there are a number of colleges and universities

Sales managers use different recruiting sources—including college and universities—to find their representatives. (Arlene Collins)

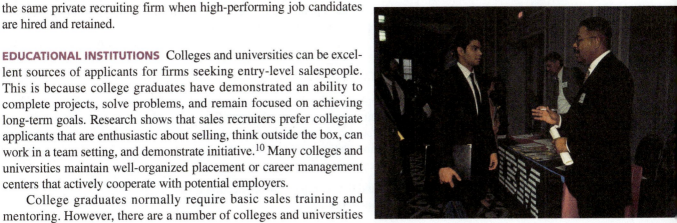

that offer undergraduate majors in professional sales. Students that major in professional sales are required to complete courses in sales management, professional selling, and business-to-business marketing, plus perform a sales internship. Firms like Hilti Corporation, an international manufacturer of construction products, are hiring new salespersons from University Sales Center Alliance (USCA) schools, a consortium of sales centers located at universities throughout the United States.[11] A recent study reported that professional sales graduates were in high demand and earned significantly higher salaries than marketing majors.[12]

JOB FAIRS/CAREER CONFERENCES AND TRADE SHOWS   **Job fairs** are career conferences jointly conducted by trade groups, student organizations, universities, cities, or business consortiums. Firms that have current or potential position openings can participate in the fairs and have sales and/or human resource representatives on hand at their booths to meet and talk with applicants. In effect, job fairs provide firms with an opportunity to conduct initial screening interviews with a large number of potential candidates and to identify a pool of individuals for formal interviews.

At trade shows, manufacturers and vendors sometimes post signs advertising open positions for distributors and sales agents. Salespeople also actively seek sales jobs at high-tech trade shows by handing out their resumes there and asking that they be passed on to the appropriate hiring person in the firm. Smart job seekers take the opportunity to ask tradeshow personnel questions to learn what it would be like to work at different firms. Recruiting reps at both job fairs/career conferences and trade shows can be accomplished at very little cost to the company.

E-RECRUITING   E-recruiting is becoming increasingly common, particularly since firms can quickly and economically generate a large pool of candidates using this method.[13] Potential applicants can go to a firm's Web site where job openings are posted on an electronic bulletin board. Job data banks are available at such sites as: www.sales.monster. com; www.acareerinsales.com; www.marketingjobs.com; www.ecruiter.com; and www. careerbuilder.com. Firms are even starting to post their job openings on Web sites, like Facebook® and MySpace®.[14]

Because the response to online ads can exceed expectations, many firms utilize key words to electronically evaluate and sort qualified from unqualified applicants. This process reduces the time managers must personally devote to the task. Of course, it is the total cost of generating applicants—finding interested personnel and screening the applications—that managers must consider when computing the cost of acquiring a pool of applicants for open sales positions. As we have pointed out repeatedly, the quality of the applicant pool is significantly more important than the size of the pool.

Selection Procedures

Once a pool of applicants for the sales position has been identified for further consideration, it is important to follow a formal interview process. An objective selection process allows the sales manager to assess the qualification levels of the applicant pool and gain essential information that is needed to select the best person for the job. The five stages of the selection process include:

- Having the candidate complete an application form.
- Testing the candidate.

- Personally interviewing the candidate.
- Verifying the candidate's background information.
- Conducting a physical exam (if necessary).

Application Forms

An **application form** is an electronic or paper form that asks the job candidate to provide a standard list of information about his or her background, education, and work experiences. Although most sales applicants initially submit an electronic or paper resume, there are a number of excellent reasons applicants are required to complete an application form. First, completed application forms provide managers with consistent information about candidates' formal education, former positions, start/stop dates, levels of responsibility, and supervisors. Also, application forms have to be signed by the candidates, thereby granting the firm legal permission to verify the information they provide.

Second, completing an application form requires a job candidate to read and follow directions, respond to questions, and express themselves, which offers sales managers an initial impression of the applicant. Some firms use screening software to check application forms submitted online for misspellings and improper grammar usage.

Third, sales managers can use the information gleaned from applications to develop personal interview questions. For example, a sales manager wanting to find out how well applicants planned during their college or university days might formulate a question as follows: "I see that you majored in English [or another subject] when you were a student at Duke University [or another University]. What motivated you to choose English as a major for your undergraduate studies?" Likewise, application forms provide sales managers with the opportunity to find inconsistencies in dates or other questionable entries that can be probed during personal interviews. An example of one area that may need further exploration during the personal interview is why someone has frequently changed employers. Studies show that a person's length of employment at one firm strongly influences how long the applicant will remain employed with a new firm.[15]

Application forms should not ask questions about an applicant's marital status, gender, religion, race, age, or handicaps. Firms and sales managers that solicit this information can be accused of illegal discrimination. Exhibit 8.5 outlines the various U.S. legislative acts that prohibit different types of discrimination. These legal standards are enforced by the Equal Employment Opportunity Commission (EEOC) and the Office of Federal Contract Compliance (OFCC). Firms can, however, inquire about an applicant's military service because they must generally report this information to the U.S. government as a condition of doing business with the government. A few applicants might deliberately add unrequested information about marital status, race, or gender on their application forms in an effort to establish a reason for not being hired. To avoid complaints of discrimination, the company should immediately inform these applicant(s) that any additional information of the sort added to the application form will result in the applicant being disqualified from further consideration.[16]

TESTING Firms test applicants to try to confirm what they have learned about candidates during the interview process. That is, testing offers managers another perspective of the applicant. A **psychological test** is a method of sampling small, representative sets of behavioral responses gathered under uniform conditions. The samples are then scored based upon predetermined rules or formulae.[17] A range of psychological tests are available to sales managers, including personality, intelligence, ability, aptitude, and emotional intelligence tests.

EXHIBIT 8.5

U.S. Legislative Acts Prohibiting Employment Discrimination

Civil Rights Act of 1964	Prohibits discrimination against any individual with respect to compensation, terms, conditions, or privileges of employment, because of race, color, religion, sex, or national origin.
Age Discrimination in Employment Act (1967)	Prohibits discrimination against an individual between 40–70 with respect to their compensation, terms, conditions, or privileges of employment.
Equal Employment Opportunity Act (1972)	Amends the Civil Rights Act of 1964 and empowers the Equal Employment Opportunity Commission (EEOC) to prevent any person from engaging in any unlawful employment practice.
Rehabilitation Act of 1973	Requires firms that employ 50 or more workers and that bid on federal contract in excess of $50,000, to affirmatively hire and promote handicapped workers.
Vietnam Era Veterans Readjustment Act (1974)	Requires employers with federal contracts or subcontracts of $25,000 or to provide equal opportunity and affirmative action for Vietnam-era veterans, special disabled veterans, and veterans who served on active duty during a war, campaign, or expedition.
Uniform Guidelines on Employee Selection Procedures (1978)	These guidelines are based upon and supersede previously issued guidelines on employee selection procedures. These guidelines have been built upon court decisions, the previously issued guidelines and practical experience of the agencies, as well as the standards of the psychological profession.
Americans with Disabilities Act (1990)	Prohibits discrimination against qualified individuals with disabilities in regard to job application procedures; hiring; advancement; or discharge of employees; employee compensation; job training; and other terms, conditions, and privileges of employment for firms with 15 or more workers.

Many sales managers utilize formal tests to identify traits they are looking for in sales candidates. (www.indexopen.com)

Personality tests are designed to measure personality traits that motivate sales applicants—traits such as empathy and ego. Since it is difficult to identify specific traits for a sales position, personality tests are the most difficult to validate. Examples of personality tests include the Multiple Personal Inventory and the Gordon Personal Profile. Firms use **intelligence tests** to estimate the quality of information acquired and used by the applicant. Intelligence tests, such as the Wonderlic Personnel Test, can be completed in 12 to 15 minutes. This test measures applicants' memory, reasoning, and verbal ability. Another intelligence test is the Otis Self-Administering Test of Mental Ability. A few firms also ask sales applicants to list their SAT Reasoning Test scores.

Ability tests are designed to estimate the current strengths and weaknesses of an applicant to effectively perform specific tasks, such as abstract reasoning and complex problem solving. For example, the Customer Contact Aptitude Series (CCAS) is an ability test that measures the core reasoning capabilities related to sales and customer service positions. **Aptitude tests**, which are similar to ability tests, measure an applicant's style of work, how

SELF-ASSESSMENT LIBRARY

There are many varieties of tests that employers utilize to screen new sales applicants. The tests look at an applicant's personality, aptitude, intelligence, ability, and emotional intelligence. Recently, firms have begun to look at an applicant's "emotional intelligence," which is a person's ability to process emotional intelligence as it relates to perception, assimilation, understanding, and management of human emotions. Have you ever wondered how adept you are at emotional intelligence? To learn how you fare in regard to emotional intelligence, go to http://www.prenhall.com/sal/, log in using the access code that came with your book. Then click on:

Assessments
 I. What About Me?
   E. Other
     1. What's My Emotional Intelligence Score?

the person interacts with other people, and whether the person has an interest in or ability to perform certain tasks, such as selling. The Campbell Interest and Skill Survey (www.pearsonassessments.com/tests/ciss.htm) is one such test. The applicant's aptitude test scores can be compared to the scores of the firm's current successful salespeople who have also taken the test. Obviously, then, aptitude testing is less appropriate for applicants who have no sales experience. Firms have started testing for **emotional intelligence**, which is an individual's ability to process emotional information as it relates to the perception, assimilation, understanding, and management of human emotion. Exhibit 8.6 provides examples of questions found on each of these tests.

Testing experts recommend that rather than relying on a single test score, like the SAT, sales managers should base their hiring decision on college grades, which are a more recent measure of a person's aptitudes.[18] In other words, grades show not only what the applicant has the ability to learn, but what he or she actually worked on and did learn. There are also additional tests that predict success in specific sales positions. One such test, pioneered by a subsidiary of International Risk Management Institute (IRMI) of Dallas, Texas, identifies the traits a salesperson needs in order to be successful. Early in the interview process, the applicant completes a 15- to 20-minute exam that identifies the person's traits. The results of the test provide interviewers with the common traits top (and bottom) sales candidates have, as well as "red flags" or concerns about the individual candidate being tested.

An IRMI spokesman claims that the exam goes beyond personality testing and determines whether candidates have the "thinking orientation to be good in sales and like it." Sales managers like the system because not only does it prevent them from hiring people with the wrong personalities for sales jobs, the test generates questions that allow them to customize the interview process for those candidates who are a good fit. The managers are also provided with appropriate answers for each question so they can compare candidates' answers.[19]

Regardless of the test administered, a firm must ensure it is "valid." That is, the test must differentiate applicants based upon who will be successful and unsuccessful on the job. If a test routinely indicates that men, women, minorities, or other members of society are less qualified, it's possible the test is biased. There are statistical procedures for validating these tests. If challenged to defend its tests in a legal venue, the firm will be required to provide this information to the courts.

EXHIBIT 8.6

Examples of Questions Asked on Different Sales Hiring Tests

Personality Test Questions

Applicants are asked to respond on a scale with anchors of Strongly Agree to Strongly Disagree

1. I get stressed out easily.
2. I put others first.

Intelligence Test Questions

Respondents answer each question as being True or False

1. Two of the following numbers add up to 13: 1, 6, 3, 5, 11.
2. A pie can be cut into more than 7 pieces by making only 4 diameter cuts through its center.

Ability Test Questions

In question 1, the answer is one-half of the previous number of .125, which is presented as a multiple-choice response.

In question 2, Grace should aim her kick at point B. This is presented as a multiple-choice response.

1. What number comes next in the following sequence? 16, 8, 4, 2, 1, .5, .25, ?
2. Grace wants to kick a ball to John. At what point below should Grace aim her kick?

```
   Grace        John
     X             X
   A     B     C     D
```

Aptitude Test Questions

Applicants are asked to respond on a scale with anchors of Strongly Agree to Strongly Disagree

1. I like to study and solve math or science problems.
2. I like to lead and persuade people and sell ideas and things.

Emotional Intelligence Test Questions

Applicants are asked to respond on a scale with anchors of Strongly Agree to Strongly Disagree

1. I do not get angry when verbally attacked.
2. In my life the stress never ends.

Sales managers are often skeptical about the likelihood of tests to predict the future sales success of candidates—and with good reason: Research has shown that no one personality or mental ability test will determine a salesperson's success.[20] This finding supports the recommendation that testing should be utilized as a confirming factor in the selection process—not an eliminating factor.[21] No applicant should be denied employment based upon a personality or mental ability test when all other factors paint an entirely different picture of the applicant.

Sales managers view the personal interview as the most important aspect of the hiring process (Chabruken/Taxi/ Getty Images)

The Personal Interview

The personal interview is considered by many people to be the most important stage in the hiring process because managers heavily rely on it—especially because testing applicants can be expensive. During **personal interviews**, job candidates appear before the firm's sales managers and other employees. In most hiring situations, sales applicants are interviewed by two to three sales managers or company personnel who use different sets of questions or role-plays to confirm that the candidate possesses the characteristics the firm desires. After completing multiple interviews, it is important for the managers to compare the information they gathered during the interviews and come to a consensus about that information. Next, we discuss a variety of different types of interviews sales managers typically conduct.

STRUCTURED INTERVIEWS A **structured interview** means that, prior to meeting with applicants, the sales manager or interview team prepares a list of questions along with a range of acceptable answers, like the ones shown in Exhibit 8.7. The questions and answers are designed to cut across an applicant's background, work experiences, formal education, sales experience, and hobbies. In a structured interview all applicants are asked the same questions.

Structured interviews have several advantages. First, if the sales manager is new at interviewing applicants, a structured interview offers confidence and "structure" to the process. Second, this approach ensures that important areas are covered during the interview because managers have a prepared list of questions to ask. Finally, standard questions make it easier to record and compare applicants' responses. When multiple interviewers conduct an interview, a structured interview more readily allows them to compare their notes and discuss the answers applicants provided.

One criticism of structured interviews is that less experienced sales managers may simply follow the questions on the list and not probe for responses that deviate from the expected answers. For example, the interviewer might focus on reading the questions and recording the applicant's responses rather than critically evaluating the applicant. After asking a question, a sales manager needs to evaluate the answer, probe further when necessary, and take sufficient notes with which to compare candidates later.

Questions:	Listen For:	List & Rate Answer +/-:
What has been your proudest achievement?	Cites examples of his or her selling success.	
Have you ever gone against others to do something you believed was right?	Yes, offers a clear example.	
What do you like about being in sales?	Independence, unlimited earning potential, helping others.	
How do you persuade reluctant buyers?	By finding and satisfying the buyer's need(s).	
Why do you want to work for this company?	He or she can help the firm grow and/or satisfy buyers' needs.	
What kind of boss do you work best with?	A boss who allows freedom, communicates expectations, and helps as needed.	
Some people like to plan their day's activities in advance. How do you do this?	Offers a specific, detailed strategy.	
What have you found to be the best way to change someone else's mind?	By appealing to their needs, feelings, and concerns.	
What is the best way to develop your specific life goal?	By focusing on family, contributing to the firm and society.	
You have a buyer who wants to buy immediately, but you are not sure the product is right for the buyer. What do you do?	Would not sell the product until certain it is what the customer needs and he or she will be truly satisfied with it.	

EXHIBIT 8.7

Structured Interview Questions and Answers

SEMI-STRUCTURED INTERVIEWS A **semi-structured interview** allows sales managers to ask a series of open-ended questions that applicants can address in their own words. An example of a semi-structured question might be: "Why are you interested in a sales position?" Then, after the interviewee answers, "I enjoy the freedom and travel," the sales manager can delve more deeply by asking: "What do you enjoy specifically about business travel?" The belief is that a semi-structured interview allows the interviewer to gain insight about the applicant as the discussion moves along a natural, logical course. Some firms extend the semi-structured interview by asking detailed questions about actual situations. For example, the interviewee might be instructed: "Tell me about a time when an irate buyer called you, what had upset them, and how you successfully handled the situation." In a semi-structured interview, the sales manager or interviewer must identify areas that require more probing and be able to redirect the discussion should it veer off course. According to one study, structured interviews are twice as reliable as semi-structured interviews in predicting how well a person will perform on the job.[22] Firms use semi-structured interviews more often when interviewing candidates for higher-level sales management jobs. The goal in this situation isn't to try to assess whether the candidate has given the "right or wrong" answers, but to gain a sense of his or her overall strategic sales vision for the firm. A semi-structured interview is more likely to lend itself to this purpose.

OTHER TYPES OF INTERVIEWS Firms often employ role-playing or field exercises during the interview process. In a **stress interview**, the interviewer places the applicant in an unstructured situation to see how well he or she will perform. For example, an applicant might be asked to sell the interviewer an item, like a pen, ashtray, or piece of furniture, to demonstrate his or her selling skills. The basic premise is that if the salesperson makes a solid attempt to sell whatever they are asked to sell, then there is a higher likelihood the applicant does not suffer from call reluctance.

A myriad of role-playing techniques can be used in a stress interview.[23] For example, the interviewer can act like a customer by ignoring the applicant, being rude and obnoxious, being inquisitive, or sitting in silence waiting for the applicant to react. It is important for sales managers to have a predetermined range of acceptable responses in mind when conducting role-plays. In other words, sales managers need to decide what the applicant must or must not do to pass the stress interview. For example, they might agree to eliminate applicants who negatively respond to confrontational "customers" (in this case, the interviewers).

A sales applicant can also find themselves in a group or panel interviews. In the **group interview**, a group of applicants for the position are placed in a group or open forum and encouraged to ask questions. Applicants are favored that ask insightful questions rather than sitting quietly in the group. A second type of **panel interview** involves placing a single applicant before a panel of two or more company representatives. In effect, the interviewers play off one another's questions. In this situation it is important for the applicant to maintain their composure and maintain eye contact with all members of the panel.[24]

Another form of stress or "surprise" interview is the field observation or "ride along." A **field observation** allows an applicant to travel with and observe a salesperson making sales calls on current and potential clients. As we explained at the beginning of the chapter, this is what Prentice Hall does. This activity gives sales force applicants a realistic view of the job for which they are applying. Is it the type of job the candidate wants to do every day, for example? Firms can also have applicants attend a social function to gauge their fit with the sales team or ask candidates to brainstorm a problem with the sales team. Stress exercises allow sales managers to observe how the applicant behaves and interacts in a day-to-day business environment. A sales manager should understand, however, that if any interview is too stressful, the applicant might become discouraged and look elsewhere for employment. Firms that use stress and role-play interviews do so in conjunction with either structured or semi-structured interviews.

Background Verification

The past performance of a candidate is, of course, a potential indicator of the person's future performance. It is not unusual, however, for candidates to exaggerate or even lie about their past performance. In fact, one study reported that human resource managers *routinely* observe job candidates exaggerating their educational requirements, salaries, or time working for former employers.[25] That's why it's so important for sales managers, human resource personnel, or independent background checking firms to verify the information candidates put on their application forms.

One way to gauge the honesty of applicants is to ask judgment-neutral questions[26] on the application form—questions such as the applicant's starting and ending dates of employment, position(s) and ranks held, accounts managed, level of sales, sales training completed, and, where permissible, salary earned. If background checks uncover the applicant has given false information, this raises questions about the applicant's basic honesty, trustfulness, and reliability. (One of the authors of this book watched a former student lose a job offer for a sales position by claiming his final collegiate grade point average was 3.20 when, in fact, it was 3.18!)

Sales managers also need to contact the references listed by candidates they are seriously considering hiring, but understand that applicants have most likely referred only those individuals who will say positive things about them. It is also helpful to require applicants to provide different categories of references. That is, business references such as former clients or employers, financial references like banks and financial institutions, and educational references such as professors or counselors. To get a more independent assessment, you can ask a reference if he or she knows anyone else you can contact—someone who is familiar with the candidate's work. Many firms routinely conduct credit checks from providers such as Equifax®. Firms that hire salespeople who are responsible for handling money are more likely to conduct credit and more extensive background checks.

Physical Exam

The final stage of the selection process is the physical exam. Firms used to require drug tests and physical exams as part of their normal hiring procedures, but the Americans with Disabilities Act of 1990 prohibits preemployment physicals. However, once the job offer has been extended, the employer can require all applicants to complete a medical exam that focuses on job-related physical requirements. It is not permissible for the firm to ask whether the applicant *has* a disability or to ask about the severity of an obvious disability.[27] A job offer may not be made conditional upon the results of a medical exam.[28] However, the firm can legally ask the following type of question if there are certain physical abilities related to the job: "The job involves lifting 25-lb. boxes on a regular basis. Is this something you would be able to accomplish?"

Making the Job Offer

Once all applicants have completed the interview process, the sales manager or interview team normally ranks each applicant in terms of their fit and potential for contributing to the firm. Then the sales manager contacts the top applicant to make a job offer. The sales manager should call the top applicant and ask if he or she is still interested in a sales position with the company. If the answer is "yes," then the sales manager should describe the position's responsibilities and make the job offer.

Sometimes applicants attempt to delay accepting the position, especially if they are highly competent, have interviewed with several firms, and are waiting on more than one job offer. That's why after talking with the applicant on the phone the sales manager should send the finalist a first-class letter containing a formal offer of employment. The letter should clearly state a deadline for accepting the position as well as information concerning the salesperson's responsibilities, starting salary, allowable moving expenses, formal training dates, time before his or her first performance review, when he or she will first be eligible for a raise, and the number of vacation days he or she has been allotted.

This completes the standardized process sales managers utilize when hiring new salespersons for their firm. As Exhibit 8.8 shows, the sales manager uses application forms, tests, formal interviews, background checks, and physicals to insure the applicants meet the standards established earlier in the process. Should an applicant not meet a standard, as shown in Exhibit 8.8, they are rejected. Even after being hired, managers must remember to evaluate the performance of new hires and then add that information to the standards they seek when they are hiring future salespeople.

Transitioning New Hires

Because of the strategic importance of hiring high-quality sales personnel, the sales manager must often go beyond simply making a job offer to the best candidate. For example, allowing high-level job offer recipients and their spouses a tour of the area in which they will be working can provide them with an understanding of what life would be like if they accepted the offer. Sales reps, like all employees, want to feel respected and assured that the company is a good fit for them. Showing that your company is a unique or exciting

EXHIBIT 8.8

Model for Selecting New Salespersons

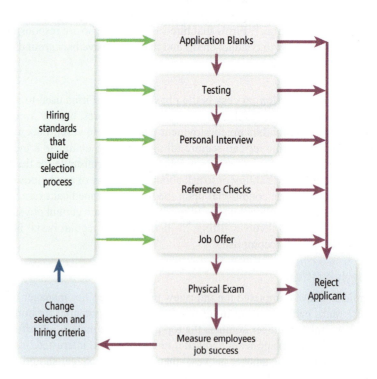

place to work can also help seal the deal. Emphasizing the selling points of the job itself and the career development opportunities that exist, as well as selling the company's image and brand, can increase the appeal of the sales opportunity.

Once a candidate accepts the job, the sales manager's role shifts to building the new sales hire's commitment to the company and enhancing his or her ability to succeed on the job. (It can also be helpful to ask what persuaded the person to say "yes" and what he or she thought of each company contact and the hiring process.) Many companies send company handbooks, product sheets, work materials, and other job and company information that can ease the new hire's transition. Sending a welcome package of apparel, pens, etc. with the company name or logo can help the new hire feel that their decision is "official" and help to build commitment. If the new hire is not scheduled to begin work for a few months, as is often the case with people who are about to graduate from college, regular telephone calls and e-mails from the new hire's coworkers and sales manager can help maintain the person's enthusiasm for the position. Lastly, if the new hire lives within a reasonable distance, inviting the new hire to celebrations, meetings, and other activities can help in transitioning the recruit to his or her new job.

Why a Diverse Sales Force Is Important

Today the growth of the U.S. population is being fueled by racial and ethnic minorities. Hispanics accounted for almost half of the population growth (40%) between 2000 and 2004, and total 41.3 million persons living in the United States. In California alone more than 10 percent of the population is Asian. The Asian population matched the Hispanic growth by 17 percent during this same period, whereas the African American population increased by more than 5 percent. Hispanic growth was driven by two factors: immigration and, perhaps more importantly, domestic births. Given these trends, sales managers and salespersons must understand that more than 110 languages are spoken in the United States today, and by 2050, non-Anglo Americans will comprise nearly half of the U.S. population.[29]

A sales manager must remain abreast of the changing marketplace and how a demographic shift increases the need to hire a more diverse sales force that reflects the buying community being served. To increase the diversity of a firm's sales force, and to prosper in a changing marketplace, firms and their sales managers must:

Good sales managers understand the many benefits of hiring a diverse sales force that mirrors the marketplace.
(Jon Feingersh/Iconica/ Getty Images)

- Institute recruiting and selection procedures that do not discriminate against candidates based upon nationality, ethnicity, age, and/or gender.
- Offer opportunities for older salespersons to work later in their lives.
- Recognize that not all families are traditional, which results in differing employee needs for parental leave, on-site childcare, job sharing, switching between full- and part-time responsibilities, and adoption support.

A number of firms have increased their partnerships with the National Black MBA Association and Historically Black Colleges and Universities (HBCU) in order to increase the level of recruitment of high-quality minority candidates.

The need to hire a diverse workforce has become even more important because so many businesses today are expanding globally to either remain or become more competitive. As the Global Sales Management feature in this chapter shows, companies look to staff their global sales forces in a variety of ways. Complicating factors for sales managers when selecting a global salesperson include culture and language. During the selection process, applicants raised in another culture are unlikely to respond the same way as local candidates. For example, in collectivist cultures—that is, cultures that are group-oriented—it is unlikely the applicant will try to sell himself. If the candidate was raised in a culture with high "power distance," or the belief that managers are of higher status, he or she is likely not to ask the hiring managers questions but rather will wait to be spoken to by the higher-status sales manager. Also, in some cultures it is considered aggressive or rude to look directly at someone for long periods of time. A U.S. sales manager might mistakenly believe that a candidate who looks away when talked to cannot be trusted.[30]

In the final analysis, however, a firm's sales effort is no better than the weakest member of the sales team. It is up to the sales manager to ensure the best qualified candidates are hired for open sales positions both domestically and abroad regardless of their age, gender, culture, marital status, race, or religion.

Avoiding Common Hiring Mistakes

Finding and hiring the "right" person for an open sales job is difficult unless the sales manager adheres to a comprehensive recruiting and selection process. Sales managers should be especially careful to avoid making the following mistakes:

RUSHING TO HIRE SOMEONE Sales managers often fall into the trap of wanting to hire someone quickly to cover open sales territories and don't look hard enough at candidates' actual capabilities and interests. Not only can such an approach result in the wrong representative being hired, it can result in the sales manager recruiting people with similar backgrounds, educational attainment, or social interests as themselves rather than diverse employees. Moreover, if the wrong person is hired and either quits or fails shortly thereafter, this leaves the sales manager in a worse position than if he or she had taken time to conduct a proper search initially.

FAILING TO CONDUCT A PROPER JOB ANALYSIS Sales managers are busy with day-to-day activities. Still, they must find time to evaluate the jobs they're trying to fill so as to identify essential skills, knowledge, and activities that the new hire should possess to succeed. This is especially true if the products and the way the firm is selling them are changing or the company's customer base is changing.

NOT GENERATING A SUFFICIENTLY LARGE APPLICANT POOL The goal is to have a large enough group of qualified individuals from which to select the best applicants to be interviewed and hired. Too often, sales managers interview only a handful of applicants because doing so is less work and consumes less time.

POOR INTERVIEW PLANNING Oftentimes sales managers interview candidates "off the cuff." This can often result in a poor set of interviews being conducted or a set of interviews that aren't easily comparable. Another pitfall can occur when multiple interviewers from the firm are used and no one takes the time to coordinate and train them to properly interview candidates.

NOT CONDUCTING A COMPREHENSIVE INTERVIEW Too often sales managers ask a few questions and then decide whether or not they will hire the candidate. They believe, incorrectly, that their own experience as a successful sales representative allows them to make accurate hiring decisions on the spot.

GLOBAL SALES MANAGEMENT

Who Should You Hire to Represent Your Company Abroad?

The people who comprise global sales forces can be classified into three categories: *expatriates*, *local nationals*, and *third-country nationals*. The positive and negative aspects of hiring salespeople from each of these groups are presented:

Expatriates

Expatriates are salespeople or managers who are transferred abroad from the home country of the firm. For example, a U.S. citizen transferred from Atlanta to London for a three-year tour fits into this category. Firms prefer expatriates because they understand the company and its policies, usually possess extensive technical experience, and have been involved in a broad range of successful projects. They also know who to contact in the home office to get things accomplished. The downside is that expatriates are more difficult to recruit and are more expensive to maintain overseas. And expatriates that do not speak or understand the local language and/or culture of the country to which they are transferred are obviously at a disadvantage.

Local Nationals

Local nationals, or personnel from the country in which the firm has a foreign operation, understand the country's marketplace and culture and are familiar with local distribution and referral systems. Because they don't need to be moved, these people are also often easier to recruit and less expensive to hire than expatriates. American companies are often able to find candidates among the ranks of foreign nationals who have earned degrees in the United States and seek positions with global firms in their home countries.

But there are disadvantages related to hiring local sales forces, too. First, the firm's personnel at headquarters sometimes ignore the suggestions local salespeople and managers provide them, perhaps because the locals are less assertive due to their cultures or have limited English language skills. And in some countries, well-qualified local hires are difficult to find. For example, one study reported that there are currently 10 openings in China for every qualified manager available there for hire. In addition, in hierarchical societies like Japan and Mexico, salespeople are viewed as being at the bottom of the social ladder. This makes it more difficult to hire the best college students for sales positions in countries such as these.

Third-Country Nationals

Third-country nationals work for a global company in a third nation. An example would be a Malaysian national, who works in the Philippines for a U.S. firm. Many third-country nationals speak several languages and understand specific industries or markets. Firms that are globalizing often like to hire these people. Not surprisingly, the number of them working for foreign companies has increased in recent years. In fact, many executives working for global firms like Coca-Cola, General Motors, and Unilever are citizens of diverse countries working in other nations. For example, Neville Isdell, the CEO of Coca-Cola, is a native of Ireland. Isdell has worked for Coca-Cola in many countries around the world, including Zambia, South Africa, Australia, the Philippines, and Germany.

The drawbacks related to hiring third-country nationals include the following: They may feel less of an allegiance to the firm than expatriates do, and initially they are less likely to possess the amount of knowledge of the company and its products than expatriates possess.

Source: Based on Earl D. Honeycutt, Jr., John B. Ford, and Antonis C. Simintiras (2003). *Sales Management: A Global Perspective*. London: Routledge.

FAILING TO PERFORM A BACKGROUND CHECK   A recent study found that as many as 20 percent of applicants fabricate facts and accomplishments on their resume and application form. When a sales manager fails to check a candidate's facts prior to offering them a sales job, this increases the likelihood of hiring someone with a dubious character. Always conduct a thorough background check.[31]

Evaluating the Success of the Firm's Sales Force Recruiting and Selection Efforts

Because recruiting and selection consume so much of the firm's resources and sales managers' time, it is imperative that an evaluation of applicant sources be performed. In effect, an evaluation allows the sales manager to determine the effectiveness of each applicant source. A matrix, similar to the one shown in Exhibit 8.9, can be used to track sales applicant sources on a computer spreadsheet program. Sales executives can also utilize the information derived from the management tool to evaluate the skills of field sales managers who are responsible for selecting and hiring new salespersons.

EXHIBIT 8.9

Using a Matrix to Evaluate the Sources of Your Applicants' Evaluation Criteria

Sales Applicant Sources	Strategic or Opportunistic Hire?	Number of Applicants Generated	Number of Applicants Hired	Percent Retained After Three Years	Cost	Number of Times Used	Percent with Above Average Performance After Two Years
Internal Applicants • Technical • Nontechnical							
Referrals • Internal • External							
Advertisements • Newspapers • Magazines							
Private Recruiters							
Educational Institution • Four-Year • Two-Year							
Electronic Web Sites • Internal • External							
Job/Career Fairs							

Summary

Hiring a salesperson is an extremely important undertaking by the firm. The five steps related to hiring are as follows: determining the number of salespersons needed; identifying the skills, knowledge, and attitudes salespersons need to succeed; attracting a sufficient number of qualified applicants; performing an interview process that assesses applicants' qualifications; and offering one or more applicants a sales position. In smaller firms, sales managers are generally responsible for these activities; however, in larger firms one or more of these activities are performed by human resource personnel.

By conducting a thorough job analysis and writing an accurate job description, a sales manager can accurately assess the qualifications needed to do a job. The job's qualifications can then be posted in advertisements designed to generate applicants. Sales managers use a variety of sources to generate applicants: referrals, advertisements, job fairs, universities, and Web job sites. The interview or selection process includes application forms, testing, personal interviews, background checks, and physical exams.

The personal interview is the most important part of the process. Sales managers can use structured and semi-structured interviews, but structured interviews have been proven to be most effective. Other personal interview techniques include role plays, stress interviews, and field observations.

Common mistakes sales managers make when managing the hiring process include rushing to fill an open sales position, failing to perform an accurate job analysis, generating too few applicants, devoting inadequate time preparing for formal interviews, conducting an abbreviated interview, and omitting background checks on finalists. Making any one of these mistakes will result in the manager hiring the wrong applicant.

Key Terms

ability tests   172
application form   171
aptitude tests   172
blind advertisements   168
emotional intelligence   173
external applicants   167
field observation   176
group interview   176
intelligence tests   172
internal applicants   166
job analysis   164
job description   165

job fairs   170
networking   167
panel interview   176
personal interviews   174
personality tests   172
psychological test   171
recruiting   166
semi-structured interview   176
stress interview   176
structured interview   175
turnover rate   163

Questions and Problems

1. Should a firm's selection process be initiated whenever there is an opening? Or should the process be ongoing? Would the hiring effort vary by firm size or industry?
2. Suppose a firm typically employees 15 salespeople. During the course of the year, 2 salespeople leave the firm for higher paying jobs, 1 salesperson is fired, and 1 salesperson retires. What will the turnover rate of the firm's salespeople be for the year?

3. Why should sales managers investigate reasons for turnover? Why is it important to compare a firm's turnover against industry turnover rates?

4. What benefits are likely to be gained by conducting a job analysis? What options does a sales manager have to analyze how a salesperson performs their duties? How is the information gathered and a job analysis utilized?

5. How are job descriptions and statements of job qualifications related? Why is it difficult to determine the necessary qualifications for a new hire?

6. How many applicants should be recruited if a firm needs to hire three salespeople, 20 percent of applicants are offered a job, but only 50 percent accept the offer?

7. What are the advantages and disadvantages of recruiting internal versus external candidates for sales positions? Discuss the four types of tests that firms rely upon when screening candidates. Why is it important for firms to validate the tests they use?

8. Why is the personal interview the most important step in the sales selection process? What are the advantages and disadvantages of structured and semi-structured interviews? What can a sales manager learn about a candidate by conducting a stress test or requiring a field observation?

9. Why is it important to conduct a background check on a candidate prior to offering them a sales position? What specific information should be verified by a background check? Can a firm require a candidate to take a physical exam prior to being offered the sales position?

10. Why is it important for sales managers to try to increase the diversity of their sales forces?

Role Play

WRT Plans for Salesperson Interviews

Howard Olsen manages the sales effort at WRT, located in Phoenix, Arizona. Next week, six finalists will visit the office for personal interviews for an open sales position. Olsen realizes that the personal interview is an extremely important component of the selection process and that in order to be as objective as possible he must have a plan to minimize subjectivity and bias during the interviews. Olsen prefers a structured interview process; he will review a list of 15 standard questions he has used in the past and make sure they are in line with the open position. He understands that he must meet with Human Resources to ensure the selection process is handled within the confines of existing laws. Olsen has also asked Larry Penley to conduct an unstructured interview with all six applicants. Lastly, Olsen wants each applicant to ride along with current salespersons to provide a stress situation that offers a different view of the applicants. The question is: How should all of these activities be planned and coordinated?

Characters in the Role Play

Howard Olsen, Sales Manager at WRT
Larry Penley, Marketing Manager at WRT
Laura Williams, Human Resource Director at WRT

Assignment

Break into groups of three, with each student in the group assuming the role of each character. Do not be concerned about matching the gender of the character with the actual gender mix of the student group. Prior to meeting as a group, work individually to review and compile your plans for conducting structured, unstructured, and ride-along interviews for each of the six finalists for the sales position at WRT. Then meet and role-play the meeting between Howard, Larry, and Laura. The goal is to conclude the meeting with an interview plan that is both logical and legal.

Caselet 8.1: Southeastern Industrial

James Johnson is regional sales manager for Southeastern Industrial, a supplier of industrial products for manufacturers of computer peripherals located in the seven southeastern U.S. states. Although Johnson's region has met its total sales and profitability goals during the past three years he has been sales manager, he is concerned about his region's turnover rate. The first year he was sales manager, the turnover rate was15 percent, followed by a rate of 18 percent the second year, and a 22 percent rate the third year.

Each of the salespeople who resigned offered good reasons for leaving. A few were old enough to retire, one or two found better paying jobs, and, unfortunately, two salespeople just did not meet our standards and had to be let go. Johnson would like to reduce the annual turnover rate to below the industry average of 12 percent per year. He plans on analyzing the situation over the next month, talking to others both inside and outside the firm, and making a proposal to upper management to revamp the recruitment and selection process.

Questions

1. What recommendations would you offer James Johnson for evaluating the current recruitment and selection process at Southeastern Industrial?
2. How would it help to compare the performance of each salesperson who either resigned or was let go?
3. Would it be helpful for Johnson to know how each salesperson was originally recruited?
4. Should Johnson scrutinize the notes from the former salespeople's personal interviews or their preemployment test scores? Assuming these items were available, what insight might they give Johnson?
5. How would you recommend that Southeastern recruit and select new salespersons?

Caselet 8.2: Harmony International

Win Ho is a Chinese American who was born in San Francisco, attended UC-Davis for his undergraduate business degree and then earned an MBA at Stanford. Ho is currently the Asian regional sales manager for Harmony International. His sales force is comprised of local hires (salespeople from the country in which they sell). One of Harmony's reps in Singapore recently left the firm to attend graduate school at the country's prestigious National University. Ho recently traveled to Singapore to interview the three finalists generated by a Singaporean search firm. The candidates were:

1. Chin Lo Wien, a Chinese Singaporean with a B.S. in Business from Nanyang University in Singapore. Although Chin has no sales experience, he has good connections in the Chinese business community. Chin answered 7 of the 10 structured interview questions correctly, attempted to sell an expensive pen when asked, and told Win Ho that the job with Harmony was his "dream job."

2. C. R. Rao, an Indian Singaporean with a B.S. in Chemical Engineering from the University of Madras. Rao has two years of newspaper advertising sales experience. However, he answered only 5 of the 10 structured questions satisfactorily and balked at selling a pen to Win Ho. Rao even appeared arrogant and admitted he had several job leads he was considering.

3. Mohammed Asri Ashraf, a Malaysian with Singaporean citizenship. Asri has an MBA from the Malaysian International University in Kuala Lumpur. He provided correct answers to 8 of the 10 structured interview questions and made a solid attempt to sell the pen to sales manager Ho. However, one thing that bothered Ho was Asri's lack of eye contact and his subservient behavior, exemplified by his answering questions by saying, "Sir, I would . . ." or "Sir, the best way to . . ."

The territory that Harmony is seeking a salesperson for is a mixture of Chinese (85%), Malaysian (10%), and Indian (5%) businesses. Based upon the limited amount of information you have, which candidate do you believe Ho should hire?

Questions

1. How helpful would a job description/qualifications be in this situation?
2. Given that the territory is predominantly Chinese, how should this influence Ho's decision?
3. Can you identify factors that might disqualify any of the finalists?
4. What explanation might you offer for Asri's behavior during the interview?
5. What is your recommendation for Ho? Why did you reach this decision?

References

1. Shamis, Barry (2007). "Have You Ever Thought About the Cost of Hiring the Wrong Salesperson?" www.salesrephire.com. Accessed May 27, 2007.
2. Jordan, Jason (2006). 2006 World Class Sales Force Benchmark Executive Summary, The HR Chally Group, www.chally.com/benchmark/index.html. Accessed 5/9/2008.
3. Burton, Scott E. (2002). "The Realization of Human Capital Advantage through Recruiting and Selection," Development Dimensions International, Inc. White Paper, 1–7.
4. Marshall, Greg W., Daniel J. Goebel, and William C. Moncrief (2003). "Hiring For Success at the Buyer-Seller Interface," *Journal of Business Research* 56, 247–255.
5. McMaster, Mark (2001). "Ask SMM," *Sales & Marketing Management* December, 58.
6. Naumann, Earl, Scott M. Widmier, and Donald W. Jackson (2000). "Examining the Relationship Between Work Attitudes and Propensity to Leave Among Expatriate Salespeople," *Journal of Personal Selling & Sales Management* Fall, 227–241.
7. Churchill, Gilbert A., Jr., Neil M. Ford, Steven W. Hartley, and Orville C. Walker, Jr. (1985). "The Determinants of Salesperson Performance: A Meta-Analysis," *Journal of Marketing Research* May, 103–118.
8. Campbell, Tricia (1999). "Finding Hidden Sales Talent," *Sales & Marketing Management*, March, 84.
9. Soltis, Cheryl (2006). "Got a Good Hire? Your Reputation May Be on the Line," *Wall Street Journal* September 26, B8.
10. Raymond, Mary Anne, Les Carlson, and Christopher D. Hopkins (2006). "Do Perceptions of Hiring Criteria Differ for Sales Managers and Sales Representatives? Implications for Marketing Education," *Journal of Marketing Education* 28 (April), 43–55.

11. Simon, Baylee (2006). "The Paper (Money) Chase," *Sales & Marketing Management* July/August, 38–40, 42–43.
12. Weilbaker, Dan C., and Michael Williams (2006). "Recruiting New Salespeople from Universities: University Sales Centers Offer a Better Alternative," *Journal of Selling & Major Account Management* 6:3 (Summer) 30–38.
13. Piturro, Marlene (2000). "The Power of E-cruiting," *Management Review* 89:1 (January) 33–37.
14. Anonymous (2007). "Recruiting with Facebook," *The Week* February 2, 5.
15. McMaster (2001).
16. Gable, Myron, Charles Hollon, and Frank Fangello (1992). "Increasing the Utility of the Application Blank: Relationship between Job Application Information and Subsequent Performance and Turnover of Salespeople," *Journal of Personal Selling & Sales Management* (Summer) 39–55.
17. Dudley, G.W. (2007). "Sales Selection: Mental Testing," Working Paper. Dallas, TX: Behavioral Science Research Press, Inc.
18. Dunham, Kemba J. (2003). "More Employers Ask Job Seekers For SAT Scores," *Wall Street Journal* October 28, B1, B10.
19. Harris, Alana (2000). "Reducing the Recruiting Risks," *Sales & Marketing Management* May 18.
20. Churchill, Ford, Hartley, and Walker (1985).
21. Dudley (2007).
22. Engle, Robert (1998). "Multi-Step, Structured Interviews to Select Sales Representatives in Russia and Eastern Europe," *European Management Journal* 16:4, 476–484; and Mak, C. (1995). "Successful People Selection in Action," *Health Manpower Management* 21, 12–17.
23. Menkes, Justin (2005). "Hiring for Smarts," *Harvard Business Review* 83:11, (November) 100–109.
24. www.jobsearchtech.about.com/interview. Accessed December 25, 2007.
25. Harris, Jim, and Joan Brannick (1999). *Finding and Keeping Great Employees.* New York: American Management Association.
26. Peck, David (2007). "Is Checking References During the Hiring Process a Waste of Time," *Sales & Marketing Management* April 12.
27. Swift, Cathy Owens, Robert Wayland, and Jane Wayland (1993). "The ADA: Implications for Sales Managers," National Conference for Sales Management Proceedings, 146–148.
28. C. David Shepherd and James C. Heartfield (1991). "Discrimination Issues in the Selection of Salespeople: A Review and Managerial Suggestions," *Journal of Personal Selling & Sales Management* Fall 71.
29. Honeycutt, Earl D., Jr., and Lew Kurtzman (2006). *Selling Outside Your Culture Zone.* Dallas: Behavioral Science Research Press.
30. Honeycutt and Kurtzman (2006).
31. Harris and Brannick (1999).

9

TRAINING AND DEVELOPING THE SALES FORCE

LEARNING OBJECTIVES

After completing this chapter, you should be able to:

- Identify factors that help determine what types of training are needed by sales personnel.
- Summarize the inputs needed to design and deliver an effective sales training program.
- Explain why it's important to assess the effectiveness of a firm's sales training and what's involved in the assessment.
- Distinguish the elements that contribute to effective and ineffective training programs.

Hiring the most talented individuals to work for your organization is only the first step toward employing a successful sales force. After salespeople are hired, they need training to deal with the challenges of the job and workplace. A poorly trained sales force will be less likely to meet the needs of potential customers, thus opening the door to your competitors. The impact of losing customers and their business ultimately affects every department in an organization. Sales managers need to take steps to ensure that their sales forces have the skills and abilities to be successful on the job. This chapter examines how sales training efforts help to accomplish this task.

ANTOINE DESTIN

SALES TRAINING MANAGER, HORMEL FOODS CORPORATION

As a territory manager selling for Hormel Foods, Antoine Destin enjoyed "the rush" he felt every time he completed a sale. However, after Destin was put in charge of Hormel's sales training, he wondered what it would be like working in a corporate environment in which he didn't have the opportunity to experience that rush. "One of the biggest adjustments I had to make was to my personal reward system," says Destin. "In the field, you can see the results of your efforts on a short-term basis. Working in training means that you have to wait six months or so before you see the fruits of your labor take hold in the success of your trainees. You have to delay gratification a bit."

Hormel's corporate sales training program for its food service division was only a year old when Destin arrived. He was the second person to fill the position. The job involved planning, executing, delivering, and evaluating the success of Hormel's sales training programs. "Determining the sales training needs of a 150-person sales force is a big challenge. Your programs have to meet the needs of three parties: management, middle managers, and the salesperson. If you aren't able to provide a product that everyone agrees to and thinks has value, you don't have a good training program," Destin explains. "Everyone has to 'buy in' to the program." Input from Hormel's sales managers is gathered during in-field visits and on-site training sessions. Input from Hormel's sales force is gathered via training conference calls with new hires.

Hormel's sales training is extensive. New hires "shadow" (accompany) other sales personnel and complete an online course during their first 18 weeks on the job. They have three formal sales training programs: new employee orientation, a sales development seminar course after about 18 months, and an advanced sales seminar after three years. As part of his job, Destin was involved in writing the content for the online course and then worked with two outside technology partners to handle its technological aspects. (Hormel is one of only a handful of companies in its industry utilizing online training, Destin says.) He was also involved in developing the content of the sales seminar, which is timed to coincide with sales representatives' careers when they are most likely to consider other employment. The sales seminars are designed to provide experienced sales representatives with new skills and improve their existing ones so as to increase their productivity and to decrease their turnover rates.

Destin says that measuring the success of Hormel's sales training program is one of the toughest aspects of his job. "Evaluating the effectiveness of training is difficult. Sure, you can tell if participants liked it. But measuring it or showing a return on the investment is tough." To help determine the effectiveness of their training programs Hormel relies on verbal feedback and on the written assessments sales representatives complete after they undergo training.

Another important component is how long it takes to get a new salesperson up to speed. One study of the insurance industry, for example, found that the average company spends as much as $120,000 (in terms of lost sales opportunities, recruiting, training, development costs, and so forth) to get a new salesperson up to speed.[1] Destin believes Hormel's online sales training has decreased the time it takes for the company's new salespeople to begin generating profitable sales levels.

To be a successful sales trainer requires several talents. "You need to have a broad base of knowledge to understand all parts of the business. This helps you to have a presence as someone who knows what they are talking about, in essence a trainer has to have credibility. You have to be a good listener. Lastly, you have to be flexible in your approach and adapt it to the needs of your learners. People have different learning styles; some may be visual learners, others focus on audio, and others more experiential."

Destin points out that good sales trainers run the risk of losing their "edge" if they stay in the office too long. They need to get in the field on a regular basis so they are aware of the challenges meeting new salespeople. The last thing a sales trainer wants to say is, "Well, this is the way we did it when I was in the field." If a sales trainer focuses on only the past, the person won't be as effective in their training efforts nor will they win many sales training accolades. "And don't underestimate the importance of the field sales manager," Destin says. Ensuring new hires are trained to be successful is ultimately the responsibility of their immediate sales managers. After working in his capacity as national sales trainer, Antoine was promoted and now is back in the field. However, this time he is responsible for their profitability and training needs of only 10 salespeople. ■

How Important Is Sales Training?

Have you ever dealt with a salesperson who wasn't knowledgeable about the product or service he or she was selling and you were extremely interested in it? It probably wasn't a reassuring experience. Organizations that utilize sales training do so because they see a number of benefits from this investment: Their sales representatives are more knowledgeable about their firm's products and services, the markets in which they operate, and the selling process than sales representatives who haven't been trained. As a result, trained representatives are able to better understand their customers and deliver better service to them. This typically results in higher sales for the company and higher incomes for the sales reps, who experience greater job satisfaction because they're successful.

Tim Owen, an agent for Northwestern Mutual Life Insurance, is a good example. Because of the sales training Owen has received, he understands the expenses associated with the long-term care of a person suffering from a chronic illness or a disabling condition. As a result, Owen is able to show how a long-term care insurance product may be of value to a baby-boomer-aged client. After graduating from college, Katrina Rademacher went to work for Tom James, an upscale clothier for executives. Because of the training she received, Rademacher knows how to provide valuable fashion advice and personalized service to her clients. Because their sales training has made them more successful, both Owen and Rademacher are satisfied with their careers and are less likely to leave their organizations. Owen and Rademacher's sales managers have benefited from the training, too, because they have to spend less time supervising the two salespeople.

When you think of it, would you want to have a relationship with a company that doesn't make an investment in the ongoing training of its sales personnel? Organizations that comment that sales training is "too expensive" or "too time consuming" seem to be ignoring the benefits of sales training. By and large, however, most companies know that training their salespeople is critical not only to their success, but to their very survival, as the following statistics show:

Selling Power magazine annually ranks the best sales companies to sell for. (Selling Power)

- Nationwide, across all industries, nearly $60 billion is spent annually on formal training efforts.[2]
- Compared with all other areas of training, sales training receives the most funding, estimated at between $4 and $14 billon yearly,[3,4] exceeding management and supervisory training.[2]
- Over 35 percent of firms report that their salespeople receive over six days of training every year.[5]
- Over 63 percent of companies will spend more than six days a year training their new salespeople, and over 30 percent will train their new salespeople for more than 15 days.[5]
- Nearly half (47%) of sales executives ranked "enhancing sales training" as the most important area in which their firm planned to make operational improvements.[5]

Every year *Selling Power* magazine publishes a list of the "50 Best Companies to Sell For" in the U.S. manufacturing and service industries.[6,7] The list includes only companies with sales forces consisting of over 500 people. The three criteria used to determine the companies included on the prestigious list are as follows: sales force compensation, career mobility, and training. The compensation category is a summary of average starting salaries, incentive pay plans, the availability of company cars, and other benefits representatives receive. The career mobility category considers the number of performance reviews sales representatives receive, a firm's sales force turnover, and the number of salespeople it promoted. The training category includes both how much time a company invests in developing the initial selling skills and product knowledge of its representatives and the follow-up training they receive. When you think about it, to a certain extent, training is the crux of these three criteria. After all, both a salesperson's compensation and career mobility are acutely affected by how well the person has been trained. With good training, a salesperson is more likely to maximize her performance, earn more money, and have greater career mobility.

Exhibits 9.1 and 9.2 show the companies on *Selling Power's* "50 Best Companies to Sell For" list ranked in terms of their training scores during the time period 2001–2007. (The companies that earned the top scores appear at the top of the lists.) Only companies that made the list in each of the years 2005, 2006, and 2007 are included. To be included in this listing is considered quite an accomplishment. Those companies listed at the top of the two charts (seven manufacturing and six service companies) made the *Selling Power* list for all seven consecutive years, which reflects their high commitment to training. Other companies, such as Microsoft and Northwestern Mutual, though not included for all seven years, should also be noted for their outstanding sales training efforts.

EXHIBIT 9.1

Training Ratings of the "Best Manufacturing Companies to Sell For" 2001–2007

A dash (-) indicates that the organization was not ranked in the "Top 25 Service Companies to Sell For" that year. (Thirty-one other companies were ranked during this period. Only those making the list for the last three consecutive years are included here.)

Source: Based on "50 Best Companies to Sell For," *Selling Power*, November/December, 2001–2007.

Company	2001	2002	2003	2004	2005	2006	2007	Total
Hormel	20	16	16	16	16	18	18	120
Novell	18	18	18	16	16	16	16	118
Abbott Laboratories	14	14	14	14	15	15	15	101
A.O. Smith	14	14	14	14	14	14	14	98
DENTSPLY Intl	14	14	14	14	14	14	14	98
Forest Labs	14	14	14	14	14	14	14	98
International Paper	14	14	14	14	14	14	14	98
Microsoft	-	-	18	18	18	18	18	90
IBM	-	16	14	14	14	14	14	86
Clayton Homes	-	13	13	13	13	13	13	78
Georgia Pacific	-	-	15	15	15	15	15	75
3M	-	-	15	15	15	15	15	75
Hoffman-LaRoche	-	-	16	15	15	14	14	74
Millipore	-	-	13	13	13	18	13	70
Ecolabs	-	-	14	14	14	14	14	70
General Electric	-	-	14	14	14	14	14	70
Tellabs	-	-	14	14	14	14	14	70
Oracle	-	-	-	14	14	14	15	57
Cisco Systems	-	-	-	14	14	14	14	56
EMC	-	-	-	14	14	14	14	56

EXHIBIT 9.2

Training Ratings of the "Best Service Companies to Sell For" 2001–2007

A dash (-) indicates that the organization was not ranked in the "Top 25 Manufacturing Companies to Sell For" that year. (Twenty-two other companies were ranked during this period. Only those making the list for the last three consecutive years are included here.)

Source: Based on "50 Best Companies to Sell For," *Selling Power*, November/December, 2001–2007.

Company	2001	2002	2003	2004	2005	2006	2007	Total
Marriott International	20	18	14	15	15	15	15	112
IKON Office Solution	20	15	14	14	14	14	14	105
United Parcel Service	16	16	16	14	14	14	14	104
Verizon	18	16	14	14	14	14	14	104
FedEx	14	14	14	14	14	14	14	98
Lawson Products	14	14	14	14	14	14	14	98
CDW	-	16	14	15	15	15	15	90
Insight Enterprises	-	15	14	13	13	13	14	83
Northwestern Mutual	-	-	14	14	15	15	15	73
Sprint Nextel	-	-	14	14	14	14	14	70
Marriot Vacation Club International	-	-	-	14	15	15	15	59
InfoUSA	-	-	-	14	14	14	15	57

The Training Process

The sales training process will be different for each firm depending upon its size, resources, and the markets in which it operates. A small organization is likely to have neither the resources, nor the level of specialization that a multi-national organization does. In smaller firms, district or regional sales managers might be in charge of their firm's sales training. However, no matter what size firm they work for, one thing all sales managers have in common is their responsibility to help train their sales teams. This training can take the form of simply providing feedback and assistance to a salesperson on a training issue, or it could involve the teaching of a course. As Mike Kapocius, a regional sales manager for Takeda Pharmaceuticals, commented, "Training doesn't end when the class is over. Training goes on all the time." This is supported by research, which has found that for sales training to be effective, managers must provide follow-up training to their representatives to reinforce what they've learned.[8]

Regardless of an organization's size or the resources it has, the process sales managers should follow to develop effective sales training programs for the personnel is the same. A four-stage sales training cycle from planning to delivery is outlined in Exhibit 9.3. Identifying the topics that need to be covered and who needs to be included in training are the first questions that must be addressed. After determining the firm's sales training needs comes the planning: what should be included in the content, who will staff the program, and what training format should be used to deliver it? Once the planning is complete, the program must be delivered in a manner that best facilitates learning. Evaluating the training effort at the individual and organizational level is the fourth stage. Next, we discuss each of these stages in more detail.

Identifying the Firm's Sales Training Needs

Most companies provide their new salespeople with training. More experienced members of sales forces generally receive training to update them on their firms' new products and other market developments. Both of these situations would seem to warrant a need for training. The latter situation would seem to be warranted when there is a difference between the outcomes the members of a firm's sales force are achieving versus what their sales managers want them to achieve. Wouldn't training correct the situation?

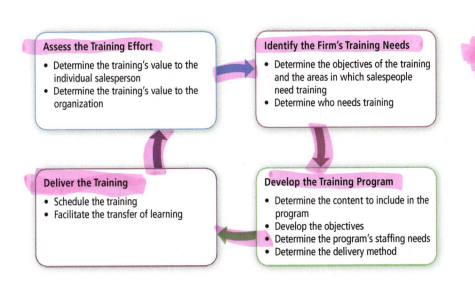

EXHIBIT 9.3

The Sales Training Cycle

Assess the Training Effort
- Determine the training's value to the individual salesperson
- Determine the training's value to the organization

Identify the Firm's Training Needs
- Determine the objectives of the training and the areas in which salespeople need training
- Determine who needs training

Deliver the Training
- Schedule the training
- Facilitate the transfer of learning

Develop the Training Program
- Determine the content to include in the program
- Develop the objectives
- Determine the program's staffing needs
- Determine the delivery method

The fact is that training is not the solution for all of the problems a sales force faces. Moreover, sales training programs can be expensive and time consuming. Before jumping to the conclusion that sales training is the "fix" you need, you must ask yourself: "Is additional training for the sales force the most appropriate response to the situation the sales force is facing?" For example, low levels of compensation, morale, motivation, and job satisfaction among representatives might be problems no amount of training will remedy.

DETERMINE SALES TRAINING OBJECTIVES Assuming the sales training appears to be warranted, most experts recommend that sales managers consider three levels of information during the training planning stage—information from the *organizational level,* the *task level,* and the *individual level.*[9] Exhibit 9.4 offers a perspective of this process. The sources of information used to determine the training needs at all three levels of assessment is displayed in Exhibit 9.5. The information should be collected through informal means, such as input provided by sales managers, upper management, training personnel, or customers; and through formal means, such as customer surveys or performance measures like sales volumes, the turnover rates among representatives, and so forth.

At the organizational level, this information should reflect the firm's mission statement, strategic initiatives, and upper management's mandates as well as the company's sales and marketing objectives.[10] Task level information can be generated from sales managers' and trainers' observations, input from customers, and from commercially available training programs. Individual level information is available from sales reps' performance reports, sales manager's observations of their representatives' performance, customers, and self-reports from sales reps.

The broadest level of analysis, the organizational analysis, should reveal which of the firm's short-term and long-term strategic goals are being met and the activities that need to be done to do so. Wausau Insurance, which provides insurance to business owners, illustrates why it's so important for a firm to match its corporate strategy with its sales training process: Because of mergers and related changes in business structures during the 1990s, Wausau's corporate strategy changed, too. Instead of focusing on small and medium-sized companies, Wausau began focusing on larger companies. As a result, Wausau's sales representatives, who had typically worked with the owners

EXHIBIT 9.4

Assessment of Training Needs at Different Levels

EXHIBIT 9.5

Sources of Training Needs Information

Input from:	Performance measures	Other
• Sales managers • Job incumbents • Upper management • Training personnel • Customers	• Sales volumes • Customers' service levels • Customer complaints • Turnover rates • Number of sales calls conducted • Profitability	• Organizational objectives • Sales training goals • Observations of salesperson's skills • Commercially available sales training programs

Determining Sales Training Needs

Sources: Based on Erffmeyer, Robert C.; Russ, Randall K. and Joseph F. Hair, Jr. (1991). "Needs Assessment and Evaluation in Sales-Training Programs," *Journal of Personal Selling & Sale Management* (11) 1, pp. 18–30; and Honeycutt, Earl D., Jr. (1996). "Conducting a Sales Training Audit," *Industrial Marketing Management* 25, pp. 105–113.

of small and medium-sized firms, found themselves working with much larger firms and more sophisticated, challenging clients. These clients required more complicated insurance products. Wausau's strategic change started the ball rolling for new types of sales training ranging from proposal development to team presentation skills. Other strategic goals a firm might uncover by doing an organizational analysis might include reducing the turnover among the company's representatives and increasing the level of the firm's overall sales or sales of certain products by offering different types of sales training.

At the task level, the focus is on identifying what level of **knowledge, skills, and abilities (KSAs)** are needed for a firm's sales jobs.[11] Job descriptions are a good place from which to acquire this information. A job description will list the KSAs and tasks a salesperson should do, with whom, why, and how often. The information might indicate that on a daily basis a sales representative must be able to collect information through an interview; analyze data in a spreadsheet; and determine what products and level of support would be best to offer a client via a written, electronic, or oral presentation. This, in turn, should affect the content presented during the training. Customer complaints can also be a great source of information when it comes to developing sales training plans. Analyzing the complaints might show that the firm's sales reps lack knowledge about certain products or services, don't take the time to follow up with customers, or that customers don't like some of the sales tactics they engage in. To remedy this, the firms might need more content training, sales process or service training, or more insight about the nature of their customers and what they expect.

DETERMINE WHO NEEDS SALES TRAINING The last level of the needs assessment is the individual level. Not all salespeople need the same sales training program. Their needs may vary depending upon their experience levels and the needs of the markets in which they sell. Sometimes groups of sales representatives who need training can be easily identified, such as newly hired representatives or newly promoted representatives. However, there will also be times when all members of a sales force need training. Such might be the case when a company, or its competitors, launches a new product or service, enters a new market, or adopts a new technology. A good needs assessment will provide an idea of what training is needed so that sales trainees get what they need to be successful—rather than too much information (which is likely to result in their boredom) or too little information (which is likely to result in their becoming frustrated). Similarly, companies with global sales forces must take into account the needs of their salespeople abroad in their sales training planning. Kodak is one company that is doing so, as the Global Sales Management feature in this chapter illustrates. Sales managers who fail to consider the cultural differences related to training their salespeople around the world face disastrous consequences

To be sure, identifying specific individuals who need training can be time consuming for a sales manager responsible for a large number of sales personnel.[12] As a result, it's not surprising that this step is often minimized, overlooked, or simply neglected. In fact, a survey of sales vice presidents reported that 34 percent of all companies said the step was a critical deficiency of their sales training programs.[13] However, information to help identify individuals can be drawn from a variety of sources. The sources include

GLOBAL SALES MANAGEMENT

The Challenges of Training a Global Sales Force

On the surface it sounds like a good idea: Develop a sales training program and then translate and launch it for use by your global sales force. But according to Mary Elliott, the worldwide director of sales and customer training for the entertainment imaging division of Kodak, you need to tailor your sales training just as you tailor your product and promotions to each country. The phrase "Think globally, but act locally" is the rule when it comes to sales training.

Customers in some countries might appreciate sales calls in which representatives immediately begin selling their products, but in other countries this would be disastrous. For example, in Asian and Latin American countries, the relationship between the buyer and the seller must first be solidified. Training salespeople to try to close a deal before the relationship is solidified would be a serious mistake in these countries. Likewise, if a culture relies heavily on social interaction, it might be more important to train representatives to focus on customer service than product features and prices.

Elliott notes that the titles of people you send to the training are particularly important in some countries. For example, in Southeast Asian cultures, such as Taiwan, if you send an assistant director to be trained, the person is likely to wonder why the director couldn't find the time to come. The way people interact with trainers is also different from country to country. In some countries, such as the United States, if there is no interaction with the trainer, the trainer assumes he or she is boring participants. In other cultures, such as Japan, interacting with the trainer and role-playing is not the norm, so participants would feel uncomfortable doing so. Nor should you assume the level of technology is the same from country to country. Start with the basics no matter who you are training or where.

The following are examples of some actual global training missteps companies have made:

- An American and British sales trainer traveled to India and planned to deliver a presentation using overhead projectors and VCRs. As often happens in India, there was an electrical blackout. Rather than changing to a different method, the trainers became very critical and frustrated, which offended the trainees because they were accustomed to power outages.[1]

- A U.S. company sent its vice president of sales to Taiwan to help the salespeople of one of its local business partners there. The salespeople were excited to finally receive the training they needed. But when the U.S. vice president met with the owner of the Taiwanese partner company, he told him that Taiwan was his company's "biggest problem in Asia." Needless to say, this created an immediate rift. The owner of the Taiwanese company promptly called the president of the U.S. company to rebut the criticism. The vice president subsequently found himself on the next plane back to the United States and was later fired. It took more than a year of apologies and a great deal of money for the U.S. company to smooth out the feathers that had been ruffled.[2]

- In Cairo, Egypt, PepsiCo combined local salespeople and those who weren't from Cairo into a large sales training program. The salespeople from "outside" of Cairo stayed in a hotel, were given free food, and were excused from certain work duties. Those from within the metropolitan area, some of whom had to travel two hours each way for the training, had to pay for their own meals and would receive calls from their bosses to take a break and solve a problem for an important customer. To say the local salespeople were frustrated and did not receive the same level of sales training is an understatement.[2]

Sources: Ramusson, Erika (1999). "A Whole New World of Training," *Sales and Marketing Management* (151) October 10: 80; Rivera, Ray J., and Andrew Paradise (2006). *2006 State of the Industry in Leading Enterprises: ASTD's Annual Review of Trends in Workplace Learning and Performance*. Alexandria, VA: The American Society for Training and Development; and Sergio, Roman, and Salvador Ruiz (2003). "A Comparative Analysis of Sales Training in Europe: Implications for International Sales Negotiations," *International Marketing Review* (20): 3, 304–328. 1. Honeycutt, Earl D., John B. Ford, and Antonis C. Simintiras (2003). *Sales Management: A Global Perspective* (2003). London: Routledge. 2. Honeycutt, Earl D., John B. Ford, and Lew Kurtzman (1996). "Potential Problems and Solutions When Hiring and Training a Worldwide Sales Team," *Journal of Business and Industrial Marketing* 11:1 (Winter), 42–53.

quantifiable performance appraisal data and customer satisfaction or CRM data to more subjective information collected from training needs surveys taken by sales managers and salespeople themselves. The latter can help build support for training programs because those who are most likely to receive the training are the individuals who identified the need for it.

After an individual's training needs are identified, they should be included in an individual training and development plan for the person. The plan should include the training courses the representative should take at scheduled career milestones, such as an advanced training course once the person has achieved a certain amount of experience. It could also include training from outside vendors, such as a software training course for a representative who struggles to use a particular type of software product. Or, it could include job rotations to ensure the representative has the opportunity to be exposed to a variety of selling experiences. Unfortunately, the attention that is needed at this stage is often

> ## S SELF-ASSESSMENT LIBRARY
>
> Successful sales managers and salespeople need to use different communication styles than those used by people in other professions, such as people in the military and people who work in the healthcare profession and other fields. Take the following self-assessment quiz to find out what your basic communication style currently is. Access the quiz by going to http://www.prenhall.com/sal/ and log in using the access code that came with your textbook. Then click on:
>
> Assessments
>   II. Working with Others
>   A. Communication Styles
>   1. What's My Face-to-Face Communication Style?
>
> Your results will be scored along a number of dimensions. Review your scores to see if you think they resemble the dimensions people need to be successful in sales and management.

minimized, overlooked, or simply neglected. A survey of sales vice presidents reported that 54 percent of companies who were shifting their sales approach—and 34 percent of all companies—identified assessing individual training and development needs as a critical deficiency of their sales training programs.[13]

Designing and Developing the Sales Training Program

WHAT CONTENT IS NEEDED? Exhibit 9.6 reflects the content areas that sales training programs cover. Product knowledge and sales skills training lead the way. Although it wasn't identified in this survey, ethics training is becoming more common. The Ethics in Sales Management feature in this chapter describes recent developments in this area.

The results of a **training assessment** need to be tailored for the target group that's being trained. Most companies identify several groups of sales personnel in need of different types of training. The training generally includes programs for new hires, ongoing training programs for established sales representatives; sales management training; and professional, or career development, programs. The training programs for new hires will often include an orientation to the company, steps and behaviors used in the selling process, product and market information, procedures used to monitor the progress of a sale, and the use of sales-related software and technology. Additionally, some organizations will include instruction on networking, or how to develop new sales contacts, and

EXHIBIT 9.6

Topics Commonly Covered in Sales Training Programs

Source: Adapted from Galea, Christine, and Carl Wiens, "Sales Training Survey (2002). *Sales & Marketing Management* 154 (7), 34–36.

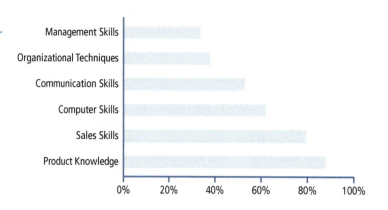

ETHICS IN SALES MANAGEMENT

Can You Teach Sales Ethics?

About 15 years ago, Dr. Robert Erffmeyer, one of the authors of this textbook, recalls talking to a sales trainer about incorporating sales ethics into his company's sales training curriculum. The trainer laughed and commented, "Why would I want to do that? I don't want to talk about things that are unethical—things that [new sales representatives] might be tempted to do to cut corners. Besides, we only hire ethical salespeople."

Times change, and attitudes gradually do, too. According to a sales and marketing management survey by Equation Research, many companies are now training their sales forces to promote their firms' ethical reputations to their clients. Ethics training specialists recommend that ethics training involve a review of a company's code of conduct and group discussions involving members of the sales force and sales management teams. The discussions should focus on specific business ethics dilemmas such as the following: selling out-of-date products, sending gifts to customers, the value and the timing of gift giving, presenting false or misleading information about your products and/or selling unproven solutions, exaggerating the extent of support your firm can offer customers, and filing inaccurate expense reports.

Participants should be encouraged to examine how certain decisions affect different stakeholders (for example, the firm's stockholders, community, managers, customers, distributors, employees, and their family members). Frequently participants are surprised by what other trainees consider to be acceptable sales practices. Ask them if the decisions would pass the *60 Minutes* test. That is, how would they explain the situation if they were asked about it in a public forum? Would the public accept the decision or be outraged? If the latter is the case, the decision should definitely be rethought.

Sources: Ferrell, O. C., J. Fraedrich, and Linda Ferrell (2002). *Business Ethics: Ethical Decision-making and Cases.* Boston: Houghton Mifflin Company, p. 444; Gilbert, Jennifer (2003). "A Matter of Trust," *Sales and Marketing Management* (155) 3, 30–36; and Weber, John A. (2007). "Business Ethics Training: Insights from Learning Theory," *Journal of Business Ethics* (70) 61–85.

instruction on time management. Many companies will bring in a group, or "class," of new hires to a central or corporate location and train them together. Depending on the start date of a new hire, a salesperson is likely to undergo training shortly after beginning his or her job or wait several months until enough new hires are in place to form a class. A number of companies have incorporated online programs that typically focus on helping reps gain product knowledge. This training can begin immediately after salespeople begin their new jobs.[14]

New hires are also likely to begin **on-the-job training (OJT)**, job shadowing, or "ride-alongs" with experienced sales personnel. This helps expose new representatives to a company's sales practices, products, and customers immediately. The idea is that the new hire will learn to model the behavior of the more experienced representative. Therefore, it is critical that the representative being "shadowed" is a good role model who is willing to train the new representative. Refresher courses for more experienced salespeople tend to cover certain advanced sales skills, including how to work with larger or more complicated customers, or advanced products and services. As we have mentioned, some companies position these courses at specific points in sales reps' careers to help prevent turnover among their salespeople.

One content area that has and will continue to be an important training area is integrating the use of technology into the sales process. Many people enter into sales professions because they enjoy interacting with people as opposed to technology. However, most sales people quickly realize how technology-driven applications such as CRM software can enhance their sales performance. Other useful technology applications include contact managers, sales call scheduling and travel route planning software, and in-house templates that automatically fill in commonly used letters, presentations, proposal information, and other documentation so that the sales rep only needs to customize or tailor it to fit his current client.

Sales managers have learned that technology can provide real benefits without resulting in unnecessary additional work.[15] Sometimes salespeople end up rejecting, or not using, the technology their sales managers provide them.[16] This usually occurs when there is a poor fit between the technology and what the salespeople need—not because the technology itself is flawed. Trainers have learned several lessons from their early efforts to train salespeople to use new technology (some of which didn't meet with success). First, the trainers must ensure that sales personnel see the potential benefits of the technology so that they will accept and use it.[17] The trainers must also thoroughly train the sales force to use the technology, both in the field and out, and provide them with adequate technical support and follow-up training if they need it.[18]

The last category of training focuses on the overall professional development of sales personnel. This might include training related to professional speaking, account management, team selling, negotiating contracts, and other advanced training conducted as part of an industry-wide seminar, for example. Category management, or managing how many different brands a retailer should carry and display, is a new area in which salespeople are receiving training. In addition, a firm's sales training programs might include enrolling in summer institutes or graduate courses offered by colleges, universities, and professional associations.

Sales representatives aren't the only people who need different types of training, though. Sales managers need training, too, especially as they transition from sales representative to sales management positions. Historically, the training needs of this group have taken a backseat to the needs of the new sales force members. Oftentimes only larger organizations have provided formal training in this area.[19] The content included in the majority of training programs for sales managers is incorporated into many of the chapters of this book. The topics include transitioning into management and coaching (Chapter 10), recruiting and interviewing (Chapter 8), conducting performance appraisals (Chapter 14), and business-to-business account management strategies (Chapters 5 and 13).[20]

Training members of the sales force is an important part of a sales manager's job. (Comstock Complete)

DEVELOPING THE OBJECTIVES OF SALES TRAINING: CHANGING IDEAS INTO ACTION After a program's training topics have been identified, the trainer needs to develop the learning objectives of the program. This will help them properly develop, execute, and evaluate the programs. Educational psychologist Benjamin Bloom outlined three different categories of intellectual behavior important for learning. The behaviors can be categorized as *cognitive, affective,* or *psychomotor behaviors.* They correspond to the KSAs we described earlier and are useful to trainers when they are writing their training objectives—that is, what they want their trainees to do in order to learn what they need to know.[21,22] The goal is to accurately describe the intent of your sales training programs in terms of these various

EXHIBIT 9.7

Using Bloom's Taxonomy (Categories) to Develop Effective Training Objectives

Source: Based on Anderson & Krathwohl, 2001, *A Taxonomy for Learning, Teaching and Assessing: A Revision of Bloom's Taxonomy of Educational Objectives.*

Cognitive/Knowledge Categories

Category (ranging from lower- to higher-level skills)	Sales Examples and *Key Words*
Remembering Recalling and restating learned information	Describe the pricing policy to a customer *List, recognize, describe, identify, name*
Understanding Interprets and translates what has been learned; explaining ideas or concepts	Summarize the pricing policy; explain the benefits of a new product to a customer *Summarize, interpret facts, infer causes, explain, classify, compare*
Applying Using information in another familiar situation	Implement the policy for a client *Administer, assess, calculate, interpret, apply, prepare, solve*
Analyzing Breaking information into parts to explore relationships	Differentiate how the pricing policies affects different types of buyers *Analyze, compare, distinguish, illustrate, infer, explain*
Evaluating Make decisions based on reflection, criticism, and assessment	Assess the viability of the pricing policy *Judge, assess, revise, recommend, convince, support, decide*
Creating Generating new ideas, products, or ways of viewing things	Create a pricing policy *Design, construct, devise, propose, develop, formulate, forecast*

Affective/Attitude Categories

Category (ranging from lower- to higher-level skills)	Sales Examples and *Key Words*
Receiving inputs Aware of and attuning to inputs	Listens to others and remembers the name of an introduced person. *Asks, describes, identifies, selects, replies*
Responding to inputs Active participation on the part of the learner	Participates in a discussion and can make a presentation *Answers, discusses presents, reports, writes*
Valuing Establishes a worth for an idea, behavior, idea	Proposes a plan or a solution that is sensitive to the needs of multiple parties *Explains, initiates, justifies, proposes, selects, shares*
Organizing Organizes values into priorities and resolves conflict between them	Prioritizes needs of customer, coworkers, and the organization *Compares, defends, explains, formulates, generalizes, modifies, integrates, relates*
Internalizing values Has a value system that controls their behavior	Revises judgments and changes behavior in light of new information. Values people for who they are *Acts, discriminates, influences, practices, proposes, qualifies, revises, serves, solves*

behaviors. Exhibit 9.7 shows the range of activities and behaviors that should be incorporated into a training program's objectives, based on Bloom's work.

Trainers should also be sure to include activities beyond the lowest level skill sets (i.e., incorporating more than just the lowest level, "remembering" in their objectives). Ultimately, training programs should show a progression of higher-level competencies and require related activities (i.e., analyzing data to make determinations, evaluating proposals to identify the most worthy one, and creating new plans). No doubt, you recall some of your earlier collegiate courses that might have included heavy doses of memorization (i.e., remembering terms on a multiple-choice test). Compare the behaviors needed to be successful in those courses to the ones that are required for upper-level courses where you are analyzing cases, writing business plans, and presenting persuasive arguments.

STAFFING THE TRAINING PROGRAM Once decisions about the content and desired outcomes of a proposed program have been determined, a number of questions about staffing of the program need to be addressed. These include internal versus external resources, time pressures, and cost considerations.

Internal versus External Staffing Resources Should the trainer come from within the company or would it be preferable to hire an outside trainer or a training vendor? This will depend on whether the firm's internal talent has the KSAs to assemble and present the program. For example, is the firm's sales process so unique that the insights and credibility an internal trainer can provide outweigh the benefits of hiring an external firm? Generally an internal trainer (one within the firm) will have more credibility than an outside trainer. There are cases, however, when an outside trainer is likely to have more credibility. For example, if a firm purchases a new information technology application, salespeople are likely to find outside trainers employed by the developer of the technology to be a more credible source of training.

Is there a dedicated sales training team within the firm that can direct the effort? Or is there a large number of people who need immediate training, which precludes using internal resources? Depending upon your answers to questions such as these, it might be more feasible to hire an outside vendor to conduct your training. Many companies today are doing just that. In fact, each year U.S. companies spend an estimated $2 billion annually on vendor-provided sales training.[23] If the training isn't extremely specific to your company—that is, if it is "generic" enough—it's possible that it can be conducted by a number of outside vendors. A number of capable vendors, including Wilson Learning, Dale Carnegie, Sales and Marketing Executives, and the Center for Creative Leadership, offer a range of programs including general sales programs and presentation and personal development programs designed for companies that lack in-house training resources. Larger firms often seek out these vendors for more specialized training, such as negotiation, category management, and leadership-development training, who often surpass what a firm's in-house training programs can offer. Or perhaps an outside technology partner is needed to help facilitate the delivery of the program via webinars, blogs, online learning, and so forth. Most companies use a combination of instructional approaches. A survey of sales companies found that 68 percent use sales managers, 58 percent have an in-house instructor, 54 percent use an outside instructor, and 20 percent indicate that the instruction is done on the computer.[24]

Time Pressures How frequently is the training needed? If it is a recurring program that is offered at regular intervals, it may warrant in-house development. Is the program needed on a regular basis or is it only needed once? Because developing an internal training program from scratch can be time consuming, offering such programs only once might not be justifiable. Also, can the program be rolled out gradually or must it be done within a short time period? When training is needed immediately and the firm's in-house resources are limited, using an external firm is likely to be beneficial. Finally, how involved should sales managers be in the training? Training programs that require the insights of a firm's sales managers might be better handled internally. If, indeed, sales managers are selected to participate in the training, will they have the time and resources to commit to the training when it needs to be conducted? Making sure sales managers are available and can dedicate the time needed to deliver the training can sometimes be a challenge. In this case, using an outside vendor might be preferable.

Costs Not to be overlooked is the cost of developing and delivering the program. If inside staff members are going to handle the program, will there be additional costs related to researching the content of the program and creating the materials for it? Are additional staffing costs required? For example, how many individuals will be delivering the training? What will it cost for them to do so? Will they have to travel to the training site? Are there enough individuals needing training to warrant the company developing and delivering the training or is it less expensive to utilize an existing vendor program? In other words, how does "outsourced" training compare price-wise to internal training? Addressing these questions will help you determine who is best positioned to staff the program.

SELECTING THE TRAINING DELIVERY METHOD There was a time when selecting the delivery format for a sales training program was very straightforward: It was generally face-to-face or **instructor-led training**. Either the sales force traveled to a central site to receive training from an instructor, or the instructor traveled to a site closer to the trainees to deliver the program. Instructor-led sales training can include many different components, including lectures, discussions, role plays, and presentations. It has the benefit of being very flexible and interactive. It also helps socialize participants and allows them to network with one another. As a result, they can consult one another for advice and support once the training has concluded, which many of them find valuable.

Historically, instructor-led training has been the method firms favor when it comes to training their salespeople. It can sometimes result in heavy doses of one-way communication, however. (You have probably experienced a long boring lecture that no one paid attention to.) This type of training also requires all participants to gather together at a particular training site, which can be expensive if representatives have to travel very far. Housing, meals, and missed selling opportunities are among the other costs companies incur by sending their representative to training.

Today, there are other alternatives to in-person, instructor-led training, however. The use of technology-based delivery methods nearly tripled between 2001 and 2006, for example.[25] In years past, technology-delivered training was simple. It might involve sending trainees printed materials and/or audio and videotapes to watch. Today, many companies allow their new sales representatives to access similar information online when and where they need to. This is referred to as **on-demand (self-paced) training**.

Instructor-led conference calls are another alternative. So are **web conferences**. Web conferencing allows a presenter to deliver information remotely to trainees' individual computers. A **webcast** is a one-way flow of communication. It is suitable for quick, worldwide training needs. A **webinar** typically is designed for a smaller audience. It incorporates a two-way flow of communication including feedback from the receivers either via phone lines and/or text messaging. Canon U.S.A. used webinars to train its large network of dealers to use new document management software complementing Canon's copier products. Dealers quickly received the training they needed at a low cost.[26]

More firms today are using webinars to provide sales training to their representatives. (istockphoto.com)

Recently two other technology-based delivery options have become available to the sales training scene: podcasting and the use of wikis. **Podcasting** involves delivering information to a salesperson's iPod™ or other similar device. Some companies send Podcast information to their representatives on a daily basis. The information might include how a new product is being accepted by customers or how competitors are working with it. Podcasts typically must be downloaded by participants, however, and they do not allow for interaction with an instructor. **Wikis** are a quick-response training vehicle (the name comes from the Hawaiian term *wiki*, which means "fast"). Wikis are web sites individual sales representatives are able to put up on short notice. A wiki allows all people who have access to a site to post material on it. Wiki participants act as instructors when they post information about how they were able to successfully sell to the firm's customers.

A key advantage of the newer approaches is their convenience; much of the coursework can be completed anytime and anywhere you have access to a personal computer. As a result, firms don't have to pay for sales representatives to travel somewhere to receive training. The new learning software is more interactive and can be tailored to the different needs of individual learners.

Exhibit 9.8 shows how frequently different general training methods are used.[27] The methods used for sales training, in particular, are similar. However, online education methods are used somewhat less often to train salespeople.[28] This might be due to the fact that teaching interpersonal and communication skills is crucial in a sales training course. However, this type of training isn't easy to transfer into an online learning format. Some companies are addressing this by incorporating a blended online (product and market knowledge) and an in-person (selling skills) approach to training. Companies such as IBM

Online training has many benefits. (Comstock Complete)

and Booz Allen Hamilton, a management strategy consulting firm, have both adopted blended approaches in their sales training. "Not every topic lends itself to e-learning," comments Melissa Chambers, a learning strategist at Booz Allen Hamilton, which has integrated 600 e-learning modules into the company's 120 classroom courses. The company's combined approach gives it the benefits distance learning affords as well as classroom participation to reinforce the lessons trainees are taught online.[29]

Roger Anderson, Home Depot's director of learning agrees that online training should not be used in all situations. Anderson says that the training is great when sales reps need the same information or "where you want all employees to hear the same message." But when you need to incorporate multiple skills for a complex job, face-to-face training is preferable.[30] A frequently used training format to handle this situation are **role-playing exercises**. Role playing requires salespeople to present information to a "client" (usually a sales trainer or another sales trainee) who has little understanding of the product and thus requires a basic presentation or who has a great deal of understanding and thus requires a very sophisticated presentation. Additionally, the demeanor of the "client" can range from pleasant to anything but pleasant. The goal is for the presenter to overcome these challenges in real time.

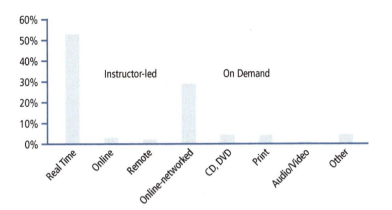

EXHIBIT 9.8

Percent of Training Delivered Using the Following Formats

Source: Based on Rivera and Paradise (2006) *State of the Industry*.

Some firms are even using avatars or computer representations of humans (like those found in the online game *Second Life*) as sales coaches. Daneielle Paden, an account manager at CDW Corp., a technology products and service company, completed a sales training course where an avatar coached her through a series of simulated phone interactions with clients. Paden was pleased with the realistic sales experience. Futuristic training such as this offers a number of benefits: (1) It provides a consistent experience with a coach who does not tire; (2) it is available any time of the day or night to sales representatives; (3) it can be used to train sales representatives individually or in groups; and (4) it can be repeated by a salesperson until he or she develops a certain level of mastery.[31]

So which training delivery method is most effective? A comparison of several instructor-led and self-paced training formats used in a new product sales training program for experienced sales representatives revealed that there was little difference in the learning outcomes representatives achieved based on the different delivery methods used.[32] A better approach would be to consider the unique challenges of each training situation—perhaps the firm's training budget is limited or there is a pressing need to train the firm's entire sales force quickly—and then choose the method that best fits the situation, depending upon factors such as these.

Delivering the Training

SCHEDULING THE TRAINING After all the planning is complete, the logistics of the program need to be addressed. If the training is instructor-led, for example, additional decisions must be made about the location of the training—whether it should take place at a centralized location, such as the company's headquarters, or a decentralized location(s), such as the territories or regions in which the trainees are located. Sales managers have to consider the travel and lodging costs that would be incurred under the different scenarios as well as the time trainees spend traveling as opposed to selling. On the one hand, a centralized site, such as a company's headquarters, is also likely to have a complete set of training resources and equipment. Centralized training also allows new sales representatives to network with other trainees outside of their districts and regions as well as the company's sales executives and in-house personnel. On the other hand, it usually involves a higher travel price tag than a decentralized sales program does. Coordinating and getting the resources and training equipment to a decentralized location can involve more work for trainers, however.

Making sure that trainees, presenters, and technical assistants have their schedules cleared and their travel and housing is also part

Avatars are finding their way into sales training situations. The virtual sales coaches are always available and never get tired. (ODD ANDERSEN/Agence France Presse/Getty Images)

of delivering the training. However, not only do the physical and logistical attributes of the training need to be ready, but the psychological "readiness" of the trainees also needs to be in place. For example, the timing of the training in the sales cycle is important. Training salespeople during a slow selling time (as opposed to bringing them in for training when they are ending a sales period) will affect how psychologically ready they are to be trained. The time salespeople need to complete any pretraining assignments you have given them also needs to be considered. Researchers have found that individuals who have a predisposition about the importance of training will transfer more into the field than those who don't.[33]

FACILITATE THE TRANSFER OF LEARNING Part of providing excellent training is ensuring that what is learned in the training program can be retained and applied in the field. This is called **learning transfer**. To help facilitate this, educational researchers suggest trainers do the following:

1. Make sure the training and field conditions, or where trainees operate, are as similar as possible.
2. Provide many opportunities to practice a new skill.
3. Provide a variety of situations to apply the new material to.
4. Identify the important features of the task.
5. Make sure the trainee has the opportunity to practice the new skills in the field.[34]

These suggestions incorporate Bloom's lower-level skill sets as well as some of the higher ones also. Learning and practicing the new behavior in a similar situation to their work environment is a critical element to ensuring the transfer of learning occurs.

Assessing the Firm's Training Efforts

The last phase of a sales training cycle is assessing the results. How effective was the firm's sales training? Were the objectives of the program accomplished? What were the gains of the program to the company? These sound like straightforward questions that should have simple answers. However, as Antoine Destin commented in the opening of the chapter, "Evaluating the effectiveness of training can be tough." Apparently, it's not just Destin who thinks so: When asked if their companies had a definitive method for measuring the value of their sales training, only 28 percent of sales trainers indicated they did.[35] This phase of training often receives the least attention despite its importance.[36]

In addition, sales trainers can't lose sight of the fact that some managers view sales training merely as an expense. As one sales professional put it: "Unlike a capital asset—which can be reused or resold—training generally can't. Therefore it is important that management clearly understand the value of this expense."[37] Clearly, evaluating the success of a firm's training effort is an area that deserves attention.

One popular assessment approach includes looking at certain reaction, learning, behavior, and ROI levels.[38] Despite some criticisms, this framework is intuitively simple and easy to apply. Exhibit 9.9 shows the different types of evaluation measures sales trainers use, their reported importance to trainers, and how frequently they use them.[39] Next, we discuss each of the four types of assessment and their strengths and weaknesses.

DETERMINE THE VALUE OF SALES TRAINING TO THE INDIVIDUAL
Reaction (Level 1) This category addresses what the trainee thought of the program by asking the person to fill out an evaluation, or what some trainers call a "happy sheet." In other words, was the trainee happy with the training? This is the most frequently used measurement. Note that in Exhibit 9.9, the four most frequently used methods—course evaluations, trainee feedback, training staff comments, and supervisory feedback—are all reaction measures. These ratings can be easily collected using end-of-course questionnaires.

EXHIBIT 9.9

Training Evaluation Measures Ranked by Their Importance and Frequency of Use

Assessment Approach	Sales Trainers' Rankings		
	Importance	Freq.	Type
Trainee Feedback	1	2	Reaction
Supervisory Appraisal	2	6	Behavior
Self-Appraisal	3	7	Behavior
Bottom-Line Measurement	4	9	Results
Customer Appraisal	5	10	Behavior
Supervisory Feedback	6	4	Reaction
Performance Tests	7	5	Learning
Training Staff Comments	8	3	Reaction
Course Evaluations	9	1	Reaction
Subordinate Appraisal	10	12	Behavior
Pre- vs. Post-Training Measurements	11	11	Learning
Coworkers Appraisal	12	13	Behavior
Knowledge Tests	13	8	Learning
Control Group	14	14	Learning

Note: Sales trainers, ratings of how important and how frequently they used each of the methods were ranked from 1 to 14.

Sources: From *Journal of Personal Selling and Sales Management*, vol. 11, no. 1, (1991): 24. Copyright C 2001 by PSE National Education Foundation. Reprinted with permission of M.E. Sharpe, Inc. All Rights Reserved. Not for reproduction. Erffmeyer, Robert C., K. Randall Russ and Joseph F. Hair, Jr. (1991). "Needs Assessment and Evaluation in Sales-Training Programs," *Journal of Personal Selling & Sale Management* (11) 1, 18–30.

Unfortunately, the assessment measures sales trainers considered most important weren't those most frequently collected.

Reaction measures have been criticized because they don't show if anything was really learned and applied back in the field. They only indicate if and how much participants liked the program. In addition, measures such as these may be unduly influenced by the training location (after a brutal winter, who wouldn't like the opportunity for training in a warm location?), the personality of the trainer, and how much the trainee values being away from work.[40] However, there is some value in collecting this information. If sales representatives like the training program, it stands to reason they will be more motivated to participate and learn from it. In sum, a good reaction rating doesn't mean learning took place. However, a negative rating reduces the chances that it occurred.

Learning (Level 2) This level involves measuring the amount of information participants mastered during the program. This can be done by testing them before and after the training and comparing the results of the two tests. However, the measurement doesn't necessarily reflect if the material can be applied in a productive manner back in the field. Both the reaction and learning level measures gauge the effectiveness of the training program at the individual level. To gain insight about the program's value at the organization level, the next two higher-level measures are needed.

Behaviors (Level 3) Level 3 measurements identify to what degree trainees applied the training principles and techniques they learned to their jobs, in essence learning transfer. The measurements can be collected by sales managers as they observe their sales personnel. They can also be collected from self-reports trainees themselves complete in journals or their contact management, or CRM, entries. Research has shown that this level of evaluation has only a few shortcomings and is particularly useful.[41]

DETERMINE THE VALUE OF SALES TRAINING TO THE ORGANIZATION

Results (Level 4) Level 4 measurements assess whether or not an organization achieved the objectives it sought by conducting the training. For example, did the program result in more sales of a new product that helped the company enter a new market? Or were fewer customer complaints received, which helped the company achieve a higher customer service rating in its industry? Measurements at this level tend to be conducted less often and, unfortunately, lend themselves to a few problems. A major problem involves determining whether the firm's objectives were achieved directly because of the training program or because of other factors—for example, because of competitors' actions, changes in the market, or changes in economic conditions.[42]

Because of the difficulties related to gauging Level 4 results, many managers assess the results of their training programs using **utility analysis**. How "useful" was the training, in other words? Although this category isn't included in the original model, it seems like a natural extension of the fourth level. Utility analysis involves looking at the economic impact the training had by examining the cost-benefit trade-offs of the training program. The costs-benefits can be measured by looking at the program's benefits—that is, the retention rates of the personnel who have been trained and the performance differences between trained and untrained employees, for example—versus what the training program cost. In other words, sales managers use utility analysis to determine the *relative* usefulness of different sales training alternatives. They want to adopt training programs that minimize the firm's costs while maximizing the important outcomes the company seeks.[43]

Completing the Sales Training Cycle

The sales training cycle is not completed until the results of training are compared with the initial objectives laid out for the program. Hopefully, the sales training objectives are met, and the program is considered a success. If this is the case, oftentimes the training program will go forward with only minor modifications and updates.

At the other extreme are those programs that do not meet their initial objectives. What might have caused these shortcomings? As you might expect, there are few companies that want to be interviewed about how their training programs didn't measure up. However, researchers investigating this area have found that the majority of companies that experience training shortcomings did not systematically set specific objectives for their training programs. Without these objectives to guide the development of their training courses, properly implementing and evaluating them will be difficult. Thus, the value of the firms' training investments would appear to be greatly diminished.[44]

Rather than an isolated event, sales training needs to be viewed as a systematic process of integrating the training curriculum into the sales force. The American Society for Training and Development regularly honors organizations for their award-winning training practices.[45] Exhibit 9.10 outlines these practices. The Professional Society for Sales & Marketing Training has identified a number of best practices for sales trainers.[46] Exhibit 9.11 consists of a "checklist" of some of these practices.

Companies that have received awards for their training programs share several characteristics. The programs:

- Include a front-end analysis of the performance, skills, and knowledge gaps of a firm's employees using both internal and external metrics, such as customer satisfaction.
- Conduct analyses, surveys, and interview of clients, customers, internal business leaders, and employees to identify the learning needs and desired outcomes at the corporate, business-unit, and individual levels.
- Link a corporation's strategic objectives to the individual objectives of its employees.
- Incorporate learning objectives in employee performance evaluations and promotional decisions.
- Use career management systems to align the competencies of the firm's employees with its functions, track the degree of employee learning, support performance reviews, and enhance productivity.
- Hold managers accountable for complying with the individual development plans of their employees.
- Use corporate universities to provide a variety of learning models in creative and dedicated learning environments.

EXHIBIT 9.10

The Best Training and Development Practices of Companies

Source: Based on Rivera, Ray J. and Andrew Paradise (2006). *2006 State of the Industry in Leading Enterprises: ASTD's Annual Review of Trends in Workplace.*

Needs Assessment

- Is the training tied to the organization's mission and vision?
- Can you understand the true nature of the problem/issue at hand, and what is needed to correct the problem?
- Is training the appropriate solution, or can the problem be corrected by other solutions, such as changing the firm's procedures, developing job aids, or modifying jobs?
- Have you determined the learning objectives that will result in the desired changes?
- Have you identified the knowledge and skills that will produce the desired new behaviors?
- Can you determine the cost/budget constraints and develop suggested solutions within these constraints?
- Can you identify the learning styles and needs of participants and incorporate them into the program's design?

Content Development

- Does the program incorporate adult learning principles into all aspects of the training?
- Does the content emphasize the essentials, not every possible detail?
- Does the program provide participants with the materials they need without overwhelming them?

Technological Proficiency

- Is the instructor up to date in the use of most current technology?
- Is the instructor able to utilize the technology that best fits the learning situation, rather than using technology for the sake of appearances?
- Can the instructor bring the course material "alive" via an effective presentation regardless of the technology used?

Personal Professional Development

- Does the instructor have an interest in participants' personal growth and learning?

Evaluation

- Does the instructor seek feedback to improve the program?
- Does the program include an evaluation process to capture information on the training's effectiveness, learning retention by participants, and the use of learning related to the firm's day-to-day business practices?

EXHIBIT 9.11

A Best-Practices "Checklist" for Sales Trainers

Sources: Based on *Training Competencies* (2006). Professional Society for Sales & Marketing Training, Retrieved January 2, 2007, from http://www.smt.org/i4a/pages/index.cfm?pageid=3325.

Summary

Every year companies invest more in the training of sales personnel than for any other occupational group, including managers and supervisors. A firm's products, services, markets, customers, and technology change rapidly. Consequently, having a sales force that is knowledgeable about these changes is critical to an organization's ability to successfully compete and survive. Regardless of the resources available to an organization, its sales training programs should follow four stages. These stages include identifying the firm's training needs, developing the training program, delivering it, and assessing its results.

Most organizations provide training for entry-level salespeople that includes selling skills, product knowledge, and technology skills; they also are more frequently including sales ethics decision-making skills. Training for more experienced sales personnel typically will include advanced decision making, sales, and presentation skills to use with larger clients. Technology and ethics training are increasingly becoming more common for sale forces.

Once the content and trainees are identified, the training program needs to be developed. Sales trainers can use Bloom's Taxonomy of Learning Behaviors to help them translate ideas into objectives that guide the development, and later evaluation, of the program. This classification framework can assist the planners in designing a program that might include only basic skills or lead to a more complex program that would include a wider range of behaviors.

The next two steps involve determining who will do the training and what delivery format best suits the program's needs. The roles sales managers play in the training process should never be overlooked because they are responsible for reinforcing the sales training on a daily basis and ultimately are responsible for the success of their representatives. Factors, such as the frequency with which the firm's training program must be conducted, the degree of specialized content the program contains, technological requirements, number of trainees, and the delivery schedule, will influence whether an outside vendor should be utilized to assist in or deliver an entire program.

Technology has expanded the methods companies have to choose from in terms of delivering training to their employees. In-person, instructor-led sessions are generally very flexible and allow participants to interact and socialize with one another, but also entail added travel costs and scheduling challenges. On-demand, or self-paced, training can involve sending printed or electronic materials and/or audio and videotapes to representatives to watch or access online. Web conferencing, webcasts, and webinars offer even more training delivery choices. With good planning and development, the delivery of the training program is often thought of as one of the most straightforward parts of training. However, logistical issues and scheduling must still be dealt with for a program to be successful. Care needs to be taken to ensure that the delivery of the material facilitates the ability of trainees to apply the content to their work environment.

Determining how successful a training program was is the final step in the sales training cycle. Most trainers use multiple measures to determine how effective their programs were. Kirkpatrick proposed a four-tier classification system that includes reaction measures, learning measures, behavioral or performance measures, and results measures. A utility analysis can be conducted to determine the cost-benefit ratios of programs. Behavior, or performance, measures offer the most valid form of assessment.

Organizations oftentimes focus on single aspects of sales training rather than viewing it as an entire process. Firms that fail to develop meaningful training objectives tend to develop programs that don't meet their needs or are impossible to assess.

Key Terms

instructor-led training 203	role-playing exercises 204
knowledge, skills, and abilities (KSAs) 195	training assessment 198
	utility analysis 208
learning transfer 206	webcast 203
on-demand (self-paced) training 203	web conferences 203
on-the-job-training (OJT) 199	webinar 203
podcasting 204	wikis 204

Questions and Problems

1. What are the limitations of a survey such as the one used by *Selling Power*?
2. In what situations does it *not* make sense to conduct sales training?
3. What is the difference between the organizational, task, and individual assessments? What are the benefits of using them?
4. Describe the concept of a KSA and how it can be used in sales training.
5. One of your friends, who just graduated from college, has accepted a sales position with a large firm. What topics do you believe should be included in a sales training course for her? Consider another friend who has accepted a position with a smaller firm that has four salespeople. How will their two experiences differ?
6. What are some of the reasons a company would consider using someone outside of the firm to train its sales force?
7. Online courses are growing. What reservations might a person have for taking sales training courses online?
8. When does in-person sales training make more sense than on-demand sales training? When does on-demand sales training make more sense than in-person sales training?
9. What sales training format do you believe holds the most promise for the future? Why?
10. "An individual should never be assigned permanently to a sales trainer's position." Develop arguments to both support and refute this statement.

Role Play

Home Fire Lights

Home Fire Lights (HFL) is a home improvement company that offers upscale outdoor living spaces complete with fireplaces, fire pits, cooking centers with islands, water-repellent furniture, heat lamps, and beautiful pergolas and columns. The company's clients range from city dwellers with small balconies to homeowners with large backyards. HFL has received good media coverage, including coverage by numerous cable networks, such as the Home Network. The growing interest in outdoor living areas among U.S. consumers has positioned the company for future growth.

Kathy Coleman, HFL's sales training manager, recently resigned. This has left the company at a crossroads: Coleman was a firm believer in taking a hands-on approach to training. She had designed a creative sales lab where trainees could work with HFL's new products and practice designing patio layouts for their customers. "Selling involves relationships, and the best way to train for that is in person, period!" Kathy had been known to say. All new hires made a trip to HFL's company headquarters for an initial two weeks of training. They returned six months later for follow-up training. A yearly new product update course has also been offered to all of the company's representatives. Because HFL is located about 110 miles from the nearest metropolitan area, trainees either drive in or fly in via a small regional airline. The president of HFL thinks this is a good time to review the company's sales training curriculum and plan for the future.

Assignment

Break into pairs or groups of three. Have one person play the role of Kathy Coleman's assistant sales trainer. This person has worked closely with Kathy for the past three years and believes HFL's training program is one of the best in the country. The role the second person plays should be that of a representative chosen by all of HFL's sales managers. A large percentage of the company's training costs are expensed to each sales manager's budget, as are the costs related to the transportation, meals, and lodging of the trainees. Moreover, many of the managers believe the time trainees spend away from the field is cutting into the firm's ability to achieve its sales and profitability goals.

The president of HFL would like the two of you to outline the direction the company's new sales training program should take. Weigh the pros and cons of the different training methods available to HFL and debate them. When you've reached an agreement, outline your suggestions for the new program. Then, share the results with your class. If you have three people, the two need to convince the president of their approach.

Sales Manager's Workshop: Identifying Training Needs

A recent e-mail from Terry, your boss, indicates that your company's headquarters is concerned about the lack of field support behind its new *Financial Project Tracking* software. As the district sales manager for Promedia, you know that one of your major responsibilities is to make sure that all your sales reps are well trained and able to sell the complete portfolio of software packages.

When the software was initially released, all Promedia's reps were fired up about selling it, and they received some training via a series of Webinars and CDs. After the introduction, a short newsletter about the usefulness of the software was published for about three months. However, no new ones have been sent since that time. That was 18 months ago.

Over the past year and a half, you have learned that the product isn't as easy to sell as headquarters initially thought it would be. It turns out it is one of the most difficult types of software to sell because of its complexity, its high cost, and the amount of competition it already faces in the marketplace. Based on the comments you've heard from your sales force, you know they would appreciate some additional training on the product. However, no one wants to go through the product's entire training program again. They really want to just know how to overcome certain problems related to selling the product.

You plan to talk with your sales reps to get their opinions about the problems they experience while trying to sell the software. However, you have decided to first review their performance in terms of selling the product to see if you can identify the areas in which they need some additional help. Conduct an opportunity analysis to identify at what stage (or stages) in the sales cycle of the product your people could use additional training.

Caselet 9.1: Justifying the Cost of a Firm's Sales Training

Chippewa Mowers has been run by the Heinz family for three generations. The mowers the company manufactures are reel mowers, often used to cut grass on golf courses and recreational fields. Chippewa's customers across the United States range from small hardware store operators to golf course owners. The company has also been slowly entering international markets.

Chippewa is capable of designing and producing custom jobs when requested. Its customers also include smaller hardware store operators who sell the mowers to homeowners looking for a more environmentally friendly way to cut their grass than gas-powered mowers. More recently, Chippewa has experienced some success using mail-order catalogs to sell to this type of homeowner.

Chippewa's geographically dispersed sales force of 15 people is composed of individuals who share an interest in working outdoors. (Most of the time they spend with their industrial accounts requires them to be outside with the people responsible for the maintenance of golf courses or recreational areas.) The representatives' backgrounds vary from mechanical engineering and agriculture to recreation and business.

Mr. Heinz was slow to authorize a purchase of laptop personal computers for Chippewa's sales force. He sees the amount of time some salespeople spend on their PCs and believes they are "time suckers." He feels that a good salesperson should be in front of the customer—not behind the screen of a computer.

Joe Hannah has been the sales manager for Chippewa Mowers for a little more than four years. His salespeople have told him they need to "keep up" with their competitors who are able to produce better-looking presentations and project proposals. Joe also knows firsthand that his salespeople have difficulties working with the company's new CRM software system. These appeared to be valid reasons for the day of training he conducted at his last meeting with his salespeople.

Mr. Heinz, who admits he doesn't know much about training, greeted Joe last week by saying, "Okay, Joe. When I invest in a new machine for production, they show me how it helps. Can you drop by next week and show me what I got for my sales training investment?"

Questions

1. How should Joe evaluate whether or not his sales training was effective?
2. What approaches should Joe consider when evaluating the effectiveness of his training programs? Discuss the merits of each.
3. What ethical considerations are involved with this decision?

Caselet 9.2: Good, Good Enough, or Not Good Enough?

Bob Sullivan works for Transcontinental Imaging Company (TIC) as a regional sales representative covering a five-county area. He has become disappointed with his position within the company because he feels he is not getting the help he needs to be successful. Specifically, he feels the sales training given by TIC is not targeting his needs. TIC is a large multinational company specializing in personal digital imaging software applications. Its customer base ranges from small individual retail store owners to large franchised photo finishing operations like Motophoto. TIC has over 1,500 commissioned sales representatives throughout the world. The average sales representative stays with TIC for four years.

TIC uses multiple methods to deliver its training, including the Internet, lectures during regional sales meetings, and infrequent regional seminars put on by outside sales consultants. The training is broken down into the following areas:

- Professional Development—Building sales skills
- Work Group Training—Understanding the business unit you work in

■ Systems and Software Training—Understanding the tools to perform your job
■ Compliance Training—Focusing on ethics.

As Bob sees it, TIC's existing training program has not been focusing on individual strengths and weaknesses. Bob expressed a need for additional training during his annual performance review, but nothing has happened. He has had three different sales managers in the past year and feels neglected. Each sales manager handles 40 to 50 salespeople. Bob keeps posting average sales numbers based on his existing customer relationships (most of which were given to him when he took over his territory three years ago), but he has difficulty penetrating new accounts. His entire pay structure is based on a commission percentage of his sales, and no benefits are offered by the company.

Bob called TIC's corporate office and expressed his concerns to Claire Boston, the corporate sales training supervisor. Her advice for him was to read some books on salesmanship and to work with his direct supervisor on any specific training needs he may have. Fed up with the lack of attention and answers, Bob decided to resign and look for another job.

Questions

1. What potential areas of weakness can you identify in TIC's approach to sales training?
2. Do you believe that TIC's sales training is appropriate for its type of business and the number of salespeople it has?
3. Did Bob Sullivan do the right thing in resigning? What other steps could he have taken to improve his current situation?
4. In this case, who should take responsibility for a salesperson who needs help to perform at a higher level? What do you think of Claire Boston's advice to Bob? What would you have said?

References

1. Wilhelm, R. (April, 2003). "Investing in New Agents: A Cost Blueprint." Windsor, CT: LIMRA International.
2. "2006 Industry Report, *Training* Magazine's Analysis of Employer-Sponsored Training in the U.S." (2006). *Training* (December) pp. 20–32.
3. *2008 Sales Training Vendor Guide* (2008). White paper published by ES Research Group, West Tisbury, MA.
4. Wilson, Phillip H., David Strutton, and M. Theodore Farris II (2002). "Investigating the Perceptual Aspect of Sales Training,"*Journal of Personal Selling and Sales Management* (22)2, 77–86.
5. Galea, Christine, and Carl Wiens."Sales Training Survey" (2002). *Sales & Marketing Management* 154(7): 34–36.
6. "Looking Up, Top Sales Priorities for 2007" (2007). *Sales and Marketing Management* 158(1), January/February, 38–39.
7. "The 50 Best Companies to Sell For" (2001–2007). *Selling Power* (Vol. 21–26) November/December.
8. Ahearne, Michael, Ronald Jelinek, and Adam Rapp (2005). "Moving Beyond the Direct Effect of SFA Adoption on Salesperson Performance: Training and Support as Key Moderating Factors," *Industrial Marketing Management* 34: 379–388.
9. Goldstein, Irwin L., and Kevin Ford (2001). *Training in Organizations: Needs Assessment, Development and Evaluation*, 4th ed. Belomont, CA: Wadsworth Publishing.

10. Attita, Ashraf M., Earl D. Honeycutt, Jr., and Mark P. Leach (2005). "A Three-Stage Model for Assessing and Improving Sales Force Training and Development," *Journal of Personal Selling & Sales Management* (25)3: 253–268.

11. Cron, William L., Greg W. Marshall, Japdip Singh, Rosann L. Spiro, and Hirsh Sujan (2005). "Salesperson Selection, Training, and Development: Trends, Implications and Research Opportunities, *Journal of Personal Selling & Sales Management* (25)2: 123–136.

12. Attia et. al. (2005). Op cit.

13. Wellins, Richard S., Charles J. Cosentino, and Bradford Thomas (Winter, 2004*). Building a Winning Sales Force. A Sales Talent Optimization Study on Hiring and Development.* Pittsburgh: Development Dimensions International.

14. Rivera, Ray J., and Andrew Paradise (2006). *2006 State of the Industry in Leading Enterprises: ASTD's Annual Review of Trends in Workplace Learning and Performance.* Alexandria, VA: American Society for Training and Development.

15. Erffmeyer, Robert, and Dale Johnson (2002). "An Exploratory Study of Sales Force Automation Practices: Expectations and Realities," *Journal of Personal Selling & Sales Management* (21)2: 167–175.

16. Speier, C., and V. Venkatesh. (2002). "The Hidden Minefields in the Automation of Sales Force Automation Technologies" *Journal of Marketing* (66)3: 98–111.

17. Robinson, Leroy, Jr., Greg W. Marshall, and Miriam B. Stamps (2005). "An Empirical Investigation of Technology Acceptance in a Field Sales Force Setting," *Industrial Marketing Management* 34, 407–415.

18. Ahearne, Michael, Roland Jelinek, and Adam Rapp (2005). "Moving Beyond the Direct Effect of SFA Adoption on Salesperson Performance: Training and Support as Key Moderating Factors," *Industrial Marketing Management* 34, 379–388.

19. Anderson, Rolph, Rajiv Mehta, and James Strong (1997). "An Empirical Investigation of Sales Management Training Programs for Sales Managers," *Journal of Personal Selling & Sales Management* (17)3: 53–66.

20. Shepherd, C. David, and Rick E. Ridnour (1996). "A Comparison of the Sales Management Training Practices of Smaller and Larger Organizations," *Journal of Business & Industrial Marketing* (11)2: 37–45.

21. Bloom, B. S. (1956). *Taxonomy of Educational Objectives, Handbook I: The Cognitive Domain.* New York: David McKay Company, Inc.

22. Anderson, L. W., and Drathwohl, D. R., eds. (2001). *A Taxonomy for Learning, Teaching and Assessing: A Revision of Bloom's Taxonomy of Educational Objectives.* New York: Longman.

23. *The 2008 Sales Training Vendors Guide.* White paper published by the ES Research Group, West Tisbury, MA.

24. Galea and Wiens (2002). Op cit.

25. Paradise, Andrew (2007). *State of the Industry Report 2007.* Alexandria, VA: American Society for Training and Development.

26. "Cannon U.S.A., Inc. Accelerates Time-to-Market with Web-Ex" (2006). White paper from Web-Ex Web site. Retrieved from: http://www.webex.com/pdf/casestudy_canon.pdf. Retrieved on November 30, 2006.

27. Riveria and Paradise (2006). Op cit.

28. 2006 Industry Report. *Training* Magazine's Analysis of Employer-Sponsored Training in the U.S. (2006). Op cit.

29. Aronauer, Rebecca (2006). "The Classroom vs. E-learning," *Sales & Marketing Management* (158)8 (October): 21.

30. Ganders, George (2007). "Companies Find Online Training Has Its Limits," *Wall Street Journal*, March 26, B3.

31. Borzo, Jeanette (2004). "Almost Human: Using Avatars for Corporate Training, Advocates Say, Can Combine the Best Parts of Face-to-Face Interaction and Computer-Based Learning." *Wall Street Journal* May 24, R4.

32. Erffmeyer, Robert, and Dale Johnson (1997). "The Future of Sales Training: Making Choices Among Six Distance Education Methods," *Journal of Business & Industrial Marketing* (12) 3/4, 185–195.

33. Wilson et. al. (2002). Op cit.

34. Goldstein and Ford (2001). Op cit.

35. Galea and Wiens (2002). Op cit.

36. Erffmeyer, Robert C., K. Randall Russ, and Joseph F. Hair, Jr. (1991). "Needs Assessment and Evaluation in Sales-Training Programs," *Journal of Personal Selling & Sales Management* (11)1: 18–30.

37. Wilson et. al. (2002). Op cit.

38. Kirkpatrick, Donald L. (1959). "Techniques for Evaluating Training Programs," *Journal of the American Society for Training and Development* 13(11): 3–9.

39. Erffmeyer, et. al. (1991). Op cit.

40. Lupton, Robert A., John E. Weiss, and Robin T. Peterson (1999). "Sales Training Evaluation Model (STEM): A Conceptual Framework. *Industrial Marketing Management* 28: 73–86.

41. Leach, Mark P., and Annie H. Liu (Fall, 2003). "Investigating Interrelationships Among Sales Training Evaluations Methods," *Journal of Personal Selling & Sales Management* (XXIII0), 4: 327–339.

42. Leach and Liu (2003). Op cit.

43. Honeycutt, Earl D., Jr., Kiran Karande, Ashraf Attia, and Steven D. Maurer (2001). "A Utility Based Framework for Evaluating the Financial Impact of Sales Force Training Programs," *Journal of Personal Selling & Sales Management* (21)3: 229–238.

44. Honeycutt, Earl D., Jr., Vince Howe, and Thomas N. Ingram (1993). "Shortcomings of Sales Training Programs," *Industrial Marketing Management* 22, 117–123.

45. Rivera, Ray J., and Andrew Paradise (2006). *2006 State of the Industry in Leading Enterprises: ASTD's Annual Review of Trends in Workplace.* Alexandria, VA: American Society for Training & Development.

46. Training Competencies (2006). Professional Society for Sales & Marketing Training. Retrieved January 2, 2007, from http://www.smt.org/i4a/pages/index.cfm?pageid=3325.

Process Management

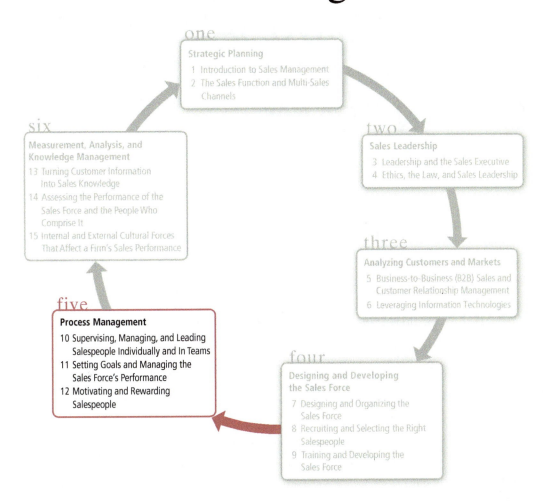

When you graduate and begin working, your first job is likely to be as a salesperson. Currently more marketing majors go into sales than any other position. The point is that you will not start as a chief sales executive or even a sales manager. Your first encounter with sales managers, then, will be as a member of the supervised.

Part Five begins with Chapter 10, *Supervising, Managing, and Leading Individually and in Teams*. In this chapter, we get more specific about those activities that make for effective management and leadership. You may not start out as a sales manager but you can certainly use this material to assess the quality of sales management you are receiving! Included in this chapter are the critical concepts of coaching, mentoring, and working in teams—both in person and virtual.

The next chapter, Chapter 11, *Setting Goals and Managing the Sales Force's Performance*, focuses on the principles of effective goal setting. Sales leaders set goals for

individual salespeople as well as for the entire sales organization. Goals are typically presented in a variety of ways reflecting effort and results of the salesperson. These goals are then tied to compensation plans, and they direct salespeople and sales managers to focus their activities on the right outcomes.

Following that discussion is Chapter 12, *Motivating and Rewarding Salespeople*. Using the goal-setting processes outlined in the previous chapter, we move into systems designed to encourage and reward achievement of those goals. Thus, this chapter describes the compensation and motivation options that companies use to motivate and reward their salespeople. Because you will likely find yourself working and managing older workers, we have included information on managing a multi-generational sales force. Sales managers need to understand and appreciate how different members of the sales force may value different rewards available to them in a work-life balance approach.

10

SUPERVISING, MANAGING, AND LEADING SALESPEOPLE INDIVIDUALLY AND IN TEAMS

LEARNING OBJECTIVES

After completing this chapter, you should be able to:

- Explain and describe the difference between sales supervision, management, and leadership.
- Identify the skills and abilities a person needs to become a good sales manager.
- Understand the elements of teamwork and how to successfully develop and work with teams, including those that are virtual.
- Recognize the ethical challenges facing leaders and teams in the sales environment.

What does it take to manage and lead salespeople individually or as a team? Do you use the same skills for a new hire that you use with an established sales veteran? It's not the same answer for every person or every occasion. A new hire might require close supervision, whereas when developing a sales proposal that involves gathering and analyzing large amounts of information from several sources, the supervision of employees might best be handled through delegation and teamwork. In other situations, the sales manager needs to take the lead and lay out the vision or plan for their sales force to follow. While there may be differences of opinion as to whether a sales manager supervises, manages, or leads his or her sales force, there is agreement that all these behaviors are needed in developing a successful sales organization.

KATHERINE TWELLS

VICE PRESIDENT, THE COCA-COLA COMPANY, CALIFORNIA SALES REGION

What surprised Katherine Twells the most about her transition from a salesperson for Coca-Cola to a leadership position might not be typical of most new sales managers. It wasn't the new title, compensation, or changes in her office space. She was surprised by how much she enjoyed working with people. "I absolutely love working with people in a teaching role and helping them develop professionally," says Twells.

Twells started out working at a bank as a management trainee and after a couple months found she was "under-challenged." With some coaxing from a college professor, she decided to accept a sales position with Coca-Cola. She initially began working a territory with 1,500 restaurants, moved into larger territories and regional accounts, and then became a sales manager. Today, she is responsible for Coca-Cola's food service division in the state of California. She manages an organization of 60 professionals, including seven area directors and a distribution manager. "I now lead leaders," she says. In her positions, Twells has been instrumental in terms of leading cross-functional teams and in developing national leadership training programs for Coca-Cola's sales associates.

This might seem like a bit of a stretch for a person who was initially a little hesitant to go into sales. With each promotion at Coca-Cola, Twells has taken on more responsibility and accountability. Ten years ago when the opportunity in sales management came along, she again needed a little coaxing to take it. She recalls asking herself, "Why do I want to manage others? I like selling!" In retrospect, this is a decision she is glad she made.

As a new manager, she found out that she had to get comfortable getting things done through others—and not doing it herself. She had to remember that everyone has a different way of doing things and that you have to learn that just because it may not be the way you would approach the situation, you can't interfere. Twells knows the importance of being a coach and developing sales representatives who can act independently and as a team. Coaching is something you do every day. Good managers are constantly coaching and giving feedback to the people who report to them directly or indirectly. You have to focus on their behaviors, and you need to be concerned about their goals. "As a sales manager, an important part of my job is to *serve* those I work with," she says.

Twells describes her leadership style as authentic, collaborative, and empowering. Good leaders really need to know and understand the people they work with as individuals. You need to learn their strengths and capitalize on them—as they work independently and in team situations. And finally, you need to trust them. There is no snap way to doing things, she says. "Leadership is an art that you work on daily."

One of the most difficult responsibilities that a new manager deals with is the performance issues of her salespeople. "You think 'I can fix this person'—but most of the time you can't. There comes a point where you risk 'over helping' someone. Sometimes people are just in the wrong job." Another area that can be a bit uncomfortable for most managers is dealing with and addressing conflict. "No one I know ever looks forward to doing that."

Twells explains that even though salespeople primarily work alone, getting them to share information and work well as a team is important. "People who operate as if they are on an island aren't successful. It is critical to be able to be a team player—you must be in touch with others." She also recommends working with and being a mentor. She has benefited from informal mentors both inside and outside of Coca-Cola. "Mentors have helped to give me perspective—I've found them to be beneficial in providing insight about how to keep my balance in situations that may lie ahead. They sometimes have the ability to look around the corner and let you know what's coming." ■

In Chapter 3 we discussed leadership theories and different approaches to conceptualizing leadership. At this point we will extend that knowledge base and explore new skill sets as you examine the activities of supervision, managing, and leading to see how they fit into a sales manager's position. Additionally, we'll examine elements of how sales managers incorporate coaching in their daily activities. Finally, as part of this discussion, we will also examine mentoring and what elements help make teamwork effective—both in person and in virtual settings.

Supervising

Supervision is generally used today to refer to time spent working with employees to be certain they are aware of the responsibilities of their job and how to perform them correctly. Because of the independent nature of the sales job, most of the supervisory activities sales managers engage in occur when they're working with new hires. This seemingly simple and potentially time-consuming task should not be taken lightly, as it is a critical element of a sales manager's responsibilities. Supervision was an important element in a manager's position when "management" was first studied, and it continues to be in the twenty-first century.

Today, the term *supervisor* is seldom heard, yet the act of supervising is no less important than it was a century ago. Sales managers—and sometimes sales trainers—spend time supervising people performing new tasks. They observe and then offer suggestions for improving their performance if needed. Their presence can help ensure that if the salesperson needs assistance, he or she gets it. Whatever you want to call it, supervising involves lots of "hands-on" time. Mark Baranczyk, the midwest regional sales manager for the Jacob Leinenkugel Brewing Company, spends about three days each week in the field with his sales representatives providing personalized supervision. During this time, he reviews the objectives of the call and helps out reps if he's needed. If a call goes well,

New hires need supervising to ensure they understand what to tell customers. (Comstock Complete)

he'll hold back on participating during the visit and offer a review of the representative's performance during a "curbside coaching and counseling" session. Sometimes Baranczyk will know the representative is having difficulties achieving an objective with a client. During calls such as these, he takes a more active role helping to answer questions, providing insight, and overcoming the client's objections. At times like these, Baranczyk needs to use coaching skills to help the salesperson identify and correct any shortcomings they have identified. We present more information about coaching later in this chapter.

Sometimes managers don't supervise new hires; more experienced sales personnel do. Some companies refer to people such as this as a *first-level manager*.[1] Another source of supervisory assistance sales managers use is technology. If a company is using a CRM system, a supervisor can track an employee's daily activities. This information can provide a sales manager with insight about how an employee is progressing with his or her customers, whether or not the person is achieving his or her objectives during calls, and using his or her time wisely.

Managing

More experienced sales personnel usually don't require supervision. They do, however, require that someone, like their sales manager, manage their work responsibilities and those of other sales force members in order to achieve the goals of their organizational unit. In this section we look at activities involved with managing a sales force from two different perspectives: from the sales manager's perspective and the sales representative's perspective.

Managing the sales force requires the sales manager to be skilled in several areas including: setting objectives, organizing the tasks necessary to achieve them, motivating the sales force, and problem solving. Although the goals of the organization are set by executive officers, most managers are charged with setting the objectives of their unit to meet the goals of the organization and developing a budget to support them. Wayne Nash is the national account sales manager for LDPI, Inc., a company that manufactures commercial lighting fixtures for hazardous, wet and clean room applications. The company's sales goals are set by LDPI's vice president of sales and marketing. Nash works with a regional sales manager, three sales engineers, and a large number of independent sales representatives and distributors located across the United States and North America. He is responsible for planning how the sales force will work to achieve the company's sales goals. He sets sales objectives for each sales unit and individual sales rep. He then allocates his budget in a manner that will support accomplishing the objectives he has laid out. If his

Managing a sales force involves planning, analysis, and organizing. (Photos.com)

company wants to increase its sales by 5 percent, Nash might, for example, look at marketing research showing potential market segments underserved by the company. To help educate potential buyers about LDPI's products, he could set aside resources to purchase advertisements in industry magazines, mail materials to a select group of customers, send personnel to participate in appropriate trade shows, and offer a financial incentive for sales made to new customers in this new market segment.

The next set of management responsibilities focuses on *organizing and staffing the sales force*. The sales manager must make decisions about how to organize the work and who is going to handle each task. This may range from broader-level decisions, such as deciding how to organize the sales force (for example, by industry, geography, or product line) to more narrow-level decisions, such as assigning specific salespeople to specific clients. It might also require making decisions about how to divide responsibilities for a team-based selling effort—for example, deciding who should handle outbound calls to qualify prospects, who should meet and present products to clients, and who should follow up to offer them sales support.

Sales managers also typically play an important role when it comes to staffing. Oftentimes they work very closely with their human resources department to recruit and select new sales force members. At other times, they leave most of the recruiting and screening activities to their human resource department, which then refers the top candidates to the sales managers for consideration and final hire or no-hire decisions.

Certainly making sure sales representatives have an incentive to do their jobs well is also an important task for the sales manager to perform (see Chapter 12); so is training and developing sales representatives (see Chapter 9) as well as coaching them.

The last set of management responsibilities involves measuring and analyzing the performance of the sales force and, when needed, taking corrective action in order to meet the initial objectives. (This aspect is discussed in more detail in Chapter 11.) In essence, this is problem solving. If LDPI was trying to capture wastewater treatment plants as potential new customers, for example, Nash would need to measure the extent of sales activities aimed at this group by determining how many inquiries resulted from the ads he placed, how many and what quality of prospects were identified at trade shows, and where potential customers were in the buying process. After analyzing the data, he might determine that although LDPI has improved its visibility among these buyers, the company's representatives still need to spend a greater amount of time familiarizing the buyers with the company. In order to help his representatives accomplish this task, he might encourage LDPI's marketing department to engage in new promotional activities, such as placing additional advertisements in other industry publications, or, for example, using a small, outbound call center to make follow-up calls to trade show attendees.

If Nash further learned that the sales force was requesting more information on the needs of the wastewater treatment industry and the regulations it's subject to, he again would have to respond. Suppose, for example, that after hearing reports such as this from the field, he learns that different chemicals are used in different climates (Florida versus Minnesota) and that different states have more stringent regulations than others. As a result of these differences, he might decide that further training of the sales representatives is needed immediately. It might be that, after overcoming these obstacles, he then learns that there are certain times of the year when municipalities are more likely to make a purchase. At this point he might decide to offer reps a 60-day bonus plan during these times of the year to motivate them to concentrate their efforts on these potential buyers. With each piece of information he gains, he *manages* his personnel and budget to accomplish the goals of his sales force.

Sources of Power

To accomplish their goals, sales managers need power, which can stem from different sources. While studying the workings of teams, two French psychologists, French and Raven, developed a classification of power bases that team leaders used to reward or punish their team members.[2] The amount of power a leader had with their team varied depending on the composition of the team and the skill set of the individual manager or leader. Some of the sources of power may be the result of a formal structure, or they may also be acquired through informal structures. Exhibit 10.1 displays the bases of power.

Formal power is given on the basis of the position a person holds in an organization. It is the authority an individual is given to accomplish his or her job. The formal bases of

EXHIBIT 10.1

Bases of Power for a
Manager and Leader

power are legitimate power, reward power, coercive power, and informational power. **Legitimate power** is the power given to a particular position. For sales managers, this typically would include the power to make decisions regarding issues of employment, budgeting, and any other decisions they need to make to accomplish the tasks under their responsibility. A national sales manager has more legitimate power than a regional sales manager, who will have more power than a district sales manager.

Reward power is the ability to distribute rewards. The rewards might include providing reps with more desirable territories (perhaps involving less travel), different compensation levels, gifts, benefits, promotions, job titles, and accoutrements related to their work environment, such as, company cars and nicer offices. Praise and recognition are also considered rewards, even more so when material rewards are not readily available. The opposite of reward power is **coercive power**. This stems from the ability of the sales manager to withhold rewards. It could also include making negative verbal comments to or about a salesperson. When coercive power is used, it typically builds resentment and resistance on the part of the recipient(s). As you might expect, it is the least effective form of power.

Informational power is power a leader derives from the ability to access and control information that other people don't have. If only the sales manager has a great deal of information about the sales process or sales organization, the person's representatives will be dependent upon the manager and will have to contact the individual for assistance at multiple points during a sales cycle. Thus, the manager will have power over the representatives. More effective organizations encourage the sharing of information throughout the sales organization. Customer relationship management systems are designed for this very purpose, in fact. The more information sales representatives have, the more empowered they are to do their jobs.

Informal power is power that an individual has as a result of his or her skills, personality, or geniality. These bases are expert power, referent power, and charismatic power. People who possess informal power can actually exert more influence over other group members than a person with only formal power. **Expert power** is power based on a person's knowledge, skills, and expertise. Sales managers who are skilled in the various aspects of selling the product, solving customer problems, and managing their accounts have expert power. **Referent power** is based on the degree to which a person is liked due to his or her personality and interpersonal skills. A sales manager who is well-liked and admired based on their personal attributes will have a high level of referent power. When an individual is strongly admired based on their personality, physical attractiveness, and other factors, that individual may have what is referred to as **charismatic power**. A person with charismatic power over their group members is often able to induce them to accomplish the most. For example, sales managers with charismatic power might have the ability to revitalize and encourage their sales forces to succeed even against seemingly insurmountable odds. However, if this power is used in a negative way, it can result in sales representatives engaging in unethical sales

ETHICS IN SALES MANAGEMENT

What Are the Traits of a Bad Leader?

Ideally, leaders work to achieve good outcomes. However, we all know of leaders who are either incapable of achieving those outcomes or work toward outcomes that benefit themselves versus their organizations or the general public. For example, in one highly publicized incident during the high-tech boom, the sales managers in a prominent brokerage firm encouraged their salespeople to sell stocks to customers that they knew weren't likely to perform well. They did so because the commissions earned on those particular stocks were higher.

- Research has shown that there are seven traits associated with bad leaders. The traits are as follows:
  - Incompetent: The leader and at least some of his or her followers lack the will or skill to sustain effective action.
  - Rigid: The leader and at least some of his or her followers are stiff, unyielding, and unwilling to adapt to new ideas, new information, or changing times.
  - Intemperate: The leader lacks self-control and is aided and abetted by followers who do not intervene.
  - Callous: The leader is uncaring or unkind and ignores or discounts the needs of the rest of the organization.
  - Corrupt: The leader lies, cheats, or steals and puts his or her self-interest above all else.
  - Insular: The leader disregards or at least minimizes the health and welfare of those outside a small center group.
  - Evil: The leader disregards the worth of others. Some leaders, and at least some followers, commit atrocities.

Source: Based on Kellerman, Barbara (2001). *Bad Leadership: What It Is, How It Happens, Why It Matters.* Harvard Business School Press.

practices, too. An example would be a manager who encouraged his or her sales force to misrepresent their firm's product characteristics to potential buyers so as to increase the company's sales volumes. The Ethics in Sales Management feature in this chapter offers some examples of this occurring.

Which form of power is most effective for a sales manager to use? Without some formal power, sales managers have a very limited ability to direct the efforts of their sales representatives. However, sales managers with only formal power might find that their sales representatives are just minimally dedicated to their jobs. Those sales managers who are able to utilize more informal power bases, in concert with their formal power bases, will likely find themselves with sales reps who actually want to work for them.

As a sales manager, you need to think about the various power bases and how you can develop and effectively use them. Bruce Hanson is a regional sales manager for Moore Wallace, a printing company with worldwide locations. Hanson utilizes a variety of types of power. He has legitimate power based on his position, reward power to affect the compensation his reps receive, the ability to hand out praise to reinforce their behaviors, and, if needed, he can use coercive power to attempt to correct the actions of representatives. Lastly, he can utilize informational power, especially with newer hires, to help guide them through a selling situation that requires a great deal of insight and experience.

Hanson is also very knowledgeable about printing and enjoys working with his sales representatives. They look to him for guidance. In other words, he has power as an expert. He makes sure that he spends time not just working with his employees but also socializing with them—whether it is over a meal, at a ballgame, or a company function. His representatives enjoy working with him and, as a result, he also has referent power and charismatic power he can use to accomplish his managerial goals.

Becoming a sales manager presents many new challenges people don't necessarily face as sales representatives. (Photos.com)

The Up-Close Perspective: Becoming the Boss

Using power is one area that new managers often struggle with as they transition into their new positions. Studies of new managers indicate that the assumptions they hold about what it is like to become the boss often are not accurate.[3] Findings indicate that the skills required to be a good manager are different from those of being a star performer. Many sales managers are promoted because of their sales ability and not their management skills. Looking back on the first group of sales representatives he managed, Dave Anderson, who was a sales manager with automotive dealerships, comments, "I am so, so sorry. I didn't know what I was doing." Anderson's comments are not that uncommon. Few new sales managers know what challenges lie ahead for them.[4]

A summary of these myths or misperceptions is contained in Exhibit 10.2. The biggest misperception of many new managers is that their jobs will revolve around implementing their own ideas. In reality, they find that it is more about working together and combining everyone's ideas. Another misperception is that power will come from their position; instead they find out that it comes more from their informal bases of power: Controlling people is not nearly as important as getting their commitment. And finally, sales managers learn that it's not just about working with individuals to keep things going, but clearing the

EXHIBIT 10.2

Perceptions of New Managers: Myths vs. Realities

	Myth	Reality
Biggest misperception of the new role:	**Authority:** "Now I will have the freedom to implement my ideas."	**Interdependency:** "It's humbling that someone who works for me could get me fired."
Source of Power:	**Based on Formal authority:** "I will finally be on top of the ladder."	**Based on Informal Power:** "Employees are wary of their managers. You really need to earn their respect."
Desired Outcome:	**Control:** "I must get compliance from my subordinates."	**Commitment:** "Compliance does not equal commitment."
Managerial Focus:	**Managing one-on-one:** "My role is to build relationships with my individual subordinates."	**Leading the team:** "I need to create a culture what will allow the group to fulfill its potential."
Key Challenge:	**Keeping the operation in working order:** "My job is to make sure the operation runs smoothly."	**Making changes that will make the team perform better:** "I am responsible for initiating changes to enhance the group's performance."

Source: Reprinted by permission of *Harvard Business Review*. From "Becoming the Boss," Linda A. Hill, Vol. 85, No. 1, January 2007, Copyright @2006 by the Harvard Business School Publishing Corporation; all rights reserved.

path of obstacles so your team will make great achievements. Recognizing these common misperceptions can help new sales managers develop into their new roles.

As a new leader, experts recommend that it is best to make a low-key entry. This gives you time to learn the ropes, develop relationships, and benefit from the wisdom of those who have preceded you. It also gives your employees time to demonstrate what they know and you a chance to show your appreciation for the contributions of each of them. As leadership expert Warren Bennis puts it, "It shows that you are a leader, not a dictator" (pp. 49).[5]

Once established in their positions, sales managers must always work to improve and expand their expertise in terms of their people management skills. There are volumes of books written on this topic. The following is a summary of one manager's suggestion of important behaviors that managers should demonstrate to the salespeople who directly report to him.[6] These are behaviors that a new sales manager should find actionable and they would serve him well.

1. *Clarify the direction your business is taking.* Managers need to communicate clearly where the business is headed, why, and how employees will contribute to it. By discussing this, people have a better perspective of the issues facing the organization and how they fit in.
2. *Set goals and objectives.* Without goals and objectives, sales managers are just making assumptions about their progress. Goals and objectives should be set at both the team and individual level. Doing a good job of establishing them will make bonus and merit incentive performance decisions clearer and easier to communicate to your individual representatives.
3. *Give frequent, specific, and immediate feedback.* This shows you are interested in the development of your representatives, how you think they are performing, and, if need be, how to improve their performance. It will also make the performance evaluation discussions go more smoothly.
4. *Be decisive and timely.* After you have the information you need, your salespeople expect you to make a decision in a timely manner. This helps your reps move forward instead of wondering how they should proceed.
5. *Be accessible.* If, as a sales manager, you expect your sales representatives to keep you informed, you need to be available when they need to see you. This can be done in person, by phone, or electronically.
6. *Demonstrate honesty and candor.* When sales managers communicate with their representatives, especially during performance appraisals, they should use language that is specific and not vague. Masking the truth doesn't help people develop.
7. *Offer an equitable compensation plan.* Good goals and clear communications will help people understand how they are being rewarded for their efforts.

The Sales Representative's Perspective: What It Takes to Be a Good Sales Manager

So what does it take to be considered a good sales manager by your sales representatives? Perspectives differ depending upon what position you are viewing things from. When groups of sales representatives were asked what characteristics help make a sales manager *good*, they were able to identify some common themes.[7,8,9,10] The following is a summary of the characteristics they identified.

1. *Is flexible.* Good sales managers need to be able to balance the demands of handling business issues one minute and then shifting gears to direct and coach people the next. They have to work through people and not do the job themselves.

2. *Is a good communicator.* This means being available to give timely and frequent feedback. When sales representatives need help, it usually means they need immediate help as opposed to feedback a couple of days later. Good managers have an open-door policy and don't mind being interrupted. They respond to e-mails the same day and return missed phone calls the day they come in.

3. *Works for the good of the team.* Good sales managers don't put their needs ahead of those of the team. They shift the spotlight from themselves so that it focuses on their team and team members. They take satisfaction from the accomplishments of their groups.

4. *Is considered trustworthy.* Over time, through actions and examples, a good sales manager is able to develop an atmosphere of trust. Sales representatives are comfortable sharing information with the manager because they know that the person will do what is best for them and will respect their individual wishes.

5. *Can motivate and lead the team.* Good sales managers help their teams conquer the challenges they face by keeping their teams motivated via informal actions (for example, by offering feedback to their reps on a personal basis) and formal actions (for example, by recognizing their representatives publicly).

Leading

Research shows that a poor sales manager can literally cost a company millions of dollars in lost sales opportunities (one research study places this number at $10 to 20 million annually). For example, two-thirds of sales vice presidents surveyed indicated that 40 percent of their sales leaders were not meeting expectations and cited a lack of leadership and coaching skills as the source of their failure. Dissatisfaction with one's boss is, in fact, the number one sales representative complaint.[11] Another study conducted by the Forum Corporation found that a firm's sales managers "figured prominently" in the success of their sales force—that a sales force whose manager thinks strategically, provides coaching and feedback to his salespeople, and creates a motivating environment perform much better than others. The respondents noted, however, that sales managers were often promoted because they were high-performing sales representatives—not because of their managerial abilities.

The qualifications required by sales managers are changing though. Firms are demanding a higher level of leadership and management skills than in the past. "We have changed the first-line sales manager's role to become more of a training and coaching/development role versus a super salesman," one survey respondent said. Given the extent to which a firm's success is determined by its sales managers, the remainder of this section examines a promising new leadership approach and some skill sets that new sales managers should develop.[12]

A New School of Managerial Thought?

In the last part of the twentieth century, leadership studies identified a classic, two-factor approach that focused on the tasks and relationship behaviors of leaders. These approaches are labeled **transactional leadership** because they focus on an exchange, of some nature, between leaders and their followers—for example, leaders giving promotions and/or bonuses to sales representatives who meet their sales goals.

More recently there has been a movement toward a **transformational leadership** approach to leadership. "It is concerned with emotions, values, ethics, standards, and long-term goals and includes assessing followers' motives, satisfying their needs, and treating them as human beings" (p. 176). Transformational leaders focus on the needs and motives of their employees and try to help them reach their fullest potential.[13] These leaders also exhibit **emotional intelligence**.[14] Emotional intelligence includes one's ability to understand and manage the emotions of other people in light of their own. The underlying premise is that people who are more sensitive to their emotions and understand the impact of their emotions on others will be more effective leaders" (p. 23).[15] Emotional intelligence includes self-awareness, self-regulation, motivation, empathy, and social skills. Exhibit 10.3 describes these abilities.[16] Leaders with high levels of emotional intelligence create environments that foster trust, reasonable amounts of risk taking, and higher levels of productivity. Low levels of emotional intelligence in a work environment foster fear and anxiety.[17] Generally, as people mature, their emotional intelligence increases.

A leader's "emotional style" impacts the culture of the person's organization or work environment. Those leaders with high levels of emotional intelligence create environments that foster trust, team building, and healthy risk taking and higher levels of productivity. Low levels of emotional intelligence in a work environment foster fear and anxiety.[16]

Note that Katherine Twells, who was profiled at the beginning of the chapter, finds her greatest rewards in being a developer of her employees' talent. In her description of her leadership style, you can see that it reflects several of the components of emotional intelligence, including self-awareness, motivation, empathy, and social skills:

> I think it is important to understand yourself and what you want from your job first. Use that as a foundation and the rest comes more easily. You have to bring in the right people, understand how to use them, create synergies, and be sincere about it. I believe that people are the best asset of an organization—but you need to understand how to motivate them to get the best results. . . . As a sales manager, an important part of my job is to *serve* those I work with.

EXHIBIT 10.3

The Hallmarks of Emotional Intelligence

Source: Reprinted by permission of Harvard Business Review. From "What Makes a Leader?" by Daniel Goleman January 1, 2004. Copyright ©2004 by the Harvard Business School Publishing Corporation; all rights reserved.

Skills or Abilities	Hallmarks
Self-Management Skills	
<u>Self-Awareness:</u> The ability to recognize and understand your moods, emotions, and what drives you, as well as how they affect others	Self-confidence Realistic self-assessment A self-deprecating sense of humor
<u>Self-Regulation:</u> The ability to control or redirect disruptive impulses and moods. The propensity to suspend judgment—to think before acting	Trustworthiness and integrity Comfort with ambiguity Openness to change
<u>Motivation:</u> A passion to work for reasons that go beyond money or status. A propensity to pursue goals with energy and persistence	A strong drive to achieve Optimism Organizational commitment
The Ability to Relate to Others	
<u>Empathy:</u> The ability to understand the emotional makeup of other people. The skill in responding to people depending upon their emotional reactions	Expertise in building and retaining talent Cross-cultural sensitivity Service to clients and customers
<u>Social Skill:</u> Proficiency in managing relationship and building networks. An ability to find common ground and build rapport	Effectiveness in leading change Persuasiveness Expertise in building and leading teams

What Leadership Competencies Do Sales Managers Need?

The studies we discussed in this chapter suggest that sales managers today need to focus on and develop better leadership skills than in the past. According to the responses of sales vice presidents, many sales managers appear to be unprepared to play this role.[18] The highest-performing sales organizations rely heavily on their sales managers to provide representatives with ongoing coaching and feedback. In fact, it is a key predictor of the success an organization will achieve. In addition to developing their coaching skills, two other leadership development methods, which have increasingly been utilized over the past 20 years are mentoring and working in teams.[19] We will look at these activities next.

Coaching

What image comes to mind when you hear the word *coaching*? Perhaps you envision someone involved in athletics or the arts. Can you imagine a performer or team trying to perfect their performance without the benefit of someone giving them feedback? No doubt you have probably tried performing some activity without the advice of a coach or teacher. Contrast that performance with one in which you received feedback. As you probably know, the value of a coach can be significant.

Coaching salespeople is not that much different than coaching athletes or performers. A study of over 1,000 firms found that salespeople who receive at least one-half day a week, one-on-one with their managers are twice as productive as other salespeople.[20] As we mentioned earlier in the chapter, Mark Baranczyk, a regional sales manager for the Jacob Leinenkugel Brewing Company, spends about three days each week in the field working with his sales representatives. During and after each of the sales calls, Mark coaches each of his representatives. This includes asking them questions about their performance, offering positive feedback and advice, perhaps setting aside time for practice, and setting future performance-related goals for them.

For sales coaching to be effective, a sales manager should follow several guidelines:[21,22]

1. *Prepare and observe.* Let your sales representatives know you are joining them to observe them and offer your feedback. Make sure you understand the objectives of the calls they are making. Watch for nonverbal communication and listen carefully.
2. *Give feedback.* Avoid asking your sales representatives "yes" or "no" questions about how well they performed. Instead, ask them open-ended questions such as the following: "What other options could you have offered the customer when she objected to the product's price?" Be specific when pointing out a person's good selling skills and those that could be improved. Telling a representative that "You should take more initiative" is not as helpful as telling the person something like the following: "When the buyer didn't know if there was a good fit between the two systems, it probably would have been a good idea to ask her to explain where the fit was 'off' or ask her to try to use our product during a no-cost trial period." Focus on improving your reps' skills rather than dwelling on things they did incorrectly. Provide the feedback as soon after the observation as possible.
3. *Be a role model.* Modeling or demonstrating the desired behaviors and letting your representatives model that behavior is a powerful way of coaching people. Explain how and why you did the things you did. Give your representatives the opportunity to use the same tactics you did.
4. *Follow-up.* Demonstrate to your representatives that you follow up—in other words, that you do what you say you will do.

5. *Trust.* When there are high levels of trust between sales representatives and their sales managers, the relationships will be more productive than those relationships that lack trust.

Sometimes it doesn't matter how great a coach a sales manager is. It still might not be enough. An example might be a case in which a sales representative is excessively absent, misses appointments and deadlines, experiences numerous customer complaints, or even is involved in auto accidents. This could indicate that the salesperson's on-the-job performance is being impacted by other factors that no amount of coaching will cure. It might be that the salesperson just needs a little time off to deal with some pressing personal issues. However, when a pattern of these behaviors develops, it may be time for the sales manager to see if the salesperson needs professional counseling. The representative could be experiencing marital or family problems, financial stress, or health or substance abuse issues. In cases such as these, the sales manager should seek the confidential assistance of his or her human resources personnel. These people can help evaluate whether the representative needs professional help, and if so, help the person get it.

Mentoring

Many firms are encouraging sales managers to not only be a mentor but to also *have* a mentor. **Mentoring** is a long-term relationship in which a senior person supports the personal and professional development of a junior person.[23] The mentor concept has its origins in Greek mythology. When King Odysseus was about to fight in the Trojan War, Mentor, an elderly friend, was charged by the king to watch over the hero's son, Telemachus. Mentor provided insights to his younger protégée that only an elder, more experienced person could.[24]

Having and being a mentor can help develop leadership skills. (Getty Images, Inc.—Stockbyte)

A *mentor* is the term used to describe a person who acts as a teacher or trustworthy advisor. The mentor typically does not have a reporting relationship with the person they are mentoring. Their relationship can be formally established by an organization or developed more informally.

Camellia Poplarski is a regional sales director for the drug maker Eli Lilly. Eli Lilly is a firm believer in the merits of being and having mentors. Typically a person being mentored benefits from being given the perspective of someone who has already "been there and done that." Mentors can help those whom they mentor with everything from the proper procedures they should follow to career advice. As Poplarski sees it, "It gives you a leg up because you learn things that are not in any book." Mentoring helps younger representatives become more knowledgeable about the marketplace, the firm for which they are selling, and its products. Having a mentor program can also give a company an advantage when it's recruiting new sales reps.[25] Experts recommend that if your organization does not have a formal mentoring program in place, you should seek out an individual several levels above you—someone whom you trust and admire and ask him or her if they would serve in a mentoring capacity to you. Mentoring "sessions" are usually very informal and occur several times a year or when needed.

Traditionally there were two times when it was thought best to have a mentoring relationship. The first was when someone was just beginning their career (they learned what to expect) and the second was when senior sales personnel had reached a plateau in their career (they benefited from offering their counsel to new hires). Research has also shown that sales managers who were mentored by managers inside their firms are less likely to leave the firm and perform better than those sales managers with peer mentors, outsider mentors, or no mentors.[26]

The Ability to Organize and Work Effectively with Teams

Historically, sales representatives have worked independently. However, with the more complex products and services firms are offering, the increased use of supply chain management, and a more global marketplace, firms are finding there are more situations in which their sales personnel must work in teams. Some organizations now assign a sales team to their key, or national accounts. To develop better product solutions for the buyer, a team might be comprised of representatives from several functional areas, such as sales, product development, operations, and customer service.[27,28]

Greg Shortell is the president and CEO of Network Engines, a company that makes server applications installed on computer hardware or packaged with it. Shortell says his company has moved from product-based sales to solution-based sales. "You need in-depth specialized knowledge . . . that goes right through all the steps from requirements to delivery—and different people have to fill those needs," he explains. For example, a "prospecting" representative might work to identify and qualify leads before handing them off to a "sales" representative who would establish face-to-face communications with prospective customers. At this point, a specialist involved with the development of the product would talk to the customers about the fit of the product with their firms. If a sale were completed, the client might then be turned over to a "customer service and follow-up" team member whose job it is to ensure that the products are delivered on time and meet the customer's quality expectations.[29]

Just working with other people does not make your group a team, however. A team is a small group of people with complementary skills, who, as such, are able to collectively complete a project in a superior way. They are committed to a common goal. Members interact with each other and the leader and depend on each other's input to perform their own work. Those teams that are empowered to handle an ongoing task are considered **self-managed teams**. A **project team** is organized around a unique task of limited duration and is disbanded when the task is completed.[30]

Sales managers working with teams will fare better if they take the time to structure and organize the teams when they are initially established. If they don't take the time to do so, the team will likely struggle. An initial "orientation" type of meeting in which the team members learn about each other's skills and the team's goals is often a good idea. The responsibilities, tasks, and leaders of the teams should be clearly assigned so that everyone

Putting together sales teams and managing them is becoming more important for a sales manager to do today. (Comstock Complete)

S   SELF-ASSESSMENT LIBRARY

No doubt in some of your courses you have had opportunities to work in small groups and teams. To develop team-building and leadership skills takes practice and experience. You can improve some of these skills with practice and by utilizing many of the behaviors discussed in this section. To assess your team-building and leadership skills, go to http://www. prenhall. com/ sal/ and log in using your access code. Then click on:

   Assessments
     II. Working with Others
       B. Leadership and Team Skills
         6. How Good Am I at Building and Leading a Team?

Your score on this instrument will provide you with a general idea of how your team-building skills compare to those of 500 business students.

understands what is expected of them and who "owns" the different aspects of different accounts or projects. Another important element of successful teams is sharing client communications. Contact management systems can be used for this purpose. Sales managers also need to make sure the team has the right people with the right skills and is only as large as it needs to be. Make sure that reward systems are in place that will motivate the individual efforts of people on the teams as well as the teams as a whole. Poorly designed reward systems for teams are a frequent reason why they fail.[31]

Being a Team Member

Once you have a team up and running, what should you expect from them—or what's expected from you as a member of a management team? Again, we will provide a short summary of some actionable behaviors a new sales manager (and team members) should consider engaging in when working with their teams.[32]

1. *Get involved.* This is particularly important when someone falls behind on their commitments, especially because of important personnel issues or crisis situations.
2. *Generate ideas.* Team members who contribute innovative and creative ideas are harder to find than those who opt not to contribute.
3. *Be willing to collaborate.* You might not enjoy working with all of your colleagues, but you need to be able to work with them for the benefit of the organization.
4. *Be willing to lead initiatives.* Future projects are full of uncertainties; being willing to take a risk is a valuable attribute.
5. *Develop leaders as you develop.* It is important to personally be involved in developing your employees.
6. *Stay current.* Know what is going on in the world and with your customers and their markets.
7. *Anticipate market changes.* Don't sit back waiting for change to occur; plan for it.
8. *Drive your own growth.* Constantly seek out education and self-development opportunities through the activities and assignments you are engaged in and in your personal relationships.
9. *Be a player for all seasons.* Be open to change in good times and bad.

VIRTUAL TEAMS Oftentimes sales managers have personnel in different geographic locations work in **virtual teams**. These people send and receive the majority of their communications electronically as opposed to in person. Some sales managers, like Katherine Twells at Coca-Cola, work virtually with their representatives and also in person with them. For others, such as Michael Muhlfelder of Pragmatech Software whose sales force is widely dispersed, working at a distance is the norm. Muhlfelder uses e-mails, instant messaging, and weekly calls to communicate with his reps. Tips for working with virtual teams include:

- Select the technology that works best for the team. Although some technologies might sound appealing, the majority of teams prefer to use an Intranet Web site with areas on team information and contacts and discussion and information posting. When needed, they will hold a teleconference.
- Communicate frequently. Most groups do so daily.
- Track down members who aren't participating. This is especially important during the early life of the team when norms are being set. The leader of the virtual team needs to ensure that all members of the virtual team are participating in the process.
- Have agreed-upon ground rules for the team's interaction. For example, require team members to answer e-mails within 24 hours, even if their replies are brief.[33,34]

Bill Febry, a former sales executive for Jacob Leinenkugel Brewing Company, says sales managers should "educate, motivate, and inspire." However, he notes that he can't do that by e-mail: "As much as I'd like to see every one of my direct reports in person, when I can't, I make an effort to pick up the phone and speak with them personally—not an e-mail, not a recording on the voice mail." In other words, in even the best virtual teams, there's no substitute for personal contact. You can't solely manage people electronically—at least not very well.

The Future of Sales Management

Whether sales managers are supervising, managing, and/or leading, they will always face challenges. Business executives have identified five challenges for future leaders:[35]

1. *Incorporate globalization/internationalization of leadership concepts.* Sales leaders must be comfortable and knowledgeable doing business in the international marketplace (see Chapter 15).

GLOBAL SALES MANAGEMENT

Developing Global Leaders

Chapter 3 identified the need for companies to engage in cross-cultural leadership research. That's a good start, but the question remains: How do companies translate those findings into action? A Conference Board study found that 79 percent of the companies it surveyed are accelerating their global leadership development activities. The survey identified several activities companies use to develop their international leaders, specifically in the Asia-Pacific area.

The top programs used to develop business leaders in the Asia-Pacific region include:

1. Internal management programs: 44 percent
2. Company training programs: 40 percent
3. International assignments greater than 2 years: 36 percent
4. Mentoring and/or coaching: 33 percent
5. Participation in cross-functional international teams: 33 percent

Some companies have gone beyond region-specific competencies to country-specific competencies. Agilent Technologies has identified the following China-specific leader competencies that will help focus both locals and expatriates working in China:

1. Persuades effectively
2. Builds networks and alliances
3. Drives operational efficiency
4. Communicates effectively
5. Balances cultural sensitivities
6. Demonstrates individual and organizational awareness.

Three recurring themes were 1.) collaboration, teamwork, communication; 2.) alignment across borders; and 3.) people development and coaching.

Source: Based on Bell, Andrew N. (2006). *Leadership Development in Asia-Pacific: Identifying and Developing Leaders for Growth.* New York: The Conference Board.

2. *Increase the integrity and character of leaders.* Sales leaders of today need to be humble, team builders, and good communicators. Transformation leadership works only when leaders have a solid moral character and a concern for others, and demonstrate these through their actions.

3. *Incorporate new ways of thinking about leadership.* Leadership is shifting from a focus of individual leaders toward developing the capacity of all group members.

4. *Integrate technology.* Technology changes how we live and work; how information is gathered, organized, and shared; and how we communicate. Leading a virtual team located in different parts of the country and globe is a reality. Leaders will clearly have to be much more engaged and comfortable with technology.

5. *Demonstrate return on investment.* Leadership development activities—just like other forms of training—must be able to demonstrate their effectiveness. Those aspiring to sales leadership positions would do well to use these challenges to guide their future directions.

Summary

In years past, many sales managers were promoted because of their excellent selling skills, with little regard for their management skills. Today, however, people know that sales managers with good managerial skills have a big impact on the success of firms. However, many organizations find that their sales managers lack these skills.

In terms of supervising their representatives, sales managers observe their representatives (more often, new hires) and then give them suggestions for improving their performance. A sales manager's presence can help ensure that if the salesperson needs assistance, he or she will get it. In some firms, more experienced sales personnel, called first-line managers, supervise new representatives.

There are a number of facets related to managing sales representatives. Although the goals of a firm are generally set by its executive officers, most sales managers are charged with setting the objectives of their unit to meet those goals and develop the budgets to support them. Sales managers are also responsible for organizing and staffing their units and analyzing the performance of their representatives to make sure they are achieving their goals. Sales managers utilize a number of sources of formal and informal power to accomplish these tasks.

Research confirms that sales managers who have strong leadership skills and who develop their sales representatives are more likely to have higher-performing sales forces than sales managers lacking these skills. Sales managers who adopt a transformational leadership style of management focus on the needs and motives of their representatives and work to develop them. Sales managers with high levels of emotional intelligence have the ability to understand and manage the emotions of other people.

Other leadership skills that have become more valued in sales managers are coaching, mentoring, and team-building. Coaching involves providing immediate feedback to your sales representatives in a positive way. Serving as a role model and demonstrating the behaviors you want your representatives to emulate is a powerful way to coach people. To successfully coach your representatives, they also need to believe they can trust you. Mentoring occurs when a senior member of a sales organization provides long-term career advice to a more junior member. This type of career guidance helps individuals gain new insights about their fit and contributions to the firm. The ability to build and develop sales teams is another skill set sales managers are increasingly being called upon to master. Because sales forces become more geographically dispersed and products and services are becoming too complex for a single individual to sell, sales representatives are increasingly working in teams to achieve their firm's sales goals. In even the best virtual teams, however, you can't solely manage people electronically. There's no substitute for personally contacting your representative either in person or on the phone.

Questions and Problems

1. Describe a situation in which a sales manager would engage in supervisory behavior? When can sales reps benefit most from supervision? Why should sales managers consider supervising a good investment of their time and efforts?
2. What activities are involved in *managing* a sales force?
3. How is a sales manager involved with organizing and staffing the sales force?
4. What bases of power available to a sales manager do you think are most effective and why? What bases of power does your favorite instructor exhibit? What about your least favorite instructor? List some examples of instructors' behaviors that illustrate each type of power.
5. Management skills are something new sales managers need to develop. What are some specific behaviors that they should engage in? What misperceptions do sales managers have about managing people?
6. Why is the concept of leadership of such importance to vice presidents of sales? What has caused their heightened concern?
7. How are transactional and transformational leadership approaches different and how are they displayed in a sales manager's behaviors? What are some of the components of emotional intelligence? Who do you know that exhibits a high level of emotional intelligence?
8. Imagine a situation in which your sales rep just had a poor sales call. What coaching principles should you make sure you follow as you provide the rep with feedback? How would you initiate such a conversation?
9. What is the value of having a mentor? Explain why you would or would not want to have one as a sales representative. Why would a salesperson want to be a mentor if it takes time away from selling to their clients?
10. Sales reps usually work independently. How would you encourage your reps to work as part of a team? What objections do you think they would have to being a team member, and how might you counter them?
11. Consider the team projects you've worked on in school. What are some of the behaviors you like to see your team members engage in? Do you believe your team members would behave differently in virtual teams?

Key Terms

charismatic power   223
coercive power   223
emotional intelligence   228
expert power   223
informational power   223
legitimate power   223
mentoring   230
project team   231

referent power   223
reward power   223
self-managed teams   231
supervision   220
transactional leadership   227
transformational leadership   227
virtual teams   232

Role Play

Outside Escapes

While she was in college, Gretchen Hutterli developed quite a reputation for the spring break vacations she planned for her friends. By the time she graduated, she had started Campus Getaways, a company that specialized in offering vacations to students. Gretchen realized, however, the limitations of working only with this market segment (lots of promotional costs, nearly complete turnover of customers, and little loyalty). In an attempt to find more loyal and profitable customers, she developed a concept for a new company called Outside Escapes. Outside Escapes offered one-week vacations involving activities (rafting, kayaking, hiking, cycling, ziplining, and so forth) in exciting locations that ranged from the Grand Canyon to Costa Rica. Outside Escapes was marketed to young (usually single) businesspeople who enjoyed an exciting vacation with social opportunities and could afford to spend several thousand dollars on a vacation for themselves. Gretchen's newest, most profitable division is Green Getaways. It is marketed to organizations as a training retreat/team-building opportunity. Both divisions sell the same vacation (although the participants are never commingled) and use the same sales force.

Gretchen's sales force has been modest in size, with three regional offices, each with five to seven sales reps and a sales manager. Each region is organized roughly by time zones (eastern, central, mountain, and Pacific) and has a sales office, but most reps work in other cities and out of their offices. Selling involves inside (telephoning contacts) sales and outside work (making corporate contacts and presentations). Reps are paid a salary and commission. Calls are forwarded to offices that are open, depending upon the time zone. Oftentimes a rep will begin working with a client in another time zone and then a different rep in the same time zone as the client will close the business. When the company's offices were small, this was not a problem. However, because its sales force has been growing geographically, it has become an issue. Gretchen has announced that she has plans to increase the company's sales by 25 percent for each of the next four years. Consequently, the problem is only likely to get worse unless it's resolved. She has brought the company's sales managers together to develop a plan.

Assignment

Divide into pairs. One of you should play the role of one sales manager who believes that dividing the work in a team fashion will improve Outside Escape's business. The second person should play the role of a sales manager who believes that each sales representative should work independently. Gretchen wants the two of you to develop a list of advantages/disadvantages of each of your approaches and suggestions on how you might proceed if your approach were implemented.

Caselet 10.1: Friend or Mentor? Deciding When to Take Action

It was spring, and Carol was waiting in a restaurant for Helen to pull up in her little red convertible. Back when Helen was a rookie and her subordinate, Carol recalled how Helen had achieved a banner year and received a big bonus. She had used the bonus to buy the "car of her dreams."

However, instead of pulling up in a little red convertible, Carol noticed Helen pulled up to the restaurant in a yellow taxi. "Where's that hot car of yours?" Carol asked her old employee.

"Oh, it's in the shop," Helen replied, and she quickly moved on to get caught up on how her friend and former boss had been since they last met about six months ago at their company's fall sales meeting. Over the past several years, both women had moved on within the company. Carol had moved into another sales management position, and Helen had moved into a position that handled larger accounts. However, the two women had managed to stay in contact with one another and have dinner together twice a year prior to their semi-annual sales meeting.

Carol had never officially been asked to mentor Helen. However, over the years Helen had sought her advice when she had difficult decisions to make. Thus, the mentoring relationship between them seemed to naturally evolve. Lately, however, Carol had heard that Helen's performance seemed to be slipping a bit. Other sales managers were talking about how she had missed appointments and meetings and had not met her deadlines. This certainly didn't seem like the Helen Carol knew.

About halfway through dinner, Carol noticed that the bottle of wine she and Helen had been sharing was empty, although Carol had consumed only one glass. Although the food was a little slow in being served, the popular "reservations only" restaurant they were dining at seemed to live up to its reputation. Nonetheless, when the women were finally served their dessert, Helen suddenly and loudly berated the waiter about his poor service. Carol was stunned. She had never seen Helen do such a thing in the past.

Carol knew a new sales management position was opening up soon and that her opinion for a new candidate would be sought. As Helen ordered "after dinner" drinks for both of them, Carol began to reconsider recommending her for the position.

Questions

1. Where should Carol's loyalties lie? What do you think is going on with Helen?
2. As her informal mentor, should Carol take it upon herself to ask Helen about her performance and what's causing it to decline? Or should she mind her own business?
3. What other actions should Carol consider taking?

Caselet 10.2: Teamwork?

The Walnut Creek Gazette started out as a small-town California newspaper. However, as the town of Walnut Creek, California, grew over the years, the paper's circulation grew, too. Nina Fong had worked her way up in the *Gazette's* advertising department. Fong had started out as a sales assistant, became a customer service rep, followed by a team leader, and finally a sales manager. In her position she is responsible for seven, 4-person teams.

The *Gazette's* sales assistants spend most of their time on the phone identifying and developing new accounts and then turning them over to account managers. Each team has two account managers who work in the field and personally contact clients. Customer service representatives make sure the *Gazette's* clients are satisfied with their published ads. Team members are compensated based both on their individual performance and the productivity of their teams as a whole.

The sales quota deadline for Nina's teams is fast approaching. Nina has just received a phone call from Bruce Nygen. Nina knows Bruce. He is the manager of a new store moving into the far edge of the *Gazette's* southwest sales territory. He had previously e-mailed Nina to check into buying some ad space. He was considering several advertising options to help him achieve certain promotional objectives, and he wanted to see how the paper could assist him.

Bruce has just explained to Nina in his phone call to her that no one from the sales department at the *Gazette* has contacted him. Nina is surprised. Lindsey Newman is a competent, senior account rep in the *Gazette's* southwest territory. Morgan Hendricks is a newer, less experienced representative who is still developing.

Nina is wrestling with the decision as to which account manager she should hand the lead to. She feels that someone as experienced as Lindsey should have already contacted Bruce as a potential new client. But Morgan has recently lost two of her accounts because her clients were not satisfied with their ad buys and the customer responses they generated. Nina knows a large sale in this territory will push this particular team over its sales goal and add to everyone's bonus, including her own.

Questions

1. What are the advantages and disadvantages of handing the lead to Morgan, the newer account manager?
2. What are the advantages and disadvantages of handing the lead to Lindsey?
3. How would you make this decision?
4. How do you think your decision would affect the rest of the members on Lindsey's and Morgan's team?

References

1. Priestland, Andreas, and Robert Hanig (2005). "Developing First-level Leaders," *Harvard Business Review* (83)6: 111–120.
2. French, J. R. P., Jr., and B. H. Raven (1959). "The Bases of Social Power," in D. Cartwright, ed., *Studies in Social Power*. Ann Arbor: University of Michigan Institute for Social Research, pp. 150–167.
3. Hill, Linda A. (2007). "Becoming the Boss," *Harvard Business Review* (85)1: 48–56.
4. Hammers, Maryann, and Gerhard Gschwandtner (2004). "Tap into the 7 Qualities of the Best Sales Managers," *Selling Power* (24)4: 61–66.
5. Bennis, Warren (2004). "The Seven Ages of the Leader," *Harvard Business Review* (82)1.
6. Bossidy, Larry (2007). "What Your Leader Expects of You—And What You Should Expect In Return," *Harvard Business Review* (85)4: 58–65.
7. Hammers, Maryann, and Gerhard Gschwandtner (2004). "Tap into the 7 Qualities of the Best Sales Managers," *Selling Power* (24)4: 61–66.
8. Kennedy, William F. (2001). "Under New Management," *Selling Power* (21)4: 71–74.
9. Gschwandtner, Lisa (2001). "What Makes an Ideal Sales Manager," *Selling Power* (21)3: 52–59.
10. Deeter-Schmelz, Dawn R., Karen Norman Kennedy, and Daniel J. Goebel (2002). "Understanding Sales Manager Effectiveness: Linking Attributes to Sales Force Values," *Industrial Marketing Management* (31): 617–626.

11. Wellins, Richard S., Charles J. Cosentino, and Bradford Thomas (2004). *Building a Winning Sales Force: A Sales Talent Optimization Study on Hiring and Development.* Pittsburg: Development Dimension International.

12. Atkinson, Thomas (2004). *How Sales Forces Sustain Competitive Advantage: Sales Force Research Report.* Boston: The Forum Corporation of North America.

13. Northouse, Peter. G. (2007). *Leadership: Theory and Practice,* 4th ed. Thousand Oaks, CA: Sage Publishers.

14. Goleman, Daniel (1998). *Working with Emotional Intelligence.* New York: Bantam.

15. Northouse, *Leadership: Theory and Practice,* p. 23.

16. Goleman, 2000. "Leadership That Gets Results," *Harvard Business Review* (78)2: 78–91.

17. Goldman, op cit. "Leadership That Gets Results," pp. 78–91.

18. Atkinson, Thomas (2004). *How Sales Forces Sustain Competitive Advantage: Sales Force Research Report.* Boston: The Forum Corporation of North America.

19. Hernez-Broome, Gina, and Richard L. Hughes (2004). "Leadership Development: Past, Present, and Future," *Human Resource Planning* (27)1: 24–32.

20. "The Chally World Class Sales Excellence Researh Report" (2007). Whitepaper produced by HR Chally Group. Dayton, OH.

21. Craumer, Martha (December 2001). "How to Coach Your Employees," *Harvard Management Communication Letter.* Boston: Harvard Business School Publishing Corporation, pp. 1–5.

22. Rich, Gregory A. (1998). "The Constructs of Sales Coaching: Supervisory Feedback, Role Modeling and Trust," *Journal of Personal Selling & Sales Management* (18)1: 52–63.

23. Hernez-Broome, and Hughes, "Leadership Development," pp. 24–32.

24. Bennis, "Seven Ages," p. 48.

25. Marchetti, Michele (2005). "A Helping Hand," *Sales & Marketing Management* (157)8: 12.

26. Brashear, Thomas C., Danny N. Bellenger, James S. Boles, Hiram C. Barksdale, Jr. (2006). "An Exploratory Study of the Relative Effectiveness of Different Types of Sales Force Mentors," *Journal of Personal Selling & Sales Management* (26)1: 7–18.

27. Jones, Eli, Andrea L. Dixon, Lawrence B. Chonko, and Joseph P. Cannon (2005). "Key Accounts and Team Selling: A Review, Framework, and Research Agenda," *Journal of Personal Selling & Sales Management* (25)2: 181–198.

28. Arnett, Dennis B., Barry A. Macy, and James B. Wilcox (2005). "The Role of Core Selling Teams in Supplier-Buyer Relationships," *Journal of Personal Selling & Sales Management* (25)2: 181–198.

29. Kinni, Theodore (2007). "The Team Solution," *Selling Power* (27)3: 27–29.

30. Polzer, Jeffrey T. (2004). *Creating Teams with an Edge.* Boston: Harvard Business School Press.

31. Ibid. pp. 108–125.

32. Bossidy, "What Your Leader Expects," 58–65.

33. Gordon, Jack (2005). "Do Your Virtual Teams Deliver Only Virtual Performance?" *Training* (42)6: 20–25.

34. Majchrzak, Ann, Arvind Malhotra, Jeffrey Stamps, and Jessica Lipnack (2004). "Can Absence Make a Team Grow Stronger?" *Harvard Business Review* (82)5: 131–137.

35. Barrett, A., and J. Beeson (2002). *Developing Business Leaders for 2010* (White paper). New York: The Conference Board.

11

SETTING GOALS AND MANAGING THE SALES FORCE'S PERFORMANCE

LEARNING OBJECTIVES

After completing this chapter, you should be able to:

- Describe how sales managers use goals to guide and control the efforts of their sales forces.
- Summarize the elements of an effective goal.
- Distinguish when different outcomes and behavioral sales goals should be used.
- Identify different resources available to capture information used for making effective decisions on goals.
- Apply goal-setting theory in order to improve managerial and motivational practices.

Companies rely on their sales forces to generate the revenues they need to stay in business. Consequently, it shouldn't surprise you that over 92 percent of companies with sales forces use some form of sales goals.[1] Setting and achieving a firm's sales goals is an extremely important and sometimes daunting responsibility of sales managers. In fact, one study reported that it is one of the top five challenges sales managers and organizations face.[2] Goal setting is a powerful sales management activity when it's done correctly. But when it's done incorrectly, not many corporate actions have a more potentially devastating consequence.

BILL FEBRY

NATIONAL TRADE MARKETING MANAGER—MILLER IMPORT AND CRAFT BRANDS, MILLER BREWING COMPANY, SAB MILLER

Bill Febry, a former sales development manager with Leinenkugel's Brewery, has always known that an important part of managing the sales force involves setting and achieving sales goals. "Working with members of the sales force to achieve sales goals is a critical element of the sales manager's position," says Febry, a seasoned sales executive promoted to the position of National Trade Marketing Manager for Miller Import and Craft Beers—SAB Miller, which now owns Leinenkugel's. "Every organization relies on this activity to help steer the course of things that will follow. The plans of the entire enterprise depend upon the ability of the sales force to meet their sales goals. If sales aren't up—something gets cut."

The brewing industry is very competitive. Although the industry's sales for traditional beers have been declining in recent years, craft beers, such as Leinenkugel's, have been growing. To improve their sales, brewers are constantly working to develop or introduce new varieties of beer. The effort requires marketing research, product and package development, promotional support, and a sales force able to sell the product. Leinenkugel's senior management team is responsible for directing the firm's overall strategic plans. But making sure those plans come to fruition in terms of revenues generated is the responsibility of the firm's sales managers and their representatives.

Leinenkugel's sales managers first consult with the company's upper managers regarding the sales goals the firm is aiming toward. They then discuss each representative's goals with the salesperson individually. Getting the salesperson's buy-in, or agreement with the goals, is extremely important, as is helping the person develop tactics to achieve those goals, says Febry. "The notion that sales managers can say 'Do it —or else' is a relic of days gone by, stupid television commercials, and bad movies," he says. "That type of an approach just doesn't work if a sales manager wants to develop and retain a professional sales force. Achieving goals should be informative to the organization and rewarded and celebrated both informally and formally with the salesperson," he says.

Leinenkugel's sales representatives are expected to plan their sales days and call on 8 to 10 retail accounts per day. Each rep is also expected to help with two promotional events per week, which can range from holding a new product sampling at an establishment to participating at a festival in which Leinenkugel's products are served. Making sure the right products get to the right

Setting goals helps focus the efforts of salespeople as well as motivates them (Shutterstock)

outlets is an important duty of the firm's salespeople, too. For example, six- or twelve-packs, bottles or cans, and cases need to be distributed to retail stores. By contrast, draft taps (kegs) need to be distributed to drinking and dining establishments.

Goal setting isn't just picking a target; it includes monitoring salespeople, market conditions, competitors' reactions, following up, and instituting corrective actions, if they are needed. Because Leinenkugel's salespeople are located throughout the country, Febry has implemented new sales technology that allows the company's sales managers to monitor a representative's activities almost in real-time. The software allows sales managers to see which actions are working and which ones are not, and they can analyze those actions by territory and region. If corrective action is needed to achieve the firm's goals, they can see that those actions are taken before it's too late. This could include adding promotional support to the firm's products, altering the sales messages related to them, focusing on different potential customers, and coaching salespeople who need help.

"When reps are having trouble achieving their goals, sales managers need to find out what types of problems they are encountering and what they can do," Febry says. "At one end of the continuum, the action might involve refining the sales message the company's sales representatives are delivering. At the other, it might involve suggesting to upper management that a major strategic initiative be overhauled."

A **sales goal (quota)** is a performance standard by which salespeople—sales representatives and sales managers alike—are measured. The primary purpose of having sales goals or quotas is to synchronize the direction and efforts of the sales force with the plans developed by a firm's top managers. Salespeople use goals to benchmark their performance within a specified time period, and, in most cases, they are compensated based on meeting those goals. Another compelling reason to use goal setting is because the achievement of those goals can and should be motivating and in most cases is tied to compensation. The first half of the chapter focuses on the sales aspects of goals and will describe why this is such an important topic, not just for the sales force but for the entire organization. The second half of the chapter concentrates on what sales managers need to do to set good goals that motivate their sales forces. ∎

Why Are Sales Goals Important to an Organization?

Sales jobs allow for a great deal of discretionary effort and time on the part of the sales representatives—especially when compared with managerial, manufacturing, and service jobs. Most sales representatives work independently and outside the immediate presence of their sales managers. Therefore, some form of goals needs to be in place to help motivate and guide their performance.

Sales personnel are not the only professionals with performance goals or quotas. Healthcare professionals operating in clinics have daily, weekly, and monthly goals in terms of patient visits. Service personnel are assigned a number of service calls they must perform during a set time period. Production workers in manufacturing have output goals. So why are achieving sales goals or quotas such a big deal?

The answer to this question can be found by examining how a firm's other departments are affected by how well the company's salespeople achieve their performance goals. As you no doubt realize, the success of the business hinges on successful sales of its products and services. Consider all the planning, the financial, production, and marketing resources and efforts that go into producing what the sales force sells. Everyone depends upon the sales force to sell the company's products and services and they eagerly anticipate knowing how things are going. If sales are going well, everyone breathes easier; if sales aren't going well, then there is reason for concern.

Using Goals to Guide and Manage the Performance of a Firm's Sales Force

Sales goals serve a variety of purposes for the sales organization. Specifically, sales goals help to:

- *Motivate the sales force.* Having achievable goals can help motivate salespeople to do their work. Goals serve as benchmarks to help them gauge how well they are doing. Tying their goals to their compensation is a common practice in North America. (However, it might surprise you that in other parts of the world, it's not, as this chapter's Global Sales Management feature explains.)

- *Focus the selling efforts of the sales force.* Goals help direct the efforts of the sales force toward certain sales activities a company wants them to engage in, such as focusing their efforts on certain products or services or target markets. For example, as more baby boomers retire and don't want to burden their children with medical expenses, many are purchasing long-term care insurance. Seeing this growing market segment, a company like Northwest Mutual Life Insurance might set a goal for its agents to contact their current life insurance policyholders, spend a certain amount of time with them to explain the product, and sell a specific number of new policies to these customers.

- *Assess the financial return on the firm's investment in its products and services.* Firms need to balance the expenditures they make on the goods and services they produce and the returns earned on them. In other words, companies want to make sure the effort they put into selling their products earns a good return. Imagine if Northwestern Mutual were to extensively promote its mutual fund product line to its existing life insurance policyholders below or above a certain income level and find this group to be a difficult sale. If the company didn't set a certain sales goal for the product and then monitor how well the goal was being met, the firm might engage in repeated efforts to capture these market segments when it's not worth the effort. When sales are falling short of expectations despite the efforts of a good sales force, it might be because the market is not receptive to the company's offerings. As a result, the firm's top managers might need to reformulate one or several of the marketing mix variables. In the case of Northwestern Mutual, the company might redirect its efforts toward selling mutual funds to new customers. Perhaps Northwestern Mutual's existing insurance clients have, on the whole, already established relationships with other brokerage firms and are reluctant to switch.

- *Compare the results achieved by salespeople in different sales territories and regions.* Gathering the results achieved in different sales territories and sales regions helps sales managers determine how the areas compare. They can then analyze the variations to determine what factors explain why sales are lower (or higher) in one territory versus another. For example, perhaps the number of competitors and the strength of each in the territories is different. Or perhaps the characteristics of the buyers in a certain area, the geographic distance between them, or the skills and efforts of the salespeople working the areas differ. Of course, as we have indicated, the performance of different salespeople can be compared, too. Performance variations are to be expected, to some extent, based on the experience and skills of different representatives as well as differences in their territories.

GLOBAL SALES MANAGEMENT:

Goals Are Goals, Right? Not Quite.

If you bring international students together, no doubt you will see both similarities and differences in dress, preferences, and behaviors. Try asking a group of them to mimic the sound a rooster makes. They will likely produce a lot of crowing sounds but each will be different and unique to their home cultures. This is what sales managers face when they're trying to manage global sales organizations. Most people agree on the big picture, but their implementation of sales management practices reflects nuances unique to their home cultures.

That said, some researchers believe that globalization is causing sales management practices to converge. In fact, information obtained from over a thousand sales managers in eight countries located across the globe have shown this to be the case. This is certainly the case in terms of the control practices sales managers exercise—that is, how they measure the performance of their salespeople and reward them.

Thus, trying to set similar goals across countries can be challenging for sales managers. For example, a sales manager in the United States is more likely to set difficult short-term goals, while in Japan the practice would be more likely to set goals that are more long term in nature. Japanese companies are less concerned with short-term goals as long as they are moving in the correct direction to achieve market share or dominance. In the Middle East, goals are conditional and usually contain the caveat "God willing." This statement allows the salesperson and the company to not meet goals and it's not their fault. Setting goals for salespeople in the European Union is similar to setting goals for salespeople in the United States. However, it can still be difficult because of differences in cultural priorities on the two continents.

The point is that although business practices are becoming more standardized around the world, there is still variation. Sales managers need to consider a sales representative's background and keep in mind that not all members of an international sales team will react to goals and the incentives for meeting them the same way.[3,4]

Sources: Cravens, David W., Nigel F. Piercy, and George S. Low (2006). "Globalization of the Sales Organization: Management Control and Its Consequences," *Organizational Dynamics* (35)3: 291–303; T. Garrison (2001). *International Business Culture.* 3rd ed. Cambridgeshire, England: ELM Publications; and Honeycutt, Earl D., John B. Ford, and Antonis C. Simintiras (2003). *Sales Management: Global Perspective.* London: Routledge.

Different Types of Goals or Quotas

Goals are based on measures of performance that occur over time. There are a variety of measurements and time periods that can be incorporated into goals. Regardless of what's being measured, however, the performance measurements, or **metrics**, should reflect what is most important in an organization's marketing strategy. Goals are often described as being either input or output based. **Input-based goals**, or **activity-based quotas**, relate to the observable selling efforts a salesperson must make—for example, the number of sales calls (by phone or in-person), presentations he or she must make, and the number of sales proposals the person writes. The number of new clients contacted by a representative is also an input goal. Input goals ensure that representatives are performing the firm's core selling activities. In the past, some of these measures have been reported by reps themselves, which made it difficult to validate their accuracy.

Customer Relation Management (CRM) systems have helped to authenticate the activities reps complete, thereby improving the validity of these measures.

Unfortunately, efforts alone don't always produce results, though. That's why output goals are important. **Output (outcome)-based goals** are the selling results a representative is expected to achieve. Examples include the number of orders the representative must receive, and the revenues, sales volumes, and profits the person must generate. Consider the hypothetical company Pickerel Lake Industries (PLI), which develops software programs for online education and training. PLI is about to introduce a new product customers might purchase based on the company's marketing research. The company has determined the revenue the product needs to earn to cover its development, production, and marketing costs, and return a profit. The number of units and the revenue associated with it are then divided among PLI's different sales divisions and then further divided among the individual sales representatives in the various divisions.

The number of presentations given can be an input goal. (Getty Images/Digital Vision)

Sales volumes generated have traditionally been the most frequent measure companies use to set goals for their salespeople. The major advantage of this approach to setting sales goals is that the measures are easily counted and analyzed, and sales representatives understand them. A disadvantage is that a sole metric may not accurately reflect the entire effort needed to produce the sales or provide a complete picture of what is being sold. For example, a Leinenkugel's salesperson might have generated a large volume of sales but very little profit because the person was discounting items or selling only items with small profit margins. Clearly, when only output is measured, it can result in a situation in which other behaviors, such as providing customer service or selling more difficult higher-margin products are being ignored or minimized by salespeople.

As a result, many organizations will utilize a combination of input and output goals. This approach can ensure that certain customer service activities are being performed and a certain amount of profitable sales are being made. For example, after PLI establishes the revenue goals for its sales representatives, it then develops the behaviors (**input goals**) they need to engage in to not only make the company's financial targets (like the number of calls and presentations they need to make) but also behaviors they need to engage in to achieve the firm's other objectives, such as, "providing the best after-sale service in the industry." This might involve, for example, requiring them to make a certain number of service calls to their customers based on the revenue each one generates.

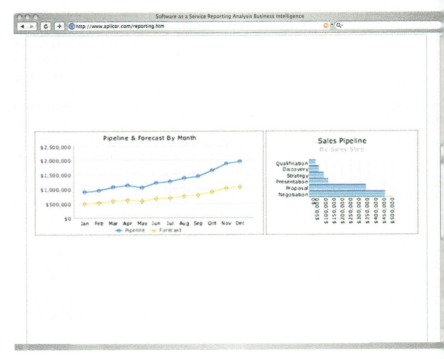

A pipeline analysis shows the stages a firm's different sales are in. (Source: Aplicor)

A newer type of measurement called a **pipeline analysis** has broken into the list of the top five measurements in recent years. It shows how well a salesperson is maintaining a stream of customers at different stages in the sales process. Exhibit 11.1 shows some of the different types of measurements firms use to

EXHIBIT 11.1

Typical Input and Output Goals Set by Firms

Input Goals	Output Goals		
Activities	**Sales Volume**	**Number of Sales**	**Ratios**
Number of telephone calls in the last 30 days	Volume in the 30-day pipeline	Number of sales made in the past 30 days	Deals closed versus deals proposed
Number of new client meetings in the last 30 days	Volume in the 90-day pipeline	Number of sales made in the past 90 days	Leads converted versus opportunities qualified
Number of presentations and demonstrations made in the last 30 days	Qualified pipeline volume	Number of qualified sales in the pipeline	
Number of proposals written in the last 30 days	Sales volume in accounts lost	Number of accounts lost	

create their sales goals. Not surprisingly, the most frequently used measurement is sales revenues generated, followed by the number of sales calls made.[5]

At the other end of the continuum are metrics related to customer service. Surprisingly, fewer than 15 percent of companies surveyed indicated that their organization included customer retention and satisfaction metrics in their goals.[5] If customer service is important, why isn't it measured and established as a goal? Could it be because customer satisfaction is difficult to measure? Does delivering good customer service simply mean a firm loses no accounts or experiences no complaints? Or is good customer service evidenced by a note from a customer to a manager commending a sales representative for going above and beyond the call of duty?

Unfortunately, sometimes it is just easier to count the number of customer complaints you receive than gauge the service your customers are getting. Perhaps an example can help illustrate this: A few years ago, one of the author's schools attempted to assess how good its marketing professors were at advising their students. The school attempted to review mandatory course evaluations ratings, count committees and service work, and count research publications and presentations. However, there was no good metric for advising the school's students. Personally interviewing them about how well they were being advised wasn't practical because of their large numbers and the large number of faculty members trying to advise them.

Nonetheless, an attempt was made to develop a measurement of some sort. Students were e-mailed a request to fill out an advisor rating slip (with three questions) and deposit it in a central location after they had met with their advisors. Advisors were also given rating slips to distribute to their advisees. (There was some concern that students who had a poor experience with their advisors would not be given slips, which is why the slips were e-mailed to students.) However, at the end of the pilot semester, only six response slips were returned to the school, even though 1,100 students received them. The advising metric project was cancelled. As it turned out, simply counting the number of complaints the department received was far easier than undertaking such a project. Unfortunately, some companies take the same approach toward measuring customer service. A more accurate, but time-consuming approach would be to develop some form of customer satisfaction measure consisting of a number of metrics, such as the number of customer complaints, the number of customers lost, the number of customer referrals, and customer satisfaction ratings.

Expense quotas are used to keep the costs associated with a representative's sales in line with what the firm thinks the representative should spend in order to be successful. The costs involved in putting on demonstrations, entertaining customers, customer sampling or trial of products, lodging, and other travel costs are among the many expenses sales representatives incur. Typically the expenses are calculated as a percentage of a representative's sales. For example, if a representative from Deere & Company is expected to generate $4,000,000 in annual sales of industrial equipment, then the representative would be expected to incur a certain percentage, say 1 to 3 percent, of that amount in expenses. The exact percentage will differ from industry to industry and even company to company. Representatives who go over the expense percentages allotted to them usually have to justify why they did so. However, salespeople whose expenses fall far short of the percentage allotted them might not be using all of the resources available to them, and they could possibly be losing sales as a result. This, too, can create a concern for their sales managers. Expense budgets are usually adjusted upward annually due to inflation.

Exhibit 11.2 displays a combination goal system for Pickerel Lake Industries (PLI). Potential customers of PLI are reluctant to seriously consider purchasing the company's software until they see it demonstrated. The worksheet below contains information on the goals for three sales representatives; the firm has set its sales volumes, net profits, the number of demonstrations, and the number of new accounts established for a certain time period. Experienced sales managers know that only after analyzing all of the data can a clear picture of the representative's entire performance come into focus.

The last step in this analysis is determining which of the goals are more important than others. PLI has assigned weights reflecting the importance of each goal. Sales volumes have been assigned a weight of 3; net profits have a weight of 4. Both number of demonstrations

EXHIBIT 11.2

Assigning Weights to Salespeople's Goals: A Worksheet

Metric	Goal	Actual (to be determined at end of sales period)	% of Goal	Weight	% of Goal × Weight
Sales Rep - Hannah Elizabeth					
Sales Vol.	$200,000		90%	3	
Net Profit	128,000		94	4	
No. Demos.	10		140	1	
New Acct.	8		120	1	
Total Score				9	
Goal score = (Goal × Weight points/weight of metric) =					
Sales Rep – Sydney Nguyen					
Sales Vol.	$250,000		112%	3	
Net Profit	172,000		102	4	
No. Demos.	11		45	1	
New Acct.	9		55	1	
Total Score				9	
Goal score = (Goal × Weight points/weight of metric) =					
Sales Rep – Moe Peterson					
Sales Vol.	300,000		103%	3	
Net Profit	190,000		84	4	
No. Demos.	9		67	1	
New Acct.	7		86	1	
Total Score				9	
Goal score = (Goal × Weight points/weight of metric) =					

and new accounts have been assigned a weight of 1. Multiplying the percent of each goal a representative ultimately achieved, by the weight of that goal yields the total weight for that factor. Adding those numbers and then dividing by the number of weights (in this case there are nine) produces the final performance score for each person.

Choosing the Right Metrics to Track

As Exhibit 11.2 indicates, adding additional metrics helped present a more complete view of the contributions of each sales representative. So, if information from four factors is better than information from just one factor, wouldn't information from 20 factors be better than just four? Most companies have multiple product lines; some will have literally hundreds. Keeping track of sales with these parameters can create headaches. As one researcher noted: "Few quota-setting procedures integrate all the relevant factors because too many parameters are required, making them extremely difficult to estimate."[6]

In fact, in a study of sales management practices, senior sales executives said that they believe their firms track too many sales performance measures. Having too many measures made it more difficult to focus on the "critical few" metrics. As one sales management executive put it: "What gets measured gets done, but only metrics that get inspected have any significant impact." Historically, most practitioners agree that having more than seven to nine metrics becomes more difficult to manage.[7]

Choosing the Right Time Period to Track

Goals need to be completed within a prescribed time period. They can be yearly, quarterly, monthly, or even weekly or hourly. Most sales organizations establish their sales goals on a yearly basis. They then break down the yearly figure into quarters and sometimes monthly units. Sales organizations that have short or rapid sales cycles, such as in-bound call centers or retail establishments, might use weekly or hourly units, for example. Textbook companies, such as Prentice Hall, for example, often set semester-long goals for their salespeople. That is, they are given two goals annually—one for the spring selling season and one for the fall selling season. Monthly goals don't work very well because after a semester starts, college bookstores place very few orders on a monthly basis.

 SELF-ASSESSMENT LIBRARY

Sales managers must make tough decisions every day. Some are based on a great deal of information and some based on limited information. Deciding which metrics to include when set goals may be based on existing information and others may need to be based more on relationships and intuitive choices. To gain some insights on your decision-making style go to

Assessments
  I. What About Me
   D. Decision-Making Insights
    5. What's My Decision-Making Style?

http://www.prenhall.com/sal/ and log in using the access code that came your book. Click on Assessments, and scroll to I. "What About Me," then to D, "Decision-Making Insights" and complete number five, "What's My Decision-Making Style?" Your results should provide you with some insights on which pattern you use most often and find most comfortable.

EXHIBIT 11.3

An Example of How Threshold, Actual, and Stretch Goals Are Set

Basic Sales Volume Goal	Threshold Goal (90%) × Goal	Actual Goal (100%) × Goal	Stretch Goal (110%) × Goal
Rep 1: $40,000	0.9 × $40,000 = **$36,000**	1 × $40,000 = **$40,000**	1.10 × $40,000 = **$44,000**
Rep 2: $100,000	0.9 × $100,000 = **$90,000**	1 × $100,000 = **$100,000**	1.10 × $100,000 = **$110,000**

What About Almost Meeting a Goal?

Should a salesperson be rewarded if they can achieve only 80 percent of their sales goal? What about 90 percent? Consider this course and your reaction to the following scenario: Over the semester you are required to interview five sales managers. Your final interview is with a company you really are interested in and are hoping to possibly work for one day. Unfortunately, at the very last minute, your interviewee has a family emergency and has no time to reschedule before your assignment is due. Consequently, you submit your four interviews, and your instructor gives you a zero because your assignment wasn't complete. Would you have preferred a grade of 80 percent for your work completed?

For the same reason illustrated above, most companies do not take an "all or none" approach. A more typical approach is to reward salespeople for reaching the 90 percent mark (what's called a **threshold goal**); the 100 percent mark (**actual goal**); or 110 percent mark (**stretch goal**). Exhibit 11.3 shows the difference of using this approach when examining sales. (The exact percentages of threshold, actual, and stretch goals will vary from company to company.)

Should Salespeople be Involved in Setting Their Own Goals?

As a student, would you prefer to be able to discuss with your instructors how your assignments and grades should be determined? If you answered "yes," you could probably guess that most salespeople feel the same way about their sales goals. Although not every organization solicits input from its sales force about the goals set for them, over 60 percent do.[8] Doing so can improve the morale of a firm's salespeople by helping their managers better understand the obstacles they face. "When the quotas are set and there's no changing them, it's de-motivating. I've seen reps cry... and leave for that reason," comments Lorena Vidaurri, a sales representative with Boise Cascade Office Products.[9] One drawback of asking salespeople for their input is, of course, that they often have an incentive to lowball their sales (make their estimates low), so they can more easily achieve their quotas. Nonetheless, some firms use a combination of a top-down and bottom-up goal setting approach. With a little negotiation, a goal that both a sales manager and representative agree on can be reached.

Threshold, actual, and stretch goals give salespeople different levels to aim for. (Shutterstock)

When is a Sale a Sale?

When do you count a product or service as sold and include it as part of the individual's sales goal? This has been a controversial topic for some time. If a sale is counted toward a sales representative's goal when a customer places an order, what happens if the customer cancels or reduces the order after 30 or 60 days? To achieve their goals, salespeople have been known to ask their clients, or otherwise to cut a deal with them to purchase products immediately, with the understanding that they can later return them.

A conservative approach would count the sale when the product is either shipped or paid for. However, this can create a problem for an item with a long sales cycle, say, an item that might not be delivered for a number of months. Many B2B sales fall into this category. For example, the sale of a commercial airplane, a highly customized product, such as a custom-built piece of industrial equipment or a personal yacht; all would have long sales cycles. Some firms deal with this problem by giving representatives partial credit (for example, 30%) when an order is placed and the remaining credit (70%) when the order is shipped.

However the sale is counted, organizations need to develop and clearly communicate this information to their representatives. Also, no matter what method is chosen, unethical sales managers (and their representatives) will have an incentive to manipulate the system, particularly because sales managers' goals (and their bonuses) are based on what their reps earn. Drug maker Bristol-Myers Squibb found itself in such a predicament. Between 1999 and 2001, the company's sales managers offered the firm's wholesalers incentives to build up their inventories of the company's products and recorded those deliveries as revenue. This allowed the company and its salespeople to meet their quarterly revenue goals. However, the U.S. Department of Justice and the Securities Exchange Commission later concluded that "loading" inventories onto wholesalers could not be recognized as revenues. The company was charged with overstating its revenues and fined.[10] The problems Bristol-Myers Squibb experienced show why sales managers (as well as a firm's top managers) need to have a strong sense of integrity.

Should Everyone Achieve Their Sales Goals?

Goals should be set with the expectation that salespeople will be able to achieve them.[11] If an organization was successful in hiring and training the best people available, this seems only reasonable. However, not every organization can hire the best or support a good training program. Some organizations, in fact, indicate that they expect between 60 percent and 80 percent of their sales force to achieve their goals.[12]

So why don't more salespeople make their goals? In some surveys conducted, the senior executives said they believed that poor skills on the part of their sales forces and sales managers were to blame.[13,14] Although a lack of skills or motivation on the part of sales personnel might be a contributing reason for their not achieving their sales goals, there are several other important factors that also should be considered. These factors include:

- Flawed sales projections based on limited marketing research
- Changes in a firm's marketing mix variables that result in inferior products or services
- An increase in the cost of supplies that are passed on to buyers in the form of higher product prices
- Promotional campaigns that don't produce the results projected
- Delays or other problems with the distribution of a firm's products
- New competitors and competing products that enter the marketplace
- Environmental factors that affect customer demand, such as slumps in the economy, natural disasters, and so forth that cause customers to postpone or cancel their purchases
- Change in laws and regulations that prevent or restrict the use of products and services or make them more expensive
- Changes in the way firms do business, for example, as a result of new technology

Do Goals Ever Get Changed or Altered?

According to surveys, most companies adjust their goals on a yearly basis to reflect changes that have occurred in the marketplace for their products. As Exhibit 11.4 shows, usually companies adjust their goals upward versus downward. Most of the respondents surveyed in the three-year time period shown said their companies increased the amount of their goals by up to 10 percent, nearly 45 percent increased the amount by over 11 percent, and 14 percent increased their quotas by over 20 percent.[15,16,17]

It is also quite common for organizations to revise their goals *during* a given year. In some cases a company's sales might exceed its expectations.[18] As a result, the firm will increase its sales goals and the goals its representatives must achieve. A number of factors

EXHIBIT 11.4

Percent of Companies That Changed Their Quotas from the Previous Year

Year	Increased Quotas	Stayed the Same	Decreased Quotas
2007	77%	18%	5%
2006	77%	19%	4%

might contribute to this; for example, a competitor might have dropped out of the market, the firm's market research might have been flawed and have underestimated a market's sales potential, or a change in economic conditions might have helped bolster buying. The opposite can also happen, though, leading a firm to lower its sales goals. Experts caution that a company shouldn't adjust its sales too many times or confusion among its sales force can result. Moreover, if the goals are being adjusted upward, salespeople will often feel cheated.[19]

What Happens When Salespeople Do Not Achieve Their Sales Goals?

Sales managers need to understand that there can be a number of reasons why salespeople don't achieve their goals. This doesn't mean that it's the end of the line for a representative. The rep's manager needs to find out why the individual didn't achieve his or her goals and help the person engage in activities that will result in success. Realize, too, that not every rep is going to meet every goal they are given each period. Even the best reps will miss some of their goals some of the time. It only becomes a problem when a rep continually or repeatedly misses goals. We'll discuss more about this aspect in Chapter 14.

The Process of Setting Good Goals

Goals can truly be a double-edged sword. When done correctly, they can motivate a sales force to succeed. However, when done incorrectly, they can be de-motivating and lead to high turnover among salespeople or tempt them to engage in unethical sales behaviors. In a series of studies, researchers found that difficult sales goals alone did not result in unethical behaviors on the part of a firm's sales force. However, they certainly helped set the stage for those behaviors. In addition, when sales representatives were given exceedingly high goals, they often focused primarily on activities that generated sales, and they delivered less customer service. The researchers also noted that a sales manager's tendency to tolerate—or not tolerate—unethical sales behaviors had a direct effect on whether their representatives would or would not engage in unethical sales behaviors.[20,21,22] The Ethics in Sales Management feature in this chapter provides additional details about the unethical sales behaviors that can occur because of poor goal setting.

Recall from Chapter 1 we discussed the importance of goal setting and the use of the SMART characteristics for developing a well-written goal (one that's specific, measurable, achievable, realistic, and time-based). That acronym is a good starting point for discussing the procedures used to set goals. After over 40 years of research on goal setting theory, it is no doubt one of the most researched, well-understood concepts in behavioral science.[25,26] After all of this study, there are two consistent findings about the use of goal setting:

- Difficult goals lead to higher levels of performance. Sales representatives will put forth more effort when their goals are somewhat difficult versus too easy or too difficult.
- Specific, difficult goals lead to higher levels of effort than general ones. Specific, difficult goals–for example, calling on eight clients a day–will lead to higher levels of performance on the part of salespeople.

ETHICS IN SALES MANAGEMENT

When Do Difficult Goals Become Too Difficult?

"I rarely give A's in the course," comments the instructor on the first day of your class. What happens in a situation such as this? It is likely that you will first feel frustrated and that the situation is unfair. Some students might feel that the situation is so unfair they decide to "do what it takes" to get a good grade—that is, they cheat.

Setting quotas so high that the average salesperson thinks they are unobtainable can result in a similar situation. For example, in the heyday of Internet advertising, the lure of a six-figure income enticed Matt Cooper to take a job selling high-cost ad campaigns to large corporations. However, the high sales goals Cooper's dot-com sales managers set for him and their "just get the job done" attitude eventually sent him over the edge: "I was misleading and lying to my customers every day," he says. Several customers even threatened him because his service didn't deliver as promised. Eventually the underhanded tactics of Cooper's company were discovered, and, like many dot.com companies, his firm died a quick death.

Even companies with a reputation for being fair to the customer can fall prey to the results of poorly set sales goals. Such was the case for Sears Automotive Centers. In the 1990s the centers hiked up their employees sales quotas in an effort to boost the division's sagging profits. Employees resorted to overcharging customers for repairs or repairs that were never done and recommending unnecessary repairs. After the California Department of Consumer Affairs began investigating the service centers, Sears apologized to its customers for having overcharged them. The company also revamped its compensation programs, Yet, in the end, its sterling reputation was still tarnished.[23,24]

Sources: Strout, Erin (2002). "To Tell the Truth," *Sales & Marketing Management* (154)7: 40–47; and Mitchell, Carol Vallone, Patricia M. Schaeffer, and Katherine A. Nelson (2005). "Rewarding Ethical Behavior," *workspan magazine* (July), Vol. 48, No. 7.

Goal setting works because it impacts people's performance in four ways:

1. Goals direct people's attention and efforts toward goal-relevant behaviors and away from other less relevant behaviors. They provide focus and direction. For example, when a new product or service comes out, more effort (and reward) needs to be placed on selling it. That's why sales managers often set specific sales goals for new products and the rewards associated with meeting those goals.
2. Goals have an energizing function. Higher goals produce more effort than goals that are set at lower levels. Knowing what level of sales is expected of them gives salespeople a target to aim for.
3. Goals affect persistence. Harder goals will prolong the expenditure of effort. Tight deadlines lead to a more rapid work pace than loose goals. When there is plenty of time, it often
   seems no one is in a hurry. With a tight schedule, step-by-step completion dates must be met, which helps the work get accomplished.
4. Goals affect people's problem-solving skills. When faced with completing difficult goals, people will seek new ways to accomplish them.

Based on goal-setting principles, here are some practical guidelines sales managers should follow when setting representatives' goals.[27]

1. Set goals that are easy for sales representatives to understand, difficult to achieve, and have exact deadlines for completion.

2. Important tasks, such as providing a high level of customer service, not included as a goal may get ignored. If an action is important, then a goal for its accomplishment should be set.

3. Having too many goals can create stress. Keep the number of goals an individual is responsible for to a reasonable number, such as three to seven. Clarify their importance so that their priorities are understood.

4. Try to get sales representatives to commit to their goals by explaining how they have been set. For example, if the representatives' goals are 6 percent higher than they were the previous year, explain why.

5. Clearly indicate how the sales performance will be measured and rewarded.

6. Provide feedback to salespeople as frequently as possible so they know if they need to redirect or increase their efforts. Encourage salespeople to use alternative approaches to sell to their customers if their initial approaches don't work.

7. Make sure people know you have confidence in their ability to achieve their goals.

8. Failing to achieve a goal should not be viewed as failure. It should be considered progress on the road to success.

In short, goals should help motivate salespeople. The next chapter describes some other ways sales managers motivate their sales forces in addition to setting goals for them.

A salesperson's goals will affect her persistence. (Michael Krasowitz/Taxi/Getty Images)

Summary

Without a plan, it's hard to tell where you may end up. Because the success of businesses hinges on the successful sales of products and services, nearly all organizations with sales forces use sales goals. The primary purpose of having sales goals, or quotas, is to synchronize the direction and efforts of the sales force with the plans developed by a firm's top managers. Keeping the efforts and activities of the sales force aligned with the firm's marketing strategies helps ensure that the firm's sales resources are being spent wisely. In addition, it allows for comparisons to be made between different sales territories and sales personnel. The results of these comparisons can then be used to determine where the company's biggest opportunities and challenges may lie.

Different types of factors can be used to set sales goals. Input factors are the efforts a salesperson is expected to make to develop relationships with customers, meet with them, and make presentations and proposals to them. Output factors are the results of what a firm expects a representative's sales efforts to yield. They include metrics such as the amount of and profitability of sales. Many organizations utilize a combination of input and output goals to ensure that their sales representatives are engaging in customer service activities as well as meeting their output goals. Expense goals are used to motivate sales representatives to keep their selling costs to a reasonable amount. Finding the correct combination of goals and not overwhelming sales representatives with too many types of goals can be a challenging task for sales managers.

The majority of organizations tie the performance of their salespeople to the compensation they receive, which is frequently based on the percentage of their goals they achieve. To help obtain their commitment to meeting their goals, sales representatives are often encouraged to provide their sales managers with input about their goals and the obstacles they face to meeting them. A firm should adjust its sales goals only as needed so as not to confuse or demoralize the company's sales representatives (especially if their goals are being increased). However, over half of sales organizations indicate they usually make at least one adjustment a year. Many people mistakenly believe that if representatives fail to achieve their goals, they are typically dismissed. Most sales experts and professionals agree, however, that the failure to meet a goal merely signals a sales manager or sales trainer to help diagnose and remedy a salesperson's selling weaknesses.

Sales goals should motivate a firm's sales force. They should be difficult, yet achievable. When they are too difficult, salespeople are more likely to behave unethically to achieve them. By contrast, when salespeople understand why their goals have been set the way they are and they are committed to them, their efforts and perseverance increase. Finally, giving their salespeople frequent and timely feedback about their progress toward their goals can help a sales manager increase or redirect their efforts.

Key Terms

activity-based quotas   244

actual goal   249

expense quotas   246

input-based goals   244

metrics   244

output (outcome)-based goals   245

pipeline analysis   245

sales goal (quota)   242

stretch goal   249

threshold goal   249

Questions and Problems

1. Based on the comments offered in the opening profile of Bill Febry, describe the different goals that you think Leinenkugel's sets for its sales force.
2. Sam is a sales manager who prefers to use output measures for goals. Melissa, another sales manager, prefers the use of input measures. Summarize the advantages and disadvantages of both approaches. What type of products/services lend themselves to each type and why?
3. Customer service receives a lot of lip service and press, but when it comes down to using it as a sales goal, it presents some problems. Develop a possible customer service goal that could be used in a B2B setting.
4. Naperville, Illinois, located southwest of downtown Chicago, has undergone rapid growth. It is now the second largest city in Illinois, next to Chicago. As a sales manager, you knew the time would come when there were more potential clients than your present sales force could handle. Your organization has authorized splitting its two Naperville sales territories under your control into four. What type of goals do you think would be the most important to focus on given the situation?
5. The sales goals for one of the territories you manage have been set at $1.1 million for the current year. There are three sales representatives in this territory: Jose, who is one

month out of training; Katie, who has five years of experience and is considered an average performer; and Kim, who has 12 years of experience and is a top performer. Set three goal levels for each representative and explain your rationale for each.

6. A number of factors can impact a salesperson's ability to achieve their goal. What are some of these factors?

7. As a student you probably have had some courses with only one or two exams or papers. Likewise you've probably encountered some courses at the other end of the spectrum where many aspects of your performance were graded. The same situation could be said to exist in sales. As a sales representative, which end of the continuum would you prefer? As a sales manager, which end would you prefer? In each case, explain your rationale.

8. How well and in what situations do "all or nothing" goals work? What problems do you think a sales manager might encounter by rewarding salespeople who only partially meet their goals?

9. Are coaching and mentoring skills involved in goal setting? If so, explain where and how they should be incorporated.

10. As a sales manager you know that goal setting can be motivational. If you are about to set goals for your sales force, what are some of the behaviors you want them to demonstrate?

Role Play

Oval Track Promotions

Oval Track Promotions (OTP) publishes a magazine about NASCAR® and other auto races. Its sales force sells advertising in the magazine and, in combination with other sales promotions, opportunities targeted toward race car enthusiasts. OTP offers six different geographic versions of its magazine (including a European version) tailored to regional interests and enthusiasts. Each geographic area has its own sales force.

Because of the rapid growth of enthusiasts' interest in racing events, OTP has seen seven straight years of continuous growth. The company's current owners want the coming year to be even better, though. Consumer research indicates that more people and families plan to spend more of their entertainment dollars on the sport in the next year. OTP's sales goals are set by the company's sales managers. They have generally agreed to provide OTP's sales reps with an ample amount of resources and expense accounts large enough for the reps to achieve their individual goals.

Assignment

Divide into pairs. One person should play the sales rep K.R. The other person should play K.R.'s sales manager. Your district is located in the part of the country with the least interest in racing. Consequently, selling promotions to this customer base is more challenging than in other areas of the country. K.R. was hired by the previous sales manager and not the current one. K.R. is a hard worker driven by compensation, who routinely meets his/her sales goals. However, she/he has an abrasive personality. Clients are generally pleased with K.R., although a couple of smaller accounts have complained about being ignored, and she/he has struggled with winning new clients.

The district's reps just received their sales goals from the company's national sales manager via e-mail, and individual meetings are being lined up between sales managers and their reps to discuss the new goals. K.R. feels that the OTP management takes advantage of her/him, and the last e-mail sent to you about her/his new sales goal reflects that sentiment. The e-mail reads as follows: "Once again you folks have set an unrealistic goal by increasing it by 10 percent over last year. You have no idea how difficult it is to make this amount. You are unfairly increasing what I need to accomplish without knowing how much work this requires on my part. I feel fully taken advantage of by this situation. I deserve better treatment than this. Policies and protocol are clearly lacking."

The other sales managers in the company recall that K.R.'s previous year's goal discussion with his/her sales manager was like a wrestling match. However, K.R. recalls the previous year's goal discussion like trying to have a discussion while being made to "walk the plank."

The goal-setting meeting is upon you both. Discuss K.R.'s new goal from your character's perspective. Explain why or why not you think it's fair.

Sales Manager's Workshop: Setting Threshold, Actual, and Stretch Goals

You received a voicemail message from your boss, Terry, discussing setting goals or quotas for the upcoming year. Terry wants to incorporate more input from your firm's sales managers and the sales reps themselves before establishing the goals. You know each of your rep's territories vary by the number of opportunities they present. In fact, you have always voiced your concern about the firm's practice of increasing reps' goals annually by a straight percentage across the board. Examine the performance of your sales representatives over the last 24 months and develop a series of threshold, actual, and stretch goals you would recommend for each of them for each of the product lines they sell.

Caselet 11.1: All In a Day's Work

Hannah Johanson manages nine sales representatives in Green Bay, Wisconsin. The majority of her sales reps are in their twenties and early thirties. Hannah was promoted to a sales manager's position, not so much because of her sales skills but because of her outgoing, caring personality. In some management circles, she is known as "Helpful Hannah" or "Happy Hannah" because of her people skills. Hannah isn't feeling very happy right now, though. She has scheduled meetings with two of her representatives to discuss their sales goals.

The first meeting will be with one of her younger sales representatives, Ella Lynn. Ella is considered to have good sales skills and is very independent. However, at times she can be a bit outspoken. In fact, after just six months with the company, she sent the vice president of sales an e-mail complaining that the vehicles the sales force drives are "gas-guzzling SUV hogs." "We don't need cars this large when all we are carrying is ourselves," the e-mail read. "Be a leader! Set the example, be green—buy us hybrids." This action certainly raised eyebrows around the company and got people talking.

By accident Hannah happened to talk with Claire Mendosa, one of Ella's larger customers over the weekend. Claire commented that she wasn't sure if she liked the new PC camera system Ella had set up for her in place of Ella's biweekly scheduled sales visits (although Ella had told her several of her other clients liked the cameras). Claire told Hannah that Ella would visit once a month and then "link up" with her for a video sales call for the other visit. Moreover, Hannah had been calling on her account for two months, prior to setting up the cameras. All this was news to Hannah. In a series of pre-meeting e-mails with Hannah, Ella explained she had purchased the PC camera with her own money. She felt that the organization's stewardship of the environment was poor, and she was doing her part to cut down on the greenhouse effect. She had planned to tell Hannah this at their meeting. Ella believes that her "video visits" are as effective as being there "in person" and should be counted the same as making a physical call on a client as part of her goals. She says she has the sales to prove it.

Hannah's second meeting will be with Syd Vance. Syd has been with the company for three years and has had some up-and-down quarters. Everyone agrees that Syd needs to increase his number of new accounts as well as improve his "adequate" customer service ratings. Hannah has heard Syd say that he had been very busy and was really working hard. Syd commented that he would like Hannah's help in establishing new goals that would help improve his performance.

Questions

1. If you were Hannah, how would you handle your meeting with Ella?
2. If you were Hannah, how would you approach your session with Syd?
3. What specific goals would you suggest for Ella and Syd to improve their performance?

Caselet 11.2: Sandwiched In

One of your better sales representatives, Devin Tyler, needs to speak to you about his goal situation. "My grandparents raised me, and I'm like an only kid. They never saved for retirement, and their Social Security checks don't go too far. If I don't look after them, nobody will. And you know we've got two kids of our own. I am a member of the sandwiched generation," lamented Devin.

Devin has come in because the quarter is over at the end of the week, and he is short of his sales goals. One of his most loyal customers, Farmer's Co-Op could buy enough to put him over his goal—if he pressed the firm to place a large order. However, he thinks a purchase of that size might not be in the company's best interests.

Devin has come to you to seek your advice. "The extra money I could make if I reached my goal would really help us out at home. But I'm concerned that Farmer's might get upset and I could lose the account," he explains.

Question

1. If you were Devin's sales manager, what would you recommend he do in this case?

References

1. Cichelli, David J., ed. (2003). 2004 Sales Compensation Trends Survey (White paper). Scottsdale, AZ: The Alexander Group.
2. Kornick, Joseph (2007). "risky BUSINESS," Sales and Marketing Management (159)5: 32–33.
3. Cravens, David W., Nigel F. Piercy, and George S. Low (2006). "Globalization of the Sales Organization: Management Control and Its Consequences," Organizational Dynamics (35)3: 291–303.
4. Honeycutt, Earl D., John B. Ford, and Antonis C. Simintiras (2003). Sales Management: A Global Perspective. London: Routledge.
5. "How Sales Forces Sustain Competitive Advantage" (2004). White paper. Boston, MA: The Forum Corporation of North America, p. 10.

6. Darmon, Rene' Y. (2001). "Optimal Sales Force Quota Plans Under Salesperson Job Equity Constraints," *Canadian Journal of Administrative Sciences* (18)2: 87–100.

7. "How Sales Forces Sustain Competitive Advantage" (2004). White paper, Boston MA: the Forum Corporation of North America, pp. 10.

8. Galea, Christine (2006). "The Rising Tide Does It Again," *Sales and Marketing Management* (158)4: 30–35.

9. Viadaurri, Lorena, and Toby Shannan (2004). "Home Office vs. the Field," *Sales & Marketing Management* (156)9: 17.

10. Taub, Steven (2005). "Bristol's Former CFO Indicted," *CFO.com*. June 16, 2005. Retrieved on April 15, 2008, from: http://www.cfo.com/article.cfm/4096065/1/c_4096737?f=related.

11. Good, David J., and Sharles H. Schwepker, Jr. (2001). "Sales Quotas: Critical Interpretations and Implications," *Review of Business* Spring (22)1/2: 32–37.

12. Cichelli, David J., ed. (2003). 2004 Sales Compensation Trends Survey (White paper). Scottsdale, AZ: The Alexander Group.

13. "How Sales Forces Sustain Competitive Advantage" (2004). Op cit.

14. Koprowski, Ron, and Tom Atkinson (2005). "The Pressure Paradox," Forum Sales Practice White paper. Boston, MA: The Forum Corporation of North American, pp. 1–5.

15. Galea, Christine (2006). "The Rising Tide Does It Again," *Sales and Marketing Management* (158)4: 30–35.

16. Kornick, Joseph, Maggie Rauch, and Rebecca Aronauer (2007). "What's It All WORTH?" *Sales & Marketing Management* (159)4: 27–39.

17. "Sales Force, Sales Compensation Programs Not Meeting Expectations According to Deloitte Consulting LLP Survey" (2005). *AP Newswire*. (June 14, 2005), p. 1. Retrieved January 11, 2006, from: http://proquest.umi.com/pdqweb?did=853422071&sid=15&Fmt=3&clientld=3840&RQT=309&VName=PQD.

18. Galea, (2006).

19. Schwepker, Charles H., Jr., and David J. Good (2004). "Understanding Sales Quotas: An Exploratory Investigation of Consequences of Failure," *Journal of Business & Industrial Marketing* (19)1: 39–48.

20. Good, David J., and Sharles H. Schwepker, J. (2001). "Sales Quotas: Critical Interpretations and Implications," *Review of Business* Spring (22)1/2: 32–37.

21. Schwepker, Charles H., and David J. Good (1999). "The Impact of Sales Quotas on Moral Judgment in the Financial Services," *Journal of Services Marketing* (13)1: 38.

22. Schwepker and Good (2004).

23. Strout, Erin (2002). "To Tell the Truth," *Sales & Marketing Management* (154)7: 40–47.

24. Mitchell, Carol Vallone, Patricia M. Schaeffer, and Katherine A. Nelson (2005). "Rewarding Ethical Behavior," *workspan magazine* (July), Vol. 48, No. 7.

25. Latham, Gary P., and Edwin A. Locke (2006). "Enhancing the Benefits and Overcoming the Pitfalls of Goal Setting," *Organizational Dynamics* (35)4: 332–340.

26. Locke, Edwin A., and Gary P. Latham (2002). "Building a Practically Useful Theory of Goal Setting and Task Motivation—A 35 Year Odyssey," *American Psychologist* (57)9: 705–717.

27. Shalley, Christina E., and Edwin A. Locke (1996). "Setting Goals to Get Innovation," *R & D Innovation* (5)10: 1–6.

12

MOTIVATING AND REWARDING SALESPEOPLE

LEARNING OBJECTIVES

At the conclusion of this chapter you should be able to:

- Summarize how motivation has been conceptualized and how the contributions of past studies can be incorporated into managerial activities.
- Explain the different models of motivation and how sales managers can utilize them.
- Identify generational differences in motivation and how to adapt motivational approaches for each group.
- Describe how managers can utilize different motivational elements available to sales organizations.
- Distinguish different situations in which financial and nonfinancial rewards should be used to motivate salespeople.
- Illustrate how compensation systems can be utilized to address different motivational needs.

No two people act the same or are driven or motivated by the same things. Motivational factors often vary at different stages of a salesperson's career. In order to help guide the activities of their sales forces as a whole, sales managers need to be able to understand what drives their individual salespeople over time. As you read this chapter, you will learn different approaches to understanding motivation. You will also explore reward mechanisms—both financial and nonfinancial compensation plans to help you guide, cajole, reward, and motivate your sales force to achieve its goals.

MICHAEL KAPOCIUS

REGIONAL ACCOUNT MANAGER,
TAKEDA PHARMACEUTICALS NORTH AMERICA, INC.

Mike Kapocius has worked in the pharmaceutical industry in a variety of positions, ranging from sales representative to sales manager to his present position as a regional account manager for Takeda Pharmaceuticals North America, Inc. (TPNA). TPNA is headquartered in Deerfield, Illinois. The company is a wholly owned U.S. subsidiary of Takeda Pharmaceutical Company Limited, a 225-year-old company and Japan's largest pharmaceutical firm.

Kapocius has always enjoyed selling and working in sales. "In college, I worked weekends as a vendor at a major league ballpark selling anything from popcorn to programs," says Kapocius. "One particularly good weekend I sold enough programs to pay for all my college expenses that year. Each time I sold a program, I knew how much of that sale was mine and that profit motivated me to sell more and more." Kapocius says that although money is still important to him, as he got older, other things, such as recognition among his peers, became more important.

Like Kapocius, most sales managers are selected because they have been successful salespeople. However, not all salespeople are equally driven by money or the prospect of advancing their careers. Making the transition from sale representative to sales manager requires that you accept that fact. Understanding exactly what it is that motivates your salespeople is therefore crucial to your success as a sales manager, Kapocius says. "You'd like to have a sales force with all exceptional salespeople, but the reality is you may not. You need to understand your reps at an individual level and learn what they want out of their careers. Then you have to structure their work so that helping them meet their goals helps you achieve your goals."

One way Kapocius learned how to do this was during his "ride alongs" with each of his 12 sales representatives. During the "ride alongs," he made an effort to learn what motivated them. Sometimes, for younger representatives, it was money. By contrast, representatives with families were often more interested in limiting their travel. As a sales manager, he had a variety of reward options he could utilize to help motivate his sales representatives. Money was important as were sales bonuses. Gift cards ranging from between $25 to $100, which sales managers could use to reward a representative's behavior on the spot, were nice to receive (no one declined them), but they were not a significant motivator. Other motivators included the opportunity to be a member of a task force or committee, to become a content expert in one area, or to attend a regional or national sales meeting. Some representatives enjoyed the chance to work a display booth at a convention. Their spouses could attend the conventions, but their travel was not covered.

But what seemed to be a particularly effective motivator for salespeople was receiving recognition that was shared with their peers. Mike would regularly send memos to his sales reps and their regional manager, praising them for accomplishing a certain activity. National top sales clubs or councils also worked well. "I recall my last year as a sale rep," says Kapocius. "I kept a photo of the location of our meeting in Hawaii under my car visor to remind me what I was shooting for and why I kept making calls late in the day." Kapocius commented that sales contests also work. However, if the rewards related to them are late in being delivered, they are not as effective as they could be. At one time, stock options were given to the firm's representatives, but those really served to help retain people over a long period of time as opposed to motivating them.

Sales managers can't be expected to know everything, so it's important to listen to and ask your representatives to help you with your "blind spots," says Kapocius. One time one of his representatives told him: "You focus too much on the final goal. You need to take time and recognize the milestones your representatives are achieving along the way." Another representative, who was particularly critical of Kapocius's style, was given the job of keeping a list of things he should have recognized, but didn't, and periodically telling him about them. This had two benefits: "I learned of things I had missed and corrected them and in the process I silenced one of my most vocal critics," Kapocius explains.

In the end, sales managers need to use their coaching skills and work with each representative individually, says Kapocius. "Your top salespeople don't need much motivation—just be sure they are getting rewarded. With your other sales representatives, you need to ask yourself: 'How can I help them achieve their goals?' Then discuss it with each person, review, revise, and revisit it," he says. ∎

What Motivates Salespeople?

Done correctly, a sales manager's motivational activities can have a positive impact on the performance and outlook of sales representatives. But the reverse is also true: Done incorrectly, the activities can actually de-motivate the sales force and be disastrous at both the individual and company level. In this chapter we'll approach it first as motivation, as we examine its different components and how they work. Then we'll look at different ways that sales managers motivate their sales forces. All of the theories have their shortcomings, and, unfortunately, none can predict what people will do in the future; however, they do offer a starting place to understand how motivation affects all of us. We will also examine the flip side of this concept, which is understanding the different types of rewards that people are motivated to achieve and the impact sales managers can have.

Understanding what needs motivate people and being able to fill those needs might, on the surface, seem like a simple thing to do. However, in practice, this requires skill in order to execute effectively—especially as your sales force grows. Let's take an example you should be familiar with. In an effort to understand what motivates the students in your class to attend a class session, your instructor may ask, "Why are you attending class today?" Possible responses from students might include:

- I want to learn how to become a sales manager.
- I'm concerned that if I'm not here I'll lose points.
- I needed a class to graduate, and this time fit my schedule.
- I have a special friend who is also taking the class, and I like to be with that person.
- I heard the instructor was fun.

What if you were to pose the same sort of question to sales representatives: Why do they go to work selling every day? The possible responses you might hear include the following:

- I like to sell, and I enjoy my job.
- It pays the bills.
- Without this job, my family would not have insurance, and we need it.
- I'm in a sales contest, and I want to win the prize in front of my peers.
- My customers are counting on me to help them solve some of their problems at work.

As you can probably guess, what motivates people ranges widely. **Intrinsic motivation factors** are those items that are done because the person finds doing the activity a reward in itself. **Extrinsic motivation factors** are external to the job and are done in order to obtain a monetary or physical reward, a social reward, or to avoid punishment. These are items, such as wages, incentives, awards, or a job title that reflects status. Those people who are motivated largely by intrinsic rewards truly love their work and take pride in the feelings of accomplishment it provides them. They have less concern or desire for economic or personal gains. Those people who are motivated primarily by extrinsic rewards are focusing on what they receive for their efforts. Their work is not of utmost importance; it's what they receive (or don't receive) for it that's important. Most people are motivated by a combination of intrinsic and extrinsic rewards. After all, it's great when you both like your job and are rewarded for doing it. Later on in the chapter we will examine how sales managers balance the intrinsic and extrinsic rewards their sales personnel seek.

Sales managers need to try to figure out what motivates their different salespeople. (Getty Images, Inc., Asian Images Group)

SELF-ASSESSMENT LIBRARY

Have you ever wondered what factors motivate you the most? Go to http://www.prenhall.com/sal/ and log in using the access code that came with your book. Then click on:

    Assessments
    I. What About Me?
      C. Motivation Insights
        1. What Motivates Me?

The results of this assessment will provide you with some insights into what factors are your strongest motivators. You might want to compare your results with other college-aged students and someone not in your age group to see if there are any differences due to age.

Motivation is a fascinating and complex topic. Sales managers need to have an understanding about what drives their sales representatives to action, how hard they are willing to work, and how long they are willing to persist. Some researchers have tried to explain motivation by identifying different *needs* of individuals or the *content* of motivation. Three of these approaches and their contributions for sales managers are outlined in Exhibit 12.1. Unfortunately, the content approach suffers from the "one-size-fits all" problem. To overcome that shortcoming, the focus shifted to understanding motivation as the process of what someone does, for how long, and at what level of intensity. Exhibit 12.2 explains how the equity and expectancy approaches work and how sales managers can use what they know about their reps to help motivate them.

EXHIBIT 12.1

**Understanding
What Motivates
Sales
Representatives—
Content
Approaches**

Maslow's Hierarchy of Needs[1]—classifies people's needs by the following levels; when the needs in one level are met; factors in the next level will motivate a person.

- Physiological—the most basic needs in order to survive: the need for air, water, food, and shelter.
- Security—the need to be safe from physical and psychological harm, the need for shelter.
- Social or Belongingness—the need to have interaction, friendships, affection, and love with individuals.
- Ego—the need to feel good about yourself, to receive recognition, appreciation, and admiration
- Self-Actualization—the need to reach one's fullest potential.

Sales managers can apply this concept by using reinforcements that meet needs at each level.

- Physiological—salary and bonuses.
- Security—insurance (for example, health, life, disability) and retirement plans.
- Social or Belongingness—programs that balance work with life and family commitments (e.g., flexible hours, job sharing, telecommuting, paid parental leave, on-site day-care, and paid sabbatical leave).
- Ego—programs that recognize individuals for their sales efforts and accomplishments.
- Self-Actualization—satisfaction with balance between accomplishments at work and the balance with home life.

McClelland's Needs Approach[2]—suggests that people are motivated by varied amounts of three needs:

- Achievement—a desire to perform challenging tasks
- Affiliation—a need to be liked and avoid confrontation
- Power—a need to take charge

Managers can apply this concept by matching reps with rewarding aspects of their job.

- Achievement—important that a sales representative who has a high amount of this drive have an interesting and stimulating job.
- Affiliation—provide friendly relationships and avoid confrontational situations or having to provide any negative feedback. As such, they are the most effective leaders.
- Power—enjoy tasks where they can lead, teach, or coach.

Herzberg's Motivation-Hygiene, or **Two-Factor Approach**[3]—suggests that sales representative needs to have a job with motivators present and hygiene factors absent or neutral.

- **Motivating factors** were found to be intrinsic to the job and included: achievement, recognition for achievement, the work itself, responsibility, advancement, or growth.
- **Hygiene factors** were found to be extrinsic to the job and included company policies and administration, supervision, relationship with supervisor, work conditions, salary, relationship with peers, status, and security.

Managers can apply this concept by considering the presence or absence of the groups of factors.

- Making sure that each sales representative finds their work interesting and challenging. As much as possible, the sales manager needs to build motivating factors such as opportunities for achievement, recognition, enjoyable work, responsibility, and advancement into each representative's activities.
- Ensure that hygiene factors, such as company policies, working conditions, and their supervisory relationship, are not considered negative and working as de-motivators.

Generational Motivational Issues

Is there a difference between what motivates salespeople based on their age? You might have noticed some differences in how someone in their sixties responds differently to situations as compared with someone in their twenties. If you work with people from multiple generations you've probably heard comments such as:

Adam's **Equity Theory**[4]—proposes that a sales rep weighs their perceived inputs and outcomes in comparison to others and decides if their effort/reward ratio is equitable or fair, and then realigns their efforts to be rewarding.

- Inputs—their perception of their training, experience, effort, hardships they endured for work, and anything else they believe they contribute to the organization.
- Outputs—their perception of their compensation, benefits, status, job security, job satisfaction, and anything else they receive.
- Balancing—a sales representative would compare their input/outcome ratio and compare it with different people. The resulting ratio could result in three possible scenarios:
  1. Equity—input/outcome ratio is equal to others' input/outcome ratio. Reps are motivated to keep doing what they do.
  2. Overpayment inequity—input/outcome ratio is greater than others. Sometimes reps will increase their efforts.
  3. Underpayment inequity—input/outcome ratio is less than others. Reps either decrease their efforts, ask for more, find different points of comparison, or leave to find more equitable job.

Sales managers can apply this concept by considering the rep's *perception* of their motivators in comparison to their peers. Sales managers need to:

- Be attentive to comments regarding concerns about fairness.
- Ask salespeople to explain their perception of how they compare with a top performer (e.g., "What would a top performer be doing? How does their performance compare to yours?"). The resulting discussion should allow all parties to view the salesperson's perception of their input/outcome ratios.

Expectancy Theory[5]—suggests that a salesperson will choose to behave in the manner that gives them the highest motivational force in order to maximize efforts they find pleasurable and minimize those that are not.

- Reps value outcomes differently (e.g., recognition, out-of-town travel, etc.).
- Reps realize that different levels of effort are required for tasks (e.g., if you prepare for a sales call you should have a better presentation, and hopefully a better chance at making a sale, to a potential client than if you did not prepare for it).
- Performances have different likelihoods of producing outcomes. Some situations are more certain than others.

Sales managers can apply this concept by focusing on the highest motivators or on how to raise the level of the lower ones. Sales managers should

- Understand what value their sales reps place on different rewards. Providing rewards reps don't want does no one much good; focus on those they value.
- Help improve reps performance. Make sure reps receive good training and are prepared and align representatives to clients whose needs are consistent with their abilities.
- Be sure to include other performance measures beyond just a sale (e.g., number of calls, presentations, and proposals) and include an incentive system that can reflect different levels of performance.

"We tried that two years ago. It won't work."

"It was a lot harder to do before technology came around."

No matter what concept or theory of motivation is developed, being able to motivate a sales force is complicated by the differences in motivation due to generational differences. For the first time in history, there are individuals from four different generations working side-by-side in the United States. The fastest growing segment of the workforce is under 27 years of age, with half of the workforce under 40 years. Younger workers are moving into important organizational positions. Yet more workers continue working past retirement age. Nearly one in four households includes a family member involved in elder care. Teams composed of multi-generational members are becoming more the norm than an exception. Understanding

Different-aged salespeople will be motivated by different things. (A Baby Boomer sales manager played by Dennis Quaid meets his new Millenial boss played by Topher Grace in the 2004 movie, *In Good Company,* Universal Pictures). (Everett Collection)

these differences and how to exploit their advantages and minimize their liabilities will be a challenge sales managers must meet.[6]

Each generational group has experienced unique events, and, as a result, each group has a different frame of reference or perspective on life. Because each generation has different sets of experiences, they have different values, expectations, and motivations. We communicate in a different manner based on our generational backgrounds and the technology that has been made available to us. Exhibit 12.3 presents the personal and lifestyle characteristics distinctive to each generation.

All of these different events, technologies, and perspectives also impact us at work—especially in terms of how sales managers need to manage, work in teams, recruit, and motivate. Consequently, each generational group is motivated by slightly different drives at work. A sales representative from the Baby Boomer generation might value money or recognition most.

By contrast, a Gen X or Millennial sales representative, although still wanting to be paid well, might put more value on having a good work-life balance. Sales representatives from the Matures appreciate more formal means of communication, whereas a Millennial desires an informal style. Exhibit 12.3 also summarizes different characterizations of the work and motivational differences of each group.

Reflecting on these composites of the different generations, consider each group and examine how managing a multi-generational sales force can affect you as a sales manager, a team member, or a leader. The benefits offered by a multi-generational sales force are significant and include an opportunity for competitive advantage. The diversity of experiences and skills that individual members can contribute can create a more versatile workforce, a group with more resources to solve problems.

Matures

Raised during the Depression and WWII, they've worked through good times and bad. They have worked in a top-down environment, know how to follow rules, and appreciate more formal communication (i.e., personal or phone over e-mail). They are hardworking, loyal, and reliable workers. They want to be respected and want a meaningful title that reflects their importance. They are admired by their Millennial counterparts and have much wisdom that they enjoy sharing with younger workers. Traditional forms of recognition (e.g., plaques, certificates, etc.) are valued. Allow them to make meaningful contributions, engage them in mentoring, and show respect for their experience.

Baby Boomers

Growing up, they have experienced economic prosperity and periods of social consciousness (e.g., civil rights and environmental). They are the dual-career couples who work long hours and, as a result, struggle to balance their family lives, which can include kids and elderly parents. They have expectations for others to work as hard as they do. Cooperative teamwork (e.g., football) and regular communication is preferred. They value promotions, leadership positions, and public recognition of their accomplishments. As they age, flexible working arrangements that help them pursue time with family and individual interests are of increasing value.

Generation X'ers

Raised by parents who both worked, they have shifted the workplace emphasis from materialism to a focus on family. They are moving into managerial positions and prefer independence over teamwork and immediate communication over structured meetings. Computer use and multi-tasking is second nature. They value work opportunities that are changing and

EXHIBIT 12.3

Generational Characteristics and Differences

	Matures	Baby Boomers	Generation X'ers	Millennials
Year born	1922–1945	1946–1964	1965–1980	1981–Present
How many	75 million	78 million	45 million	80 million
Workplace composition	5%	45%	40%	10%
Defining events and trends	Great Depression New Deal Labor Unions World War II Korean War	Suburbia Space Race Focus on Youth Vietnam War Assassinations Equal Opportunity for All Earth Day	MTV AIDS Personal Computers Fall of Berlin Wall Challenger Wall Street Frenzy	Gulf Wars Clinton/Lewinsky School Shootings Corporate Scandals 9/11 Iraq Facebook
Workplace characteristics	Organizational loyalty Respect authority Sacrifice Duty before fun Adhere to rules	Idealistic Workaholics Time stressed Personal fulfillment Question authority	Individual contractor Entrepreneurial Flexible Seeking work-life balance Media/Info./Tech Savvy Sets own rules	Multi-tasker Entrepreneurial Well educated and well-traveled Team-oriented Socially/politically conscious Media/Info./ Tech Savvy
Work Preference	Individual	Committee within unit	Matrix	Global
Diversity	Non-existent. White males only	Politically correct and legislated	Valued and sought out	Expected—way of life
Work Technology	Mimeograph machine Mainframe	Copiers Desktop	Paperless office Laptop	Wireless office iPhone®
Communication Style	Formal Memo	In person	Direct, via e-mail	Immediate, via instant messaging
Leadership Style	Authoritative Command-and-control	Benevolent dictator Participative	Straightforward Everyone is the same with equal input	Relationship and team building via group meetings and technology
Reward Preferences and Motivators	Larger office and other perks Public recognition that their contribution is valued Money	Promotion Opportunities for leadership Money	Workplace flexibility Latest technology Freedom to set own rules and/or work on own projects Opportunities for learning & development Opportunities to work with other bright, creative people	Workplace flexibility Latest technology Time off for travel and philanthropic work Opportunities to work with other bright, creative people Opportunities to move up and contribute

allow for the opportunity to grow. Flexibility in working arrangements is critical as family time is more important than time at work. Bonus days off may be valued more than the traditional monetary bonus.

Millennials

Soon to be the largest group in the workforce. Some have experienced tight job markets and moved home. They've been counseled to find a good job that's right for them. They follow the X'ers in their requirement of a work-life balance. They have a high level of social consciousness and responsibility and desire an employer who incorporates and displays these values in their work. Being individuals in a team is valued. These people like immediate feedback and rewards. They want meaningful work experiences and mentors or coaches who can help them achieve their goals and contribute to their companies. Flexibility in their work environment is a must.

No doubt managing someone who is your parents' or grandparents' age might initially seem a little daunting. (Having someone their child or grandchild's age managing them may initially be a bit uncomfortable to them also.) Keep in mind that everyone—no matter what the person's age is, has something valuable to offer a sales organization. It's a sales manager's job to figure out what that is. Listen to what different people have to say, ask questions, and determine what motivates them.

The Dos and Don'ts of Motivating Your Sales Representatives

The following section summarizes some of the suggestions sales managers can use to motivate their sales forces.

- Hire self-motivated people: The old adage "Surround yourself with good people and you'll never have any problems too big to achieve" would seem to fit. When you are hiring, be sure to look for individuals who demonstrate a "can-do" approach to work.
- Show trust: Sales managers need to demonstrate trust with their employees and will gain it in return. Those managers who don't won't get any in return from their salespeople.[7]
- Capitalize on unique strengths of each member of the sales force. Great managers discover the unique characteristics each employee has, then capitalize on them.[8]
- Encourage some people to become experts. Having someone designated as a specialist in an area demonstrates that you trust the person and want to recognize the person's contribution to the team.
- Empower salespeople to make their own decisions. When you feel like you "own" some aspect of your work, you become more motivated to be responsible for it. Likewise, empowering salespeople to make decisions helps develop and motivate them.
- Ensure that you offer rewards that are valued by all of the members of your sales force, regardless of their age, gender, and years of experience.
- Develop or remove deadbeats: Nothing can put a damper on things faster than a full-time complainer whose attitude sours others. Coach those salespeople who are open to becoming more positive about their jobs, and dismiss those who aren't.[9] If a person is not the right fit for the job, help him or her realize as much.

When good performing sales representatives are no longer demonstrating their past levels of achievement and their performance has leveled out, they may have reached a **plateau** in their careers. This is not an uncommon event for someone who has had a successful career for a long period of time. In essence they are still capable of performing at a high level but might no longer be driven by their current mix of rewards.

Peter Gundy, principal and director of sales compensation at Buck Consultants, notes: "You end up with salespeople who may not have that fire in their bellies anymore, so you have to find other ways of motivating them. Certainly the challenge and thrill of the hunt are still part of the job," comments Gundy. Gundy recommends mixing up their reward plans to possibly include new responsibilities, such as training and coaching newer representatives. Alternately you could develop a plan based on tenure, where you recognize salespeople who earn 110 percent of their quota for so many years in a row.[10]

Having a good understanding of what motivates salespeople is really half the picture. A good sales manager has to have this underlying base of information to build on. The second half of the picture is ensuring that your salespeople are rewarded for their efforts. The next section discusses the various financial and nonfinancial rewards available to sales personnel and insights that sales managers need to know to administer them.

Financial and Nonfinancial Rewards

Imagine that you just won a contest your instructor held as part of your sales management class or in the personal selling class. How would you like to be rewarded for your efforts? Would you like your reward to be an award, extra points to improve your grade, a meal at a nice restaurant, public recognition, a day off from class, an opportunity to attend a training seminar, a weekend trip, or merchandise? With so many choices to choose from, how could your instructor go wrong? Let's consider a few things:

- If you've received about as many certificates or awards as your wall can hold, then another piece of paper or a trophy might really turn you off. But if you really need something of the sort to make your resume look good, then such a reward might be great.
- If you've already nailed down the grade you want to get in the course, additional points won't help you much. However, if you're really struggling in the course, extra points might be wonderful.
- If you work at a fancy restaurant or a resort, then a fancy meal or a weekend stay might not be so valuable because you have access to them already. But if you wanted to take someone special out to thank them for the things they've done for you, this could be a good reward.
- Public recognition in class is nice. However, if you've already done a couple of activities that resulted in your being recognized, you might be uncomfortable receiving more recognition. That said, if you thrive on positive feedback, you'll want even more.

As you can probably tell from this discussion, there are many ways to reward performance. *Sales and Marketing Management Magazine* has run a monthly column discussing what motivates salespeople. Exhibit 12.4 shows a sampling of what some individuals had to say about what motivates them.[11]

What Motivates You as a Salesperson?
- "Achieving a team goal and all of us going on a four-day cruise."
- "Receiving a gift from the company president at a company-wide meeting."
- "The owner's verbal recognition."
- "A work environment that lets me work part of the day at home to balance my family needs."
- "A trip to Hawaii for reaching a sales goal."
- "A personal gift selected for me by the company president."
- "Sending me to a seminar that helps me become more productive."
- "A trip to a special spa."
- "Quarterly bonuses. The extra money helps with the bills."
- "Being selected for the President's club (and the ring or trip that comes with it)."

EXHIBIT 12.4

Salesperson Motivation

Not only do the rewards salespeople desire differ from person to person, they also differ from country to country. The Global Sales Management feature in this chapter examines the findings of researchers who looked at the importance of different types of rewards in different countries and how they motivated salespeople there.

GLOBAL SALES MANAGEMENT

"We're All in It for the Money, Right?"

A common assumption about salespeople, regardless of where they live, is that they enter the profession because of the high monetary rewards associated with it. But does this type of motivation drive sales personnel worldwide? In a study conducted in 2003, salespeople in nine countries were asked the following question: "(What) one thing would you most like to obtain from your career?"

The findings of the study indicated that although sales representatives in different countries responded similarly, there were some meaningful differences. The response "to earn a lot of money" was the motivator listed first in Singapore, the U.K., and the United States. However, in Australia, Canada, New Zealand, and Norway, salespeople said their number one motivator was being able to "use (my) special abilities." Both of these responses were the top motivators for salespeople in Chile and Sweden.

Another factor listed among the top motivators was having the opportunity to "do new and exciting things." The opportunity to "go into management" received mixed ratings depending upon the country in which the question was asked. Although it was a more popular motivator in Singapore, Australia, and the U.K., it was a much less popular response in Sweden, Canada, and the United States.

So, if what motivates salespeople isn't the same worldwide, then shouldn't compensation plans be adjusted to reflect as much? The researchers noted that although the same motivators are essentially important in all of the countries the study examined, the individual country differences needed to be considered by managers. This is particularly true when it comes to sales contests. For example, in some countries, such as Japan, recognizing the accomplishments of individual salespeople to a greater degree than the accomplishments of one's sales force as a whole is not considered to be in good form.[12]

Source: Tanner, John F., Jr., and George W. Dudley (2003). "International Differences: Examining Two Assumptions about Selling," in *Advances in Marketing*, William J. Kehoe and Linda K. Whitten, eds., Society for Marketing Advances, pp. 236–239.

The Components of a Reward Program

With so many options that can be used to motivate sales personnel, the task for putting together a complete program, or **total rewards program**, initially might seem daunting. We use the term *total rewards* to include all of the options a sales manager should utilize to reward performance rather than just compensation and benefits. Exhibit 12.5 depicts the different factors that affect the rewards sales managers choose to use.[13,14] As you consider the different factors involved in a reward system, you can appreciate the complexity of administering them. Human resource personnel are likely to be involved in administering the program. Typically top sales management executives will help structure components critical to salespeople. The programs need to be designed so that salespeople receive rewards that keep them motivated but don't cause a financial burden to the firm. Of course, the plan needs to be in line with what others in your industry and area are paying. Otherwise you risk losing reps to your competitors offering better pay and benefits.

Now let's look at each of the different reward factors used to motivate salespeople.

The **marketplace environment** includes factors such as the level of industry competition, the use of technology, the financial resources firms in the industry have available to them, the competition for sales personnel, and the level of training salespeople require. Companies with limited competition in the marketplace and desirable products and services are likely to have more resources available to them to reward their salespeople than companies selling undifferentiated products and services in highly competitive markets. Similarly, to recruit salespeople who live in high-cost locations, a firm might need to offer them higher compensation levels. Firms might also have to adjust their reward levels in order to retain and recruit for positions for which there are few qualified or trainable salespeople. Kevin Powell, the president of Werner Electric Supply of Minnesota, knows, for example, that to find a sales representative with a sales or business background and some experience selling electrical products, he will likely have to pay the person more than someone who lacks as much.

Many organizations make a conscious effort to strengthen their **organizational culture** by choosing certain rewards to offer their sales representatives. Take, for instance, New Belgium Brewing Company, a Fort Collins, Colorado, company that prides itself on its environmental responsibility, philanthropy, and the fact that it's a great place to work (see website photo on opposite page). The company has its own water treatment plant and wind farm that produces its energy, and it has taken the 3Rs of reduce, reuse, and recycle to extremes. In addition to donating $1 for each keg it sells to the communities in which they were purchased, the company believes work should be fun. To keep things fun, it gives each of its employees a "cruiser bicycle" (one with fat tires) after they have been employed by the company for one year. After five years, the company gives them a trip to Belgium.

The **business strategy** a company utilizes also affects the rewards it will use to motivate its salespeople. If a company's plan includes achieving aggressive growth in new markets, landing new accounts needs to be rewarded. If serving a firm's existing customers and expanding their accounts is important, salespeople's customer service efforts need to be rewarded. The latter was the case when IBM began selling information services as well as computer hardware; IBM realized that its sales force would have to make changes as well. The company wanted to make its salespeople experts in the industry—that is, it wanted them to sell solutions to customers and not just products. To achieve this goal, IBM reorganized its sales force and reduced the number of customers each salesperson serves. IBM salesperson Elizabeth Cook now has fewer customers, but spends more time with each of them. "I'm now more accessible and visible to them," says Cook. In the past, IBM salespeople spent up to six hours each week in company meetings. Now they only meet for

EXHIBIT 12.5

Factors That Affect an Organization's Total Rewards Program

MARKETPLACE ENVIRONMENT
How do market and industry factors affect the rewards a firm offers its salespeople?

ORGANIZATIONAL CULTURE
How does an organization's culture affect the rewards the firm offers its salespeople?

BUSINESS STRATEGIES
How does the strategy of a business affect the rewards a firm offers its salespeople?

TOTAL REWARDS STRATEGY
Compensation
Benefits
Work-Life Rewards
Recognition
Development

MOTIVATES

SALESPERSON

A company's organizational culture impacts the rewards it offers its employees. New Belgium Brewery's website exemplifies its unique organizational culture: http://www.followyourfolly.com/index.html.

30 minutes a week with their sales managers. Additionally, IBM's sales force is encouraged to work as part of a team that has more responsibility and accountability.[15]

These three factors then influence the **total rewards strategy**, particularly the compensation and benefits, that sales managers use to motivate their personnel. The five major categories of a total rewards approach include compensation, benefits, work-life programs, performance and recognition elements, and development and career opportunities. Exhibit 12.6 outlines different elements or programs compiled by the nonprofit association WorldatWork, which could be used in a total rewards program.[16] The remainder of this chapter will discuss each of the categories and some of the major elements of each category.

Compensation

The first category of rewards is compensation, which often includes a **base salary** and different forms of **variable pay** (or *incentive pay*). Some sales positions are all salary or all incentive or commission-based; however, the majority of salespeople are compensated under a **combination plan**, which includes a salary component and a variable pay component. Combination pay plans are used by over 60 percent of firms, followed by straight salary plans, which are used by nearly 20 percent of firms. Commission-only plans are used by about 10 percent of firms.[17] Historically, salespeople in the financial industry have been among the highest paid salespersons, followed by salespeople selling in manufacturing and the service industries. The details behind all these plans are usually developed at headquarters by top executives from sales, marketing, finance, and human resources. Sales managers are charged with making certain that the various programs are implemented in a manner to achieve company objectives, including personal development and sales goals.

As important a role as it plays, it seems surprising to find that, when asked to describe what their company's compensation program was designed to do, only about one-third of employees could accurately do so.[18] Obviously, if you design a compensation program so as to motivate your employees and truly use it as such, they need to understand how it works.

BASE SALARY A base salary is a fixed amount of compensation an individual receives. It will depend upon a combination of factors. A newly hired graduate's salary is likely to take into account the person's unique skills (languages spoken, for example), past experiences (for example, whether he or she completed a sales internship; held a selling job; or participated in a local, regional, or the National Collegiate Sales Contest), and future potential. As we have explained, higher living costs in some locations can also influence the salary levels firms offer their salespeople. Differential pay based on this factor is called a **cost-of-living allowance (COLA)**, or adjustment. (There are several Internet calculators that allow a person to compare the cost of living of one location versus another. The calculator at http://cgi.money.cnn.com/tools/costofliving/costofliving.html is one such calculator.)

Some positions, particularly those requiring a salesperson to offer high support levels to a firm's customers, will be entirely salaried or **straight salary**. For example, some automotive dealerships, such as Saturn, have moved their salespeople to salary-only plans to encourage them to offer exceptional service to customers. This plan also works well when salespeople are just getting established and developing their own clientele, or **book of business**. It might also work in situations where it is difficult to trace what role in the sale

EXHIBIT 12.6

A Total Rewards Inventory

Compensation	Benefits	Work-Life	Performance Recognition	Development & Career Opportunities
Base Wages • Salary Pay **Variable Pay** • Commissions • Team-Based Pay • Bonus Programs • Incentive Pay Short term • Profit Sharing • Individual Performance-Based Incentives • Performance-Sharing Incentives Long term • Stock Options/Grants	**Legally Required/Mandated** • Unemployment Insurance • Workers' Compensation Insurance • Social Security Insurance • Medicare • State Disability Insurance (if applicable) **Health & Welfare** • Medicare Plan • Dental Plan • Vision Plan • Prescription Drug Plan • Flexible Spending Accounts (FSAs) • Health Reimbursement Accounts (HRAs) • Health Savings Accounts (HSAs) • Mental Health Plan • Life Insurance • Spouse/Dependent Life Insurance • Short Term/Long Term Disability Insurance	**Workplace Flexibility/Alternative Work Arrangements** • Flextime • Flexible Schedules • Telecommuting • Alternative Work Sites • Compressed Workweek • Job Sharing • Part-time Employment • Seasonal Schedules **Paid and Unpaid Time Off** • Maternity/Paternity Leave • Adoption Leave • Sabbaticals **Health and Wellness** • Employee Assistance Programs • On-site Fitness Facilities • Discounted Fitness Club Rates • Preventive Care Programs • Weight Management Programs • Smoking Cessation Assistance • On-site Massages • Stress Management Programs **Caring for Dependents** • Dependent Care Reimbursement Accounts • Dependent Care Travel Related Expense Reimbursement • Childcare Subsidies • On-site Caregiver Support Groups • On-site Dependent Care • Adoption Assistance Services • After-School Care Programs • College/Scholarship Information • Scholarships • Mother's Privacy Rooms • Summer Camps and Activities	**Performance Recognition** • Service Awards • Retirement Awards • Peer Recognition Awards • Spot Awards • Managerial Recognition Programs • Organization-wide Recognition Programs • Exceeding Performance Awards • Employee of the Month/Year Awards • Appreciation Luncheons, Outings, Formal Events • Goal-Specific Awards (Quality, Efficiency, Cost Savings, Productivity, Safety) • Employee Suggestion Programs	**Learning Opportunities** • Tuition Reimbursement • Tuition Discounts • Corporate Universities • New Technology Training • On-the-Job Learning • Attendance at Outside Seminars and Conferences • Access to Virtual Learning, Podcasts, Webinars • Self-Development Tools • Corporate Athletic Programs **Coaching/Mentoring** • Leadership Training • Exposure to Resident Experts • Access to Information Networks • Formal or Informal Mentoring Programs **Advancement Opportunities** • Internships • Apprenticeships • Overseas Assignments • Internal Job Postings • Job Advancement/ Promotion

continued

EXHIBIT 12.6 (*continued*)

A Total Rewards Inventory

Compensation	Benefits	Work-Life	Performance Recognition	Development & Career Opportunities
	Retirement • Defined Benefit Plan • Defined Contribution Plan • Profit Sharing Plan **Pay for Time Not Worked** • Vacation • Holiday • Sick Leave • Bereavement Leave • Leaves of Absence (Military, Personal, Medical, Family Medical)	• Voluntary Immunization Clinics • Wellness Initiatives • Health Screenings • Nutritional Counseling • On-site Nurse • Business Travel Health Services • Occupational Health Programs • Disability Management • Return to Work Programs • Reproductive Health/Pregnancy Programs **Community Involvement** • Community Volunteer Programs • Matching Gift Programs • Shared Leave Programs • Disaster Relief Funds • Sponsorships/Grants • In-Kind Donations	**Financial Support** • Financial Planning Services and Education • Adoption Reimbursement • Transit Subsidies • 529 Plans **Voluntary Benefits** • Long-Term Care • Auto/Home Insurance • Identity Theft Insurance • Employee Discounts • Concierge Services • Transit Passes • Parking		• Career Ladders and Pathways • Succession Planning • On/Off Ramps Through Career Life Cycle • Job Rotations

Source: © 2007. Adapted and reprinted with permission from WorldatWork. Content is licensed for use by purchase only. No part of this work may be reproduced, excerpted or redistributed in any form without express written permission from WorldatWork.

each individual played, for example, when B2B sales involved a large capital purchase by a customer and a team-selling approach was utilized to close the sale. The advantage of this for salespeople is that they can count on receiving a steady stream of income for their efforts—even when their firms' sales are slow. The disadvantage is that if the salespeople have been very productive, they will receive no additional income. The benefit for the organization is that the amount of income it must pay is predictable. The drawback is that the firm's sales representatives might be interested in only producing the minimum levels of work required and that their sales managers may have limited control when it comes to motivating them. However, the effective use of goals and quotas can help offset these disadvantages. This form of pay is particularly useful when a salesperson is developing their expertise and skills, at which time they will often transition to a combination plan. For the more experienced salesperson, variable pay will likely play a more significant role.

VARIABLE (INCENTIVE) PAY Variable pay acts as an incentive for the salesperson. For those salespeople who are particularly motivated, they know that their extra effort will be rewarded. Bonuses and commissions are two examples of incentive plans. A **bonus** is a lump sum of cash used to reward sales personnel and sales managers for achieving varying sales levels. Some companies have several types of bonuses and they are administered on either a quarterly, semiannual, or annual basis. For example, some organizations give their salespeople **stock options**, which allow them to purchase their companies' shares at reduced prices. After holding the stock for a minimum time period, they have the opportunity to sell it or include it in their retirement packages. The intent of this form of compensation is to encourage salespeople to make a long-term commitment to the organization. A bonus is usually a great motivating reward, even though a salesperson might not know how large it will be. A yearly bonus versus, for example, a monthly or quarterly bonus might lose some of its potential to motivate salespeople due to the long period of time they have to wait to earn it. **Team-based pay** is another type of bonus that rewards salespeople for their group productivity. IBM uses a team approach to selling. Its teams consist of inside representatives, products specialists, product consultants, and other experts. They earn compensation based on their individual goals and additional bonuses when their teams achieve their goals.

A **commission** is a percentage of the price of the product or service that salespeople earn for their selling efforts. Most commission programs are **progressive plans**. Progressive plans increase the percentage of commission a firm's sales representatives earn for each progressive level of sales. These plans encourage representatives to sell as much as possible. **Regressive plans** decrease the percentage commission a firm's sales representatives earn when they sell more products and services. A plan such as this allows an organization to limit the amount sales representatives can earn when selling an easy-to-sell product or service—one that perhaps has been extensively pre-sold via advertising campaigns, so the representative is merely acting as an order taker. Of course, such a system can result in some motivational problems. For example, if sales representatives have met or exceeded their goals, they may be motivated to "coast" or slow down for the rest of the sales period. Exhibit 12.7 shows the amount of commission a salesperson would make for selling $500,000 worth of products and/or services under a progressive versus regressive plan.

Some sales positions may be entirely commission based. A firm with restricted cash flow, those with new products that need a strong push, and those in very competitive industries might opt for this approach. Advertising sales positions, some types of insurance sales, and some automobile sales positions are examples. The advantage of this approach is that firms pay only for successful sales efforts—they don't have to pay salespeople who are doing a poor job or are not contributing to the firm's profit. The disadvantages lie at both extremes: If a firm's sales are slow, then its sales representatives will experience low levels

EXHIBIT 12.7

An Example of a
Salesperson's
Compensation
Based on a
Progressive versus
a Regressive Plan

Amount Sold	Progressive Plan		Regressive Plan	
	Percent	Amount	Percent	Amount
$0–$100,000	5%	$5,000	15%	$15,000
$100,001–$200,000	8%	8,000	10%	10,000
$200,001–$300,000	10%	10,000	8%	8,000
>$300,000	15%	30,000	5%	10,000
Total commission		$53,000		$43,000

of income. When this happens, the company's better salespeople will tend to leave the organization to sell products and services that earn them better pay. The other extreme is an organization that has a strong product or service that takes little effort to sell. In this case, the firm's salespeople will earn a great deal of money without much effort on their part.

An additional disadvantage of commission-only pay is that a firm runs the risk of its salespeople focusing solely on activities that will earn them the largest commission. For example, they may focus their energies on products and services that are easiest to sell and ignore new or higher-margin products that are more difficult to sell. Additionally, salespeople are more likely to ignore smaller, less lucrative accounts and customer service activities. The Ethics in Sales Management feature in this chapter describes how a commission-focused compensation system put a salesperson in a position that resulted in him compromising his ethical standards.

ETHICS IN SALES MANAGEMENT

What Do You Do If Your Company's Compensation System Encourages Unethical Behavior?

Note: The following is an account by one of the authors' former students about a situation in which he found himself as a sales representative. The student and company's identities have been withheld to allow them to remain anonymous. After reading the person's account, decide whether an alternative compensation plan would have been more ethical. Do you think such a plan could realistically be implemented at this company? Finally, what would you do if you were to find yourself in a similar situation?

Just after I graduated from college, I worked for a mobile medical services firm. I was second in charge of a department that offered various tests to identify individuals with osteoporosis. Generally speaking, the machines that we used and the tests that we performed were beneficial to the right group of patients.

Mainly I was responsible for operating the equipment and training new employees to give the tests. On occasion, I would be asked to go to doctors' offices to "market" our services. I was young, had no marketing background, and was given little to no instruction on how to ethically "sell" our service to prospective clients (doctors). So I went with what I knew; I focused on what drove me at the time—money. I was driven by my compensation system.

I would go to a doctor's office, set up my company's equipment, show the doctor how our product worked and what it diagnosed, and I would reveal that it administered a low-level (small dose) X-ray. I knew the equipment well and the disease that it diagnosed. I'd go into detail about the type of patient that would be at risk, and, if diagnosed with osteoporosis, what medications were available on the market to treat it.

Oftentimes I would ask if the doctor had a volunteer that I could give an exam to. This would show that the exam was non-invasive, quick, easy, and painless. After the ethical demo, I'd take the doctor into a private room and tell him about the pricing. This is where the shades of gray come in. Everything prior to this conversation I felt positive about. However, in this conversation, instead of just going over our pricing for a full- or half-day's screening, I'd delve a little deeper into the economics than what might have been ethical.

I told the doctor about our fees and then went into great detail about the amount of money that would be reimbursed by various insurance companies for the exam. Basically, I would lay out in gory detail how much profit a doctor could make by bringing in our services and giving us a maximum patient load while we were there. Although I'd previously told the doctor who the "right" group of at-risk patients were, at this point I'd tell him or her that the insurance companies paid for the exam annually and that some of our current clients (doctors) were running every single one of their patients through the exam so as to establish a "baseline." Using the baseline, the doctor could see the bone density of their patients today and compare them to what they were a few years later. Of course, this would involve retesting their patients and collecting money again from insurance companies.

I can't recall a client that we didn't close the deal with. Some doctors brought us in once a week for a full day and sent along every patient that they had. We worked off a flat rate for the day or half-day, so even if a patient's insurance was not very good, there was little or no risk to his or her doctor because there were no incremental costs related to testing more patients. The only thing the doctor might miss out on was the opportunity cost incurred if another patient with better insurance could have been tested instead.

We worked in quite a few gynecologists' offices and often scanned every client that came to see them that day. I didn't feel bad about this because these clients really constituted our "at-risk" group—that is, people who were truly at risk of developing osteoporosis. However, other general practice doctors did not use our services quite so ethically. I actually scanned one doctor every year for a few years so that he could bill his own insurance company for his own tests!

In the end, I still question my method of pitching that product, and the fact that I'm questioning it probably means that it wasn't quite right. I comfort myself by knowing that I did provide doctors with all the positive, good information that they needed to know about the tests. Ultimately it was up to them to whom they prescribed the exams.

Would a "code of ethics" at this company have changed my marketing strategy for this product? First off, this was a company driven by the dollar (and, at the time, so was I). Consequently, the busier I kept our equipment, the more I'd work the more I'd make. So, if the code were in place, I don't think I'd have followed it, and I doubt anyone would have ever found out. Even if an example was given in the code of ethics regarding the tactic I was using, I probably would have found a way to rationalize to myself that I was somehow in compliance with the code, as I told the doctors the truth about everything. And finally the owner of the company was, I believe, a shady character to begin with. As a result, I know that the code, if created, would never have truly had the support of the company's top managers.

COMBINATION PLANS Because of the problems noted above, many firms use combination plans that include both salaries and incentives. Combination plans are designed to capitalize on the advantages a base salary and incentive programs offer and to minimize their disadvantages. These plans are particularly beneficial for new salespeople. A base salary gives sales representatives the security of knowing that in bad times, they will have income to fall back on, which can help minimize their turnover. An incentive component of the plan then serves to further motivate them. Oftentimes representatives can take a **draw**, or advance, on their incentive pay as well. The plans can be designed so that new sales representatives start out earning lower-percentage commissions but then gradually earn higher percentage commissions as they become more experienced. The percentage for each pay component varies depending on the company's objectives. For example, a well-established firm with high service requirements might offer a combination plan that consists of 80 percent salary and 20 percent commission. A split such as this ensures that each account will receive the service the firm wants it to, but reps are given enough of an incentive to try to sell more. By contrast, a less established firm might set up a combination plan that consists of 60 percent salary and 40 percent commission because the company wants its sales force to spend more effort on closing sales. Exhibit 12.8 displays the average level of combination pay (base and bonus plus commission) U.S. salespeople earned in the years 2004–2006, depending upon their productivity.[19]

According to Melaney Barba, a sales manager for Liberty Mutual Insurance, the company uses a combination plan that includes a salary, commission, and a variety of bonuses. "Our system allows the rep the security of a steady income when they start, which transforms to more incentive bases as their skills and customer base develops," explains Barba. New sales representatives start out with a base salary for their 15 weeks of training. Over the course of three years, the salary levels they earn decrease as they sell to new accounts and begin to build their commissions. At the seven-year mark, their salaries are completely phased out. At this point, their salaries are replaced by their commissions and bonuses coming from the renewals of the policies they've sold in the past. Liberty Mutual Insurance representatives can also take a draw on their commissions, which many of them do as they begin their careers.

EXHIBIT 12.8

Total Salaries (Base and Bonus on the Bottom Plus Commission on the Top) for Sales Personnel for the Years 2004-2006.

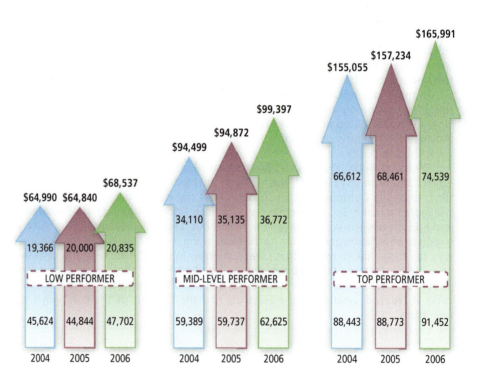

Benefits

Benefits provide security for members of an organization. They are becoming increasingly more expensive, representing approximately 40 percent of a firm's payroll costs, on average. There are several different types of benefit programs that companies provide. Some programs are required by law. The programs legally required in the United States include Social Security, a government retirement program; workers' compensation that provides income to employees hurt or disabled on the job; unemployment insurance; and family and medical leave programs that give employees time away from their jobs to care for family members. Firms are not required to pay employees while they are on family leave. They need only guarantee that their jobs will be available for them when they return to work. Legally required programs constitute about 20 percent of all benefit payments employers make.[20]

Employers can choose to provide their employees with a number of other benefit programs. The most costly and most valued programs are health insurance programs that can include eye, dental, life, disability, and other forms of insurance. Some programs cover employees only. Other plans cover the families of a firm's employees, too. Health insurance payments constitute nearly 25 percent of the average employer's benefit payments.[21]

Many companies also provide their salespeople with **retirement or pension benefit programs** that give them income after they retire. Sometimes referred to as *defined benefit programs,* they specify the exact amounts employees will be paid once they retire. The amount will vary from company to company and from employee to employee, depending on their tenure. Usually it is based on the average compensation the employee received during their last three to five years. Employees that stay for less than a certain number of years (usually 25 to 35 years) are entitled to less than the full amount. Some companies also provide a **defined contribution program**, jointly funded by an employer and the employee. 401(k) savings accounts, IRAs (individual retirement accounts), and profit-sharing programs are examples. However, today many are moving away from defined contribution programs. Retirement plans constitute about 15 percent of the average employer's benefit payments.[22]

The last category of benefit programs is **paid time off** from work. This includes payment for vacations, holidays, sick days, and other time away from work. Most organizations give each one of their salespeople one to two weeks of paid vacation after having worked for their firms for one year. This can gradually increase to four weeks a year. Paid time off programs account for about 25 percent of the benefit payments the average employer makes. Other programs, such as lunches and breaks, account for the remaining 15 percent firms spend on benefit payments, on average.[23]

Work-Life Rewards

As Exhibit 12.6 shows, there are a variety of reward programs that help employees find a balance between their work and life (away from work). As noted earlier in the chapter, each generational group may value these differently. **Workplace flexibility programs** are designed to help employees schedule where and when they work. Many salespeople work out of their homes and at irregular hours to accommodate the needs of their clients. Some employers will pay for **leaves of absence** for births, adoptions, and for sabbaticals. **Health-and-wellness programs** focus on maintaining or improving the health and fitness levels of salespeople. Healthy employees have lower insurance costs than those who are not healthy. Two examples are corporate fitness facilities and employee assistance programs, which are designed to help salespeople with drug and alcohol problems they might have.

Flextime can be a valuable benefit for salespeople and other employees. (Photos.com)

Community involvement programs compensate or partially compensate employees during the time they volunteer. Programs that focus on **care for dependents** provide support for employees with childcare or dependent needs. **Financial support programs** offer employees assistance for a variety of purposes, including education costs, adoption costs, costs related to elder care, and so forth. Other benefits offered voluntarily by firms vary by the organization and can range from travel and transit assistance to employee discounts.

Recognition Programs

Benefits and work-life programs are largely determined at a firm's corporate level and/or human resources level. However, most sales managers have a great deal of flexibility when it comes to implementing recognition rewards. Eighty-five percent of companies reported that their sales managers use recognition rewards to enhance the individual performance of sales representatives; 43 percent of firms say their sales managers use them in team-selling situations.[24] The rewards can be very informal and handled at a personal level between the sales representative and the sales manager. Or, they can be very formal and handled in front of the entire sales force or company. Recognition is often used to reinforce the short-term behavior of sales representatives.

Exhibit 12.9 displays the frequency of the use of different incentives.[25] Other rewards might include a dinner at a special location, a hotel room upgrade (from sharing a room to a single room), or an appointment to a desirable committee in the firm. Sales managers who want to reinforce good selling behaviors on the spot often will award gift cards or free meal cards to their representatives, as Mike Kapocius explained in the opening profile. Retail salespeople who sell many manufacturers' products are sometimes encouraged by the manufacturers to promote their particular brands through the use of **sales promotion incentive funds (SPIFs)**. For each selected product they sell, they receive money or merchandise as a reward.

Perhaps the most widely used form of recognition is done through local, regional, or organization-wide sales contests. The amount of influence a sales manager has in developing these events depends upon where they originate. The contests can be based on a time period (for example, weekly, monthly, quarterly, or yearly) or around the launch of a new product or service. Melaney Barba, with Liberty Mutual Insurance, comments that her sales representatives thrive on competition. "I use local sales contests to help support our organization-wide Liberty Leaders Contest. We have monthly winners who have their pictures displayed and names engraved on our permanent plaque." Sales managers should make sure that sales contests are implemented correctly and are fair. Most experts agree that you want to make sure that your contests allow salespeople to be winners without branding other salespeople as losers. One way of doing this is to design your contest so that there are

EXHIBIT 12.9

Frequency of the Use of Different Sales Incentives

Source: Based on Kornik, Joseph (2007). "What's It All Worth? 2007 Compensation Survey," *Sales & Marketing Management* Vol. 159, No. 4, pp. 27–39.

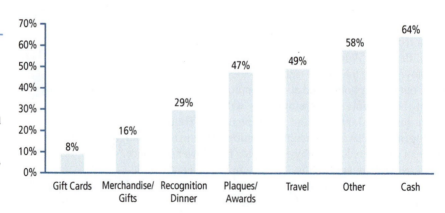

- Use them sparingly. If you use contests too frequently or on a predictable schedule, salespeople might hold back on their selling until the contest starts.
- Be selective in what products/services to include. Including new, unproven products and services helps motivate salespeople's to learn about them and sell them.
- Make the rewards you offer attractive to salespeople of all ages and experience levels. In other words, use rewards that motivate all groups.

EXHIBIT 12.10

Recommendations for Successful Sales Contests

multiple winners, depending upon the amount of product a rep sells. The top-selling rep would be awarded the most lucrative prize, and other high-achieving reps would be awarded lesser prizes. Firms such as Maritz Incentives are frequently hired by firms to assist their sales managers with their contests. Companies like Maritz do everything from helping to choose the types of rewards to offer, communicating them to representatives, and distributing them to winners. Exhibit 12.10 outlines some suggestions for planning and implementing sales contests.

Similarly, Kapocius recalls the importance of being inducted in the top sellers club: "These [programs] can be very motivating because reps receive a great trip (partner included) and typically meet and are recognized by the organization's top leaders. Giving your input to the company's leaders can be very motivating, especially to an established rep." Being included in a top sales recognition group is typically based on several criteria, including a certain level of sales success. However, many organizations will also consider other activities such as a salesperson's teamwork, leadership, and community service. In some organizations, membership is determined by a vote of the sales representatives themselves.

It should be noted that if a company relies exclusively on external or extrinsic rewards, it runs the risk of having trained or motivated its sales force to perform only when they are given "goodies" rather than relying on intrinsic motivators, such as satisfaction with their work. The following analogy demonstrates how tying extrinsic motivators to an intrinsically motivating activity can destroy what normally would motivate a sales representative.

There was a small baker with a good business and regular customers who noticed his sales had fallen off drastically in the late afternoon. Stepping outside his store, he spotted a group of very menacing boys who were harassing everyone who walked by and scaring off his customers. After politely asking the group to stop bothering his customers, the boys laughed and said, "Make us move, little man!" They then continued to harass and ultimately chased off the remaining bakery customers for the day.

The next day the boys arrived and began harassing customers again. The baker quickly went out and handed each boy five dollars and said he had changed his mind. He told them that he actually liked their insults and was going to pay them for insulting him. The boys thought he was nuts and began making nasty comments about the baker and his "lousy" rolls and other products. After a few minutes, the baker said, "That's fine. Thanks for your efforts," and returned to work.

The next day the boys arrived again. The baker apologized to them, saying that he had only enough to pay each of them four dollars to make their mean comments to him and harass his customers. After a couple of minutes listening to the boys complain about their diminished pay, they began again to sling their insults.

The following day, the baker lowered the amount to only three dollars per boy. The day after that, he paid them only two dollars a day. On the fifth day, the baker said he could pay them only one dollar for their comments. The boys looked at the one-dollar bills and with great disgust said, "If you are only going to pay us one dollar each—it's not worth our time and effort!" With that they left and didn't return.

The moral of this story is that organizations should be cautious about the extrinsic rewards they use and the frequency with which they administer them. This is especially true of sales contests. A contest should be held for a short period of time and should motivate reps to do something they are not already doing or are supposed to be doing. What exactly is the "ideal" frequency with which awards should be administered, you might be wondering? Research by behavioral scientists has demonstrated that when we are learning a new behavior, a constant reinforcement schedule works best. For example, if you do something correctly, you should be rewarded every time. However, when no one is around to constantly reward your behavior, it will quickly diminish. The reward schedule that seems to best reinforce behavior is an intermittent or variable schedule in which the performer does not know exactly when he or she will get the reinforcement. In sum, reinforcing the behaviors you want your salespeople to exhibit—on an intermittent schedule—is a fine way to reward and motivate them.

Expense Accounts

Not included in Exhibit 12.6 were **expense accounts**. Salespeople incur a whole host of costs. Controlling the rising price of fuel and transportation costs is becoming a battle for many sales managers. According to the American Express Global Business Travel Forecast, the average cost of a domestic business trip, including airfare, lodging, and car rentals, is $1,110 while an international trip is $3,171.[26] These numbers will surely increase as the price of fuel rises. Many organizations work with firms that specialize in securing corporate discounts from airlines and other transportation-related companies. Organizations also work with firms to determine when companies should provide sales reps with leased vehicles or reimburse reps for the personal use of their vehicles.

The majority of firms either supply or reimburse their salespeople for their home office expenses that can include the cost of their laptops and software, cell phones, office supplies and printers, Internet charges, and voice and data communications systems. Experts say the median costs of these offices are nearly $5,000 in direct and support costs. Another significant expense is lodging and food that vary widely depending upon where you are conducting business. For example, the average cost for a meal and lodging is over $532 in New York City versus $150 in Peoria, Illinois.[27] The most frequently used method to reimburse travel expenses is an **unlimited plan** under which all of the sales rep's expenses are covered. This is in contrast to a **per diem plan** where a rep is allocated a certain amount of money for each day traveled. A third method is a **limited plan** where the exact amounts for each meal and travel expense are set. Exhibit 12.11 outlines the advantages and disadvantages of each plan in terms of management control, flexibility, record keeping, and administration costs.

Expense accounts should be designed to be a neutral factor in a reward system. That is, salespeople should not be placed in a position where they use their own income to cover the costs of making a sale. Likewise, they should not be using the extra income from these funds for their personal use.

Personal Development and Career Opportunities

The last category of rewards, career development and opportunities, addresses the question, "What do my salespeople want out of their careers, and how can I help them achieve it?" **Learning opportunities** include access to new educational experiences. These can range from coursework to a summer training experience to the completion of a graduate program. One new area is the development of the "corporate athlete." Programs such as this are based on the premise that to be in optimum "condition," salespeople must learn how to combine their busy schedules with healthy living practices and exercise. Via a training regimen,

	Unlimited	Per Diem	Limited
Advantages	- All expenses covered - Very flexible - Simple administration	- Simple to administer - Low costs - Sales managers can control and forecast expenses - Limits abuse	- Sales managers can control and forecast expenses - Little abuse
Disadvantages	- Potential for abuse is high - No incentive to be economical - Sales managers cannot forecast costs - Amounts that exceed federal limits are subject to withholding and payroll taxes - Higher administrative costs	- Not flexible, may have costs exceeding limits	- Higher administrative costs - Not flexible

EXHIBIT 12.11

A Comparison of Expense Account Plans

attendees learn how to balance these demands and, by doing so, have the energy and attitude they need to sustain their efforts and succeed.[28, 29]

One form of a learning opportunity unique to salespeople is a **sales meeting**. Often held on a yearly or semiannual basis (although some organizations hold them daily, weekly, or monthly), these gatherings are meant to be educational and motivational experiences for participants. Typically new product and/or service information and training updates are covered. Sales meetings can be held on a local, regional, or national level. National meetings are often held at attractive locations and include opportunities for socializing. Sometimes motivational speakers are brought in. For example, salesman Chris Gardner, whose rags-to-riches story was portrayed in the best-selling book and film *The Pursuit of Happyness*, has addressed a number of sales forces on the importance of perseverance.

Encouraging sales representatives to mentor or coach less-experienced reps can also be a powerful motivator. A program such as this publicly recognizes experienced sales representatives for their skills and expertise, thereby offering them a measure of prestige. Providing your sales representatives with advancement opportunities and allowing them to participate in succession planning so they can get the experience they need to further their careers can also be a powerful motivator.

Sales managers often offer their representatives different travel opportunities as a way to reward them. (Comstock Complete)

Summary

Making certain that the sales force is motivated and receiving the rewards they value is an important part of a sales manager's job. It would be an easy job if every salesperson were motivated by the same rewards—but they aren't. Some salespeople are driven by internal or intrinsic factors and others by more material extrinsic factors. Content approaches have attempted to explain motivation by delineating the factors that make up a person's motivation. Process approaches have examined the steps individuals go through to be motivated. In today's workplace, there are four different generations working side-by-side. Some of the differences in terms of how to motivate salespeople can be explained by their generational experiences and values. The "Matures" grew up in a time of world conflict and limited technology. These salespeople tend to place a higher value on traditional rewards. Baby Boomers were raised in a period of social strife. These salespeople tend to integrate technology into their work and place a heavy value on leadership. Salespeople from Generation X learned from their parents to place only limited trust in their employers. These salespeople enjoy using technology and value family above work. The fourth generation, the Millennials, have grown up with limited trust in government and employers. Using technology is second nature to these salespeople. They oftentimes seek a balance between their lives and their work. Sales managers need to understand the differences between the groups and strive to satisfy the motivational needs of each.

Because the values of salespeople are changing, many sales managers now take a total rewards approach to motivate them. The compensation elements of a total rewards program include a base salary and incentive, or variable, pay. Benefits programs are designed to provide for the health and retirement security needs of a sales force. The work-life elements of a total rewards program include programs that allow salespeople to choose when and where they work as well as to balance their health and family needs. Rewarding salespeople by recognizing them on a district-, regional-, or organizational-wide basis is a particularly good motivator. Salespeople can receive praise, cash, merchandise, travel benefits, or membership in a top performers' club as part of a reward program. The final category of rewards, development and career opportunities, attempts to help the individual salesperson identify their future career aspirations and lay out a path for their attainment.

Key Terms

base salary   272
benefits   279
bonus   275
book of business   272
business strategy   271
care for dependents programs   280
combination plan   272
commission   275
community involvement programs   280
cost-of-living allowance (COLA)   272
defined contribution program   279
draw   278
expense accounts   282
extrinsic motivation factors   263
financial support programs   280
health-and-wellness programs   279
intrinsic motivation factors   263
learning opportunities   282
leaves of absence   279
limited plan   282

marketplace environment   271
organizational culture   271
paid time off   279
per diem plan   282
plateau   268
progressive plans   275
regressive plans   275
retirement or pension benefit program   279
sales meeting   283
sales promotion incentive funds (SPIFs)   280
straight salary   272
stock options   275
team-based pay   275
total rewards program   270
total rewards strategy   272
unlimited plan   282
variable pay   272
workplace flexibility programs   279

Questions and Problems

1. What intrinsic and extrinsic factors motivate you as a student? What intrinsic and extrinsic factors do you think would motivate you as a salesperson? What about as a sales manager?

2. As a sales manager, how can you apply the findings of the content approaches? How can you apply the findings of the process approaches? Which do you think makes the most significant contributions and why?

3. Sales manager Gretchen Anderson recalls a "ride along" with one of her sales representatives, Bill, who consistently struggled to reach his quota. They reached their first destination at 10:50 a.m., and Bill said, "Let's eat some lunch." The two had lunch, met the client at 1 p.m., and were done at 1:20 p.m. Bill then told Gretchen he had no other sales calls planned. "I started early today, so I'm knocking off when we get back," Bill told her. In terms of equity theory, describe what is going on from Bill's perspective and from Gretchen's perspective. If you were Gretchen, how would you handle this situation?

4. Given the information below, what insights do you have about the following representatives and what is or isn't motivating them?

	2007 Sales	2008 Sales	2009 Sales	Comments
Dustin	$80,000	$86,000	$94,500	Three years of experience; named outstanding trainee three years ago
Jessica	$104,000	$111,000	$119,000	Ten years of experience; three years in the $100,000 Club and also had a baby!
Deborah	$109,000	$103,000	$97,500	Twenty years of experience; 2009 is the first time the rep didn't make the $100,000 Club in 10 years

5. As a sales manager, what are some behaviors and actions you would try to use to motivate your personnel?

6. The intent behind a COLA is to help salespeople who live in and work in high-cost locations. Find an online cost-of-living calculator or use the one at http://cgi.money.cnn.com/tools/costofliving/costofliving.html. Compare the living costs in Minneapolis–St. Paul; Raleigh–Durham, North Carolina; Dallas–Fort Worth, and San Francisco. Which area has the highest and lowest cost of living? Compare these costs with a small city near you. How much (more or less) would you need to earn as a sales representative in order to move from one locale to another? Consider two members of the sales force that are producing identical results. Is it fair that one sales representative living in a large metropolitan area is compensated more than another one living in a smaller town just because the costs of living in one location are higher than the other?

7. Some students have doubts about being able to support themselves under an incentive-only system. What advice would you offer them?

8. Which three work-life programs do you find most attractive? Which three do you think someone your parents' age would find most attractive? What about your grandparents' age?

9. If you were to hold a sales contest and offer a trip as an award, what location would you pick? For each generation, identify a location that you believe they would find particularly motivating and explain why.

10. What type of performance recognition program would motivate you the most? The least?

11. Some sales managers give cash cards worth about $25 each to their sales representatives when they perform a new skill. What do you think the pros and cons of this practice are?

12. How could a recognition program for marketing students work within your college's business-education department? What would you use as motivators if you had an unlimited budget? What if your budget were $250?

Role Play

BioIDs

BioIDs specializes in incorporating biometrics (such as fingerprints, retinal scans, body measurements, and so forth) into ID cards so that a person's identification can be immediately verified. BioIDs' business has been growing because more organizations ranging from the U.S. Department of Homeland Security to local school districts are needing to verify the identities of people. Government organizations have been the company's largest segment. Selling to them is often a long process that involves a large number of people in a buying center. Salespeople have to be prepared to work with multiple people and be available on short notice to work with buying committees.

BioIDs' sales goals have always been aggressive because the company's products and services have a stellar reputation and the sales force has achieved an impressive record of growth and customer satisfaction. However, the company has also seen its competition grow both in terms of revenues captured and competing products and services being offered. Nonetheless, BioIDs has worked to keep the organization the leader in its industry by providing great compensation and benefits to everyone in its sales force.

However, with only a few weeks remaining in the sales year, it appears that one particular BioIDs district, District Six, will be lucky if it reaches its threshold goals, let alone its actual goals. Two salespeople are clearly coming in below goal. Both have lost major accounts in the last quarter, and neither has a pipeline that is full. One of them is Jerry Thibodeaux. Just a few years ago, Jerry was a member of the President's Club for his outstanding record. However, 18 months ago, his elderly mother moved in with his family, so he is often unavailable to clients. About the same time, another award-winner sales rep, Rachel Simon, had a baby. It's the couple's first child and has developed complications that require Rachel to have to come home immediately if the caretaker she has hired requests her to do so. Both Jerry and Rachel barely made their threshold goals last year, and, despite taking work home, they aren't going to make it this year. To make matters worse, customer satisfaction ratings among the district's customers have fallen off.

Assignment

Split into pairs. One of you is the sales manager for District Six and the other the regional manager. Both of you stand to lose $10,000 in bonuses, and other sales representatives in District Six will lose $4,000 in bonuses if the goals aren't met. In situations such as these, the national sales manager will request an action plan for the future. Outline the plan the two of you propose to the national sales manager to improve sales. What types of reward programs might you propose?

Caselet 12.1: Adjusting Your Compensation Plan to Motivate Your Sales Representatives

Pelican Pharmaceutical Company is having difficulty retaining quality, experienced salespeople. The problem started three years ago when the patent for the firm's most popular drug expired, and other low-cost drug producers began manufacturing and selling similar drugs under generic names. Pelican has a board of directors that is fiscally conservative and only believes in rewarding sales performance based on profitability. So, as the firm's sales slumped, so did the incomes of Pelican's sales representatives and sales managers. Frank Killey was hired last year as the new director of sales at Pelican. Frank has been struggling with motivation and reward issues for a sales force that is again failing to make its yearly sales quota.

Pelican still has numerous viable drugs to sell but does not have a "blockbuster" drug in its research pipeline. Last week, one of Frank's senior sales managers came into his office and resigned, telling Frank that he planned to take early retirement because the industry is changing, and he had had enough.

Pelican provides both its sales representatives and sales managers with modest salaries, company cars, and full benefits, which are some of the best in the industry. The company pays commissions based on salespeople surpassing their previous year's sales totals. An escalating reward system kicks in once a sales representative achieves 80 percent of his or her sales quota. There are also special sales contests related to selling the company's most profitable drugs. The rewards for these contests usually consist of trips or merchandise.

However, the average salesperson at Pelican is only achieving 75 percent of his or her sales quota, which means the person earns no commission. Those who do earn bonuses are usually only a few percentage points over quota, so their commission checks are marginal. The sales quotas were set by Pelican's board of directors and are based on the company's overall operations overhead and the return the company's shareholders expect.

Frank is very concerned about the downward spiral he is seeing in his sales force. He thinks changing the commission structure would solve the problem. His goal is to kick off Pelican's upcoming annual sales meeting with a presentation outlining the company's new and improved commission structure. To implement the new commission plan, he will have to make a proposal to the board of directors to lower the quotas reps must achieve by 10 percent. That way, at least 50 percent of the sales representatives would have an opportunity to achieve and exceed their quotas. He also plans to highlight the company's existing total rewards package, including Pelican's generous company-car usage policy and valuable benefits package.

Questions

1. What problems do you anticipate Frank will run into when he presents his revised commission structure plan to Pelican's board of directors?
2. If Pelican were a low-cost, generic pharmaceutical company, how would you as a sales manager reward and motivate sales representatives?
3. What other motivational tools could Frank have used to retain and motivate employees other than adjusting the sales quota downward?
4. Identify other areas within the company that will be affected if Frank's plan is approved by the board of directors.
5. Do you feel the company should have adjusted its commission structure before the patent for its best-selling drug expired? Is it fair to penalize the sales force with lower commissions for an outside competitive factor they cannot control? Explain your answer.

Caselet 12.2: Which Is Better? A Market Share–Based Incentive System or a Revenue-Based Incentive System?

Phil Lehman, a very successful salesperson, started working for Lextron Corporation right out of college. Phil has been with Lextron, a major manufacturer of sterilized medical equipment, for over 10 years. During his first 10 years with the company, he won numerous sales awards, was a sales dollar leader in most product categories, and never missed his sales quota, which increased by approximately 10 percent each year.

Lextron's customers are major hospitals and medical centers across the country. The company currently has a 40 percent market share in the United States, which is double its nearest competitor. Territories are divided up by metropolitan areas, and commissions are paid based on sales volume. Phil had been working in the Atlanta, Georgia, territory his entire career.

Two years ago Phil's wife, Marcia, who is a physician, had an opportunity to take a new position in Milwaukee, Wisconsin. The position would have enabled her to do more research, which is one of her passions. Coupled with this offer was the fact that both Phil and Marcia are from the Milwaukee area. Thus, Phil's company agreed to transfer him to the Milwaukee territory, which had recently opened up.

The move back to Milwaukee started out great. Phil's wife enjoyed her new job, and he worked hard making new contacts in the medical community. He opened up six new major accounts in his first year and another three in his second year. However, Phil was running out of new account prospects. He figured he had doubled his market share since he started working in Milwaukee, and he speculated that his products were in 80 percent of the hospitals and clinics within his territory. Despite his hard work, he was making less money in commissions and not winning sales contests like he did when he was in Atlanta.

Mark Green, a regional sales manager for Lextron, is Phil's direct supervisor. Mark has agreed to visit Phil in his territory to discuss a pressing issue Phil has not yet disclosed to him. At lunch Phil asks Mark several questions about his sales performance over the past two years. Mark praises Phil for doing an excellent job and encourages him to keep up the good work.

Phil then asks Mark why he is not being compensated for his efforts. Mark is puzzled. He tells Phil he is paid on a commission like every other sales representative in the country. Phil then lays out the compensation he received in Atlanta for capturing just 40 percent of the market and the compensation he receives now in Milwaukee for capturing 80 percent of the market—double what he had in Atlanta.

Questions

1. How do you think Mark Green should react to Phil's argument about market share and compensation? (Remember, he just told Phil he was doing an excellent job.)
2. Do you believe Phil has been fairly compensated since his move to Milwaukee? What other compensation programs could the company have put in place to avoid this situation?
3. Should Lextron Corporation consider changing its commission structure from one that is revenue-based to one that is market–share based? If so, how might this affect the firm's other territories. Explain your answer.
4. How do you think the size and speed of growth in a metropolitan area like Atlanta affect commissioned salespeople with territories in areas such as this? What about commissioned salespeople with territories with shrinking population bases, such as Milwaukee?

5. Should the territory Phil was working in Atlanta have been split in two—to allow Lextron to capture more market share and keep the market share of different territories around the country and the compensation associated with on par with one another?

6. Should the existing salesperson in a territory to be split receive any additional compensation of future lost wages because the territory is going to be smaller? Explain your answer.

References

1. Maslow, Abraham H. (1943). "A Theory of Human Motivation," *Psychological Review* July, pp. 370–396.
2. McClelland, David C. (1965). "Toward a Theory of Motive Acquisition," *American Psychologist* May, pp. 321–333.
3. Herzberg, Fredrick (1968). "One More Time: How Do You Motivate Employees?" *Harvard Business Review* January–February, Vol. 46, No. 1, pp. 53–62.
4. Adams, John S. (1963). "Toward an Understanding of Inequity," *Journal of Abnormal and Social Psychology* (67): 422–436.
5. Vroom, Victor (1964). *Work and Motivation.* New York: John Wiley & Sons.
6. *Aligning a Multi-Generational Workforce with Your Business Goals* (2005). Executive Brief. Milwaukee, WI: Versant Works.
7. Buckingham, Marcus (2005). "What Great Managers Do," *Harvard Business Review* March, (83)3: 70–79.
8. "Motivation: The Not-so-Secret Ingredient of High Performance" (2006). Chapter of *Performance Management.* Boston: Harvard Business School Publishing.
9. Ibid.
10. Strout, Erin (2003). "Veteran Sales Slackers," *Sales and Marketing Management* (155)7: 26.
11. "What Motivates Me?" (2005) *Sales & Marketing Management* (157)5: 18.
12. Tanner, John F., Jr., and George W. Dudley (2003). "International Differences: Examining Two Assumptions About Selling," in *Advances in Marketing*, William J. Kehoe and Linda K. Whitten, eds. Society for Marketing Advances, pp. 236–239.
13. Jensen, Doug; McMullen, Tom and Mel Stark (2007), *The Manager's Guide to Rewards*, New York: American Management Association, p. 72.
14. WorldatWork, http://www.worldatwork.org/waw/home/html/home.jsp. Retrieved on June 13, 2007.
15. Strout, Erin (2003). "Blue Skies Ahead?" *Sales & Marketing Management* March, (155)3: 24–30.
16. WorldatWork, http://www.worldatwork.org/pub/TR_Inventory040207.pdf. Retrieved on June 13, 2007.
17. Heide, Christen P. (1997). "What America's Small Companies Pay Their Sales Forces, and How They Make It Pay Off," Chicago, IL: Dartnell Corporation, p. 36.
18. Jensen, McMullen, and Stark, Op cit.
19. Kornik, Joseph (2007). "What's It All Worth? 2007 Compensation Survey," *Sales & Marketing Management* (159)4: 27–40.
20. *Employee Benefits* (2006). Washington D.C.: United States Chamber of Commerce.
21. Ibid.
22. Ibid.
23. Ibid.
24. Kornik (2007).
25. Ibid.

26. Reeves, Dan (2007, December 3), "Business Travel Expenses Expected to Rise 6% Next Year," *USA Today*. Retrieved on January 2, 2008, from: http://www.usatoday.com/money/ industries/travel/2007-12-03-business-travel-costs_N.htm?csp=34.

27. "10 Costliest U.S. Cities: Per Diem Costs" (2005). *Sales and Marketing Management* September, (157)9: 31.

28. Groppel, Jack, and Bob Andelman (2000). *The Corporate Athlete: How to Achieve Maximum Performance in Business and Life*. New York: John Wiley & Sons.

29. Loehr, Jim, and Tony Schwart (2001). "The Making of a Corporate Athlete," *Harvard Business Review* (79)1: 120–128.

Measurement, Analysis, and Knowledge Management

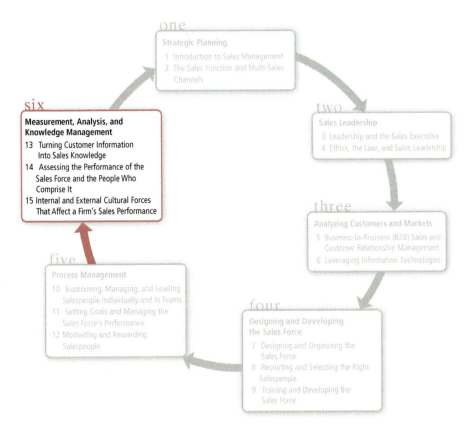

one
Strategic Planning
1 Introduction to Sales Management
2 The Sales Function and Multi-Sales Channels

two
Sales Leadership
3 Leadership and the Sales Executive
4 Ethics, the Law, and Sales Leadership

three
Analyzing Customers and Markets
5 Business-to-Business (B2B) Sales and Customer Relationship Management
6 Leveraging Information Technologies

four
Designing and Developing the Sales Force
7 Designing and Organizing the Sales Force
8 Recruiting and Selecting the Right Salespeople
9 Training and Developing the Sales Force

five
Process Management
10 Supervising, Managing, and Leading Salespeople Individually and in Teams
11 Setting Goals and Managing the Sales Force's Performance
12 Motivating and Rewarding Salespeople

six
Measurement, Analysis, and Knowledge Management
13 Turning Customer Information Into Sales Knowledge
14 Assessing the Performance of the Sales Force and the People Who Comprise It
15 Internal and External Cultural Forces That Affect a Firm's Sales Performance

In previous parts of this book, you came to understand how sales managers supervise, manage, and lead individual and sales team efforts. This includes setting goals, managing performance, motivating, and rewarding sales personnel.

But now how much can we sell? In Chapter 13, *Turning Customer Information into Sales Knowledge*, we explore processes that make customer data more useful. Specifically, we examine how forecasts are created and used. Further, customer data integration processes are also developed. Data regarding customers comes from a number of sources other than salespeople. Combining that data so that it can become useful knowledge is an important aspect of customer data technology.

Chapter 14, *Assessing the Performance of the Sales Force and the People Who Comprise It*, discusses the importance of assessing sales performance at both the individual and team levels. Without assessing or evaluating sales efforts,

it is impossible to know what is or is not working and, most importantly, why? When performance falls below expectations, the sales manager investigates whether expectations are unrealistic or the sales team needs managerial guidance to reach their goals. Individually, sales managers consider how hard a salesperson works, how successful they are, how profitable they are, and their personal development.

Chapter 15, *Internal and External Cultural Forces That Affect a Firm's Sales Performance*, offers an insight into the importance of culture, both internal and external, to the sales firm. For sales firms with misaligned internal cultures, sales personnel spend 30 to 40 percent of their time working on activities that are not valued by customers. The sales manager plays a huge role in aligning the sales culture with customer expectations. Sales personnel engage with buyers from different cultures, genders, religions, and orientations. To succeed, salespersons must be aware of these differences and must tailor their behavior so that the buyer is not offended.

13

TURNING CUSTOMER INFORMATION INTO SALES KNOWLEDGE

LEARNING OBJECTIVES

After completing this chapter, you should be able to:

- Identify the major elements of customer data integration.
- Explain how documented, accessible customer information benefits a firm's various functional groups.
- Create sales forecasts using the various types of forecasting methods prominently implemented in sales settings.

Salespeople are in the unique position of conversing face-to-face, by phone, and by e-mail with customers over a long period of time. The quality of information they collect is very high, but often the knowledge that is created by those conversations rarely moves beyond the sales rep's head. Yet such knowledge is vital for organizations that want to provide the right services and products, develop marketing campaigns that engage clients, and grow their customers' account shares over time. In this chapter, we explore the use of technology and customer information. Specifically, we focus on the sales force's responsibility to provide high-quality information to other areas of the firm and the benefits in doing so.

JEFFREY BAILEY

SENIOR SALES MANAGER, ORACLE CORPORATION

Jeffrey Bailey, a senior sales manager with Oracle Corporation, has salespeople calling on companies smaller than $500 million in annual sales. His sales team, divided into three regions, covers 16 southeastern states. Bailey recalls, "When I first began selling to what we call the mid-market, Oracle really had no idea how much we would sell. We hit our annual quota in just a few months, ending the year at twice the original quota. The next year, we finished 150 percent of the plan."

Although such success is always sweet, it created a lot of problems for the organization. "We don't make a product (the company sells software to businesses), but we do have to hire people to serve clients and to work with the sales team to help sell deals." With sales outstripping forecasts, staying fully staffed was a major problem.

As the market matured, salespeople remained optimistic. Quickly, forecasts became inaccurate, but now sales were being over-forecasted rather than under-forecasted. "We had to learn to be pessimistic in our forecasting. Sarbanes-Oxley and Wall Street value accuracy over optimism. My salespeople now forecast a sales number they are willing to commit to called 'commit numbers,' which represent a most-likely scenario; then they add to that deals that are possible but not probable, called 'upside.' Finally, they also put into the system all of the deals they are working on, whether they believe the deals will close sooner, later, or never. These are called 'pure pipeline.'" Bailey then gives this number to his manager, who adds all of the other senior managers' forecasts and presents it to the executive team.

"My job involves managing resources—making sure we have enough people working on the right deals so we can meet our quota," says Bailey. "We also watch how much forecasts change. Things can go badly quickly, such as when oil prices rise or markets become hot. When deals suddenly drop out at a high rate or go from a million dollars to $200,000, we need to find out why quickly so we can make the right decisions."

Because it takes a team of people to close a sale at Oracle, Bailey has several people he can go to for more information about any particular sale. "The issue is accuracy—we don't want any surprises." To his salespeople, it is a matter of professional pride. "If they know their business, their forecast should be accurate." ■

The engineers for HealthLink, a Jacksonville, Florida, company that manufactures medical and surgical supplies and equipment, are considering whether to add features to the company's autoclave. An *autoclave* is a device used to sterilize medical instruments used in surgery. Sales for HealthLink's autoclave have been good, but Marc Hanna, the company's vice president of sales, believes that several opportunities exist to grow the business if certain features are added to the device. If those features are added, how many additional autoclaves will be sold? he wonders.

John Buchy, the vice president of sales for Buchy Food Service in Greensville, Ohio, is in a similar situation as Hanna. Buchy is looking at a new line of products from Pepperidge Farm. His company supplies restaurants with many products, including baked goods from several bakeries. Which restaurants will be interested in Pepperidge Farm's new line of baked goods? How much of Buchy's current product sales would be lost or "cannibalized" by the new line versus the sales the company would gain? More importantly, how can Hanna and Buchy begin to answer questions such as these?

Sales executives often find themselves in the critical position of estimating the demand for their firms' products and services. Accuracy is important. If the executives overestimate the demand, the company could end up investing in manufacturing and distribution assets it won't need. For example, Caterpillar overestimated the demand for its construction equipment. The company bought a manufacturing facility in Texas and filled it full of manufacturing equipment only to let it sit dormant for two years after the firm's forecasts changed. The situation could have been much worse: Caterpillar could have hired many employees only to lay them off when the demand for the new equipment did not materialize.

Underestimating demand can be just as devastating. When a company introduces a new product, marketing and sales campaigns are launched to create demand. If the campaigns are successful but the firm's manufacturing unit isn't making enough of the product to meet that demand, then the door is open for competitors to launch "copycat" products and steal market share. For example, IBM's inability to meet demand for Thinkpad laptop computers left the market open for Dell to catch up and pass IBM.

Forecasting demand, though, is only part of understanding customers. Consider Hanna's dilemma regarding which features to add to the autoclave. A stronger understanding of customers can lead to better product design, too. In addition, if Hanna understands the value that doctors will place on those additional features, he will be able to set a price that reflects that value, maximizing the return on his company's investment.

The better Marc Hanna understands doctors, the better his company can develop solutions for their needs. (Comstock Complete)

Yet, even with all of the customer knowledge needed to determine which features to add and what price to charge, Hanna has to also be concerned with a number of other factors. For example, which competitor is most likely to react by cutting its prices? Which distributors are most likely to feature the new product, and which distributors will need additional training and support in order to effectively sell the new product? When the product is launched, who are the experts that can help solve any technical problems? As problems arise, what are the fixes? Answers to all of these questions are important individually. Taken together, they could prove to be the difference between success and failure.

Knowledge Generated by the Firm's Sales Force

One important goal for organizations is to develop a **customer knowledge competence**, or the ability to gather, analyze, and utilize customer knowledge *effectively* at the organizational level. Developing

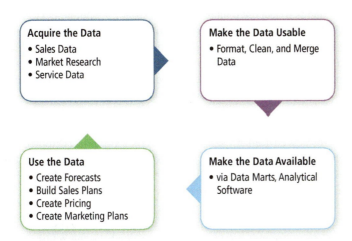

EXHIBIT 13.1

The Customer Data Integration Process

such a competence first requires integrating customer data from the many locations across the firm. Exhibit 13.1 illustrates the process of **customer data integration** (CDI), which is the technical process of gathering data and making it useful and available. CDI is not a software application per se but a set of rules for this process. There are, however, companies that do provide different types of data management software (like Teradata's data management tool).

The first step is to simply acquire the data. This sounds simple, but actually the process of gathering data can be quite difficult. For example, the sales data might reside in a contact management or CRM software program and not merge well with data from the firm's accounting or shipping systems. In addition, market research data can be overlaid with the information to provide sales managers with greater insight. For example, a company might only know how much of a product customers purchased. However, the firm's marketing research department can then research the total purchases made in the market for that product category, adding up all of the competitors' products which can then be used to calculate the market share of the company captured.

After acquiring the data, it has to be integrated and put into a usable format. For example, how does a company keep track of a client? By name? Seems simple enough, but firms sometimes go by initials and sometimes by the entire name. Or, divisions might be listed under a company's divisional name, not the corporate name. Furthermore, a company's shipping location might be different than the location to which its invoices should be mailed. Other considerations also have to be determined, like what is an account. Is an account a person who makes a decision, a location who receives a shipment, or the company that buys? Making decisions such as these is an important element in making data useful but that is only part of the step; cleaning the data and making it accurate is also important.

The next step is to make the data available to decision makers. Sales executives trying to create a sales strategy would benefit from better market segmentation models, for example. Those models, though, require additional marketing research data. So, for example, if the executives only have access to their firm's contact management data, they cannot take advantage of the segmentation models. One approach is to take data from various sources and compile it into a **data mart**, which is a specialized database designed for a specific purpose. In this instance, the purpose is to support the decision making of the firm's sales executives. Consequently, the data mart would include the data these people need the most.

Data has to be made available to decision makers or it provides no value. Data warehouses centralize data; data marts make the data available in a useful format to sales managers and their personnel. (Comstock Complete)

The final step is to use the data to develop a strategy. This process could include sales forecasting, determining pricing strategies, looking for new product opportunities, and so forth. As you can probably tell, to have a customer-knowledge competence, you need more than data: You need people trained to analyze the data properly and processes in place that encourage employees to act upon the data. In other words, a competence cannot be purchased like software can; it has to be developed, just like sales skills have to be developed.

Salespeople generate a great deal of data. From the name of the receptionist to the strategic plans of key customers, salespeople become privy to customer knowledge of all types. The challenge is to organize that data and make it available and useful to other parts of the organization, including a firm's marketing, manufacturing, finance, and other functions. Let's explore how those other areas use sales-generated knowledge.

MANUFACTURING Manufacturing departments rely heavily on the information generated by their firms' sales forces. In some businesses, such as the retail furniture business, salespeople sell products that are then accumulated into group orders and subsequently manufactured. In other industries, a firm's manufacturing department makes products and stockpiles them until they are sold. In both cases, though, salespeople's forecasts are important inputs into how much the firms should make.

PRODUCT DEVELOPMENT Who knows more about what consumers want than salespeople? Based upon what their customers are asking for, salespeople provide the product developers in their firms with recommendations about new products, different feature combinations, and even stripped-down versions of existing products. A firm's salespeople are often the first in the company to run across competitors' new products, and they can convey that information to product developers, too.

Marvin Wagner, a global engineer for the equipment manufacturer Deere & Company, spends a great deal of time in the field with farmers testing the products he and his team design. But Wagner's team also spends time with the salespeople who sell Deere's equipment to farmers to get a feel for what their priorities really are: Farmers might say they "want" every feature they can get, but the salespeople at the dealerships can provide insight about the features they will actually pay for.

FINANCE AND ACCOUNTING A company's credit policies affect its salespeople. Loose credit policies mean more sales and more bad debts; tight credit policies mean fewer sales but fewer bad debts. Salespeople can provide information to finance and accounting so that the company's credit policies are competitive. In many business-to-business markets, determining competitors' true prices can't be done by surveying the shelves of retail stores. In those situations, salespeople are the best source of this information. In addition, salespeople can report on market conditions that cause customers to buy instead of lease products or vice versa. Reports like these can be useful in terms of the firm's pricing or capital needs—for example, whether it needs to finance new facilities if people are spending freely or cut back on its expansion plans if people are limiting their spending.

MARKETING The marketing department creates sales and marketing campaigns that should boost the firm's sales. Any increase in sales due to a campaign is called **lift**. Salespeople contribute important information both before and after the campaign. Before the campaign, the information they provide can help design a good campaign. At Alcatel, a French telecommunications company, Marketing Manager Andrea Wharton talks to Alcatel's salespeople to hear the "language" they use to sell products. She then incorporates that language into the design of her trade-show campaigns.

During a campaign, salespeople provide marketing with information about how well the campaign is working. That's what Sales Manager Tricia Jennings does, along with her salespeople at Merck Pharmaceuticals. During a campaign, the reports from Jennings' salespeople (and the rest of Merck's sales representatives) are compiled to assess how the campaign's going. Keep in mind that Merck's salespeople do not actually close sales on the spot; they have to wait for doctors to prescribe Merck drugs to patients before they know if they were truly successful. For that reason, tracking actual sales to a specific campaign can be very difficult. That's why Merck's sales and marketing planners rely heavily on the company's salespeople to tell them what doctors are saying about the drugs being promoted—even before they are prescribed.

Marketing departments need customer information from salespeople so that they can design better marketing support programs. (Redux Pictures)

SALES MANAGEMENT Of course, sales management also uses information from salespeople. Information such as how hard or easy it is to sell a product can lead to decisions about the training that relates to the product, which products should be emphasized, whether sales managers should push for a price cut or product enhancement, how many salespeople to hire, and a host of other decisions. This type of information should reside in the customer records that salespeople keep and the reports they make to their managers. Sales managers are important users of this information, yet they must help other users sift through it and use it as well. For example, when salespeople complain that the firm's prices are too high, sales managers can help employees in the firm's finance department understand if the complaints are prevalent and legitimate or not.

HUMAN RESOURCES A firm's human resource department is directly affected by the information sales reps impart to the firm. For example, if they report that sales are grim, this will have implications for the firm's hiring plans. Perhaps more salespeople will have to be hired to improve the level of sales or perhaps the firm's workforce will have to be downsized. For example, Mark Prude is a human resources director for Granite Construction. As Granite Construction grows, Prude pays close attention to the firm's sales forecasts so that he has enough new employees coming on board at the right time, with enough of the right training so they can be productive quickly.

In the next section, we examine sales forecasts—how they are created and how they are used. Forecasting is just one specialized use of customer knowledge, albeit an important one, as you should have already concluded.

Sales Forecasting

Forecasting how much a company will sell can be a daunting task. As you can see in Exhibit 13.2, the process can seem complex. A forecast is not only an estimate of what consumers' demand will be for certain products, but how much of them the firm can produce and sell at certain prices, and how its competitors and customers will respond to those prices. Thus, a sales forecast is actually a function of a number of estimates.

One of the first estimates that companies try to make is that of **market potential**, or the total, industry-wide sales expected for a product category for a period of time. Market potential is often estimated by research companies who then sell their data to the various companies in the market. For example, if you want to know the market potential for CRM software, the Gartner Group (www.gartner.com) is one company that can provide estimates for you.

Note that market potential is what can reasonably be sold by all companies in a market, not how many companies or individuals comprise the market you hope to sell to. In the first half of the 1900s, Carl Crowe was the leading Western expert on China. During the Great Depression, Crowe argued that America could pull itself out of the Depression by simply selling one product to each person in China. Of course, a lot of assumptions had to hold true for his plan to work, one of which is that each person in China wanted something the United States had to offer and could pay for it. This fallacy to which many executives fall prey is known as "Chinese Marketing." In other words, how much a firm can sell in a market is not solely a function of the number of customers in a market. Nor is a firm's penetration of it guaranteed. Thus, the executive has to know more than the market potential in order to make a reasonably good forecast. Among other things, she has to understand the firm's sales potential. The firm's **sales potential** is the maximum market share the company can reasonably expect to achieve. It is typically represented as a percentage of a market's total sales.

From this estimate, an executive can then create a **sales forecast** of either the revenue or units his or her firm expects to sell and then allocates the revenue or units to individual salespeople in the form of sales quotas. Exhibit 13.2 illustrates the relationship between market potential, sales potential, and quota.

Note that sales for the company in the exhibit grew at relatively the same rate as the market in which it competed. In other words, the company's share of the market was stable. The one year in which the company increased its market share was 2008. Perhaps the company engaged in marketing and sales activities that were very unique and successful in 2008. Or perhaps it introduced a new product or one of its competitors went out of business in 2008.

Note, too, that except for the year 2010, the firm's New York sales office grew at the same rate as the company did. In that year, the office experienced higher sales—perhaps as a result of having a really good sales manager or any of a number of other reasons. Because it did so well, the New York sales office was given a quota for 2011 that rose at the same rate as the company's forecast and the market forecast. The company could have just as likely given the New York office a higher growth rate for its sales quota for many reasons. This might have been done, for example, if the firm's customer base in the New York area was growing at a faster rate than the rest of the country. Now let's go back and look at how managers estimate the size of each of the "pieces" in the sales forecast "puzzle." We will begin first with market potential.

EXHIBIT 13.2

An Example of a Firm's Market Potential, Sales Potential, Sales Forecast, and Sample Sales Quota

The lines represent actual sales for the years 2007 through 2010. The top line is the total market sales, the middle is the company's sales, and the bottom is the New York City office's sales. Note that the company increased market share in 2008, whereas the New York City office grew at a slightly faster rate than either the market or the company for 2010.

Estimating Market Potential

Factors external to a firm can influence the demand for products. Economic factors, such as the Iraq War and Hurricanes Katrina and Rita, which destroyed several oil refineries, combined to boost oil prices. The increased manufacturing occurring in China in recent years has also created additional demand for oil as have the increasing number of people in China driving automobiles.

Other forces, such as technology, can affect the market potential for products, too—especially if the technology increases the availability of substitute products. For example, the improved process of fracturing has made it easier and cheaper to extract natural gas from rock. Because oil can sometimes be substituted by natural gas, the potential market for it climbed: Entire cities converted their bus and truck fleets to natural gas, and many manufacturing facilities converted their heating systems from oil to natural gas.

The boom for natural gas also led to increased drilling in Texas during 2006 and 2007, which, in turn, resulted in a shortage of natural-gas drilling rigs. If your company manufactured drilling bits for the gas rigs during the boom, the demand for your product shot up very quickly. This example illustrates the nature of **derived demand**, which means that the demand for drill bits was actually created by (or derived from) the demand for a product further down the supply chain. In other words, when people wanted more natural gas, demand was created for drilling rigs, which increased the demand for drill bits. Derived demand can cause wide swings in the demand for a company's product.

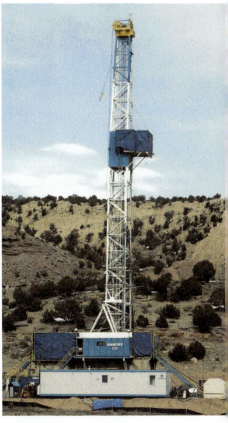

For example, suppose you work for Advanced Micro Devices, an Austin, Texas–based company that makes computer-chip manufacturing machines. The demand for your machines is a function of the demand for chips, which is a function of the demand for computers, including computers in your car, your refrigerator, your television, and so forth. Suppose your only account is Texas Instruments (TI), which owns 50 computer-chip manufacturing machines. Each year, TI routinely replaces 20 percent of those machines with your machines. Now suppose TI's 20 percent annual demand for machines increases by 5 percent in a particular year (to 25 percent total). If this is the case, the company will need 53 machines. But the machines you must supply to TI will go from 10 machines (the normal replacement rate when TI's demand is steady) to 13 machines (the number of machines TI normally needs to replace, plus the number it needs to meet the additional demand). The increase isn't 5 percent for you, but 30 percent! (See Exhibit 13.3 for the math.) How will you meet this greater demand? This is an example of the volatility caused by derived demand, a factor that must be considered when forecasting market potential.

The demand for natural gas is derived from the demand for many products because natural gas is used to operate so many different types of equipment. The demand for drilling rigs like this one, however, is derived from the demand for natural gas. (AP Wide World Photos)

Demand is also influenced by **elasticity**, or the degree to which a product's price affects its sales. **Inelastic demand** occurs when there are few or no substitutes for the product and people have to have it, no matter the price. In other words, the demand for it does not change if its price changes. Few products are truly inelastic. Even when gasoline prices rise, for example, most of us find ways to reduce our driving or get better gas mileage. If, however, there are many substitutes for a product, such as reliable public transportation, then consumers can simply shift their preferences when prices change. Other factors affect a market's potential as well, including the following:

■ Laws and Regulations: Laws and regulations can affect the demand for products by making them, increasing the costs associated with them, and imposing tariffs and trade restrictions on them. For example, in 2007, Congress considered banning incandescent lightbulbs, with the ban reducing the number that could be produced each year until the bulbs were no longer manufactured at all. If that law was passed, then demand for compact fluorescent bulbs, which are more energy efficient, will skyrocket, and the demand for incandescent lightbulbs will fall dramatically.

EXHIBIT 13.3

An Example of the Volatility of Derived Demand

At the beginning of Year 1, 50 machines are required based on forecasted sales. At the end of the year, 10 are worn out but 7 are purchased because only 47 are needed. During Year 2, 7 machines wear out, but 52 are needed, so 10 are purchased.

Year	Demand for Chips	Machines Needed to Handle Demand	Worn-out Machines	Machines Available	New Purchases
1	100%	50			
2	95%	47	10	40	7
3	105%	53	7	40	12
4	100%	50	13	40	10

ETHICS IN SALES MANAGEMENT

Forecasts are not just for a company's internal use. Executives of public companies provide forecasts to Wall Street analysts who then use those forecasts to recommend buying or selling stocks to consumers and institutional investors. The more positive the forecast, the better the stock price, assuming, of course, that the analysts believe the company executives.

In addition to analysts, suppliers often use their customers' forecasts to build their own forecasts. For example, Bose makes car stereos for General Motors (GM) and relies on GM forecasts to make plans for the future. Bose has other customers and other markets so if GM's forecast is wrong, not too much damage is done to Bose. But StraightSource, a consulting company in Dallas, has one customer that accounts for over 50 percent of the company's business. If that one customer's forecast is off by a large degree, the damage to StraightSource could be significant.

So why would a company lie about a forecast? Because of the potential effect on stock price. If an executive can influence stock price upward with a rosy forecast and that executive has significant compensation tied to stock price, the temptation is there to exaggerate the company's future prospects. The benefit, of course, is only short term if the company can't deliver the sales it forecasted.

Some of the bigger scandals in business began with booking false sales in order to maintain or increase the stock price. Mattel, for example, once booked tentative orders as confirmed sales in order to meet an overly optimistic forecast. The resulting scandal cost the CEO her job. Enron's spiral downward began with forecasts of continued growth—growth that could only occur due to questionable business practices.

One of our students described a similar process at his company as the reason why he left. "Part of the unofficial code of conduct was to put in fake orders or release blanket orders three to six months in advance and then cancel those releases after the month ended. This practice ensured that salespeople and their managers got their monthly sales bonuses."

As we have explained, a forecast is, at best, nothing more than an educated guess. As such, forecasts are rarely right. The temptation to lie about something that is going to be wrong anyway may loom large for some executives. They see it as a little lie. The problem is that little lies lead to big lies. A false forecast leads to an Enron.

■ Social Factors: Social factors are general fashions and trends within a society. For example, consumers might choose to avoid products from a country that has a reputation for failing to monitor the quality of its products. Chinese toys laden with lead are an example. Even fashionable colors are influencing corporate laptop purchases.

■ Demographic Trends: Demographic trends can have a major impact on a product's market potential. The fact that people in developing countries are having fewer children has affected the market potential for baby-related products such as diapers, for example. In the United States, generational differences between Millennials (those born after 1980), Boomers, and Generation X'ers (just about all other working adults) can make selling from one group to the other more difficult. Millennials, for example, might find it preferable to communicate with their customers via handheld devices, whereas Boomers or X'ers might prefer telephone calls or personal visits.

Exhibit 13.4 provides a list of various factors external to the firm and how they can affect a market's potential. Clearly, a firm's ability to forecast market demand is a function of its ability to identify and estimate the influence of these market factors.

A company's sales potential is a function of the market potential and the company's ability to capture a share of that market. External factors, though, can favor one competitor over another. The social trend toward reducing trans fats bodes well for brands that have always been made without them. Similarly, a change in trade laws can make a competitor with overseas plants more cost effective or vice versa.

Sales executives also have to consider the impact of their own actions—internal factors, that is. The introduction of new products, the ability to find new uses for old products, and improving one's production processes to lower prices are among the internal activities that can influence a company's sales potential.

Forecasting Methods

As Exhibit 13.5 illustrates, forecasts, by and large, are generated using information gathered internally by the firm or externally generated by others, such as research firms and the government. In addition, the forecasts are either qualitative (subjective) or quantitative (objective). To some extent, the forecasts are all combinations of people's best guesses as to what will happen in the future. Although some of these methods can be used to forecast both market potential and sales potential, others are specific to just one or another. We'll point out which is which as we describe each one.

TIME SERIES TECHNIQUES Time series techniques are a group of statistical methods used to examine sales patterns over time. One simple method is a **trend analysis**, which involves determining the rate at which a company's sales have grown in the past and then using that rate to estimate future sales. This is also called a **naïve forecast**. For example, look back at Exhibit 13.2. You can see how the sales for this particular firm have trended upward; if you simply extended the line into 2011, you'd have a forecast based on the historical data. Trend analysis is just one of several time series techniques that use historical data to estimate sales. Trend analysis, though, can also be used for determining market potential.

Trend analysis can be useful when changes in a market are few and not very dramatic. But when the market does change frequently, you might overestimate sales after a period of rapid growth or underestimate sales following a brief downturn using trend analysis. For example, as the trend away from trans fats began to take hold, some products became very popular, and the sales of them increased quite quickly. Snackwell's cookies are a good example. For a time, the product experienced sharply rising demand. Eventually, however, the high rate of increase could not be sustained, and the sales growth of the product eventually flattened out (although the sales are still much higher than they were before the anti-trans-fat trend).

EXHIBIT 13.4

Factors That Affect Market Potential

Factor	Influence on Potential
Economy	Economic influences can make market potential greater or smaller; for example, China's increased manufacturing base increased the demand for petroleum products, particularly as the buying power of the Chinese population increased demand for plastic products as well as gas-powered vehicles
Technology	New technology can create substitute products, lowering demand for the original product; change price structure, making products more affordable and increasing demand; create new uses, expanding market demand; for example, new drilling technology had made drilling for natural gas affordable in certain parts of Texas
Legal and Regulatory	Laws can make products illegal; increase the costs associated with the product (such as by increasing a firm's waste restrictions during manufacturing); and make them more or less competitive as a result of tariffs and subsidies imposed, for example
Social Factors	Changes in trends and fashions affect demand. For example, new research on the health hazards of trans fats significantly reduced the demand for some cooking oils and products made with trans fats
Demographic Trends	Demographic trends can shift demand. For example, retiring baby boomers increased the demand for vacation homes, which then influenced demand for lumber and other building supplies

Trend analysis can still be useful in cases such as this if you make some adjustments to them. One adjustment is to use a **moving average**, where the rate of change for the past few periods is averaged. **Exponential smoothing** is a type of moving average that puts more emphasis on the most recent period. Exhibit 13.6 provides an example as well as an example of exponential smoothing.

Determining how much weight to place on the most recent period is a decision the executive has to make based upon such factors as changes in the market that might make more recent data more useful.

Correlational analysis is a form of trend analysis, but instead of using past sales (or past sales only), sales forecasts are based on the trends of other variables. Preferably, the sales executive wants to find a variable that leads, or happens before, the sales of the company's product, called a **leading indicator**. The Conference Board, for example, publishes a single number that represents a composite of commonly used leading indicators.

One common indicator is housing starts (the number of houses that are beginning to be built); for example, it is a leading indicator of home appliance sales. When new homes are built, they are filled with new appliances, so housing starts precede the purchase of appliances. Whirlpool uses housing starts to predict market potential. The company further considers housing starts by the size of the house being constructed to break the market down into segments such as luxury homes, mid-level homes, and starter and vacation homes (for which consumers typically buy low-end appliances. In fact, so many businesses depend on housing starts that the variable is an important predicting variable for the entire economy.

Most organizations do not depend on a single variable such as housing starts for forecasting; rather, they build more sophisticated statistical models incorporating the trends for many variables. For example, a regression analysis allows the sales executive to include a number of variables. The influence of each variable is estimated and weighted to determine its impact, and the effects are summed to provide a single estimate of sales. Cessna Aircraft Company, for example, builds complex statistical models to estimate the sales for the small planes it makes. The models include variables such as the number of miles flown in a market,

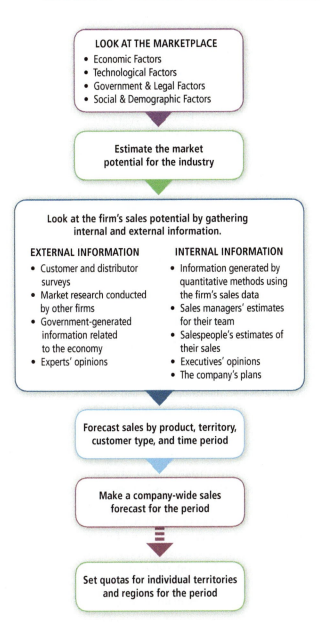

EXHIBIT 13.5

The Forecasting Process

Factors in the marketplace can influence market and sales potentials differently. The same factor can have the opposite effect on one company's sales versus another company's, too. The dashed line to quota refers to the fact that quotas are influenced by other objectives, in addition to sales forecasts.

interest rates, fuel prices, corporate profit indicators, and other variables that influence airplane sales. These types of variables can be useful in predicting market potential, from which Cessna could then derive sales potential based on its own availability of new aircraft, market penetration, marketing plans, and other variables.

CONSUMER SPENDING CORRELATES Other variables used for correlational forecasts are variables that predict how much consumers will spend overall. The Consumer Confidence Index, a measure of how confident consumers are that the economy is favorable, is one that has been shown to lead consumer spending. Similarly, the Conference Board Index of Leading Indicators mentioned earlier is another.

Claritas, a marketing research company (www.claritas.com), publishes a Consumer Buying Power model that companies can use to determine how much consumers can buy

EXHIBIT 13.6

Examples of Trend Forecasts

A simple trend analysis might look like the solid line, resulting in no forecasted change in the growth of the firm's sales rate from 2010 to 2011. By contrast, an exponential smoothing analysis could weight the last two years more heavily, as illustrated by the dashed line. This would result in a sales forecast for 2011 that's nearly double that of 2010. A moving average (assuming that the company was in business for many years before 2006) would result in a forecast in between the two. In times of rapid change, the different types of trend forecasts can yield very different results.

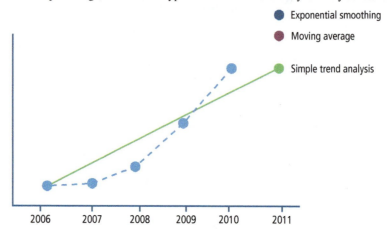

• Exponential smoothing

• Moving average

• Simple trend analysis

2006   2007   2008   2009   2010   2011

in a particular market. Sales executives can then use this as a powerful correlate to purchases for their own product. For example, the model has been used to forecast household repair service purchases, mobile telephone sales, and vitamin sales.

BUSINESS SPENDING CORRELATES Similar to the variables listed above, companies that sell to other businesses can find variables that are useful in correlational analysis. For example, the U.S. Census of Manufacturers is a survey of companies conducted by the federal government every five years. The survey combines businesses into the North American Industry Classification System (**NAICS**, rhymes with "snakes"), according to the products or services offered. The company could forecast demand using NAICS data, such as the number of workers in an industry or a region; if there were 12 machines sold for every 1,000 workers and a region had 100,000 workers in a particular industry, the 1,200 machines should be sold. Thus, NAICS could be used for both market potential and sales potential if the company knew how many it sold per 1,000 workers compared to the overall industry.

RESPONSE MODELS **Response models** are another form of sophisticated statistical models. Rather than considering the influence of market factors over time, these models examine how customers respond to sales and marketing strategies. Hewlett Packard (HP), for example, uses regression analysis and other statistical models to predict the demand for its products based on variables such as the firm's pricing promotions and advertising budgets. Via CDI, response models can be built using data HP maintains on its customers, including what they bought, at what price, in what month, and so forth. The model helps HP see how many customers are price-sensitive, for example, and only buy when products are on sale or which customers always buy at the beginning and end of a budget year; this method is used primarily for sales potential. The model is very useful in terms of planning HP's sales and marketing actions because it allows the company to determine the potential return it can earn by pursuing alternative plans.

MARKET TESTS One response model that's especially useful when firms are trying to figure out how well a new product or service is likely to be accepted is to conduct a market test. A **market test** is an experiment in which a company launches an offering in a limited market in order to learn how the market will react to the product. The demand can then be extrapolated to the full market. However, market tests can also alert your competitors to the new offering, and they, in turn, can undertake actions, such as drastic price cuts, to skew the results of your market test.

Acxiom is a company that makes software to help firms with their CDI and marketing efforts. Acxiom's Web site (www.acxiom.com) claims the following cities are the best test markets for U.S. companies: Birmingham, Alabama; Greensboro–Winston-Salem, North Carolina; Newburgh, New York; Savannah, Georgia; and Memphis, Tennessee. These cities were chosen because their populations are very similar to the entire United States. Companies can launch their products in these cities and get a good idea of whether their marketing plans will work nationwide.

JUDGMENT TECHNIQUES Although all forecasts rely on someone's judgment, some techniques involve judgments by someone of the actual forecast and these are considered **judgment techniques**. Judgment techniques include executive or expert opinions, surveys of customers' (or channel members') intentions or estimates, and estimates by salespeople.

EXECUTIVE OPINION Executive opinion is exactly what the name implies. It is simply the best-guess estimates of a company's executives. Each executive submits an estimate of the market potential and the company's sales potential, which are then averaged to form the overall sales forecast. This method of estimating sales is easy to implement and costs little; in addition, there is something of a psychic commitment to achieving the forecast because no one wants their predictions to be proven wrong. The disadvantages of the method include the possibility that the opinions are biased because executives frequently aren't out selling in the field. In other words, the more an executive is removed from the market, the less accurate his estimate is likely to be. Factors within the organization can also lead to judgmental bias. For example, if executives know their quotas will be set based on their forecasts, they will attempt to lower them to make their quotas more achievable. Or, for example, an executive might overestimate the sales of a certain product because higher-level executives have pinned their hopes on it, and he doesn't want to upset them.

EXPERT OPINION Expert opinion is similar to executive opinion except that the expert is usually someone outside of the company. Carl Crowe, whom we mentioned earlier in the chapter, is one example. As far back as the early twentieth century, he was asked to estimate sales in China. Today, Paul Greenberg, Jill Dyché, and Bruce Culbert are experts in the CRM software market. Often they are asked to estimate the sales for the software of different companies.

In many instances, opinions such as these, along with those of executives, are used in conjunction with more quantitative methods. For example, once a company has conducted a trend analysis, an expert might be consulted. The expert might suggest that some methods for estimating might be better than others under certain circumstances or that certain market factors should be given more or less weight. As a sole method of forecasting, however, expert opinions are often not very useful. Just consider, for example, how difficult it is for so-called sports experts to predict the team that will become the national champion.

CUSTOMER AND CHANNEL SURVEYS In some markets, including the CRM software market, research companies ask customers how much they plan to spend in the coming year on certain products. Similarly, surveys are done for products sold through distributors.

Companies then buy the surveys from the research companies to use as a starting point for their forecasting. Surveys are better at estimating market potential rather than sales potential, however. Plus, they can be costly.

Many companies do their own surveys of their customers. American Airlines regularly surveys passengers about their plans to fly to estimate its future sales. It also routinely surveys corporate travel departments about their travel budgets. Similarly, Microsoft conducts annual surveys to gauge future business-software spending. The company also conducts focus groups, which involve bringing groups of customers together to discuss their business trends as well as what they do and do not like about particular products.

Channel surveys are similar in that manufacturers ask their distributors or retailers how much they expect to sell. Surveys such as this can account for varying local market conditions as well as changes in the competitive environment. Delta Faucet is one company that surveys its distributors in order to estimate its sales. The company combines this estimate with an estimate from plumbers (end users) to increase the accuracy of its forecasts.

SALES FORCE COMPOSITE A similar method is to ask the members of your sales force what they think they can sell. Salespeople, though, are often not aware of the company's plans to introduce new products, new promotions, or new pricing strategies. Thus, they cannot account for these plans in their estimates. They also tend to be optimistic about what they think they can sell—unless they realize that their estimates are being used to set their sales quotas. If this is the case, they will likely lower their estimates.

A more common approach is to use sales force composites for shorter-range forecasts. Every week, for example, Richard Langlotz, branch general manager for Konica-Minolta in Fort Worth, Texas, asks his salespeople how many copiers and digital printers they expect to sell in the coming week and month. He then uses this information to plan his inventory. The company, though, uses other methods to forecast sales for the next quarter or the next year.

The Limitations of Forecasting

Forecasting is an attempt to predict the future. So, no matter how much time and effort a company puts into forecasting, the forecast is likely to be wrong. The question is how wrong will it be? And how will that affect the actions the company takes and its competitive position? Although the company might not get its forecast exactly right, the firm wants to get it close enough that company goals can be achieved. Some factors, though, can greatly influence forecasting accuracy.

 SELF-ASSESSMENT LIBRARY

No forecast is 100 percent accurate. The future can be very ambiguous, yet tolerating ambiguity is not something that we all do equally well. How well do you tolerate ambiguity? Go to http://www.prenhall.com/sal/ and log in using the access code that came with your book. Then click on:

> Assessments
> I. What About Me?
> A. Personality Insights
>   5. How Well Do I Handle Ambiguity?

Your overall score will give you an indication of your ability to tolerate, and even enjoy, ambiguous situations. You might even get an indication of whether you will look forward to or dread working with forecasts!

DATA QUALITY One major factor affecting forecasting accuracy is the quality of data used to forecast. For example, suppose a company asked its distributors: "How many decorator faucets do you hope to sell in the next quarter?" and an optimistic answer would be given. But if asked: "How many decorator faucets will you sell next quarter?" a distributor might respond less optimistically. The difference might be slight—until added up over a thousand distributors.

Similarly, recall our discussion about CDI earlier and the need to define and cleanse data. If the customer data set does not combine all locations of customers together well, then the estimates for market segments based on the company's size could be way off. CDI is important for data quality, which in turn affects sales managers' forecasting.

RAPID CHANGE The best forecasts are usually those that include as much information as possible. That means using as many methods as possible and creating multiple forecasts for multiple conditions. When an executive places too much emphasis on one forecast or one method, then the likelihood of an accurate forecast is diminished, particularly if conditions are changing rapidly.

GLOBAL SALES MANAGEMENT

Forecasting or Fortune Telling?

The challenges of forecasting demand in developing countries can be tremendous. For example, gold can be mined in South America, but unstable governments have made such mining impossible. Companies that own the mines are afraid to invest and start production if a government takeover of the mine seems likely. Not a problem to most people, unless you are responsible for selling supplies to gold mines.

Even when governments are stable, the lack of availability of data from trustworthy sources can make forecasts difficult. Governments and universities in developing countries do not routinely collect data such as the Consumer Price Index, durable good sales, housing starts, and the like.

In fast-growing countries, such as India and China, the problem isn't always availability of data but reliability. Changes are so rapid that the conditions under which demand was forecasted become quickly obsolete.

For example, in 2004, the number of call center jobs in India serving U.S. customers tripled, following a year in which the number had doubled. In 2002, the growth in call center positions in India was about 15 percent. Companies such as Alcatel suddenly found sales for India impossible to forecast. The only data they could get were estimates in the United States of outsourcing plans.

In fact, economic growth in India has been so rapid since the turn of the century that predicting consumer spending, for example, has been almost impossible. In high-growth areas like Hyderabad, Madras, Pune, and Bangalore, the quandary for consumer companies is determining how much capacity to add. Procter & Gamble, for example, is building a new detergent plant in Bangalore to serve this market, but the question is how big to build it. The answer to that question is a function of other questions: How long will the market grow at the current rate? What factors are driving that growth and how will these factors change? The quality of data available to answer those questions is suspect, making any investment decisions a gamble.

LENGTH OF THE HORIZON In the last 20 years, weather predictors have gotten pretty good at forecasting the weather for the next day or two, and they are getting better. However, it's much harder for them to predict what the weather will do for the next 90 days or the next year. It's the same reason why experts can't seem to agree whether or not global warming is occurring. The longer the forecasting horizon is, the less accurate the forecast is likely to be. The same is true for sales executives—accurately estimating next week's sales might be relatively easy; accurately estimating sales five years from now will likely be much more difficult.

TIME AND COST Forecasting takes time. The longer it takes to get a forecast, the less time you have to act on that information before the forecasting period has passed and conditions change again. Forecasting also costs money. So, for example, if a window of opportunity is open for just a short period of time, doing a costly, time-consuming market survey might not be money well spent. Rather, it might make more sense to do a rough forecast and call a few customers and salespeople to quickly get their opinions about the forecast. Then after the company has taken action, the firm's managers will have more information they can use to adjust the rough forecast.

Guidelines for Forecasting

As we've discussed, forecasting is not an exact science. There are, however, guidelines that can improve the quality of forecasts. The first is to commit to accuracy. Some firms even reward managers for being accurate.

Making a commitment to accurate forecasting requires using the forecast properly. In fact, many sales executives believe that there is no direct connection between a sales forecast and its associated quota. Paul Nelson of IBM, for example, says, "My quota is a function of what my company *needs* me to sell, which can be independent of sales forecasts." What Nelson is saying is that even if IBM were to predict its sales were going to be low, it might need to assign higher quotas to its sales force for certain reasons—say, to meet the revenue targets being demanded by IBM's shareholders based on what the firm's competition is earning. Or maybe IBM simply wants to motivate its sales force to outdo itself. Nelson recognizes that it's his job to find a way to achieve his quota regardless of what the firm thinks it can sell. So, he accepts this disconnect. As he says, "Achieving goals, setting sales records, capturing market share—those are things I want to accomplish, and I would not want to work somewhere where they didn't want to grow." Yet others argue that this practice is a misuse of forecasts. If a sales manager creates a forecast and then finds that upper management increased that forecast for the purpose of setting a quota, the next forecast will be neither as optimistic nor as accurate. Why? Because the sales manager is likely to **sandbag**, or fail to forecast sales as high as they should be for fear that the forecast will be used against him. One manager, who asked to remain anonymous, said he provides an estimate to upper management every quarter. The company then adds 10 to 15 percent to his estimate and makes that his quota. This gives him an incentive to forecast lower sales levels. Is it any wonder that his forecast is always 15 percent low?

USE MULTIPLE METHODS As you might guess from reading about the limitations of forecasting, one way to achieve more accurate forecasts is to use multiple methods—that is, to create forecasts from surveys and trends and then utilize expert opinions to estimate a range of sales. Another is to simply keep at it. The first time a manager creates a forecast, it is likely to be wrong; in fact, forecasts are usually inaccurate to some degree. That said, the second time you do anything, you usually do it better than the first time. Forecasting is no different. After a certain amount of experience they will be better able to fine-tune a forecast and minimize its inaccuracy.

PICK THE RIGHT METHOD(S) FOR YOUR BUSINESS Although it may seem obvious, picking the right method for the business is important. A business with a long sales cycle and derived demand, for example, may find naïve forecasts less useful because volatility in demand could swing the trend in either direction. A firm that sells consumer packaged goods (like Campbell's Soup or Suave shampoo) might find trend analysis very useful for short-term forecasts but might need to use other methods for longer-term forecasts.

USE AS MUCH INFORMATION AS YOU CAN Use as much information as possible to generate forecasts. For example, by forecasting the sales for the company's different regions and managers separately, managers can sometimes account for local conditions that can change the firm's overall national forecast. When American Airlines conducts a customer survey, it forecasts each segment of its customers independently by their frequent flier status. Thus, the Platinum Executive (American's most frequent flier) is forecasted separately from the Gold Advantage member (American's lowest level of frequent flier). In addition, the company also does trend analyses for each segment separately; note how CDI is involved because the statuses of the company's frequent fliers have to be integrated with the forecasting model. All of these individual forecasts are blended together, just as HP blends together the forecasts for its individual products. HP has many product lines, such as computers, printers, and servers. By forecasting each separately, as well as overall sales, more information is used and should result in a more accurate final forecast.

PLAN FOR MULTIPLE SCENARIOS What happens if the environmental factors the firm's facing vary greatly? Does the company's sales forecast also change greatly? For example, if you are working at Whirlpool, perhaps you consider forecasts under multiple housing-start scenarios. If housing-start estimates increase by 15 percent more than is expected or by 15 percent less than is expected, what happens to your company's appliance sales? This is what you want to find out. Then, as the year develops, you can adjust your sales estimates based on what actually happens to housing starts.

TRACK YOUR PROGRESS AND ADJUST THE FORECAST As time goes on, forecasts should be adjusted to reflect reality. For example, DeAnn Bartlett, sales manager for HP, had a forecast of about 10 percent growth for 2007. After the first quarter, though, it was clear that her team would do much better because market acceptance of a new pricing strategy was greater than expected. The forecast was then adjusted to reflect the new reality. In addition, she and her sales team record win/loss data in their CRM system (they use Siebel). When a big sale is won, the salesperson records why; conversely, when a sale is lost, the reason is also recorded. With this information, she and her sales executives can adjust strategies in order to adapt to changing market and environmental conditions. Those changes in strategies influence forecasts.

Summary

Understanding what to offer to what market requires understanding customers, but making that understanding actionable requires more. Creating a customer knowledge competence, or the ability to gather, analyze, and utilize customer knowledge effectively at the organizational level is an important goal to which salespeople can contribute. A first step in developing that competence is customer data integration or CDI.

Many areas of the firm rely on customer data gathered by salespeople and through other means. Manufacturing, product development, marketing, sales management, human resources, and others rely on such data in order to create forecasts for their area of operations. Sales forecasting, then, is an important role for the sales force.

One of the first estimates a company tries to make is an estimate of the market's potential or overall demand. Overall demand is influenced by a number of factors, such as elasticity, but also by the economy, laws and regulations, social factors, demographic factors, and others. Sales potential, or what the company could sell if all went well, is another estimate. In addition, executives also forecast what is likely to be sold.

The methods used to generate these estimates are time series techniques, including trend analysis, moving averages, and the use of exponential smoothing. Correlational analysis is a form of trend analysis but instead of basing the trend on past sales, the trends of other variables are correlated. Variables that trend ahead of sales are called leading indicators. Some of the correlates are variables such as the Consumer Confidence Index.

Response modeling is a growing area of forecasting. These are statistical models that consider the influence of marketing factors, such as how much the company is planning to spend on advertising and sales efforts. A specific form of response modeling is to conduct a market test, or a trial of all of the marketing factors, and see how customers respond.

Judgment techniques are also used, including expert or executive opinions and surveys of customers or channel members. Even sales force composites are considered judgments of the sales team.

Forecasts are limited by the quality of data used to create the forecasts, the degree to how rapid things change, length of the planning horizon, and how much the company wants to spend on creating a forecast. No matter how much money and time is made available, forecasting is not an exact science. To improve forecast accuracy, companies should make a commitment to forecasting accurately. In addition, forecasting accuracy can be improved by using multiple methods, picking the right methods for the business, using as much information as possible, planning for multiple scenarios, and adjusting the forecast as things change.

Key Terms

correlational analysis 302	market potential 297
customer data integration 295	market test 305
customer knowledge competence 294	moving average 302
data mart 295	NAICS 304
derived demand 299	naïve forecast 301
elasticity 299	response models 304
exponential smoothing 302	sales forecast 298
inelastic demand 299	sales potential 298
judgment techniques 305	sandbag 308
leading indicator 302	trend analysis 301
lift 296	

Questions and Problems

1. Suppose your company sells plastic injection machines that are used to inject plastic into molds so companies can make plastic bottles. From what consumer products is the demand for your machines derived? How volatile would you expect your demand to be, and why?

2. What are the best and worst methods for forecasting the sales of the following products and services? Why?

    a. A new dorm for your campus (how big should it be?)
    b. Street sweepers
    c. Tax consulting services for small businesses
    d. A new laboratory device used in physics experiments

3. Your boss says, "All we have to do is sell one of these new products to each of our current customers and it will be successful!" What assumptions have to hold true for her wish to come true? Is she guilty of Chinese Marketing? What problems could arise if she treats that statement as a forecast?

4. What is the difference between a forecast and a quota? Is the difference large? Is it important to recognize the difference?

5. A sales executive has a difficult time forecasting sales without knowing how many salespeople the firm will employ (an aspect we looked at in Chapter 7). Yet, the size of the sales force can be enlarged or shrunk depending on the forecast. Similarly, advertising drives sales: If the firm increases its advertising, its sales should increase; if it decreases advertising, its sales should fall. Yet advertising budgets are often based on a percentage of sales. How can these circular problems be tackled?

6. For the following products and services, what factor(s) would you use to estimate market potential?

    a. Campbell's Soup
    b. Fossil watches
    c. Pontiac sports cars
    d. Bose Wave radios
    e. Viagra
    f. Calvin Klein men's suits

7. You just took over as the chief sales officer of Lombardi Trophy Co., a company you've worked at for almost 20 years. You know the firm's sales forecasts are inaccurate because the company has annually added 20 percent to the quotas assigned to the firm's salespeople, which collectively they have always met or exceeded. But you need an accurate forecast for various purposes, including budgeting. How would you change the situation so you get accurate forecasts?

Sales Manager's Workshop

Making Forecasts

You just got the following e-mail from the regional vice president, your boss. In it, she says:

"Revenue has fallen off about 10 percent this month, which is a poor start to the quarter. With two months left in the quarter, I'd like a forecast from each of you. We will then meet by conference call this Friday at 8 a.m. EST to discuss. Call the WebEx conference number and have your PowerPoints loaded so we can review each forecast."

You know from experience that you have to use several different methods to generate your forecast. Using the Aplicor data set, create three different forecasts using different methods, then combine them into one brief PowerPoint presentation.

Caselet 13.1: Englander Container

Englander Container manufactures cardboard boxes used to ship products, not package them. The company makes boxes for U-Haul, Mayflower Moving and Storage, and other shipping companies such as Fed-Ex and UPS. Englander also sells direct to companies that ship the products they make, such as Procter & Gamble. The company's sales figures for the past 20 quarters are provided in the following table:

Quarter	Shipping Company Sales (000,000)	Industrial User Sales (000,000)	Government Sales (000)
1	43.0	48.0	-0-
2	44.5	50.5	-0-
3	46.0	52.0	-0-
4	48.0	53.0	-0-
5	49.0	55.0	-0-
6	50.5	57.5	-0-
7	49.5	59.0	-0-
8	50.5	61.0	-0-
9	50.0	60.0	-0-
10	51.0	60.5	-0-
11	52.0	57.0	-0-
12	53.0	59.0	-0-
13	54.5	61.0	-0-
14	56.0	61.5	-0-
15	55.5	62.0	-0-
16	56.5	60.5	-0-
17	58.0	63.0	-0-
18	59.0	64.0	-0-
19	60.5	64.5	-0-
20	60.0	66.0	0.50

Late this year, the company was able to secure a General Services Administration contract to provide containers to the U.S. government. The contract enabled the company to bid on special packaging needs for the U.S. military. Currently, the company has almost $100 million in four bids on military contracts that will be decided upon in the first quarter of next year. It expects to bid on another $300 million in additional government contracts that will be decided upon later during the year.

Questions

1. Use two different trend analysis methods and determine how much the company will sell next year. How confident are you that this is an accurate forecast? What additional information or methods would you like to incorporate in your forecast?
2. Assume that the company is manufacturing at 90 percent of its capacity in order to meet its current sales levels. If it wins every U.S. government contract it's bid on, what impact will that have?

Caselet 13.2: Freud Testing Services

Freud Testing Services (FTS) conducts psychological profile testing for companies who are looking to hire new salespeople. FTS claims that these tests are accurate 9 out of 10 times, meaning that if FTS says to hire someone, the chances are 90 percent that the person will become a successful sales rep. The company sells its product through independent distributors, which retail the tests for $95 per person being tested.

There are currently 22 distributors selling FTS testing products, along with other testing products and sales training and consulting services. The sales of FTS products generated by each distributor range from $10,000 (generated by a small distributor in Arizona) to almost $100,000 (generated by a distributor in New York City). The average annual FTS sales per distributor are about $22,000. The total sales for FTS are about $4 million per year.

George Shannon, the owner of FTS, would like to grow the business by another million dollars in two years. The question is, how? George has considered adapting the tests so they could be used to screen retail salespeople. Right now, they are used only to screen business-to-business salespeople. The tests could also be translated into different languages and sold in other countries. Or perhaps George could simply look for additional distributors. He has called you and asked how he should go about determining the potential of each of these markets.

Questions

1. In a perfect world, how would you answer George?
2. Assuming George had no cash to spend, how would your answer change?

14

ASSESSING THE PERFORMANCE OF THE SALES FORCE AND THE PEOPLE WHO COMPRISE IT

LEARNING OBJECTIVES

After completing this chapter, you should be able to:

- Explain why it is important to evaluate the overall performance of the firm's sales force.

- List the advantages and disadvantages of sales, cost, and profit analyses.

- Understand the importance of profitability and the application of ROI and ROAM.

- Explain both input and output objective sales performance measures.

- Explain the differences between performance and effectiveness.

- Compare formal and informal evaluations.

- Describe how the sales manager can implement an effective performance review.

TOM SHERRILL

DIVISION SALES MANAGER, B.W. WILSON PAPER COMPANY

B.W. Wilson, which has office locations in North Carolina and Virginia, is a medium-sized distributor that sells a wide range of paper products to commercial printers, publishers, and government print facilities. According to Tom Sherrill, a division sales manager for B.W. Wilson, the print industry is one of the world's largest manufacturing sectors. Moreover, a printing firm will generally form a close relationship with its largest paper supplier, such as a company like B.W. Wilson. The sales rep for the distributor is the key liaison in this relationship and must be an effective performer for B.W. Wilson to succeed.

Traditionally, paper distributors compensate sales reps on a straight commission basis. However, sales trainees initially receive a guaranteed salary for 9 to 18 months, and experienced hires are paid a salary for 3 to 9 months. B.W. Wilson gradually transitions its new salespeople from a salary to a straight-commission pay system by using a temporarily inflated commission rate as the rep moves to the standard commission plan. The standard commission plan pays representatives a percentage of the gross profits derived from their monthly sales, and representatives are evaluated on those profits. There is no salary draw, and only a minimal expense allowance is paid. The goal of the pay plan is to motivate sales personnel to increase their sales volumes, avoid discounting the company's products, and sell more profitable items.

Although the compensation plan gives B.W. Wilson's sales representatives a powerful incentive to increase their sales and gross profits, the firm considers other performance measures to be important to its goals, too. Consequently, at the beginning of each fiscal year Sherrill meets with his sales reps to set mutually agreed upon goals for that year that include their gross sales, gross profit percentages, and gross profit dollars. These goals are then compiled to set a total sales forecast for his division. At the same meetings, Sherrill and B.W. Wilson's other sales executives set goals for the company's key accounts, identify specific product lines for those accounts, and peg their sales and profit potential. Sherrill and the sales reps also adopt strategies to grow accounts. The strategies can include increasing the number of sales calls and service levels an account receives, developing specific inventory or discount programs for customers, distributing paper manufacturers' advertising to customers, and jointly calling on accounts in tandem with a manufacturer's sales, rep, and other methods that strengthen account relationships.

315

In addition to expanding the sales at the firm's existing accounts, sales reps are also expected to open new accounts. However, rapid advances in printing technology have forced printers to merge or shut down. As a result, the number of clients at many paper distributors is dwindling. Nonetheless, it is critical that sales reps open new accounts to replace the lost ones, and this measure is included in the annual reviews B.W. Wilson's reps receive.

Sherrill requires his new, salaried reps to submit call reports to him. However, he does not always require his commissioned reps to submit reports. However, all reps are advised to keep their call reports, which are evaluated when there are problems. The call reports not only reveal the number of sales calls reps are making but also indicate how effectively they are using their valuable time. They have a natural tendency to spend quite a bit of time with the accounts they have successfully sold to because doing so affords them a certain comfort level. Of course, the sales representatives employed by other firms are competing for the time and attention of the largest printers in the market. Consequently, it is a greater challenge for B.W. Wilson's sales reps to schedule and plan the calls made to these companies. Sherrill therefore monitors the number of calls made to each account to ensure his sales representatives are appropriately allocating time to their accounts.

At the end of each quarter, Sherrill meets with his sales reps to evaluate their actual results compared to their sales goals. Because the profit margins of paper distributors have gotten squeezed in recent years, most distributors the size of B.W. Wilson no longer employ sales managers. Instead, they expect their division managers to manage their sales representatives. Today, most commissioned sales reps are treated more like "independent contractors"—they either produce results or do not survive in the business. This can hinder a sales team's efforts as well as the communication between a firm's sales, operations, and management groups. However, most of the full-commission reps nonetheless value the constructive feedback, joint goal setting, and performance evaluations and incentives B.W. Wilson provides them. Sherrill also believes that his sales reps need to receive performance appraisal feedback from the firm's internal customer service, shipping, and accounting groups to determine whether the reps have good communication skills and exhibit proper attitudes and behaviors.

Evaluation Helps the Sales Manager Know What Is Working and Why

Sales managers are responsible for planning, implementing, and controlling a firm's sales activities. To control the sales effort so that the firm's goals are accomplished, sales managers must continually monitor and evaluate the performance levels of both the individuals who comprise the sales force and the sales force as a whole. For example, if the sales force's goal is to increase the number of a firm's new customers by 5 percent over the course of 12 months, sales managers must develop a specific plan for how that level of sales growth will occur. Perhaps the sales team will be instructed to call upon customers in a different market segment or new geographical location. Based upon this strategy, the sales manager might also decide to offer training sessions to ensure that individual members of the sales force are prepared to successfully serve new customers or perhaps hire additional salespeople for the expanded territory.

Without conducting evaluations, it will be nearly impossible for sales managers to know what about the new strategy is or is not working, why, and, most importantly, what should be done about it. Comprehensive evaluations also help managers determine whether the deviations uncovered are attributable to incorrectly set goals or a weak performance on the part of the firm's salespeople. Said differently, did the sales team fail to meet expectations or did the firm's managers set inappropriate goals?[1] The firm's planning efforts, of course, set forth what the sales force should do; and evaluation efforts document what actually took place. This means that the value of planning is limited unless sales managers perform an evaluation to document what actually worked. In turn, information derived from the evaluations will affect the firm's sales planning in future periods.

Evaluating the individual sales representatives responsible for executing the firm's strategy can be quite complex because they call on different buyers in different territories and often have distinct goals and different experience levels. The process requires the sales manager to select and compare, at regular intervals, both objective and subjective information about all sales personnel. To accomplish this, sales managers utilize a combination of input activities, output results, profitability measures, and qualitative assessments. Once completed, sales managers utilize the results of evaluations to manage the sales force by assigning raises, promoting salespeople to managerial positions, recommending training to remedy identified shortcomings related to a sales representative's performance, and, when necessary, replacing low performing sales force members. In summary, conducting a comprehensive evaluation of the firm's sales team and individual salespeople allows sales managers to do the following:

- Identify deviations from the firm's goals and the goals set for the firm's individual salespeople that have resulted
- Determine the causes of the deviations
- Adjust the firm's sales territories as needed
- Determine the training and development the sales force and individual representatives need
- Motivate salespeople and establish work expectations for them
- Link the compensation and rewards given salespeople to their actual performance
- Identify individuals for promotion, further training, or termination
- Help salespeople set and work toward their career goals
- Provide information for the planning activities conducted by the firm's human resources group
- Establish recruiting criteria for salespeople

The purpose of this chapter is to explain exactly how sales managers evaluate both their individual salespeople and their entire sales force. First, we discuss various evaluation techniques. Second, we explain how to evaluate the sales force's activities and outcomes, with the goal of identifying deviations from standard or expected performance. Last, we consider how to assess the performance of the firm's individual salespeople. ■

Evaluating the Performance of the Sales Force as a Whole

In general, sales managers evaluate the overall performance of their sales teams by comparing and analyzing different types of information. Because firms set myriad goals, multiple measures are used to assess whether or not the company's objectives were achieved. Different evaluation criteria are necessary because there is no single measure of a sales force's effectiveness. The three most common forms of sales team analysis focus on sales, costs, and profitability. We discuss each type of analysis next.

Evaluating the sales force allows a sales manager to know what is and what is not working. (Comstock Complete)

Sales Analysis

Conducting a **sales analysis** involves gathering, sorting, assessing, and making decisions based upon a company's sales revenue. Sales revenue information can be gathered via the firm's point-of-sale records, sales reports, field reports, and customer feedback.[2] Sales information is routinely gathered for accounting purposes; however, it probably is not organized in a form that's useful for conducting a sales analysis. As Exhibit 14.1 shows, the sales manager must organize the sales data so that market and salesperson deviations are apparent. For

EXHIBIT 14.1

Analyzing a Firm's Overall Sales

Analysis by U.S. Region

REGION	QUOTA	ACTUAL	DIFFERENCE	PERFORMANCE
Northeast	$4,861,500	$4,948,920	$87,420	102%
Mid-Atlantic	$5,093,000	$5,209,880	$116,880	102%
Southeast	$4,167,000	$4,147,400	−$19,600	99.5%
Southwest	$3,588,250	$3,425,100	−$163,150	95%
Mid-Central	$3,472,500	$3,698,875	$226,375	107%
Western	$5,112,750	$5,120,250	$7,500	100%
Total	$26,295,000	$26,550,425	$255,425	101%

Analysis by Salesperson (Southwest Region)

SALESPERSON	QUOTA	ACTUAL	DIFFERENCE	PERFORMANCE
Albert (West Texas)	$804,000	$810,000	+ $6,000	101%
John (Colorado)	$868,000	$851,000	− $17,000	98%
Claudia (Arizona)	$609,000	$631,000	+ $22,000	104%
George (Oklahoma)	$592,000	$416,000	− $176,000	70%
Julie (New Mexico)	$345,000	$345,000	0	100%
Martin (Nevada)	$370,000	$372,000	+ $2,000	103%
Total	$3,588,000	$3,425,000	− $163,000	95%

Analysis by Product (George—Oklahoma)

PRODUCT	QUOTA	ACTUAL	DIFFERENCE	PERFORMANCE
A	$143,000	$149,000	$6,000	104%
B	$244,000	$160,000	− $8,400	66%
C	$118,000	$42,000	− $760	36%
D	$87,000	$65,000	− $220	75%
Total	$592,000	$416,000	− $176	70%

example, the sales manager will want to understand if the firm's revenues are increasing or decreasing, how well different products are selling in each sales territory, and how different sales regions and salespeople are performing compared to previous periods.[3]

Returning to Exhibit 14.1, it is apparent that the southwest region is significantly below quota, or its expected sales. The sales manager should investigate what caused the deviation of −5 percent ($163,500) in that region. Breaking down the analysis by the six sales representatives assigned to the southwest region shows that George, in Oklahoma, sold only 70 percent of his quota for the period. By segmenting the next four product lines sold by George, it is clear that he fared poorly, selling three out of four product lines during the evaluation period. Thus, based upon the sales analysis, the sales manager has identified that George's substandard performance in the Oklahoma territory is the source of the significant deviation from the southwest region's expected performance. Now the sales manager must investigate further to determine whether George's performance is due to a lack of ability, personal problems, increased competition, or another reason that requires managerial intervention.

To perform consistent evaluations, managers must ensure that two points related to sales are standardized. First, firms must accurately define when a product is "sold." As we explained in Chapter 11, some firms consider a product "sold" when the item is ordered, others when the product ships, and still others wait until the customer remits payment for the product. Second, in periods of inflation, firms can actually sell fewer items but still increase their sales revenues if the product's price continues to increase. By analyzing both the firm's sales revenues *and* the number of units sold, a sales manager will more clearly understand when such a phenomenon has occurred. A sales and unit analysis alone seldom provides sales managers with all of the information they need. Moreover, the information extracted can at times be misleading. For example, a firm might experience an increase in its revenues, but if its costs skyrocketed as a result, this wouldn't be apparent to managers looking at a sales analysis alone. That's why additional measures, like costs, are needed.

Cost Analysis

Sales managers conduct a **cost analysis** to figure out what the relationship was between the sales that the firm generated during a given period and the costs that were incurred to make those sales. (Recall again that we first discussed sales budgets, or quotas, in Chapter 11.) Sales costs can be stated as a percentage of sales to assess whether or not the sales-cost relationship remained constant or whether relative to the sales generated, the firm's selling costs increased or decreased. For example, if a company's sales were $1.5 million and its selling expenses were $150,000, then sales costs would be 10 percent of the revenues generated. Costs, as a percentage of sales, will also vary by industry and location. For example, the expenses related to selling oil drilling equipment might be higher than the expenses related to selling pharmaceutical products. Managers also understand that a firm's selling expenses in New York City are going to be higher than they are in Omaha, Nebraska.

As Exhibit 14.2 shows, a cost analysis allows the sales manager to calculate the variance between actual and budgeted selling expenses for all of the firm's sales regions. Any

EXHIBIT 14.2

Analyzing a Sales Force's Costs

	Compensation Costs			Training Costs		
	Budgeted Costs	Actual Costs	Variance	Budgeted Costs	Actual Costs	Variance
Northeast	$429,000	$472,500	$43,500	$237,600	$263,250	$25,650
Mid-Atlantic	$396,000	$411,750	$15,750	$113,300	$110,812	($2,488)
Southeast	$407,000	$393,750	($13,250)	$224,400	$237,375	$12,975
Mid-Central	$374,000	$354,375	($19,625)	$116,600	$93,375	($23,225)
Southwest	$308,550	$301,218	($7,332)	$96,195	$79,368	($16,827)
West	$425,000	$421,000	($4,000)	$215,000	$221,000	$6,000
Total	$2,339,550	$2,354,593	$15,043	$1,003,095	$1,005,180	$2,085

	Compensation Costs		Training Costs	
	Budgeted % Sales	Actual % Sales	Budgeted % Sales	Actual % Sales
Northeast	9.5%	8.7%	5.3%	4.8%
Mid-Atlantic	7.9%	7.6%	2.1%	2.2%
Southeast	9.5%	9.8%	5.7%	5.4%
Mid-Central	10.3%	10.9%	2.7%	3.4%
Southwest	8.1%	8.3%	2.1%	2.6%
West	9.5%	9.1%	2.8%	2.7%
Total	9.0%	8.9%	3.7%	3.7%

territory in which actual costs exceed budgeted costs should receive further scrutiny. For example, in Exhibit 14.2 the northeast territory's actual compensation costs exceeded the compensation budget by $25,000 and the sales manager should identify the cause of this deviation.

Cost data allow a firm to set pricing levels and budgets. For example, a sales manager can plan costs for training, travel, entertainment, salaries, and samples when constructing a sales budget. When a sales manager conducts a cost analysis, this permits her to determine which market segments are most expensive to serve, identify inefficient company functions that appear to cost more than they are worth, assess whether the cost of a sales call is increasing, and decide when it is time to modify the commission rates paid salespeople for selling different products.

Another method of analyzing costs is to consider the differences related to each product line. A product expense analysis allows the sales manager to gauge the level of profits each product line is contributing and how much it costs to sell the product. As Exhibit 14.3 shows, WRT, Inc., sells three different computer product lines: computers, monitors, and routers. Looking at the expense analysis, you can see that costs associated with each product line differ. The cost of goods sold and the commission for selling computers amounts to 62 percent of the sales price, 70 percent of the sales price for monitors, and 25 percent of the sales price for routers. Based upon the available expense information, WRT's sales managers will want to consider whether: (1) competition is driving the selling price lower for computers and monitors and/or (2) the sales force is lowering prices to close sales quickly.

The cost analysis conducted for sales evaluation purposes differs significantly, however, from the cost accounting related to the firm's production processes—the ones you learned about in your introductory accounting courses. Instead of the costs associated with the production of products, many of which are standardized, the sales manager must examine the expenses incurred by salespeople performing nonstandardized interactions with buyers. For example, some sales representatives spend dramatically more than others. This can take the form of higher meals, more expensive hotels, and expensive relationship-building activities like golf to close a sale. A few salespersons may appear to spend a lot of money to "buy the business." To minimize this behavior, some firms, including Massachusetts Financial Services of Boston, analyze their salespeople's expenses in great detail using very sophisticated methods.

Because of the availability of data, sales and cost analyses are the two most frequently used methods of evaluating a sales force's effectiveness. Even with improvements in computer systems and software, analyzing sales costs still consumes time, money, and sales managers' time. Sales managers face a major problem when conducting a cost analysis because there is often no clear method of allocating direct and indirect selling costs. For example, should sales executives' salaries, which are an indirect cost of the selling process,

EXHIBIT 14.3

WRT, Inc: An Example of an Expense Analysis by Product Line

Product Line	2006 Sales (000)	Cost of Goods & Commission	Cost of Goods % of Sales	Contribution Margin	Contribution Margin (%)
Computers	$36,400	$22,800	62%	13,600	38%
Monitors	10,400	7,200	70	3,200	30
Routers	5,200	1,300	25	3,900	75
Totals	$52,000	$31,300	60%	20,700	40%

be apportioned to each territory when computing "sales" expenses or not? The senior executives in firms make these decisions to ensure there is consistency in all territories when they are conducting a cost analysis. That said, once a decision is made, the cost allocations must be performed consistently in future periods so the firm's managers can readily compare the data from one period to other periods.

Profit Analysis

Sales managers conduct a **profitability analysis** by combining sales and cost data in the equation: sales – costs = profit. By computing a profitability analysis, the sales manager can identify unprofitable product lines, territories, and customer segments; evaluate territory and product performance by profitability; and calculate year-end sales team bonuses. Advances in information technology have made it easier for sales managers to conduct profitability analysis, which is now a key measure tracked by companies that follow a relationship marketing approach to business. As we discussed in Chapter 5, CRM-focused firms use profitability analyses to compute the lifetime value of their customers as a basis for selecting which ones to serve. Sales managers should strive to conduct as thorough an analysis of their sales forces as possible with the understanding that profitability analyses can be time consuming and costly.

An illustration of profitability analysis, shown in Exhibit 14.4, compares the profits of the same three product lines—computers, monitors, and routers—we looked at in the previous cost analysis section. Although all three product lines made a positive contribution toward the firm's fixed costs of between 30 to 40 percent, two of the products returned a profit to the company whereas the other, the sale of monitors, actually lost money! Once the sales manager understands that a product line, customer, or territory is losing money, she can devise a strategy to return the category to profitability. For example, based upon the information in Exhibit 14.4, the sales manager might try to reduce the selling expenses associated with the line or work with her firm's marketing department to increase the line's advertising so as to improve its sales. As you can see, only by computing the profitability of a company's product lines can the sales manager identify problems such as these.

Ratio Measures for Evaluating the Sales Force

Sales managers employ ratios or relationships between activities and performance or assets and performance to standardize the way salespersons or sales managers are evaluated. Ratios are computed at standard intervals—quarterly or annually—to identify sales force performance trends. Listed below are two ratios appropriate for such evaluations.

	Totals	Computers	Monitors	Routers
Sales	$52,000	36,400	10,400	5,200
Cost of Goods Sold	$27,900	20,000	6,900	1,000
Gross Margin	$24,100	16,400	3,500	4,200
Other Expenses:				
Selling	$6,800	4,000	2,000	800
Administrative	$8,000	5,600	1,600	800
Total Other Expenses	$14,800	9,600	3,600	1,600
Net Profit (Loss)	$9,300	6,800	(100)	2,600

EXHIBIT 14.4

WRT, Inc: An Example of a Profitability Analysis by Product Line ($000)

RETURN ON INVESTMENT (ROI) Analyzing the **return on investment (ROI)** is a useful tool managers can use to evaluate the performance of their sales force. Sales managers compute ROI using the following formula:

$$\text{ROI} = \frac{\text{Net Profit}}{\text{Sales}} \times \frac{\text{Sales}}{\text{Investment}}$$

By dividing the firm's net profit by its sales, it is possible to compute the profitability rate for sales. The second step is to divide sales revenue by investment—that is, the total assets listed on a firm's year-end balance sheet. Managers are concerned with the total assets they manage regardless of their origin—whether the assets consisted of investments made by the firm's shareholders, loans the firm has secured, or earnings the firm has retained. Although the formula appears to show that the sales component in each part of the ROI equation can cancel one another out, there are two separate elements at work: (1) the rate of sales profit and (2) the rate of capital turnover. The rate of sales profit is a result of the firm's sales volume, product mix, product prices, and promotional activity. Capital turnover is a financial relationship that considers the sales volume and assets being managed by the firm. Therefore each component is calculated separately and then multiplied, as shown below:

$$\text{ROI} = \frac{\text{Net Profit }\$200,000}{\text{Sales }\$1,500,000} \times \frac{\text{Sales }\$1,500,000}{\text{Investment }\$1,000,000}$$

$$13.33 \qquad \times \qquad 1.5 \qquad = 19.995\%$$

As you can see from the calculation, the profit for the sales team is 13.33 percent, and the capital turnover is 150 percent, resulting in an ROI of nearly 20 percent. If the firm's capital invested in its assets (inventory and so forth) costs 8 percent, an ROI of 20 percent is excellent. This means that the firm is paying 8 percent to finance its assets, but is earning a 20 percent return on them, for a difference of 12 percent. In other words, the firm is using its assets efficiently to earn money. By contrast, if the firm's ROI were just 9 percent, its managers would perceive that performance was poor. Why? Because the firm is paying 8 percent to finance its assets, but the return on its investment (9 percent) is barely above that cost. A low ROI suggests that the sales force needs to increase its total sales and/or increase the average price of each sale.

Firms are computing ROI in increasing numbers, but in conjunction with business initiatives like customer loyalty and retention. For example, Hewlett Packard has increased its awareness of how its gains in customer loyalty affect the company's ROI across various buyer segments. At HP, ROI is more about tying sales activities to business results.[4]

RETURN ON ASSETS MANAGED (ROAM) Another form of return on investments is **Return on Assets Managed (ROAM)**. The ratio is a popular way for upper-level managers to evaluate the performance of sales managers at all levels. Basically, ROAM tells executives how well a firm's sales managers in different territories are managing the firm's assets individually (versus the firm as a whole) so as to generate profits.[5] ROAM utilizes different components than ROI, as shown in the following equation:

$$\text{ROAM} = \frac{\text{Contribution Margin}}{\text{District Sales Revenue}} \times \frac{\text{District Sales Revenue}}{\text{Average Accounts Receivable} + \text{Inventory}}$$

The **contribution margin** is computed by taking the selling price of a product and subtracting the cost of goods sold (what the product cost the firm) and the sales commission. For example, if Product A has an average selling price of $25, the cost of goods sold is $10, the selling expenses related to the product are $5, and the contribution margin of that product is $10. It is the dollar amount that is "contributed" toward the firm's fixed costs until the company's breakeven point is reached. Once this point is reached, all contribution margins become profits. The district's sales revenue is the total sales revenue generated by the district. The assets managed are the firm's total accounts receivable, or money owed the firm, and goods held in inventory.

As an evaluative measure, ROAM should only be employed when the sales manager controls the assets (accounts receivable or goods held in inventory). For example, ROAM is a more useful performance measure at small and medium-sized wholesale firms in which sales managers approve sales made on credit and manage inventory levels. However, if the firm's inventory levels and credit approval functions are centrally managed, ROAM is not an appropriate metric for evaluating a sales manager. Individual salespersons should never be evaluated using ROAM unless they control the firm's assets or accounts receivable.

Relating the Performance of the Sales Force to the Firm's Salespeople

The sales manager next collects and organizes data in order to interpret the findings. Typically, sales managers want to understand why an organization's sales goals were or were not met—especially sales revenue goals. Too often, and without a systematic evaluation process, a simplistic answer is that the sales force did not work hard enough to reach the goal. However, in addition to insufficient salesperson effort or an unrealistic sales forecast, there are other possible reasons for a sales revenue shortfall:

- The firm's pricing isn't competitive.
- The firm's products suffer from quality or delivery problems.
- The firm's salespeople lack sales ability or need additional training.

Next, the sales manager lists the possible explanations for the missed performance objectives and analyzes each reason. If a lack of sales ability is suspected, then the manager should examine the activities (number of calls made, for example) of the firm's salespeople to ensure that at least they invested a sufficient amount of sales effort. If that's not the problem, then the manager should examine the previous performance of the sales force. If just as many sales calls were made to customers in the past, how many of the calls resulted in actual sales? If, for example, the firm's product quality and/or delivery are problematic, then more than one salesperson will exhibit low sales for that one product.

When an initial analysis fails to pinpoint the source of the deviation, the sales manager should consider the possibility that the company is experiencing increased competition and identify the territories in which this is occurring. Sales managers must also question whether sales quotas for the firm's representatives were correctly set to begin with and if future quotas should be determined using a different approach. The sales manager might also want to interview former customers, salespeople, and sales managers to learn why the business was lost. Once apparent explanations are uncovered, the sales manager should verify this information against salespeople's reports or other sales data to confirm that their hypothesis is valid.

Evaluating Individual Sales Representatives

Most firms appraise their individual salespeople on a regular schedule. One survey of U.S. salespeople found that about 40 percent of reps receive evaluations at least quarterly, 13 percent receive them quarterly to biannually, and 25 percent are assessed biannually to annually. However, nearly one in five (19 percent) of the salespeople surveyed said they did not receive a formal performance evaluation.[6]

EXHIBIT 14.5

Most Popular Metrics Used to Construct Sales Goals

Rank	% Using	Input	Output
1	40%		Revenues generated
2	31%		Number of calls made and leads
3	29%		Profits generated
4	24%		Number of orders received
5	18%		Number of customers in the pipeline

Firms report the following evaluation practices:

- Most firms examine both quantitative and qualitative criteria when it comes to evaluating their salespeople. However, a greater emphasis is placed on output (quantitative) measures, like the sales revenues they generate.
- The input of salespeople is sought, to varying degrees, before their quotas or performance standards are set.
- The sales goals of different salespeople differ based upon their activities and territories.
- Companies utilize multiple information sources to perform evaluations.
- Most salespeople receive a written evaluation conducted in an office setting.[7]

You might be wondering, at this point, which evaluation measures firms use most often. Exhibit 14.5 displays the results of a survey that was conducted to answer that question. Not surprisingly, the most frequently used measurement was sales revenue generated. A new type of measurement called a *pipeline analysis* has broken into the list of the top five measurements in recent years. A **pipeline analysis** shows how well a salesperson is maintaining a stream of customers at different stages in the sales process. At the other end of the continuum are metrics related to customer service.

A sales manager's performance appraisals should cover a wide range of evaluative areas that mirror the salesperson's diverse range of duties and responsibilities. This can result in assessment of four separate appraisal areas: *input measures*, *outcomes*, *profitability*, and *personal development*. In combination, these four areas comprise a comprehensive performance appraisal process. That is, each set of criteria provides the sales manager with differing insights about how the salesperson is performing and how they can be more effectively directed. An example of a comprehensive evaluation form that addresses each of these four areas is shown in Table 14.1.

Information on these and many other metrics are becoming more readily available to sales managers through the use of CRM software systems—especially the number of customers in the sales pipeline.[8] The more information that is collected, the more likely the sales manager will have an accurate record of each salesperson's activities and sales effectiveness. However, there are limits about how much information is useful for sales managers and how much is too much. You can lose sight of the "forest" if you look at too many "trees." That's why many firms concentrate on the sales revenues their sales forces generated.

Handheld devices and other technology allow sales managers today to evaluate their personnel in near real time. (Shutterstock)

Leveraging Technology to Manage Sales Rep Performance

In decades past, sales representatives mailed, phoned, faxed, and e-mailed their call reports to their sales manager who, when they found time, would enter the information into databases or spreadsheets in order to assess how their representatives were doing. Sometimes, this process took days or even weeks. "We'd have the information, but it was always like looking in a rearview mirror," comments Ken Deakman, a sales manager with

Skipka–Deakman Associates, a company that sells mobile sales-data gathering devices. "As a sales manager, you'd never be looking at where you were headed, only where you had been."

Deakman's perspective is different now.[9] In today's competitive marketplace, the lifespan of a new product might be only 60 days. During that time the new product must gain market share or it won't be around long. Having immediate feedback from the sales force about how well the product is selling or what objections they are hearing from buyers can mean the difference between determining a winning approach or withdrawing a new product shortly after its launch. Deakman, a former sales manager himself, has been

TABLE 14.1

PERFORMANCE APPRAISAL FORM FOR A SALES REPRESENTATIVE		
NAME: Joe Smith	Manager: Sally Jones	
TERR: 1AB	Hire Date: 01/05/05	
Judgement		
Problem-Solving Skills		
Commuication w/Manager		
Expense Vouchers		
Dirstrict Other Reports		

PERFORMANCE SUMMARY   Overall Achievement Rating (value of 1 to 6)

AREAS REQUIRING IMMEDIATE ATTENTION

PROFESSIONAL DEVELOPMENT GOALS AND OBJECTIVES

PERFORMANCE VS. GOALS AND OBJECTIVES

SUPERVISOR SIGNATURE: DATE:

EMPLOYEE COMMENTS

EMPLOYEE SIGNATURE: DATE:

continued

TABLE 14.1 (*continued*)

PERFORMANCE APPRAISAL FORM FOR A SALES REPRESENTATIVE

| NAME: Joe Smith | | Manager: Sally Jones |
| TERR: 1AB | | Hire Date: 01/05/05 |

2009 SALES	2009 TE (Travel & Expense)	2009 PRODUCT SAMPLING
09 $ Inc	09 TE:	09 Sampling:
09 % Inc	09 TE Bdgt:	09 Samp Bdgt:
09 vs. Goal	09 % Bdgt:	09 % Bdgt:

2008 SALES
08 $ Inc
08 % Inc
08 vs. Goal

2008 SALES RATE	
Specialization	15
Region	31

Achievement Levels:

Outstanding = 1; Exceeds Requirements = 2; Meets Requirements = 3; Needs Improvement

PERFORMANCE AREAS	ACHIEVEMENT LEVELS	SUPPORTING COMMENTS
ORGANIZATION		
Macro Planning		
Micro Planning		
Setting Priorities		
Across-the-Board Coverage		
Mktg Materials/Sales Tools		
Self Sampling		
Follow-up Systems		
SALES INTERVIEW		
Rapport, Customer Relations		
Questioning Techniques		
Establishing Priorities		
Listening		
Sells from Product		
Trial Close		
Gets Commitment for Action		
Closing Skills		
Product Knowledge		
Use of Mktg Materials		
Technology Demos		
Sell-Through		
Servicing of Accounts		
Appropriate Amt of Field Time		
Length of Calls		
# Calls per Day		
Key Closing Strategies		
Coverage of Product Lines		
Custom Products Presented		
TEAMWORK		
Communication with Office		
Competitive Information Shared		
Impact on District Success		
Drives National Programs		
SAMPLING OF PRODUCTS		
Thoroughness of Coverage		
Accuracy of Coverage		
Timeliness		
Judgment		
TRACKING		
Accuracy		
Timeliness		
Pending Totals		
Closed Totals		
Used for Planning		
CUSTOMER RELATIONS		
Rapport, Customer Relations		
Promoting Company Programs		
Discounting Strategies		
Troubleshooting		
LAPTOP USE		
Frequency of Communication		
Use of CC:Mail		
Creative Applications		
GENERAL/ADMINISTRATIVE		
Attitude and Morale		
Initiative		
Consistency of Effort		

working to help give sales managers a technological advantage. Exhibit 14.6 shows a handheld computer that uses software to move data, in real time, from salespeople in the field back to their sales managers at headquarters. As Exhibit 14.6 shows, sales managers receive real-time information on their representatives' accounts, including their competitive position relative to those accounts, sales to them, activities they have pursued to obtain those sales, and their sales-visit notes. Using the unit allows a geographically dispersed or a small sales force to be more nimble and respond quickly to change. As a result, geography and time are no longer adversaries to efficient operations.

Deakman notes that some organizations periodically send their sales managers into the field to verify whether their sales representatives are working or not. Sadly, some of them aren't. Being able to access their sales representatives' call report information daily has lessened the need for field visits and has also made salespeople more accountable. Initially Deakman was concerned that sales representatives would be reluctant to use the mobile devices for fear they would be constantly monitored by their sales managers. Instead he encountered two types of reactions to the devices: (1) higher-performing salespeople using the handheld devices viewed them as an opportunity to improve their sales practices and (2) lower-performing sales representatives who viewed the devices as an invasion of their privacy. Studies have shown that salespeople are reluctant to adopt technology unless they can see the benefits to be gained from the new devices.[10]

Many people mistakenly believe that if a sales representative fails to achieve their goals, they are typically dismissed. Most sales experts and sales professionals agree, however,

EXHIBIT 14.6

Using Handhelds to Capture Performance

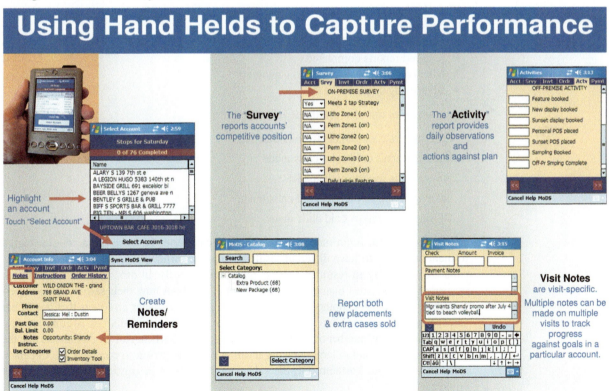

Source: Ken Deakman.

that the failure to meet a goal merely signals that a sales manager or sales trainer needs to help diagnose and remedy a salesperson's selling weakness(es). Simply by sharing the data with their employees, sales managers can help them discover for themselves what they're doing well and what they might improve upon to be more successful. One of the great things about sales is that it's very quantitative—even seemingly subjective criteria can often be quantified. So, for example, if you're doing a great job as a sales representative and your numbers show it, no one can take that away from you.

Input Measures

We first discussed input measures in Chapter 11 when we introduced setting goals for salespeople. Recall that input measures gauge the effort put forth by the salesperson to contact, work with, and sell to buyers. For example, when a salesperson at the pharmaceutical firm AstraZeneca completes five sales calls a day, the sales manager can infer that the salesperson is making sufficient effort to succeed. Conversely, when the sales manager observes that too few product demonstrations and phone calls are being made to potential customers, this implies the salesperson is not investing a necessary amount of effort to engage buyers. Input measures are considered important because they are directly controlled by sales representatives. By contrast, closing sales depends a great deal upon what buyers decide to do—an aspect that sales representatives are far less able to control. The following are among the input measures sales managers use to assess a salesperson's performance:

- number of days worked
- sales calls per day, week, or month
- sales calls per customer
- service calls
- dealer meetings
- customer training sessions conducted
- product demonstrations conducted
- required reports completed
- letters or phone calls made to customers
- advertising displays set up

Sales managers can also subdivide input measures by:

Current versus potential customers called

Planned versus cold sales calls made

Sales versus service calls made

Telephone versus on-site sales calls made

Closing calls versus cold calls made

Firms segment input measures into distinct categories because the activities related to them are likely to have different results or portend different things. For example, cold calls are less likely to result in success than planned calls. In other words, the different measures provide sales managers with distinct clues about how their salespeople are performing their jobs. As another example, suppose a sales manager discovers that one of her salespersons is not making a sufficient amount of in-person calls but is completing a higher-than-average number of phone calls to customers. This behavior might indicate that the rep's sales territory is too large, making it difficult for the person to complete the in-person sales calls assigned to them. Or, the salesperson may not be putting forth an adequate amount of effort.

Managers also examine how salespeople allocate their time, including the time they spend on their sales calls. For example, sales managers often contrast how their firms' top performers are spending their time versus less productive sales members. Deviations between high and low performing groups can help the sales manager coach less productive salespeople to spend their time more efficiently and improve the effectiveness of their sales calls. The recommendations might include specific sales approaches top performers utilize, including the type(s) of questions they ask buyers and the amount of time they spend on different types of calls.

Input measures also tell sales managers about the sales strategies their representatives are using. For example, relationship-oriented companies might expect a number of sales calls to be made to their customers and a rapport developed with them prior to a sale being made. By contrast, less relationship-oriented firms will expect their salespeople to make one or a few sales calls to customers before trying to close the deal. In this case, sales managers can look at the number of calls their representatives are making to see which of the two strategies are being pursued. Sales managers understand, too, that the quality of sales representatives' efforts can differ. This is evident when two salespeople make an equal number of customer calls and spend the same amount of time with their customers, but one of the representatives closes a significantly higher level of sales than the other. The perceptive manager will realize that training and coaching can help the marginal salesperson achieve higher quality and more effective sales calls.

Outcome Measures

Recall from Chapter 11 that **outcome measures** are the actual results of salespeople's efforts. Outcome measures provide an indication of the salesperson's ability to close a sale. The number of new customer accounts opened and the sales revenue to new customers are, for example, evidence of a representative's sales efforts. Cancelled orders are another output measure. If a sales representative has a large number of cancelled orders, it may indicate that the salesperson used high-pressure tactics or acted deceptively in garnering the sale. Lost accounts also call into question whether the salesperson was addressing the needs of the customer firm. The following is a list of output measures sales managers use to assess their representatives:

- Sales revenues generated
- Sales revenues generated per account
- Sales revenue generated as a percentage of a salesperson's territory potential
- Number of orders generated
- Number of new customers won
- Number of sales to new customers
- Cancelled orders
- Lost accounts

Keep in mind that output measures can be misleading when a sales cycle, or the time to move through the sales process, extends over several quarters of a year. Exhibit 14.7 shows various output performance measures and the percentage of U.S. firms that use them to evaluate their salespeople.[11] Sales managers closely monitor these measures to ensure that their sales representatives are getting results and achieving their goals. However, many sales managers believe that sales representatives' output measures are highest when they devote a sufficient amount of time and quality to their input measures. A growing number of salespeople today use their laptop computer and CRM system to ensure a quality sales call is made. In fact, one study concluded that working hard was equally as important as working smart.[12]

EXHIBIT 14.7

Output Measures U.S. Firms Use to Evaluate Their Sale Forces

Measure	% of Firms Using*	Measure	% of Firms Using*
Sales		Profit	
Sales Volume	79%	Net Profit	69%
Sales Volume/ Previous Year's Sales	76	Gross Margin Percentage	34
Sales to Quota	65	Return on Investment	33
Sales Growth	55	Orders	
Accounts		Number of Orders	47
Number New Accounts	69	Average Order Size	22
Number Lost Accounts	33	Order per Call Ratio	14

*Percentage of firms that use this measure to assess the performance of their sales force.

Remember the three salespersons Moe, Sydney, and Hannah who set sales goals in Chapter 11? Look at Exhibit 14.8 to see how well the three salespersons performed during a sales period. If sales volume sold (actual/goal) were the sole focus of Pickerel Lake Industries' (PLI) sales evaluations, Moe would be considered to be performing better than Sydney, followed by Hannah. Using only profitability (net profit/goals), Sydney ranks the highest, with Hannah and Moe switching positions. Both sales volume and profitability are output evaluations and reflect what has been sold. However, by adding input metrics, a more complete picture comes into focus. The number of demonstrations is considered an important input factor because it helps customers grasp how the features of PLI's products benefit them. Moreover, nearly all customers need to experience the benefits of the software before they will purchase it. Looking only at this metric, Hannah would be rated first, followed by Moe and Sydney. Lastly, the number of new accounts opened in this period reflects the activities and follow-through required to get a purchase order guided through some potentially long and complex purchase channels. Again, Hannah is first, followed by Moe and Sydney.

The last step in this analysis is determining which of the performance measures are more important than others. PLI has assigned weights reflecting the importance of each goal. Sales volumes have been assigned a weight of 3, and net profits a weight of 4. Both number of demonstrations and new accounts have been given a weight of 1. Multiplying the percent of each goal a representative achieved by the weight assigned to him yields the total weight for that factor. Adding those numbers and dividing by the number of weights (in this case there are nine) produces the final performance score for each person: At 100.6 percent of goal, Hannah's performance ranks first, followed by Sydney at 93.7 percent, and Moe at 88.1 percent of goal. As you can see, each of the sales representatives appears to have strengths and weaknesses. Only after a sales manager evaluates a number of factors will she have a more complete understanding of each salesperson's performance.

Profitability Measures

Firms are placing increased emphasis on *profitability* measures like:

- Net profit as a percentage of sales
- Net profit contribution
- Net profit dollars
- Return on investment
- Gross margin

Metric	Goal	Actual	% of Goal	Weight	Goal × Weight
Sales Rep—Hannah Elizabeth					
Sales Vol.	200,000	180,000	90	3	270
Net Profit	128,000	120,000	94	4	376
No. Demos.	10	14	140	1	140
New Acct.	8	10	120	1	120
Total Score				9	906
Goal score = (Goal × Weight points/weight of metric) = 906/9 = 100.6%					
Sales Rep—Sydney Nguyen					
Sales Vol.	250,000	280,112	112	3	336
Net Profit	172,000	175,000	102	4	408
No. Demos.	11	5	45	1	45
New Acct.	9	5	55	1	55
Total Score				9	844
Goal score = (Goal × Weight points/weight of metric) = 844/9 = 93.7%					
Sales Rep—Moe Peterson					
Sales Vol.	300,000	310,000	103	3	303
Net Profit	190,000	160,000	84	4	336
No. Demos.	9	6	67	1	67
New Acct.	7	6	86	1	86
Total Score				9	793
Goal score = (Goal × Weight points/weight of metric) = 793/9 = 88.1%					

EXHIBIT 14.8

Weighting and Combining Salespeople's Performance: A Worksheet

The salesperson can impact the firm's profitability through the: (1) specific products sold and (2) final prices negotiated for them. This means that two salespeople can sell the same sales revenue levels and meet the exact quota requirements. However, based upon the mix of products sold and prices they negotiated, one salesperson could produce higher gross sales margins for the firm. Likewise, the expenses salespeople accumulate, such as their travel and entertainment expenses, impact their firms' profitability. For example, to improve their firm's profitability, salespeople could opt to take clients to less costly luncheon meetings instead of more expensive dinners. Sales managers evaluate their representatives on these criteria too. Profitability criteria are, in fact, increasingly being incorporated into salespeople's assessments and can directly impact a salesperson's quota and bonuses. During times of slow growth and heavy competition, profitability is critically important to firms.

Ratio Measures for Performance Appraisals

Sales managers should also be familiar with **ratio measures** computed for individual performance appraisals by combining various input and output data. A list of commonly used sales ratio measures is presented in Exhibit 14.9. **Sales volume per call** is a ratio that assesses a salesperson's efficiency. It is computed by dividing the total revenue generated by the salesperson by the total number of sales calls he or she made during a particular period. A low sales volume per call suggests that the salesperson is either devoting excessive time to small accounts or is not giving a sufficient amount of attention to larger

EXHIBIT 14.9

Common Ratios Used to Evaluate Salespersons

Expense Ratios:

Sales expense ratio = Expenses/Sales
Cost per call ratio = Total costs/Number of calls

Account Penetration and Servicing Ratios:

Account penetration ratio = Accounts sold/Total accounts in market
New account conversion ratio = Number of new accounts/Total number of accounts
Lost account ratio = Prior accounts not sold/Total number of accounts
Sales per account ratio = Sales dollar volume/Total number of accounts
Average order size ratio = Sales dollar volume/Total number of orders
Order cancellation ratio = Number of cancelled orders/Total number of orders
Strike rate = Number of orders/Number of quotations

Call Productivity Ratios:

Calls per day ratio = Number of calls/Number of days worked
Calls per account ratio = Number of calls/Number of accounts
Planned call ratio = Number of planned calls/Total number of calls
Orders per call (batting average) ratio = Number of orders/Total number of calls
Profit per call ratio = Total profit/Number of calls made

accounts. Or, perhaps the salesperson is deliberately generating a larger number of small sales rather than a smaller number of large sales because the large sales have already been closed by his or her competitors. Another commonly employed ratio is the **order per call**, or salesperson's "batting average." It is computed by dividing the total number of sales a person closes by the total number of sales calls he or she made. For example, if a salesperson is successful 30 times out of 100 sales calls, then the person's batting average is .300 (30/100). All other things being equal, the higher a salesperson's batting average and sales volume per call are, the greater is the person's sales efficiency. A third ratio is the **average cost per sales call**, which is a salesperson's total sales expenses divided by the total number of calls made by the salesperson. This relates back to the profitability measures we just discussed. A low cost per call ratio, when all other measures are satisfactory, signals efficiency on the part of a salesperson. However, when a sales manager observes both a low sales volume *and* a low cost per call ratio, this suggests that the representative is making too few sales calls and is not devoting sufficient time and effort to establish relationships with the firm's customers.

Additional ratios sales managers use to evaluate their salespeople include the **close rate** and the **profit per call**. These ratios are calculated as follows:

$$\text{Close rate} = \frac{\text{Number of orders}}{\text{Number of quotations}} \qquad \text{Profit per call} = \frac{\text{Total profit}}{\text{Number of calls made}}$$

The close rate is essentially how well the salesperson can close once she has attempted to "seal the deal" by giving customers price quotes on the firm's products. The profit per call ratio represents the total profit derived from an account divided by the number of calls needed to make the sale. For example, if a salesperson made a sale of $10,000 and $3,000 in profit after five sales calls, the profit per call would be $600. Ratios can provide sales managers with additional insight about why a salesperson is or is not reaching her goals. Like other measures of performance, ratios indicate what aspects of the salesperson need to be further investigated—for example, whether the person is a poor closer, as indicated by his or her close rate, or is offering too many discounts to customers, as indicated by his or her profit per call ratio.[13]

The Four-Factor Model of Evaluation

As discussed throughout the chapter, managers employ both behavioral and outcome-based factors to evaluate sales. Because a person's sales performance is a multi-dimensional outcome, it may be beneficial to examine the four-factor model. The four-factor model is comprised of four performance factors: two input activities (days worked and calls rate) and two output measures (batting average and average order size). These factors are combined to give the following equation:

$$\text{Sales} = \text{Days Worked} \times \text{Call Rate} \times \text{Batting Average} \times \text{Average Order Size}$$

The four-factor model shows that sales can be increased by working more days, calling upon more customers per day, closing higher rates of sales per call, and selling larger orders when making a sale. If a salesperson is not meeting his or her quota, then the likely explanation can be found in one or more of these four factors. That is, if the salesperson is working full days and calling upon the expected number of accounts, then the problem might lie in the quality of the person's sales calls (batting average). Or if the order size is below the expected level, this indicates the salesperson is concentrating excessively on small accounts rather than on larger ones. The four-factor model should be used with caution, however, since the four factors are correlated. For example, a higher call rate is positively correlated with higher sales but negatively correlated with average order size. In other words, there are trade-offs among the factors that have to be considered. The factors therefore can't be considered in isolation from one another.

Qualitative Performance Measures

Sales managers also examine **qualitative performance measures** or judgments made by salespeople's supervisors about their performance or abilities. Common qualitative performance measures utilized for performance appraisals include:

- salespeople's job knowledge
- problem-solving skills
- creativity
- attitude and morale
- internal and external relationships
- initiative and judgment
- communications with management
- timeliness in completing reports

Companies evaluate a salesperson's company, product, market knowledge, personal appearance, and motivation against that of an ideal salesperson.[14]

Sales managers can use a variety of methods and tools to perform the qualitative part of a salesperson's evaluation:

- *The essay technique* is a brief statement written by the sales manager to describe the overall salesperson's performance level. However, since there is generally no standardized format for what is discussed and how ratings are assigned using the essay technique, it is difficult to compare evaluations across individual salespersons. Go to Exhibit 14.1 and look at the "performance summary" section of the assessment form to see an essay technique evaluation.
- *Rating scales* utilize phrases or terms as anchors that describe the salesperson's personal characteristics or performance. A variety of rating scales can be used to

evaluate the sales force, such as graphic rating/checklist methods. An example of this type of scale is shown below:

> "Maintains outstanding relationships with customers."
> Almost Never   1   2   3   4   5   6   7   Almost Always

■ *Force ranking* occurs when each salesperson's performance is ordered from "highest" to "lowest" within a district or region. The sales manager bases his or her final rankings on relevant performance characteristics. This technique provides sales representatives with little feedback about how to actually improve their sales; however, it can be useful for sales managers selecting people for promotion. General Electric and Ford force rank their managers.[15]

■ *Management by objectives* (MBO) is a goal setting and evaluative process that results in mutually agreed upon performance measures and assessments between a supervisor and an employee. Specifically, MBO is a three-step process: (1) setting mutually agreed upon, well-defined, and measurable objectives to be achieved within a specified time frame; (2) managing the activities the employee performs within the time period to achieve the objectives; and (3) assessing the employee's performance against the objectives. A major problem of MBO is that sales managers must invest a significant amount of time to make it work.

■ *A behaviorally anchored rating scale* (BARS), as seen in Exhibit 14.10, is a set of scaled statements that describe the level of performance a salesperson received in terms of various job behaviors. The linking of behaviors and results become the basis for evaluating a salesperson's performance. Implementing a BARS evaluation system requires the sales manager to identify key behaviors related to a salesperson's success and rank salespeople on each one. The design of such an instrument is both time consuming and expensive. In addition, all ranking scales, including BARS, can undervalue and overvalue important areas of a salesperson's performance.

Of course, the overall goal for conducting individual appraisals is to improve the future performance of sales representatives. Some of the more immediate *qualitative* goals include counseling, training, and developing salespeople. Some of the more immediate *quantitative*, or output, goals include establishing the compensation and raises salespeople

EXHIBIT 14.10

Behaviorally Anchored Rating Scale

Very High		
More often than not,	10.0	Promptly submitted all field reports even in difficult situations
salesperson submitted	9.0	Promptly met deadlines in most
accurate and needed	8.0	report completion situations
sales reports	7.0	Usually on time when submitting
Moderate		properly formatted sales reports
Regularity in submitting	6.0	Expected to regularly be tardy in submitting
accurate and needed	1.0	field sales reports
field sales reports	4.0	Expected to be tardy and submit inaccurate
Very Low		field sales reports
Irregular and unacceptable	3.0	Disregarded due dates for almost all reports
promptness and accuracy	2.0	Never filed field sales reports and resisted
of field sales reports	1.0	managerial guidance to improve performance
	0.0	

are to receive or promoting or terminating them. The specific purpose of any assessment must be clearly defined because each goal involves distinct evaluation techniques and measures. Said differently, the items used to evaluate sales representatives depend upon the objectives of the appraisal. For example, if the objective of the evaluation is to gauge a salesperson's suitability for a management position, then items on organizing, planning, working with others, and acceptance of responsibility are important. Conversely, if the goal of the evaluation is to improve a salesperson's performance, then the items utilized should objectively rate the person's duties and key responsibilities. The evaluation items used by sales managers will vary by culture, as the Global Sales Management feature explains.

GLOBAL SALES MANAGEMENT

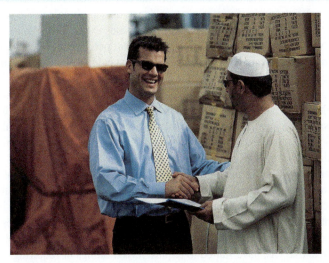

The evaluation criteria and work expectations sales managers have varies by culture. (Getty Images/Digital Vision)

Evaluating Salespeople Working Overseas

Evaluating salespeople assigned to positions abroad is a more complex undertaking than assessing domestic salespeople. Many additional factors come into play, including a salesperson's ability to adjust to the living conditions and culture of a foreign country, assuming she has relocated abroad. The criteria U.S. firms use to evaluate their salespeople working abroad include: technical ability, cultural empathy, adaptability, flexibility, diplomacy, and language skills. A salesperson's cultural skills are often more important than their technical capabilities, however. Even when a salesperson is native to the country he or she is selling in, cultures vary considerably and so do people's perceptions of what does or what does not constitute satisfactory performance. For example, in collectivist societies like Japan, teamwork is favored over individual accomplishments. As a result, a Japanese salesperson's evaluation focuses more on contributions to team efforts and furthering company goals than individual performance.

Source: Based on Money, R. Bruce, and John L. Graham (1999). "Salesperson Performance, Pay, and Job Satisfaction: Tests of a Model Using Data Collected in the U.S. and Japan," *Journal of International Business Studies* 30(1): 149–172.

The Problem of Evaluation Bias

Evaluation bias is defined as *a systematic tendency toward a lack of objectivity, fairness, or impartiality on the part of the evaluator that is based upon personal preferences and beliefs or a systematic error in the assessment instrument and procedures or in the interpretation and evaluation process*. To minimize evaluation bias, firms try to implement systematic assessment processes where a sales manager applies performance standards that directly relate to an employee's job description. This means that an appraisal system is based upon a salesperson's behavior or results rather than on the salesperson's traits or personal characteristics. For example, if the salesperson is instructed to complete four sales calls a day, this should be the work standard the person is held to, regardless of what the sales manager thinks of the sales representative personally or the job they are doing. In other words, sales managers must evaluate the members of their sales teams from as close to a point of neutrality as possible.

Sales managers are prone to at least five types of evaluation bias. **Halo effect** occurs when a sales manager allows one or more evaluation categories that are perceived to be important to influence the overall assessment of the salesperson. An example of halo effect occurs when a sales manager focuses on a salesperson's high sales revenue, but fails to assign low ratings for customer complaints and high sales expenses! In this example, meeting the sales revenue goal overshadows other important performance measures.

A second bias the sales manager must guard against is **leniency or harshness tendency** that occurs when a salesperson is rated at the extremes—either outstanding or below average on most or all performance attributes. The reason that sales managers rate at the extremes is attributable to their personalities or their own beliefs about how to define each level of performance. When sales managers utilize their own perspective of performance, rather than using clearly defined performance standards, the entire evaluation system is jeopardized because across a large number of salespersons similar ratings are dissimilar!

Central tendency bias, or the practice by managers to rate in the center of the scale, can be just as detrimental to salespersons and human resource follow-up because little information is provided since everyone appears to be average. As a result of no variability in ratings, it is difficult to identify true differences in performance and should it become necessary to terminate a salesperson, existing evaluations will be of little value. To combat central tendency bias a number of firms, like GE, have started to require forced ratings or requiring sales managers to place at least 10 percent of the sales force in the lowest overall performance category.

A fourth form of subjectivity that enters the evaluation process is **interpersonal bias**, which occurs when a manager's performance ratings are influenced by how much they like or dislike the individual being evaluated. For example, if a salesperson is too outspoken or dresses too casually or too formally, a manager may unconsciously lower (or raise) the person's evaluation rating. Some salespersons may try to employ their selling skills to positively influence the sales manager's perception of them as being likeable and thus bias their evaluations upward.

Finally, **outcome bias**, or allowing the results of an action to influence the manager's assessment, can impact overall evaluations. An example would be a sales manager who rates a salesperson who has closed a large, important sale higher than a salesperson who failed to close such a large sale, even though both people did an equally good job. In other words, the ultimate decision to buy or not buy largely depended on the different buyers involved—not the sales representative's behaviors.

Informal Evaluations

A few sales managers claim that formal sales force evaluations are unnecessary because they assess their salesperson's performance on a daily or "as needed" basis. However, it's not hard to argue that evaluations such as these are highly biased. For example, say that a salesperson wins a company golf tournament. One sales manager will view this as a positive achievement, whereas another manager might ask how it was possible for the salesperson to work 55 to 60 hours each week and still excel at the game of golf. Second, informal evaluations result in sales managers assessing differing amounts and quality of information about each salesperson. For example, one salesperson might request that their customers write letters of appreciation and provide positive feedback to their sales manager. Conversely, another salesperson might be reluctant to ask their customers for this type of assistance. If the sales managers don't evaluate the two representatives using hard, detailed criteria, biased evaluations are likely to occur. In other words, when a sales manager engages in informal evaluations, she is unable to evaluate her sales force either consistently or comparatively. Thus, *formal* evaluation systems are more likely to produce objective appraisals and minimize the number of demoralized sales reps that ultimately leave the firm or go so far as to file suit against it claiming their appraisals were biased.

Sales managers who appraise their personnel informally risk not being taken seriously and tend to produce evaluations that are not objective. (Getty Images)

Reducing Sales Management Errors in Performance Evaluations

To minimize the effects of evaluation bias when completing performance appraisals, the sales manager should take the following actions:

1. Before completing the evaluation forms, read and be familiar with each trait listed on the form.
2. Do not allow one factor to influence others.
3. Base your ratings on actual performance, not potential.
4. Don't overrate salespeople—evaluate them based on an objective, unbiased standard.
5. Rate the salesperson on his or her performance over the evaluation period, not a specific incident.
6. List sound reasons for all performance appraisal ratings.[16]

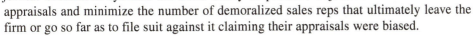

SELF-ASSESSMENT LIBRARY

One purpose of performance appraisals is to help salespeople meet or exceed their goals. An important part of the performance appraisal process is providing accurate feedback to the salesperson in a way that motivates the person to improve. How good are you at giving performance feedback and coaching an employee to higher levels of performance? To learn how good you might be at providing performance feedback to members of a sales team, go to http://www. prenhall. com/ sal/ and log in using the access code that came with your book. Then click on:

  Assessments
    III. Life in Organizations
      A. Organization Structure
        3. How Good Am I at Giving Performance Feedback?

What Happens When Salespeople Don't Achieve Their Sales Goals?

"Off with their heads," yelled the Queen of Hearts. Fortunately, things aren't as bad for salespeople who don't reach their goals as it was for Alice, in Lewis Carroll's *Adventures of Alice in Wonderland*. In fact, sales managers, researchers, and consultants agree that salespeople who don't achieve their goals aren't at the end of the line. As we have explained, there can be a number of reasons why a salesperson does not achieve 100 percent of their sales goals. When salespeople do not reach their sales goals, their performance is measured against other local representatives and national averages. If a representative is an **outlier**—that is, the person's sales are out of line with everyone else's—the representative is typically put under closer scrutiny. Not meeting a goal signals the representative's sales manager to work more closely with the salesperson to find out what activities or practices the person needs to engage in to be successful.

> **Ethical Sidebar**
>
> Imagine working for a sales manager who deliberately or unknowingly biases his sales force evaluations. That is, consider how destructive it is for a sales manager to evaluate his sales team based primarily on personal feelings or friendship. Salespersons in many organizations often complain that it is their relationship, rather than their performance, that gets evaluated by the boss. Other criticisms that appear to influence annual evaluations and subsequent salary increases include: length of time on the job, social activities like golf or dinners that take place away from work, and where or if one attends religious services. It is natural for a sales manager to prefer the company of some salespersons over others; however, the sales manager must do their best to evaluate their sales team based on set standards from a point of neutrality. Biased evaluations are unethical and in many instances they are ruled illegal when challenged in court!

Should a salesperson continue to under-perform during the next time unit (for some companies it might be the next quarter; for others the next year), they will then be placed on probation. Sales reps who work solely on commission will probably realize their performance is low, based upon their low pay, and look for opportunities elsewhere. Sales representatives receiving a salary and commission who continue to fall short of their quotas eventually face termination.[17,18]

Developing and Reallocating Salespeople's Skills and Efforts

If it is determined that a salesperson requires additional personal development, this should be clearly communicated to them. This is why some firms employ MBO systems to help salespersons set mutually agreed upon goals that they work to accomplish. Should the evaluation confirm that shifting the salesperson's priority from one activity to another will improve his or her performance, this must also be communicated to the salesperson. For example, if it is apparent the salesperson has not been devoting sufficient time to selling high profit margin products, the sales manager must redirect the salesperson's efforts. Likewise, sales managers could be spending excessive time selling instead of managing the sales force. In such circumstances the sales manager must devote more field time to coaching the sales force.

Modifying the Performance Setting

The firm's performance appraisals might also indicate that changes are needed in sales procedures or methods. Perhaps the sales training program has not adequately prepared the sales force for success in the field. When this occurs, firms must consider modifying their training programs. For example, as new products are introduced or selling strategies change, firms might add high-tech training programs to prepare the sales force for marketplace changes.[19] If the analysis shows the sales force is weak at making sales presentations, for example, this must be communicated to the sales team, and proper training must be implemented to correct the deficiency. Alternately, the firm might need to hire more experienced and successful salespeople. The analysis might also confirm that the firm's products need to be improved or new products need to be added to the company's product lineup. Lastly, the appraisals might indicate that the company's marketing strategies and/or credit policies need to be changed.

Summary

Sales managers evaluate the activities and accomplishments of their sales forces in order to know what is working, what is not, and, most importantly, why. This information shapes the daily decisions the sales manager makes to improve the performance of the sales force. Of course, the quality of the decisions they make will be higher if the information emanates from objective evaluation efforts.

To increase the probability that the sales force will reach its goals, sales managers analyze their firms' sales, costs, and profitability measures. Sales information provides managers with an understanding of the revenue the firm generated. Cost figures relate the company's sales expense to its sales goals. Profitability figures tell supervisors if the sales effort was worthwhile. The analyses help managers identify deviations from the firm's plans that can then be further investigated to understand why they occurred. If the firm's plans and goals are not achieved, sales managers must determine whether the plans were incorrectly set and/or if the sales force did not perform up to par. Finally, based upon the results of their analyses, sales managers can decide what aspects of the sales function and the firm as a whole need to be changed.

To ensure their sales representatives are on track, sales managers continually monitor their performance. Formal appraisals of representatives are usually conducted once or twice annually to understand their performance, potential for advancement, and qualifications for reward. Because the duties of salespeople are complex, they are generally evaluated based upon a broad set of metrics that include their inputs, or efforts they make to sell the firm's products, plus the outcomes they achieve, such as the revenues and profits they actually generate. Professional development criteria are also included in the evaluations. By utilizing multiple measures, sales managers gain a more comprehensive picture of their salespeople. Sales managers must also be aware of the potential for bias to enter into the assessment process and take steps to prevent it.

When sales managers perform regular, objective, and comprehensive evaluations, they will be more cognizant of both their sales forces and the markets for their products. This will allow them to make more informed decisions and improve the odds that they, their salespeople, and the firm as a whole succeed.

Key Terms

average cost per sales call   332
central tendency bias   336
close rate   332
contribution margin   322
cost analysis   319
evaluation bias   336

halo effect   336
interpersonal bias   336
leniency or harshness tendency   336
order per call   332
outcome bias   336
outcome measures   329

Questions and Problems

1. What is the relationship between managerial control and sales team evaluations? When managers make decisions without the benefit of accurate information, what is the likely outcome?

2. When a sales manager detects a deviation from the performance expected by the firm, what are the two most common aspects they investigate?

3. What are the different goals of evaluation and assessment? That is, what types of decisions must a sales manager make, and how are these decisions linked to the type of evaluation information needed?

4. Why is sales revenue the most common data used? What are some limitations of considering only sales revenue generated?

5. List three managerial decisions that are possible based upon a cost analysis.

6. Review the data presented for Hannah, Moe, and Sydney in Exhibit 14.8. What areas do they excel in? Which areas, as their sales manager, would concern you?

7. The handheld mini-PCs discussed in the chapter can be upgraded with Global Positioning Systems (GPS) to allow a sales manager to track exactly where each sales representative has been and is currently. What do you think the pros and cons of using this technology might be? As a sales manager, would you use it?

8. If a salesperson received 32 purchase orders during the month based upon 123 sales calls, what is his order per call, or "close rate"?

9. In what ways can salespeople influence the profitability of their territories?

10. Sales managers should assess qualitative measures against what standard? Why?

11. What challenges are posed when firms evaluate a global sales force's efforts?

12. Explain the common types of bias to which sales managers can fall victim.

Role Play

Johnson Controls Considers Changing Its Assessment Criteria

Rhonda Jones is sales manager for Johnson Controls, a manufacturer of switches and thermostats for industrial HVAC (heating, ventilation, and air conditioning) systems. Until recently, Johnson Controls utilized its sales force to push its products through its distribution chain. As a result, the firm's sales force members were evaluated in terms of the sales revenues they generated, number of new accounts they opened, and the extent to which they increased the sales they made to their existing accounts. Recently, however, Johnson Controls' senior managers have switched to a customer-centric strategy that focuses on the firm's best customers. Jones wonders if the categories on the company's performance appraisal forms used to evaluate the firm's representatives should also be modified. She thinks that rather than sales revenues generated, the appraisals should take other evaluation criteria into account. Despite the change in the sales force's strategy, Jones would find it troubling not to expect the members of the firm's sales force to meet certain sales revenue levels. Jones has scheduled a meeting with Fred Mader, president and Sue Maloney, operations manager at Johnson Controls to discuss potential changes in the firm's evaluation policy.

Characters in the Role Play

Rhonda Jones, sales manager at Johnson Controls

Fred Mader, president at Johnson Controls

Sue Maloney, operations manager at Johnson Controls

Assignment

Break into groups of three, with each student in the group playing each character. Do not be concerned about matching the gender of the character with the actual gender mix of the student group. Prior to meeting in the group, work individually to summarize and support your own recommendations for a new set of objective and subjective measures of performance for the sales force at Johnson Controls. Then meet and role-play the meeting between Rhonda, Fred, and Sue. The goal is to conclude the meeting with a unified plan for modifying the evaluation system for salespersons at Johnson Controls.

Sales Manager's Workshop

Promedia Technology (PMT) Analyzing the Performance of Your Sales Representatives

As Promedia's district sales manager, it is time to conduct an end-of-the-year evaluation of your five salespeople. After reviewing the evaluation criteria discussed in this chapter, go to the Applicor data and analyze the performance of your five salespeople. Consider looking at several activity, outcome, and profitability figures. Based upon the performance of each salesperson, write a short report to the national sales manager detailing their performance and also justify the raise you recommend for each. When you are satisfied with your report, if it's requested, turn it in to your sales management professor.

Caselet 14.1: "Happy Hannah:" Did the Sales Reps Meet Their Goals?

Recall in Chapter 11 when our sales manager "Happy" Hannah Johanson helped establish goals for two of her sales reps: the outspoken Ella Lynn and the on-again-off-again Syd Vance. Three sales quarters have passed since that meeting and Hannah has collected the performance measures for both of the reps outlined in Figure 1 below. She'll be meeting with both reps tomorrow and needs to prepare for the feedback sessions tonight for the mid-morning meeting tomorrow.

Ella has continued to be the firm's "sustainability" advocate. Her efforts, combined with the rising price of fuel, have resulted in her being in a small group of reps piloting several brands of hybid vehicles for possible adoption by the entire sales force. This has pleased Ella immensely.

As Hannah skimmed her local newspaper, she saw Syd's picture on the sports page. "Star Pitcher Takes Team to Nationals," read the headline. Syd's team, sponsored by Honker's—a popular tavern near a local wildlife preserve, had gone 45–5 over the last

FIGURE 1

Last 3 Sales Quarters: Actual vs. Goal Figures

Sales Goals and Actual Quarter	Ella's Sales Figures			Syd's Sales Figures		
Sales Vol. Goal	125,000	125,000	125,000	150,000	150,000	150,000
Sales Vol. Actual	120,000	128,000	118,000	140,000	130,000	105,000
Demonstrations Goal	9	7	11	10	8	6
Demonstrations Actual	8	8	8	10	10	10
New Account Goal	4	3	5	4	3	2
New Account Actual	4	4	4	5	5	5

4½ months, won the regionals, and was headed to the national play-offs. Based upon the newspaper article, Syd has a great pitching arm.

Questions

1. Based on the performance data in Figure 1, what "deviations" would you focus on during your meeting with Ella?
2. Based on the performance data, what factors would you focus on during your meeting with Syd? What approach would you take in your meeting with Syd?
3. Would your response differ if Syd's team was sponsored by a religious or a civic organization?

Caselet 14.2: Ligon Industrial

Ligon Industrial, which is located in Athens, Georgia, manufactures customized truck bodies for utility firms located in the state. Ligon's sales manager, Fred Stephenson, recently ranked each of the company's five salespeople in five performance areas. The rankings were as follows:

Salesperson	Sales Revenue	New Accts.	Lost Accts.	Expenses	Profitability
Ford	1	5	3	2	4
Smith	5	4	1	3	2
Glassman	3	1	5	4	3
Whitbeck	2	3	4	1	5
Thelen	4	2	2	5	1

However, once Stephenson had ranked his sales staff, it was hard for him to identify the salesperson who should receive the top rating. He also wondered how he could utilize the information to coach each salesperson to improve his or her performance.

Questions

1. Are all five categories used for ranking the sales force equal in importance?
2. What are the advantages and disadvantages of a ranking system?
3. Under what conditions is it appropriate to rank one's sales force?
4. What can be concluded if each category receives an importance weight?
5. What recommendations would you offer Fred Stephenson?

References

1. Wotruba, Thomas R., and Edwin K. Simpson (1992). *Sales Management*. Boston: PWS-Kent.
2. Hymowitz, Carol (2001). "Ranking Systems Gain Popularity but Have Many Staffers Riled," *Wall Street Journal* May 15, B1.
3. Terpstra, Vern, and Ravi Sarathy (1997). *International Marketing*. Ft. Worth: Dryden Press.
4. Owens, Darryl E. (2007) "Metrics Need a Link to Results, Exec Buy-in, Momentum," *Marketing News* March 1, pp. 13, 22.
5. Cron, William L., and Michael Levy (1987). "Sales Management Performance Evaluation: A Residual Income Perspective," *Journal of Personal Selling & Sales Management* August, 57–66.
6. Pettijohn, Linda S., R. Stephen Parker, Charles E. Pettijohn, and John L. Kent (2001). "Performance Appraisals: Usage, Criteria, and Observations," *Journal of Management Development* (20)9: 754–771.
7. Jackson, Donald, Jr., John Schlacter, and William Wolfe (1995). "Examining the Bases Utilized for Evaluating Salespeople's Performance, *Journal of Personal Selling & Sales Management* (Fall)15: 57–65.
8. Stein, David (2007). "Do You Really Measure Performance?" *Sales & Marketing Management* April, p. 9.
9. Personal interview conducted with Ken Deakman, Slipka-Deakman Associate, Inc. Centerville, MN. June 26, 2007.
10. Honeycutt, Earl D., Jr., Tanya Thelen, Shawn T. Thelen, and Sharon K. Hodge (2005). "Impediments to Sales Force Automation," *Industrial Marketing Management* (34)4: 313–322.
11. Marshall, Greg, John Mowen, and Keith Fabes (1992). "The Impact of Territory Difficulty and Self versus Other Ratings on Managerial Evaluations of Sales Performance," *Journal of Personal Selling & Sales Management* (Fall)12: 35–48.
12. Leong, Siew Meng, Donna M. Randall, and Joseph A. Cote (1994). "Exploring the Organizational Commitment—Performance Linkage in Marketing: A Study of Life Insurance Salespeople," *Journal of Business Research* (29)1: 57–63.
13. Jobber, David, and Geoff Lancaster (2000). *Selling and Sales Management*. Harlow, England: Financial Times Prentice Hall.
14. Hill, John S., and Arthur W. Allaway (1993). "How U.S.-based Companies Manage Sales in Foreign Countries," *Industrial Marketing Management* 22, 7–16.
15. Hymnowitz (2001).
16. Marshall, Mowen, and Fabes (1992).
17. Schwepker, Charles H., Jr., and David J. Good (2004). "Understanding Sales Quotas: An Exploratory Investigation of Consequences of Failure," *The Journal of Business & Industrial Marketing* (19)1: 39–48.
18. Good, David J., and Sharles H. Schwepker, Jr. (2001). "Sales Quotas: Critical Interpretations and Implications," *Review of Business* Spring, 22, 1 & 2, pp. 32–37.
19. Jackson, Schlacter, and Wolfe (1995).

15

INTERNAL AND EXTERNAL CULTURAL FORCES THAT AFFECT A FIRM'S SALES PERFORMANCE

LEARNING OBJECTIVES

After completing this chapter, you should be able to:

- Explain what characterizes an organization's corporate culture.
- List and explain different cultural categories that guide organizations.
- Discuss how a firm's culture impacts its sales effort.
- Offer a strategy for modifying a firm's culture.
- Discuss the impact global, national, and local cultures have on sales management.
- Contrast the differences related to managing domestic versus overseas sales personnel.
- Explain why having a diverse sales force is important to the success of today's sales organizations.

KEVIN YODER

DISTRICT MANAGER, ASTRAZENECA P.L.C.

Kevin Yoder is district sales manager for AstraZeneca P.L.C. (AZ), a global pharmaceutical firm that believes its culture is what makes it a great company and a great employer. For example, only by working responsibly can the company earn and maintain the trust and confidence that make such a vital contribution to their corporate reputation and license to do business.

As a result, AstraZeneca works hard to ensure its high-level values are translated into consistent and appropriate actions and behavior worldwide on the part of its sales representatives. The company emphasizes that actions and behaviors—not just words—shape its culture. It focuses on:

- Respect for the individual and diversity
- Openness, honesty, trust, and support of one another
- Integrity and high ethical standards
- Leadership by example at all levels

AstraZeneca also creates a level of enthusiasm and determination among its sales representatives that keeps them focused on the company's internal and external customers.

Yoder believes that the firm's corporate culture and values are, in fact, an extremely important factor for his sales team's success in the marketplace. He feels that he can leverage tools like performance reviews and recognition systems because they are aligned with the corporation's culture and strategy.

Two examples serve to support the importance of aligning a firm's performance and recognition systems to its corporate culture.

- First, AstraZeneca utilizes a balanced scorecard. Within an employee's scorecard, each goal is tied to "organizational behaviors." This allows sales managers to use ongoing and yearly performance appraisals to link a person's individual performance with the firm's culture and strategy.
- Second, field representatives are expected to work collaboratively with internal and external customers. Professional development, training, mentoring, and ongoing feedback by the sales manager helps develop and refine this skill set.

As a manager, Yoder believes in several key elements that contribute to his team environment. They include:

- *Accountability* for delivering all aspects of the job correctly and on time.
- *Communications* that are shared and understood by all who make and are impacted by a decision.
- *A customer and business focus* that is professional for internal and external customers.
- *Team spirit* that constructively addresses roadblocks and maximizes the accountability of employees.
- *Continuous improvement* that encourages innovation and taking calculated risks.
- *Valuing diversity* by enhancing and encouraging diversity and fostering a climate of mutual respect.
- *Resolving conflict* by focusing on facts and behavior.
- *Personal pride* that is evident to internal and external customers.

By diligently aligning his representatives' values with AstraZeneca's external strategies, Yoder strives to achieve more successful outcomes for the people he and his team serve. ■

As you will learn in this chapter, firms like AstraZeneca take symbolic and substantive actions to communicate and reinforce their culture to their employees. **Culture** refers to the traditions and beliefs held by people. The role culture plays in the business world continues to expand as global trade, cross-cultural selling, and the diversity of customers and employees increases. Sales managers and salespersons must understand this impact. The composition of the U.S. workplace is changing rapidly, too, to include workers from diverse backgrounds. If organizations are to succeed in the future, the diversity that exists in day-to-day life must be reflected in their sales forces. The goal of this chapter is to explain how culture—both internal and external to the firm—impacts the way sales forces operate and how people's cultural beliefs and practices influence their alliances, customer relationships, and management practices.

How the Corporate Culture of a Firm Affects Its Sales Force

A firm's **corporate culture** is characterized by the beliefs, attitudes, values, assumptions, and ways of doing things the company's members share and teach new members.[1] A company's corporate culture will influence:

- The firm's ethical standards and policies.
- The firm's attitudes toward diversity and multiculturalism.
- How a firm's managers and employees communicate and behave.
- The tone of the work environment.
- The stories employees tell about the firm's successes and failures.[2]

Corporate culture has also been described as "the water in the fishbowl of any business,"[3] because salespersons are immersed and operate in it, but are unaware of the firm's culture until something changes.

The Firm's Marketplace Orientation

The way organizations operate and the corporate cultures that result from them are often manifested by an organization's orientation to the marketplace.[4] A firm's marketplace orientation may evolve in ways that reflect its founder's values, its initial product offerings, its geographical locale, or its competitive environment. There are five basic orientations a company may assume: a production, product, sales, marketing, or relationship orientation.

Firms that are **production oriented** are most concerned with mass-producing products at low prices to achieve economies of scale. This approach allows a firm to offer a limited number of reasonably priced products at multiple locations. As a functional area of the production-oriented firm, sales is seldom consulted before product or pricing decisions are made. These changes are determined by production and financial executives. In a production-oriented firm, the sales force is more of an afterthought. The company's managers believe that the sales force's job is to communicate with potential buyers about the specifications of the firm's products and their availability and to take customers' orders. Production-oriented firms are more likely to prosper when market demand for their products exceeds their ability to supply them.

A **product-oriented** company focuses on the newest technology or latest product feature. Sometimes called the "better mousetrap syndrome," the firm's goal is to differentiate its products from those of its competitors by constantly upgrading the products. In product-oriented firms, engineering and research and development (R&D) are accorded superior status, and the firm's focus centers on the product rather than the buyer. The role of the sales force is to notify buyers that the latest product models have been released and convince buyers that they are better than competing products.

When the supply of products exceeds the demand for them, firms often become **sales oriented**. For example, when multiple competitors enter the marketplace and there are few noticeable differences between their products, customers tend to focus on the prices of the products. As a result, some sales managers will coach their salespeople to practice "hard sell" tactics regardless of customer needs. Management is likely to use a "carrot and stick" approach to motivate the sales force. In this company culture, salespeople receive bonuses for reaching their assigned sales goals, but face punishment or dismissal when desired sales levels are not reached!

By contrast, a **market-oriented** firm pursues the dual goals of satisfying their buyers while maximizing the profits of their firms. In market-oriented companies, senior executives are more active in sales and customer activities. As a result, salespeople are expected to satisfy the needs of their buyers in addition to meeting their sales goals. These goals can come into conflict, however, whenever short-term sales goals are achieved at the expense of customer satisfaction.

As we have explained in Chapter 5, more firms have become **relationship marketing oriented**, whereby they seek to establish long-term relationships with their customers. Salespeople are expected to act as consultants to fully understand their buyers' long-term needs.[5] Relationship-oriented firms expect their sales force to provide high levels of service to profitable accounts and grow business with buyers who are willing to pay higher margins for greater service and the meeting of their needs.

When a firm's organizational culture is aligned with its marketplace strategy, the company's sales managers and the sales force are more likely to be successful. Thus, each type of orientation we've just discussed is appropriate when it is aligned with the market in which the firm operates. For example, in many developing markets in Asia and Africa today, consumers are interested in purchasing high-quality items at affordable prices. However, in more developed nations, like the United States, Europe, and Japan, buyers expect customized solutions to their problems, and they have the economic power to purchase those solutions. The problem arises when the marketplace changes and firms do not adjust their orientations and internal cultures to match the needs of the marketplace. In fact, experts estimate that about 30 percent of salespeople fail to meet the performance levels that their firms expect of them because there is a misalignment between internal culture and marketplace realities.[6]

Low- versus High-Performance Cultures

A company's culture determines the way the company addresses the external marketplace via the firm's vision, mission statement, strategies, and metrics that are selected to define success. A firm's internal culture also determines how a company responds to situations both inside and outside the organization; how power, status, and resources are bestowed within the organization; how resources are allocated; what the membership of the firm's various groups is; and the firm's policies and procedures. In turn, a firm's corporate culture guides the behavior of its employees, salespeople, and new hires by influencing how they conduct business with the company's customers.[7]

Behavior that is culturally sanctioned thrives and is rewarded, whereas unapproved cultural behavior is frowned upon or even punished. Internal cohesion is achieved via a system of informal rules and peer pressure that shape the behavior of the firm's employees.[8] As a result, the sales force feels better about its work, cooperates as a team, and sustains its behavior. A firm's culture also determines how it adapts to changes in the external marketplace—for example, how the company responds to the changing needs of buyers or competitors' actions.

A firm's culture can be weak or strong and revolves around the amount of agreement workers have about specific values and ways things get done. As seen in Exhibit 15.1, when a firm has a strong culture, this signals that there is widespread agreement about the firm's key norms and values. Conversely, a firm with a weak internal culture lacks a consensus about what is important. An environment characterized by weak values often results in negative behavior that includes gossiping, manipulation, favoritism, communication breakdowns, and dysfunctional internal competition. These practices are exacerbated when sales managers and their employees lack a sense of unity about the firm's vision and strategy. An excellent example of a firm that lacked a sense of unity between management and workers was the energy giant Enron, which went bankrupt.

LOW-PERFORMANCE CULTURES   Firms with weak cultures are associated with lower financial performance, and they exhibit a number of unhealthy characteristics that include:

- *Insular thinking:* Members are inward thinking, believing all answers for the firm's problems exist within the firm. As a result, they avoid looking outside the firm for best practices. Managers may behave arrogantly.
- *Resistance to change:* There is a desire to maintain the status quo. There is little support for new ideas and the firm's leaders discourage change.
- *Politicized internal environment:* Problems are resolved, and decisions are made based upon the individual power of the firm's managers and executives. Rather than doing what is best for the firm, the decisions are based upon what is best personally for individual managers.
- *Unhealthy promotion practices:* Promotions are made without the skills and capabilities of the candidates being seriously considered or matched to the positions to which they are being promoted. For example, a hardworking or long-serving sales representative might be promoted to a managerial position even though the person has no long-range vision or ability to create a new culture.

EXHIBIT 15.1

The Characteristics of Low-Performing versus High-Performing Corporate Cultures

Low-Performing Culture	High-Performing Cultures
Are inward thinking	Are people oriented
Are resistant to change	Are results oriented
Are characterized by a politicized environment	Stress achievement and excellence
Exhibit unhealthy performance practices	Reinforce the firm's cultural beliefs

When Bill George assumed the top spot at the medical equipment giant Medtronic, he inherited a corporate culture that was extremely value-centered but plagued by a lack of accountability and conflict avoidance. George knew that most of the "old-timers" at Medtronic felt that the firm was successful and that culture change was unnecessary. In contrast, George understood that a cultural shift had to occur or Medtronic would lose out to more aggressive competitors that had coordinated their internal culture and external strategy.[9]

HIGH-PERFORMANCE CULTURES By contrast, companies with a strong corporate culture tend to be results oriented and associated with healthy cultural attributes like those listed below:

- *People oriented:* Workers are treated with respect and their achievements are celebrated. A full range of rewards and punishments are employed to encourage high-performance standards, and managers at all levels are held responsible for developing workers under their care.
- *Results oriented:* Workers who excel are identified and rewarded; control systems are developed to collect, analyze, and interpret performance; and sales managers/salespersons who do not meet standards are replaced.
- *Stress achievement and excellence:* Salespersons feel a constructive pressure to be the best, sales managers pursue programs that motivate workers to perform at their highest level, and excellence links cultural metrics to performance measures.
- *Reinforce cultural beliefs:* The firm's ceremonies, symbols, language, and policies lead to superior results achieved by average workers. Meaningful slogans are utilized to communicate the firm's values.

At Medtronic, Bill George learned that sales goals were routinely missed, budgets were exceeded, and new products were delayed—all without consequence to the firm's managers. The first change George made was "empowering" managers to achieve goals and holding them responsible for meeting their goals.[10] As a result, Medtronic's sales and profits increased significantly.

Achieving Internal Alignment

Sales executives realize that culture can be a source of competitive advantage when firms align their internal cultures with a strong external market strategy. Firms that successfully align their internal culture with their external market strategy also report higher levels of financial performance.[11,12] Many firm's sales and marketing efforts often lack alignment. This misalignment is explainable by two factors: economics and culture.[13] First, the sales and marketing areas often compete over how the company's budget is divided, each believing the other receives too much of the budget. Second, sales and marketing workers tend to exhibit different job cultures. That is, marketers tend to be more analytical, data oriented, and project focused. The sales team, on the other hand, is comprised of members who are action oriented, relationship driven, and short-term focused.[14] Perhaps most importantly, the two areas of business are judged differently in regard to their performance. The sales team is often evaluated based upon results—closing sales. Conversely, marketers are judged by the programs they propose, and their success or failure takes much longer to discern. Each group may believe that their contributions are more important than that of other functions.[15] Given these fundamental differences, it is hardly surprising that the marketing and sales areas of the firm find it difficult to work together.[16] Sales and marketing departments often move through a four-stage alignment, as shown in Exhibit 15.2.

Undefined Sales and marketing work independently, on their own agendas, with little knowledge of what the other functional area is doing. There is a duplication of work, and some efforts go undone. Resolving conflicts comprises the bulk of the interactions between the groups.

↓

Defined Sales and marketing establish rules to minimize conflicts. Each functional area understands what it's supposed to do and meetings between the groups are more reflective. Both areas work together at trade shows and customer conferences. However, there can be a duplication of efforts.

↓

Aligned Clear but flexible boundaries exist between the two areas. Sales and marketing engage in joint planning and training activities and confer about sales efforts to the firm's major accounts.

↓

Integrated As the two functional areas integrate, the boundary lines between them become blurred. Marketers assume joint responsibility for major accounts and shared evaluation, incentive, and reward metrics are adopted.

Misalignment and Entropy

When there is an alignment gap within an organization, entropy occurs. **Entropy** is the amount of energy employees expend engaging in nonproductive activities as a result of this mismatch. Four cultural gaps contribute to entropy:[17]

- *A lack of personal alignment:* Gaps that exist between employees' stated values and their behaviors. An example is when sales leaders do not "walk the talk" or demand that the sales team "do as I say, not as I do." Likewise, a salesperson might not be honest with a sales manager about what happened on a sales call or the reason a customer cancelled an order. Any gap in personal alignment leads to a lack of trust between sales managers and their sales teams.
- *A lack of structural alignment:* Gaps that exist between the firm's stated values and the rules, regulations, and managerial systems it puts in place. For example, if a firm says that it encourages its salespeople to behave ethically but then fails to reward ethical behavior when it comes to the reps' raises and promotions, the sales team will become cynical.
- *A lack of a values alignment:* Incongruence exists between employees' personal values and the collective values of the groups within which they work. For example, there will be a lack of a values alignment when a salesperson's ethical values are higher or lower than the overall ethical values of the group within which he or she works. Incongruent employees and collective values can lead to role conflict where the salesperson is unable to satisfy the firm's values without violating his or her own.[18]
- *A lack of mission alignment:* Gaps that exist when the objectives of the members of the sales team fail to align with the firm's goals. For example, a lack of mission alignment exists when a firm instructs its sales team to devote time to relationship-building, but its sales force members continue to sell products that maximize their income at the expense of those relationships. Mission alignment gaps can detract from a sales manager's ability to channel the efforts of his or her sales team in a unified direction.

Sometimes a country's laws and the global selling environment the firm is trying to compete in create a cultural misalignment, as the following Ethics in Sales Management sidebar shows.

ETHICS IN SALES MANAGEMENT

What Constitutes a Bribe?

What is and what is not ethical behavior varies widely based upon one's culture and the legal system within which one operates. For example, in Japan, a salesperson is expected to give a buyer a gift in order to expand their friendship. However, in the United States, buyers do not expect and are apprehensive about accepting gifts from salespersons. One reason U.S. firms are careful about giving or receiving gifts from current or actual business partners relates to the Foreign Corruption Practices Act (FCPA) of 1977 and 1988. Although the expectation of bribes or "grease" is an accepted tradition in many cultures, the FCPA forbids U.S. firms from paying bribes to receive an order. However, the FCPA does allow an exception to the bribery prohibition that allows payments to be made for routine governmental actions such as permits, documents, utilities, inspections, and other "similar" actions. What is significant to understand about cross-cultural sales situations is that in certain cultures sales representatives are expected to offer gifts at appropriate times. When "appropriate" gifts are not offered, the buyer is likely to become offended and break off negotiations!

When a firm experiences cultural entropy, managers have two choices—change the sales strategy to fit the culture or alter the firm's culture to fit the sales strategy. For example, when Hewlett-Packard (HP) adopted a customer-centric sales approach, CEO Mark Hurd introduced HP's Total Customer Experience® program, which measured a number of customer satisfaction components that included the promise fulfillment of representatives, their follow-up, and customer support levels. The new customer-oriented goals and firm orientation required HP to undergo a cultural shift.[19]

Sales Managers as Culture Creators

Modifying a firm's culture so that it aligns with strategy is a difficult undertaking for any manager.[20] There are several actions a sales manager can take to create a strong, high-performing culture that encourages internal unity and an ability to adapt to external changes. First, the sales manager must determine which parts of the firm's current culture support the firm's strategy and which do not. Second, the sales manager must communicate honestly and openly to all workers the cultural areas that need to be modified or whether a completely new culture is required. Lastly, the sales manager must take visible actions that communicate a transformation of the existing culture.

For example, in 2001 Dow Corning wanted to move to a more entrepreneurial sales force culture. To make the cultural shift, its top managers determined that the sales force needed more time to meet and think creatively. To free up blocks of time for the sales team, Dow Corning's managers purchased a new CRM system that transferred information to the Web and created virtual ways for the sales members to share information with one another. As a result, the Dow Corning sales team identified and penetrated new accounts that they had not previously pursued.[21]

Managers who want to change firm culture can take two actions: primary (substantive) or secondary (symbolic).[22] **Symbolic actions** communicate shifts in an organization's culture, whereas **substantive actions** demonstrate that a sales leader is serious about changing the firm's culture. Managers who take symbolic actions communicate the kinds of behavior they are encouraging. For example, the CEO at infoUSA, a company that maintains and

EXHIBIT 15.3

Sales Management Actions That Shape a Firm's Corporate Culture

Symbolic Actions:
- Serve as a role model for the sales force
- Hold ceremonies and make special appearances

Substantive Actions:
- Replace salespeople unwilling or unable to accept changes
- Change dysfunctional policies and practices
- Realign rewards and incentives and resource allocations
- Redesign work spaces
- Pen a written values statement

sells databases of North American businesses and consumers, takes symbolic action by meeting regularly with the firm's sales and marketing managers to ask for ideas for business growth.[23] Likewise, a sales manager who wants to encourage a customer orientation might symbolically assume responsibility for a major account while substantively modifying the evaluation criteria for the sales team to include customer satisfaction ratings. A number of actions available to sales managers, as listed in Exhibit 15.3, can be divided into symbolic and substantive categories.'

A substantive action might include replacing sales members who are reluctant or unable to embrace a new culture by new sales team members. Being willing to make personnel changes is a key substantive action that demonstrates the sales manager's seriousness about change. If senior salespersons are fiercely competitive, unwilling to work in a team setting, and are unable to convert to a relationship strategy, their "early retirement" or "transfer to another opportunity" informs everyone in the firm that the sales culture is being transformed.

Of course, the changes sales managers make must result in a strategy-culture fit. That is, the sales manager must modify the firm's strategy to fit the company's culture or change the company's culture to match the firm's strategy. Otherwise, the gap between culture and strategy will cause entropy and impede its execution. In addition, sales managers must modify policies and practices that impede the successful execution of a new strategy. For example, sales managers will provide sales training to ensure the sales team possesses the skills, knowledge, and attitudes necessary to succeed in the field. Likewise, the sales manager will need to coordinate with other managers in the firm to ensure destructive subcultures don't flourish within the accounting, marketing, operations, finance, or engineering groups and that the firm's credit policies, return policies, and customer service levels, for example, are synchronized with and support the firm's sales efforts. In this way, sales managers work to create **internal alignment**. A case in point: When IBM integrated its sales and marketing areas, the move resulted in lower sales costs, reduced market-entry costs, and shorter sales cycles.[24] IBM even went so far as to modify its physical facilities by assigning its sales and marketing departments to a common office space.

Finally, the allocation of the firm's rewards, incentives, and resources must be based upon the new culture and a new values statement must be written, clearly stating the new cultural values. In the early 1990s, for example, the North American branch of Alberto-Culver, which manufactures Alberto VO5 and other personal care products, developed a list of 10 cultural imperatives: honesty, ownership, trust, customer orientation, commitment, fun, innovation, risk-taking, speed and urgency, and teamwork. After the list of imperatives was agreed upon, one group member suggested the acronym HOT CC FIRST, which made these values easier to remember.[25] Perhaps most importantly, cultural values have to be put into practice at all levels. Otherwise, all the time and money invested in culture change will be in vain.

How External Cultures Affect a Firm's Sales Force

To be successful in the global marketplace, sales organizations and sales managers have to understand and work in national cultures that are characterized by distinct values, norms, and attitudes. The increasing level of global business occurring around the world requires that sales managers and their employees understand cultural differences in order to work together and prosper. The key is to understand cultural differences and take advantage of the broader perspectives they offer in terms of finding managerial solutions. For example, sales managers must understand that in the United States, workers are generally encouraged to act individually, whereas in most Asian societies, group business decisions are more likely to be made. Also, it is considered healthy behavior in Western societies to compete for promotions and incentives. In other cultures, however, salespeople try to maintain group harmony rather than competing with one another.[26]

The likelihood of developing interpersonal relationships increases when salespersons and managers are sensitive to different cultural practices. For example, when a salesperson enters a sales meeting with a potential customer from a different culture with a general understanding of that person's cultural beliefs, the salesperson's words, actions, and body language can be tailored to maximize the potential of successfully interacting with that individual. Likewise, understanding other cultures allows sales managers to behave correctly in global sales situations, which will minimize conflicts and build better relationships with both customers and their sales team.

The Different Levels of Culture

A level of **global culture** appears to be emerging as consumers worldwide are exposed to the same movies, the Internet, cable/satellite television, MTV®, and magazines that advertise global brand products. This creates a class of consumers who possess similar knowledge, needs, and wants about the goods they purchase. However, when selling to potential buyers from distinct cultures, it is naive to believe they purchase in exactly the same way and for the same reasons. For example, even though consumers the world over know about and desire global brands like Gateway®, Lexus®, and Cartier®, they are most likely to purchase these products based upon distinct influences and purchase processes learned in their home or national cultures.

National culture has the greatest impact on buyer behavior and, as Exhibit 15.4 shows, consists of five distinct dimensions common to all countries.[27]

- Power distance is the acceptance of unequal power and authority relations in society. Some cultures, such as China, Malaysia, Slovakia, and the Philippines, accept larger power distances between members of society and the organization, which impacts buyer-seller relationships and selling contexts. In other words, some cultures view the parties involved in social interactions to be equal or unequal. Power distance levels define the roles played by members of that culture, including those played by salespeople. When dealing with owners, managers, or scientists from cultures with large power distances, it is imperative for a salesperson to act respectfully and use formal titles unless instructed otherwise. U.S. egalitarianism does not play well in these cultures.

EXHIBIT 15.4

Dimensions of National Culture

- **Uncertainty avoidance** defines how a society reacts to uncertainty and ambiguity. The higher the level of perceived ambiguity, the greater the society's need for well-defined rules dictating people's behavior. For example, in Japan, Greece, and Portugal, all aspects of a business arrangement must be clearly stated and all eventualities explored before a deal is finalized. In these countries, a firm will be reluctant to change suppliers until it is convinced a potential new partner is trustworthy and dependable. In other cultures, like Singapore, Denmark, or Sweden, there is less fear of uncertainty. By contrast, in Asia, lower-level managers will agree to a business arrangement, after which there will be a banquet attended by the firm's top executives, who sign or ratify the formal agreement.

- **Individualism/collectivism** means that some cultures are more group oriented than others in their decision process. Individualism is a major characteristic of U.S. culture, but in Asian cultures group cohesion and safety are important aspects of business decisions. Thus, no single manager will make a decision unless the group has been consulted and consensus is reached. There is an old Chinese proverb: "The duck that flies in front of the formation gets shot down," which provides insight about how people feel about individualism in that culture. Buyers from cultures that rate high in collectivism are unlikely to accept "hard closing" salespersons.

- **Masculinity/femininity** describes the traits valued by a society. Masculine traits are stressed in China and Slovakia and include strength, success, and confidence. Feminine traits are most commonly found in Sweden and Norway, and they encompass nurturing, relationship-building, and improving one's quality of life. In masculine cultures, individuals view wealth-building as a primary goal—a goal that's less important in feminine cultures. As a result, salespeople from masculine cultures tend to be more responsive to financial sales incentives than sales reps from feminine cultures.

- **Long-term orientation** focuses on virtues oriented toward future rewards, like thrift and perseverance.[28] Asian cultures rate highest on long-term orientation. For example, firms in the United States focus on short-term sales and profits, like those earned during the current quarter or year. By contrast, in Japan, corporate goals and views are more long term, meaning 5 or 10 years into the future. Thus, gaining trust and forming relationships does not occur quickly in long-term-oriented Asian cultures.

Although sales managers and salespersons often have a broad understanding of different national cultures, they are surprised when cultural dilemmas fall outside the five dimensions we discussed earlier. Three examples provide a clearer understanding of behavior that falls outside national cultural norms: First, the culture of the United States is characterized by low uncertainty avoidance. By contrast, Japanese culture is high on uncertainty avoidance. However, when legal agreements are drawn up by Japanese firms, there are intentional ambiguous clauses written into the agreements; conversely, U.S. agreements are written by attorneys, and every potential contingency is covered. Second, U.S. culture ranks as one of the highest for individualism, yet U.S. citizens report the highest rate of philanthropy in the world.[29] Lastly, although Japanese culture is rated high in collectivism, visitors to Japan are often surprised to see Japanese businessmen on subways reading magazines that contain nude photos and violent stories. Therefore, rather than expecting Hofstede's general dimensions to precisely explain individual behavior, you need to take the specific context of the situation into account.[30]

Local culture is found in different geographical regions, cities, and neighborhoods. It, too, influences the behavior of buyers and sellers. For example, when selling to New Yorkers, the buyer will likely want the salesperson to quickly state the point of the meeting so as not to waste their time. By contrast, getting to the point too quickly in traditional southern U.S. culture without first making small talk is more likely to be considered acting rudely. Telemarketers who call upon different regions of the United States learn this cultural practice very quickly!

The Components of Culture

It is very helpful for a sales manager and their salespersons to understand the following eight components that characterize a culture before attempting to sell or manage in it. The aspects include the culture's:

1. Communication style(s)
2. Religion(s)
3. Education levels
4. Aesthetics
5. Social Organizations
6. Technology
7. Time
8. Values and Norms

Communication Style

A major area of cultural conflict is attributable to ineffective communications. Communication problems are sure to occur unless the sender of the message understands the receiver's culture. How people communicate varies widely within and between cultures. Across cultures, words and phrases are utilized differently. For example, in the Philippine culture, "yes" can mean "yes, I will consider your product" to "yes, I hear you." Also, members of certain subcultures may speak more loudly or with more emotion. Think about animated discussions that occur between African-, Jewish-, or Italian-Americans. Americans from different backgrounds often perceive discussions like these to be hostile rather than exciting conversations between friends![31]

CROSS-CULTURAL COMMUNICATION PROBLEMS A number of common communication problems complicate cross-cultural interactions: carelessness, multiple meaning words, idioms, and slang. *Carelessness* occurs when the salesperson is not properly prepared and speaks extemporaneously—almost ensuring the likelihood of misspeaking. In this situation, an unprepared salesperson uses a word not understood by the customer or makes insensitive remarks. Words can also have *multiple meanings* in different cultures. For example, if you were to say *the motor runs smoothly* in the United States, few people would misunderstand you. In other cultures, buyers would take you literally by wondering, for example, how it was possible for a Chevrolet "Nova" to run smoothly when "nova" translates to "no go" in Spanish. *Idioms* are words that have no literal translation. If a salesperson were to say, "Our product is the Cadillac of the industry," "it is raining cats and dogs," or "I'm under the weather," these phrases have no translatable meaning to someone from another culture. Likewise, "comparing apples and oranges" is a common sales metaphor that can be translated literally by a buyer who has yet to master the American lexicon. Lastly, there is *slang*. An example occurs when a buyer asks the seller: "What's the *damage* for the product?" meaning how much does the product cost? When salespersons employ careless words, use inappropriate words, idioms, or slang, *noise* is generated that reduces the efficiency of communication between individuals from different cultures.

Other differences that a sales manager or salesperson must understand and consider when engaging in cross-cultural communications include:

- The tone of voice: refers to loudness, tone, and clarity of response. In certain subcultures, bargaining between buyer and seller is loud and emotional. Conversely, most Asian cultures perceive loud, emotional discussions as being inappropriate.
- The timing of responses: the length of time one takes to consider the question asked. In the United States, waiting too long to respond may be considered a sign of dishonesty; however, people in Asian cultures generally pause and reflect on an issue before responding.
- Interruptions: Asian cultures in general regard interruptions to be rude. By contrast, French, Italian, and Middle Eastern cultures are comfortable when multiple people talk at once and interrupt each other at will.
- Degree of directness: Asians, Hispanics, and East Indians tend to soften negative responses. Similarly, Japanese buyers might ask a question rather than answer "no." By contrast, many Americans believe that business discussions should be direct, no-holds-barred, discussions.
- Degree of embellishment: In Italian or Middle Eastern cultures, flowery, embellished statements are considered an artistic form of expression. By contrast Americans tend to be more reserved in their language.

A key when communicating with someone who has been raised in another culture is not to breach that culture's rules of etiquette. In other words, it is best for the seller to mirror the buyer's communications behavior. If the buyer speaks slowly, listens intently, is less direct, and does not embellish, the seller should mirror their presentation to the buyer's communication pattern.

Also, cross-cultural communications can differ depending upon the directness of the words. In **low-context cultures**, like the United States, words are used exclusively to communicate what is meant. If something is left unstated, the receiver of the message does not necessarily assume that they should read between the lines. In high-context cultures, like those found in Asia and the Middle East, details and specifics are left unsaid, and the receiver must gain insight through nonverbal communication.

When humans communicate nonverbally, the unstated is often as, or more, important than what is clearly articulated. Nonverbal communications are therefore important for both the buyer and seller and can include:

- Appearance: different cultures have distinct expectations about facial hair and attire that includes formality of dress. Europeans tend to dress more formally than Americans.
- Posture: involves how a person sits or stands. In Asian cultures, a person of lesser status does not tower over or turn their back on a superior. In low power distance societies, like Scandinavia, such actions are viewed to be less important.
- Space/Distance: the physical distance between the customer and the salesperson. Americans generally prefer a larger "zone of comfort" around their bodies than do Latin Americans, for example. Middle Eastern males and Hispanics operate in spaces of 0 to 18 inches. By contrast, most Americans and Western Europeans feel comfortable in zones of 18 inches to three feet. Asians generally prefer a space of three feet or greater.
- Sense of smell: refers to body odors and colognes/perfumes. In certain cultures, strong body odor is accepted; in other cultures, body odors are viewed as being offensive.

- Hand gestures: can mean something other than intended. The O.K. sign in the United States is considered offensive in most European nations. When conducting business or eating with customers from Arab nations, using your left hand is considered rude.
- Handshakes: Americans are more likely to shake hands firmly, whereas the British are more likely to shake hands softly. Hispanics are more likely to offer a moderate handshake and a frequently repeated grasp.
- Physical contact: in Spanish cultures, friends touch constantly. However, in most Asian nations, touching is seldom observed and almost never practiced on the head. This is particularly true in Thailand.
- Eye contact: prolonged or direct eye contact is considered aggressive in some cultures, while it is a sign of honesty in others.
- Body angles: refers to how one positions themselves relative to others. For example, in Japan, the person with the least status, such as the salesperson, bows lower than the customer. In addition, one should never turn one's back on or tower over a superior in Asia.

There is little doubt that the better informed and educated salespersons and sales managers are about verbal and nonverbal customer communications, the fewer mistakes will be made. The goal in all sales encounters is to avoid words or actions the customer might perceive to be offensive or inappropriate. Once you offend a customer, no matter how unintentional, it can be very difficult and expensive to repair the damage. By understanding nonverbal communication patterns, the seller can not only better comprehend what the buyer says, but what they mean, especially during negotiations.[32]

Religion

Your religious beliefs have an important bearing on your actions, including what you drink, eat, the hours or days you're available for work, and how as a buyer you interact with salespeople, your coworkers, and members of the opposite gender. This means that a Moslem or Jewish customer observes or celebrates different holidays than Christian salespersons. For example, buyers who abstain from consuming specific foods and drinks due to their religious beliefs will need to be taken to restaurants that offer vegetarian and kosher meal choices. This topic could be incorporated into sales training sessions based upon the cultural composition of the marketplace. It is also recommended that the salesperson ask the customer where they would like to eat or if the intended restaurant is acceptable for lunch or dinner.

Educational Levels

In some cultures, a salesperson will not be accepted unless they possess an educational level similar to the buyer. This attitude exists because education, social class, and occupation are mutually inclusive in most cultures.[33] Customers from these cultural backgrounds expect their salesperson to be equally educated so that complex issues can be discussed and potential solutions can be offered. For example, one German-born researcher at a prestigious institution refused to speak with salespeople who did not possess a Ph.D. in chemistry. If a salesperson sells to cross-cultural customers who are influenced by education, they should consider earning a certified sales designation, such as "Certified Professional Salesperson," and ensure that their degree and certification—if it is relevant—are clearly displayed on their business cards.

Aesthetics

Each culture perceives different objects to be beautiful and visually appealing. Thus, how a person dresses, appreciates artwork, and presents food is impacted by one's

Sales managers need to coach their salespeople to be aware of the fact that their customers' religious beliefs and customs could be very different than their own. (Shutterstock)

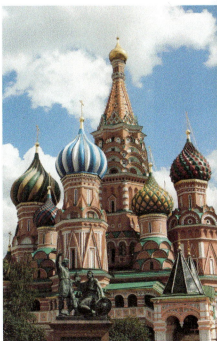

In terms of the presentations they make to their customers, salespeople need to realize that aesthetics like colors, shapes, and what's considered to be beautiful and visually appealing differ from culture to culture. (Shutterstock)

culture. When a salesperson makes a sales presentation or develops sales promotional materials, cultural aesthetics like colors and shapes should be carefully considered. For example, several U.S. firms placed Arabic writing and the flag of Saudi Arabia on products and advertisements, only to learn that *Allah* had been blasphemed! This means that colors, styles, and shapes must be carefully considered before making a presentation or printing proposals that could offend the potential customer. For example, in Asian countries, white is the primary funeral color, whereas gold and yellow colors suggest wealth, authority, and longevity.[34]

Social Organizations

Social organizations comprise the social groups to which a person belongs. These associations include one's family, community groups, special interest groups, and work groups. In cultures that rate high on collectivism, membership in the correct social groups is extremely important. Difficulties can arise when a salesperson from a blue-collar area calls upon primarily white-collar customers. When this happens, the words used and social graces employed can severely strain a potential working relationship. This means that in certain cultures, buyers will only purchase from salespeople that have been accepted into their inner circle.

Technology

It is important for the salesperson to understand the technological sophistication and limitations of potential customers. In many corporations today, engineers who occupy technical positions within global firms have emigrated from other nations. To improve the chances of selling successfully to these people, it is important for salespersons to possess at least a similar level of technological expertise. Moreover, some cultures favor hard work over modern conveniences. For example, immigrants from Asian and Eastern European countries expect to work long and hard hours to succeed and are not impressed by the latest electronics that promise to save them time.

Not all cultures are as impressed by technological gadgets as are Americans. (Photo Researchers, Inc.)

Time

The observation of time varies by culture. In modern cultures with efficient transportation systems, it is important to arrive promptly for meetings. However, in less developed cultures, time is viewed more relatively. This means the customer is less concerned about time, so the salesperson must be adaptable and understanding when the customer forgets appointments or arrives late. One salesperson was surprised, when arriving early for an appointment with a Panamanian-born customer, to learn that the buyer was still out for lunch and wasn't expected back for at least half an hour!

This cultural component can also include the time it takes for buyers and sellers to form a relationship, develop trust, and conduct business with one another. For example, female Hispanic business owners take more time to make decisions. Minorities also tend to take longer to make decisions, but pass on more referrals. Thus, a salesperson should expect to make additional calls to minority decision makers before attempting to close a sale![35] Italian business managers are likely to spend a considerable amount of time on small talk during sales meetings. By contrast, Scandinavians prefer a short, formal introduction immediately proceeded by a business discussion.[36]

Values and Norms

All cultures have rules or norms of acceptable and unacceptable behavior that can include:[37]

- Hard work as opposed to relaxation or leisure.
- Egalitarian decision making as compared to patriarchal decision making.
- Conservatism in contrast to liberalism.
- Female submissiveness versus female liberation.
- Ethnocentrism as opposed to polycentrism.
- Youthfulness versus maturity.

Sales managers and salespeople must be sensitive to the distinct values and norms practiced by buyers from different cultures. In general, a number of cultures view female salespeople as less credible. This means that customers from the Middle East or certain Asian cultures may have more difficulty interacting with female sales managers. For example, in Japan there is a saying: "Women are like the air, absolutely essential, but they should remain invisible." However, research shows that U.S. female expatriates are just as successful as their male counterparts overseas, even in male-dominated cultures like Korea and Japan![38]

Many cultures view their way of doing business as being the only way (ethnocentric) rather than one of many ways of conducting commerce (polycentric). Buyers and sellers who are **ethnocentric** are more rigid, whereas those who are **polycentric** are more flexible in their business dealings. A form of **corporate ethnocentrism** also exists within very large firms where sellers are expected to adopt the Wal-Mart® or General Motors® way of doing things.

Ethnocentrism occurs when we interpret the actions of others in the context of our own culture. For example, mainline American culture suggests that a dishonest person will avert looking directly into another person's eyes. However, in Asian cultures, a common cultural belief is that it is aggressive to look someone directly in the eyes for an extended period of time. When we evaluate the behavior of others based upon what we know, we use a **self-reference criterion**. The self-reference criterion through which we evaluate others is composed of our customs, institutions, and ways of thinking. Thus, we evaluate others based upon what we have learned and come to believe is true in our own culture.

There is nothing inappropriate about preferring our own cultural practices, but potential problems arise when we distort how we view others. This is especially true for salespeople who call upon buyers from other cultures and, as a result of their ethnocentrism, misinterpret what is said or not said. For example, in the United States, it is considered "normal" to make friends quickly and share intimate details of our lives with our new friends. In other cultures, however, friendships are formed very slowly. Consequently, attempting to form a new friendship so casually is viewed as being frivolous or even rude.

How does one overcome ethnocentrism? The first way to reduce ethnocentrism is to learn about other cultures. That is, learning to recognize and understand the values that motivate people from different cultures to behave the way they do. With this knowledge, it becomes easier to apply what you have learned to future sales situations you encounter. This awareness allows you to understand why an Asian- or African-American buyer takes longer to form a relationship rather than prematurely dismissing the potential customer as someone who is not ready to commit to a relationship with you and your company. A second way to overcome ethnocentrism is to become more aware of the beliefs that can distort your perceptions and cause you to misinterpret your customers or sales team. In effect, learning about your own cultural beliefs allows you to recognize the incorrect analysis that we engage in when we encounter behavior influenced by another culture.

Managing the Global Sales Force

As the forces of globalization expand the scope of international marketing and commerce, sales managers find themselves supervising salespersons from different cultures that reside around the globe. For example, a U.S. firm might be headquartered in New Jersey with branch offices located in London, Paris, Berlin, Delhi, Singapore, and Tokyo. As discussed in the first section of this chapter, aligning a firm's internal culture with the marketplace is not easy. Operating in multiple locations, with managers and salespersons representing myriad cultures, makes it difficult to employ a single system to supervise salespersons. This is due to different behaviors and motivations that exist in countries and cultures. Even with diverse personnel and practices, sales managers are expected to supervise diverse sales forces from afar with expertise and aplomb. This section presents major differences that arise when sales managers are called upon to design, select, train, motivate, compensate, and evaluate a global sales force.

Designing the Global Sales Force

Sales managers must initially base their decisions on how best to organize a global sales force by understanding the needs of current and potential customers, the targeted market, competitors, and the firm's strengths and resources. Although these criteria mirror the information used to design the sales force in the home market, sales managers must decide whether it would be more beneficial to employ expatriates, local hires, or third-country salespersons to work in global locations. Each category of salesperson offers advantages and disadvantages for the global sales force.

Expatriates are salespersons who move from the home country to an overseas location. An example would be a British citizen who worked for a British firm being reassigned to Nairobi, Kenya, to oversee the sales efforts in that African nation. The benefit of employing an expatriate salesperson in a foreign market is their knowledge of the product line and familiarity with company policies. The major disadvantages of employing an expatriate salesperson are lack of culture/market knowledge and cost. The vice president of Coca-Cola® Japan stated that the cost of assigning him to Tokyo in the early 2000s exceeded more than $1 million annually. **Local hire salespersons** are individuals who live in the country where business is conducted. For example, Procter & Gamble® could hire a salesperson from Shanghai, China, to work in the local marketplace. Advantages of local salespersons include lower costs and higher cultural and market knowledge. Disadvantages include poor product and company knowledge. The final category of salesperson to work in a global marketplace is a **third-country salesperson** or an individual hired who was born outside both the firm's home and targeted markets. For example, a Japanese firm might hire a salesperson from the Philippines to work in Singapore. Third-country salespersons normally possess a higher-level understanding of the marketplace and culture than expatriates and are willing to work for a lower salary. Disadvantages of third-country salespersons include less influence with the home office and potential burnout from working overseas for extended periods.

A few generalizations can be made in regard to designing and entering overseas sales territories. When establishing new territories in emerging markets that are undeveloped and small in sales volume, firms often partner with local sales firms to handle their product line. Partners save the external company money because they know and are known in the marketplace. If the marketplace is large enough to sustain a company sales force, firms may begin with a geographical organization that utilizes a general salesperson to sell a narrow product line. However, as the market grows or if different cultures/languages are spoken, the sales organization must be reorganized as a product or market sales force to match different buyer needs.[39]

Because of different cultural practices, the way personal selling is organized has to match local expectations.[40] For example, automobiles have been sold door-to-door in Japan for decades, and Russian banks recently assigned salespersons to sell credit in appliance stores. Also, more than 100,000 citizens of Singapore participate in multi-level marketing product sales.[41]

Selecting Sales Personnel

In global sales situations, the attributes of an effective salesperson may rival that of a diplomat! Therefore, it is essential for sales managers to precisely define what they are looking for in a global salesperson. Attributes that come to mind include maturity, flexibility, breadth of knowledge, cultural empathy, and a positive outlook. Most of these skills and attitudes can be assessed during the personal interview and during role-playing exercises. The few studies that have been conducted in the hiring of global salespersons suggest that selection criteria should be localized.[42] A major problem encountered by global firms is that in many cultures sales is not viewed as a professional occupation. As a result, highly qualified individuals will often not apply for sales positions.

In the United States sales applicants are expected to sell themselves during the personal interview. When U.S. sales managers conduct a personal interview with a candidate from another culture and expect the applicant to ask for the job, they are likely to be disappointed. This is because in many cultures the applicant only speaks when the interviewer asks a direct question. Secondly, the applicant may not make or maintain direct eye contact with the interviewer. As stated earlier in this chapter, staring at strangers may be viewed as an aggressive act.

Hiring mistakes are extremely costly in international sales situations. When a global salesperson does not work out, hundreds of thousands of dollars and significant amounts of time are wasted. Recent research found that a manager's cultural knowledge affects personnel decisions. That is, given identical personnel information, German and Austrian managers were more likely to hire compatriots than were Italian managers.[43] This finding suggests the need for additional research to be conducted to improve our understanding of global hiring practices.

S   **SELF-ASSESSMENT LIBRARY**

It is extremely expensive and time consuming for a company to select and transfer a sales manager and his or her family abroad. What happens all too often is the sales manager or the person's family is unhappy in their new assignment, and, as a result, the manager either leaves the firm or fails to complete the two- to three-year assignment abroad. Have you ever considered how well you would do while working in another country or culture? To learn your suitability for an overseas assignment, go to http://www.prenhall.com/sal/ and log in using the access code that came with your book. Then click on:

Assessments
   III. Life in Organizations
     B. Careers
       5. Am I Well-Suited for a Career as a Global Manager?

Training Global Salespeople

International sales training can be either standardized or localized. That is, when a local or third-country salesperson is hired, sales training must provide them with product knowledge, company information, and sales skills. Even after receiving training, it is common for local salespersons to cling to local culture as is seen today in China and Russia.[44] Trainers must also employ different instructional methods when teaching sales methods in other cultures. For example, American trainers observed that Japanese trainees would not voluntarily respond to questions addressed to the entire class for fear of being labeled a "show-off." However, when asked directly, the Japanese trainees would answer so as not to embarrass their American trainers.[45] For expatriates who are selected to sell in an overseas market, their training must focus on understanding culture and special sales problems.

Technology now allows global sales forces to be trained more efficiently. Sales personnel can study modules on the Internet and then complete an interactive assessment test. Sun Micro Systems states that employing the Internet can shorten training time by up to 75 percent. Also, in nations where there are limited communication systems, firms have adopted CD ROM–based training approaches.[46] Technology is best used to transfer standardized information, such as product information, but it is more appropriate to localize and personally teach sales techniques.[47]

Motivating Global Sales Personnel

Devising a motivation system for global sales personnel is complicated by the presence of distinct cultures, sources, and philosophies.[48] Global sales managers and salespersons work hard and, like all personnel, experience frustrations when traveling, interacting with buyers from other cultures, and being away from their families. No matter, the global salesperson must remain motivated to perform at high levels. It is important, therefore, that a firm's motivation system be designed for global sales personnel based upon their national culture.

Remember earlier when we discussed Hofstede's components of national culture? A major difference between sales personnel in different cultures can be observed in the individualism/collectivism component of national culture. In the United States, firms motivate salespersons by appealing to their individual ability to work hard and succeed. As a result, Western companies focus on individual pay systems and rewards to motivate their sales personnel. In Asian cultures, however, collectivism or a group orientation plays a major role and a willingness to compete against one's peers is less acceptable. As a result, most Asian salespersons are paid a straight salary and can earn a bonus for group achievements. Individual commission systems are rarely implemented in collectivistic cultures.

The opportunity for growth within the company is also a motivating factor. Therefore, it is important for global sales personnel and managers to understand that success in the current job will lead to an attractive position within the firm once an overseas assignment is completed. For example, in 2007, the consumer goods giant Unilever began slashing 20,000 employees from its ranks worldwide. As a result, salespersons began wondering, "Where have all the jobs gone?" Unilever is in a quandary about how to make the needed personnel cuts while keeping their managers and salespersons motivated.[49] It is also wise for headquarters to communicate with global sales managers and to seek their input about decisions that affect them. Nearly all managers feel more motivated when they believe they are well informed and that their opinions are important. However, in global sales the forces of language, culture, and communication styles can complicate effective communication between managers and sales reps.[50]

Compensating Global Sales Personnel

Because global firms operate in multiple locations, it is nearly impossible to offer a single compensation plan that is fair, balanced, and flexible. As a result, compensation plans for American companies vary widely.[51] Most salespersons and sales managers expect to receive a higher salary in overseas posts than they make in the United States. One important reason that expatriates receive higher salaries is that they often have to maintain two homes or places of residence—one in the location abroad and another in the home country. Global firms realize that it is important for expatriates to receive a salary that reflects their new responsibility, allows the family to live comfortably in a secure area of the overseas country, and permits the expatriate to entertain local employees and customers.

However, the firm incurs a number of additional expenses that include international schools for the expatriate's children, annual vacation travel to the United States, helping the expatriate maintain their U.S. home, and providing added security in certain overseas locations. In contrast, European sales managers receive higher benefits and deferred compensation in their salary packages.[52]

Evaluating Global Sales Personnel

In many overseas markets, the sales force is evaluated based upon their performance as a team rather than as an individual. In contrast, most U.S. sales personnel are given a quota and then they are evaluated based upon their performance compared to expected performance. As a result of this difference in sales situations, global sales managers must accompany the salesperson on sales calls to observe their performance and seek inputs from buyers, other salespersons, and supervisors. Unlike U.S. sales managers, global sales managers may view individual performance measures as being less important.

In one study that contrasted U.S. and Japanese sales managers' evaluations of their salespersons using the same performance scales, American sales managers rated most of their sales staff in the middle of the scale with a few high performers and no low performers. Japanese sales managers, on the other hand, rated their sales team along a normally distributed curve: a few high, a few low, and most salespersons placed in the center of the scale. What is instructive from this study is that poorly performing U.S. sales personnel are forced to leave the firm—either voluntarily or involuntarily. In Japan, firms continue to employ lower-performing sales personnel. A problem for Japanese sales managers, not faced by most American sales managers, is how to motivate poor performers.[53]

Lastly, domestic sales managers often have trouble understanding expatriate situations or accurately measuring their contribution to the organization. Until recently the physical distances between sales manager and expatriate made direct communication difficult. This problem has been minimized by affordable telephone services, e-mail, instant messaging, and company CRM systems. Even with greater sources of information, firms resort to measuring "easy" criteria like profitability, productivity, or market share to measure expatriate success rather than considering the expatriate's full range of responsibility. Thus, especially in global sales situations, different sales goals require different assessment criteria.[54]

Changing Demographics and Diversity in the Sales Force

In the United States and other industrialized countries of the world, **multiculturalism** or the presence of multiple groups of people that are representative of different cultures, races, languages, and religions live together in a single country or area of the nation. For example, by 2050 less than half the U.S. population will be Caucasian in comparison to 69 percent in 2000.[55] Hispanics have become the largest U.S. "minority" group, moving

Sales managers today know that to sell successfully to a more diverse customer base, they need a diverse sales force. (Compassionate Eye Foundation/Robert Kent/Getty Images/Digital Vision)

past African-Americans who for hundreds of years comprised the largest minority group. To date, little research has evaluated the performance of minority salespeople. However, anecdotal reports suggest that minority salespeople perform similar to salespeople as a whole and that more minority salespeople are being promoted to management positions.

Multiculturalism is prompting the senior managers of firms to adopt **diversity initiatives**—initiatives aimed at doing business with and hiring people from multiple cultures. CEOs know that as the demographics of a nation shift, to remain competitive they must diversify in order to meet the needs of their diverse customer bases. Business scholars suggest that there is a relationship between a diverse workforce and firm performance[56] and that when managed correctly diversity leads to competitive advantage.[57] For example, Coca-Cola® and other U.S. firms have long selected senior executives from among their best global managers.

Previous generations of immigrants to the United States pursued a strategy of assimilation that revolved around blending into the majority culture and becoming "American." Today, however, U.S. residents from other nations are culturally integrating without losing their identities. As a result, most firms view multiculturalism as a strength that allows the company to consider and resolve opportunities from multiple viewpoints and implement strategies that are appropriate for a multicultural marketplace. In this way the firm can maximize the entire range of talent and experience of a diverse workforce.

Most companies understand that demographic shifts in the population and the global economy result in a more diverse workplace and the need to engage customers and workers from different cultures. Globalization means that more firms are developing, manufacturing, and marketing products and services worldwide. In response to global business and the need to understand and succeed in different cultures, many firms have formed strategic alliances to pursue common goals. Likewise, workers in the global economy are encountering more diverse customers and employees than in the past. The crucible for sales executives is to recognize that, based upon their unique backgrounds, salespeople from diverse cultures bring added value and strength to the sales team—even though managing a diverse group of individuals is more complicated.[58]

The Benefits of Embracing Diversity

There are multiple reasons that firms and their sales forces should embrace diversity. From an ethical and moral perspective, embracing diversity is the right thing to do because it is inclusive and fair. Also, embracing diversity is a legal requirement in the United States, with historical precedents—firms may not discriminate based upon race, gender, or national origin.[59] Also important is the fact that shifting demographics and globalization forces have changed the composition of firms' sales forces and customer bases. As a result, firms are feeling pressure to change their perspectives and practices toward diversity. Other benefits are as follows:

- Hiring a diverse workforce can offer the firm a sales and marketing advantage. Managers today believe that a diverse sales force can better understand and serve a diverse customer base. Sellers who share similar cultural traits with buyers often form stronger relationships.[60]
- Supporting diversity can reduce a firm's total costs. Salespeople who feel valued for what they can contribute will experience greater job satisfaction and longevity with their firms. Thus turnover and hiring costs should be lower.

■ Hiring a diverse workforce is believed to lead to more creative problem solving and decision making. This is because diverse groups of workers are more likely to suggest creative solutions to problems than homogeneous groups. One study reported that innovative companies reported higher levels of diversity than noninnovative firms.[61]

Despite these benefits, diversity can cause negative outcomes unless a firm's strategy is properly managed. This is because the greater the percentage of diverse workers, the higher the likelihood of cultural conflict taking place. Oftentimes people from minority and majority groups feel more comfortable interacting with individuals similar to themselves. However, in a business organization, all workers—regardless of their race, gender, religion, or sexual orientation—must interact and work together or a firm's effectiveness suffers. When cultural interpersonal conflicts occur, the sales manager must spend valuable time resolving them. Thus, being able to effectively manage conflict is a requirement for firms that aspire to perform at a high level and profit as a result of their diversity. To overcome the obstacles to diversity that exist, the following are measures sales managers must take:

■ The barriers of prejudice, stereotyping, and ethnocentrism that were discussed earlier in this chapter must be replaced by a philosophy of equal opportunity and value.
■ The firm's human resource policies, its hiring, training, promotion, compensation, and retirement policies, must be evaluated to ensure they are culturally and gender neutral. When the policies prevent a diverse workforce from succeeding, changes must be made. HR programs must be initiated that offer minorities an opportunity to move into upper management.
■ Managers must ensure that minorities, both salespersons and sales managers, are invited to participate in activities both within and outside the company. Otherwise minority employees will feel alienated and their rate of turnover will accelerate.

To individual salespeople, an organization's climate refers to how the work environment "feels" to them. For example, do they feel like they fit in? Do they feel like they have an equal chance to succeed? One study suggests that 50 to 70 percent of a firm's climate is attributable to its leadership.[62] Therefore, sales managers are encouraged to assume a leadership role of embracing, supporting, and advancing diversity in the workplace.

Summary

Culture is both a micro- and a macro-force that influences how a firm operates in today's global economy. That is, from a micro perspective, a firm's internal culture determines sales team attitudes and behaviors, the work environment, the treatment of new salespersons, and how managers interact with their employees. When a firm's internal culture is aligned with its external strategy, studies show that firms are more profitable. Likewise, a firm's internal culture determines attitudes toward embracing diversity and ensuring that cultural differences are factored into work rules, policies, and managerial practices. From a macro perspective, national culture impacts everything we do. Stated differently, national culture determines how employees and customers think, act, and purchase. As the United States becomes more diverse and engages in increasing levels of global trade, the cultural impact on most business relationships will increase.

Sales managers play important roles in aligning internal cultures with external strategies. Sales managers align internal sales cultures by taking symbolic actions and making substantive decisions. For example, a sales manager might symbolically adopt a major customer to provide outstanding service while modifying internal policies and replacing current salespersons that do not possess needed skills, knowledge, and attitudes necessary for future success.

Sales managers and salespersons are more likely to succeed in today's diverse marketplace when they understand their own ethnocentrism; they must also be aware that culture impacts how buyers view sales calls, interpersonal communications, and relationships. This is particularly true for sales managers who direct and control sales assets that are located around the globe. Cultural differences complicate the design, selection, training, motivation, compensation, and evaluation of overseas salespersons and sales managers. Lastly, the sales force, customers, and partners are becoming more diverse as the demographics of the U.S. population continue to change. As demographics shift, company policies and practices must remain current in order to offer equal opportunity to all sales personnel. If a firm is to succeed in the diverse marketplace of the future, the sales force must be a reflection of the buyers that they serve.

Key Terms

corporate culture 346	market-oriented 347
corporate ethnocentrism 359	masculinity/femininity 354
culture 346	multiculturalism 363
diversity initiatives 364	national culture 353
entropy 350	polycentric 359
ethnocentric 359	power distance 353
expatriates 360	product oriented 347
global culture 353	production-oriented 347
high-performance culture 348	relationship marketing oriented 347
individualism/collectivism 354	sales oriented 347
internal alignment 352	substantive actions 351
local culture 355	symbolic actions 351
local hire salespersons 360	self-reference criterion 359
long-term orientation 354	third-country salesperson 360
low-context culture 355	uncertainty avoidance 354

Questions and Problems

1. Explain what constitutes a corporate culture. Why might some employees view culture as the "water in the fishbowl" of their daily activities?
2. Explain the five orientations a firm can adopt and the impact they have on its sales force. What impact will they have on the sales force's relationships with other functional areas within the firm and the firm's customers?
3. Why might a firm's sales and marketing functions be misaligned? What are the consequences of a misaligned culture?
4. When a sales force's group values differ from the rules, regulations, and managerial systems in place within the firm, describe the type of gap that can develop.
5. Contrast how firms with high-performance corporate cultures operate versus firms with low-performance cultures. How does a sales manager change a low-performance culture to a high-performance culture?
6. Explain the role sales managers play as creators of culture.

7. What types of actions can a sales manager take to increase the probability of successfully interacting with someone from a different culture?
8. Discuss how nonverbal communication might impact sales situations.
9. Why is it important for sales managers to understand their own tendencies to be ethnocentric?
10. How does culture impact the management of the global sales force in regard to designing a sales organization, selecting, training, motivating, compensating, and evaluating outside the home country?
11. How will the increasing diversity of the U.S. population affect how firms hire and manage their sales personnel and sell to potential clients?
12. Offer several reasons why a sales manager should embrace diversity.

Role Play

Expatriate Pay and Benefits at RPG, Inc.

James Ford is the global sales manager for RPG, Inc., a company that manufactures consumer goods in the United States and Europe. For the past decade RPG has assigned expatriates to sites in Europe that include London, Madrid, Rome, and Oslo. When the dollar was strong, most expatriate sales managers were able to live comfortably in their respective locales. However, with the adoption of the euro in most EU countries and the decline of the dollar, expatriate sales managers are complaining loudly about the "difficulty" of living overseas.

Ford realized he was no expert on expatriate expenses and compensation, so he approached an expatriate consulting firm in Boston, World Assignments. Currently each expatriate manager receives a salary that is 40 percent higher than their U.S. salary that is increased by an inflation factor each year. For example, last year the inflation increase was 4.2 percent. The managers also receive a housing and food allowance. The four expatriate sales managers recently sent a joint letter to Ford expressing their frustration with their inadequate salaries and asking that some action be taken as soon as possible to rectify their situation.

Ford is sympathetic to the complaints of the expatriate sales managers, but he also feels living abroad for three years in choice assignments should be perceived as a reward in itself. Ford has scheduled a meeting with Gerry Jones, RPG's human resource director, and Helen Rheil, a consulting manager at World Assignments to analyze the current compensation system and recommend changes to the firm's overseas pay policy, if warranted.

Characters in the Role Play

James Ford, global sales manager at RPG, Inc.

Gerry Jones, human resource director at RPG, Inc.

Helen Rheil, expatriate consultant at World Assignments

Assignment

Break into groups of three, with one student in the group playing each character. Do not be concerned about matching the gender of the character with the actual gender mix of the student group. Prior to meeting as a group, work individually to summarize and support your own recommendations for a revised compensation system for expatriate sales managers at RPG, Inc. Then meet as a group and role-play the meeting between James,

Gerry, and Helen. The goal is to conclude the meeting with a unified recommendation for offering a fair and equitable compensation system to RPG's sales managers in Europe.

Caselet 15.1: Long Island Manufacturing

Jim Johnson is the new sales manager for Long Island Manufacturing (LIM), a supplier of products for restaurants in the greater New York City area. Johnson spent the first month of his tenure at LIM analyzing the culture of his new firm. He's noticed that although the company sets annual and quarterly goals for its sales force, penalties aren't imposed when the goals are not met. Also, salespeople appear to meet their sales goals late in the performance period by negotiating lower prices with their customers. In addition, accounts often receive poor customer service. Jim Johnson realizes that if he is to change the firm's sales culture, he must take action.

Questions

1. What actions would you recommend that Johnson take?
2. How difficult will it be for Johnson as he attempts to realign the internal culture with LIM's external strategy if the firm's upper managers don't support his actions?

Caselet 15.2: China Enterprises N.A.

China Enterprises N.A. is a distributor of goods manufactured in China. The company sells its products to U.S. wholesalers and "big box" retailers like Wal-Mart, Target, and Kmart. China Enterprises is located near the Port of Los Angeles and employs 32 salespeople who are geographically assigned across the United States. When the firm first opened, experienced salespeople were hired who had existing relationships with wholesalers. Later, as China Enterprises began to sell to big-box retailers, employees were assigned to work at the headquarters of these corporations.

After more than 20 years, China Enterprises has a number of field salespeople who are of Hispanic and Asian heritage. Likewise, a large number of customer service and support employees within the China Enterprise's Los Angeles headquarters are first- or second-generation Americans whose parents immigrated to the United States from Asia and Mexico. The national sales manager at China Enterprises is John Aquino, a first-generation Filipino-American. Aquino is a proud American. All three of his children are college graduates of prestigious U.S. universities, and he feels that his sales team and customer service reps are hardworking and want to advance within the firm. Because it's an international firm, China Enterprises has embraced diversity and always hires the best candidate for the job, regardless of the person's race, gender, religion, or national origin. However, Aquino feels he needs to analyze the firm's HR policies and practices to ensure that current and future salespersons will not be discriminated against and that everyone has opportunity for advancement within the firm.

Questions

1. What policies should Aquino examine with regard to hiring, training, evaluating, and compensating his sales force and customer service employees?
2. What managerial practices should Aquino consider?
3. What other functional areas within the firm should Aquino work with during and after the study is complete?
4. Why is such a study necessary?

References

1. Gunn, B. (2000). "Illuminating Culture," *Strategic Finance Magazine* April, (18)10: 14–16.
2. McLarney, C., and E. Chung (2000). "What Happened is Prologue: Creative Divergence and Corporate Culture Fabrication," *Management Decisions* (38)6: 410–419.
3. Featherly, Kevin (2006). "Culture Shock," *Sales & Marketing Management* January/February, 45–48.
4. Honeycutt, Earl D., Jr., John B. Ford, and Antonis Simintiras (2003). *Sales Management: A Global Perspective*. London: Routledge.
5. Jap, Sandy D. (2001). "The Strategic Role of the Salesforce in Developing Customer Satisfaction across the Relationship Cycle," *Journal of Personal Selling & Sales Management* Spring, (21)2: 95–108.
6. Wellins, Richard S., Charles J. Cosentino, and Bradford Thomas (2004). "Building a Winning Sales Force," *Development Dimensions International, Inc.* Winter, 6.
7. Duncan, W. Jack (1989). "Organizational Culture: Getting a 'Fix' on an Elusive Concept," *Academy of Management Executive* 3, 229–236.
8. Sherwood, J. J. (1988). "Creating Work Cultures with Competitive Advantage," *Organizational Dynamics* (winter), 5–27.
9. George, Bill (2003). *Authentic Leadership*. San Francisco: Jossey-Bass.
10. Ibid.
11. Sorensen, J. B. (2002). "The Strength of Corporate Culture and the Reliability of Firm Performance," *Administrative Science Quarterly* March, (47)1: 70–91.
12. Beaudan, E., and G. Smith "Corporate Culture: Asset or Liability? Merging Two Cultures," *Ivey Business Journal* March–April, (64)4: 14–16.
13. Kotler, Philip, Neil Rackham, and Suj Krishnaswamy (2006). "Ending the War between Sales & Marketing" *Harvard Business Review* July–August, 68–78.
14. Shapiro, Benson (2002). "Want a Happy Customer? Coordinate Sales and Marketing," *Harvard Business School Working Knowledge* October 22, 2007. Retrieved on April 19, 2007, from: http://hbswk.edu/item/3154.html.
15. Schemerhorn, John R., Jr. (2008) *Management*, 9th ed. Hoboken, NJ: John Wiley & Sons, p. 94.
16. Kotler, Rackham, and Krishnaswamy (2006).
17. Barrett, Richard (2006). *Building a Values-Driven Organization*. Amsterdam: Butterworth-Heineman.
18. Chonko, Lawrence B., and John J. Burnett (1983). "Measuring the Importance of Ethical Situations as a Source of Role Conflict: A Survey of Salespeople," *Journal of Personal Selling and Sales Management* (3)1: 41–47.
19. Hosford, Christopher (2006). "Rebooting Hewlett-Packard," *Sales & Marketing Management* July/August, 32–35.
20. Sims, R. R. (2000). "Changing an Organization's Culture Under New Leadership," *Journal of Business Ethics* May, (25)1: 65–78.
21. Neuborne, Ellen (2003). "Bright Ideas," *Sales & Marketing Management* August, 26, 28–30.
22. Schein, E. H. (1992). *Organizational Culture and Leadership,* 2nd ed. San Francisco: Jossey-Bass.
23. Neuborne (2003).
24. Kotler, Rackham, and Krishnaswamy (2006).
25. Bernick, Carol Lavin (2001). "When Your Culture Needs a Makeover," *Harvard Business Review* June, (79)6: 53–61.

26. Honeycutt, Earl D., and Lew Kurtzman (2006). *Selling Outside Your Culture Zone.* Dallas, TX: Behavioral Science Research Press.
27. Hofstede, G. H. (1984). *Culture's Consequences: International Differences in Work-related Values.* Thousand Oaks, CA: Sage.
28. Hofstede, G. H. (2001). *Culture's Consequences: Comparing Values, Behaviors, Institutions, and Organizations across Nations.* Thousand Oaks, CA: Sage.
29. Lussier, Robert N., and Christopher F. Achua (2003). *Leadership: Theory, Application, Skill Development.* Eagan, MN: Thomson Corporation.
30. Osland, J. S., and A. Bird (2000). "Beyond Sophisticated Stereotyping: Cultural Sense-making in Context," *Academy of Management Executive* (14)1: 65–79.
31. DuPraw, Marcelle E., and Marya Axner (1997). "Working on Common Cross-Cultural Challenges," Topsfield Foundation. Retrieved May 28, 2008, from: http://www.pbs.org/ampu/crosscult.html.
32. Reynolds, Nina, and Antonis Simintiras (2000). "Toward an Understanding of the Role of Cross-Cultural Equivalence in International Personal Selling," *Journal of Marketing Management* 16, 829–851.
33. Hofstede, Geert (1991). *Cultures and Organizations.* London: McGraw-Hill.
34. Hodge, Sheida (1998) "Feng Shui: A Realtors' Guide for Increased Sales to Asians," *Professional Training Worldwide.*
35. Chang, Julia (2003). "Multicultural Selling," *Sales & Marketing Management* October, 26.
36. Lewis, Richard D. (1996). *When Cultures Collide: Managing Successfully Across Cultures,* Boston: MA: Nicholas Brealey Publishing Limited.
37. Jandt, Fred E. (2004). *An Introduction to Intercultural Communication.* Thousand Oaks, CA: Sage.
38. Caligiuri, Paula M., and Rosalie L. Tung (1999). "Comparing the Success of Male and Female Expatriates from a U.S.-based Multinational Company," *International Journal of Human Resource Management* October, (10)5: 763–782.
39. Honeycutt, Ford, and Simintiras (2003).
40. Johansson, Johny K., and Ikujiro Nonanka (1997). *Relentless: The Japanese Way of Marketing.* New York: Harper Business.
41. Cateora, Philip R., and John L. Graham (2007). *International Marketing.* Boston: McGraw-Hill Irwin, p. 502.
42. Ibid.
43. Rouzies, Dominique, Michael Segalla, and Barton A. Weitz (2003). "Cultural Impact on European Staffing Decisions in Sales Management," *International Journal of Research in Marketing* (20)1: 67–85.
44. Cateora and Graham (2007).
45. Marken, James A., and Earl D. Honeycutt, Jr. (2008). "Utilizing Activity Theory to Plan Cross-Cultural Sales Training," *National Conference in Sales Management Proceedings,* 1–6.
46. Cateora and Graham (2007).
47. Jantan, M. Asri, Earl D. Honeycutt, Jr., Shawn T. Thelen, and Ashraf M. Attia (2004). "Managerial Perceptions of Training and Performance," *Industrial Marketing Management* October, 33, 667–673.
48. Neelankavil, James P., Anil Mathur, and Yong Zang (2000). "Determinants of Managerial Performance: A Cross-Cultural Comparison of the Perceptions of Middle-Level Managers in Four Countries," *Journal of International Business Studies* (31)1: 121–140.
49. Ball, Deborah, and Aaron O. Patrick (2007). "How a Unilever Executive is Thinning the Ranks," *Wall Street Journal* November 27, B1, B3.

50. Mintu-Wimsatt, Alma, and Julie B. Gassenheimer (2000). "The Moderating Effects of Cultural Context in Buyer-Seller Negotiation," *Journal of Personal Selling & Sales Management* Winter, (20)1: 1–9.

51. Piercy, Nigel F., George S. Low, and David W. Cravens (2004). "Consequences of Sales Management's Behavior- and Compensation-Based Control Strategies in Developing Countries," *Journal of International Marketing* (12)3: 36–57.

52. Honeycutt, Ford, and Simintiras (2003).

53. Money, R. Bruce, and John L. Graham (1999). "Salesperson Performance, Pay, and Job Satisfaction: Tests of a Model Using Data Collected in the U.S. and Japan," *Journal of International Business Studies* (30)1: 149–172.

54. Bohlander, George W., and Scott A. Snell *Managing Human Resources,* 14th ed. Mason, OH: South-Western, pp. 670–673.

55. U.S. Census Bureau (2004). "U.S. Interim Projections of Age, Sex, Race, and Hispanic Origin," www.Cenus.gov/ipc/www/usinterimproj/.

56. Kahn, J. (2001). "Diversity Trumps the Downturn," *Fortune* July, (144)1: 114–116.

57. Gilbert, Jacqueline A, and John M. Ivancevich (1999). "Organizational Diplomacy: The Bridge for Managing Diversity," *Human Resource Planning* (22)3.

58. Honeycutt, Ford, and Simintiras (2003).

59. Orlando, R. C. (2000). "Racial Diversity, Business Strategy, and Firm Performance: A Resource-Based View," *Academy of Management Journal* (43)2: 164–177.

60. Berta, D. (2002). "Mixing it Up: Diversity Good for Business, Confab Finds," *Nation's Restaurant News* August, (36)34: 1, 103.

61. Kahn (2001).

62. Watkins, C. (2001). "How to Improve Organizational Climate," *People Management* June, (7)13: 52–53.

PART SEVEN

CASES

Jerry Kollross contributed many of the cases in this section of the textbook. Kollross is the president and owner of Top Golf Products and an adjunct instructor at the University of Wisconsin, Eau Claire, and the University of Wisconsin, Stout. He has held sales and sales executive positions with a number of U.S. firms, including Innomark Communications, Golf USA, *The Bradenton Herald,* and the American Printing Company.

Case Studies

Case Study 1
The Plantation
Planning, Setting Goals, and Team Selling

Case Study 2
Lexington Industries
Conducting Business Ethically in the Pacific Rim

Case Study 3
The San Francisco Giants
A CRM Case Analysis

Case Study 4
TIP Financial Services Corporation
Managing a Field Sales Force

Case Study 5
Wellco Distributors
Considering a Diversity Program

Case Study 6
Pacific Medical Supply Company
Hiring, Motivating, and Retaining Good Salespeople

Case Study 7
Southeastern Sales Associations
Evaluating and Coaching Salespeople to Improve Their Performance

Case Study 8
Afgar Corporation
Managing Multi-channel Sales

Case Study 9
Freedom Telecom
Setting New Sales Goals to Turn the Sales Force Around

Case Study 10
The Sarasota Journal
Inevitable Change and the Restructuring of the Sales Force

Case Study 11
Concord and Associates
Evaluating a Sales Territory

Case Study 12
Cannon Associates
Achieving Internal Alignment among Your Old and New Sales Forces

CASE STUDY 1

The Plantation
Planning, Setting Goals, and Team Selling

Roger Owens was the successful owner of 50 Jiffy Lube oil change stations in the Atlanta area. He built his business from the ground up over a 30-year period and always considered himself to be a savvy businessperson until now. Despite Roger's success in the oil change business, he was on the brink of filing bankruptcy. His financial difficulties stemmed from his involvement as the only stakeholder in a golf course residential property being developed near Lake Oconee, Georgia, which is located about an hour east of Atlanta.

Roger owned a cabin on Lake Oconee for many years where his wife and three daughters spent their weekends during the summer. Before the property values in and around the lake started to rise, Roger bought a large piece of land with 1,000 feet of lakeshore frontage as an investment. His speculation that land values would rise paid off 15 years later when he sold the parcel for a substantial profit to the Ritz Carlton Hotel chain. A five-star Ritz Carlton resort now sits on the property.

With the profits Roger made from his land sale, he reinvested in a 300-acre property that had limited access to Lake Oconee but offered panoramic views of it. It was Roger's dream to build a golf course and housing development on the property for Atlanta families looking for summer recreation and second homes. The name of his development was the Lake Oconee Plantation, and it was to be his legacy.

During the research and development phase of Lake Oconee Plantation, Roger solicited experts in their field for advice but chose to manage the development of the project himself and keep the costs to a minimum whenever he could. He built his oil change business by being as efficient as possible, and he was using this same business formula in his new venture as a developer. His first priority was to build a golf course and clubhouse that would serve as a magnet to attract second-home buyers to the area. The 230 half-acre home sites were to be located on and around the pristine and lush 18-hole manicured layout, which he aptly named The Plantation Course.

The signature hole of the course was carved out of the sandy soil right next to the valuable lakeshore frontage of Lake Oconee. The large, white, plantation-style clubhouse had views of the lake from the dining room and pro shop. When The Plantation Course and clubhouse opened to the public, it was considered one of the best new courses in eastern Georgia and made *Golf Digest*'s Top 100 new course list. The cost of constructing the lots, course, and clubhouse and putting in roads stretched Roger financially. Unforeseen cost overruns and upgrades to the course and an irrigation system had cost millions of dollars. Everything Roger owned was leveraged against the Lake Oconee Plantation development.

In the first year the course opened, it sold 22,000 rounds of golf and 20 club memberships. However, it still failed to break even and lost $200,000. The second year saw a slight increase in rounds played and memberships, but the financial results were similar to the first year. This put Roger further into the red. The housing sites around the course were selling slowly at a clip of only two per month. At the current sales rate, it would take over nine years to sell out the remaining home sites. Only six homes were completed or under construction on the 30 home sites that had been sold.

Roger did not have nine years to wait for the balance of the home sites to be sold. He was under pressure from the bank to generate more revenue; otherwise they were going to foreclose on the property and force Roger to sell all of his assets as part of the personal guarantee he signed when he took out the loan. Roger's relationship with the bank had become very contentious. What started out as a professional business relationship with high hopes of wealth for both sides had become a nightmare and created sleepless nights for Roger. Communications between Roger and the bank were taking place by registered letters sent to Roger's attorney. Roger had hired a bankruptcy attorney to examine the language of his loan and to better measure his financial options. The bottom line according to Roger's attorney was that cash was needed, and the sooner the better. For the first time in Roger's long successful career, his back was to the wall.

Roger's window of opportunity to turn around his fortunes was small. If he could increase the sales rate of the home sites to eight to ten per month, he could keep up on his bank payments and fulfill his loan obligation. Additional revenues would also be generated as more homes were built on the vacant lots and residents became members of the club. The new residents would help to increase the food and beverage sales in the clubhouse and would also increase the total rounds of golf sold. If everything fell into place and memberships increased, the golf course operations could start to make a profit within two years.

Beth Owens, Roger's daughter, graduated two years ago from the University of Georgia in nearby Athens. She had a business administration degree with an emphasis in marketing. Beth had worked for her dad since graduation. Her role was to market and sell the home sites in the Lake Oconee Plantation Development. Roger had promised Beth a position in his development venture years ago when things were still in the idea stage. Most of the communication between Beth and her father was centered on how difficult things were in the second-home market. Increasing interest rates, falling home values, and ballooning adjustable rate mortgages were putting pressure on the market. Beth had no idea on how to counter this economic trend.

Roger had insulated Beth from the full seriousness of the situation, however. He never put any pressure or time frames on her for selling the home sites. He kept all of his financial difficulties to himself and painted everything in a positive light to his family and friends. Even Roger's wife Irene had no clue that everything they owned was on the line and about to come crashing down. Roger loved his daughter and thought the world of her, but he knew a drastic change needed to be made in the sales and marketing of the home sites if his dream was going to pay off. Beth would need to be replaced with some experienced sales and marketing professionals.

After interviewing four different real estate sales and marketing firms, Roger decided to hire the Royal Group out of Augusta, Georgia. The Royal Group was owned and operated by Dan Cross. Dan and his wife started their company 10 years ago and, in that time, had worked on over 20 different successful developments across Georgia and South Carolina. Roger liked Dan's confidence and the team approach to selling he laid out in his presentation during the interview.

Dan looked younger than his 45 years and dressed impeccably. He was a consummate salesperson, a good listener, and spoke with a great deal of thought. He assured Roger he would be the one doing most of the closings on the housing sites. This gave Roger great confidence. During the interview, Roger was very upfront on what needed to be done and the critical time line he was under. It was the first time Roger really admitted to someone other than his attorney that he was in financial trouble. Roger also explained that the home sites were competitively priced for the area, and the target market he was trying to capture was young, affluent families who golfed.

At no point during the interview did Dan ever waver in his confidence that the sales targets Roger laid out could not be accomplished in two years, given the pricing structure of the lots and current market conditions. Dan laid out his fee structure to Roger. The

Royal Group would be paid a 15 percent straight commission on all closed sales and a $10,000 per month retainer that would be renewable every six months during the two-year contract, providing Roger's sales goals were being met. The Royal Group would also be allowed to solicit area builders to build spec homes at a discount of 20 percent on 20 of the remaining lots. Finally, any lot that sold at a $10,000 premium would receive a golf-course membership that would be attached to the deed of the land. The normal cost of a full golf membership was $20,000.

Roger agreed to all of the terms of the contract with the Royal Group after consulting with his attorney and reviewing the numbers. If the contract with the Royal Group continued for the entire two years and all of the lots sold, Roger could fulfill his loan obligations and own the course outright. With the contract signed, Dan's team went to work on implementing their plan to sell the remaining 200 home sites in a 24-month time frame.

The Royal Group was a lean operation that consisted of Dan, his wife Sara, Jim Thompson, and Kimberly Southworth. Each of the four members played an important role in the success of the business. Dan and his wife were the field team who spent much of their time (Wednesday through Sunday) on-site. Sara greeted customers and gave tours at the property site, while Dan was the closer and deal maker. Jim and Kimberly worked back in the Augusta home office on the marketing and customer service of the properties they represented. Jim had expertise in design and print production as well as Web site development expertise. Everything that had to do with marketing the property would be driven by Jim. Kimberly was in charge of all incoming calls and mailings. She acted as the point person to direct inquires or questions to Dan or Sara.

All four team members worked seven days a week. If a call came in outside of normal business hours, it rolled over from the main number to the cell phone of whoever was on call that day. The group had a rule that a prospect would always hear a live friendly voice answer the phone. Everything within the organization was built on gaining the trust of customers to the point where they became members of the Royal Group family. When Dan and his wife started the company 10 years ago, they realized the key to a successful sales operation was to treat each customer lead like it was their only one. The other part of their ongoing success was a goal to close 50 percent of the customers who visited their properties. Dan believed that if prospective customers said "no," they simply meant not now. He also had quite an ego when it came to sales. He felt like he could close anyone if given enough time. He measured his closing ratio on every development. He had a solid 43 percent closing ratio over his last five development contracts.

The first step the sales team took was to develop a strategic sales and marketing action plan for the Lake Oconee Plantation development. A quick start was needed to meet the goal of selling 200 home sites in only 24 months. In order to develop an effective plan, Dan needed to know what had transpired over the past two years while Beth Owens was in charge of The Plantation's sales and marketing efforts. Dan worked through Roger to set up a meeting with Beth at the sales trailer located on the property. Dan knew this would be a difficult and uncomfortable meeting, but he needed to find out what kind of information Beth had compiled that may help his team develop its strategic plan. He spent the first hour of the meeting just getting to know Beth. He had her talking about her days at school in Athens, her interest in Braves baseball, and her upcoming wedding, which was going to take place on The Plantation grounds.

As part of Dan's meeting plan, he put together a list of questions he needed answered. His goal was not to seem threatening but to make Beth feel she had all the answers. Once she warmed up to him, she was a wealth of information. She provided him with all of the answers to his list of questions. She had also recorded the resort's customer traffic per day and even had the weather conditions of each day summarized. Beth provided records of bulk mailings, prospect phone calls, pending contracts, current property owners, local builders, and three sets of lead lists (a hot list, a warm list, a cool list). Each of her three lists had copious notes about the prospective buyers. Between all three lists there were over 80 names.

By the time Dan left the meeting with Beth, he sensed she was relieved to turn over all of the information to Dan. Although Beth was well organized and thorough in her role in sales and marketing, Dan hypothesized that the problem might lie with her lack of sales ability. Beth was very young and very much entitled; everything that came out of her mouth was pretentious. She even referred to herself in the third person, saying, "Beth will have a wedding everyone will be talking about." Dan concluded that customers probably got turned off by Beth and her "it's about me" attitude.

Based on the information provided by Beth, the members of the Royal Group team broke the needed sales down into a month-by-month plan so they knew exactly how the ebbs and flows of sales would take place. For example, after working through the following lead data provided by Beth (see the following chart), they forecasted they could close 30 sales per month (one per day in the busy summer months of July and August) and only five sales per month in slower months like December and January.

Beth's Qualified Sales Leads by Month (from previous year)

Jan	Feb	Mar	Apr	May	Jun	Jul	Aug	Sep	Oct	Nov	Dec
10	16	28	32	41	66	102	98	30	12	15	9

As the following chart shows, they also set their goals based on how many quality leads it would take to sell 200 home sites in two years and ranked the leads on a low- (25 percent), medium- (35 percent), and high- (50 percent) probability closing ratio. They always planned for a worst-case (low) closing scenario when developing their marketing budget.

Royal Group's 12-Month Sales Goals Based on Sales Leads Generated and a 25 Percent Closing Ratio

Jan	Feb	Mar	Apr	May	Jun	Jul	Aug	Sep	Oct	Nov	Dec
Total Sales Leads Generated											
20	30	40	45	50	80	120	120	40	20	20	20
Total Sales Leads Closed											
5	7	10	11	12	20	30	30	10	5	5	5

The team would regularly review and adjust its marketing budget as sales started to come in because each property had its own unique characteristics. As a general rule, most of the marketing budget was spent on the front end to generate a buzz around the property. The initial budget would always include a new Web site, brochures, and the purchase of a clean lead database that was segmented by a customer's income, age, and profession. After the lots started selling, a referral program with existing buyers was used to generate high-quality leads. The referral leads were contacted by Dan or Sarah by phone and with customized mailings or e-mails as a follow-up.

The second step the team members employed was to create a hook to get things off to a fast start. The goal they laid out was to sell 150 of the home sites during the first 12 months, so getting things off on the right foot was paramount to their success. Dan referred to this as the "cowbell" effect. He had grown up in Wisconsin and, as a child, witnessed how when one cow discovered something fascinating or tasty, the other cows quickly followed. Dan had used his cowbell theory in many of his other residential development sales plans with success.

In the case of this property, he would use two approaches. His first was to sell local builders lots at a 20 percent discount on a first-come, first-served basis, if they would start building spec homes on their purchased properties within six months. The second part of his plan was to attach a 50 percent discount golf-course membership to 20 of the best available properties. The memberships would be attached to the deeds of the properties, so anyone who bought an existing home in the future would have an automatic membership to The Plantation Course. Dan was not concerned about any competitive influences in the area or the slump in the housing and financial markets. He felt strongly that if his company stuck to its strategic plan and made adjustments to its marketing as necessary, all of the home sites would be sold within the two years Roger wanted.

The third step in the team's action plan was to spruce up the grounds around the point of sale. Rather than greet customers in the sales trailer Roger's daughter worked out of, they made a quick deal with a local builder to construct a spec home by granting a 20 percent discount on the land and a free membership. The spec home would be rented (cost equal to the mortgage) by the Royal Group for two years and then be turned back over to the builder. The builder had 90 days to complete the home, which would be used as the new sales office. The home would also be landscaped, and area decorators and furniture stores would provide furnishings at no cost to the model for visitors to view. The Royal Group also staked the properties with more visible markers and put up premium custom-wood signs to replace the flimsy small plastic signs that were previously planted on the lots.

The next-to-last step was to plan the sales process. This included the pre-approach, approach, tour, close, and follow-up of potential clients. Even though the Royal Group team members were experienced in real estate sales, this step was always tailored for each property they worked at. The final phase of the sales plan was "The Dan and Sara Show," as Kimberly and Jim put it: Once potential customers contacted Dan or Sara, they would receive a handwritten note from either Dana or Sara inviting them to the area. The note also included a very clear set of directions to the property and a map.

Customers were then telephoned following the correspondence as the bond- and rapport-building process began in earnest. Once prospective customers arrived on the grounds, both Dan and Sara greeted them like family and offered them coffee or tea with fresh fruit, cheese, and crackers. Sara even made fresh-baked cookies on some occasions. They focused their conversations on the customers' needs and desires. Once Sara toured the available properties with the customers, they were invited to come back and sit down with Dan to discuss the specifics of owning a property.

Dan was the master closer once Sara left the room after giving him some indication of the customer's interest in a property. Sometimes it was just her eye contact that told Dan what he wanted to know. Everything was done to make the customer feel comfortable. However, Dan was clearly in charge of the close at all times. The follow-up after the sale fell into Sara's hands. She would send a plant or a bottle of wine with a card welcoming the new families to The Plantation. The card always contained both Dan and Sarah's cell phone numbers, which customers were told they could call at any time if they had questions.

Part of Dan's philosophy when he built his sales team was to have all team members do what they enjoy most. He figured most people enjoy what they do best, so it made sense to have each person on his team become great at doing a specific task. For Sarah it was meeting new people and the bond and rapport process, for Jim it was the creative process, and for Kim the role of traffic controller suited her fine. Dan, of course, was the ultimate closer.

QUESTIONS

1. Do you believe the team sales approach in this case would work in other sales organizations? Why or why not?

2. Are past sales successes of an organization always good indicators of new sales opportunities? What questions would you have asked Dan Cross during the interview process if you were Roger Owens?

3. How well would the "cowbell" theory used by Dan Cross work in other sales and marketing organizations? Give an example of such an organization.

4. How critical is it to know what your sales goals are before a sales action plan is put together? Why do Dan and his team members reengineer their sales process for every property they are involved in?

5. Do you agree with Dan's assessment that competition and other outside influences like interest rates have little impact on sales if everything in the sales and marketing action plan is executed to perfection? Explain your answer.

6. Dan surrounds himself with experts who love what they do and do it well. What are some possible negative effects the group could experience as a result of being so specialized?

7. Is Roger Owens the ultimate customer in this case for the Royal Group? Or are there others? Explain your answer.

CASE STUDY 2

Lexington Industries
Conducting Business Ethically in the Pacific Rim

"These illicit payments have to stop!" Those were the exact words Ted Harrison, a sales representative for Lexington Industries, said as he dined with his wife Susan at a five-star restaurant in Taipei, Taiwan's exclusive business district. Harrison was not speaking of illicit payments (bribes) by his own company, but rather the business practices of his foreign competitors. In the last two years alone, he had lost 80 percent of the bids he submitted in Pacific Rim countries for rebar steel contracts. Rebar is a common steel reinforcing bar, an important component of reinforced concrete and reinforced masonry structures, like bridges and buildings.

Ted had seen plenty of his foreign competitors' corruption during his time overseas. The playing field was not level because his company was based in the United States and had to comply with the U.S. Foreign Corrupt Practices Act, which prohibits businesspeople from offering bribes to win sales contracts or gain influence. Ted and Susan had been living in Taiwan for three years and had witnessed the growing U.S. business presence there. He also had seen many U.S. companies leave the region because they were unwilling to risk the legal repercussions that might result from offering bribes and kickbacks to foreign governments and companies in China. Ted estimated the amount of lost business for U.S. companies in the region to be in the tens of billions of dollars in just the last three years.

Lexington Industries was a major steel producer in the United States and wanted to expand into China and other Pacific Rim countries that were building and using a lot of steel rebar to construct buildings and infrastructure. Lexington was a midsized, nimble steel company that had grown its business by using recycled steel from aftermarket steel suppliers and lean manufacturing principles. The firm had grown rapidly. However, in recent years the growth had slowed, and investors were putting pressure on the company's executives to deliver higher returns on their stock holdings.

At one time, Ted was Lexington Industries' top domestic salesperson. He was considered a master at developing business relationships and was dubbed the "rainmaker" by executives because of the way he brought in business—like rain. Ted was well compensated for his sales efforts and for his move to Taiwan. He was determined to be as successful in the global marketplace as he was in the U.S. market.

Ray McMahon was the vice president of sales for Lexington Industries and was growing impatient with the lack of contracts coming out of Ted's territory in the Pacific Rim. Ray sent Ted an e-mail expressing his dissatisfaction. He also said some of the company's top-level executives were starting to doubt Ted's abilities and were questioning his generous compensation package and expense account. Ted fired back an e-mail the next day reminding Ray that the lack of sales was not due to the lack of opportunities to bid on contracts, but his inability to bribe officials to secure the contracts. He finished his e-mail by saying he was afraid his hands were tied. "Untie your hands and just get it done," Ray wrote back.

Feeling that he had just been given the green light to conduct business on a level playing field, Ted wasted no time contacting one of his customers, Fiju Construction. He had just submitted a bid to Fiju the day before, and the contract was still pending. Over the phone, Ted asked his customer what it would take to guarantee his getting the contract. "1 million Chinese yuan," said his customer.

"Done," Ted replied. The contract was signed and delivered to Ted the next day. He then sent an e-mail to Ray telling him that the Fiju contract was accepted, and he would need $127,364 (the equivalent of 1 million yuan) wired to Fiju Construction no later than the end of the week.

Ted did not hear from Ray. Friday came and went, so he attempted to call Ray at his office on Monday morning. After reaching Ray's assistant, he found out Ray had been fired. Ted also learned Ray was under investigation for conspiracy to commit fraud in a domestic bribery case. His assistant went on to say she thought Ray was the only person under investigation at this point, but officials were still investigating and had seized his computer.

After Ted hung up the phone, he wondered when the other shoe would drop.

QUESTIONS

1. How can U.S. companies compete globally if laws such as the Foreign Corrupt Practices Act are in place?

2. Do you think Ted Harrison should have bribed Fiju Construction? Should he tell his company what he did? Explain your answer.

3. Do you believe Ted should have disregarded Ray's e-mail message telling him to "untie his hands"? Or should he have clarified its implications with Ray? Explain your answer.

4. Research how U.S. companies that bribe their customers are brought to justice. What is the likelihood of their being caught?

5. What other foreign-market entry barriers might U.S. companies run up against? Do you think it's possible other cultural barriers hampered Ted's sales in Taiwan?

6. From a management standpoint, how much time should a salesperson be allowed to penetrate a new market? Was Ray being fair in questioning Ted's skills as a salesperson after only three years? Explain your answer. Would your answer be different if the salesperson were attempting to penetrate a domestic market? Explain your answer.

7. Look up the Web site for the Organisation for Economic C-operation and Development (OECD) at www.oced.org and explain what actions they take to reduce the corruption related to foreign transactions.

CASE STUDY 3

The San Francisco Giants
A CRM Case Analysis*

The San Francisco Giants mission statement reads:

> "The San Francisco Giants represent innovation, professionalism, and excellence on and off the field. We're dedicated to serving our customers, providing a high-quality entertainment experience, and enhancing our value as a community asset."

On April 11, 2000, the San Francisco Giants moved into their new home ballpark, AT&T Park. AT&T Park is the first privately financed ballpark in major league baseball since the Dodger stadium in 1962. The Giants' president joined the executive vice president and chief operating officer to implement an ambitious financing plan that concluded with 29,500 season ticket holders, including 15,000 charter seat members (only three other times in the franchise history had the Giants sold more than 10,000 season tickets). The stadium seats a total of 41,503 people. Dan Quill, like everyone in the Giants organization, has responsibility for some customers, but his primary responsibility is information technology (IT). In that role, he manages the Giants' CRM implementation in the club's ticket office, which is in charge of Giants ticket sales. Other ticketed events held at AT&T Park are outsourced to other companies.

Sales Force and Marketing for the Giants

The Giants, sales force is divided into three different departments. The downstairs group works with renewal accounts (old season ticket holders). Their job is to retain existing season ticket holders. There are currently six sales representatives in the renewal group who are responsible for reselling 10,000 season ticket holders. The average revenue from renewal season ticket sales is $21 million. The ballpark is broken into six sections acting as the sales representatives' territories, so each rep is tasked with filling a section in the stadium.

Next, the upstairs group is in charge of new season ticket sales and group sales (new ticket sales). This group develops new leads, converting as many as possible into new season ticket sales or selling group events. The upstairs group operates more under a sales automation system versus a CRM solution.

At times, the needs of the two ticket groups are the same, but most often they are different. For example, the renewal group customer list doesn't change very often, whereas the sales group changes all the time. The last group is a separate sales team that works with sponsorships related to the Giants. Since the number of accounts they manage is rather small, Dan has not worked on any technology solution for this team.

The History of the Giants' CRM System

In 2000, 10 reps were dealing with a pool of 10,000 season ticket holders. The Giants were using a CRM system called Pandesic that the team had purchased. This system was used by both ticket sales groups, although it was mostly oriented toward the renewal

---

*This case was prepared by Scott Stack and Jacqueline Simpson under the direction of Dr. John F. Tanner, Jr. Some information has been changed to enhance the pedagogical value of the case.

group. Pandesic gathered customer data, such as e-mail addresses and other customer data. Before 2000, the 10 reps had only 15 percent of their season ticket holders' e-mail addresses. After Pandesic was introduced, the number of season ticket holders' e-mail addresses kept on record had increased to 80 percent. Pandesic had a feature that allowed season ticket holders to resell tickets. The Giants called this feature The Double Play Ticket Window, but season ticket holders had to provide a valid e-mail address to participate. This was why the number of valid e-mails increased so quickly.

Shortly after the Giants began using the Pandesic system, the company selling Pandesic phased out the Pandesic line, leaving the Giants with massive amounts of customer data but no way to manipulate it. The company essentially lost all of the data they had. Management learned through their Pandesic experience that the organization and their sales representatives can benefit through a CRM system, but at the same time, they were leery of purchasing anything to replace it. Since they could not use Pandesic anymore, they created a custom CRM system called Profiler 1 for the Giants' renewal group.

Profiler 1 was introduced during 2001–2002. To reduce costs and because of the increased functionality of Profiler 1, the Giants' sales renewal group was reduced to six salespeople who were still responsible for 10,000 total seats. At this point, reps were given customer territories by seating area. Profiler 1 was designed to gather customer information for the Giants' renewal sales group so that they could use the data to increase sales productivity. Examples of the data collected can be seen in Exhibit 1.

As Dan reflected on that experience, a number of problems that were encountered during Profiler 1's implementation came to mind. First, a few salespeople were not utilizing the system as expected. Instead, they were using paper and their own notes as they were before any CRM applications were introduced. So information that could be helpful to other representatives or other departments could not be accessed.

The organization gained participation through persistent mid-process bosses who required the salespeople to use the system. For example, the organization implemented a campaign, based on analyzing data in the Profiler 1 database. A campaign is a subset of people who have particular needs and are targeted for renewal with a specific offer. Reps then had to make calls using the system while keeping the data accurate. Examples of campaigns can be seen in Exhibit 2. The program was made more useful through additional features. Adding campaign features allowed the renewal group to manipulate relevant customer information in order to prioritize the call list. Reps would target specific customers, which ultimately improved renewal sales. The representatives could update customer information, such as e-mail addresses. Also, each call campaign had a beginning date and an end date that was set before the campaign started.

Ultimately the sales representatives were having trouble viewing the data and interacting with the CRM system. As they gained experience, they began demanding more from the system than it was designed to deliver. Through the implementation of

---

EXHIBIT 1

CRM Data Collected in Profiler 1

Customer bio info (name, address)
Customer contact history (all e-mail, outbound phone, inbound phone, in-park visits)
Customer seats
Customer purchasing habits
All bulk e-mail communications, including whether or not customers opened the e-mail and clicked the link (both individually and in aggregate)
Customer seat preferences and upgrade information
All campaigns the customer is active in (as well as historical)
Aggregate reporting on where customers are (i.e., reports on what reps are doing what in summary)
Current sales numbers (tells the reps where they are in relation to their previously set goals)

EXHIBIT 2

Campaigns Conducted within Profiler 1

FRZ Resv—Outbound calls to reservations

Mar05 Buyer—Outbound calls to buyers who purchased in March 2005, but hadn't purchased yet

No Money—Outbound calls to nonpayers

Past Y06—Outbound calls to people who indicated they were interested in season tickets in 2005

Phase—No e-mail: Outbound calls to customers with no e-mail addresses

Phase—No read: Outbound calls to customers who don't have good e-mail addresses

POD—Outbound calls to priority-on-deck customers (these people paid for seasons ahead of getting them)

Reg On Deck—Outbound calls to on-deck customers

Renewal Phase 1—Outbound calls to renewal customers in the first phase of our group sales

Renewal Phase 2—Outbound calls to renewal customers in the second phase of our group sales

Renewal Phase 3—Outbound calls to renewal customers in the third phase of our group sales

Season Leads—Outbound calls to past season ticket holders

Survey Identify—Outbound calls to people who said they were interested in tickets from 2005 questionnaire

Survey Issues—Outbound calls to people who had problems with their seats in 2005

Profiler 1, the Giants recognized the limitations of the system and began designing Profiler 2, which was introduced at the end of 2003. Profiler 1 limited salespeople's productivity because they had trouble manipulating their customers' information. The salespeople needed a system that was more campaign friendly and had better user interfaces.

Profiler 2 included improved interfaces. One helpful addition was text mining. Text mining allows the system to search the customer e-mail database for particular words or phrases. The system saves e-mail as records that can then be searched. As an example, any customer with the words "playoff tickets" in an old e-mail could be e-mailed with a playoff ticket promotion. Text mining such as this allows representatives to select a specific group of customers who could be qualified for different campaigns. The initial training with Profiler 2 was done by an outside agency over a couple of days. Even though the new system had improved functionality, it was again difficult to get the renewal group to use the new system. Dan found that the representatives were not utilizing the information provided by customers' e-mails and were not using the channel as an effective way to communicate. Taking the time to update customer information isn't always useful to a representative, but it is useful to other departments in the organization. Management had to explain how the new system would not only help the ticket organization as a whole, but also the renewal representatives' performance. Even so, since they often did not directly benefit from keeping the data current, the sales teams were reluctant to spend time on data management that could be spent talking to customers. Obviously, all the representatives needed to use the system or the success of the new Profiler would struggle. The Giants had to find incentives for their staff to actively participate.

One strategy involved the creation of a special position called the advocate. The Giants' staff designated one of the six renewal reps as an advocate, and this rep began using the new system six months before it was implemented. As the rep's performance increased, the others naturally wanted to use the improved system.

At the beginning, not all salespeople were equally interested. In some instances, reps were leaving out key data or simply not using the system at all. Managers still had to be firm with some representatives to ensure that full participation was reached. With management oversight, the group fully utilized the system, which led to the completion of 12 different campaigns during the first year. The renewal sales team was vital to the success of Profiler 2. Technical limitations, though, still plagued the system and bothered Dan. Speed within the e-mail application was limiting the representatives' performance. Management functions were also needed, such as reporting mechanisms that allow the tracking of sales rep performance within each campaign. The current system has no reporting capabilities. Dan feels that most of the limitations to Profiler 2 boil down to making data more available to management. For that reason, he is considering a new system, Profiler 3.

Developing a New Sales and CRM Strategy

A key component to any customer retention strategy is to focus on high-risk customers—those that are most likely to stop doing business with the company. By targeting the high-risk customers, the company produces greater sales returns and improves its sales forecast accuracy. However, there was no obvious way to identify those customers most likely to leave.

At the same time, there was little data to identify those who were most loyal. One challenge has been to target the right customers for upgrades, meaning upgrading to a higher-quality season ticket. The season ticket plan prices are as follows: Lower Box $2,772, Left Field Lower Box $2,436, Arcade $2,268, View Box $2,184, View Reserve $1,512, Left Field Bleachers $1,428, Gamer Section (Sections 328–330) $840, and Center Field Bleachers $1,008. One fear is that the Giants are leaving money on the table by not targeting upgrades more effectively. Similarly, Quill's counterpart in marketing, Valerie Stanhof, believes that there are other ways to generate revenue from season ticket holders, through camps, special events, "Bring a Friend" promotions for extra single-game tickets, merchandise, and the like. Right now, the sales reps do not use Profiler 2 for anything other than selling season tickets.

Going into the Giant's seventh year at AT&T Park the Profiler 2 system is at the outer end of its useful life. Although Profiler 2 helped increase the renewal rate of season ticket holders to over 90 percent by the six salespeople, the organization is concerned about managing churn or customer turnover and wants to find a way to keep customers coming to the ballpark.

QUESTIONS

1. What suggestions would you have for Dan to help ensure Profiler 3 is more functional and more smoothly implemented than Profiler 2?

2. What should Dan think about in order to build a system that's more useful across his entire organization? Should the renewal group's CRM system be integrated with other ticket sales departments?

3. What strategies could be used to increase the Giants' customer loyalty? Can you think of a strategy that could be used to increase the Giants' sales revenues outside of the San Francisco area?

CASE STUDY 4

TIP Financial Services Corporation
Managing a Field Sales Force

It was Tuesday, June 1. Don Krane had just left the office of Jack Jensen, his firm's regional vice president of sales. Jack has been the regional vice president for TIP Financial Services in Kansas City, Kansas, for over 20 years. Don manages 50 of TIP's sales associates covering the state of Iowa. He has worked for Jack for the past three years.

During his three-hour drive back to his home in Des Moines, Iowa, Don thought about what had just transpired during his afternoon-long meeting with Jack. The meeting was scheduled by Jack, and the agenda was meant to serve as a wake-up call for Don. He was under pressure to turn things around in his district, which had experienced steadily declining sales during his tenure.

Despite having prepared for the meeting and outlining reasons for why his district was failing and what he was going to do about the problem, Don was told in no uncertain terms that unless things actually turned around in Iowa, he would be let go before the end of the year. As he drove across the Iowa state line, he had pretty much convinced himself that there was no way he could fight the trends plaguing the traditional financial services industry in which he worked. Still, he kept replaying the words Jack expressed to him as he left the meeting. "In my view, *potential* is just wasted talent," he had said. "I still believe in your talent. I like the ideas you presented and am anxious to see if they can work for you." Don appreciated Jack's parting vote of confidence and felt deep down inside that he was a winner and a talented leader. However, he really needed his new plan to "right the ship" in his district.

Background

After graduating with a finance degree from Iowa State, Don had climbed up the corporate ladder while working for an independent, single-branch bank in Des Moines. He started out as a teller and worked his way through a plethora of jobs, including a chief loan officer position and a wealth counselor position. At age 40, he became the bank's president and was featured in several Iowa business journals as a rising star in the state's banking industry.

It looked like Don and his family were leading storybook lives until he learned that his bank was being acquired by a larger national banking institution, and his position would be eliminated. With two kids almost ready to go off to college and a sizable mortgage on a new house built the previous year, Don was determined to use the opportunity to restart his career. He was a firm believer in fate and that when one door closed, another one opened.

Although he was offered several opportunities with other banks in the area, Don wanted to get out of the banking industry because he saw too much consolidation going on. Within two months of being laid off, he accepted a position working for TIP Financial Services as a sales manager for the state of Iowa. Although he had no experience directly selling insurance and financial products, he was very knowledgeable about various financial products from his years in the banking business. He also knew the state of Iowa like the back of his hand, having spent his entire life there. Don embraced the new challenge and was determined to work hard to be an effective sales manager.

TIP Financial Services is based in Chicago, Illinois. It was founded in 1930 as an insurance company that primarily served farm families in the Midwest. Today the company does business in 17 states, although the bulk of business—80 percent—still comes from customers in the Midwest. The firm manages over $20 billion in assets via a network of 4,500 independent contractor agents (called financial consultants) and more than 6,000 support employees. Its financial products include home and property insurance, business insurance, 401k plans, stocks and mutual funds, long-term care insurance, annuities, and financial planning and trust services.

TIP Financial Services is also a member of the Insurance Marketplace Standards Association (IMSA). IMSA's goal is to promote a documented set of high standards covering various aspects of the insurance industry. TIP was a founding member of IMSA. The company even helped write the association's original policies and procedures related to treating insurance customers honestly, fairly, and with integrity.

TIP, in fact, is an acronym for Trust, Integrity, and Performance. The three words still appear in the company's advertising campaigns and are the cornerstone of its selling strategy—providing people in small towns with financial services via qualified financial consultants that live in their communities. The company's financial consultants are well trained, professional, and provide an extraordinary level of service. Having a relationship with one's customers is a top priority for TIP's financial consultants. Every consultant is trained to learn about their customers' needs and goals before identifying potential products to help them meet their objectives.

This was exactly what enticed Don Krane to take the position as sales manager with TIP Financial Services. He was a big believer in high ethical standards and felt the opportunity to work for the company was an excellent fit for him. In his first year, he spent a lot of time traveling to all of the small towns in Iowa meeting the consultants he managed. His group of 50 financial consultants consisted of 47 men and 3 women. Collectively they were a solid group with a few top performers. As is often the case with sales, the 80–20 principle definitely applied in his district: 80 percent of the business was closed by just 20 percent of his financial consultants.

Year Two

By Don's second year, 20 members of his team had turned over. The turnover was simply due to a lack of selling success on the part of consultants. He either fired them, or they left of their own accord. Most of Don's time was now spent recruiting and training new consultants. Very little of his time was spent in the field with his experienced consultants. Still, sales were increasing by 5 percent yearly, and Don was only traveling two days a week as opposed to the four days a week he traveled in his first year, which made things easier on his family. More and more of his communications with his team were being done over the phone or via e-mail rather than through personal visits. Usually the communications were related to problems with existing accounts or changes in policies being dictated by headquarters.

Year Three

In Don's third year, the sales in his district were flat, and he had to replace another 15 consultants. Of the 15 consultants Don replaced in year three, 12 were people he had hired less than 18 months earlier. He had enlisted the use of a recruiter to help him find qualified candidates, but there were fewer and fewer qualified candidates who wanted to relocate to small towns in Iowa.

Year Four

May marked Don's four-year anniversary with TIP Financial Services. It was during this month he learned his job was in jeopardy. He was feeling a lot of stress and starting to lose sleep at night ruminating about work. When the company's first-quarter sales results were released earlier in the month, Don's district ranked dead last sales-wise. To make matters worse, he had just received a disturbing telephone call from his longtime customer Bruce Bowen. Bruce owned a window manufacturing company located in Davenport, Iowa. All of Bruce's business insurance was written with TIP as was his personal life insurance and annuities. Many of his 150 employees were also TIP customers through a 401k TIP offered. Bruce had met Don on one of his many trips to Davenport, and the two hit it off immediately. Both men were golfers and huge Iowa State University Cyclone fans, having attended the college about the same time. They would often meet up to tailgate at Cyclone football games and to play golf.

Bruce was very blunt with Don on the phone. He expressed his displeasure about the young, uninformed TIP representative now servicing his company. He went on to say that the man was his third sales representative in three years, and he questioned why Don couldn't find someone more seasoned who would take the time to learn his business and try to understand his needs. He felt like he was in constant transition when working with TIP Financial Services and needed stability from the firm. Finally, he lowered the boom and told Don he was moving his business to another financial services provider. He just wanted to make sure there were no hard feelings. It was just business, after all.

Shortly after the phone call from Bruce, Don received an e-mail from Jack Jensen requesting a meeting at his office to discuss the status of the Iowa district. In the two weeks leading up to the meeting with Jack, Don did a lot of soul searching as to why his last two years with TIP Financial Services had spiraled downward. After some thought, he came up with three major reasons:

First, it was the financial industry itself. The Internet had spawned many newly formed financial companies offering cut-rate fees. Don felt his company was clinging to a dying business model. Using the Internet, clients could gather information and make transactions anywhere in just seconds. They didn't have to wait for a TIPS consultant to pay them a visit. Indeed, customers were becoming increasingly savvy, and transaction fees within the industry were shrinking. By contrast, TIP Financial Services' overhead remained high as were the commissions its consultants earned.

Second, his younger subordinates weren't willing to work as hard and put in long hours to achieve success. Although Don regularly put in 50- to 60-hour workweeks, many of the consultants working for him reached a certain pay level, became complacent, and would not push for new business. He believed most of his reps probably worked, on average, 30 to 35 hours a week. He called these consultants "silos" because they did just enough to get by and didn't want to be bothered by management. They drove Don crazy.

Financial consultants were expected to make 100 phone calls a day and conduct 15 to 20 personal visits to existing customers or new prospects each week. Many of these visits had to take place from 4 p.m. to 9 p.m. after clients had arrived home from work. Despite the high income a rep could potentially earn—some of the top-performing financial consultants in the Iowa district made $250,000 a year, which nearly equaled Don's compensation—the job simply required more dedication than most people were willing to give.

The third and final reason was turnover. It was easy to figure out why the turnover rate was so high. It was hard for a new consultant to come into a territory. They were first required to go through rigorous training, then learned about their existing customers, and, finally, were expected to grow their client bases by winning new accounts.

Many of Don's new hires burned out on the long hours and the rejection that often came with prospecting for new business. Very few had the thick skin necessary for a career in financial services sales.

The turnover was also a problem because it occupied so much of Don's time. He estimated he spent 60 percent of his time recruiting and training new financial consultants. Don spent the other 40 percent of his time conducting performance appraisals, filling out travel expense forms, corresponding with TIP's corporate office, and helping his consultants with their field problems. He was surprised by how little time he spent working with his experienced consultants and spending "face time" with their customers, who represented the bulk of his business.

Don believed his experienced, successful consultants held the key to his hiring the right people, so he began to create a "profile" of them. He asked himself two questions: Who would I want calling on me? And who would I want to be my mentor if I were just starting out in this business? With these two questions in mind, Don put together his "perfect financial consultant" list of traits, which were as follows:

- Self-motivated and able to work with little supervision
- Knowledgeable about financial products
- Possess an undergraduate degree in finance
- Mature and able to establish relationships with older, wealthy clients
- Has local ties to the community in which he or she works (is a member of the Chamber of Commerce, Kiwanis, Masons, school board, and so forth)
- Service-focused and willing to go the extra mile at all times
- Resilient when times got tough (thick-skinned)
- Ethical and trustworthy
- Financially motivated

Don was ready for his June 1 meeting with Jack Jenson, which was scheduled to last most of the afternoon. He planned to present the three reasons why he believed his district was failing and to lay out a new plan to turn his district around. The plan included having his experienced, successful financial consultants mentor and partner with new consultants to help them close new business. He believed his plan was simple and straightforward. The veteran financial consultants would split commissions with their less experienced coworkers on any new business they jointly closed. The new financial consultants would be responsible for "bird-dogging," or uncovering, new business leads and setting up meetings with potential clients.

Another part of Don's plan was to wait a while to assign new hires to TIP's existing customers. They could be assigned existing accounts, but only if they successfully generated new business during their first year, In the interim, the veteran consultants would handle the business until the time was right to turn it over to the new hires. This would help prevent the situation that cost Don his friend Bruce Bowen's business.

The third part of Don's plan was to hire two different recruiters to bring in new talent. Don would only conduct final interviews. He intended to spend more time in the field (back to the four days a week he spent during his first year with TIP). One recruiter would focus on college-aged graduates. The other recruiter would spend time finding more mature candidates. The idea was to hire more mature individuals and women for Don's team.

Don had done a careful analysis of the demographics of customers buying financial services from local institutions like TIP Financial Services. He discovered that most of the customers were Baby Boomers (ages 40 to 70). In addition, he discovered that just under 40 percent of the clients were women. Don realized he needed consultants that could relate better to this generation (and gender). He had learned over the past four years that young men and women just out of college with little experience had trouble convincing seasoned buyers to purchase products from them. Although the young men and women college graduates were very aggressive on the phone, they often had difficulty gaining credibility with clients in person. This is why Don thought his mentoring and team-selling idea would pay big dividends.

QUESTIONS

1. Identify the selling strategy used in the financial service industry. How are traditional and on-line financial service sales different?

2. What issues does Don Krane face? What could he be doing better?

3. Do you believe Don's collaborative selling approach will work? What are some potential problems he could face? What would you do differently if you were him?

4. What corporate growth strategies could TIP Financial Services use to help increase its consultants' sales in territories like Iowa?

5. You have replaced Don Krane as sales manager in the Iowa district. What sales strategy will you pursue during your first year in the position?

CASE STUDY 5

Wellco Distributors
Considering a Diversity Program

Background

Wellco Distributors is a manufacturers' distributor that sells hydraulic industrial supplies to original equipment manufacturers (OEMs) and retailers in the five Midwestern states of Ohio, Illinois, Indiana, Iowa, and Missouri. Wellco represents 10 different hydraulic manufacturers and employs 25 sales representatives or approximately five for each state it serves. The sales executive who oversees the 25 reps is Colin Furr. Furr started his sales career with Procter & Gamble (P&G) in Cincinnati, Ohio, after graduating from the Professional Sales Program at Ball State University in Muncie, Indiana. Furr feels that the training and systems approach he learned at P&G has been a large factor in his successful sales career. However, after selling for P&G for 10 years, he took a job with Wellco managing a sales territory in Indiana and earned significantly more money. Five years ago, Furr became Wellco's top sales manager and relocated to the firm's main office located in Chicago.

The Problem

Overall, sales revenues have stagnated at many of the larger firms Wellco calls upon. It is apparent to Furr that Wellco's buyers and its customer base have changed since he began working for the company a decade ago. More firms are now foreign-owned, especially those located in large cities like Cleveland, Chicago, Indianapolis, and St. Louis. Also, Wellco's salespeople report that they are calling upon more women and minority buyers when visiting major accounts. During a recent sales call to a manufacturer in St. Louis to discuss the account's large decline in purchases from Wellco, a minority purchasing manager remarked to Furr that Wellco's sales force looked pretty "white bread" in comparison to the company's competitors. Furr was aware that Wellco's sales force was not very diverse, but this comment took him by surprise.

As Furr drove back to his office in Chicago, he kept replaying the remark in his head. He reflected on the composition of the 25 salespersons that worked for Wellco: Most, if not all, appeared to be Caucasian, middle-aged, and male. Stated bluntly, a diverse sales force had yet to come to Wellco Distributors.

Furr believes this is a key problem. The next morning he called Wellco's human resource manager and asked for demographic statistics on the company's current sales force, along with information regarding female, African-American, Asian, and Hispanic salespersons that may have worked for Wellco in the past decade. The next day the human resources department forwarded Furr the information shown in Exhibit 1. As the exhibit shows, all of Wellco's current salespersons are male. The average age is 49, with a mean of 12 years tenure with the firm. Six of the salespersons are military veterans and two are Vietnam veterans.

Since the inception of the firm, Wellco has hired two African-American salespersons. Both left the firm after their initial performance reviews. Another salesperson reported he was Asian, and one female had worked in sales 10 years ago. Both the Asian and the female salesperson left Wellco for reportedly higher salaries with competitors. For the five years that Furr has managed the Wellco sales force, no minority salespeople had been hired, and none had left the sales force.

EXHIBIT 1

Demographic Statistics of Wellco's Sales Force

Number of salespersons: 22
Average age: 49 (range 26 to 65)
Time with firm: 12 years (range 1 to 26)
Gender: Men, 22; Women, 0
Education: Graduate degree, 2; Bachelor's degree, 14; Attended college, 6
Veterans: 6
Vietnam veterans: 2
Disabled veterans: 0
Caucasian: 22
African-American: 0
Asian: 0
Hispanic: 0

Currently Wellco has three open sales positions. The first position is located in Chicago, where the salesperson calls upon and interacts with a number of managers from Japan, Germany, and Great Britain. In addition, a significant number of engineers and buyers are either foreign-born or minority Americans. The second open sales territory is located in Muncie, Indiana, and most contacts in this territory are native-born U.S. citizens. In the third territory, located in St. Louis, Missouri, the demographics of the territory are similar to the managers, engineers, and buyers found in Chicago.

Furr ponders what he should do to increase the level of diversity within Wellco's sales force. What benefits and complications would such a change generate? Furr also knows that any formal change in personnel policies would have to be approved by Wellco's senior managers. How would he pitch the idea to them?

Furr also has a number of other decisions to make in order to diversify his sales force. First, what proportion of the 25 sales rep positions should be occupied by women and persons of color? Currently there are three open sales positions, and the average turnover rate at Wellco is 10 to 15 percent each year. Consequently, Furr wonders whether he should hire only minority salespersons for the next few years or selectively add high-quality minority salespersons. Would it be best to hire the top sales candidate regardless of their race, gender, religion, or national origin, but, when all other things are equal, give additional weight to diversity candidates? Furr also wonders how difficult it would be to attract experienced sales reps versus relatively new sales candidates who recently completed their undergraduate education.

A second dilemma for Furr is how Wellco should go about attracting applications for open positions from minority sales candidates. Previously, candidates for open positions either mailed their resumes to the company's human resources department or Wellco's salespeople referred candidates for open sales positions. Furr wants to ensure that potential high-quality minority candidates are reached, but he is unsure how and where to recruit them. At a recent seminar, a guest speaker who teaches professional sales at Northern Illinois University recommended that Wellco affiliate with the university's Professional Selling Program and offer summer internships to minority and women undergraduate students. Furr wonders if this is a good way to attract diverse applicants.

A third area of concern is the hiring process. Furr feels that managers need diversity training to ensure they are culturally sensitive to candidates from different backgrounds and cultures, especially when they are being interviewed. What types of questions should be asked of minority candidates and how might interviewees react to questions based on their culture?

While reading a book entitled *Selling Outside Your Culture Zone*, Furr learned that buyers from diverse cultures react differently based on their national culture. If this is true for buyers, would the same expectations not also hold true for sales position applicants? In other words, should sales managers expect minority candidates to exhibit the same behaviors and responses to questions as nonminority applicants?

Wellco currently offers new salespeople formal sales training that consists of formal classes and on-the-job training. Since most of the company's salespeople are white, the training program is structured for white men. Furr wonders how the sales training program should be restructured to give salespeople from different cultures and backgrounds the tools they need to succeed at Wellco. Said differently, do trainees from distinct cultural backgrounds differ in the ways they participate and learn?

Lastly, what actions need to be taken by Wellco to minimize the turnover rate of these new sales representatives? It is one thing to hire highly qualified minority salespersons, but how can Wellco ensure the new sales reps remain on the job? Furr is considering assigning mentors to each minority salesperson, but this strategy requires careful thought and selection. Currently, new salespersons are on their own after the formal training program and two weeks of on-the-job sales training from their sales managers and Wellco's sales trainer. Furr also wants to spend as much time as possible with each new minority salesperson, but he is afraid this might distract him from allocating time to all the other important things he is required to do to help the sales force succeed.

As Furr drives home in his new Toyota Prius, listening to the Dixie Chicks on his iPod, he wonders why personnel issues have become so complex. Hiring and managing salespeople seemed like it was much simpler when he studied sales at Ball State two decades ago; and Procter & Gamble's managers seemed to worry very little about the diversity of the firm's sales force when he worked for them. Furr thinks to himself: "Why me, and why now?"

QUESTIONS

1. What arguments should Furr make to Wellco's senior managers to gain their support for increasing the diversity of the firm's sales force?

2. Does Wellco's current sales force composition pose a legal problem for the company?

3. Would you recommend that Furr hire salespeople from diverse backgrounds all at once or slowly over several years? What is your rationale for your recommendation?

4. In what media outlets should Furr advertise to reach more diverse sales applicants? Write up an advertisement Furr could use to attract highly qualified applicants.

5. How would you recommend Furr modify Wellco's hiring process? What about its sales training program?

6. Why might highly qualified applicants leave their jobs even though their performance is satisfactory? What programs can Furr and Wellco undertake to retain minority sales reps hired by the company?

CASE STUDY 6

Pacific Medical Supply Company
Hiring, Motivating, and Retaining Good Salespeople

Jim Shine had some big problems on his hands as the owner and sales manager of Pacific Medical Supply Company. But these are the types of problems owners of a successful small business like Jim's like to have. Jim's problems involved his most junior salesperson, Nicole Landis. Nicole's impact on Pacific Medical Supply's sales was huge, despite the fact that the company hired her right out of college. The specific problems Jim faced as a result of Nicole's extraordinary sales efforts involved professional jealousy among his sales staff, the discovery of an out-of-whack sales commission structure, and a customer service department that was tired of being dumped on by the salesperson they nicknamed the "Land Shark." The company's sales commission structure is as follows:

Pacific Medical Supply Company pays a commission on customer orders based on the tiered commission rates shown in Table 1.

Table 1 Pacific Medical Supply
Company Sales Commission Rates

Sales per Month	% of Sales
Less than $100,000	8.5%
$100,001 to $200,000	10.0%
$200,001 to $300,000	13.0%
$300,001 to $400,000	18.0%
$400,001 to $500,000	25.0%

Example: Monthly sales of $120,000 would result in a monthly commission of $10,500.00 ($100,000 × .085 + $20,000 × .10). This commission level, if sustained, would equate to $126,000 in annual income.

Note: If all the orders were new business, $1,200 per month or $14,400 per year would be added to the salesperson's commission.

Pacific Medical Supply's Sales Commission Structure

- Commissions are paid on each month's sales orders by the 5th day of the following month.
- One percentage point is added to new business for a term of 12 months
- New business is defined as an account that has not placed an order with Pacific Medical Supply for a two-year period.
- If an order is placed by one account and the product ships to an account of another salesperson, the commission is split 50/50 between the two salespeople.
- A guaranteed draw on commission will be granted for salespeople who are working their first two years with the company. The amount of the draw will be negotiated at the time of a person's hiring. In rare cases, the draw may be extended.

Pacific Medical Supply had been experiencing record profits since Nicole was hired. The profits are as follows:

Table 2   Pacific Medical Supply Company's Sales Revenues

Year 1	$2,500,000
Year 2	$3,000,000
Year 3	$4,000,000
Year 4	$4,500,000
Year 5	$5,000,000
Year 6	$5,500,000
Year 7	$6,250,000 (Nicole Landis hired in May)
Year 8	$7,000,000
Year 9	$10,000,000
Year 10	$12,500,000 (projected)

However, the once laid-back culture of the company Jim founded was now a place in which tension and anxiety existed. Changes needed to be made, but Jim was not going to upset his star salesperson to appease some disgruntled employees.

Jim founded his company as a sole proprietorship 10 years ago. He had worked as a salesman for a larger medical supply company in the Southern California market for 15 years before starting his own business, aptly named Shine Medical Supply. Before Jim began his sales career, he was a lifeguard on the beaches of Santa Monica, California. He had no formal sales training, but knew everything there was to know about waves, surfing, and working with people.

Jim's first year in business was lean, however. He worked out of the basement in his Long Beach, California, residence until he had enough money to finance the purchase of a small building, which just happened to be five blocks from the ocean. After the move, Jim renamed his business Pacific Medical Supply Company and incorporated. He also hired his first employee (his wife). His business steadily grew, and Jim added employees and sales staff as warranted. As the company expanded over the years, his role within his company changed from being sales-oriented to involving day-to-day operations management. However, he still kept tabs on all of his customers; he considered them to be his friends. The business was still small enough where Jim knew all of the customers by name. Many of Jim's initial customers still considered him their salesperson, even though he rarely made outside sales calls anymore.

The business model Jim adopted when he started his company was to supply hospitals and clinics name-brand medical supplies at fair-market prices in the Southern California market, which included Los Angeles. His goal was not to offer the lowest prices, but rather offer the best service and delivery on products. For this reason Jim spent much of his time making sure the operations and distribution side of the business was run to perfection.

Over time, the product lines offered by Pacific Medical Supply grew from offering only a handful of products, like disposable masks, gloves, and blood collection vials, to product offerings that numbered in the hundreds. Disposable plastic instruments and syringes imported directly from a manufacturer in China became the company's bestsellers, representing 20 percent of Pacific Medical Supply's total sales, which generated an 80 percent profit margin. Other products in their line averaged a profit margin ranging from 40 to 50 percent.

The company's customer base also grew in conjunction with the number of products offered. Other avenues of sales for Pacific Medical Supply included health maintenance organizations (HMOs), the U.S. military, and Fortune 500 companies. To keep customers coming back for reorders, the company prided itself on promising 100 percent customer satisfaction and next-day delivery. The golden rule for retaining customers in the medical supply business was always having the products they wanted on hand. This basic principle was what Jim saw as the key to the company's success and growth over his first six years in business. To keep his customers supplied and happy, Jim's major investments during that time included expanding his company's warehouse space and purchasing new delivery vehicles.

Four years ago, Jim Shine had a by-chance encounter with Nicole Landis on a flight from San Francisco to Los Angeles. The two were seated next to each other and struck up a conversation during the short trip. Nicole was a senior on the California State Fullerton gymnastics team. She and her teammates were returning from a competition during the winter semester break. At first glance, Jim noticed Nicole was very fit and attractive (the prototypical "California girl"). After 10 minutes into their conversation, he felt like they were longtime friends. Jim learned Nicole was a business major and was going to be graduating in May with a degree in marketing. As they exited the plane, Jim handed Nicole one of his business cards and told her that if she was interested in working for him as a salesperson to give him a call after graduation.

Five months later, Jim received a call from Nicole. She inquired if the offer he had made was still available. Jim said it was. Within a week Nicole was on board at Pacific Medical Supply and learning about the products she would be selling. During her first week, she worked with the company's in-house customer service personnel, who processed orders and took in-coming customer phone calls. In her second week, she observed the sales side of the business by traveling for a day with each of the company's five salespeople on staff.

Nicole found it odd that she was the only female salesperson working for Pacific Medical Supply. She also thought it was rather strange that Jim, who was the owner and sales manager, was not involved with her training other than to set her up with her training itinerary and sales leads. After 10 days on the job, she headed out with a list of past customers who had *not* done business with Pacific Medical Supply for at least a two-year period. The prospecting phase of her sales career was about to begin.

Nicole was a natural in sales if there ever was one. She could bond and rapport with anyone from purchasing agents to doctors. Her sales style was to nurture her customers by being honest and prepared. She approached her sales role as an expert consultant who could solve customers' problems and fulfill needs with her products. The formula worked. Jim's hiring of Nicole was a boon for his business. Within her first six months in sales, Nicole was already covering her $50,000 annual draw on her commission. After two years, she was the company's third leading salesperson and at times during the year was making over $20,000 a month in commissions. By her third year, Nicole had broken the bank and was making over $300,000 a year as the top salesperson in the company. Her income history is as follows:

Table 3   Annual Income—Nicole Landis

Year	Sales	Income
1 (6 months)	$295,000	$28,000
2	$1,550,000	$130,000
3	$2,975,000	$315,000
4 (projected)	$3,825,000	$430,000

Nicole enjoyed her newfound wealth; with her student loans paid off, she spent her hard-earned income on a new BMW convertible and took out a mortgage on a beachfront condo in Long Beach, California. Even with her busy work schedule, Nicole had some balance to her life. She still found time to volunteer as a part-time coach for a local youth gymnastic center. She was gracious in her newfound success and wealth, but she was still intensely competitive and wanted to work even harder. She knew the support she received from the company employees who processed and filled her orders accurately made her success possible, and she was very vocal in thanking everyone for their hard work on her orders.

The many years Nicole spent in gymnastics had taught her that discipline and hard work would be the path to success in life, and she was making the lesson she learned pay big dividends now in her sales career. Her work habits while out in the field were legendary (averaging 10 personal calls and 50 phone contacts a day), and her attention to detail was nothing short of perfection (she rarely made a mistake). When she was in the office, she was talking to customers, e-mailing proposals to purchasing agents, or checking orders. Her Saturday mornings were spent in the office catching up on paperwork and making up her call list plan for the following week. As an owner, Jim could not have been more pleased with the effort and results posted by Nicole. He was happy to see Nicole and his company's income benefit from her sales successes over her three-and-a-half years with the company.

Jim sat down one day and started to dissect Nicole's sales numbers. He calculated that in the next 12 months she could be making almost $450,000 a year in commissions if her new business continued to build at the same rate. His first thought after this discovery was one of great news because he would also personally be making more money. However, when taking a second look at his commission structure, Jim saw there was a flaw in the top end of his commission schedule that would need to be addressed. Nicole had already benefited from a mistake in the company's commission structure. Jim also had a morale problem within his sales team. He had been hands-off as a sales manager and pretty much let his salespeople do their own thing, as long as sales kept increasing.

Until Nicole arrived, he felt his salespeople did a relatively nice job keeping customers satisfied. Three of the five salespeople made low six-figure incomes and were honest, hardworking individuals. The other two were just treading water and selling enough to cover their draw and get small commission checks every month. Nicole's success opened Jim's eyes to what might be possible if his sales force were comprised of five more Nicoles. He also thought it might be time for him to look for a professional sales manager to light a fire under some of the "deadwood" on his sales team.

Jim never had to replace a salesperson in his 10 years in business because all of them had left on their own accord. However, he thought now might be the time for a shake-up because a few salespeople were being real jerks to Nicole, which Jim interpreted as professional jealousy. Many of the accounts Nicole was now selling to were all accounts the existing salespeople had given up on. Her success made them look foolish.

One day Jim overheard one of his salespeople say to Nicole: "I better hide my laptop from you before you download all my accounts." The salesperson also belittled her for "cherry picking" the product line. Jim saw that these crass comments really upset Nicole, but Jim did nothing to address the inappropriate behavior for fear of getting in the middle of a fight.

There were also some grumblings about Nicole from the women who worked in customer service. Because of Nicole's large load of orders, they had to become more productive and had less time to socialize among themselves. Nicole also was in the habit of spot-checking many of her orders after they were processed by customer service. Often there were quite a few mistakes. Nicole was very polite and diplomatic when she pointed out the errors, but it still rubbed the customer service people the wrong way. It seemed to Jim this problem was beginning to fester. It was no secret around the company that the entire customer service team gossiped about the "Land Shark"—little miss pretty Nicole Landis.

Everything came to a head on a Friday afternoon as Jim was driving up the Santa Ana Freeway to Los Angeles for a long weekend with his wife. That's when he received a phone call from Nicole. Jim could tell from her voice that she was upset and not her usual upbeat cheerful self. She explained that the past few months have been unbearable for her around the office, and she felt like she was on an "island" all alone and employees were making it difficult for her to do her job properly. Nicole went on to say that she felt underappreciated for her efforts, and it would be nice to have someone say you are doing a good job now and then. In closing, she said she was burned out and was going to take next week off to assess her work situation and life in general.

QUESTIONS

1. Are people like Nicole born to be natural salespeople? Or can good sales managers help them become better salespeople? Is there a way Jim might enlist Nicole to help Pacific Medical Supply in this regard?

2. Can you find the flaw in Pacific Medical Supply's sales commission structure that might be adversely affecting its lower performers? How, as a sales manager, would you change the plan to better motivate them?

3. Should the profit margin of the product play a role in the commission structure? What if a salesperson predominantly sold products with an 80 percent profit margin? Should the person be paid more than someone who predominant sold products with a 40 percent profit margin?

4. In your opinion, what should Jim do to try to retain and motivate Nicole?

CASE STUDY 7

Southeastern Sales Associations
Evaluating and Coaching Salespeople to Improve Their Performance

Southeastern Sales Associates, headquartered in Raleigh, North Carolina, is a manufacturers' representative firm that sells air-conditioning supplies to firms in approximately 35 counties in eastern North Carolina. The company partners exclusively with Bryant® Home Comfort Systems, which manufactures gas furnaces; heat pumps; state-of-the-art thermostats that control temperature, humidity, air quality, fan speed, and ventilation; air purifiers; ventilators; and humidifiers. Bryant® is known for manufacturing high-quality heating and cooling products and offering high-quality customer service and a 10 year warranty on the major components of its products. Southeastern has a good working relationship with Bryant®.

Frieda Johnson is completing her first year as sales manager for Southeastern Sales Associates. In 2004, Frieda completed her B.S.B.A. with a sales concentration at Elon University, and during the summer between her junior and senior years, she completed an internship at Southeastern. A few months before her graduation, the owner of Southeastern called Frieda and offered her a full-time sales position managing customer accounts in the coastal counties of Brunswick and New Hanover. Both counties were experiencing significant growth and development because of their proximity to the Atlantic Ocean and the influx of retirees moving there. The area was also growing because of its closeness to the resort cities of Wilmington, North Carolina, and Myrtle Beach, South Carolina. There are large numbers of golf courses in the area, a major medical center located in Wilmington, and housing prices—while escalating—are still lower than those found in the northeastern United States. Thus, many new residents believe the area offers a high quality of life at an affordable price.

Because of the warm weather and high humidity, residents must have air-conditioning. However, as a result of the area's proximity to the ocean and the high humidity, external air-conditioning and heat pump units deteriorate more quickly than in other parts of the country. In units placed near the ocean, the coils could begin deteriorating in as little as one year.

After a one-month intensive training program, Frieda moved to Wilmington to service her accounts. The accounts were comprised of builders, independent air-conditioning contractors, distributors, and "big-box" retail stores. Her job as a sales rep was to meet with builders and contractors to convince them of the quality of Bryant® heating and air-conditioning systems. This resulted in the builders and contractors recommending Bryant® systems to their customers who contracted with them to build new homes, remodel older homes, or replace outdated and less efficient systems. Likewise, Frieda called upon distributors and retailers to provide them with training regarding the use of Bryant's products, resolve any complaints they might have, and maintain close working relationships with them.

It took Frieda about six months to form relationships and refine her knowledge of the broad HVAC (heating, ventilation, air-conditioning) product line. Her first year in the region resulted in a 10 percent increase in sales and 12 percent increase in profits for Southeastern Sales Associates. Frieda acknowledged that her success was also due to the high quality of the products, Bryant's coordinated marketing program, and high-quality customer service provided by the manufacturer. Frieda's sales increased by 8 percent the following year, then 12 percent, and 18 percent the fourth year. As a result, she was the top sales rep within the firm, earning high commissions, bonuses, and trips to Hawaii and London for winning sales contests. She was subsequently promoted to her position as a sales manager.

As sales manager, Frieda travels with each of her eight sales representatives once a month. This means she drives from Raleigh, for no more than three hours each way, to one of the eight territories. When Frieda travels to the Outer Banks or Wilmington, she normally spends the night prior to riding along with the local sales representative. Otherwise, she leaves at 6:30 in the morning and meets the sales rep for breakfast around 8:30 to discuss the call schedule that day over breakfast. Frieda feels she is a natural when it comes to coaching her sales team. This is because most sales reps want to learn how to improve their performance in order to earn higher salaries.

On a recent field visit with Robert Weston in the Fayetteville territory, Frieda observed that Robert needed additional product knowledge about the most recently introduced heat pump by Bryant, the Evolution Series®. It was obvious he did not have the knowledge he should have had to answer the questions the owner of the largest independent HVAC firm in Fayetteville, North Carolina, was asking him. A similar event occurred in Goldsboro, North Carolina, when Susan Hartwell stumbled badly on questions posed by the manager of a Lowe's store who was having problems answering customers' questions about Bryant's warranty.

Frieda was also thinking about another problem she had uncovered. It appeared that some of her salespeople were turning in questionable expenses. For example, several salespersons had taken relatively new clients and their spouses to very expensive restaurants. Frieda understands the importance of building relationships, but she wants her salespeople to make sure there will be a return for investing in relationships. A few other salespersons appear to be charging more gas for their company cars than seems feasible. Either the salespersons are driving their company car for personal business or they are filling up their spouses' vehicles.

Lastly, a few salespersons appear to spend most of their time with their best buyers with whom they have comfortable relationships, while steering clear of difficult accounts. Again, Frieda has no problem with her salespeople spending time with their best buyers in order to maintain and grow their relationships with them. However, if they are to grow their territories, they must make every effort to win back buyers who were lost to competitors. Frieda wonders whether she should hire an experienced salesperson to handle lost accounts rather than expecting the reps who lost them to try to reestablish them.

What is frustrating for Frieda is that if she were the salesperson assigned to any one of the territories, she could quickly correct and manage any of these situations. That is, Frieda would spend her nights and weekends reviewing Bryant's product specifications, minimize her travel and entertainment expenses, and appropriate the correct amount of time to spend with current and lost accounts. However, Frieda understands that she is a sales manager and that her job differs from that of the sales force. Namely, she must organize and manage the sales force in ways that result in maximum performance. Realizing that she must take action, she ponders the best way to improve her eight-member sales team.

QUESTIONS

1. How might Frieda evaluate whether or not the shortcomings she observes in her salespeople are a serious problem?

2. Rate the situations detailed by Frieda from most serious to least serious. What course of action should Frieda take to address each, and when?

3. Can Frieda compare her understanding and anticipated actions with that of her salespeople? Why or why not?

4. Do you believe Frieda has an accurate understanding of her role as a sales manager?

CASE STUDY 8

Afgar Corporation
Managing Multi-channel Sales

Background

Afgar Corporation is a multi-national corporation headquartered in Sweden that specializes in manufacturing products sold to the printing industry. The company's products include printing plates, inks, UV and aqueous coatings, digital equipment, and graphics software for image scanning and manipulation. After dominating the European market for a quarter of a century, Afgar entered the U.S. market in 2005, by acquiring Digitsoft Industries. Digitsoft was based in Boston and specialized in prepress digital equipment and software. By purchasing Digitsoft, Afgar captured immediate market share in the United States. The size and financial strength of Afgar also helped pull Digitsoft out of a difficult financial situation at the time. That is, the company had been unable to properly fund research and design at a time when the technology in its industry was rapidly changing. The acquisition has been deemed a success by Afgar's managers mainly due to deals that allowed Digitsoft's hardware and software to be bundled with Afgar's inks, coatings, and printing plates. Afgar's customers were now being provided with one-stop shopping.

One of the benefits for the old Digitsoft employees who were retained after the acquisition was the generous vacation and holiday time Afgar offered them. As is the custom with many European companies, all employees were given an automatic four weeks of vacation per year. By contrast, Digitsoft had offered its first-year employees no vacation time, one week of vacation after a year's service, and two weeks after five years with the company.

Afgar's liberal vacation policy was obviously embraced by the company's old Digitsoft employees. However, sales representatives rarely used up their vacation time because their salaries were relatively small compared to the commissions they earned. Being on the phone constantly with customers and in the field selling every day meant higher pay checks for them. Thus, for the sales force, taking time off for vacations was often not an option. In addition to the salaries and commissions reps earned, Afgar held a host of sales competitions to promote different products. Some of the sales contest prizes included 10-day cruises for two, European family vacations, and home theater systems. Needless to say, the competition to win the prizes was fierce.

Business-to-business sales in the printing industry are similar to business-to-business sales in other industries. With so many printing companies to call upon, Afgar relied on distributors to purchase and inventory its consumable products and then sell them directly to printing companies. Deliveries to printers were made daily on a "just-in-time" basis. A typical distributor, on average, serviced 500 to 600 customers in a geographical territory and had a sales staff of 8 to 10 sales representatives. Because the printing distribution industry is generally a low-profit-margin, high-quantity sales enterprise, competition is fierce. To succeed as a distributor, you must acquire new customers; retain existing customers; offer excellent customer service; and maintain loyal, long-term relationships with both your customers and suppliers. Each of Afgar's territories had at least three to four distributors calling on the same printers.

Afgar's field sales representatives (FSRs) acted as missionary salespeople, demonstrating the company's product to end users (printers). The reps demonstrated products like graphics software, tested consumable products like inks and printing plates, or flew customers to Boston for new equipment demonstrations. Once a product was adequately demonstrated and won a printer's approval, the printer would get a price for the product from its distributor of choice.

Because the distributors were selling commodity items from multiple manufacturers, price and payment terms were often their main selling point, and printers often played one distributor against another. From a manufacturer's standpoint, such as Afgar, performance and quality is where their salespeople tried to make their products stand out. However, both old and new printing customers were constantly being "poached," which made for a lack of trust between distributors and the field sales representatives of manufacturers like Afgar. This was especially difficult for Afgar because it was the newest player trying to gain market share. When Afgar would try to get new customers to use its products and distributors, the existing distributor and manufacturer would drop its prices to protect their business.

Throughout the industry, distributors offered their customers rebates based on their quarterly or year-end sales totals. The rebates could be redeemed for free products or credit. In some cases, manufacturers recommended distributors to customers if they had a "favored" relationship with them or were paying them back for a new lead. Because distributors' sales representatives called upon the same customers as manufacturers' representatives did, they would often bring new business leads to the manufacturers. Therefore, paybacks like these were not uncommon.

Once a sale was made, it was the responsibility of the manufacturer's field rep to make sure all of the products were working in the customer's facility. Each field rep spent approximately three weeks a year in product training seminars back at the home office. These training sessions were not optional, and attendance was strictly enforced by the training department.

In addition to its field representatives in 20 different territories across the United States, Afgar also had a team of telephone sales representatives (TSRs), who sold the firm's consumable products directly to printers. Each territory had a designated TSR. The TSR's job was to call upon the printers' personnel who order the ink, printing plates, and coatings to make sure they were not running low. The TSRs worked off a database provided by the FSRs. The database included the names of the end customers, preferred distributors from which to purchase products, and type of products they would likely order. An average customer might order $1,000 worth of product a week; a large customer could order $10,000 a week.

In the beginning, the TSRs were an asset for the FSRs because they kept tabs on the many smaller accounts using Afgar's products. Small accounts were only visited once a month by the FSRs, so the TSRs calling upon them was a good way for the accounts to get cost effective services. The problem was that because of their commission structure, the TSRs also started calling on larger accounts, sometimes two and three times a day: Every time a TSR took an order, which was in turn e-mailed or faxed to a distributor, the person received a small commission. In time, the TSRs realized they could cherry-pick the customers they called on and get one large order by making one phone call in a few minutes as opposed to making 20 calls over the course of a couple of hours to get the same result.

The resulting firestorm of "service" phone calls made to Afgar's large customers began to create problems between the company's FSRs and TSRs. In one instance the owner of the largest printer in Cincinnati, using all of Afgar's products, told his FSR: "If that woman [TSR] from your company calls my purchasing agent one more time this week, I'm pulling all of your equipment and products out of my shop."

A Sales Manager's Dilemma

Paul Welton had just finished his first week working as the regional sales manager in Afgar's Ohio-Kentucky-Indiana territory. It was a turbulent week. In addition to living out of a hotel room and working with a realtor to find a house for his family, Paul's top sales-person resigned abruptly after having been offered a better job with one of his customers.

Paul was new to the territory, but a proven leader and five-year veteran with Afgar. Before his arrival, he had worked in Afgar's North American headquarters in Boston, where he worked his way up from a telephone service representative (TSR) to a manager in the firm's telemarketing department. During Paul's three-year tenure as a telemarketing manager for Afgar, his team of 20 grew its new business by 150 percent and increased the sales to its existing customer base by 50 percent. His telemarketing team consisted of 18 women; two of them made, on average, 150 customer phone calls per day.

In his new role as regional sales manager, Paul was responsible for supervising five field sales reps (FSRs), each with about 15 years of sales experience in the field. Coming into this position, Paul also knew he was going to be managing a rogue bunch of men who were known as the "gun slingers" back in Boston. The men had earned the reputation because of the way they did business under their previous manager, Wyatt Fullmore. Wyatt was a West Texas transplant who had made a name for himself by turning the Ohio-Kentucky-Indiana territory around. The territory quickly went from being Afgar's lowest revenue-generating territory to its number-one territory in the country.

Wyatt's brash attitude, combined with his slow southern drawl and good-old-boy sense of humor, galvanized Wyatt with his sales team and distributors. Wyatt was a win-at-all-costs sales manager who was known for pushing the envelope on company policies, which didn't sit well with Afgar's upper managers. He mostly let his reps deal with the customers, and Wyatt made sure the group's distribution partners were satisfied. However, he was always available to support his reps when they needed him, especially when they needed his help to close a deal. Although he enjoyed high-level meetings where the decisions were made, he was frustrated by customers who waffled on making buying decisions. Thus, when he was called to help out with a deal, he was determined to get it done. He was the ultimate closer.

Paul was also well aware of the disdain his FSRs had for the aggressive telemarket-ing sales campaign originating from Afgar's corporate headquarters. But he knew the strategy worked because executives praised the additional revenue the TSR's generated, and they marveled at the incredible return on investment the department provided. Competitors were also starting to use the same "phone-in" tactics, which meant Afgar's telemarketing sales were here to stay.

Paul believed his success as a field sales manager was to lead by using some of the same principles he implemented as a telemarketing manager. These tactics were to work harder and smarter than the competition, set individual and team goals with his FSRs, and celebrate the victories. His first goal as the leader was to repair the ill will between the field representatives he now managed and the telemarketing representative for his terri-tory. Before he left his previous position, he transferred the top TSR from his team to his new territory to ensure he had the best individual working for him on the inside. He knew who the big players were in his territory, and he was well aware that the distributors had made a lot of money off the telemarketing efforts he managed. Telemarketing was going to continue to help his FSRs make their sales quotas.

What Paul didn't know was what Wyatt Fullmore had been doing while managing the territory he was now inheriting. All he knew about Wyatt was that he always had a funny or risqué story to tell, which always ended with him letting out hearty belly laughs, but you could never get a straight answer from him when you needed one. Wyatt was also unceremoniously fired two weeks before Paul took over the territory. Paul was given very few details as to why Wyatt was let go, however. A memo put out by the company simply stated that Wyatt was no longer with the company "effective immediately."

"From hero to zero overnight," Paul thought to himself after reading the memo. He tried calling Wyatt after he received the memo, but his cell and office phone were already disconnected. In the previous year Wyatt was considered the "rainmaker" at Afgar's corporate headquarters for taking his territory to number one in such a short time. Now he was gone. Was the gun slinger ambushed?

A month later, Paul Welton had started to settle into his new role. He had made an offer to purchase a house in an upscale Cincinnati neighborhood, and it had been accepted. In a couple of weeks his wife and child would be joining him in Cincinnati. He would not miss flying home on the weekends. He even had things "flying" on the business side of things. He was putting in 14-hour days traveling with his FSRs, visiting existing customers and distributors. He even made some new business calls that seemed to be very promising. The interviews were moving along to add another FSR, and the candidates were proving to be excellent. In an effort to heal the rift with telemarketing, Paul flew the new TSR for his territory, Betty McManners, out for a regional sales meeting so she could meet his sales team.

Everything was going along pretty well in Paul's mind until he attended a dinner meeting with Frank Tappen. Frank was the owner of Tappen Distributors, Afgar's largest account in the territory. The company had been in business for 50 years and was well respected for their sales staff's product knowledge, excellent customer service, and professionalism.

Frank held nothing back during his dinner meeting with Paul. Paul learned there were some rebate credit payments due Tappen for persuading one of its largest printing customers to use Afgar's equipment and consumable products. Rebates were not an uncommon sales tactic for distributors to give to their printers. However, this was the first Paul had heard about manufacturers like Afgar using rebates with their distributors. Frank went on to explain how Wyatt structured these so-called distributor rebates: To help Tappen sell Afgar's high-priced equipment to printers, Wyatt issued credits to Tappen. Tappen would then make the payments on the equipment. Printers weren't aware of the details of the arrangement. They just thought that they were getting the use and ownership of free equipment for simply switching the purchase of their consumable products to Afgar's products. Afgar was not the leading seller of consumables, but its products performed well enough when tested that the switch was an easy one for most printers to make. Financially speaking, it was a "no brainer." There also was no need for the printer to switch distributors because Tappen carried different manufacturers' products, including Afgar's.

Paul was perplexed. How did Wyatt issue credits back to Tappen, which in turn converted the credits to cash to pay the banknote on the customer's equipment? Paul assured Frank that Afgar wanted to keep their relationship strong, take care of this specific printer, and continue to grow their business together. Paul told Frank that this was the first deal of this type he had ever heard of, and he needed time to talk with his boss back in Boston to find out what to do.

"The sooner the better," Frank said. He needed to make a payment on one of the loans on Monday. He went on to say he had two other banknotes outstanding that would require payments at the end of the month. Paul asked Frank if he could get copies of the signed agreements on the contacts. Frank replied, "Are you kidding me, Paul? Everything was done on a handshake with Wyatt. There are no written agreements."

A week later, Paul uncovered how Wyatt was able to issue rebates to Tappan. It turned out that Wyatt had company-approved, unchecked authority to give distributors credit for faulty Afgar products. Wyatt used the rebates at his discretion to appease printers and distributors. However, he was only required to send back partially defective product samples (for example, one bad printing plate from a batch of 40) for the credit to be approved. To avoid incurring shipping and handling costs, the rest of the faulty products were to be scrapped.

Paul discovered the credit pool by questioning why he was receiving weekly shipments of bad printing plates and contaminated ink containers from his FSRs. Paul asked them why they weren't shipping the products back to Boston. The reps informed Paul that Wyatt had always written up the returns and approved the final authorizations for credits. After further examination, Paul found out that his territory last year had issued $1,400,000 in faulty product credits—four times what the average Afgar territory issued. Paul had no idea of how big this problem was or how many customers and distributors were involved. He also wondered if his FSRs knew about the rebate scheme.

QUESTIONS

1. How should Paul proceed to resolve this problem?

2. Should Paul restructure his district's TSR/FSR sales strategies? If so, how?

3. What ethical issues have been breached in this case, if any? Were any laws broken, to your knowledge?

4. What kind of leader was Wyatt Fullmore?

CASE STUDY 9

Freedom Telecom
Setting New Sales Goals to Turn the Sales Force Around

Mark Phillips, Regional Sales Manager, Commercial Accounts

Did you ever feel like you were paddling upstream against a Class 3 rapid? This was what Mark Phillips told his wife he felt like. Mark and his wife, Beth, were discussing what had transpired during the workweek during their regular Friday night dinner out in downtown Omaha, Nebraska. As usual, the conversation revolved around Mark's continuous battle to stay afloat in his job with Freedom Telecom.

Beth and Mark had been married for 35 years, had put four sons through college, and thought by now they would be enjoying their lives as empty nesters. Five years ago, not only were they sure they would be empty nesters by now, Mark was even looking forward to early retirement after 30 years of service with Freedom Telecom. He was 55 years old and making over $100,000 a year in salary and commissions. His plan was to retire from his longtime employer under the rule of 85 (age + years of service) and collect a pension that would have covered all of his and Beth's healthcare costs and pay him 50 percent of his salary annually for the rest of his life.

Freedom Telecom's outstanding retirement benefits package was one of the main reasons Mark and his colleagues were so loyal to the company over the years. They even referred to their pension benefits as the "golden handcuffs." Employees rarely left the company because finding a benefits package as generous as Freedom Telecom's anywhere else in the industry was next to impossible.

Unfortunately, however, things weren't turning out the way Mark and Beth thought they would. Freedom Telecom had experienced problems, and the company was in trouble. Mark's pension was now gone, revoked because of Freedom Telecom's financial difficulties and rising national healthcare costs. Mark now knew he was going to have to work until at least age 67. That's when Medicare would kick in and cover some of his healthcare costs. Despite his troubles, Mark summed up the situation after dinner: "The past is the past. I have a duty to give the company my best until I decide or they decide my services are no longer needed," he told Beth.

Freedom Telecom's financial difficulties were well documented on the front pages of newspapers and business magazines across the country. First, there was the scandal involving inflated revenues that forced Freedom Telecom to restate its profits going back four years. Following a major plunge in the company's stock price and a federal indictment, the firm's CEO, CFO, and financial auditors took a very public and humiliating fall from the corporate tower. Although none of the company's officers served jail time for their actions, the damage to the Freedom Telecom brand name was significant. As a result, customers jumped ship like it was the Titanic.

With a public relations mess on its hands and bleeding red ink, Freedom Telecom faced the challenge of re-branding itself and moving forward with significantly smaller lines of credit. In response, competitors took advantage of the company's weak stature and doubled their efforts to gain market share. Making matters worse was the major drain of young talent Freedom Telecom experienced. Most employees under the age of 40 left for smoother waters. In just a few years, Freedom Telecom went from a vibrant company trumpeted by investors to an oft-used "don't do this" case study in college business ethics classes.

Mark lived all the ups and downs Freedom Telecom had experienced. As one of the company's regional sales managers for commercial accounts, he had a unique vantage point. He often joked that he needed all of his fingers and toes to count how many times he had to apologize each business day to his sales group for problems that were a result of a waning company. Mark maintained his wry sense of humor and a penchant for using analogies that involved boats and water. His latest e-mail to his reps was a good example:

> Crew, it seems we find ourselves in quite a predicament in the middle of an ocean of issues. We have an old navigation system, the motor is in need of repair, the captain jumped overboard, the sky is full of clouds ready to open up with a major storm, and we are faced with finding our way to land before we sink or are shot out of the water by a pirate. Did I mention that we also are taking on water? I need your attention now more than ever to focus on the here and now and work together to right this ship. Once we find land, I am confident we can start to build customer relationships again on solid ground. Please forward me your individual action plan on how we can find land in the next 30 days. I will be sharing with you our region's first-quarter goals once you give me some solid ideas.
>
> —*Mark "Skipper" Phillips*

Freedom Telecom was one of the many spin-off companies that emerged out of the breakup of the once-monopolistic U.S. telecommunications industry. After the federal government broke up the monopoly "Ma Bell" in the1970s, several firms like Freedom Telecom sprung up and prospered by leasing Ma Bell's existing phone line infrastructure and focusing on niche regional business markets. Early on, Freedom Telecom primarily served rural residential customers in the northern plain states. The company established its headquarters in Omaha, and over the course of 30 years, grew into the third-largest telecommunication company in the United States.

For many years, Freedom Telecom touted the sales slogan: "Freedom to choose with dependable service." Indeed, early on, the firm grew by persuading residential customers to switch from their existing local- and long-distance service providers to the company's "freedom plan." With no capital invested in infrastructure, Freedom Telecom was able to use a low-price pitch with great success to attract customers. The plan offered customers a 50 percent discount off of their previous monthly phone bills and soon became one of the most popular plans in the Midwest.

However, as the industry became flooded with competitors, it became increasingly difficult for Freedom Telecom to be the low-price leader in its market. As a result of shrinking residential market share, Freedom Telecom started to target commercial business customers. The top salespeople and managers in the residential sales group were moved to a newly created commercial division.

Mark was on board in the commercial division beginning day one. In a few short years he worked his way up to sales manager, and in 1995, he was promoted to his current position as Freedom Telecom's regional sales manager in charge of commercial business accounts. During his tenure, the commercial division grew to become the most profitable division within Freedom Telecom. The profits from Mark's region alone represented 10 percent of the company's overall profits last year.

The success of the commercial sales division was based on three solid fundamentals Mark developed: (1) every contract had to be written to provide Freedom Telecom with long-term profits; (2) innovation had to be at the forefront of every new service offered; and (3) customers had to be treated like family members, be shown respect, and given honest answers to their questions. One of the reasons Mark was so successful in his position was the fact that he truly believed in these three business principles and lived his daily life by them. Mark also felt people should enjoy what they do, and he always brought a sense of adventure and fun to everything he was involved in. Not surprisingly, he was well liked by everyone, including the 12 salespeople who reported to him.

Over the years Mark pushed for new cutting-edge services and deals like partnering with Motorola on equipment offerings, bundling phone and Internet access, offering direct connect services (two-way direct communications), and introducing technical service and systems installation products to Freedom Telecom's service offerings. But aside from a few old-timers in the repair division, not many current employees remembered Mark's long-standing contributions to the company.

Wendy Maxwell, Vice President of Sales

Attendees of Freedom Telecom's last shareholder meeting were led to believe Wendy Maxwell, aged 43, would be the new savior of the company. Wendy had a very successful 20-year sales career in the pharmaceutical industry and was brought in to fill Freedom Telecom's vacant vice president of sales position. Mark would be one of her direct reports as a regional sales manager.

Mark learned shortly after her arrival that Wendy had hit the ground running in her new position. In her first week as vice president, she changed the Freedom Telecom's commission structure, developed rigorous customer contact goals that had to be verified and, like Jack Welch, the renowned former CEO of GE, terminated the lowest-producing 10 percent of the sales force.

Mark finally met Wendy two weeks after she had been hired. During the meeting, Mark made every effort to understand what Wendy was trying to accomplish and how she defined her long-term sales goals. Mark had not lost any of his representatives to Wendy's cuts, and he saw an opportunity for his region to make more money under her commission structure. Most of Mark's questions for Wendy surrounded her new call reporting edict:

"It's been my observation from looking at the commercial accounts division that your salespeople must be wasting time calling on the same customers they have called on for years," Wendy responded. "They never push to make contacts higher up within the new organizations they're trying to sell to—to reach executives who make major decisions. They are missing additional sales opportunities by not having these high-level relationships. I want each of your salespeople to make at least two calls a month at the executive level, and I have a list of titles that qualify as executives." Wendy went on to explain that Mark was to monitor his representatives' call reports and spot-check their phone calls to verify the visits took place. In addition to the two in-person executive calls, 10 mid-level personal calls, and 20 low-level personal calls were to be made each month by each salesperson.

Mark explained to Wendy the way his region was structured and how it might be difficult to make her new call reporting system work for his salespeople. "I'm not making excuses," Mark said. "However, I have specialists within my region that have different strengths. Frank Wood is extremely good at opening doors at the executive level, so he would have no difficulty reaching two executives a month. He might even meet that goal every week. Rick Sutton is my technical salesperson. I send him in to work with the customer's information systems representatives to answer questions that no one else in my region can answer. His expertise is networking-based. I would not call him a salesperson, but most of the sales our region has made are due in part to Rick making customers feel comfortable with the technology. I also have Matt Moore, who has only been in my group for two years. But this guy is an icebreaker. He gets into customers we couldn't crack for years. Once he is in the front door, I team him up with Frank, and they work their magic."

"Stop right there," interrupted Wendy. "I'm not looking for some magic sales formula. I am trying to employ a proven sales plan that if executed correctly will give this company a quantifiable amount of sales, month in, month out. If salespeople cannot make the numbers I set forth, then HR will hire new salespeople who can. Now are you going to implement my structured call reporting plan and make sure your salespeople are meeting their goals? Or do I need to find someone else who will?"

After a brief pause, Mark caught his breath. He did not answer Wendy's question because he thought it was rhetorical anyway. "Wendy, if my salespeople reach their sales call goals, how will you translate those calls into final sales numbers?"

"If our sales call quotas are met and we maintain the industry average of closing sales, which is 20 percent, we should increase our overall annual sales by 15 percent," answered Wendy. "To help us increase our closing ratio, I also plan on instituting a mandatory five-day, in-house sales training course that each sales representative will need to pass once a year. I have already enlisted an outside sales consultant I have worked with in the past to run the sales training program for us. You and the other regional sales managers will also need to complete and pass the sales training."

Mark did a quick calculation in his head of what his region's closing ratio was and came up with 10 percent—not 20 percent. He also knew it sometimes took years to fully develop a relationship with customers before they would enter into contracts. "What do you consider a closed sale?" he asked Wendy.

"A closed sale is a 12-month signed contract for one or more of our services," Wendy replied.

"What about long-term contracts?" Mark inquired.

"There's little or no customer loyalty in the telecom industry, Mark," she replied. "We are in a fast-paced cutthroat industry. Either you get eaten or you eat someone else and live to survive another day. Right now, Freedom Telecom is on the verge of being eaten. Unless I can increase our sales in the next six to nine months, it is likely we both will be working for someone else."

Mark pondered the situation. He supervises four teams in his region, each of which consists of three individuals. Each team is located in a different city: Denver, Kansas City, Oklahoma City, and Little Rock, Arkansas, and is given a sales quota based on its previous year's sales. In previous years, the company expected a 10 percent increase in sales each year for his 12-member group. In addition to nine regular salespeople, Mark has one technical salesperson, one salesperson dedicated to new business, and one salesperson dedicated to growing the services sold to existing accounts. Occasionally, Mark sends different team members into another team's city if he thinks a better relationship might be formed with a certain customer. However, in most cases, he has only done this when an existing account was in jeopardy.

Mark spends at least five days a month working with each of the four teams he manages (20 days a month in the field). He often shares the experiences he's had with one team with his other teams to help his entire group succeed. Mark knows all of Freedom Telecom's key commercial customers in all four cities by name and was involved in closing most of the larger sales contracts. An average customer contract is worth approximately $250,000 a year, and Mark's 12 salespeople are managing about $72,000,000 in annual contracts. Broken down by salesperson, this represents about $6,000,000 (24 accounts × $250,000) per salesperson. A full 80 percent of existing contracts have been in existence for two years or more.

Each salesperson is paid a salary based upon his or her years of industry experience and receives a yearly cost-of-living increase. As Exhibit 1 shows, a bonus has been paid to the group based upon it achieving a certain percentage of its sales goal and is equally divided among the 12 members in Mark's region and Mark himself. He shares the regional bonus as an equal member, in other words. In past years, the region's bonuses, when broken out individually, were 20 to 30 percent of a person's salary (depending on the salary an individual salesperson was earning).

EXHIBIT 1

Former Regional Bonus Structure (based on % over previous year's final sales figure)

1 percent over sales quota ($25,000 bonus)
2 percent over sales quota ($50,000 bonus)
3 percent over sales quota ($75,000 bonus)
4 percent over sales quota ($100,000 bonus)
5 percent over sales quota ($125,000 bonus)
6 percent over sales quota ($150,000 bonus)
7 percent over sales quota ($175,000 bonus)
8 percent over sales quota ($200,000 bonus)
9 percent over sales quota ($225,000 bonus)
10 percent over sales quota ($250,000 bonus)

Each additional percentage increase in sales results in earning a sales bonus of $25,000. For example, coming in 12 percent over sales quota would result in a $300,000 bonus; coming in 13 percent over sales quota would result in a $325,000 bonus; and so on.

Last year Mark's region sold 8 percent more than the previous year, earned a $200,000 bonus that they split equally among the 12 members and Mark. Thus, the 13 people each earned a $15,384 bonus. Exhibit 2 outlines Wendy Maxwell's new bonus structure.

Mark calculates what he thinks his salespeople's new bonuses would be under Wendy Maxwell's new commission plan. This is shown in Exhibit 3.

After calculating the potential commission available for each of his sales reps, Mark sees they could, indeed, earn more under Wendy's new plan. Even though Mark is not in total agreement with Wendy's new sales strategy, there was a potential upside to her pay plan for those salespersons who achieved what was asked of them.

EXHIBIT 2

New Bonus Structure for Representatives

Each salesperson will be rewarded individually based upon the number of calls he or she makes and his or her closing percentage. To encourage reps to close business early in the year, a premium commission will be paid on sales closed in the 1st and 2nd quarters.

Monthly sales call quotas:
2 Executive Level
10 Mid-manager Level
20 Low Level

Closing ratio per call: Goal: 20 percent

- Existing contracts that are renewed earn 50 percent of full commissions
- Monthly bonus for a rep achieving his sales call quota: $500.00
- Monthly bonus for a rep achieving a 20 percent closing ratio: $500.00
- Monthly bonus for active contracts:
  - .030 percent of the customer's monthly bill during the first 12 months of a new contract
  - .015 percent of the customer's monthly bill on a renewed contract
  - All contracts signed in the 1st quarter will result in the signing rep receiving a .005 percent bonus on monthly billings
  - All contracts signed in the 2nd quarter will result in the signing rep receiving a .0025 percent bonus on monthly billings

EXHIBIT 3

Potential Annual Bonus per Representative

Total monthly bonuses for achieving sales call quota:	$4,000
Total monthly bonuses for achieving closing ratio quota:	$0
Total monthly bonuses for monthly billing:	$3,600
Total monthly bonuses for renewed contracts:	$7,200
Total monthly bonuses for early contracts:	$3,000
Total anticipated annual bonus per rep	$17,800

QUESTIONS

1. Has the telecom industry passed up Mark Phillips? What are some of the realities outlined by Wendy Maxwell that may make Mark change the way he manages his sales teams?

2. Mark seems like a nice guy, is well liked by his sales teams, and has a good sense of humor. Despite losing most of his long-term company benefits, he seems to have a positive attitude toward his job. Is there a place in Freedom Telecom for Mark under Wendy Maxwell's leadership?

3. The case went into great depth to document the trials and tribulations faced by Freedom Telecom and the telecom industry in general. Despite the great pains Mark Phillips and his sales team have faced, they have been relatively successful as a unit. Should there be exceptions made within Wendy's new call reporting structure to appease Mark and his team? Explain.

4. Do you agree or disagree with Wendy's approach to increasing sales based upon the number of calls and closing ratios representatives achieve? Does this regimented form of sales management and going by industry average closing ratios make sense for the telecom industry as it exists today?

5. Who would you prefer to work for, Mark or Wendy? Explain why. Which of the two do you think will make the company more money in the short run? How about in the long run?

6. Do you believe a sales manager can be effective by using humor in situations that might need to be treated more seriously? In other words, was Mark's e-mail using boat and water references appropriate for a sales force facing serious issues that need immediate attention? Explain your answer.

7. Leading and managing sales teams and individuals is often a balancing act. Which of the two compensation packages do you think will better motivate Freedom Telecom's commercial accounts group? Which approach is more quantifiable? Which approach makes it easier to implement clear goals for which individual reps are accountable?

CASE STUDY 10

The Sarasota Journal
Inevitable Change and the Restructuring of the Sales Force

It was late in the afternoon on a Friday. Wilma Collins sat behind her desk looking out a window across Sarasota Bay on the Gulf Coast of Florida. She could see Long Boat Key in the distance and longed for the day when she could retire and not have to deal with the problems she was currently facing as sales manager. Earlier in the afternoon, another 20 termination slips were delivered to *Sarasota Journal* employees. Most of the cuts this time around were in the newspaper's press room and circulation department. Wilma had a brief scare earlier in the afternoon when she received an e-mail marked "URGENT." For a moment she thought she was being let go. However, the e-mail instead alerted her about an 8 A.M. meeting on Monday for all of the *Journal*'s managers. The e-mail was sent by Bob Bowen, the paper's president and editor in chief.

In the past five years the *Sarasota Journal* had seen its employee base cut in half while undergoing two different buyouts and management changes. Rumors were rampant that the daily paper was going to be sold again before the end of the year. It was even rumored that bankruptcy was imminent for the 100-year-old daily paper. Wilma was three years from retirement and was hoping she could hang on a few more years. She was fearful of losing her health benefits and pension before she was old enough to qualify for Medicare and Social Security benefits. She was especially concerned about her healthcare benefits because she suffered from rheumatoid arthritis and always had some form of constant pain in one of her joints.

Background

Wilma had spent her entire 35-year career in the newspaper business since graduating from Florida State University with a recreation degree. She began her career as a telemarketer selling classified advertising for a small weekly paper in Tallahassee, Florida, and then moved to Tampa, Florida, where she worked for most of her career as a circulation manager for a large newspaper there. In 1998, she moved to the smaller Sarasota, Florida, market to take a sales management position in the retail and classified advertising department of the *Sarasota Journal.* In her role as sales manager, she led a team of eight sales consultants (see Exhibit 1).

Wilma liked new challenges and considered each new position to be a career advancement move. She also enjoyed the fast-paced environment and the connection to the community the newspaper business provided. Wilma had never married and considered the newspaper and its employees her family. She lived for her job, so it truly pained her to see friends let go due to changing economic conditions surrounding the newspaper business. Wilma longed for the old days when the business was less cutthroat, and employees were not worried about whether or not they had a job when they came to work everyday.

It was about the same time Wilma moved to Sarasota that the changes in the newspaper business started to take place. In 1998, Internet Web sites were just beginning to generate advertising revenues by selling banner ads. However, at the time, this was having little competitive impact on newspapers. In most cases, the cost of Internet advertising wasn't generating a high return on the investment made by advertisers. Other

Tom Freeman—$1,200,000 in Sales (20% in online advertising), 10 years, Auto/Boat/Cycle Dealerships and Real Estate/Developers

Frank Jackson—$900,000 in Sales (10% online advertising), 18 years, Large Retail Accounts

Betty Freeman—$875,000 in Sales (30% in online advertising), 3 years, Mom and Pop Stores (under 500,000 in sales) and Service Businesses

John Ackerman—$600,000 in Sales (50% in online advertising), 2 years, Local Resorts/Fitness and Travel-Related Businesses

Francis Rosen—$450,000 in Sales (5% online advertising), 25 years, calls exclusively on Bradenton, Florida, businesses 15 miles north of Sarasota

Joan Archer, Carrie Wilson, and Ann Carter—$2,100,000 total (15% online classified advertising); 15 years, 20 years, and 1 year; All Classified advertising accounts that call in (phone sales only)

Total Advertising Sales: $6,125,000 ($1,230,000 in online advertising—20%)

EXHIBIT 1

Sales Totals, Years of Service, and Markets Served by the *Sarasota Journal*'s Retail and Classified Sales Consultants

mass media like newspapers, magazines, radio, and television still had a grip on the demographic audiences companies targeted to sell their products and services.

However, as the Internet expanded, online advertising space became more available and drove online advertising prices down. The Internet sites also developed sophisticated software that targeted potential customers depending on the Web sites they visited and search words they typed in. The style of ads available on the Internet also grew and started to come in different formats other than banner ads, including pop-up ads; sidebar ads; floating ads; and Unicast ads, which are TV-like commercials that run in pop-up windows. As Internet Web sites became more popular with consumers, Internet companies began to promote their sites with the greater advertising revenues they were earning. This increased the site's popularity, siphoning a significant amount of business away from the mature newspaper industry.

Over the past five years, the *Sarasota Journal* has fought to stay profitable by cutting back on staff, tailoring its product, purchasing new technologies to gain efficiencies, and trying to take advantage of its brand name by introducing a news Web site. In the early years of the Internet, the paper's managers had purchased valuable domain names and had recently launched several Web-only initiatives to increase revenues. The *Journal*'s online newspaper division had been experiencing annual growth rates of 30 percent and had been able to increase its advertising rates by 10 percent. In an internal memo to the company's employees, Bob Bowen wrote:

> "We must embrace the benefits of the Internet and its positive impact on our local newspaper rather than the negative aspects. There are some positive signs we are seeing within our Internet division that makes me optimistic about our future. Unfortunately, we do not need the number of staff to run this division as we do our daily printed newspaper; therefore, you will continue to see a reduction in our employee base. We also need our current and new employees to have different skill sets than in the past if we are to survive."

Wilma had embraced computers and was a very savvy Internet user. As a sales manager, she needed to be on top of the newest technologies. As of late, much of her time was spent looking at what the *Journal*'s competitors were doing and asking newspaper advertisers what they wanted when it came to placing ads on the Internet. She was very much in tune with the market and the competition her sales consultants faced in terms of selling both newspaper and digital ads.

While researching the local market, Wilma discovered the competition from local television and radio stations was her main competitor for retail advertising. The stations ran ads during their broadcasts as they had traditionally done. However, like the *Journal,* they had also developed slick Web sites where they also ran ads. For classified advertising, the local market was much cloudier. The Sarasota area had 10 different used auto/truck/boat trader Web sites, and all of the area's new car dealerships had Web sites of their own. In the lucrative area of employment classifieds, national competitors like monster.com and hotjobs.com were getting most of the business from larger local firms looking to advertise for new employees.

Every day it seemed Wilma would discover another nimble Internet competitor. Many days she would come home from working a 10-hour day with her head spinning. Deep down she felt there was no way the existing business model of the newspaper business could compete against smaller niche Internet companies for advertising dollars. The legacy ties and overhead of the newspaper business were just not set up to compete against start-up Internet companies run out of someone's kitchen.

The previous month Wilma had received a telephone call from John Franks, who worked as a sales consultant for her from 1998–2003. John left the *Sarasota Journal* after 10 years to work for a start-up local Internet advertising firm called Gulf Coast Living, which sells retirement communities along Florida's Gulf Coast. John had called to offer Wilma a position selling Internet advertising to local developers and existing retirement communities. The position would require Wilma to travel and have three or four overnights a week. John was very persuasive. He told Wilma how his company's business was exploding, and he went on to list all of the innovative revenue streams the company provided. The average salesperson's commission was three times what Wilma was currently making. The company was small with only 12 employees, but its sales were almost half the *Sarasota Journal*'s advertising revenues.

The low overhead and sales-driven business model of John's company intrigued Wilma. It was difficult, but after a few days of pondering the offer, she politely told John she was not ready to make a change at this point in her life, and she felt the travel requirement would take too much of a toll on her physically. John was disappointed but understanding and left the offer on the table if she decided to change her mind.

Monday Morning

The manager's meeting was about to begin on Monday morning. The lights in the room were dimmed, and a laptop computer with a high-definition digital projector sat in the middle of the massive oak conference table. The blinds were closed and the room was quiet when Bob Bowen entered it at precisely 8 a.m. Bob was a proud Ivy League graduate about the same age as Wilma. Having begun his career as a beat writer in New York City, he had followed his father's footsteps into the newspaper business. His father was a journalist who had won a Pulitzer Prize for covering WWII while working for the *New York Times*. Bob was respected and well liked by the *Journal*'s employees, despite the difficult times the newspaper was experiencing. After thanking everyone for attending, he began making a PowerPoint slide presentation. The first group of slides recapped the *Sarasota Journal*'s circulation numbers and other prominent newspapers' numbers during the previous six months. The slides presented the following statistics:

- Circulation for daily papers across the country has fallen 2.1 percent, and Sunday papers, 3.1 percent in the past six months (*Sarasota Journal*'s numbers declined 2.5 percent daily and 3.6 percent for Sunday).
- Six of the 10 highest selling dailies and an additional 555 daily newspapers registered declines in the past six months.

- Some of the largest newspapers in the country experienced even greater circulation declines (*Los Angeles Times* lost 4.25 percent, the *Washington Post* lost 3.5 percent, and the *Chicago Tribune* lost 3 percent).

As always, Bob was the eternal optimist. Despite the dire numbers, he focused on the positive aspects of the newspaper business. He cited a recent study by an independent research group that surveyed shoppers to assess the strength of newspapers as an advertising medium. He presented the following numbers from the study:

- 52 percent of consumers said they read advertisements in the newspaper—more than any other medium.
- 46 percent said newspapers were their preferred medium for getting ad information (for television, the figure was just 10 percent).
- 50 percent considered newspaper ads valuable for planning their shopping (the figure was just 13 percent for the Internet).
- 72 percent of readers surveyed enjoyed reading the newspaper.
- Only 19 percent of newspaper readers found ads intrusive versus 38 percent of television viewers.
- 40 percent of readers trusted newspaper ads (the figure was only 23 percent for television ads and 18 percent for radio ads).
- 80 percent of newspaper readers visited a store or showroom after seeing an ad and bought something that was advertised.

The rest of Bob's presentation outlined his vision for the *Sarasota Journal* over the course of the next three years. Bob acknowledged that the paper's circulation numbers probably hadn't yet bottomed out, but he made it clear that his strategy for the future would be to invest in digital technology to reach *Sarasota*'s online audience. As he closed the meeting, he spoke of newspapers' great heritage in American society and the *Sarasota Journal*'s heritage in particular:

> . . . we have a great responsibility to deliver the local news in an accurate manner, and we are entrusted to provide a product to our audience that is both compelling and innovative. If the digital revolution we find ourselves in dictates the paper part of our product becomes obsolete, then so be it. The *Sarasota Journal* has been a brand that has delivered trustworthy news and advertising to our local customers for over 100 years, and we are at a crossroads to make sure we deliver the same benefits to our audience for the next 100 years.

As he closed the meeting, Bob challenged all of the *Journal*'s managers to come up with a three-year plan on how to organize and manage their departments to embrace the changes occurring in the marketplace. He warned the managers that the assignment would require making difficult decisions about the newspaper's personnel, and would test the abilities of the managers. Bob wanted each of the manager's plans to focus on personnel, training, execution, competitors' reaction, compatibility with other departments, and revenue streams. A rough draft of each manager's plan was due on his desk in 30 days. The deadline for the final draft was due in 60 days.

QUESTIONS

1. Is Wilma Collins the right person for the sales manager position at the *Sarasota Journal*? Given her background, health issues, and age, does she have the qualifications and energy to identify what changes need to be made and to implement them within the sales department?

2. Compare Bob Bowen's optimism and leadership to that of Wilma Collins. How important is it for a sales manager to provide a positive outlook when leading a sales team? Explain.

3. If you were Wilma, explain how you would stay focused on your job knowing you had a better job offer on the table with another organization not in turmoil.

4. If you were Wilma, what organizational changes would you present to Bob? Make your suggestions based on the sales staff performance data shown in Exhibit 1. What other information about the staff might be beneficial for you to know before making your recommendations?

5. What impact does the Internet have on the sales profession? Are all old market organizations (like newspapers) going to become obsolete? Who needs to drive the need for cultural change within an organization?

6. Describe the perfect salesperson for the *Sarasota Journal*. As a sales manager, how would you find and recruit this person and what types of training and development would you provide them?

Concord and Associates
Evaluating a Sales Territory

Emily Murray was a regional sales manager at Concord and Associates, a firm selling manufacturers' computer peripheral equipment to firms using Dell®, Acer®, Apple®, and Lenovo® systems. The computer peripheral industry encompasses computer displays and projectors, computer input drives and speakers, personal storage drives, and printing and imaging equipment.

Emily's territory included Southern California, Arizona, and New Mexico. She had been the southwest regional sales manager for Concord and Associates for two years. Prior to assuming her current position, Emily was the top salesperson in Phoenix, Arizona, for four of the seven years she had held that position. She also completed an evening MBA program at Arizona State University while she lived in Phoenix. When the regional sales manager's position opened up due to an early retirement, she was offered the job, which she accepted immediately.

Emily was known by her six sales reps to be smart, cool under fire, yet demanding. She was always available to help them find information, devise a strategy for a customer, or help solve a personal or family problem. What the sales team did not know was that Emily held herself to even higher standards than she did her workers!

On November 10, Emily Murray sent out the following e-mail to her six sales representatives:

Team,

As you know the end of the year is fast approaching! This year has been another successful one for Concord and Associates, with sales revenues slightly exceeding our forecasts. Therefore, as is the practice each year, please call or e-mail my secretary Sally to set up an appointment during the week of December 8th–15th so that we can discuss your formal evaluation for the year. I will forward a copy of the forecasts that we agreed to last January and a list of questions for you to answer that will guide our discussion during the review meeting. Thank you again for your hard work on behalf of Concord and Associates and your clients. I look forward to seeing you in Los Angeles the second week of December.

Best,
Em

Emily knew she would be busy over the next month preparing for the formal evaluations. In her many years in sales, she had experienced several sales managers who put little time into preparing for the evaluations. Instead, these managers "shot from the hip." They would look at the revenues their salespeople generated relative to their quotas and authorize a raise and bonus for them based upon their "making their numbers."

Although Emily knew that making one's quotas was important, she understood there were many things to be learned from "slicing and dicing" the numbers. Said differently, analyzing quantitative numbers was both an art and a science. One needed to understand the science of statistics but also be able to go more deeply into when, where, and how those numbers occurred. She knew that if her sales team were to improve each year, she would have to truly understand not only what their sales were, but why the results were what they were.

The following week Emily had her secretary, Sally, e-mail her salespeople their forecasts and agreed-upon goals for the year. In a separate attachment, Sally asked each of them to respond to the following questions and return their answers to Emily by December 1:

1. What were the purchasing trends in your territory over the past year?
2. What strategies have your competitors employed over the past year?
3. What factors do you attribute to your success (or shortfall) this year?
4. Are there any other factors, either business or personal, that Emily needs to be aware of, that directly impact your performance in your territory?

Over the Thanksgiving holiday, Emily went to her office several mornings to begin looking through the numbers for each of her salespersons. The first analysis that she gathered from her CRM system offered the following snapshot of her regional sales force's performance during the year.

As Emily stated in her e-mail, her sales team had surpassed its quota by $135,000. However, this amounted to less than 1 percent over the forecast. Given the slowdown in the economy and the increase in interest rates, she was glad her sales team's overall performance had exceeded expectations. While she was thinking about the implications of Exhibit 1, she was reminded of how the sales process goes: A few salespeople seem to exceed their quotas, whereas others struggle and never find their niche. This year, four of her salespeople had achieved or exceeded their goals, and two had fallen short. Susan, in Los Angeles, was slightly below goal. Jose, who managed the Phoenix/Tucson territory, was short by $300,000 or nearly 18 percent! Emily was aware that Jose was struggling, but she wanted to understand why. She decided to generate the information shown in Exhibit 2 to see if she could better understand what was going on.

Although Jose had exceeded expectations in terms of selling Product A, he had fallen short of his quota selling products B, C, and D. Again, Emily needed more information about her sales team to gain a more accurate understanding of the situation not only in the Arizona territory, but in the other five territories in the region.

EXHIBIT 1

Sales Compared to Quota, by Territory

Territory	Quota (000)	Sales (000)	Variance (000)
Bob—San Diego	$2,200	$2,315	$+115
Susan—LA	$2,800	$2,795	$−5
Omar—Anaheim	$3,100	$3,500	$+400
Jose—Phoenix/Tucson	$1,950	$1,600	$−350
Robert—New Mexico	$2,100	$2,110	$+10
Marites—Simi Valley	$2,950	$2,965	$+15
Totals	$15,100	$15,285	$+135

EXHIBIT 2

Sales by Product Line for Phoenix/Tucson Territory (Jose)

Product Line	Quota (000)	Sales (000)	Variance (000)
A	$800	$900	$+100
B	$200	$175	$−25
C	$550	$200	$−350
D	$400	$325	$−75
Totals	$1,950	$1,600	$−350

After a little thought and clicking on her computer, additional information was provided for each salesperson that included:

Utilizing the information provided in Exhibits 1 and 3, Emily computed the average order size and travel and entertainment cost per sale. She also decided it would be helpful to look at additional information that could be easily generated by her CRM system. She was always amazed at how much information was available if you knew what to look for. Exhibit 4 shows the information she was able to extract from the database.

Emily also perused each salesperson's personnel file for notes she had made after returning from days in the field with them. Here are the notes on Jose when she made sales calls with him in the Arizona sales territory.

Call Notes—Jose: Arizona Territory

1/15: Traveled with Jose to two accounts in Phoenix, after which we drove for three hours to one account located in Tucson. Suggested to Jose that it would be more efficient to schedule calls in either Phoenix or Tucson and drive in the evening when possible. Call quality was satisfactory, but Jose did not appear to be as familiar with the accounts as he should be. This concern, along with suggestions for reviewing customer files prior to a visit, was discussed with Jose.

3/18: Jose met me at the Tucson airport, and we visited four accounts. Three calls that Jose selected went well, but the fourth call (a company that I had selected) was clearly upset about a late delivery. Jose assigned blame for the misunderstanding on production. I was able to resolve the issue with the buyer, and when I raised the problem with the production manager, she informed me that Jose had promised the customer an unrealistic delivery date. I called Jose and told him not to promise delivery dates sooner than available from our manufacturing facility.

Territory	Days Worked	Sales Calls per Day	Total # Sales Made	Expenses
Bob—San Diego	220	4	65	$26,400
Susan—LA	225	4.2	98	$30,200
Omar—Anaheim	218	5	105	$21,200
Jose—Phoenix/Tucson	210	3	68	$30,500
Robert—New Mexico	222	3.5	59	$27,800
Marites—Simi Valley	230	5	108	$19,600
Averages	**220.8**	**4.12**	**83.8**	**$25,950**

EXHIBIT 3

Inputs by Territory

Territory	Gross Margin (%)	Miles per Sales Call	Rush Orders (%)	Number of Complaints
Bob—San Diego	35	31.2	4.00	5
Susan—LA	33	28.5	5.25	8
Omar—Anaheim	34.7	25.3	6.10	4
Jose—Phoenix/Tucson	29	45.6	10.50	16
Robert—New Mexico	34.3	47.8	5.75	7
Marites—Simi Valley	35.5	25.1	8.00	3
Averages	**33.58%**	**33.92**	**6.60%**	**7.17**

EXHIBIT 4

Additional Information by Territory

6/22: Called on four firms in Phoenix. Good calls, well planned, and Jose was well prepared. Told Jose how pleased I was with the calls and to keep up the good work.

8/08: Spent two days with Jose. First day in Tucson and the second, after driving from 5 to 8 P.M., was in Phoenix. Glad to see that Jose was following my suggestions about minimizing drive time during work hours. Calls were satisfactory and revolved around gathering information about upcoming request for quotations and resolving a few requests for minor changes to orders. Overall a satisfactory performance.

9/31: Visited for one day in Phoenix. Went to see our largest customer there and learned that we had been outbid by our major competitor on a major new contract. Jose seemed shocked at this news. I asked Jose how we had lost the contract to our largest competitor without knowing we were in danger of losing the account. He seemed embarrassed and said he did not know. This is a big blow to our region's sales and to Jose's expected sales for the year.

Emily read through the call summaries again and mulled these events over in her mind while thinking about the quantitative data she had already analyzed. Her task now was to meld the two—quantitative and qualitative—analyses into a coherent performance appraisal for a struggling member of her sales team.

Jose has scheduled his annual review for December 14 at 2 P.M. Emily has a week to prepare her formal evaluation of Jose's performance for this year. Based upon your understanding of performance appraisal and the information provided above, what should Emily say to Jose? That is, what can be deduced from the year's performance records? Lastly, what specific recommendations would you make to Jose for improving his performance in the coming year?

QUESTIONS

1. There is little doubt that there are negative trends in regard to Jose's annual performance. Analyze the data to uncover the specific behaviors that contributed to his level of performance.

2. Are any other salespersons that work for Emily Murray having potential problems in any performance areas? If so, what are they?

3. Based upon the information presented in the case, what strategy or approach does Jose appear to be taking when meeting with his customers?

4. Compute several ratios discussed in the evaluation chapter to help you compare and contrast the six salespersons managed by Emily Murray. Are these ratios helpful in your evaluation? How so?

5. What reasons might Jose offer to rebut a negative annual performance appraisal? How might Emily Murray respond to his rebuttal?

6. Write a formal narrative to Jose to explain your evaluation of his performance. Remember the importance of being factual and objective.

CASE STUDY 12

Cannon Associates
Achieving Internal Alignment among Your Old and New Sales Forces

Rick James is sales manager at Cannon Associates, a sales firm located in Richmond, Virginia. Rick graduated from Old Dominion University (ODU), where he earned a B.S. degree in marketing and sales in 1990. He began his sales career at Cannon in 1995, after completing five years' of service in the U.S. Air Force as an electronics officer. After performing successfully for a number of years as Cannon's sales rep in Northern Virginia and Washington, D.C., the company promoted him to the position of sales manager.

Currently, Rick James manages 16 Cannon sales associates working geographical territories in the states of North Carolina, Virginia, Maryland, Pennsylvania, and in Washington, D.C. Cannon also employs eight inside sales reps, many of whom eventually strive to move to outside sales positions as they become available. The ages of the company's salespeople range from mid-20s to the early 60s.

As a sales manager, Rick has always been willing to take a chance on hiring young, less experienced salespeople who demonstrate high potential. Perhaps this is because he had little sales experience when he was hired by Cannon Sales Manager Nancy Williams after he left the Air Force. Rick sees in new hires what he believes Nancy saw in him: bright, highly motivated, and goal-oriented new additions to the company. In his opinion, these new hires require training and mentoring to help them become the next generation of successful salespeople.

To Rick's frustration, however, he has noticed a growing gap between Cannon's older sales veterans and its new hires—to the extent that it threatens the firm's team-selling strategy. More recently, Rick seems to field more and more gripes from both groups. That is, the older account managers complain that the newer salespersons don't take direction well, want to be given more responsibility without earning it, and they try to rationalize their failures as being beyond their control. On the other side, the younger inside sales reps complain that the veterans are condescending when they talk with them, appear to mistrust their work ethic, and hog all the glory for success with the accounts.

Complaints have become so bad Rick feels he has become a referee who spends all his time smoothing over internal arguments about account management. As of yet, he is not aware of any accounts being lost by this internal strife; however, Sally Jenkins, one of Cannon's customers, called from Abba Enterprises and told him she had observed tension between Cannon's inside and field sales personnel. Rick is afraid that if he does not act soon, sales will be lost. Moreover, he has little doubt that several younger sales personnel, who have less invested in their Cannon Associates careers, will start looking for opportunities elsewhere.

After 12 years with Cannon Associates, Rick James feels more like a sales veteran than a new sales hire. However, he can see both viewpoints. That said, no matter how hard James has tried to communicate to his reps that criticizing one another is not a good way to resolve their different viewpoints, neither side has been willing to admit fault or make concessions.

About a month ago, Rick hired a management consulting firm to come in and conduct a team-building exercise for his sales personnel. The all-day workshop consisted of breaking his salespeople into teams of four, consisting of both inside and outside reps, and having them work on problem-solving and group exercises. The goal was to show them that working together led to superior results. Rick then hosted a dinner for his sales reps at a nice restaurant in Richmond, where he handed out training certificates to the sales team.

After the workshop and dinner, the bickering and complaints seemed to disappear, and Rick was relieved. Then he received another call from Sally Jenkins. Apparently the senior sales rep who manages her account had taken an order that was supposed to ship on the 15th of the month. When Sally called inside sales/customer service and asked about the order, the inside salesperson began laughing about how the senior sales rep, who thought he knew everything, had entered the order incorrectly. Sally told the inside rep she didn't care who or what had happened, but from where she sat, she had placed an order with Cannon Associates that was needed by her company, and she had been let down. The inside sales rep reassured Sally, and told her that thanks to him, her order would indeed arrive the next day.

Rick also talked to Sally and reassured her that her order would arrive the next day, He then immediately called the inside sales rep into his office and asked for his side of the story. In effect, the inside sales rep corroborated what Sally Jenkins had told him. Rick told the inside sales rep that he did the right thing by expediting Sally's order. However, he also explained to him that it was unprofessional and unacceptable to criticize or make negative comments about anyone at Cannon Associates, including Sally's field rep.

Rick then called the senior sales rep by phone and asked for his side of the story. After listening, he concluded that the rep had told the inside salesperson, in no uncertain terms, not to "mess with his orders." In effect, it was evident that little had changed between the old and new groups.

Rick understands that he must do something to resolve the "us vs. them" mentality that is taking a toll on his group's sales and customer satisfaction goals. The question is, what? He has already tried a team-building effort to encourage the members of his sales team to interact with one another more productively. However, he now realizes that a more major action is needed to resolve these conflicts once and for all.

After mulling the situation over, Rick walks outside Cannon Associates' corporate offices, which overlook the James River. Life seems so peaceful from this vantage point, but he knows he must devise a plan to minimize the internal conflicts his group is experiencing and maximize their cooperation. Otherwise, sales will be lost, and most likely, sales personnel will be lost. Rick considers a number of possible alternatives. They include the following:

Admonishing the sales team. Rick could send out a letter admonishing the team and discussing the incident and its negative consequences.

Reorganizing the sales team. Perhaps the sales team needs to be reorganized with clear lines of authority that include the inside sales reps reporting to Cannon's most senior field sales reps.

Firing reps for poor performance. Rick could set an example by firing the inside sales rep involved in the incident or the field reps who didn't follow through.

Bring in another consulting team. Perhaps a consulting team that specializes in corporate culture change can provide more detailed guidance. This would be expensive, but it might just be what the doctor ordered.

Holding regular team-building meetings. Rick feels that much of the problem revolves around a lack of trust and communication. The younger sales associates want to take on more responsibility, but the senior sales reps are used to working alone. Moreover, they do not want to share the "spotlight" with reps who have not "earned their stripes."

Shifting the corporate culture. Perhaps Rick needs to restructure expectations, rewards, and training for the sales team. This, however, needs to be a comprehensive restructuring. What if his sales team doesn't buy into the changes he suggests? Then what will happen to their sales and turnover?

Later that evening, Rick and his wife, Pilar, drove down I-64E toward their getaway home at Duck, North Carolina, on the Outer Banks. He is still contemplating how to put into place a culture change at Cannon Associates. There are lots of ways of addressing this very insidious situation; he needs to identify the most opportune way. As he and Pilar sit eating steak and lobster that night, Rick believes that he has come up with a solution for ending the stalemate. First thing Monday morning, he will begin to "rough out" a plan to present to the owner of Cannon Associates by the following Friday at the latest. On the short ride back to their beach house Rick realizes that he now has only one more day at Duck to enjoy the beautiful beaches and surf the big waves. Then, back to work!

QUESTIONS

1. If you were Rick James, what plan would you rough out on Monday morning and present to the owner of Cannon Associates?

2. What do you see the major problem to be between the old and new sales reps?

3. Explain why each group might feel the way they do?

4. What other possible alternatives to the current situation can you suggest?

5. What immediate and long-term consequences do you see occurring if the problem is not fixed?

Name Index

Subject Index

427